Major Problems
in the
Civil War and Reconstruction

MAJOR PROBLEMS IN AMERICAN HISTORY SERIES

GENERAL EDITOR
THOMAS G. PATERSON

Major Problems
in the
Civil War and Reconstruction

DOCUMENTS AND ESSAYS

SECOND EDITION

EDITED BY
MICHAEL PERMAN
UNIVERSITY OF ILLINOIS AT CHICAGO

HOUGHTON MIFFLIN COMPANY   Boston   New York

Editor-in-Chief: Jean L. Woy
Senior Associate Editor: Frances Gay
Senior Project Editor: Janet Young
Editorial Assistant: Carolyn Wagner
Associate Production/Design Coordinator: Jodi O'Rourke
Assistant Manufacturing Coordinator: Andrea Wagner
Marketing Manager: Sandra McGuire

Cover design: Sarah Melhado

Cover art: *Battle of Shiloh*, 1888, L. Prang & Company, a chromolithograph by Prang
after painting by deThulstrup, Library of Congress

Printed in the U.S.A.

Library of Congress Catalog Number: 97-72533

ISBN: 0-395-86849-1

123456789-DH-02 01 00 99 98

Contents

I put this in "Behind the Lines" week — because of emancipation except pp. 156–158.

CHAPTER 7
The Northern Home Front
Page 186

CHAPTER 8
The Southern Home Front
Page 215

CHAPTER 11
Congress's Terms for the Defeated South
Page 311

CHAPTER 12
Political and Economic Change in the Reconstruction South
Page 342

CHAPTER 13
Southern Republicans and the Problems of Reconstruction
Page 377

CHAPTER 14
The Northern Retreat from Reconstruction
Page 401

CHAPTER 15
The Impact and Significance of the Sectional Conflict
Page 431

Preface

The sectional conflict of the mid-nineteenth century, many scholars have argued, ranks as the greatest crisis in the history of the United States. Courses on this momentous episode—usually called "Civil War and Reconstruction"—have become a staple and necessary feature of the history curriculum in American colleges and universities. And, since the Civil War has probably been written about more than any other event in the nation's history, the amount of literature and documentation about it is simply immense.

This book, a volume in the Major Problems in American History Series, is intended to provide students and instructors with essential, readable, and provocative documents and essays on the issues of the period. Essays were selected because of their quality as pieces of historical writing and interpretation as well as their contribution to ongoing debates among historians. For the documents, the aim was to choose those important ones that either served as examples in the essays or that conveyed the spirit of contemporary issues. Some of these documents are very well known and so significant that they could not be excluded. Most of them, however, are less familiar, and several have not been previously published.

Like the other volumes in the series, *Major Problems in the Civil War and Reconstruction* is organized into chapters, each one of which covers a significant topic or aspect of the period. Every chapter opens with a brief introduction that sets the scene and defines the central issues. The documents and essays, introduced by headnotes, aim to provide evidence and interpretation that will enable readers to develop their own understanding and assessment of the topic. Each chapter closes with a list of books and articles for further reading.

The chapter topics reveal the diversity and richness of the history of the Civil War and Reconstruction. Because the national crisis from roughly 1840 until 1880 centered on questions of government and public policy, it was essentially political in nature. While politics may have shaped the crisis, however, social, cultural, and economic developments coursed through it. So this book includes topics on a variety of aspects of the era to reflect historical reality as a whole, not just one or two facets of it.

Although the era covered by this volume seems to consist of two parts, the Civil War and Reconstruction, it actually has three components: the causes of the war, the war itself, and the consequences of the war. The war is the central event, but why it happened and what its results were can only be explained in terms of the entire period of sectional crisis. In this book, the coming of the war (its causes) is covered in Chapters 1 through 3. The war, which actually lasted only four years, is treated in Chapters 4 through 9. And the aftermath of the war (its consequences) is discussed in Chapters 10 through 14. A final chapter assesses the conflict and its impact.

This second edition is organized like the first, but two features are different this time around. First, the historical literature on the period has shifted in focus since this volume appeared in 1991. The war itself has assumed greater significance than before. This is primarily because the military history of the event has moved in a new direction. Historians are now treating the fighting of the war as an aspect of social history—that is, the war as experienced by the ordinary people who, as soldiers, struggled through it. Another recent emphasis stemming from social history is found in the writing on the experiences of noncombatants in both the Union and the Confederacy. To reflect this growing scholarly interest, chapters on the home front in both the North and South have been added, and the chapter on emancipation now highlights the ways the slaves contributed to and participated in that momentous event. But political issues continue to attract historical inquiry, and so this second edition includes new chapters on Abraham Lincoln as wartime president and on the retreat of the North from Reconstruction. The chapter on the significance of the sectional conflict has been moved to the conclusion of the book so as to enable readers to evaluate the entire episode after studying all its elements and features in the preceding chapters.

Another change in this edition amounts to a shift in approach. Because of the emergence of these new topics and changes in emphasis, the selections in some of the chapters do not necessarily disagree with or directly contest each other. Instead, they represent differing aspects of, or ways to think about, the topics, rather than contrasting interpretations. This shift is largely the result of a development in historical scholarship, which is becoming less disputatious and more descriptive than previously.

In developing a book like this, the editor needs advice and warning from other historians who know the field and teach the subject to students. I would like to thank the following historians who were consulted by the editorial staff at Houghton Mifflin and provided very helpful comments and suggestions on the table of contents: Gabor Boritt, Gettysburg College; Leslie A. Schwalm, University of Iowa; Brooks D. Simpson, Arizona State University; and Mitchell Snay, Denison University. At a later stage, Leslie Rowland of the University of Maryland at College Park and Phil Paludan of the University of Kansas also offered suggestions.

At Houghton Mifflin, Jean Woy, editor-in-chief, helped plan the new edition, and Frances Gay, senior associate editor, helped guide the book through the revision process. My thanks to both of them. Also to be thanked are Thomas G. Paterson, general editor of the series; Diane Kraut of DK Research, who handled the permissions most effectively; and Carrie Wagner, editorial assistant.

And last, I thank my wife, Karen, for her love and support.

M. P.

Major Problems
in the
Civil War and Reconstruction

CHAPTER
1

The North and South Compared

The conflict in mid-nineteenth-century America was waged by two separate geographical regions. It was therefore significantly different from the internal wars in England in the 1640s and 1650s, known as the English Civil War, and those in France in the late eighteenth century and Russia in the early twentieth century, known as the French and Russian Revolutions. On the other hand, the attempt by the South to break away and form an independent country was quite similar to the contemporaneous secession movements within the Austro-Hungarian Empire in the 1860s and 1870s that contributed to the creation of the new nations of Germany and Italy.

By withdrawing from the United States, the Confederacy was in effect embarking on a parallel course of nation-making. And the embryonic Confederate States of America seemed to possess all the ingredients of a nation. Its people spoke a common language—English. They practiced a common religion—Protestant Christianity. The majority of them possessed a common ancestry and ethnicity—Scots-Irish and English. And they shared a common political outlook—the profession and practice of republicanism, federalism, representative government, and broad-based electoral participation. Few nations that endured for any length of time have been endowed with so many widely shared features.

Ironically, however, most of these values and characteristics were also true of the United States from which the Southerners were trying to distance and separate themselves. Thus the question arises as to why the Southern states felt so acutely conscious of their difficulties and distinctiveness that they took the drastic step of seeking their independence. Perhaps there was just a conflict of interests, rather than of basic beliefs and attitudes. If so, why could they not be reconciled? After all, every sovereign state or nation contains within its confines divergent interests, such as antagonistic social classes or competing economic groups and occupational sectors. Yet these differences can usually be accommodated or surmounted.

Perhaps the two regions were different in such a subtle way that points of friction such as these could not be assuaged. Maybe the differences that did exist became exaggerated or blown out of proportion somehow, and then proved impossible to reconcile. Whatever the circumstances, people at the time were apparently convinced that accommodation between the regions was out of reach. But historians have to examine and ponder the reasons for this if they are to explain why war was the final outcome.

⊨ *D O C U M E N T S*

Among contemporaries, the nature and degree of the contrast between the two sections was the subject of a good deal of comment as well as polemic. The selections that follow demonstrate this. The first four criticize the South, while the last three are forcefully defensive of it.

The first document is from *An Appeal in Favor of That Class of Americans Called Africans,* a very early abolitionist book published by Lydia Marie Child in 1833. The second observation comes from Frederick Law Olmsted, a northern journalist and later a famous urban planner, who undertook several tours of the Southern states in the 1850s. Here, in a *New York Times* article of January 12, 1854, he points out how sharply divergent were the values and self-images of the South's ruling class. The third selection is from Hinton Rowan Helper's extremely controversial *The Impending Crisis of the South: How to Meet It* (1857), in which the author, a nonslaveowning North Carolinian, claims that slavery has made the South economically backward, and urges his fellow nonslaveholders to acknowledge the problem and do something about it. Olmsted is the author of the fourth selection, from his book, *The Cotton Kingdom* (1861), in which he emphasizes the rapidity of material change and improvement in the Northern states compared with the South.

The fifth selection is from the first of two public letters written in 1845 by James Henry Hammond, a future governor and U.S. senator from South Carolina, to Thomas Clarkson, a leading English abolitionist. In this extract, Hammond points out his region's cultural superiority in relation to the North. In the sixth selection, this boast is carried to an extreme by George Fitzhugh, the South's most provocative polemicist, in his *Sociology for the South* (1854). In the seventh document, an extract from the pamphlet, "The Non-Slaveholders of the South," James D. B. DeBow, a leading Southern nationalist, demonstrates why he thinks Southerners who have no apparent interest in maintaining slavery can be relied upon to support it.

Lydia Maria Child Describes How Slavery Harms the South, 1833

Political economists found their systems on those broad and general principles, the application of which has been proved by reason and experience to produce the greatest possible happiness to the greatest number of people. All writers of this class, I believe without exception, prefer free labor to slave labor.

Indeed a very brief glance will show that slavery is inconsistent with *economy,* whether domestic, or political.

The slave is bought, sometimes at a very high price; in free labor there is no such investment of capital.—When the slave is ill, a physician must be paid by the owner; the free laborer defrays his own expenses. The children of the slave must be supported by his master; the free man maintains his own. The slave is to be taken care of in his old age, which his previous habits render peculiarly helpless; the free laborer is hired when he is wanted, and then returns to his home. The slave does not care how slowly or carelessly he works; it is the free man's interest to do his business well and quickly. The slave is indifferent how many tools he spoils; the free man has a motive to be careful. The slave's clothing is indeed very cheap, but it is of no consequence to him how fast it is destroyed—his master *must* keep him covered, and that is all he is likely to do; the hired laborer pays more for his garments, but makes them last three times as long. The free man will be honest for reputation's sake; but reputation will make the slave none

From Lydia Maria Child, *An Appeal in Favor of That Class of Americans Called Africans,* Carolyn L. Karcher, ed. (University of Massachusetts Press, 1996), pp. 72–73.

the richer, nor invest him with any of the privileges of a human being—while his poverty and sense of wrong both urge him to steal from his master. A salary must be paid to an overseer to compel the slave to work; the free man is impelled by the desire of increasing the comforts of himself and family. Two hired laborers will perform as much work as three slaves; by some it is supposed to be a more correct estimate that slaves perform only *half* as much labor as the same number of free laborers. Finally, *where* slaves are employed, manual industry is a degradation to white people, and indolence becomes the prevailing characteristic.

Slave owners have indeed frequently shown great adroitness in defending this bad system; but, with few exceptions, they base their arguments upon the necessity of continuing slavery because it is already begun. Many of them have openly acknowledged that it was highly injurious to the prosperity of the State.

Frederick Law Olmsted Observes Southern Lassitude, 1854

. . . The direct influence of Slavery is, I think, to make the Southerner indifferent to small things; in some relations, we should say rightly, *superior* to small things; prodigal, improvident, and ostentatiously generous. His ordinarily uncontrolled authority, (and from infancy the Southerner is more free from control, in all respects, I should judge, than any other person in the world,) leads him to be habitually impulsive, impetuous, and enthusiastic: gives him self-respect and dignity of character, and makes him bold, confident, and true. Yet it has not appeared to me that the Southerner was frank as he is, I believe, commonly thought to be. He seems to me to be very secretive, or at least reserved, on topics which most nearly concern himself. He minds his own business, and lets alone that of others; not in the English way, but in a way peculiarly his own; resulting partly, perhaps, from want of curiosity, in part from habits formed by such constant intercourse as he has with his inferiors, (negroes,) and partly from the caution in conversation which the "rules of honor" are calculated to give. Not, I said, in the English way, because he meets a stranger easily, and without timidity, or thought of how he is himself appearing, and is ready and usually accomplished in conversation. He is much given to vague and careless generalization, and greatly disinclined to exact and careful reasoning. He follows his natural impulses nobly, has nothing to be ashamed of, and is, therefore, habitually truthful; but his carelessness, impulsiveness, vagueness, and want of exactness in everything, make him speak from his mouth that which is in point of fact untrue, rather more often than any one else.

From early intimacy with the negro, (an association fruitful in other respects of evil,) he has acquired much of his ready, artless and superficial benevolence, good nature and geniality. The comparatively solitary nature and somewhat monotonous duties of plantation life, make guests usually exceedingly welcome, while the abundance of servants at command, and other circumstances, make the ordinary duties of hospitality very light. The Southerner, however, is greatly wanting in hospitality of mind, closing his doors to all opinions and schemes to which he has been bred a stranger, with a contempt and bigotry which sometimes seems incompatible with his character as a gentleman. He has a large but unexpansive mind.

From Frederick Law Olmsted, *The Cotton Kingdom,* Arthur M. Schlesinger, ed. (Knopf, 1953), pp. 615–617.

The Southerner has no pleasure in labor except with reference to a result. He enjoys life itself. He is content with being. Here is the grand distinction between him and the Northerner; for the Northerner enjoys progress in itself. He finds his happiness in doing. Rest, in itself, is irksome and offensive to him, and however graceful or beatific that rest may be, he values it only with reference to the power of future progress it will bring him. Heaven itself will be dull and stupid to him, if there is no work to be done in it—nothing to struggle for—if he reaches perfection at a jump, and has no chance to make an improvement.

The Southerner cares for the end only; he is impatient of the means. He is passionate, and labors passionately, fitfully, with the energy and strength of anger, rather than of resolute will. He fights rather than works to carry his purpose. He has the intensity of character which belongs to Americans in general, and therefore enjoys excitement and is fond of novelty. But he has much less curiosity than the Northerner; less originating genius, less inventive talent, less patient and persevering energy. And I think this all comes from his want of aptitude for close observation and his dislike for application to small details. And this, I think, may be reasonably supposed to be mainly the result of habitually leaving all matters not either of grand and exciting importance, or of immediate consequence to his comfort, to his slaves, and of being accustomed to see them slighted or neglected as much as he will, in his indolence, allow them to be by them.

Of course, I have been speaking of the general tendencies only of character in the North and the South. There are individuals in both communities in whom these extreme characteristics are reversed, as there are graceful Englishmen and awkward Frenchmen. There are, also, in each, those in whom they are more or less harmoniously blended. Those in whom they are the most enviably so—the happiest and the most useful in the social sphere—are equally common, so far as I know, in both; and the grand distinction remains in the mass—manifesting itself, by strikingly contrasting symptoms, in our religion, politics and social life.

In no way more than this: The South endeavors to close its eyes to every evil the removal of which will require self-denial, labor and skill. If, however, an evil is too glaring to be passed by unnoticed, it is immediately declared to be constitutional, or providential, and its removal is declared to be either treasonable or impious—usually both; and, what is worse, it is improper, impolite, ungentlemanly, unmanlike. And so it is ended at the South. But, at the North this sort of opposition only serves to develop the reform, by ridding it of useless weight and drapery. . . .

Hinton Rowan Helper Exposes Southern Economic Backwardness, 1857

And now that we have come to the very heart and soul of our subject, we feel no disposition to mince matters, but mean to speak plainly, and to the point, without any equivocation, mental reservation, or secret evasion whatever. The son of a venerated parent, who, while he lived, was a considerate and merciful slaveholder, a native of the South, born and bred in North Carolina, of a family whose home has been in the valley of the Yadkin for nearly a century and a half, a Southerner by instinct and by all the influences of thought, habits, and kindred, and with the desire and fixed purpose to reside

---

From Hinton Rowan Helper, *The Impending Crisis of the South* (Burdick Bros., 1857), pp. 24–25, 60–61.

permanently within the limits of the South, and with the expectation of dying there also—we feel that we have the right to express our opinion, however humble or unimportant it may be, on any and every question that affects the public good; and, so help us God, "sink or swim, live or die, survive or perish," we are determined to exercise that right with manly firmness, and without fear, favor or affection.

And now to the point. In our opinion, an opinion which has been formed from data obtained by assiduous researches, and comparisons, from laborious investigation, logical reasoning, and earnest reflection, the causes which have impeded the progress and prosperity of the South, which have dwindled our commerce, and other similar pursuits, into the most contemptible insignificance; sunk a large majority of our people in galling poverty and ignorance, rendered a small minority conceited and tyrannical, and driven the rest away from their homes; entailed upon us a humiliating dependence on the Free States; disgraced us in the recesses of our own souls, and brought us under reproach in the eyes of all civilized and enlightened nations—may all be traced to one common source, and there find solution in the most hateful and horrible word, that was ever incorporated into the vocabulary of human economy—*Slavery!* . . .

To undeceive the people of the South, to bring them to a knowledge of the inferior and disreputable position which they occupy as a component part of the Union, and to give prominence and popularity to those plans which, if adopted, will elevate us to an equality, socially, morally, intellectually, industrially, politically, and financially, with the most flourishing and refined nation in the world, and, if possible, to place us in the van of even that, is the object of this work. Slaveholders, either from ignorance or from a wilful disposition to propagate error, contend that the South has nothing to be ashamed of, that slavery has proved a blessing to her, and that her superiority over the North in an agricultural point of view makes amends for all her shortcomings in other respects. On the other hand, we contend that many years of continual blushing and severe penance would not suffice to cancel or annul the shame and disgrace that justly attaches to the South in consequence of slavery—the direst evil that e'er befell the land—that the South bears nothing like even a respectable approximation to the North in navigation, commerce, or manufactures, and that, contrary to the opinion entertained by ninety-nine hundredths of her people, she is far behind the free States in the only thing of which she has ever dared to boast—agriculture. We submit the question to the arbitration of figures, which, it is said, do not lie. With regard to the bushel-measure products of the soil, of which we have already taken an inventory, we have seen that there is a balance against the South in favor of the North of *seventeen million four hundred and twenty-three thousand one hundred and fifty-two bushels,* and a difference in the value of the same, also in favor of the North, of *forty-four million seven hundred and eighty-two thousand six hundred and thirty-six dollars.* It is certainly a most novel kind of agricultural superiority that the South claims on that score! . . .

Frederick Law Olmsted Criticizes the South's Lack of Material Progress, 1861

. . . One of the grand errors, out of which this rebellion has grown, came from supposing that whatever nourishes wealth and gives power to an ordinary civilized community must

From Frederick Law Olmsted, *The Cotton Kingdom,* Arthur M. Schlesinger, ed. (Knopf, 1953), pp. 615–617.

command as much for a slave-holding community. The truth has been overlooked that the accumulation of wealth and the power of a nation are contingent not merely upon the primary value of the surplus of productions of which it has to dispose, but very largely also upon the way in which the income from its surplus is distributed and reinvested. Let a man be absent from almost any part of the North twenty years, and he is struck, on his return, by what we call the "improvements" which have been made. Better buildings, churches, school-houses, mills, railroads, etc. In New York city alone, for instance, at least two hundred millions of dollars have been reinvested merely in an improved housing of the people; in labour-saving machinery, waterworks, gasworks, etc., and much more. It is not difficult to see where the profits of our manufacturers and merchants are. Again, go into the country, and there is no end of substantial proof of twenty years of agricultural prosperity, not alone in roads, canals, bridges, dwellings, barns and fences, but in books and furniture, and gardens, and pictures, and in the better dress and evidently higher education of the people. But where will the returning traveller see the accumulated cotton profits of twenty years in Mississippi? Ask the cotton-planter for them, and he will point in reply, not to dwellings, libraries, churches, school-houses, mills, railroads, or anything of the kind; he will point to his negroes—to almost nothing else. Negroes such as stood for five hundred dollars once, now represent a thousand dollars. We must look then in Virginia and those Northern Slave States which have the monopoly of supplying negroes, for the real wealth which the sale of cotton has brought to the South. But where is the evidence of it? where anything to compare with the evidence of accumulated profits to be seen in any Free State? If certain portions of Virginia have been a little improving, others unquestionably have been deteriorating, growing shabbier, more comfortless, less convenient. The total increase in wealth of the population during the last twenty years shows for almost nothing. One year's improvements of a Free State exceed it all. . . .

[handwritten margin note: South reinvests in slaves— North in material progress.]

James Henry Hammond Claims Southern Cultural Superiority, 1845

. . . In a social point of view the abolitionists pronounce Slavery to be a monstrous evil. If it was so, it would be our own peculiar concern, and superfluous benevolence in them to lament over it. Seeing their bitter hostility to us, they might leave us to cope with our own calamities. But they make war upon us out of excess of charity, and attempt to purify by covering us with calumny. You have read and assisted to circulate a great deal about affrays, duels and murders, occurring here, and all attributed to the terrible demoralization of Slavery. Not a single event of this sort takes place among us, but it is caught up by the abolitionists, and paraded over the world, with endless comments, variations and exaggerations. You should not take what reaches you as a mere sample, and infer that there is a vast deal more you never hear. You hear all, and more than all, the truth.

It is true that the point of honor is recognized throughout the slave region, and that disputes of certain classes are frequently referred for adjustment, to the "trial by combat." It would not be appropriate for me to enter, in this letter, into a defence of the practice of duelling, nor to maintain at length, that it does not tarnish the character of a people to acknowledge a standard of honor. Whatever evils may arise from it, however, they

From James Henry Hammond, "Letter to an English Abolitionist, 1845," in *The Ideology of Slavery,* Drew Gilpin Faust, ed. (Louisiana State University Press, 1981), pp. 179–191.

cannot be attributed to Slavery, since the same custom prevails both in France and England. . . . Slavery has nothing to do with these things. Stability and peace are the first desires of every slave-holder, and the true tendency of the system. It could not possibly exist amid the eternal anarchy and civil broils of the ancient Spanish dominions in America. And for this very reason, domestic Slavery has ceased there. So far from encouraging strife, such scenes of riot and bloodshed, as have within the last few years disgraced our Northern cities, and as you have lately witnessed in Birmingham and Bristol and Wales, not only never have occurred, but I will venture to say, never will occur in our slave-holding States. The only thing that can create a mob (as you might call it) here, is the appearance of an abolitionist, whom the people assemble to chastise. And this is no more of a mob, than a rally of shepherds to chase a wolf out of their pastures would be one. . . .

It is roundly asserted, that we are not so well educated nor so religious here as elsewhere. I will not go into tedious statistical statements on these subjects. Nor have I, to tell the truth, much confidence in the details of what are commonly set forth as statistics. As to education, you will probably admit that slave-holders should have more leisure for mental culture than most people. And I believe it is charged against them, that they are peculiarly fond of power, and ambitious of honors. If this be so, as all the power and honors of this country are won mainly by intellectual superiority, it might be fairly presumed, that slave-holders would not be neglectful of education. In proof of the accuracy of this presumption, I point you to the facts, that our Presidential chair has been occupied for forty-four out of fifty-six years, by slave-holders; that another has been recently elected to fill it for four more, over an opponent who was a slave-holder also; and that in the Federal Offices and both Houses of Congress, considerably more than a due proportion of those acknowledged to stand in the first rank are from the South. In this arena, the intellects of the free and slave States meet in full and fair competition. Nature must have been unusually bountiful to us, or we have been at least reasonably assiduous in the cultivation of such gifts as she has bestowed—unless indeed you refer our superiority to moral qualities, which I am sure *you* will not. More wealthy we are not; nor would mere wealth avail in such rivalry.

The piety of the South is unobtrusive. We think it proves but little, though it is a confident thing for a man to claim that he stands higher in the estimation of his Creator, and is less a sinner than his neighbor. If vociferation is to carry the question of religion, the North, and probably the Scotch, have it. Our sects are few, harmonious, pretty much united among themselves, and pursue their avocations in humble peace. In fact, our professors of religion seem to think—whether correctly or not—that it is their duty "to do good in secret," and to carry their holy comforts to the heart of each individual, without reference to class *or color,* for his special enjoyment, and not with a view to exhibit their zeal before the world. So far as numbers are concerned, I believe our clergymen, when called on to make a showing, have never had occasion to blush, if comparisons were drawn between the free and slave States. And although our presses do not teem with controversial pamphlets, nor our pulpits shake with excommunicating thunders, the daily walk of our religious communicants furnishes, apparently, as little food for gossip as is to be found in most other regions. It may be regarded as a mark of our want of excitability—though that is a quality accredited to us in an eminent degree—that few of the remarkable religious *Isms* of the present day have taken root among us. We have been so irreverent as to laugh at Mormonism and Millerism, which have created such commotions farther North; and modern prophets have no honor in our country. Shakers,

Rappists, Dunkers, Socialists, Fourrierists and the like, keep themselves afar off. Even Puseyism has not yet moved us. You may attribute this to our domestic Slavery if you choose. I believe you would do so justly. There is no material here for such characters to operate upon. . . .

George Fitzhugh
Praises Southern Society, 1854

. . . At the slaveholding South all is peace, quiet, plenty and contentment. We have no mobs, no trades unions, no strikes for higher wages, no armed resistance to the law, but little jealousy of the rich by the poor. We have but few in our jails, and fewer in our poor houses. We produce enough of the comforts and necessaries of life for a population three or four times as numerous as ours. We are wholly exempt from the torrent of pauperism, crime, agrarianism, and infidelity which Europe is pouring from her jails and alms houses, on the already crowded North. Population increases slowly, wealth rapidly. In the tide water region of Eastern Virginia, as far as our experience extends, the crops have doubled in fifteen years, whilst the population has been almost stationary. In the same period the lands, owing to improvements of the soil and the many fine houses erected in the country, have nearly doubled in value. This ratio of improvement has been approximated or exceeded wherever in the South slaves are numerous. We have enough for the present, and no Malthusian* spectres frightening us for the future. Wealth is more equally distributed than at the North, where a few millionaires own most of the property of the country. (These millionaires are men of cold hearts and weak minds; they know how to make money, but not how to use it, either for the benefit of themselves or of others.) High intellectual and moral attainments, refinement of head and heart, give standing to a man in the South, however poor he may be. Money is, with few exceptions, the only thing that ennobles at the North. We have poor among us, but none who are over-worked and under-fed. We do not crowd cities because lands are abundant and their owners kind, merciful and hospitable. The poor are as hospitable as the rich, the negro as the white man. Nobody dreams of turning a friend, a relative, or a stranger from his door. The very negro who deems it no crime to steal, would scorn to sell his hospitality. We have no loafers, because the poor relative or friend who borrows our horse, or spends a week under our roof, is a welcome guest. The loose economy, the wasteful mode of living at the South, is a blessing when rightly considered; it keeps want, scarcity and famine at a distance, because it leaves room for retrenchment. The nice, accurate economy of France, England and New England, keeps society always on the verge of famine, because it leaves no room to retrench, that is to live on a part only of what they now consume. Our society exhibits no appearance of precocity, no symptoms of decay. A long course of continuing improvement is in prospect before us, with no limits which human foresight can descry. Actual liberty and equality with our white population has been approached much nearer than in the free States. Few of our whites ever work as day laborers, none as cooks, scullions, ostlers, body servants, or in other menial capacities. One free citizen does not lord it over another; hence that feeling of independence and equality that distinguishes

---

*Reverend Thomas Malthus was a British economic philosopher who, in 1798, argued that there was a tendency in nature for populations to exceed their means of subsistence and resources, resulting in disease, famine, and other suffering.

From George Fitzhugh, *Sociology for the South, or the Failure of Free Society* (Richmond, Va: A. Morris, 1854), Appendix, pp. 253–255.

us; hence that pride of character, that self-respect, that give us ascendancy when we come in contact with Northerners. It is a distinction to be a Southerner, as it was once to be a Roman citizen. . . .

J. D. B. DeBow Explains Why Nonslaveholders Should Support Slavery, 1860

. . . Having then followed out, step by step, and seen to what amounts the so much paraded competition and conflict between the non-slaveholding and slaveholding interests of the South; I will proceed to present several general considerations which must be found powerful enough to influence the non-slaveholders, if the claims of patriotism were inadequate, to resist any attempt to overthrow the institutions and industry of the section to which they belong.

1. *The non-slaveholder of the South is assured that the remuneration afforded by his labor, over and above the expense of living, is larger than that which is afforded by the same labor in the free States.* To be convinced of this he has only to compare the value of labor in the Southern cities with those of the North, and to take note annually of the large number of laborers who are represented to be out of employment there, and who migrate to our shores, as well as to other sections. No white laborer in return has been forced to leave our midst or remain without employment. Such as have left, have immigrated from States where slavery was less productive. Those who come among us are enabled soon to retire to their homes with a handsome competency. The statement is nearly as true for the agricultural as for other interests, as the statistics will show. . . .

2. *The non-slaveholders, as a class, are not reduced by the necessity of our condition, as is the case in the free States, to find employment in crowded cities and come into competition in close and sickly workshops and factories, with remorseless and untiring machinery.* They have but to compare their condition in this particular with the mining and manufacturing operatives of the North and Europe, to be thankful that God has reserved them for a better fate. Tender women, aged men, delicate children, toil and labor there from early dawn until after candle light, from one year to another, for a miserable pittance, scarcely above the starvation point and without hope of amelioration. The records of British free labor have long exhibited this and those of our own manufacturing States are rapidly reaching it and would have reached it long ago, but for the excessive bounties which in the way of tariffs have been paid to it, without an equivalent by the slaveholding and non-slaveholding laborer of the South. Let this tariff cease to be paid for a single year and the truth of what is stated will be abundantly shown. . . .

[3.] *The non-slaveholder of the South preserves the status of the white man, and is not regarded as an inferior or a dependent.* He is not told that the Declaration of Independence, when it says that all men are born free and equal, refers to the negro equally with himself. It is not proposed to him that the free negro's vote shall weigh

From J. D. B. DeBow, "The Non-Slaveholders of the South," in DeBow et al., *The Interest in Slavery of the Southern Non-Slaveholder. The Right of Secession. Slavery in the Bible.* (Evans and Cogswell, 1860), pp. 3–12. This selection is also available in *Democracy on Trial, 1845–1877* Robert W. Johannsen, ed. (Harcourt, Brace, 1966), pp. 50–54.

equally with his own at the ballot-box, and that the little children of both colors shall be mixed in the classes and benches of the school-house, and embrace each other filially in its outside sports. It never occurs to him, that a white man could be degraded enough to boast in a public assembly, as was recently done in New York, of having actually slept with a negro. And his patriotic ire would crush with a blow the free negro who would dare, in his presence, as is done in the free States, to characterize the father of the country as a "scoundrel." No white man at the South serves another as a body servant, to clean his boots, wait on his table, and perform the menial services of his household. His blood revolts against this, and his necessities never drive him to it. He is a companion and an equal. When in the employ of the slaveholder, or in intercourse with him, he enters his hall, and has a seat at his table. If a distinction exists, it is only that which education and refinement may give, and this is so courteously exhibited as scarcely to strike attention. The poor white laborer at the North is at the bottom of the social ladder, whilst his brother here has ascended several steps and can look down upon those who are beneath him, at an infinite remove.

[4.] *The non-slaveholder knows that as soon as his savings will admit, he can become a slaveholder, and thus relieve his wife from the necessities of the kitchen and the laundry, and his children from the labors of the field.* This, with ordinary frugality, can, in general, be accomplished in a few years, and is a process continually going on. Perhaps twice the number of poor men at the South own a slave to what owned a slave ten years ago. The universal disposition is to purchase. It is the first use for savings, and the negro purchased is the last possession to be parted with. If a woman, her children become heir-looms and make the nucleus of an estate. It is within my knowledge, that a plantation of fifty or sixty persons has been established, from the descendants of a single female, in the course of the lifetime of the original purchaser.

[5.] *The large slaveholders and proprietors of the South begin life in great part as non-slaveholders.* It is the nature of property to change hands. Luxury, liberality, extravagance, depreciated land, low prices, debt, distribution among children, are continually breaking up estates. All over the new States of the Southwest enormous estates are in the hands of men who began life as overseers or city clerks, traders or merchants. Often the overseer marries the widow. Cheap lands, abundant harvests, high prices, give the poor man soon a negro. His ten bales of cotton bring him another, and second crop increases his purchases, and so he goes on opening land and adding labor until in a few years his draft for $20,000 upon his merchant becomes a very marketable commodity. . . .

E S S A Y S

The evaluations of the differences between the sections that were proffered by contemporaries were, of course, part of a propaganda war. The historian's task is to discover the reality behind the polemics. The first selection reprinted here comes from the late Edward Pessen of the City University of New York. He finds that a comparison of the social structures, economic systems, and political practices of the two regions reveals that the similarities outweigh the differences. By contrast, James M. McPherson of Princeton University concludes that the South was very different from the rest of the country, yet was more in step with contemporary European societies than were other areas of the United States.

The Similarities between the Antebellum North and South

EDWARD PESSEN

How different from each other were the North and South before the Civil War? Recent work by historians of antebellum America throws interesting new light on this old question. Since some of these studies deal with individual communities, others with single themes of antebellum life, they are in a sense Pirandelloan pieces of evidence in search of an overarching synthesis that will relate them to one another and to earlier findings and interpretations. My modest hope is that the discussion that follows will be useful to historians in pursuit of such a synthesis.

The terms "North" and "South" are, of course, figures of speech that distort and oversimplify a complex reality, implying homogeneity in geographical sections that, in fact, were highly variegated. Each section embraced a variety of regions and communities that were dissimilar in climatic, topographical, demographic, and social characteristics. If, as Bennett H. Wall has written, "there never has been the 'one' South described by many historians," neither has there been the one North. Historians who have compared the antebellum South and North without referring to the diversity of each have not necessarily been unaware of this diversity. Their premise, in speaking of the North and South, is that the Mason-Dixon line divided two distinctive civilizations, the basic similarities within each of which transcended its internal differences.

The modern discussion is a continuation of a scholarly controversy that has engaged some of the giants of the American historical profession. Charles A. Beard, Ulrich B. Phillips, Allan Nevins, David M. Potter, C. Vann Woodward, and other scholars of stature have been drawn to the theme because it is inextricably related to perhaps the most fascinating of all questions in American history: the causes of the Civil War. Many historians attribute that "irrepressible conflict" to the fundamental differences between the two civilizations that were parties to it. Even those scholars who have played down the role of sectional differences in bringing on the war have found themselves unable to avoid comparing the ways of life and thought of the two belligerents.

Unsurprisingly, the discussion has produced a variety of interpretations. Some scholars have emphasized the similarities of the North and South, a much greater number have stressed their dissimilarities, and others have judiciously alluded to their significant likenesses—"commonalities," in Potter's terminology—and unlikenesses. The greater popularity, among scholars and laity alike, of comparisons that emphasize differences is doubtless due, in part, to the fact that the war heightened our perceptions of those supposedly irreconcilable differences and, in part, to the fact that several dissimilarities were so striking, so unarguable, so obviously significant. While much of the scholarly controversy has concerned subtle sectional distinctions, whether in values, ideals, or other complex intangibles that might be read one way or the other, depending on the predilections of the interpreter, other disparities transcend subjectivity, based as they are on hard, quantifiable evidence.

From "How Different from Each Other Were the Antebellum North and South?" by Edward Pessen, *American Historical Review,* Vol. 85, No. 5, December 1980, pp. 1119–1143, 1147–1149. Reprinted by permission of Edward Pessen, Distinguished Professor of History, Baruch College and the Graduate School at University Center, the City University of New York.

Here were two sections containing roughly equal areas for human settlement. Yet on the eve of the Civil War the population of the North was more than 50 percent greater than that of the South. The most dramatic disparity concerned racial balance: roughly one-quarter of a million Northern blacks comprised slightly more than 1 percent of the Northern population; the more than four million blacks in the South constituted one-third of the Southern population. And almost 95 percent of Southern blacks were slaves. Although the value of agricultural products in the two sections was almost equal, Northern superiority in manufactures, railroad mileage, and commercial profits was overwhelming, far surpassing the Northern advantage in population. Similarly, Northern urban development outdistanced Southern, whether measured by the number of cities or by the size and proportions of the population within them. What did these and other, harder to measure, differences signify? To what extent were they balanced out by important sectional similarities? These are among the questions this essay will consider.

In comparing the great antebellum sections, it is useful to remember that all powerful, complex, and viable contemporaneous societies are likely to converge or be similar in some respects, dissimilar in others. It would be lovely were we able to estimate precisely the relative significance of the various criteria of comparison, the points at which similarities or differences become critical, and the nature of the balance between likenesses and unlikenesses that would justify appraising two societies as "essentially" different or similar. Alas, we cannot. A society or civilization is a complex Gestalt. The subtle reciprocity binding together its elements cannot be understood by mechanically attempting to weigh the significance of each of these elements and then adding up the total. The impossibility of contriving a simplistic calculus for measuring societies does not, of course, mean that a sensible comparison is impossible. It means only that such a comparison will inevitably be subjective and serve, at best, as a point of departure to those who evaluate the evidence differently.

A comprehensive comparison of the two sections would overlook nothing, not even the weather, which, according to Phillips, "has been the chief agency in making the South distinctive." In the space available here I shall focus on what our sociological friends might call three social indicators: (1) the economy, (2) the social structure, and (3) politics and power. In selecting these matters for examination, I do not mean to suggest that they are more important than values, ideals, the life of the mind, or any number of other features of antebellum life. Tangible phenomena may be easier to measure than intangible, but they offer no better clue to the essential character of a place and a people. I emphasize economic, social, and political themes because all of them are clearly important, the evidence on them is substantial, and each has recently been re-examined to interesting effect. [The selection on politics has been omitted.]

The economic practices of each section—one hesitates to call them economic "systems" in the face of the contradictory and largely planless if not improvisatory nature of these practices—were similarly complex. Northerners and Southerners alike made their living primarily in agriculture. Guided by the unique weather and the unequal length of the growing seasons in their sections, Northern and Southern farmers increasingly specialized, but in dissimilar crops. Tobacco and, above all, rice, sugar, and cotton were largely unknown to the North. Yet in the South, as in the North, farmers—whether large or small—sought and for the most part achieved self-sufficiency. They produced more grains and corn than anything else and in both sections raised and kept domestic animals roughly equal in quantity and, it has recently been claimed, comparable in quality. In view of the regularity with which Northern farmers brushed aside the lonely voices in their midst who urged subordination of profits to the "long-range needs of the soil," their money-mindedness in planting wheat (their own great dollar earner) year after year, and their unsentimental readiness to dispose of "family land" so long as the price was right, what Stanley L. Engerman has said about Southern planters seems to apply equally well to Northern agriculturalists: they were certainly not "non-calculating individuals not concerned with money."

The enduring popularity of *Gone with the Wind* suggests that the American popular mind continues to believe that the Old South was a land of large plantations populated by masters both honorable and courtly, cruel and sinful, by Southern belles "beautiful, graceful . . . , bewitching in coquetry, yet strangely steadfast," by loyal, lovable, comic, but sometimes surly Negroes, and by white trash or "po' buckra." American historians have, however, known for at least half a century that the plantation legend "is one of great inaccuracy"—false to the character of Southern society, to the diversity of Southern whites, and to the realities of black life. Great plantations centering on splendid mansions did exist in the Old South but not in very great numbers.

The most distinctive feature of the antebellum Southern economy, as of Southern life as a whole, was, of course, its "peculiar institution." Slavery had not been unknown in the North, flourishing through much of the seventeenth and eighteenth centuries and persisting in New Jersey until 1846. But it had involved relatively few blacks and had had slight effect on Northern life and thought. Northern public opinion, better represented by the authors of the Federal Constitution in 1787 and the Missouri Compromise in 1820 than by the abolitionists of the antebellum decades, accepted slavery, approved of doing business with those who controlled it, abhorred its black victims, and loathed Northern whites who agitated against it. Northern acquiescence in Southern slavery does not erase this most crucial difference between the sections, but it does argue for the complementarity and economic interdependence of North and South.

The profitability and other economic implications of antebellum slavery have become the subjects of intense recent debate, stimulating the development of cliometrics or the new economic history. Since slavery was more than a labor system, historians have also searchingly investigated its noneconomic implications for both blacks and whites. A fair reading of the recent evidence and argument is that, while more slaves by far worked as field hands, slaves also performed with great efficiency a great variety of other jobs, many of them skilled, allowing for significant economic differentiation within the slave community. And, as exemplary workers and as costly and valuable properties, skilled slaves were ordinarily spared gratuitous maltreatment or deprivation. Despite the inevitable brutality of the system, slaves appear to have managed to maintain the integrity of their personalities, customs, values, and family ties.

Several trade unionists in the antebellum North agreed with slavery's apologists that not only the working and living conditions but in some respects the "liberty" enjoyed by Northern hirelings compared unfavorably with the situation of slaves. These were patently self-serving arguments, designed to put the lot of the Northern worker in the worst possible light. The fact remains that the economic gap between enslaved black and free white workers in antebellum South and North was narrower than historians once thought. Evidence bearing on the conditions of white Northern as well as black Southern labor demonstrates that during the middle decades of the nineteenth century the real wages of Northern workingmen declined and their living conditions remained bleak, their job security was reduced, their skills were increasingly devalued, and in many respects their lives became more insecure and precarious.

At mid-century industrial workers in the South as in the North worked primarily in small shops and households rather than in factories. Trade unionists in Baltimore, Louisville, St. Louis, and New Orleans were with few exceptions skilled and semi-skilled white artisans, precisely as they were in Philadelphia, New York, Boston, and Pittsburgh. In Southern as in Northern towns and cities, the least skilled and prestigious jobs were those done preponderantly by Catholic immigrants rather than by older Protestant, ethnic groups. Significantly, the South attracted far fewer of the antebellum era's "new immigrants"—that is, Germans and Irish—than did the North. For all of their smaller numbers in the South, European immigrants played an economic and social role there that was not dissimilar to what it was in the North. Diverse measurable evidence indicates that the pattern of immigrant life in the United States was national, rather than distinctly regional, in character. A similar point can be made about Southern urbanism and manufacturing—namely, quantitative distinctiveness (or deficiency), qualitative similarity to the North. Although the value of Southern manufactured products was usually less than one-fifth of the national total during the antebellum decades, the South was hardly a region devoid of industrial production. Articulate Southerners "crusade[d] to bring the cotton mills to the cotton fields," and, whether due to their exhortations or to the play of market forces, the amount of capital the slave states invested in cotton manufacturing doubled between 1840 and 1860, surpassing their rate of population growth. Because the South nevertheless lagged far behind the Northeast in manufacturing, one influential school of historians has described the antebellum economy—and, for that matter, Southern society as a whole—as noncapitalist, prebourgeois, or "seigneurial."

Some historians have criticized Southern deficiencies in commerce, finance, transportation, and manufacturing as manifestations of economic wrongheadedness and irrationality and have attributed to these deficiencies the South's defeat in the Civil War. A number of modern economic historians, cliometricians for the most part, have interpreted the evidence somewhat differently. Invoking the old argument of "comparative advantage," they have noted that heavy investment in cotton, the nation's great dollar earner in international trade, was hardly irrational, since it enabled the South to equal the national rate of profit during the era. Southerners who did invest in Southern factories got a return that compared favorably with industrial profits elsewhere. (Why, ask the critics, didn't they invest more of their capital that way?) If Southern manufacturing was outdistanced by that in the Northeast, it compared favorably with industrial production in the Northwest and, for that matter, in Continental Europe in the mid-nineteenth century. If the South suffered inordinately in the wake of the financial panics of 1837 and 1839, it was, as Reginald C. McGrane noted long ago, precisely because the South had speculated excessively in transportation projects and land acquisition as well as other investments. The South's "unusually favorable system of navigable streams and rivers" has been cited to explain its lag in railroads. Yet in the 1840s Southern railroads "equalled or exceeded the national average capitalization per mile." The views of many scholars are expressed in Gavin Wright's recent observation that "before the War the South was wealthy, prosperous, expanding geographically, and gaining economically at rates that compared favorably to those of the rest of the country."

Antebellum Northern investors, like their counterparts in the South and in Europe, put their money into American products, industrial and agricultural, solid and flimsy, drawn almost entirely by the profit margin likely to result from their investment. Investors in all latitudes appear to have been indifferent to possible long-range consequences of their financial transactions, acting rather on the principle that the "rational" investment was the one likely to pay off. That the railroads, the diversified industry, and the commercial superiority of the North turned out to have important military implications in the 1860s could hardly have been anticipated by earlier profit-seekers. When the commercial magnates known as the Boston Associates invested heavily in factories built in the new suburbs of Boston, they hardly had in mind outfitting Union troops a generation later; they were much more concerned about maintaining close ties with Southern cotton magnates on whose raw materials they were so heavily dependent. There is something bizarre in historians, more than a century after the event, scrutinizing the economic behavior of antebellum capitalists and subjecting that behavior to unrealistic tests of rationality and farsightedness that these men themselves would have found farfetched.

To argue, however, as several historians have, that a substantial Southern lag— whether in railroad mileage or urban growth—is not as great when it is measured in *per capita* rather than absolute terms explains away rather than explains these fundamental sectional differences. For it can reasonably be maintained that the antebellum South's comparatively small white population (which accounted for its high *per capita* rates) was not due to historical accident but to significant features, if not failings, in Southern civilization. That all differences between two communities indubitably have a historical explanation—be it the smaller population, the hotter climate, or the prevalence of enslaved blacks—in no sense detracts from the significance of those differences. The burden of my argument is not that antebellum economic developments in the states south of the Potomac were almost exactly like, let alone a mirror image of, those in the states north of the river but rather that the economies were similar in significant ways that are often taken for granted, as, for example, in the similar operation of the profit motive or the similarity of the laws of inheritance in the two sections. And even where, as in industrial production and labor systems, the South and North differed most glaringly, modern evidence has reduced and placed in a somewhat different perspective the gulf between them. As for the recent suggestion that the South was not capitalistic, I shall defer comment until I have first dealt with social and political matters, since capitalism concerns more than economic arrangements alone.

only 2 classes

Historians have long known that a society's social structure offers an important clue to its character. The kind of social classes that exist, the gulf between them, their roles in society, the ease or difficulty of access to higher from lower rungs on the social ladder, and the relationships between the classes tell as much about a civilization as do any other phenomena. What distinguishes modern from earlier historians in their treatment of social class is the extent to which they have borrowed from social scientists both in theorizing about class and in the methodology used for measurement. Employing these new approaches, historians have drastically modified earlier notions of antebellum society.

The ancient belief that the white antebellum South consisted of two classes, wealthy planters at the top and a great mass of poor whites below, may continue to command some popular acceptance. That belief has been so long dead among historians, however, that as early as 1946 Fabian Linden could remark that "the debunking of the 'two class' fallacy" had "become the tedious cliché." For, beginning in 1940 and continuing steadily thereafter, Frank L. Owsley and a group of scholars influenced by his work utilized hitherto neglected primary sources to reveal that the most typical white Southerners by far were small farmers working the modest acreage they owned with few, if any, slaves.

The too neat portrait that the Owsley school drew of the white Southern social structure was quite similar to the picture of *Northern* society accepted by historians less than a generation ago. The white population was ostensibly composed primarily of the great "middling orders," hard-working, proud, and not unprosperous farmers for the most part, whose chance to rise even higher socially matched the opportunities an increasingly democratic society gave them to exert political influence and power. Small groups of rich men—great planters in the one clime and merchants and industrialists in the other—occupied the highest social plateau; professionals who served the rich were slightly above the middle, which was occupied by small business people and independent farmers, skilled artisans, and clerks; and below them stood industrial and landless agricultural laborers. Since class is determined not by bread alone, blacks—whether slave or free and regardless of how much individuals among them had managed to accumulate—were universally relegated to the lowest levels of the social structure, scorned even by white vagrants and frequently unemployed workers, urban and rural, who constituted America's equivalent of a propertyless proletariat.

The achievement of recent research is its transformation of what was a rather blurred image of social groups, whose membership and possessions were both unclear, into a more sharply focused picture. By digging deeper, particularly in nineteenth-century data on wealth and property, historians have come close to knowing the numbers of families belonging to different wealth strata and the amount of wealth these families owned. The beauty of the new evidence on who and how many owned what and how much is that in the antebellum era wealth appears to have been the surest sign of social, as well as of economic, position. Antebellum wealth was almost invariably made in socially acceptable ways. Modern scholars have found that "the social divisions of antebellum America were essentially wealth-holding categories." The upper class did not comprise so much the families who "controlled the means of production" as it did the families who "controlled the vast wealth created largely through the exchange of goods produced." Degree of wealth was the surest sign of the quality of housing, furnishings, and household goods a family could afford, of its style of living and uses of leisure, and of the social circle within which it moved and its individual members married. Gathering from the manuscript census schedules, probate inventories, and tax assessors' reports statistically valid samples or, in some cases, evidence on every family in the community under study, modern scholars have been able to arrange the antebellum Southern and Northern populations on a wealth-holding scale. While it is close to a statistical inevitability that the distribution of wealth in the South and North would not be precisely the same, the most striking feature of the evidence is how similarly wealth was distributed—or maldistributed—in the two sections.

On the eve of the Civil War one-half of the free adult males in both the South and the North held less than 1 percent of the real and personal property. In contrast, the richest 1 percent owned 27 percent of the wealth. Turning from the remarkable similarity in sectional patterns of wealth-holding at the bottom and the very top, the richest 5 to 10 percent of propertyowners controlled a somewhat greater share of the South's wealth, while what might be called the upper middle deciles (those below the top tenth) held a slightly smaller share in the North. The South also came close to monopolizing wealthy counties, the per capita wealth of which was $4,000 or more and, despite its smaller population, the South, according to the 1860 census, contained almost two-thirds of those persons in the nation whose worth was at least $110,000. According to Lee Soltow, the leading student of this evidence, these sectional disparities "could be attributed almost entirely to slave values. . . . If one could eliminate slave market value from the distribution of wealth in 1860 . . . , the inequality levels in the North and South were similar."

In view of the centrality of slavery to the antebellum South, it is idle to speak of "eliminating the market value" of slaves from the sectional comparison. Northern free labor, rural and industrial, also represented a form of "sectional wealth," if a much overlooked form. Although as individual human beings they did not add to their own private wealth or to the wealth of the employers they served, their labor created wealth for themselves and for these same capitalists at rates of productivity that, I believe, even Robert W. Fogel and Stanley L. Engerman would concede compared favorably with the rates of the most efficient slaves. In other words, the North had access to a form of wealth, free labor, that was roughly as valuable per capita as was slave wealth, however absent this Northern wealth was from the reports prepared by census takers and assessors. Given the known habits of these officials to overlook small property holdings—precisely the kind of holdings that would have been owned by Northern working people—and to accept as true the lies people swore to as their worth, it is likely that the fairly substantial cumulative wealth owned by small farmers and modest wage earners was almost entirely omitted from the wealth equation. Such groups were far more numerous in the North than in the South. Had slaves been treated as part of the potential property-owning Southern population to which they actually belonged, instead of being treated as property pure and simple, the total wealth of the antebellum South would have been diminished by several billion dollars: the product of multiplying the number of slaves by the average market price of almost $1,000 per slave. The addition of nearly four million very poor black people to the number of potential propertyowners in the South would have increased its rate of inequality (and the Gini coefficient of concentration that measures it), although not everywhere to the same extent.

Wealth in both sections was distributed more equally—perhaps the more apt phrase is less unequally—in the countryside than in towns and cities. While the rural North has been less intensively investigated than its Southern counterpart, enough research has been completed to disclose that the North was hardly a haven of egalitarian distribution of property. Rural Wisconsin (which had a Gini coefficient of inequality as high as that of antebellum Texas), the Michigan frontier, and northwestern New York State were centers of inequality and poverty. At mid-century, the proportion of white men who owned land in any amount was substantially lower in the Northwest than in the South. The percentage of free males owning land in the North as a whole was slightly smaller than in the South. Owing to the absence of slaves and to the relative paucity of very large farms, wealth was somewhat less unequally distributed in the rural North than in the South.

In investigating the distribution of wealth in the antebellum rural South, scholars have probed data on different states, counties, and regions. The patterns throughout are remarkably similar, whether for wealth in general, land and real estate, or personal and slave property. Accentuating the maldistribution of landed wealth—whether in Alabama, Mississippi, Louisiana, Texas, the "cotton South," or the agricultural South as a whole— was a fact of life that the Owsley school neglected: the dollar value per acre of large farms owned by slave-owning planters was substantially greater than the value per acre of the small farm. And yet, regardless of the nature of the soil or the proportion of large farms in a given region, the rates of wealth concentration were remarkably similar as well as constant during the decades before the war. Paralleling the recent finding that in antebellum Texas, no matter what the differences were "in climate, soil, and extent of settlement, the most striking fact is . . . the high degree of concentration in wealthholding across all the regions," another recent study reports no great differences in "the degree of inequality" between the cotton South and the other "major agricultural regions" of grain, tobacco, sugar, and rice production in 1860.

The distribution of slave wealth closely followed the pattern of other forms of Southern wealth. During the decade before the war, slaveownership was confined to between 20 and 25 percent of white families, and maldistribution of this form of property was the rule within the slave-owning population. Half of all slaveowners owned five or fewer slaves, with only one-tenth owning the twenty or more slaves that by Ulrich B. Phillips' definition made them "planters." Less than one-half of 1 percent owned one hundred or more slaves. As with other forms of wealth, the concentration of slave wealth increased slightly between 1850 and 1860.

While the South had long lagged behind the North in urban development, recent scholarship has unearthed evidence that Southern cities grew at a remarkable rate during the antebellum decades. If the Southern rate of urban expansion still did not match the Northern quantitatively, Southern cities, old and new, were qualitatively not unlike their Northern counterparts. Antebellum cities in all latitudes were amazingly similar in the roles they played in the political, administrative, financial, economic, artistic, and intellectual affairs of their regions. Antebellum cities were also alike in the types of men who ran them, in the underlying social philosophies guiding those men, and in their "social configurations." Not the least of the similarities of cities in both great sections was in their distribution of wealth.

Three things can be said about the distribution of wealth in the towns and cities of the Old South. Property ownership was even more concentrated there than in rural areas. Riches became more unequally distributed with the passage of time, with the proportion of the propertyless increasing sharply between 1850 and 1860. There was an increase too in the proportion of urban wealth owned by the largest wealthholders—at least for the dozen communities measured to date. And the patterns of wealth distribution in Southern cities were very much like those that obtained in the North.

The pattern of wealth distribution in Providence and Newport (Rhode Island), Pelham and Ware (Massachusetts), Newark, Pittsburgh, Cleveland, Milwaukee, the great cities on the Northeastern seaboard, and a dozen other Northern urban centers was impressively consistent and glaringly unequal. The sharp maldistribution of the 1820s and 1830s became more widely skewed with the passage of time (the Gini coefficients of inequality for 1860 matched those prevalent in the South). On the eve of the Civil War, the wealth of most cities, while greatly augmented, was "less widely dispersed than it had been earlier"; the propertyless groups in Stonington (Connecticut) and Chicago, for example, comprised between two-thirds and three-fourths of all households by the outbreak of the war.

Nor do sectional rates of vertical mobility appear to have been much different. In 1856 Cassius M. Clay told an Ohio audience that "the northern laboring man could, and frequently did, rise above the condition [into] which he was born to the first rank of society and wealth," but he "never knew such an instance in the South." Recently unearthed evidence on the social origins of the men in the "first rank" does not sustain Clay's surmise, so popular with contemporary yeasayers. In the South, "increasing barriers to slaveownership resulting from higher slave prices and the growing concentration of wealth" left "lesser planters," not to mention laboring men, with their "aspiration thwarted." And in the North—whether in Wayne County (Michigan), Newport, Stonington, small towns in Massachusetts, Chicago, and Brooklyn, or the great cities of New York, Boston, and Philadelphia—eminent and rich men of humble birth were a rarity. Evidence on the more likely movement from a lower social position to an adjacent one, rather than to the very top, remains in pitifully short supply. In antebellum Philadelphia, small New England counties, and rural Georgia, even the modest movement from one plebian level to another appears to have seldom occurred.

Throwing important, if indirect, light on the relatively slight opportunities for upward social and economic movement antebellum America offered to poor or economically marginal men is the era's high rate of physical or geographical mobility. In rural as well as urban communities, in large cities and small, and on both sides of the Mason-Dixon line, armies of footloose Americans were on the move, following trails never dreamed of in the Turner thesis. One-half of the residents, primarily the poorer and propertyless, left those communities from one decade to another in their search for a more acceptable living. I have no doubt that future research will yet disclose that, during what was a period of economic expansion in both sections, significant numbers of Americans improved their lot, even if modestly. To date, however, the data reveal equally slight rates of social mobility and high rates of geographical mobility on both sides of the Mason-Dixon line.

Carl Degler has recently observed that Southern society "differed from northern in that the social hierarchy culminated in the planter, not the industrialist." At mid-century, great Northern fortunes, in fact, owed more to commerce and finance than to manufacturing. What is perhaps more important is that a sharply differentiated social hierarchy obtained in both sections. In Degler's phrase, planter status was "the ideal to which other white southerners aspired." A good case can be made for the equally magnetic attraction that exalted merchant status had for Northerners. If the fragmentary evidence on Virginia, Georgia, and the Carolinas, which Jane H. Pease has so effectively exploited, is any indication, then great planters lived less sybaritically and consumed less conspicuously than historians have previously thought. If Philip Hone's marvelous diary—two dozen full-to-the-brim volumes of life among the swells during the antebellum decades—has broader implication, then the Northeastern social and economic elite commanded a lifestyle of an elegance and costliness that, among other things, proved irresistibly attractive to the aristocratic Southerners who graced Hone's table, pursued diversion with other members of Hone's set, and married into its families—the Gardiners, Coolidges, Coldens, Bayards, Gouverneurs, and Kortrights.

That the social structures of the antebellum South and North were in some important respects similar does not, of course, make them carbon copies of one another. In this as in other respects the chief difference between the sections was that one of them harbored a huge class of enslaved blacks. John C. Calhoun, James H. Hammond, George Fitzhugh, and other influential Southern champions of white supremacy never ceased reminding their antebellum audiences, therefore, that in the South "the two great divisions of society [were] not the rich and the poor, but white and black, and all the former, the poor as well as the rich, belong to the upper classes." Several historians have recently agreed that great planters and small white farmers in the South shared common interests, for all the disparity in their condition. The interests of the different social classes will be considered in the discussion of influence and power that follows. Whatever these interests may have been, Southern whites, rural and urban, lived as did Northerners—in a stratified society marked by great inequalities in status, material condition, and opportunity. . . .

The striking similarities of the two antebellum sections of the nation neither erase their equally striking dissimilarities nor detract from the significance of these dissimilarities. Whether in climate, diet, work habits, uses of leisure, speech and diction, health and disease, mood, habits, ideals, self-image, or labor systems, profound differences separated the antebellum North and South. One suspects that antebellum Americans regarded these matters as the vital stuff of life. The point need not be labored that a society, one-third of whose members were slaves (and slaves of a distinctive "race"), is most unlike a society of free men and women. An essay focusing on these rather than on the themes emphasized here would highlight the vital disparities between the antebellum South and North. And yet the striking dissimilarities of the two antebellum sections do not erase their equally striking similarities, nor do they detract from the significance of these similarities.

The antebellum North and South were far more alike than the conventional scholarly wisdom has led us to believe. Beguiled by the charming version of Northern society and politics composed by Tocqueville, the young Marx, and other influential antebellum commentators, historians have until recently believed that the Northern social structure was far more egalitarian and offered far greater opportunity for upward social movement than did its Southern counterpart and that white men of humble position had far more power in the Old North than they did in the Old South. In disclosing that the reality of the antebellum North fell far short of the egalitarian ideal, modern studies of social structure sharply narrow the gulf between the antebellum North and South. Without being replicas of one another, both sections were relatively rich, powerful, aggressive, and assertive communities, socially stratified and governed by equally—and disconcertingly—oligarchic internal arrangements. That they were drawn into the most terrible of all American wars may have been due, as is often the case when great powers fight, as much to their similarities as to their differences. The war owed more, I believe, to the inevitably opposed but similarly selfish interests—or perceived interests—of North and South than to differences in their cultures and institutions.

It is a commonplace in the history of international politics that nations and societies quite similar to one another in their political, social, and economic arrangements have nevertheless gone to war, while nations profoundly different from one another in their laws of property or their fundamental moral and philosophical beliefs have managed to remain at peace. The Peloponnesian War, which, like the American Civil War, was a bitter and protracted struggle between two branches of the same people whose societies were in vital respects dissimilar from one another, appears to have owed little to these differences. In Thucydides' great account, Athens and the Athenians were profoundly unlike Sparta and the Lacedæ monians, whether in "national" character, wealth, economic life, ideals and values, system of justice, attitudes toward freedom, or life-style. But to Thucydides, as to the leading spokesmen for the two sides, these dissimilarities were one thing, the causes of the war quite another. Athens and Sparta fell out primarily because both were great imperial powers. "The real cause of the war," concluded Thucydides, "was formally . . . kept out of sight. The growth of the power of Athens and the alarm which this inspired in Lacedæmon, made war inevitable." None of this is to say that sectional differences had no influence whatever on the actions of those influential men that in April 1861 culminated in the outbreak of the American Civil War. The point rather is that, insofar as the Peloponnesian War throws any light whatever on the matter, wars between strikingly dissimilar antagonists break out not necessarily because of their differences, important as these are, but because of their equally significant similarities.

Late in the Civil War, William King of Cobb County, Georgia, reported that invading Union officers had told him, "We are one people, [with] the same language, habits, and religion, and ought to be one people." The officers might have added that on the spiritual plane Southerners shared with Northerners many ideals and aspirations and had contributed heavily to those historical experiences the memory and symbols of which tie a people together as a nation. For all of their distinctiveness, the Old South and North were complementary elements in an American society that was everywhere primarily rural, capitalistic, materialistic, and socially stratified, racially, ethnically, and religiously heterogeneous, and stridently chauvinistic and expansionist—a society whose practice fell far short of, when it was not totally in conflict with, its lofty theory.

The Differences between the Antebellum North and South

JAMES M. McPHERSON

The notion of American Exceptionalism has received quite a drubbing since the heyday of the exceptionalist thesis among the consensus school of historians in the 1950s. Interpreters of the American experience then argued that something special about the American experience—whether it was abundance, free land on the frontier, the absence of a feudal past, exceptional mobility and the relative lack of class conflict, or the pragmatic and consensual liberalism of our politics—set the American people apart from the rest of mankind. Historians writing since the 1950s, by contrast, have demonstrated the existence of class and class conflict, ideological politics, land speculation, and patterns of economic and industrial development similar to those of Western Europe which placed the United States in the mainstream of modern North Atlantic history, not on a special and privileged fringe.

If the theme of American Exceptionalism has suffered heavy and perhaps irreparable damage, the idea of Southern Exceptionalism still flourishes—though also subjected to repeated challenges. In this essay, "Southern Exceptionalism" refers to the belief that the South has "possessed a separate and unique identity . . . which appeared to be out of the mainstream of American experience." Or as Quentin Compson (in William Faulkner's

From James M. McPherson, "Antebellum Southern Exceptionalism: A New Look at an Old Question," *Civil War History,* Volume 29, #3, 1983, pp. 230–244. Copyright © 1983. Reprinted by permission of The Kent State University Press.

Absalom, Absalom!) expressed it in a reply to his Canadian-born college roommate's question about what made Southerners tick: "You can't understand it. You would have to be born there." . . .

Many antebellum Americans certainly thought that North and South had evolved separate societies with institutions, interests, values, and ideologies so incompatible, so much in deadly conflict that they could no longer live together in the same nation. Traveling through the South in the spring of 1861, London *Times* correspondent William Howard Russell encountered this Conflict of Civilizations theme everywhere he went. "The tone in which [Southerners] alluded to the whole of the Northern people indicated the clear conviction that trade, commerce, the pursuit of gain, manufacture, and the base mechanical arts, had so degraded the whole race" that Southerners could no longer tolerate association with them, wrote Russell. "There is a degree of something like ferocity in the Southern mind [especially] toward New England which exceeds belief." A South Carolinian told Russell: "We are an agricultural people, pursuing our own system, and working out our own destiny, breeding up women and men with some other purpose than to make them vulgar, fanatical, cheating Yankees." Louis Wigfall of Texas, a former U.S. senator, told Russell: "We are a peculiar people, sir! . . . We are an agricultural people. . . . We have no cities—we don't want them. . . . We want no manufactures: we desire no trading, no mechanical or manufacturing classes. . . . As long as we have our rice, our sugar, our tobacco, and our cotton, we can command wealth to purchase all we want. . . . But with the Yankees we will never trade—never. Not one pound of cotton shall ever go from the South to their accursed cities."

Such opinions were not universal in the South, of course, but in the fevered atmosphere of the late 1850s they were widely shared. "Free Society!" exclaimed a Georgia newspaper. "We sicken at the name. What is it but a conglomeration of greasy mechanics, filthy operatives, small-fisted farmers, and moon-struck theorists . . . hardly fit for association with a southern gentleman's body servant." In 1861 the *Southern Literary Messenger* explained to its readers: "It is not a question of slavery alone that we are called upon to decide. It is free society which we must shun or embrace." In the same year Charles Colcock Jones, Jr.—no fire-eater, for after all he had graduated from Princeton and from Harvard Law School—spoke of the development of antagonistic cultures in North and South: "In this country have arisen two races [i.e., Northerners and Southerners] which, although claiming a common parentage, have been so entirely separated by climate, by morals, by religion, and by estimates so totally opposite to all that constitutes honor, truth, and manliness, that they cannot longer exist under the same government."

Spokesmen for the free-labor ideology—which had become the dominant political force in the North by 1860—reciprocated these sentiments. The South, said Theodore Parker, was "the foe to Northern Industry—to our mines, our manufactures, and our commerce. . . . She is the foe to our institutions—to our democratic politics in the State, our democratic culture in the school, our democratic work in the community, our democratic equality in the family." Slavery, said William H. Seward, undermined "intelligence, vigor, and energy" in both blacks and whites. It produced "an exhausted soil, old and decaying towns, wretchedly neglected roads . . . an absence of enterprise and improvement." Slavery was therefore "incompatible with all . . . the elements of the security, welfare, and greatness of nations." The struggle between free labor and slavery, between North and South, said Seward in his most famous speech, was "an irrepressible conflict between two opposing and enduring forces." The United States was therefore two nations, but it could not remain forever so: it "must and will, sooner or later, become either entirely a slaveholding nation, or entirely a free-labor nation." Abraham Lincoln expressed exactly the same theme in his House Divided speech. Many other Republicans echoed this argument that the struggle, in the words of an Ohio congressman, was "between systems, between civilizations."

These sentiments were no more confined to fire-breathing Northern radicals than were Southern exceptionalist viewpoints confined to fire-eaters. Lincoln represented the mainstream of his party, which commanded a majority of votes in the North by 1860. The dominant elements in the North and in the lower South believed the United States to be composed of two incompatible civilizations. Southerners believed that survival of their special civilization could be assured only in a separate nation. The creation of the Confederacy was merely a political ratification of an irrevocable separation that had already taken place in the hearts and minds of the people.

The proponents of an assimilationist rather than exceptionalist interpretation of Southern history might object that this concept of a separate and unique South existed *only* in hearts and minds. It was a subjective reality, they might argue, not an objective one. Objectively, they would insist, North and South were one people. They shared the same language, the same Constitution, the same legal system, the same commitment to republican political institutions, an interconnected economy, the same predominantly Protestant religion and British ethnic heritage, the same history, the same shared memories of a common struggle for nationhood.

Two recent proponents of the objective similarity thesis are [the late] Edward Pessen and the late David Potter. In a long article entitled "How Different from Each Other Were the Antebellum North and South?" Pessen concludes that they "were far more alike than the conventional scholarly wisdom has led us to believe." His evidence for this conclusion consists mainly of quantitative measures of the distribution of wealth and of the socioeconomic status of political officeholders in North and South. He finds that wealth was distributed in a similarly unequal fashion in both sections, that voting requirements were similar, and that voters in both sections elected a similarly disproportionate number of men from the upper economic strata to office. The problem with this argument, of course, is that it could be used to prove many obviously different societies to be similar. France and Germany in 1914 and in 1932 had about the same distribution of wealth and similar habits of electing men from the upper strata to the Assembly or the Reichstag. England and France had a comparable distribution of wealth during most of the eighteenth century. Turkey and Russia were not dissimilar in these respects in the nineteenth century. And so on.

David Potter's contention that commonalities of language, religion, law, and political system outweighed differences in other areas is more convincing than the Pessen argument. But the Potter thesis nevertheless begs some important questions. The same similarities prevailed between England and her North American colonies in 1776, but they did not prevent the development of a separate nationalism in the latter. It is not language or law alone that are important, but the uses to which they are put. In the United States of the 1850s, Northerners and Southerners spoke the same language, to be sure, but they were increasingly using this language to revile each other. Language became an instrument of division, not unity. The same was true of the political system. So also of the law: Northern states passed personal liberty laws to defy a national Fugitive Slave

Law supported by the South; a Southern-dominated Supreme Court denied the right of Congress to exclude slavery from the territories, a ruling that most Northerners considered an infamous distortion of the Constitution. As for a shared commitment to Protestantism, this too had become a divisive rather than unifying factor, with the two largest denominations—Methodist and Baptist—having split into hostile Southern and Northern churches over the question of slavery, and the third largest—Presbyterian—having split partly along sectional lines and partly on the question of slavery. As for a shared historical commitment to republicanism, by the 1850s this too was more divisive than unifying. Northern Republicans interpreted this commitment in a free-soil context, while most Southerners continued to insist that one of the most cherished tenets of republican liberty was the right of property—including property in slaves.

There is another dimension of the Potter thesis—or perhaps it would be more accurate to call it a separate Potter thesis—that might put us on the right track to solving the puzzle of Southern exceptionalism. After challenging most notions of Southern distinctiveness, Potter concluded that the principal characteristic distinguishing the South from the rest of the country was the persistence of a "folk culture" in the South. This gemeinschaft society, with its emphasis on tradition, rural life, close kinship ties, a hierarchical social structure, ascribed status, patterns of deference, and masculine codes of honor and chivalry, persisted in the South long after the North began moving toward a gesellschaft society with its impersonal, bureaucratic meritocratic, urbanizing, commercial, industrializing, mobile, and rootless characteristics. Above all, the South's folk culture valued tradition and stability and felt threatened by change; the North's modernizing culture enshrined change as progress and condemned the South as backward.

A critic of this gemeinschaft-gesellschaft dichotomy might contend that it was more myth than reality. One might respond to such criticism by pointing out that human behavior is often governed more by myth—that is, by people's perceptions of the world—than by objective reality. Moreover, there *were* real and important differences between North and South by the mid-nineteenth century, differences that might support the gemeinschaft-gesellschaft contrast.

The North was more urban than the South and was urbanizing at a faster rate. In 1820, 10 percent of the free-state residents lived in urban areas compared with 5 percent in the slave states; by 1860 the figures were 26 percent and 10 percent, respectively. Even more striking was the growing contrast between farm and non-farm occupations in the two sections. In 1800, 82 percent of the Southern labor force worked in agriculture compared with 68 percent in the free states. By 1860 the Northern share had dropped to 40 percent while the Southern proportion had actually increased slightly, to 84 percent. Southern agriculture remained traditionally labor-intensive while Northern agriculture became increasingly capital-intensive and mechanized. By 1860 the free states had nearly twice the value of farm machinery per acre and per farm worker as the slave states. And the pace of industrialization in the North far outstripped that in the South. In 1810 the slave states had an estimated 31 percent of the capital invested in manufacturing in the United States; by 1840 this had declined to 20 percent and by 1860 to 16 percent. In 1810 the North had two and a half times the amount per capita invested in manufacturing as the South; by 1860 this had increased to three and a half times as much.

A critic of the inferences drawn from these data might point out that in many respects the differences between the free states east and west of the Appalachians were nearly or virtually as great as those between North and South, yet these differences did not produce a sense of separate nationality in East and West. This point is true—as far as it goes. While the western free states at midcentury did have a higher proportion of workers employed in non-farm occupations than the South, they had about the same percentage of urban population and the same amount per capita invested in manufacturing. But the crucial factor was *the rate of change.* The West was urbanizing and industrializing more rapidly than either the Northeast or the South. Therefore while North and South as a whole were growing relatively farther apart, the eastern and western free states were drawing closer together. This frustrated Southern hopes for an alliance with the Old Northwest on grounds of similarity of agrarian interests. From 1840 to 1860 the rate of urbanization in the West was three times greater than in the Northeast and four times greater than in the South. The amount of capital invested in manufacturing grew twice as fast in the West as in the Northeast and nearly three times as fast as in the South. The same was true of employment in non-farm occupations. The railroad-building boom of the 1850s tied the Northwest to the Northeast with links of iron and shifted the dominant pattern of inland trade from a North-South to an East-West orientation. The remarkable growth of cities like Chicago, Cincinnati, Cleveland, and Detroit with their farm-machinery, food-processing, machine-tool, and railroad-equipment industries fore-shadowed the emergence of the industrial Midwest and helped to assure that when the crisis of the Union came in 1861 the West joined the East instead of the South.

According to the most recent study of antebellum Southern industry, the Southern lag in this category of development resulted not from any inherent economic disadvan-tages—not shortage of capital, nor low rates of return, nor non-adaptability of slave labor—but from the choices of Southerners who had money to invest it in agriculture and slaves rather than in manufacturing. In the 1780s Thomas Jefferson had praised farmers as the "peculiar deposit for substantial and genuine virtue" and warned against the industrial classes in cities as sores on the body politic. In 1860 many Southern leaders still felt the same way; as Louis Wigfall put it in the passage quoted earlier, "we want no manufactures; we desire no trading, no mechanical or manufacturing classes."

Partly as a consequence of this attitude, the South received only a trickle of the great antebellum stream of immigration. Fewer than one-eighth of the immigrants settled in slave states, where the foreign-born percentage of the population was less than a fourth of the North's percentage. The South's white population was ethnically more homoge-neous and less cosmopolitan than the North's. The traditional patriarchal family and tight kinship networks typical of gemeinschaft societies, reinforced in the South by a relatively high rate of cousin marriages, also persisted much more strongly in the nineteenth-century South than in the North.

The greater volume of immigration to the free states contributed to the faster rate of population growth there than in the South. Another factor in this differential growth rate was out-migration from the South. During the middle decades of the nineteenth century, twice as many whites left the South for the North as vice versa. These facts did not go unnoticed at the time; indeed, they formed the topic of much public comment. North-erners cited the differential in population growth as evidence for the superiority of the free-labor system; Southerners perceived it with alarm as evidence of their declining minority status in the nation. These perceptions became important factors in the growing sectional self-consciousness that led to secession.

The most crucial demographic difference between North and South, of course, resulted from slavery. Ninety-five percent of the country's black people lived in the slave states, where blacks constituted one-third of the population in contrast to their one percent of the Northern population. The implications of this for the economy and social structure of the two sections, not to mention their ideologies and politics, are obvious and require little elaboration here. Two brief points are worth emphasizing, however. First, historians in recent years have discovered the viability of Afro-American culture under slavery. They have noted that black music, folklore, speech patterns, religion, and other manifestations of this culture influenced white society in the South. Since the Afro-American culture was preeminently a folk culture with an emphasis on oral tradition and other non-literate forms of ritual and communication, it reinforced the persistence of a traditional, gemeinschaft, folk-oriented society in the South.

Second, a number of recent historians have maintained that Northerners were as committed to white supremacy as Southerners. This may have been true, but the scale of concern with this matter in the South was so much greater as to constitute a different order of magnitude and to contribute more than any other factor to the difference between North and South. And of course slavery was more than an institution of racial control. Its centrality to many aspects of life focused Southern politics almost exclusively on defense of the institution—to the point that, in the words of the *Charleston Mercury* in 1858, "on the subject of slavery . . . the North and South . . . are not only two Peoples, but they are rival, hostile Peoples."

The fear that slavery was being hemmed in and threatened with destruction contributed to the defensive-aggressive style of Southern political behavior. This aggressiveness sometimes took physical form. Southern whites were more likely to carry weapons and to use them against other human beings than Northerners were. The homicide rate was higher in the South. The phenomenon of dueling persisted longer there. Bertram Wyatt-Brown attributes this to the unique Southern code of honor based on traditional patriarchal values of courtesy, status, courage, family, and the symbiosis of shame and pride. The enforcement of order through the threat and practice of violence also resulted from the felt need to control a large slave population.

Martial values and practices were more pervasive in the South than in the North. Marcus Cunliffe has argued to the contrary, but the evidence confutes him. Cunliffe's argument is based mainly on two sets of data: the prevalence of militia and volunteer military companies in the free as well as in the slave states; and the proportion of West Pointers and regular army officers from the two sections. Yet the first set of data does not support his thesis, and the second contradicts it. Cunliffe does present evidence on the popularity of military companies in Northern cities, but nowhere does he estimate the comparative numbers of such companies in North and South or the number of men in proportion to population who belonged to them. If such comparative evidence could be assembled, it would probably support the traditional view of a higher concentration of such companies in the South. What Northern city, for example, could compare with Charleston, which had no fewer than twenty-two military companies in the late 1850s— one for every two hundred white men of military age? Another important quasi-military institution in the South with no Northern counterpart escaped Cunliffe's attention—the slave patrol, which gave tens of thousands of Southerners a more practical form of military experience than the often ceremonial functions of volunteer drill companies could do.

As for the West Point alumni and regular army officers it is true, as Cunliffe points out, that about 60 percent of these were from the North and only 40 percent from the South in the late antebellum decades. What he fails to note is that the South had only about 30 percent of the nation's white population during this era, so that on a proportional basis the South was overrepresented in these categories. Moreover, from 1849 to 1861 all of the secretaries of war were Southerners, as were the general in chief of the army, two of the three brigadier generals, all but one commander of the army's geographical departments of the eve of the Civil War, the authors of the two manuals on infantry tactics and of the artillery manual used at West Point, and the professor who taught tactics and strategy at the military academy.

Other evidence supports the thesis of a significant martial tradition in the South contrasted with a concentration in different professions in the North. More than three-fifths of the volunteer soldiers in the Mexican War came from the slave states—on a per capita basis, four times the proportion of free-state volunteers. Seven of the eight military "colleges" (not including West Point and Annapolis) listed in the 1860 census were in the slave states. A study of the occupations of antebellum men chronicled in the *Dictionary of American Biography* found that the military profession claimed twice the percentage of Southerners as of Northerners, while this ratio was reversed for men distinguished in literature, art, medicine, and education. In business the per capita proportion of Yankees was three times as great, and among engineers and inventors it was six times as large. When Southerners labeled themselves a nation of warriors and Yankees a nation of shopkeepers—a common comparison in 1860—or when Jefferson Davis told a London *Times* correspondent in 1861 that "we are a military people," they were not just whistling Dixie.

One final comparison of objective differences is in order—a comparison of education and literacy in North and South. Contemporaries perceived this as a matter of importance. The South's alleged backwardness in schooling and its large numbers of illiterates framed one of the principal free-soil indictments of slavery. This was one area in which a good many Southerners admitted inferiority and tried to do something about it. But in 1860, after a decade of school reform in the South, the slave states still had only half the North's proportion of white children enrolled in public and private schools, and the length of the annual school term in the South was only a little more than half as long as in the North. Of course education did not take place solely in school. But other forms of education—in the home, at church, through lyceums and public lectures, by apprenticeship, and so on—were also more active in North than South. According to the census of 1860, per capita newspaper circulation was three times greater in the North, and the number of library volumes per white person was nearly twice as large.

The proportion of illiterate white people was three times greater in the South than in the North; if the black population is included, as indeed it should be, the percentage of illiterates was seven or eight times as high in the South. In the free states, what two recent historians have termed an "ideology of literacy" prevailed—a commitment to education as an instrument of social mobility, economic prosperity, progress, and freedom. While this ideology also existed in the South, especially in the 1850s, it was much weaker there and made slow headway against the inertia of a rural folk culture. "The Creator did not intend that every individual human being should be highly cultivated," wrote William Harper of South Carolina. "It is better that a part should be fully and highly educated and the rest utterly ignorant." Commenting on a demand by

Northern workingmen for universal public education, the *Southern Review* asked: "Is this the way to produce producers? To make every child in the state a literary character would not be a good qualification for those who must live by manual labor."

The ideology of literacy in the North was part of a larger ferment which produced an astonishing number of reform movements that aroused both contempt and fear in the South; Southern whites viewed the most dynamic of these movements—abolitionism— as a threat to their very existence. Southerners came to distrust the whole concept of "progress" as it seemed to be understood in the North. *DeBow's Review* declared in 1851: "Southern life, habits, thoughts, and aims, are so essentially different from those of the North, that here a different character of books . . . and training is required." A Richmond newspaper warned in 1855 that Southerners must stop reading Northern newspapers and books and stop sending their sons to colleges in the North, where "every village has its press and its lecture room, and each lecturer and editor, unchecked by a healthy public opinion, opens up for discussion all the received dogmas of faith," where unwary youth are "exposed to the danger of imbibing doctrines subversive of all old institutions." Young men should be educated instead in the South "where their training would be moral, religious, and conservative, and they would never learn, or read a word in school or out of school, inconsistent with orthodox Christianity, pure morality, the right of property, and sacredness of marriage."

In all of the areas discussed above—urbanization, industrialization, labor force, demographic structure, violence and martial values, education, and attitudes toward change—contemporaries accurately perceived significant differences between North and South, differences that in most respects were increasing over time. The question remains: were these differences crucial enough to make the South an exception to generalizations about antebellum America?

This essay concludes by suggesting a tentative answer to the question: perhaps it was the *North* that was "different," the North that departed from the mainstream of historical development; and perhaps therefore we should speak not of Southern excep- tionalism but of Northern exceptionalism. This idea is borrowed shamelessly from C. Vann Woodward, who applied it, however, to the post–Civil War United States. In essays written during the 1950s on "The Irony of Southern History" and "The Search for Southern Identity," Woodward suggested that, unlike other Americans but like most people in the rest of the world, Southerners had experienced poverty, failure, defeat, and had a skepticism about "progress" that grows out of such experiences. The South thus shared a bond with the rest of humankind that other Americans did not share. This theme of Northern exceptionalism might well be applied also to the antebellum United States— not for Woodward's categories of defeat, poverty, and failure, but for the categories of a persistent folk culture discussed in this essay.

At the beginning of the republic the North and South were less different in most of these categories than they became later. Nearly all Northern states had slavery in 1776, and the institution persisted in some of them for decades thereafter. The ethnic homoge- neity of Northern and Southern whites was quite similar before 1830. The proportion of urban dwellers was similarly small and the percentage of the labor force employed in agriculture similarly large in 1800. The Northern predominance in commerce and manufacturing was not so great as it later became. Nor was the contrast in education and literacy as great as it subsequently became. A belief in progress and commitments to reform or radicalism were no more prevalent in the North than in the South in 1800—

indeed, they may have been less so. In 1776, in 1800, even as late as 1820, similarity in values and institutions was the salient fact. Within the next generation, difference and conflict became prominent. This happened primarily because of developments in the North. The South changed relatively little, and because so many Northern changes seemed threatening, the South developed a defensive ideology that resisted change.

In most of these respects the South resembled a majority of the societies in the world more than the changing North did. Despite the abolition of legal slavery or serfdom throughout much of the western hemisphere and western Europe, much of the world—like the South—had an unfree or quasi-free labor force. Most societies in the world remained predominantly rural, agricultural, and labor-intensive; most, including even several European countries, had illiteracy rates as high or higher than the South's 45 percent; most like the South remained bound by traditional values and networks of family, kinship, hierarchy, and patriarchy. The North—along with a few countries in northwestern Europe—hurtled forward eagerly toward a future that many Southerners found distasteful if not frightening; the South remained proudly and even defiantly rooted in the past.

Thus when secessionists protested in 1861 that they were acting to preserve traditional rights and values, they were correct. They fought to protect their constitutional liberties against the perceived Northern threat to overthrow them. The South's concept of republicanism had not changed in three-quarters of a century; the North's had. With complete sincerity the South fought to preserve its version of the republic of the founding fathers—a government of limited powers that protected the rights of property and whose constituency comprised an independent gentry and yeomanry of the white race undisturbed by large cities, heartless factories, restless free workers, and class conflict. The accession to power of the Republican party, with its ideology of competitive, egalitarian, free-labor capitalism, was a signal to the South that the Northern majority had turned irrevocably toward this frightening, revolutionary future. Indeed, the Black Republican party appeared to the eyes of many Southerners as "essentially a revolutionary party" composed of "a motley throng of Sans culottes . . . Infidels and freelovers, interspersed by Bloomer women, fugitive slaves, and amalgamationists." Therefore secession was a preemptive counter-revolution to prevent the Black Republican revolution from engulfing the South. "*We* are not revolutionists," insisted James D. B. DeBow and Jefferson Davis during the Civil War. "We are resisting revolution. . . . We are not engaged in a Quixotic fight for the rights of man; our struggle is for inherited rights. . . . We are upholding the true doctrines of the Federal Constitution. We are conservative."

Union victory in the war destroyed the Southern vision of America and insured that the Northern vision would become the American vision. Until 1861, however, it was the North that was out of the mainstream, not the South. Of course the Northern states, along with Britain and a few countries in northwestern Europe, were cutting a new channel in world history that would doubtless have become the mainstream even if the American Civil War had not happened. But it did happen, and for Americans it marked the turning point. A Louisiana planter who returned home sadly after the war wrote in 1865: "Society has been completely changed by the war. The [French] revolution of '89 did not produce a greater change in the 'Ancien Regime' than has this in our social life." And four years later George Ticknor, a retired Harvard professor, concluded that the Civil War had created a "great gulf between what happened before in our century and what has happened since, or what is likely to happen hereafter. It does not seem to me as if I were living in the country in which I was born." From the war sprang the great flood that wrenched the stream of American history into a new channel and transferred the burden of exceptionalism from North to South.

FURTHER READING

Clement Eaton, *The Growth of Southern Civilization, 1790–1861* (1961)
Robert W. Fogel and Stanley L. Engerman, *Time on the Cross: The Economics of American Negro Slavery* (1974), chaps. 1–3
Eugene D. Genovese, *The Political Economy of Slavery* (1965)
——, *The World the Slaveholders Made* (1969)
Fletcher M. Green, "Democracy in the Old South," *Journal of Southern History* 12 (1946), 3–23
Peter Kolchin, *Unfree Labor: American Slavery and Russian Serfdom* (1987)
Leon Litwack, *North of Slavery: The Negro in the Free States, 1790–1860* (1961)
Douglass C. North, *The Economic Growth of the United States, 1790–1860* (1961)
James Oakes, *The Ruling Race: A History of American Slaveholders* (1982)
Rollin Osterweiss, *Romanticism and Nationalism in the Old South* (1949)
Frank L. Owsley and Harriet C. Owsley, "The Economic Basis of Society in the Late Ante-bellum South," *Journal of Southern History* 6 (1940), 24–45
David M. Potter, "The Historian's Use of Nationalism and Vice Versa," in *The South and the Sectional Conflict* (1968), 34–83
——, "The Nature of Southern Separatism," in *The Impending Crisis, 1848–1861* (1976)
Charles G. Sellers, Jr., "The Travail of Slavery," in Sellers, ed., *The Southerner As American* (1960), 40–71
Mitchell Snay, *Gospel of Disunion: Religion and Separatism in the Antebellum South* (1993)
Charles S. Sydnor, "The Southerner and the Laws," *Journal of Southern History* 6 (1940), 3–23
Harry Watson, "Slavery and Development in a Dual Economy: The South and the Market Revolution," in Melvyn Stokes and Stephen Conway, eds., *The Market Revolution in America* (1996)
Gavin Wright, *The Political Economy of the Cotton South* (1978)
Bertram Wyatt-Brown, *Southern Honor: Ethics and Behavior in the Old South* (1982)

CHAPTER 2

Sectional Politics

in the 1850s

A small cadre of activists advocating the immediate and unconditional abolition of slavery emerged in the 1830s. From the start, they encountered massive opposition. Not only were they resisted vigorously by the Southern slaveholding interest, but they also encountered Northerners' fears that agitation to end slavery would almost certainly destabilize the fragile Union and could result in the liberation of millions of black slaves, who would then migrate northward. Also, the abolitionists soon faced the reality that the federal government could not legally intervene in the internal affairs of member states and so could not abolish slavery outright.

For the next fifteen years or so, the abolitionists labored, with some success, to change public opinion and to pressure public officials and governments to take antislavery stands. But in the late 1840s and early 1850s, the debate over slavery changed course when the United States acquired immense tracts of western land as a result of the war against Mexico from 1846 to 1847. The annexation of Texas had caused some strain between the sections earlier in the decade, but now the southwest region that encompassed what was later to become the states of California, Utah, New Mexico, and Arizona was added, and the status of the new territories as either slave or free would soon have to be decided. Would the nation allow slavery to go into these vast areas, or simply exclude it? An issue that had been somewhat theoretical had now become practical and immediate, since decisions about slavery's legitimacy as an American institution could no longer be postponed. On the other hand, it was also true that the question of slavery's status in the new territories diluted, and even diverted, the campaign for abolishing it. Because the territorial issue focused on slavery's restriction, it left the institution untouched where it already existed.

The test case for determining the status of slavery in the unorganized territories was the sparsely settled area of Kansas. Although located to the east of the Mexican Cession, Kansas was not yet ready for statehood. From 1854, when the Kansas-Nebraska bill was introduced, until 1858, when the proslavery Lecompton Constitution was defeated, Kansas was the focus of national politics, with each section resolved to control the emergent state. Why did Southerners stake so much on a contest they could not expect to win? And why were Northerners so fearful of losing Kansas? Were both sides perhaps overreacting? Whatever one might conclude, examination of this issue as seen

*by each of the protagonists reveals much about the priorities and concerns of both sides
as well as about the state of political feeling in the nation by the mid-1850s.*

DOCUMENTS

Sectional dissension had quieted down somewhat after the Compromise of 1850, but it was rekindled by Senator Stephen Douglas's Kansas-Nebraska proposal and would intensify during
the remainder of the decade. The first document reprinted here, the Appeal of the Independent
Democrats of January 19, 1854, is an angry response to Douglas's initiative on the part of leading antislavery Democrats, among them Salmon P. Chase and Charles Sumner. In the second selection, Douglas explains the objectives of his bill in a letter to the editor of the *State Capitol
Reporter* of Concord (N.H.) on February 16, 1854. Sumner's inflammatory speech on "Bleeding Kansas," delivered in the Senate on May 20, 1856, is the third document. In this extract, he
attacks the reputation of Andrew P. Butler, the veteran senator from South Carolina, whose kinsman, Congressman Preston Brooks, took it upon himself to avenge this insult by physically assaulting Sumner. The fourth selection is from a speech in the House on July 11, 1856, by
Thomas S. Bocock of Virginia, defending Brooks's act.

The fifth document is from the famous speech of Senator William Henry Seward of New
York, given in Rochester, New York, on October 25, 1858. Seward described the sectional dispute as an "irrepressible conflict," a phrase that haunted him in his campaign for the Republican nomination in 1860 and has haunted historians ever since. The sixth and final piece is from
a speech in the Senate on December 19, 1859, by Albert G. Brown of Mississippi, indicating
how Southern slaveholders felt about restrictions on their rights.

Independent Democrats Protest
the Kansas-Nebraska Act, January 1854

As Senators and Representatives in the Congress of the United States it is our duty to
warn our constituents, whenever imminent danger menaces the freedom of our institutions or the permanency of the Union.

Such danger, as we firmly believe, now impends, and we earnestly solicit your
prompt attention to it.

At the last session of Congress a bill for the organization of the Territory of Nebraska
passed the House of Representatives by an overwhelming majority. That bill was based
on the principle of excluding slavery from the new Territory. It was not taken up for
consideration in the Senate and consequently failed to become a law.

At the present session a new Nebraska bill has been reported by the Senate
Committee on Territories, which, should it unhappily receive the sanction of Congress,
will open all the unorganized Territories of the Union to the ingress of slavery.

We arraign this bill as a gross violation of a sacred pledge; as a criminal betrayal of
precious rights; as part and parcel of an atrocious plot to exclude from a vast unoccupied
region immigrants from the Old World and free laborers from our own States, and convert
it into a dreary region of despotism, inhabited by masters and slaves.

From "Appeal of the Independent Democrats," January 19, 1854, in Richard Hofstadter, ed. *Great Issues in
American History* (Random House, 1958), pp. 355–359.

Take your maps, fellow citizens, we entreat you, and see what country it is which this bill gratuitously and recklessly proposes to open to slavery. . . .

This immense region, occupying the very heart of the North American Continent, and larger, by thirty-three thousand square miles, than all the existing free States— including California . . . this immense region the bill now before the Senate, without reason and without excuse, but in flagrant disregard of sound policy and sacred faith, purposes to open to slavery. . . .

Nothing is more certain in history than the fact that Missouri could not have been admitted as a slave State had not certain members from the free States been reconciled to the measure by the incorporation of this prohibition [the Missouri Compromise of 1820] into the act of admission. Nothing is more certain than that this prohibition has been regarded and accepted by the whole country as a solemn compact against the extension of slavery into any part of the territory acquired from France [under the Louisiana Purchase] lying north of 36° 30', and not included in the new State of Missouri. The same act—let it be ever remembered—which authorized the formation of a constitution by the State, without a clause forbidding slavery, consecrated, beyond question and beyond honest recall, the whole remainder of the Territory to freedom and free institutions forever. For more than thirty years—during more than half our national existence under our present Constitution—this compact has been universally regarded and acted upon as inviolable American law. In conformity with it, Iowa was admitted as a free State and Minnesota has been organized as a free Territory.

It is a strange and ominous fact, well calculated to awaken the worst apprehensions and the most fearful forebodings of future calamities, that it is now deliberately proposed to repeal this prohibition, by implication or directly—the latter certainly the manlier way—and thus to subvert the compact, and allow slavery in all the yet unorganized territory. . . .

We appeal to the people. We warn you that the dearest interests of freedom and the Union are in imminent peril. Demagogues may tell you that the Union can be maintained only by submitting to the demands of slavery. We tell you that the Union can only be maintained by the full recognition of the just claims of freedom and man. The Union was formed to establish justice and secure the blessings of liberty. When it fails to accomplish these ends it will be worthless, and when it becomes worthless it cannot long endure.

We entreat you to be mindful of that fundamental maxim of Democracy—EQUAL RIGHTS AND EXACT JUSTICE FOR ALL MEN. Do not submit to become agents in extending legalized oppression and systematized injustice over a vast territory yet exempt from these terrible evils.

We implore Christians and Christian ministers to interpose. Their divine religion requires them to behold in every man a brother, and to labor for the advancement and regeneration of the human race.

Whatever apologies may be offered for the toleration of slavery in the States, none can be offered for its extension into Territories where it does not exist, and where that extension involves the repeal of ancient law and the violation of solemn compact. Let all protest, earnestly and emphatically, by correspondence, through the press, by memorials, by resolutions of public meetings and legislative bodies, and in whatever other mode may seem expedient, against this enormous crime.

For ourselves, we shall resist it by speech and vote, and with all the abilities which God has given us. Even if overcome in the impending struggle, we shall not submit. We shall go home to our constituents, erect anew the standard of freedom, and call on the people to come to the rescue of the country from the domination of slavery. We will not despair; for the cause of human freedom is the cause of God.

S. P. Chase

Charles Sumner

J. R. Giddings

Edward Wade

Gerritt Smith

Alexander De Witt

January 19, 1854

Senator Stephen Douglas Explains the Objectives of His Bill, February 1854

. . . The bill provides in words as specific and unequivocal as our language affords, that the *true intent and meaning* of the act is NOT to legislate slavery into any Territory or State. The bill, therefore, does not introduce slavery; does not revive it; does not establish it; does not contain any clause designed to produce that result, or which by any possible construction can have that legal effect.

"Non-intervention by Congress with slavery in the States and Territories" is expressly declared to be the principle upon which the bill is constructed. The great fundamental principle of self-government, which authorizes the people to regulate their own domestic concerns, as recognized in the Compromise measure of 1850, and affirmed by the Democratic national convention, and reaffirmed by the Whig convention at Baltimore, is declared in this bill to be the rule of action in the formation of territorial governments. The two great political parties of the country are solemnly pledged to a strict adherence to this principle as a final settlement of the slavery agitation. How can that settlement be final, unless the principle be preserved and carried out in all new territorial organizations? . . .

But, sir, I fear I have already made this letter too long. If so, my apology therefore is to be found in the great importance of the subject, and my earnest desire that no honest mind be misled with regard to the provisions of the bill or the principles involved in it. Every intelligent man knows that it is a matter of no practical importance, so far as the question of slavery is concerned. The cry of the extension of slavery has been raised for mere party purposes by the abolition confederates and disappointed office-seekers. All candid men who understand the subject admit that the laws of climate, and production, and of physical geography, (to use the language of one of New England's greatest statesmen,) have excluded slavery from that country. This was admitted by Mr. Everett in his speech against the bill, and because slavery could not go there, he appealed to southern Senators not to insist upon applying the provisions of the Utah bill to Nebraska, when they would derive no advantages from it. The same admission and appeal were made by Mr. Smith, of Connecticut, in his speech against the bill. To-day Mr. Badger, of North Carolina, replied to these appeals by the distinct declaration that he and his southern friends did not expect that slavery would go there; that the climate and

Letter, Stephen A. Douglas to Editor of Concord *State Capitol Reporter,* January, 1854, in *The Letters of Stephen A. Douglas,* Robert W. Johannsen, ed. (University of Illinois Press, 1961), pp. 288–289.

productions were not adapted to slave labor; but they insisted upon it as a matter of principle, and of principle alone. In short, all candid and intelligent men make the same admission, and present the naked question as a matter of principle, whether the people shall be allowed to regulate their domestic concerns in their own way or not. In conclusion, I may be permitted to add, that the Democratic party, as well as the country, have a deep interest in this manner. Is our party to be again divided and rent asunder upon this vexed question of slavery? . . .

Senator Charles Sumner of Massachusetts Ridicules the Southern Gentry, May 1856

My task will be divided under three different heads: *first,* THE CRIME AGAINST KANSAS, in its origin and extent; *secondly,* THE APOLOGIES FOR THE CRIME; and, *thirdly,* THE TRUE REMEDY.

Before entering upon the argument, I must say something of a general character, particularly in response to what has fallen from Senators who have raised themselves to eminence on this floor in championship of human wrong: I mean the Senator from South Carolina [Mr. BUTLER] and the Senator from Illinois [Mr. DOUGLAS], who, though unlike as Don Quixote and Sancho Panza, yet, like this couple, sally forth together in the same adventure. I regret much to miss the elder Senator from his seat; but the cause against which he has run a tilt, with such ebullition of animosity, demands that the opportunity of exposing him should not be lost; and it is for the cause that I speak. The Senator from South Carolina has read many books of chivalry, and believes himself a chivalrous knight, with sentiments of honor and courage. Of course he has chosen a mistress to whom he has made his vows, and who, though ugly to others, is always lovely to him,—though polluted in the sight of the world, is chaste in his sight: I mean the harlot Slavery. For her his tongue is always profuse in words. Let her be impeached in character, or any proposition be made to shut her out from the extension of her wantonness, and no extravagance of manner or hardihood of assertion is then too great for this Senator. The frenzy of Don Quixote in behalf of his wench Dulcinea del Toboso is all surpassed. The asserted rights of Slavery, which shock equality of all kinds, are cloaked by a fantastic claim of equality. If the Slave States cannot enjoy what, in mockery of the great fathers of the Republic, he misnames Equality under the Constitution,—in other words, the full power in the National Territories to compel fellow-men to unpaid toil, to separate husband and wife, and to sell little children at the auction-block,—then, Sir, the chivalric Senator will conduct the State of South Carolina out of the Union! Heroic knight! Exalted Senator! A second Moses come for a second exodus!

Not content with this poor menace, which we have been twice told was "measured," the Senator, in the unrestrained chivalry of his nature, has undertaken to apply opprobrious words to those who differ from him on this floor. He calls them "sectional and fanatical"; and resistance to the Usurpation of Kansas he denounces as "an uncalculating fanaticism." To be sure, these charges lack all grace of originality and all sentiment of truth; but the adventurous Senator does not hesitate. He is the uncompromising, unblush-

From Charles Sumner, "The Crime Against Kansas," in *Charles Sumner: His Complete Works,* George Frisbie Hoar, ed. (Negro Universities Press, 1969 [1900]), Vol. 5, pp. 144–146.

ing representative on this floor of a flagrant *sectionalism,* now domineering over the Republic,—and yet, with a ludicrous ignorance of his own position, unable to see himself as others see him, or with an effrontery which even his white head ought not to protect from rebuke, he applies to those here who resist his *sectionalism* the very epithet which designates himself. The men who strive to bring back the Government to its original policy, when Freedom and not Slavery was national, while Slavery and not Freedom was sectional, he arraigns as *sectional.* This will not do. It involves too great a perversion of terms. I tell that Senator that it is to himself, and to the "organization" of which he is the "committed advocate," that this epithet belongs. I now fasten it upon them. For myself, I care little for names; but, since the question is raised here, I affirm that the Republican party of the Union is in no just sense *sectional,* but, more than any other party, *national,*—and that it now goes forth to dislodge from the high places that tyrannical sectionalism of which the Senator from South Carolina is one of the maddest zealots. . . .

Congressman Thomas S. Bocock of Virginia Defends Preston Brooks, July 1856

. . . Thus far have I considered it as a question of law. I come now to investigate it as a question of right and justice. Because we happen to be members of Congress, will it be pretended that we are at liberty to rise in our places, and, with absolute impunity, abuse, malign, and slander each other, or any other person we may choose? The doctrine is absolutely monstrous. Nor is its meanness diminished by saying that a majority in framing their rules must properly restrict debate. We know too well that rules are often broken now-a-days. How many of the speeches delivered on this question have conformed to our rule, which requires the debate to relate strictly to the subject under consideration? Scarcely one.

Besides, the gentlemen of the North are largely in the majority on this floor. Sectional feeling runs high. It may be agreeable to them to abuse the southern members—their constituents, their institutions, their families, &c. Shall we be required to submit to it all, and be utterly without redress? Surely not; it is impossible. We have no such right, and could not enjoy it, if it were given. Say by express law, if you choose, that members of Congress shall enjoy perfect freedom of debate, and may abuse, and traduce, and malign whomsoever they choose. The right will be worth but little. There can be no royal prerogative of slander in this country. You may draw around it the strongest muniments of legal defense; you may make the sheriff and his *posse* the warders on the tower; you may make instruments of punishment to bristle on the walls, still the immunity will not be perfect. When it begins to throw its venom fiercely around, injured sensibility will revolt, and aroused manhood will still occasionally break over and inflict condign punishment. A broken head will still pay the penalty for a foul tongue.

Think, sir, of American character, how sensitive, yet how brave; how easily wounded, yet how quick to avenge the injury! Better death than disgrace! Can you, then, by legislation make American gentlemen submit to traduction with composure? Never!

From John S. Bocock, speech in U.S. House, July 11, 1856, *Congressional Globe* 34 Cong. 1 Sess., Vol. 25, Pt. 3, pp. 819–820.

never, sir! You must first tame our high hearts, and teach them the low beat of servility; you must make our Anglo-Saxon blood run milk and water in our veins; you must tear from the records of history the pages which tell the deeds of our heroic ancestry, and persuade us that we have descended of drabs and shrews. When you have done that, and changed Billingsgate into rhetoric, and railing into eloquence, you may then convert the Senate and the House of Representatives into two great Schools for scandal [a reference to Richard Brinsley Sheridan's famous play], in which your Backbites and your Crabtrees may strut their "*hour*" on the stage and feel happy. Then, too, you may build up your great doctrine of woman's rights; for whereever your Backbites and your Crabtrees are the prominent actors, the Lady Sneerwells and Mrs. Candors should take their parts to make the play complete. If this is your doctrine, gentlemen, bring on your Theodore Parkers, and your Ward Beechers [two leading abolitionists], and your strong-minded women, and have a good time of it here and in the Senate. *Gentlemen* will retire voluntarily from both without the process of expulsion.

Slander never can, (in this country,) under any guise, in any form of authority, enjoy perfect immunity, and have

> "As large a character as the wind,
> To blow on whom it pleases."

Surely there has been no disposition or intention to give it such immunity or liberty heretofore; and any such construction is in the teeth of law and in the face of justice.

This, then, being the doctrine of law and justice, let me apply it to the case in hand.

I believe that Mr. SUMNER's speech was made "*contra morem parliamentarium*"; that under guise of debating the Kansas bill, he sought occasion to pour out his private resentments, and vent his personal malice. In thus stepping beyond his parliamentary right, he lost his constitutional protection, and became liable as any other citizen would be. The assault and battery committed on him occupies, in this regard, the same ground, not lower, not higher, than the same assault and battery upon any other person.

It has been asked, if Mr. SUMNER was liable to an action of libel, why not pursue him in the courts of justice? That question may as well be asked in any other case of assault and battery. If a man insults you in a public crowd, or traduces your wife or daughter, and you knock him down, it may be asked, why not sue him? That, surely, is the legal course. But there are offenses of such a nature, that men cannot always wait for redress on the slow and uncertain course of legal proceedings. The courts are then to inquire how much is to be pardoned to the weakness of human nature under the circumstances?

This is the great case of "the violation of the freedom of speech" in the person of Mr. SUMNER. He wantonly gave an insult, and was punished, rashly perhaps, for it. Why, then, Mr. Speaker, should Massachusetts become so much excited on the subject? Will she adopt the quarrels and take up the fights of her sons wherever they go? Freedom of speech is a right of the private man as well as of the public man. Whenever a son of hers gives an insult and gets a knock, is she to rush forth and cry out "that the freedom of speech has been violated?" I have known parents who identified themselves with their children in all their quarrels and broils with their schoolfellows and playmates; and the consequence in such cases always is, that the parent gets the more ill-will, and the children the more ill-treatment. . . .

Senator William H. Seward of New York Warns of an Irrepressible Conflict, October 1858

. . . The slave system is one of constant danger, distrust, suspicion, and watchfulness. It debases those whose toil alone can produce wealth and resources for defense, to the lowest degree of which human nature is capable, to guard against mutiny and insurrection, and thus wastes energies which otherwise might be employed in national development and aggrandizement.

The free-labor system educates all alike, and by opening all the fields of industrial employment, and all the departments of authority, to the unchecked and equal rivalry of all classes of men, at once secures universal contentment, and brings into the highest possible activity all the physical, moral and social energies of the whole state. In states where the slave system prevails, the masters, directly or indirectly, secure all political power, and constitute a ruling aristocracy. In states where the free-labor system prevails, universal suffrage necessarily obtains, and the state inevitably becomes, sooner or later, a republic or democracy.

Russia yet maintains slavery, and is a despotism. Most of the other European states have abolished slavery, and adopted the system of free labor. It was the antagonistic political tendencies of the two systems which the first Napoleon was contemplating when he predicted that Europe would ultimately be either all Cossack or all republican. Never did human sagacity utter a more pregnant truth. The two systems are at once perceived to be incongruous. But they are more than incongruous—they are incompatible. They never have permanently existed together in one country, and they never can. It would be easy to demonstrate this impossibility, from the irreconcilable contrast between their great principles and characteristics. But the experience of mankind has conclusively established it. Slavery, as I have already intimated, existed in every state in Europe. Free labor has supplanted it everywhere except in Russia and Turkey. State necessities developed in modern times, are now obliging even those two nations to encourage and employ free labor; and already, despotic as they are, we find them engaged in abolishing slavery. In the United States, slavery came into collision with free labor at the close of the last century, and fell before it in New England, New York, New Jersey and Pennsylvania, but triumphed over it effectually, and excluded it for a period yet undetermined, from Virginia, the Carolinas and Georgia. Indeed, so incompatible are the two systems, that every new state which is organized within our ever extending domain makes its first political act a choice of the one and the exclusion of the other, even at the cost of civil war, if necessary. The slave states, without law, at the last national election, successfully forbade, within their own limits, even the casting of votes for a candidate for president of the United States supposed to be favorable to the establishment of the free-labor system in new states.

Hitherto, the two systems have existed in different states, but side by side within the American Union. This has happened because the Union is a confederation of states. But in another aspect the United States constitute only one nation. Increase of population, which is filling the states out to their very borders, together with a new and extended net-work of railroads and other avenues, and an internal commerce which daily becomes more intimate, is rapidly bringing the states into a higher and more perfect social unity

From William H. Seward, "The Irrepressible Conflict," Rochester, N.Y., October 25, 1858, *The Works of William H. Seward,* George E. Baker, ed. (Houghton Mifflin, 1884), Vol. 4, pp. 290–292. This selection is also available in reprint by AMS Press, 1972.

or consolidation. Thus, these antagonistic systems are continually coming into closer contact, and collision results.

Shall I tell you what this collision means? They who think that it is accidental, unnecessary, the work of interested or fanatical agitators, and therefore ephemeral, mistake the case altogether. It is an irrepressible conflict between opposing and enduring forces, and it means that the United States must and will, sooner or later, become either entirely a slaveholding nation, or entirely a free-labor nation. Either the cotton and rice-fields of South Carolina and the sugar plantations of Louisiana will ultimately be tilled by free labor, and Charleston and New Orleans become marts for legitimate merchandise alone, or else the rye-fields and wheat-fields of Massachusetts and New York must again be surrendered by their farmers to slave culture and to the production of slaves, and Boston and New York become once more markets for trade in the bodies and souls of men. It is the failure to apprehend this great truth that induces so many unsuccessful attempts at final compromise between the slave and free states, and it is the existence of this great fact that renders all such pretended compromises, when made, vain and ephemeral. Startling as this saying may appear to you, fellow citizens, it is by no means an original or even a moderate one. Our forefathers knew it to be true, and unanimously acted upon it when they framed the constitution of the United States. They regarded the existence of the servile system in so many of the states with sorrow and shame, which they openly confessed, and they looked upon the collision between them, which was then just revealing itself, and which we are now accustomed to deplore, with favor and hope. They knew that either the one or the other system must exclusively prevail. . . .

Senator Albert G. Brown of Mississippi Renounces the Protection of the Union, December 1859

. . . All we ask—and, in asking that, we shall never cease—is, that our property, under the common Government, be put upon the same footing with other people's property; that this Government of ours shall be allowed to draw no insulting discrimination between slave property and any other kind of property; that wherever the authority of the Government extends, it shall be given to us in an equal degree with anybody else; and, by that, I say again, I mean given to the extent of affording us adequate and sufficient protection. Who does not know that, in the last two or three years, emigrant trains were robbed in Utah by the Mormons; not robbed of slaves, but robbed of other kinds of property. What was done? An army was promptly sent to repair the injury, at an expense, I dare say, when we shall sum up the bill and pay it, of $20,000,000. Who believes that if the property had been our slaves, any reparation would have been insisted upon? Is the Government so prompt to send armies to protect us against the underground process? No. Twenty millions of property may be stolen from us, and the Government stands by and contents itself with simply remonstrating, with giving gentle hints that it is all wrong. When I say this is done by the Government, I do not mean the government of James Buchanan, or Franklin Pierce, or Millard Fillmore; but I mean the Government in whosever hands it happened to rest. Justice has never been done us; our property has never been treated like the property of other people; has never received the same sort of

From Albert G. Brown, Speech in U.S. Senate, December 19, 1859, *Congressional Globe* 36 Cong., 1 Sess., Vol. 29, Pt. 1, p. 187.

protection, the same kind of security. While the Government has been ready to protect other people's property on the high seas and in the Territories; while it has been ready to make war at home and declare war against foreign countries for the protection of other people's property, we have received no such guarantees from it. I demand them. I demand to be treated as an equal. If you will insist upon taxing me as an equal, I do not feel disposed to come up and pay my taxes, simply to know the Government through its power to make exactions on me. I do not choose to perform military service, and spill my blood and risk my life and lay down the lives of my people for the common protection, in defense of a Government which only knows me through its powers to tax me. I claim the same right to protection on the part of my people as I concede to you. Wherever your property is on the face of God's habitable globe, on the sea or on the land, I claim that the arms and power of this Government must go to protect and defend it. For that was the great object of creating the Government; and when it falls short of that object, it fails in its great mission, the great purpose for which it was created.

I know of no mission which this Government has to perform except to protect the citizen in his life, his liberty, and his property. When it fails in these great essentials, it has failed in everything; and I stand even in this august presence to say, as I have said in the more august presence of my immediate constituents, the Legislature of my State— and if they choose to repudiate me for saying it, I am willing to be repudiated—that whenever the Government fails, I do not ask it to refuse, but when it fails to protect me and my people in our lives, our liberties, and our property, upon the high seas or upon the land, it ought to be abolished. If that be treason, gentlemen, make the most of it. That is all I have said; and by that proposition living or dying, sinking or swimming, surviving or perishing, I mean to stand here and elsewhere.

Those who have served with me in this House and in the other House of Congress, know, or ought to know, that I am deeply and earnestly and at heart devoted to the Democratic party. I am devoted to it, because I have always regarded it as a party that dispensed equal and exact justice to every part of the country. I am a Democrat because I have always felt that this Government would dispense to Massachusetts the same measure of justice that it gave to Mississippi; that it would give to Pennsylvania no more than it gave to Virginia; and I should be as ready to despise it if I thought it would give more to my State than to any other State in the Confederacy. While I say this, I am equally free to say, that I would, if it were in my power, rend it into ten thousand fragments, if it exacted of me to do that for Massachusetts which the Senator from Massachusetts would not do for Mississippi. If I have asked, in all this, anything more for my country, for my State, or for my section, than I would give to any other State or section, show me in what, and I am ready to submit. I ask nothing for my section that I am not willing to yield to any other.

Now, Mr. President, thanking the Republican benches for the patient and polite attention which they have given me, I take my seat. [Laughter, every seat on the Republican side being vacant.] . . .

ESSAYS

The issues of "Bleeding Kansas" and "Bleeding Sumner" were interrelated, and they contributed significantly to the climax of the sectional crisis in the late 1850s. In the first essay, William E. Gienapp of Harvard University points out how Brooks's caning of Sumner was a decisive incident that hardened Northerners' distaste for and hostility toward the South and its values. The accompanying piece, by Don E. Fehrenbacher of Stanford University, is an analysis of the Kansas episode and how it confirmed Southerners' fears that the North did not respect their rights and interests.

The Caning of Charles Sumner and the Rise of the Republican Party

WILLIAM E. GIENAPP

When the Republican party elected its first President, Abraham Lincoln, in 1860, only six years had elapsed since its formation, and only four years since the creation of its national organization. Despite this remarkable achievement, the party had a precarious early existence, and emerged as the principal opposition to the Democrats only after a severe and difficult struggle with the rival American or Know Nothing party. It certainly was anything but clear initially that the Republicans would become a permanent fixture in the two party system. In fact, the 1855 state elections were a serious setback for the fledgling party. With only one year remaining until the 1856 presidential election, the Know Nothings were the Democrats' most formidable opponent. Indeed, in several Northern states the Know Nothings were so strong the Republican party did not even exist.

In late November 1855, as he surveyed the political disorder of the previous two years, former New York Governor Washington Hunt expressed strong doubts about the permanence of the Republican party. He remained hopeful that the Whig party could be revived. Still, he admitted that he was uneasy. With an eye to the convening of a new Congress, now less than two weeks away, he predicted that the Republicans, hoping for new outrages in Kansas and in Washington to bolster their party's sagging fortunes, would try to provoke Southerners with insults and bravado. "We must be prepared for high words and stormy scenes," he warned, "but we will hope that there will be sense and moderation enough to prevent any desperate deeds, or any violent action in Congress." Hunt's fears were as well taken as his optimism misplaced. The most dramatic event of the session was the caning of Senator Charles Sumner of Massachusetts by Representative Preston S. Brooks of South Carolina. This was precisely the kind of event Hunt had feared: it inflamed popular emotions in both the North and the South, intensified sectional animosity, and destroyed the cherished hopes of men such as himself for the preservation of a national conservative party.

Most historians, in seeking to explain the rise of the Republican party, have emphasized, sometimes almost without qualification, the Kansas issue. There is no doubt that the repeal of the Missouri Compromise and the ensuing troubles in the Kansas Territory were critical to the party's increasing strength. Nevertheless, if this issue were primarily responsible for the party's growth, one must ask why, despite the persistence of the Kansas crisis and the vigorous efforts of Republicans to capitalize on it, the party had remained so weak. Why did the party's spectacular growth occur in the late spring and summer of 1856, and not earlier? This is a complex question, but one reason that has not received the emphasis it deserves is Brooks' attack on Sumner.

From William E. Gienapp, "The Crime Against Sumner: The Caning of Charles Sumner and the Rise of the Republican Party," *Civil War History*, Vol. 25, No. 3, September 1979, pp. 218–245. Reprinted with permission of The Kent State University Press.

When Congress convened in December, 1855, observers quickly noticed an intensified animosity between antislavery men and Southerners. The continuing troubles in Kansas, where free-state men had established their own government in opposition to the recognized territorial authorities, greatly contributed to this hardening of feeling. "We have before us a long session of excitement, & ribald debate," Sumner commented when debate over Kansas opened in the Senate. A staunch antislavery man, Sumner immediately began preparing to speak on affairs in Kansas. On May 19 and 20, 1856 he delivered a carefully rehearsed speech on "The Crime Against Kansas," in which he severely lashed the Administration, the South, and the proslavery men in Kansas. The Republican leader also made scathing personal attacks on several prominent Democrats, including Senator Andrew P. Butler of South Carolina, then absent from the Senate. Sumner's attack on the sixty year old Butler, a kindly man of charm and grace who was widely admired and respected in Washington, produced considerable resentment.

No one was more angered by Sumner's comments than Preston S. Brooks. A distant relative of Butler's, Brooks was a proud, aristocratic South Carolina congressman now serving his second term. He considered Sumner's speech an insult to his aged relative and his state, for which he decided to chastise the Massachusetts senator, as a Southern gentleman would any inferior. When the Senate adjourned on May 22, Brooks entered the Senate Chamber. Sumner was seated at his desk, writing letters and franking copies of his speech. When the Chamber was clear of ladies, Brooks walked up to Sumner's desk and, pronouncing the speech a libel on South Carolina and on Butler, began to strike the Senator over the head with a gutta percha cane. In his excitement Brooks forgot his original intention merely to flog Sumner, and began to hit him with all his strength. Sumner, stunned and blinded by blood, vainly tried to ward off the blows to his head. Brooks continued the attack, even after his cane had shattered, until he was seized by a Northern congressman who had rushed to the scene of the attack. Brooks' friends then quietly led him away. Sumner lay on the floor, unconscious and bleeding profusely. The following day Brooks informed his brother that he gave Sumner "about 30 first rate stripes" with the cane. "Every lick went where I intended," he wrote triumphantly. It was four years before Sumner returned to his seat in the Senate.

At the insistence of the Republican members, the Senate established a special committee of investigation. Lacking a single Republican member, it met and promptly decided that it had no jurisdiction over the matter. Attention thus turned to the Republican dominated House of Representatives. Although the House voted to appoint a committee of investigation, only two Southern members, both border state men, supported the majority. Speaker Nathaniel P. Banks of Massachusetts appointed a committee which recommended by a straight party vote to expel Brooks. After a heated debate the House voted for expulsion by 121 to 95, but as it required a two-thirds vote, the motion failed. Only one Southern congressman voted against Brooks. Following the vote, Brooks made a defiant speech in defense of his action and resigned, confident that his constituents would support him. Unanimously re-elected, he triumphantly returned to the session. Ultimately the only punishment Brooks received was a $300 fine for assault levied by a Washington court.

Though the focus of this essay is on the Northern reaction to the caning, it is necessary to examine briefly the Southern response, for the former can be understood fully only against the background of the latter. Some Southerners privately expressed disapproval of Brooks' action. A handful even wrote letters of sympathy to Sumner. Other

Southerners, while not disapproving of the caning, criticized Brooks for assaulting Sumner on the floor of the Senate. Senator James Mason of Virginia, despite his belief that Sumner "did not get a lick amiss," added that "for appearances it would have been better, had it lighted on him outside the Chamber." Public criticism, however, was rare. The general Southern response was one of strong approval. A virtual unknown before the incident, Brooks returned home a hero and a celebrity. Resolutions endorsing the assault were passed at meetings in the South and a number of souvenir canes were ostentatiously presented to him. "Every Southern man sustains me," Brooks boasted after the caning. "The fragments of the stick are begged for as *sacred relicts.*"

Meanwhile, Southern editors vied with each other in the enthusiasm of their endorsements of Brooks. This praise was not confined to South Carolina, where the press was unanimous in its approval. The influential Richmond *Enquirer* declared:

> We consider the act good in conception, better in execution, and best of all in consequence. The vulgar Abolitionists in the Senate are getting above themselves. . . . They have grown saucy, and dare to be impudent to gentlemen! . . . The truth is, they have been suffered to run too long without collars. They must be lashed into submission.

It went on to suggest that Republican Senators Henry Wilson and John P. Hale would benefit from a similar beating. In another issue it demanded that the Republicans in Congress be silenced if the Union were to survive. The rival Richmond *Whig* hailed the assault as "A Good Deed," and suggested that William H. Seward, another prominent Republican Senator, "should catch it next," while the Richmond *Examiner* maintained that Brooks' example should be followed by other Southern gentlemen whose feelings were outraged. With the reckless bravado that increasingly characterized Southern politics in this decade, the Southern press deliberately taunted Northerners by their endorsements of Brooks, phrasing them in a manner best designed to humiliate Northern sensibilities.

Even before the Southern reaction was known, news of the attack on Sumner electrified the North. Statements of shock and outrage poured in to the stricken Senator from sympathizers. A Boston clergyman declared, "I have experienced more moral misery in thinking on the assault than any other event ever excited in me," while a prominent German leader in Chicago testified that news of the attack "perfectly overwhelmed me with indignation and rage." Horace Mann, the famous educator, eloquently expressed Northern sentiment when he wrote Sumner: "We are all not only shocked at the outrage committed upon you, but we are wounded in your wounds, & bleed in your bleeding." Richard Henry Dana, Jr., perhaps best described the impact of the assault when he told Sumner, "When Brooks brought his cane in contact with your head, he completed the circuit of electricity to 30 millions!"

The depth of feeling and the level of excitement in the North surpassed anything observers had witnessed. A western correspondent assured Sumner that he had never seen men so aroused before; William H. Furness, the prominent clergyman, observed the same response in Philadelphia. A New York man told Banks that no event in the history of Congress had produced so much excitement. The greatest indignation naturally was felt in Massachusetts, where conservatives were badly shaken by the depth of the sectional animosity they observed. "You can have little idea of the depth & intensity of the feeling which has been excited in New England," Robert C. Winthrop warned Senator John J. Crittenden of Kentucky after the assault. Edward Everett, a sober, level-headed observer, affirmed that "when the intelligence of the assault on Mr. Sumner . . . reached Boston, it produced an excitement in the public mind deeper and more dangerous than I have ever witnessed. It was the opinion of some persons that if a leader daring & reckless enough had presented himself, he might have raised any number of men to march on Washington."

Public indignation over the Sumner-Brooks affair inevitably increased when news arrived that the town of Lawrence, Kansas, headquarters of the free-state movement, had been "sacked" by a proslavery army the day before the attack on Sumner. Historians now know that the reports of the attack on Lawrence were grossly exaggerated. Still, as the first accounts arrived, Republican newspapers shrilly proclaimed that yet another proslavery outrage had occurred. The coincidental timing of these two events served to magnify northern indignation. Winthrop reported with alarm that the "concurrence of the Kansas horrors" with the Sumner caning "has wrought up the masses to a state of fearful exasperation." Winthrop's fellow conservative Bostonian, Amos A. Lawrence, noted that the invasion of Lawrence and the assault on Sumner had excited the people of the country more than he had ever seen.

During the initial outcry over the caning, a handful of Republicans believed that the Kansas outrages were more important. This view, however, was decidedly the exception among seasoned political observers. Despite the attack on Lawrence, most politicians in the North agreed that, at least during the first weeks immediately following these two events, the Sumner assault was more important in producing northern indignation. Meetings to protest the caning dwarfed Kansas meetings in size, they attracted many more non-Republicans, both in the audience and as participants, and revealed more widespread excitement and deeply felt anger. There are several reasons why this was the case. Unlike accounts of the Sumner-Brooks incident, the news from Kansas was invariably fragmentary, uncertain, and contradictory; the deliberate attack on a senator for words spoken in debate seemed an attack on the Constitution, and as such it was much more ominous and threatening than events in a distant, sparsely settled territory. "The Kansas murders are on the border and border men are always represented and known to be often desperate but to see a senator assaulted in the Senate Chamber no one can find any excuse for it," one Northerner explained. Not only did Brooks' act undermine the basic principles of the American political system, but Northerners were keenly aware of the deliberately insulting nature of the caning. "We all or *nearly* all felt that we had been personally maltreated & insulted," a Boston man told Sumner afterwards. Men who had listened for over a year to stories of Kansas outrages without feeling that drastic action was necessary were suddenly shaken from their complacency by the Sumner affair. "The Northern blood is boiling at the outrage upon you," a New York Republican wrote Sumner. "It really sinks Kansas out of sight."

Nothing better demonstrated the almost universal extent of the outrage over the assault than the indignation meetings held in the North in late May and early June. Countless meetings, in small towns as well as large cities, in the West as well as the East, protested the caning. The two most significant meetings were held in New York City and Boston.

In New York [for example] a large group assembled at the Broadway Tabernacle to condemn the assault. The impulse for the meeting came largely from conservatives. Aware of the harmful consequences of making the meeting a partisan gathering, Republicans quietly encouraged its organization but shrewdly left its direction to others. The

Tabernacle was jammed to overflowing, with perhaps as many as 5,000 people inside, and thousands more outside, unable to gain entrance. The conservative influence at the meeting was readily apparent. George Griswold, one of the city's most respected merchants, presided. Vice presidents included such notable conservatives as Luther Bradish, William Kent, James A. Hamilton, and William F. Havemeyer. Among the speakers were Daniel Lord, a leading member of the bar; Samuel B. Ruggles, a prominent Know Nothing and former Whig; John A. Stevens, President of the Bank of Commerce; and Charles King, President of Columbia College. The crowd cheered as Lord defended free speech and denounced the Senate for failing to uphold its privileges; as King declared that the time had come for the North to act as well as talk; as Stevens called for "union at the ballot box" to stop these outrages; and as Ruggles asserted that if Congress would not maintain its dignity, then "force must be met by force." At the end of the meeting, the audience roared its approval of the moderately worded resolutions. Yet observers noted that the crowd was prepared for even stronger language.

Describing this meeting as "the most remarkable & significant assembly I ever attended," publisher George Putnam asserted that "no public demonstration has ever equalled this denunciation of the alarming crime. . . . The feeling was *deep,* calm, but resolute." Another observer noted that the vast multitude was "earnest, unanimous, and made up of people who don't often attend political gatherings." It was led by men "not given to fits of enthusiasm or generous sympathy, unlike[ly] to be prominent in anything wherein the general voice of the community does not sustain them."

Commentators immediately recognized the significance of the meeting. Antislavery sentiment had never been strong in New York City, where conservatives had persistently sought grounds of political accommodation with the South. In the aftermath of the assault on Sumner—a man for whom they had no political sympathy—they suddenly found themselves using language which previously they would have thought inflammatory. The New York *Tribune* was struck by this change in public sentiment. Men who had always been "conservative and cotton loving to the last degree," it noted, were now denouncing the Slave Power: "At no period since the formation of the Constitution has the public mind of this city been wrought to such a pitch of feeling and indignation as at the present moment." Putnam excitedly proclaimed that "*a new era* is inaugurated. . . . Never in my life have I felt anything like the stirring excitement & earnest determination which has been roused up by the blows of that bludgeon." . . .

In the wake of these indignation meetings, many men described the North as united in condemnation of Brooks. [Richard Henry Dana, Jr.], for example, reported that "it looks . . . as though the North was going all one way." Yet this appearance of unanimity was misleading. A few Northerners openly approved of Brooks' course, and more expressed such sentiments privately. Several prominent newspapers tempered their criticism of the assault with the assertion that Sumner had provoked it by his speech. Although in a more limited way than in the South, Northern public opinion on the caning was coercive, a situation Republicans used to pressure reluctant conservatives to cooperate with the party. A full month after the assault Everett, who had good reason to know, commented that the caning of Sumner "threw the entire north . . . into a frenzy of excitement . . . & no one dares speak aloud on the subject except to echo the popular voice." Former Governor Emory Washburne of Massachusetts made a similar complaint about Republican pressure after the assault: "It is not enough that you agree with them. You must say your creed in their words with their intonation and just when they bid you or they hang or burn you as a heretic." Some observers, especially conservatives frightened by the increasing sectionalism of American politics, vainly argued that the assault was purely a personal affair between Brooks and Sumner. But the enthusiastic and widespread support of Brooks in the South, and the ardent championing of Sumner in the North, necessarily made it a sectional incident. "That which hitherto has been an issue between the Southern Senators and Mr. Sumner," the New York *Tribune* asserted, "they have now made an issue between them and the great body of the people of the North. . . ."

Although Northern indignation meetings were non-partisan, "Bleeding Sumner" inevitably became a Republican issue. It was an ideal issue in several respects. Freedom of speech had always been a sacred American principle. Northerners, after years of abolitionist agitation, were keenly aware that, at least on the slavery issue, freedom of speech had long ago ceased in the South. Now it seemed directly under attack in Congress. The fact that the Constitution specifically protected congressional freedom of debate made the assault more startling. A conservative Republican organ, the *Illinois State Journal,* which was not given to exaggeration, characterized the assault as "the most direct blow to freedom of speech ever made in this country." "The great thing before the free states is the fact that freedom of debate is practically destroyed in Congress," one Massachusetts Republican solemnly proclaimed: "The inmost essence of the Constitution, that which gives it life and meaning, has been struck at, and grievously wounded, if not killed." This attack on free speech, and the subsequent failure of the Senate to defend its privileges, was the theme of Lord's widely reprinted speech at the New York meeting. Republicans lost no time in linking this issue with the assault, and the defense of free speech with their party. Free Soil, Free Labor, Free Men, Free Speech, and Frémont, chanted the party faithful in 1856.

According to Republicans, Brooks' attack was ominous because it was part of a conspiracy to destroy free speech and liberty everywhere. In explaining why the Sumner assault had aroused "a deeper feeling in the public heart of the North than any other event of the past ten years," the staid New York *Times* commented:

> The great body of the people, without distinction of party, feel that *their* rights have been assailed in a vital point,—that the blow struck at SUMNER takes effect upon Freedom of Speech in that spot where, without freedom of speech, there can be no freedom of any kind. . . .

This issue could be linked effectively to the Kansas outrages for, according to Republicans, free-state men in Kansas had been murdered and terrorized, and free-state newspapers destroyed, because they opposed slavery. The infamous code of laws enacted by the proslavery territorial legislature had even made it a crime to assert that slavery did not legally exist in Kansas. Both in Kansas and in the nation's capital, men seemed to be attacked for what they said. Slavery propagandists, the Cincinnati *Gazette* asserted, "cannot tolerate free speech anywhere, and would stifle it in Washington with the bludgeon and the bowie-knife, as they are now trying to stifle it in Kansas by massacre, rapine and murder." Other Republican newspapers echoed this theme. Nor was this threat to liberty confined to Washington and Kansas. "It seems that the Missouri Kansas Statutes, with additions, are to be established throughout the Union," one Indiana man wrote to Sumner. Henry Ward Beecher concisely brought these themes together in a powerful article on the caning entitled "Silence Must be Nationalized." Such events were part of a "long-formed, deeply-laid plan, of destroying free speech in the Republic, and making SILENCE NATIONAL!" he argued. Brooks "was the arm, but the whole South was the body!"

This linking of the Sumner and Kansas outrages was an extremely important aspect of the Republicans' use of the caning as a campaign issue. Republicans, far from viewing the Sumner assault as competing with the Kansas crisis for public attention, viewed them as mutually reinforcing. Historians have recognized that Bleeding Sumner and Bleeding Kansas were very powerful Republican symbols in the 1856 campaign. However, the manner in which the Sumner outrage gave credence to Bleeding Kansas has not been sufficiently emphasized. "It may seem hard to think but still it is true that the north needed in order to *see* the slave aggression, one of its best men Butchered in Congress, or something else as wicked which could be brought home to them. Had it not been for your poor head, the Kansas outrage would not have been felt at the North . . . ," one supporter consoled Sumner. Despite a year of agitation by the Republican press over the situation in Kansas, many Northerners, especially conservative former Whigs, remained skeptical of Republican claims. Such men were naturally suspicious of agitation and abolitionism anyway, and it was difficult to decide what was the truth about Kansas. This changed with the Sumner assault. Men were now more easily convinced that Southern aggression was a fact, that the South was capable of any atrocity to maintain its national power. "Soon men will be convinced Kansas difficulties are real, not stories circulated without foundation, for mere political capital," a correspondent assured Congressman Edwin B. Morgan after the caning. A Vermont Republican agreed: "*Brooks* has knocked the scales from the eyes of the blind, and they now *see!*"

At the same time, the Sumner assault gave the Republican party another means of increasing anti-Southern sentiment in the North. This was consistent with the party's primary goal, which was more to check the political power and arrogance of the South than to attack slavery. When confronted with united Southern opinion, it was only a short step from condemning Brooks to condemning the South. The Republican view of the South as a backward, degraded, barbaric society built on brutality and depravity, gained increased credibility as Southerners rallied to the defense of Brooks, the symbol of everything that Northerners despised in Southern chivalry. Brooks, in Republican rhetoric, became the inevitable product of a slave society. The North was the symbol of civilization, the South of barbarism. "The symbol of the North is the pen; the symbol of the South is the bludgeon," Beecher thundered at the New York meeting to tremendous cheering. A prominent New York conservative, earlier sympathetic to the South, now denied that Southerners were the cultivated aristocrats so often pictured: "they are, in fact, a race of lazy, ignorant, coarse, sensual, swaggering, sordid, beggarly barbarians, bullying white men and breeding little niggers for sale." This had been a common abolitionist theme, but Northerners generally had resisted endorsing it. Now it did not appear so extreme. . . .

The ideological significance of the Sumner caning was not the new ideas it developed, but the way it strengthened the persuasiveness of already existing Republican themes. Republicans used the Sumner assault and the incidents in Kansas to support their basic contention that the South, or more accurately, the Slave Power, had united in a design to stamp out all liberties of Northern white men. This became one of the most important and persuasive themes in the Republican campaign of 1856. Northern liberties, Northern manhood, Northern equality were all under assault by the Slave Power, party spokesmen argued. By such rhetoric, Republicans made the threat posed by the Slave

Power seem much more real and personal. They used the symbol of slavery, the essence of everything Northerners feared and hated, to express this threat. Thus the New York *Evening Post* asked after the caning:

> Has it come to this, that we must speak with bated breath in the presence of our Southern masters . . . ? If we venture to laugh at them, or to question their logic, or dispute their facts, are we to be chastised as they chastise their slaves? Are we too, slaves, slaves for life, a target for their brutal blows, when we do not comport ourselves to please them?

Brooks' blows were directed at every Northern freeman and must be resisted, contended a conservative New York minister after attending the meeting at the Tabernacle. "If the South appeal to the rod of the slave for argument with the North," he sternly insisted, "no way is left for the North, but to strike back, or be slaves." The Slave Power, arrogant and domineering, was determined to rule the country at all costs, the New York *Times* declared. The Sumner assault helped confirm the impression that "it will stop at no extremity of violence in order to subdue the people of the Free States and force them into a tame subserviency of its own domination."

To the modern reader, these Republican claims seem grossly exaggerated. Yet they struck a responsive chord in the minds of countless Northerners. Historians have not given sufficient attention to the manner in which Republicans utilized the civil liberties issue in the 1850s. Most Northerners had no sympathy for a crusade to abolish slavery in the South. But from their perspective the South, not the North, was acting aggressively, and Northern rights, not Southern, were under attack. After the Civil War a Republican journalist argued, with some justice, that the slavery issue would not have been so precipitated "but for the fatuity of the slaveholders, exhibited in their persistent demand that there should be no discussion." Avery Craven is only partially correct when he says that the sectional conflict "assumed the form of a conflict between *right* and *rights*." For Republicans, as well as Southerners, the issue was one of rights.

Some Democrats, such as the distinguished Pennsylvania jurist Jeremiah S. Black, charged the Republicans with hypocrisy on this issue. Such criticism was not totally without foundation. The fact that it was a leading Republican Senator who had been struck down, rather than someone else, influenced the response of *both* parties, Republican *and* Democratic. No doubt Republicans exploited the assault for political advantage, and such agitation did nothing to improve understanding between sections. Still their protests cannot be dismissed as mere party rhetoric. If these outrages had been isolated incidents, it would have been impossible to convince Northern public opinion that a real threat existed. What made the Republican view compelling was the fact that these latest outrages were part of a long series of what were perceived as assaults on Northern civil liberties, beginning with the gag rule in the 1830s. This cumulative effect, coupled with the particularly dramatic nature of the assault on Sumner and the sack of Lawrence, convinced many Northerners that these charges were more than political propaganda. After explaining that he had paid little attention to political matters in the past, one of Seward's correspondents confessed that the Sumner and Kansas outrages "startled me as tho a thunderbolt has fallen at my feet." The assault on Sumner was "not merely an *incident*, but a *demonstration*," Hannibal Hamlin's father-in-law asserted. Citing the repeal of the Missouri Compromise, the invasions of Kansas, the behavior of Southern congressmen, the policy of the Administration, and all the acts of violence of the period, he concluded:

bring all the proofs together & do they not furnish a clear demonstration of a settled purpose to annihilate freedom. . . . It seems to me the demonstration is as certain as any demonstration in mathematics. Incidents are no longer incidents—they are links in the chain of demonstration, infallible, plain, conclusive.

Republican strategists were acutely aware that concern for the welfare of blacks, free or slave, had never been a strong sentiment in the free states, and that appeals based on the immorality of slavery were not calculated to bring political success. The symbols of Bleeding Sumner and Bleeding Kansas allowed Republicans to attack the South without attacking slavery. By appropriating the great abolitionist symbol of the Slave Power, and linking it to the threat to Northern rights, Republicans made a much more powerful appeal to Northern sensibilities than they could have otherwise. As John Van Buren warned James Buchanan during the campaign, this appeal was especially strong among old Jacksonian Democrats. Such men coupled an intense hatred of the slave with a bitter animosity against slaveholders. The acrimonious struggle between the Van Buren Democrats and Southern political leaders in the previous decade had made them especially sensitive to charges of Southern arrogance and dictation. They were quite willing to enter a movement to check the political power of the South, but not to strike at slavery. One rank-and-file Democrat who joined the Republican party after the Sumner caning denied that he had any sympathy for abolitionism, or that his views on the social position of blacks had changed. But he was no longer willing to tolerate the aggressions of the Slave Power in Congress, in Kansas, and in the country generally: "Had the Slave power been less *insolently aggressive,* I would have been content to see it extend . . . but when it seeks to extend its sway by fire & sword . . . I am ready to say hold enough!" "Reserve no place for me," he told a long-time Democratic associate, "*I shall not come back.*" . . .

Republicans were incalculably aided by the South's foolish course in endorsing Brooks' action. Had the South repudiated Brooks, it would have helped retard (at least temporarily) the growth of anti-Southern sentiment in the North. Immediately after the caning, some leading conservatives confidently predicted that Southerners, both at home and in Congress, would not sustain Brooks. Events mocked their prediction and destroyed their influence. Conservatives vainly implored Southern congressmen not to endorse Brooks. A prominent Southern banker in New York City warned Howell Cobb, the leading Southern member of the House investigating committee, that the assault was unjustifiable and any attempt by the South to sustain it "will prove disastrous in the extreme." The Southern defense of Brooks came as a great shock to many calm, responsible Northerners. "It was not the act itself (horrible as that was) that excited me," a prominent New York conservative told Hamilton Fish, "but the tone of the Southern Press, & the approbation, apparently, of the whole Southern People." Similarly, Daniel Lord wrote after the Senate report on the assault: "On this subject our Southern friends have a folly rising to madness. Instead of cutting from it as a miserable indiscretion and meeting it as such, they tie themselves to it and it will sink them." The New York *Times,* in an editorial titled "Stupidity of the South," spoke of "the fatuous blindness" of Southerners in approving Brooks' conduct:

> There never was so good an opportunity offered to the South, before, to make capital for itself, as in this case of the ruffian BROOKS; but, true to their instincts, and blinded by the madness that must lead to their utter defeat, they have chosen to defend the outrageous

scoundrelism of their self-appointed champion and have thus made themselves responsible for his acts.

When Sumner returned to the Senate four years later, the Boston *Evening Transcript* declared that Southerners had only themselves to blame for his increased influence.

Confronted with Southern unity, Republicans argued that Northern unity was the only defense against aggression. The time for compromise had passed. The South's only hope was in Northern division. In making this appeal, Republicans sought to accomplish two objectives. First, by emphasizing sectional issues, they portrayed the American party, which sought to avoid them, as irrelevant in the present crisis. The contest was strictly between Republicans and Democrats. Second, they identified Northern Democrats with the unpopular policies and actions of their Southern allies. "Old party names must be forgotten, old party ties surrendered, organizations based upon secondary issues abandoned," Samuel Bowles' Springfield *Republican* proclaimed after the Sumner assault. The solution was for the people to unite and vote out of office those men who upheld these outrages, and this could be done only by supporting the Republican party. . . .

Just as the Sumner assault allowed Republicans to moderate and broaden their appeal, so it proved a powerful stimulus in driving moderates and conservatives into the Republican party. What made the Sumner caning of vital importance was not its effect on committed antislavery men, who had already gone into the Republican party, but its impact on moderates and conservatives, who had previously held aloof from the party out of fear that it was too radical and threatened to disrupt the Union. For many of these men, the Sumner assault was critical in their decision to join the Republican party. From New York Morgan reported after the Sumner protest meeting: "The Straight Whigs and conservatives are fast finding their places. . . . The doubtful and hesitating men are more excited now—than those who took the right ground early." Observers in other areas noted the same phenomenon: conservatives were most aroused by the assault, and they were now vehement in their denunciations of the South. . . .

No single event or issue can account for the remarkable Republican vote in the 1856 presidential election. Still, by helping to bring Whigs, Democrats, and Know Nothings into the Republican party, the Sumner assault was critical to the party's vote. Reflecting on the repeal of the Missouri Compromise, the attempt to subjugate Kansas, and the assault on Sumner, one Northerner concluded that Southerners were mad: in all their ingenuity they could not have devised a better means of uniting the North against them than this series of outrages. Democrats were badly shaken by the defections to the Republican party that they observed. Brooks' attack was doing the party "vast injury," a prominent New York Democrat warned Stephen A. Douglas. "You can scarcely imagine how much steam they are getting up on the subject." Democrats and Republicans alike concurred that the caning caused many antislavery Democrats to break finally with their party and go over to the Republicans. The Pennsylvania Republican wheelhorse Alexander McClure maintained that the party's most effective issue with such Democrats was Brooks and his bludgeon. Secretary of the Treasury James Guthrie agreed. From Washington he warned John C. Breckinridge, the Democratic Vice Presidential nominee: "This nomination of Freemont & Sumner excitement will give the free States against us with few exceptions . . . N[ew] York is gone in the opinion of many of our best Politicians here and the Sumner Beating has done it in this early stage of the Game." William L. Marcy, a shrewd observer of Northern public opinion, predicted that the Sumner-Brooks affair would cost the Democratic party 200,000 votes in the fall election. Guthrie believed that such losses were even greater.

The impact of the Sumner caning on the [Millard] Fillmore movement was devastating. By bringing conservatives into the Republican party—men whose support Fillmore [presidential nominee of the American, or Know Nothing, party] absolutely needed if he were to have any hope of election—the Sumner assault, along with the Kansas outrages, destroyed Fillmore's chances of carrying a single Northern state. This was the most important political consequence of the caning. Fillmore's weakness in the North, in the wake of these events, severely crippled his strength in the South, as many of his supporters, believing that the election was now reduced to a contest between Buchanan and Frémont, deserted Fillmore to vote for Buchanan. At the same time, these events caused countless Northern antislavery Know Nothings to join the Republican party. Fillmore's supporters became despondent as they saw his strength eroded by events. As he helplessly watched these developments, Winthrop insisted that "Brooks & Douglas deserve Statues from the Free Soil [Republican] party. The cane of the former & the Kansas bill of the latter . . . have secured a success to the Agitators which they never could have accomplished without them." Fillmore himself reinforced this feeling. "Brooks' attack upon Sumner has done more for Freemont than any 20 of his warmest friends North have been able to accomplish," he complained during the campaign. "If Freemont is elected, he will owe his election entirely to the troubles in Kansas, and the martyrdom of Sumner . . . the Republicans ought to pension Brooks for life. . . ." . . .

Despite the caning of Sumner and the Kansas violence, Frémont was defeated in November, as Fillmore polled enough votes nationally to give Buchanan a plurality and victory. The Republican party was unable to overcome the handicaps under which it commenced the campaign. Yet even in defeat, Republicans expressed optimism about the future. What was remarkable in the election results was not that Frémont lost, but that he did so well. From the beginning of the campaign the most prescient Republican leaders had believed that there was little chance of victory in their party's first national contest. The Republican party lacked an efficient national organization; in several Northern states the party had not even existed prior to 1856; Fillmore's candidacy would divide the opposition vote; the Democrats were well organized and well financed. Faced with these problems, Republican leaders had hoped to establish a sound national organization and, by crushing the American party, emerge as the only significant opposition party to the Democrats. In view of these difficulties, the Republican performance in the 1856 election was astounding. With a vote in the free states which exceeded that of either opponent, Frémont managed to carry all but five Northern states. Moreover, the American party had been destroyed as a viable national organization. It was clear in the aftermath of the 1856 election that the Republican party constituted the major opposition to the Democracy. Far from being discouraged, most Republicans were heartened by the results. With four years to strengthen their party organization and clarify their program, they were confident of victory in 1860. . . .

Throughout the summer and fall of 1856, as the presidential campaign rolled on and his disability continued, Sumner impatiently chafed at his incapacity to campaign for Frémont. He wrote letter after letter bemoaning his inability to speak now, when so much was at stake. More sagacious friends tried to console him. The old Jacksonian editor Francis P. Blair, now a prominent Republican manager, urged Sumner not to exert himself until he was fully recovered. "You have . . . done more to gain the victory than any other," he comforted the Senator with his sharp eye for the currents of popular feeling. Other Republicans provided similar testimony of his unique service to the party. Sumner did more for his party by his suffering than he ever had done by his speeches. The Brooks assault was of critical importance in transforming the struggling Republican party into a major political force. "By great odds the most effective deliverance made by any man to advance the Republican party was made by the bludgeon of Preston S. Brooks," McClure acutely concluded in retrospect. The caning of Charles Sumner was a major landmark on the road to civil war.

Kansas, Republicanism, and the Crisis of the Union

DON E. FEHRENBACHER

"All Christendom is leagued against the South upon this question of domestic slavery," said James Buchanan on the Senate floor in 1842. "They have no other allies to sustain their constitutional rights, except the Democracy of the North. . . . In my own State, we inscribe upon our banners hostility to abolition. It is there one of the cardinal principles of the Democratic party."

The crisis of 1850 once again confirmed the crucial importance of northern Democrats in the southern strategy of defense, and it also revealed the extent to which that defense might be breached by an unsympathetic president. The South accordingly appears to have benefited more from the political consequences of the Compromise of 1850 than from any of its specific provisions. For a reunited Democratic party, pledging faithful adherence to the Compromise, swept to victory in the presidential election of 1852 and also won a two-thirds majority in the House of Representatives.

During the next eight years, under Franklin Pierce and his successor, James Buchanan, southern influence dominated the executive branch of the federal government through the agency of northern doughfaces [Northern politicians sympathetic to the South] like Caleb Cushing and Jeremiah S. Black, as well as southerners like Jefferson Davis and Howell Cobb. Throughout the period, the Senate remained safely Democratic and therefore safely prosouthern on slavery questions. In the House of Representatives, three of the five speakers serving between 1850 and 1860 were Democrats from Georgia, Kentucky, and South Carolina. Seven of the nine members of the Supreme Court were Democrats; and in 1857, six of them declared the Missouri Compromise restriction unconstitutional on the ground that Congress had no power to prohibit slavery in the territories.

Of course, these were things that southerners had come to expect. In 1861, Alexander H. Stephens reminded his fellow Georgians: "We have had a majority of the Presidents chosen from the South; as well as the control and management of most of those chosen from the North." Then he went on to name other offices in which southerners had outnumbered northerners: Supreme Court justices, 18 to 11; speakers of the House, 23 to 12; presidents pro tem of the Senate, 24 to 11; attorneys general, 14 to 5; foreign ministers, 86 to 54; and in the appointment of some 3,000 clerks, auditors, and controllers, better than a two-to-one advantage.

From "Kansas, Republicanism, and the Crisis of the Union," reprinted by permission of Louisiana State University Press from *The South and the Sectional Crisis*, pp. 46–65 by Don E. Fehrenbacher. Copyright © 1980 by Louisiana State University Press.

The extraordinary power traditionally exercised by southerners in national affairs constituted one of the principal deterrents to disunion; for as long as it endured, the South had better reason to remain in the Union than to leave. It was the loss of a substantial part of that power in 1860 that drove the seven states of the Lower South into secession, and the critical element in the loss was the weakened condition of the South's only ally in Christendom—the northern Democracy.

The structure of southern power in national politics during the 1850s was a kind of holding-company arrangement in which the South held majority control of the Democratic party, and the Democrats were the majority party in the nation. The same pattern had prevailed during much of the preceding half century, and the recent experience with Zachary Taylor had revealed that the Whig party could *not* be brought under southern control—not even when it was headed by a southern slaveholder. In any case, the distress of the Whig party soon left the Democrats as the only national party organization through which the South could exercise national power.

Nothing, then, was more vital to southern security within the Union than maintaining the majority status of the Democratic party. And in this respect, the Democratic victory in 1852 was not as overwhelming as it appeared on the surface, especially in the North. Although Pierce carried fourteen out of the sixteen free states, he did so with only a plurality of their popular vote. The structure of southern political power therefore resembled a bridge that rested at one end on an insecure foundation. To be sure, Democratic mastery seemed firm enough in 1853, with the presidency recaptured and the party controlling both houses of the incoming Congress by huge majorities. But this flush of prosperity proved to be ominous, in a way, and also treacherous—ominous because of what it signified about the condition of the Whig party, and treacherous because it encouraged the disastrous blunder of the Kansas-Nebraska Act.

The disintegration of the Whig party, and thus of the second American party system, began with the alienation of southern Whigs from Taylor in 1849–1850 and was largely completed by 1855. Historians continue to ponder the question of why the Whig party perished in the 1850s while the Democratic party, though presumably subject to the same disruptive pressures, managed to survive. It may be, simply, that the Whigs lacked the symbolic appeal, the tradition of victory, and the degree of cohesion necessary for survival in the 1850s. Another explanation is that Whiggery was in a sense absorbed by the burgeoning nativist movement, which then failed in *its* efforts to become a major, bisectional party. But in addition, it appears that differences of sectional balance *within* the two parties may account for the greater vulnerability of the Whigs. Since the South was much more united than the North on the issue of slavery, it was accordingly easier for many northern Democrats to remain within a party increasingly dominated by proslavery southerners than it was for southern Whigs to remain within a party increasingly dominated by antislavery northerners. That is probably why the disruption of the second American party system started with the collapse of Whiggery in several states of the Lower South.

Why the Whig organization did not at least survive in the North as a major antislavery party, instead of giving way to the Republicans, is another question and need not be answered here. The point is that the death of the Whig party as a national organization proved harmful to the health of the Democratic party and thus to the structure of southern political power. For the Democrats, during the later 1850s, were opposed in both the North and the South by sectional or local parties that did not have to make any concessions to intersectional accommodation within their organizations. The cross-pressures of party and section upon northern Democrats became much more severe when the Whigs were replaced by a more aggressively antislavery party that stood to profit organizationally from continued agitation of the slavery issue. The challenge of Republicanism compelled men like Stephen A. Douglas, in the interest of political survival, to show more independence of southern influence where slavery was concerned, and this necessity could not fail to place heavy strains upon party unity.

And even in the South, where the Democrats themselves were supposedly the radical party on sectional issues, they came under cross-pressure from the post-Whig opposition parties, which, as a matter of political strategy, often tried to outdo them in proslavery extremism. It was the southern opposition press, for instance, that started the attacks on Buchanan's Kansas policy in the summer of 1857, and it was the southern opposition press that set up the loudest clamor for a territorial slave code two years later. As John V. Mering has pointed out, "Only in Tennessee among southern states that had elections for governor in 1859 did the Opposition refrain from taking a stronger stand on behalf of slavery in the territories than the Democrats."

But the first baneful consequence of the Whig decline was passage of the Kansas-Nebraska bill, which never could have been accomplished if the Democrats had not held such large majorities in both houses of Congress. The bill received the support of nearly nine-tenths of all southern members casting votes and nearly three-fourths of all Democrats. It was an official party measure, endorsed and vigorously promoted by the Pierce administration, but its disruptive influence is strikingly illustrated by the fact that in the House of Representatives, northern Democrats were divided, 44 in favor and 44 against. The political aftermath turned into a Democratic nightmare, with waves of popular indignation sweeping through the free states, 66 out of 91 House seats held by northern Democrats lost in the midterm elections, and the emergence of a broad anti-Nebraska coalition that would soon crystallize into the Republican party.

The struggle over the Kansas-Nebraska bill was the most egregious of several instances in which southerners, during the 1850s, traded some of their power advantage for empty sectional victories. Although its momentous consequences are plain to see, the struggle is of interest not only because of what it did *to* the South, but also because of what it revealed *about* the South.

Historians differ about the degree to which southerners of the 1850s were committed to the further expansion of slavery. The South delineated by William L. Barney, for instance, was a society in constant need of more room for its growing slave population and of new land to replace its easily depleted soils. "The continual maturation of slavery within a fixed geographical area," he writes, "created class and racial stresses that could be relieved only through expansion." Furthermore, "as long as the option of adding slave territory was kept open, Southerners could delude themselves with the comforting belief that eventually slavery and its terrible racial dilemma could vanish slowly and painlessly, by a diffusion of all the blacks out of the American South into the tropics of Central and South America."

On the other hand, there are historians disposed to believe that the sectional controversy of the 1850s had less to do with the further expansion of slavery than with the future of slavery in modern America. In their view, the pernicious and seemingly useless quarrel over the territories was primarily a symbolic struggle laden with implication—or, as has been said, "merely the skirmish line of a larger and more fundamental conflict."

No doubt there is room enough for both interpretations in any comprehensive explanation of the coming of the Civil War, but southern expansionism hardly seems to have been the animating spirit of the Kansas-Nebraska Act. The measure, by repealing the 36° 30′ restriction of the Missouri Compromise, admitted slavery into an area unsuited for it and in no way facilitated the expansion of slavery southward into areas that *were* suited for it.

It is true that some southerners cherished the hope of making Kansas the sixteenth slave state, but even if they had succeeded, it would have been a nominal and temporary triumph gained at excessive cost. Proslavery imperialism became an absurdity in Kansas, and, as far as southern political power was concerned, it would have been much better strategy to settle for the admission of Kansas as a free but *Democratic* state, like the three states actually admitted in the 1850s—California, Minnesota, and Oregon. That was precisely the strategy adopted by Robert J. Walker as governor of Kansas in 1857, but the South rose up in revolt against it and saw Kansas admitted just a few years later as a Republican state instead.

The bitterest irony in the Kansas-Nebraska Act was that its sponsors justified it as a logical and reconciliatory extension of the Compromise of 1850. They insisted, erroneously, that the old dividing-line policy had been replaced with a new, uniform national policy of nonintervention [Douglas's theory of popular sovereignty, whereby the voters of a territory rather than Congress would determine whether slavery should be admitted] and that, accordingly, to retain the slavery restriction north of 36° 30′ in the organization of new territories would violate the letter and spirit of the recent Compromise. Actually, however, the popularity of the Compromise of 1850 resulted largely from its general pacificatory effect, not from any principles that could be inferred from its specific provisions. In short, the clearest violation of the spirit of the Compromise would be *any* legislative action that revived the slavery controversy. And the political power of the South, depending as it did upon the strength and unity of the Democratic party, likewise stood to suffer grievously from any renewal of slavery agitation. Southerners must have realized as well as Douglas that repeal of the Missouri Compromise restriction would, in his words, "raise a hell of a storm." Why, then, did they risk so much for so little to be gained?

For one thing, it appears that the southern members of Congress more or less drifted into the Kansas-Nebraska struggle without giving it much thought beforehand. Certainly there was no strong pressure on them from home to secure the repeal at that time, and it is notable that members from the Lower South were not prominent in the early stages of the affair. In fact, the senator who initiated the move to make the repeal explicit was a Kentucky Whig—the successor of Henry Clay.

Southern press support for the Kansas-Nebraska bill was relatively restrained, as Avery O. Craven has shown. "It is difficult for us to comprehend, or credit the excitement . . . in the North on account of the Nebraska question," wrote an Alabaman in the summer of 1854. "Here," he continued, "there is no excitement, no fever, on the subject. It is seldom alluded to in private or public and so far as the introduction of slavery [into Kansas and Nebraska] is concerned, such a consummation is hardly hoped for." But the savage northern denunciation of the measure encouraged southern members to close ranks on the issue, and they supplied more than 60 percent of the votes cast for passage.

With sectional violence thereafter erupting and becoming chronic on the prairies of Kansas, the South's emotional investment in the proslavery cause in Kansas grew to enormous proportions, even while the chances of gaining anything of practical importance were steadily dwindling.

Southern attitudes throughout the Kansas controversy demonstrate the intensely reactive nature of southern sectionalism. That is, the South did not so much respond to the Kansas-Nebraska issue itself as react to the northern response to the issue; and much the same thing happened four years later in the struggle over the Lecompton constitution. Similarly, what angered southerners most about John Brown's raid on Harpers Ferry was the amount of applause it received in the North.

The language of antislavery denunciation had a cumulative effect by the 1850s, and southern skin, far from toughening under attack, had become increasingly sensitive. According to Senator Judah P. Benjamin of Louisiana, the heart of the matter was not so much what the abolitionists and Republicans had *done* or might *do* to the South, as it was "the things they *said*" about the South—and the moral arrogance with which they said them. Southerners, though often emphatically denying it, in fact cared deeply about northern opinion of the South and its people. They wanted, above all, an end to being treated as moral inferiors, and thus an end to the fear of eventually *accepting* the badge of inferiority. The result, says Charles G. Sellers, was a "series of constantly mounting demands for symbolic acts by which the North would say that slavery was all right."

The most conspicuous badge of sectional inferiority was overt federal prohibition of slavery in the territories. For many southerners by the 1850s, such exclusion had become a moral reproach of unbearable weight. When Douglas offered them the opportunity to erase a large part of the stigma by repealing the Missouri Compromise restriction, they could scarcely do otherwise than grasp it.

The symbolic victory thus achieved in the Kansas-Nebraska Act was not really expected to bring any tangible benefits. But the course of events in Kansas did conspire to offer the South a chance in 1858 to win another victory of the same kind—that is, the admission of Kansas as a nominal slaveholding state under the Lecompton constitution. Once again, and in an even more dubious cause, southern members of Congress closed ranks. Knowing that the constitution did not represent the will of the territorial population, knowing that Kansas was destined to be a free state whatever the formal terms of her admission might be, and knowing that the issue would surely cause havoc among the northern Democracy, they nevertheless voted almost unanimously for the Lecompton bill.

Again there appeared to be an important principle at stake. For here was an opportunity to test one of the items in the Georgia platform of 1850—namely, whether a slave state could ever again be admitted to the Union, now that an antislavery party had become predominant in the North. There had *been* no such admission, after all, since that of Texas twelve years earlier. The test came, moreover, in the aftermath of the Dred Scott decision, when southerners were again reacting to a northern reaction and also discarding the notion that the Constitution, of its own force, gave them any protection against antislavery attack.

As it became increasingly clear that the Lecompton bill, with half of the northern Democrats opposing it, could not command a majority in the House, another secession crisis developed. The ultimatum "Lecompton or disunion" reverberated in the halls of Congress, in the southern press, and in southern legislatures. With Alabama leading the way, contingent steps toward secession were officially taken by several states. "Upon the action of this Congress, must depend the union or disunion of this great Confederacy," a Georgia congressman warned. The people of the South were determined, he said, "to have equality in this Union or independence out of it . . . you must admit Kansas . . . with the Lecompton constitution." "The equilibrium in the balance of power is already lost," declared a member from Mississippi. "Reject Kansas and the cordon is then completed. . . . Against this final act of degradation I believe the South will resist—resist with arms." "Save the Union, if you can," wrote a South Carolinian to Senator James H. Hammond. "But rather than have Kansas refused admission under the Lecompton Constitution, let it perish in blood and fire."

The symbolic importance of the issue was not diminished but rather was enhanced by the fact that the South had nothing material to gain from the admission. As Buchanan's pro-Lecompton message to Congress perceptively argued: "In considering this question, it should never be forgotten that in proportion to its insignificance . . . the rejection of the constitution will be so much the more keenly felt by the people of . . . the States of this Union, where slavery is recognized." So, paradoxically, the very futility of the proslavery cause in Kansas made the Lecompton question more clearly a "point of honor" and a meaningful test of how *little* could be expected from the North in the way of concessions. In the words of one South Carolinian, it would have been "dirt cheap" for the free states to yield.

Once again, however, a legislative crisis ended in a legislative compromise—or rather, in this case, a pseudocompromise that did not conceal the reality of southern defeat. The critical question was whether the Lecompton bill should be passed as it was or be amended to allow resubmission of the constitution to the voters of Kansas, which would surely mean rejection. With the House of Representatives this time standing its ground, southern members of Congress ended by accepting the so-called "English compromise," which provided for an indirect resubmission of the constitution and thus allowed them to save face a little with their constituents.

For this miserable achievement the South paid dearly. The Democratic party, split by an anti-Lecompton revolt with Douglas at its head, suffered another election defeat in 1858 and became the minority party in virtually every northern state. From that point on, the odds favored election of a Republican president in 1860. Moreover, the English compromise was so obviously a southern backdown from the threat of disunion that it encouraged Republicans to regard later secession threats as mere resumption of a game of bluff.

The compromise nevertheless satisfied many southerners, even some aiming at disunion, because it enabled them to retreat from a shaky limb. The Lecompton constitution, for a number of reasons, provided a very dubious basis for a sectional ultimatum. Governor Joseph E. Brown of Georgia, who was ready at the time to inaugurate a secession movement, later acknowledged that an outright defeat of the Lecompton bill would have caused "great confusion," and that "the democratic party of the state would have been divided and distracted." It appears, then, that in 1858 there was some possibility of an *unsuccessful* secession movement that might have thrown secessionism generally into disrepute and thus, like a small earthquake, taken off some of the underlying stress.

The Lecompton affair proved to be the last full-dress legislative crisis and compromise in the tradition of 1819–1821, 1832–1833, and 1846–1850. Reflecting upon the pattern of events from the introduction of the Tallmadge proviso [a House amendment to the bill of 1819 to admit Missouri to statehood, which, if enacted, would have prohibited further introduction of slaves into Missouri] to the hollow triumph of the English compromise, one is disposed to doubt that legislative crisis was ever the proper fuse for setting off a civil war in the United States. A crisis arising in Congress could usually be controlled by Congress. The greatest danger in 1850, for instance, had been that presidential intervention might take matters out of congressional hands.

The end of the Lecompton controversy in fact marked the end of the territorial issue as a serious threat to the Union. Kansas ceased to be disputed ground and was admitted quietly as a free state in 1861. There was no other sectional issue with which Congress seemed likely, in the near future, to create another legislative crisis. Certainly not the agitation for a reopening of the African slave trade; for that had only minority support even in the Lower South. And certainly not the issue of a slave code for the territories, which provoked so much congressional debate in 1859 and 1860. That was not a southern demand upon Congress for legislation, but rather a southern Democratic demand upon Douglas for renunciation of his apostasy or withdrawal from the approaching presidential race.

James Buchanan had entered the presidency in 1857 determined to end the conflict in Kansas and thereby restore sectional peace. He hoped that "geographical parties," as he phrased it in his inaugural, would then "speedily become extinct." His efforts ended in a curious mixture of success and failure; for the resolution of the Kansas problem, by the very manner in which it was accomplished, substantially increased the strength of the Republican party. . . .

The disintegration of the Whig party, and hence the breakup of the second American party system, had begun before 1854, but it was the Kansas-Nebraska Act, more than anything else, that determined the character of the third party system in its early years. If the sectional truce of 1850 had remained more or less in effect, the Whig party might well have been succeeded by the Native American or Know-Nothing party. Instead, with the slavery controversy reopened to the point of violence, the anti-Nebraska coalition of 1854 swiftly converted itself into the nation's first major party organized on antislavery principles. Suddenly, the South faced a new menace and a new potential cause for secession—the possibility that a Republican might be elected to the presidency.

The causes for secession listed in the Georgia platform of 1850 [a list of six eventualities drawn up by a Georgia state convention, any one of which would be sufficient cause for disunion] had all been legislative acts that might be passed by Congress. The sectional crises of 1820, 1833, 1850, and 1858 had all been precipitated by such legislation, enacted or proposed. But, beginning in 1856, the election of a Republican president became a more probable occasion for disunion than any legislative proposal likely to receive serious consideration in Congress. Beginning in 1856, a different finger was on the trigger mechanism. Control passed from the professional politician to the ordinary voter, particularly the northern voter. And if worse should come to worst, how did one go about compromising the results of a presidential election?

It was difficult for the people of the South to view Republicans as merely a political opposition. "If they should succeed in this contest," said a North Carolina newspaper in September 1856, "the result will be a separation of the States. No human power can prevent it. . . . They would create insurrection and servile war in the South—they would put the torch to our dwellings and the knife to our throats. They are, therefore, our enemies."

We should perhaps pay more attention to the fact that 1856 was a year of genuine secession crisis, mitigated only by the general belief that the Republicans had but an outside chance of capturing the presidency. For southerners, the outcome of the election spelled temporary relief but very little reassurance. The Democrats did elect James Buchanan to succeed Franklin Pierce, and they did recapture control of the House of Representatives. Buchanan triumphed by sweeping the South, except for Maryland, and by carrying also the five free states of New Jersey, Pennsylvania, Indiana, Illinois, and California. But only two of those five states gave him popular majorities—Indiana, 50.4 percent, and his own Pennsylvania, 50.1 percent. The Democratic share of the free-state vote fell from 50.7 percent in 1852 to 41.4 percent in 1856. John C. Frémont, the Republican candidate, outpolled Buchanan in the North by more than a hundred thousand votes. Frémont and Millard Fillmore, the American party candidate, together outpolled him by more than a half million votes in the North. There was little difficulty visualizing what would happen to the Democratic party in the free states if its divided opposition should become united. The party had, in fact, hung on to the presidency with its fingertips; and the loss of that precarious hold, even many conservative southerners agreed, would mean a prompt disruption of the Union.

In these circumstances, the all-out drive to make Kansas a slave state under the Lecompton constitution was plain political folly. And the midterm congressional elections of 1858 accordingly proved disastrous for the Democrats because of what happened in those same northern states that Buchanan had carried two years earlier. The Republicans increased their share of the total vote in New Jersey, Pennsylvania, Indiana, and Illinois from 35 percent in 1856 to 52 percent in 1858. The most stunning reversal came in Pennsylvania. There, just the year before, the Democrats had elected a governor by more than forty thousand votes, but in 1858 they lost nearly all of their congressional seats and were outpolled by twenty-five thousand votes. "We have met the enemy in Pennsylvania," said Buchanan, "and we are theirs."

From the Lecompton struggle onward, all the signs of the times pointed to a Republican victory in 1860 and to some kind of secession movement as a consequence. Yet the Democratic party, instead of reuniting to meet the danger, became increasingly a house divided against itself. The quarrel between Douglas and the South, aside from its strong influence on the shape of the final crisis, deserves attention because of what it reveals about the psychological escalation of the sectional conflict.

Douglas in 1856 had been the favorite presidential nominee of the South, and especially of the Lower South, which gave him thirty-eight of its forty-seven votes at the Cincinnati convention. Four years later at Charleston, however, delegates from the Lower South walked out of the convention rather than accept his leadership of the party. In the interval, Douglas made his fight against the Lecompton constitution, opposing even the English compromise; he issued the Freeport doctrine [that slavery could not exist anywhere without the support of local police regulations] during the debates with Lincoln as a means of salvaging the principle of popular sovereignty while at the same time endorsing the Dred Scott decision [that slavery had to be permitted in the territories]; and, presumably as a consequence of those actions, he managed to win reelection to the Senate against the Republican tide that swept so many northern Democrats out of office in 1858.

It was success at the polls that the South needed most from its northern allies, but what southern Democratic leaders proceeded to insist upon instead was party orthodoxy, as they defined it. Ignoring the plain fact that for Douglas, opposition to the Lecompton constitution had been a matter, not only of principle, but also of political survival, they branded him a traitor. And ignoring the fact that the Freeport doctrine was actually of southern origin, they branded him a heretic. As punishment, the Senate Democratic leadership in December 1858 stripped him of his chairmanship of the committee on territories, a position that he had held continuously for more than ten years.

Douglas responded with his usual vigor and combativeness. The southern Democrats, in turn, set out to make approval of a territorial slave code the supreme test of party loyalty. That was the ostensible issue that eventually disrupted the party at Charleston, but the real issue was Douglas, and the purpose of the slave-code agitation was to destroy him as a presidential candidate.

Of course, the South never approached unanimity in such matters, and the Little Giant continued to have supporters in every southern state right down to 1860. Even the Lower South gave him 11 percent of its total popular vote for president that year. One is nevertheless struck by the volume and intensity of southern hatred for Douglas in the period 1858–1860. He was with us, the indictment ran, "until the time of trial came; then he deceived and betrayed us." He "placed himself at the head of the Black column and gave the word of command," thereby becoming "stained with the dishonor of treachery without a parallel in the political history of the country." And now, covered with the "odium of . . . detestable heresies" and the "filth of his defiant recreancy," he would receive what southern patriots had always given northern enemies—"war to the knife." Then, "away with him to the tomb which he is digging for his political corpse."

In retrospect, it appears that the only hope of preventing a Republican presidential victory lay in uniting the Democratic party behind Douglas. Yet, by 1860, southern hostility toward Douglas had taken on a life of its own and become implacable. The motives of southern leaders at this point are not easily fathomed or summarized. Perhaps as many as a score of them harbored serious presidential aspirations and so had personal reasons for wanting Douglas out of the way. There were also committed secessionists working openly to disrupt the Democratic party and welcoming the likelihood of a Republican presidential victory as the best means of achieving disunion. Covertly or subconsciously allied with them was a larger group of southerners (including Jefferson Davis, for example) who continued to call secession a "last resort," while conducting themselves in a way that tended to eliminate other choices. Their "conditional Unionism" with impossible conditions amounted to secessionism in the end.

But in addition to all the purposes visible in southern attitudes toward Douglas, his defection had an important symbolic meaning that weighed heavily on the southern spirit. The theme of betrayal and fear of betrayal runs prominently through much of the southern rhetoric of alienation. The South had been betrayed, in a sense, by its own ancestors who first accepted the role of slaveholder. It felt betrayed by New England, whose abolitionist zealots now made war on an institution introduced into the country by New England slave traders. It felt betrayed by Taylor as president and by Walker as territorial governor of Kansas. Southerners also feared treachery from their slaves and free blacks. They distrusted the sectional loyalty of nonslaveholding southern whites, and in the Lower South there was strong doubt that the border states could be depended upon in a crisis.

In such a context, the defection of Douglas was an especially painful blow. Perhaps no single event contributed so much to the southern sense of being isolated in a hostile world. "[It] has done more than all else," wrote a South Carolinian, "to shake my confidence in Northern men on the slavery issue, for I have long regarded him as one of our . . . most reliable friends." A correspondent of the Charleston *Mercury* put it more tersely: "If he proved false, whom can you trust?" To despair of Douglas was virtually to despair of the Union itself. At the Charleston convention in the spring of 1860, the states of the Lower South withdrew from the Democratic party organization rather than submit to the nomination of Douglas. Who could then doubt that those same states would withdraw from the Union rather than submit to the election of a Republican president? In this respect, the dramatic walkout of delegates at Charleston was a dress rehearsal for secession.

The final crisis of the Union is commonly thought of as starting with the election of Lincoln in November 1860, but the entire presidential campaign had taken place in an atmosphere of crisis that extended back into the preceding year. When the Thirty-sixth Congress convened on December 5, 1859, John Brown was just three days in his grave, and the storm of emotion caused by his adventure at Harpers Ferry had not yet begun to abate. The House of Representatives plunged immediately into a two-month-long speakership contest of such bitterness that many members of Congress armed themselves for protection against assault. One senator, with grim hyperbole, said that the only persons not carrying a revolver and a knife were those carrying two revolvers.

Then, after an angry renewal of the slave-code debate in the Senate, there came the splitting of the Democratic party at Charleston. By midsummer, many southerners recognized that the odds strongly favored a Republican victory, and they began, in their minds, at least, to prepare for it. October elections for state offices in Pennsylvania and Indiana turned probability almost into certainty, and still there was another month left for preparation.

Meanwhile, with the apprehension aroused by John Brown still keenly felt, a new wave of fear swept through the South. There were reports of slaves in revolt, of conspiracies uncovered just in time, of mass poisonings attempted, of whole towns burned, and of abolitionist agents caught and hung. And the full terror, presumably, still lay ahead. "If such things come upon us," said a Georgia newspaper, "with only the *prospect* of an Abolition ruler, what will be our condition when he is *actually in power?*" The very vagueness of the prospect made it all the more ominous. Fear of Republican rule was to no small degree a fear of the unknown. Chief Justice Roger B. Taney was not alone in believing that the news of Lincoln's election might be the signal for a general slave uprising. But other prophets of doom, like the editors of the Richmond *Enquirer,* pictured Republican purposes working out in more insidious ways:

> Upon the accession of Lincoln to power, we would apprehend no direct act of violence against negro property, but by the use of federal office, contracts, power and patronage, the building up in every Southern State of a Black Republican party, the ally and stipendiary of Northern fanaticism, to become in a few short years the open advocates of abolition. . . . No act of violence may ever be committed, no servile war waged, and yet the ruin and degradation of Virginia will be as fully and fatally accomplished, as though bloodshed and rapine ravished the land.

One wonders how often in history rebellions and other cataclysmic events have not occurred, even in the presence of adequate causes, simply because there was no practical point of impulse where feeling and belief could be translated into action. For southerners, the presidential election of 1860 was just such a point of impulse—its date fixed on the calendar, its outcome predictable and not subject to compromise, its expected conse-quences vague but terrible. All the passion of the sectional conflict became concentrated, like the sun's rays by a magnifying glass, on one moment of decision that could come only once in history—that is, the *first* election of a Republican president. If secessionists had not seized the moment but instead had somehow been persuaded to let it pass, such a clear signal for action might never again have sounded.

Yet, even under these optimum conditions created by Lincoln's election, the southern will to act was but partly energized. The South, though long united in defense of slavery, had never been close to unity on the subject of secession. And so, in the end, the best fuse available set off only half of the accumulated charge. Just the seven states of the Lower South broke away from the Union in the winter of 1860–1861, although their very number, as I have already suggested, probably had a critical influence on the subsequent course of events.

But if only the Lower South seceded, the entire Slaveholding South had contributed heavily to the event that activated the secession movement—that is, to the Republican capture of the presidency. In 1852, the Free Soil Candidate for president received only 7 percent of the popular vote in the free states and did not come close to winning a single electoral vote. Just eight years later, Lincoln won 55 percent of the popular vote in the free states and 98 percent of their electoral vote. It is difficult to believe that a political revolution of such magnitude would have occurred if southerners had not chosen to pursue the will-o'-the-wisp of Kansas, sacrificing the realities of power to an inner need for reassurance of their equal status and moral respectability in the face of antislavery censure.

The Charleston *Mercury,* commenting on the Dred Scott decision in 1857, said that it was "a victory more fatal, perhaps, than defeat," because the antislavery forces always rose up stronger after each sectional confrontation and, in fact, seemed to feed on adversity. Pursuing the same theme more than a century later, David M. Potter wrote:

> For ten years the Union had witnessed a constant succession of crises; always these ended in some kind of "victory" for the South, each of which left the South with an empty prize and left the Union in a weaker condition than before. . . . Not one of [the victories] added anything to the area, the strength, the influence, or even the security of the southern system. Yet each had cost the South a high price, both in alienating the public opinion of the nation and in weakening . . . the Democratic party, which alone stood between the South and sectional domination by the Republicans.

Yet the victories of the South, though useless, were not meaningless. Important values seemed to be at stake—values associated, above all, with regional and personal self-respect. More than one southern political leader insisted that the fight for the Lecompton constitution had to be made because it was a "point of honor." With the same sensitivity about honor and the same disregard for possible consequences, many a southerner had faced his opponent on the dueling ground.

In the spring of 1861, with secession accomplished and the Confederate States of America a functioning reality, there remained still another point of honor to be settled, another empty prize to be won at exorbitant cost. It appears now that the Confederacy's best hope of survival may have been to avoid war and consolidate its independent status as long as possible, rather than trying to win a war against a stronger enemy. But the stars and stripes still flying on a fortified island in Charleston Harbor had become an infuriating symbol of southern independence unrecognized and thus another instance of southern honor degraded. So, in the early morning of April 12, 1861, southerners once again did what they had to do. They opened fire on Fort Sumter and this time gained a military victory more disastrous, perhaps, than any of their later military defeats.

FURTHER READING

Tyler Anbinder, *Nativism and Slavery: The Northern Know Nothings and the Politics of the 1850s* (1992)

John Ashworth, *Slavery, Capitalism and Politics in the Antebellum Republic, Vol. 1, Commerce and Compromise, 1820–1850* (1995)

William L. Barney, *The Road to Secession: A New Perspective on the Old South* (1972)

William J. Cooper, Jr., *The South and the Politics of Slavery, 1828–1856* (1978)

David Donald, *Charles Sumner and the Coming of the Civil War* (1960)

Don E. Fehrenbacher, *Prelude to Greatness: Lincoln in the 1850s* (1962)

———, *The Dred Scott Case: Its Significance in American Law and Politics* (1978)

Eric Foner, *Free Soil, Free Labor, Free Men: The Ideology of the Republican Party before the Civil War* (1970), 77–93

———, "Racial Attitudes of the New York Free Soilers," in *Politics and Ideology in the Age of the Civil War* (1980)

William E. Gienapp, *The Origins of the Republican Party, 1852–1856* (1987)

Michael F. Holt, *The Political Crisis of the 1850s* (1978)

Harry V. Jaffa, *Crisis of the House Divided: An Interpretation of the Lincoln-Douglas Debates* (1959)

Robert W. Johannsen, ed., *The Lincoln-Douglas Debates of 1858* (1965)

———, *Stephen A. Douglas* (1973)

Marc W. Kruman, *Parties and Politics in North Carolina, 1836–1865* (1983)

John McCardell, *The Idea of a Southern Nation: Southern Nationalists and Southern Nationalism, 1830–1860* (1979)

Michael Perman, ed., *The Coming of the American Civil War, 3rd ed.* (1993)

David M. Potter, *The Impending Crisis, 1848–1861* (1976)

James A. Rawley, *Race and Politics: "Bleeding Kansas" and the Coming of the Civil War* (1969)

Thomas Schott, *Alexander H. Stephens: A Biography* (1988)

Richard H. Sewell, *Ballots for Freedom: Antislavery Politics in the United States, 1837–1860* (1976)

Kenneth M. Stampp, *America in 1857: A Nation on the Brink* (1990)

J. Mills Thornton, III, *Politics and Power in a Slave Society: Alabama, 1800–1860* (1978)

CHAPTER
3

The Secession Crisis

As President-elect Abraham Lincoln journeyed from Springfield, Illinois, to Washington in February 1861, negotiations and conferences to stall and reverse the movement for Southern secession were still taking place in the capital. Even if they failed, contemporaries believed, war was not the only possible outcome, and so the situation remained quite fluid. Or was this perception just an illusion? Perhaps too much had already transpired, not only in the few months following Lincoln's election but in the previous quarter-century of sectional wrangling, for the momentum to be stopped.

Secession had been urged for roughly a decade by a group of Southern politicians who recognized that there was no permanent security within the Union for the South's way of life, based as it was on the "peculiar institution." They had maneuvered and organized to prepare the South for the break that had now arrived as a result of the disintegration of the Democratic party and the attainment of the presidency by the antislavery Republicans. But most Southern voters were not convinced. Secession was closely contested in Texas as well as in Alabama and Georgia, with many in those states feeling that withdrawal was completely ill advised, or else that it was premature until Lincoln demonstrated hostile intentions with an overt act.

Meanwhile, in the Upper South—Virginia, Tennessee, North Carolina, and Arkansas—secession had been voted down or not even put to a vote at all. These Upper South states were less committed to slavery than the Deep South, and they also had valuable economic ties to the North. Their inhabitants concluded that not only would secession be a risky undertaking, it might also jeopardize their own interests.

When Lincoln took office, only the seven Lower South states had seceded. A conciliatory approach might therefore have confined the Confederacy to a remnant that was not likely to survive as an independent nation. But what could the president offer without undermining his party and betraying the voters who had elected him? Historians continue to debate whether an opportunity was lost during the secession crisis or whether the die had already been cast.

DOCUMENTS

With the Deep South states in the process of seceding, the new Republican administration, headed by Abraham Lincoln, deliberated over the course it should pursue. The first selection reprinted here has two parts, both showing how firm Lincoln's position was on the meaning of the 1860 election; they are letters to Senator Lyman Trumbull of Illinois on December 10, and to Congressman John A. Gilmer of North Carolina on December 15, 1860. Representative Gilmer, a Unionist from the Upper South, became an important spokesman for those resisting secession in Virginia, North Carolina, and Tennessee. The second document is Gilmer's letter to Secretary of State William H. Seward of March 8, 1861, imploring him to continue the strategy of conciliation, which Gilmer believed could keep these states from leaving the Union and perhaps also stop the entire movement in its tracks. The third item is from Seward's memorandum of March 15, 1861, on the resupply of Fort Sumter, which he had submitted to the new president in response to his request for the written views of all the members of the cabinet.

The next three documents, when added to Gilmer's letter, give a sense of the views and sentiments of leading Southerners. The first two are extracts from speeches given in the Georgia Hall of Representatives during November and December 1860 by the state's foremost political leaders, who were presenting the issues and alternatives facing Georgia. Alexander H. Stephens, a former congressman and the future vice president of the Confederacy, urged the state not to secede. His friend Robert Toombs was an ardent secessionist who had insisted on secession in his fiery speech the evening before, November 13, 1860. And the last extract is from an editorial in the Raleigh *North Carolina Standard* on December 5, 1861, suggesting that honor was not necessarily incompatible with caution over secession.

President-Elect Lincoln Explains What Is at Stake, December 1860

I.

Private, & confidential.

Springfield, Ills. Dec. 10, 1860

Hon. L. Trumbull.

My dear Sir: Let there be no compromise on the question of *extending* slavery. If there be, all our labor is lost, and, ere long, must be done again. The dangerous ground—that into which some of our friends have a hankering to run—is Pop. Sov. Have none of it. Stand firm. The tug has to come, & better now, than any time hereafter. Yours as ever,

A. Lincoln

II.

Strictly confidential.

Springfield, Ill. Dec 15, 1860.

Hon. John A. Gilmer:

My dear Sir—Yours of the 10th is received. I am greatly disinclined to write a letter on the subject embraced in yours; and I would not do so, even privately as I do, were it not that I fear you might misconstrue my silence. Is it desired that I shall shift the ground upon which I have been elected? I cannot do it. You need only to acquaint yourself with that ground, and press it on the attention of the South. It is all in print and easy of access. May I be pardoned if I ask whether even you have ever attempted to procure the reading of the Republican platform, or my speeches, by the Southern people? If not, what reason

Letters from *Abraham Lincoln, Speeches and Writings,* Don E. Fehrenbacher, ed. (Library of America, 1989), Vol. 2, pp. 190–192.

have I to expect that any additional production of mine would meet a better fate? It would make me appear as if I repented for the crime of having been elected, and was anxious to apologize and beg forgiveness. To so represent me, would be the principal use made of any letter I might now thrust upon the public. My old record cannot be so used; and that is precisely the reason that some new declaration is so much sought.

Now, my dear sir, be assured, that I am not questioning *your* candor; I am only pointing out, that, while a new letter would hurt the cause which I think a just one, you can quite as well effect every patriotic object with the old record. Carefully read pages 18, 19, 74, 75, 88, 89, & 267 of the volume of Joint Debates between Senator Douglas and myself, with the Republican Platform adopted at Chicago, and all your questions will be substantially answered. I have no thought of recommending the abolition of slavery in the District of Columbia, nor the slave trade among the slave states, even on the conditions indicated; and if I were to make such recommendation, it is quite clear Congress would not follow it.

As to employing slaves in Arsenals and Dockyards, it is a thing I never thought of in my life, to my recollection, till I saw your letter; and I may say of it, precisely as I have said of the two points above.

As to the use of patronage in the slave states, where there are few or no Republicans, I do not expect to inquire for the politics of the appointee, or whether he does or not own slaves. I intend in that matter to accommodate the people in the several localities, if they themselves will allow me to accommodate them. In one word, I never have been, am not now, and probably never shall be, in a mood of harassing the people, either North or South.

On the territorial question, I am inflexible, as you see my position in the book. On that, there is a difference between you and us; and it is the only substantial difference. You think slavery is right and ought to be extended; we think it is wrong and ought to be restricted. For this, neither has any just occasion to be angry with the other.

As to the state laws, mentioned in your sixth question, I really know very little of them. I never have read one. If any of them are in conflict with the fugitive slave clause, or any other part of the constitution, I certainly should be glad of their repeal; but I could hardly be justified, as a citizen of Illinois, or as President of the United States, to recommend the repeal of a statute of Vermont, or South Carolina.

With the assurance of my highest regards I subscribe myself

Your obt. Servt.,

A. Lincoln

Congressman John A. Gilmer of North Carolina Urges Delay and Conciliation, March 1861

Confidential.

Greensboro, N.C., March 8th

Since the defeat of the secessionists on the 28th in this state they have become furious. Our Governor went down to Wilmington on last Saturday among his fellow

Letter, John A. Gilmer to William H. Seward, March 8, 1861, in Frederic Bancroft, *The Life of William H. Seward* (Harper and Brothers, 1900), Vol. 2, appendix, pp. 546–547.

disunionists, was called, and made a speech to a large crowd of disunionists. He was bold, and defiant. He said that circumstances would soon occur, which would induce N.C. to retrace her steps, and that she would be out of the Union soon.

The only hope of the secessionists now is that some sort of collision will be brought about between federal and state forces in one of the seceding states. I have full confidence that you in some way wiser and better than I can devise or suggest can prevent this.

If you can do this, I believe I can say that Virginia can be kept from secession. You can do much to quiet Virginia. If the Virginia convention can adjourn without harm to the peace of the country, a great point will be gained. If the border states can be retained, Mississippi, Louisiana and Texas will soon be back. If the others never come back, there will be no great loss. But I believe Georgia and Alabama will also soon want to return.

If for any decent excuse the Govt. could withdraw the troops from all the southern fortifications, the moment this is known N.C., Va., Md., Del., Ky., Tenn., Md. and I believe Arkansas are certainly retained. The only thing now that gives the secessionists the advantage of the conservatives is the cry of coercion—that the whipping of a slave state, is the whipping of slavery.

When these states come back as many of them will they will come with the fortifications. If they do not find it to their interest to return let them keep their plunder—or if any whipping is to be done let it be after the other slave states have certainly determined to remain.

The present excitement should be allowed to pass away as soon as possible without fighting.

Secretary of State William H. Seward Advises Restraint, March 1861

. . . The policy of the time, therefore, has seemed to me to consist in conciliation, which should deny to disunionists any new provocation or apparent offence, while it would enable the Unionists in the slave states to maintain with truth and with effect that the alarms and apprehensions put forth by the disunionists are groundless and false.

I have not been ignorant of the objections that the administration was elected through the activity of the Republican party; that it must continue to deserve and retain the confidence of that party; while conciliation toward the slave states tends to demoralize the Republican party itself, on which party the main responsibility of maintaining the Union must rest.

But it has seemed to me a sufficient answer—first, that the administration could not demoralize the Republican party without making some sacrifice of its essential principles, while no such sacrifice is necessary, or is anywhere authoritatively proposed; and secondly, if it be indeed true that pacification is necessary to prevent dismemberment of the Union and civil war, or either of them, no patriot and lover of humanity could hesitate to surrender party for the higher interests of country and humanity.

Partly by design, partly by chance, this policy has been hitherto pursued by the late administration of the Federal government, and by the Republican party in its corporate action. It is by this policy, thus pursued, I think, that the progress of dismemberment has

From William H. Seward, "A Cabinet Paper," March 15, 1861, in *The Works of William H. Seward,* George E. Baker, ed. (Houghton Mifflin, 1884), Vol. 5, pp. 607–608. This selection is also available in AME Press, 1972 reprint.

been arrested after the seven Gulf states had seceded, and the border states yet remain, although they do so uneasily, in the Union.

It is to a perseverance in this policy for a short time longer that I look as the only peaceful means of assuring the continuance of Virginia, Maryland, North Carolina, Kentucky, Tennessee, Missouri, and Arkansas, or most of those states in the Union. It is through their good and patriotic offices that I look to see the Union sentiment revived and brought once more into activity in the seceding states, and through this agency those states themselves returning into the Union. . . .

The fact, then, is that while the people of the border states desire to be loyal, they are at the same time sadly, though temporarily, demoralized by a sympathy for the slave states, which makes them forget their loyalty whenever there are any grounds for apprehending that the Federal government will resort to military coercion against the seceding states, even though such coercion should be necessary to maintain the authority, or even the integrity, of the Union. This sympathy is unreasonable, unwise, and danger-ous, and therefore cannot, if left undisturbed, be permanent. It can be banished, however, only in one way, and that is by giving time for it to wear out, and for reason to resume its sway. Time will do this, if it be not hindered by new alarms and provocations. . . .

The question submitted to us, then, practically is: Supposing it to be possible to reinforce and supply Fort Sumter, is it wise now to attempt it, instead of withdrawing the garrison?

The most that could be done by any means now in our hands would be to throw two hundred and fifty to four hundred men into the garrison, with provisions for supplying it five or six months. In this active and enlightened country, in this season of excitement, with a daily press, daily mails, and an incessantly operating telegraph, the design to reinforce and supply the garrison must become known to the opposite party at Charleston as soon at least as preparation for it should begin. The garrison would then almost certainly fall by assault before the expedition could reach the harbor of Charleston. But supposing the secret kept, the expedition must engage in conflict on entering the harbor of Charleston; suppose it to be overpowered and destroyed, is that new outrage to be avenged, or are we then to return to our attitude of immobility? Should we be allowed to do so? Moreover, in that event, what becomes of the garrison?

I suppose the expedition successful. We have then a garrison in Fort Sumter that can defy assault for six months. What is it to do then? Is it to make war by opening its batteries and attempting to demolish the defences of the Carolinians? Can it demolish them if it tries? If it cannot, what is the advantage we shall have gained? If it can, how will it serve to check or prevent disunion?

In either case, it seems to me that we will have inaugurated a civil war by our own act, without an adequate object, after which reunion will be hopeless, at least under this administration, or in any other way than by a popular disavowal both of the war and of the administration which unnecessarily commenced it. Fraternity is the element of union; war is the very element of disunion. Fraternity, if practised by this administration, will rescue the Union from all its dangers. If this administration, on the other hand, take up the sword, then an opposite party will offer the olive branch, and will, as it ought, profit by the restoration of peace and union. . . .

Former Congressman Alexander H. Stephens of Georgia Advises against Secession, November 1860

. . . I am for exhausting all that patriotism demands before taking the last step. I would invite, therefore, South Carolina to a conference. I would ask the same of all the Southern States, so that if the evil has got beyond our control, which God in His mercy grant may not be the case, we may not be divided among ourselves; but, if possible, secure the united co-operation of all the Southern States, and then in the face of the civilized world we may justify our action, and with the wrong all on the other side, we can appeal to the God of battles, if it comes to that, to aid us in our cause. But do nothing in which any portion of our people may charge you with rash or hasty action. It is certainly a matter of great importance to tear this Government asunder. You were not sent here for that purpose. I would wish the whole South to be united if this is to be done; and I believe if we pursue the policy which I have vindicated, this can be effected.

In this way our sister Southern States can be induced to act with us; and I have but little doubt that the States of New York, Pennsylvania, Ohio, and the other Western States will compel their Legislatures to recede from their hostile attitude, if the others do not. Then, with these, we would go on without New England, if she chose to stay out.

(**A voice.**—"We will kick them out.")

No; I would not kick them out. But if they chose to stay out, they might. I think, moreover, that these Northern States, being principally engaged in manufactures, would find that they had as much interest in the Union under the Constitution as we, and that they would return to their constitutional duty,—this would be my hope. If they should not, and if the Middle States and Western States do not join us, we should at least have an undivided South. I am, as you clearly perceive, for maintaining the Union as it is, if possible. I will exhaust every means thus to maintain it with an equality in it.

My position, then, in conclusion, is for the maintenance of the honor, the rights, the equality, the security, and the glory of my native State in the Union if possible; but if these cannot be maintained in the Union, then I am for their maintenance, at all hazards, out of it. Next to the honor and glory of Georgia, the land of my birth, I hold the honor and glory of our common country. In Savannah I was made to say by the reporters, who very often make me say things which I never did, that I was first for the glory of the whole country and next for that of Georgia. I said the exact reverse of this. I am proud of her history, of her present standing. I am proud even of her motto, which I would have duly respected at the present time by all her sons,—"Wisdom, Justice, and Moderation." I would have her rights and those of the Southern States maintained now upon these principles. Her position now is just what it was in 1850, with respect to the Southern States. Her platform then established was subsequently adopted by most, if not all, the other Southern States. Now I would add but one additional plank to that platform, which I have stated, and one which time has shown to be necessary; and if that shall likewise be adopted in substance by all the Southern States, all may yet be well. But if all this fails, we shall at least have the satisfaction of knowing that we have done our duty and all that patriotism could require.

From Alexander H. Stephens, speech, December 1860, in Richard M. Johnston and William H. Browne, *Life of Alexander H. Stephens* (Philadelphia, 1878), pp. 579–580.

Senator Robert Toombs of Georgia Defends His Own and His State's Honor, November 1860

. . . But we are told that secession would destroy the fairest fabric of liberty the world ever saw, and that we are the most prosperous people in the world under it. The arguments of tyranny as well as its acts, always reenact themselves. The arguments I now hear in favor of this Northern connection are identical in substance, and almost in the same words as those which were used in 1775 and 1776 to sustain the British connection. We won liberty, sovereignty, and independence by the American Revolution—we endeavored to secure and perpetuate these blessings by means of our Constitution. The very men who use these arguments admit that this Constitution, this compact, is violated, broken and trampled underfoot by the abolition party. Shall we surrender the jewels because their robbers and incendiaries have broken the casket? Is this the way to preserve liberty? I would as lief surrender it back to the British crown as to the abolitionists. I will defend it from both. Our purpose is to defend those liberties. What baser fate could befall us or this great experiment of free government than to have written upon its tomb: "Fell by the hands of abolitionists and the cowardice of its natural defenders." If we quail now, this will be its epitaph.

We are said to be a happy and prosperous people. We have been, because we have hitherto maintained our ancient rights and liberties—we will be until we surrender them. They are in danger; come, freemen, to the rescue. If we are prosperous, it is due to God, ourselves, and the wisdom of our State government. We have an executive, legislative, and judicial department at home, possessing and entitled to the confidence of the people. I have already vainly asked for the law of the Federal Government that promotes our prosperity. I have shown you many that retard that prosperity—many that drain our coffers for the benefit of our bitterest foes. I say bitterest foes—show me the nation in the world that hates, despises, villifies, or plunders us like our abolition "brethren" in the North. There is none. I can go to England or France, or any other country in Europe with my slave, without molestation or violating any law. I can go anywhere except in my own country, whilom [i.e., at one time] called "the glorious Union;" here alone am I stigmatized as a felon; here alone am I an outlaw; here alone am I under the ban of the empire; here alone I have neither security nor tranquillity; here alone are organized governments ready to protect the incendiary, the assassin who burns my dwelling or takes my life or those of my wife and children; here alone are hired emissaries paid by brethren to glide through the domestic circle and intrigue insurrection with all of its nameless horrors. My countrymen, "if you have nature in you, bear it not." Withdraw yourselves from such a confederacy; it is your right to do so—your duty to do so. I know not why the abolitionists should object to it, unless they want to torture and plunder you. If they resist this great sovereign right, make another war of independence, for that then will be the question; fight its battles over again—reconquer liberty and independence. As for me, I will take any place in the great conflict for rights which you may assign. I will take none in the Federal Government during Mr. Lincoln's administration.

If you desire a Senator after the fourth of March, you must elect one in my place. I have served you in the State and national councils for nearly a quarter of a century without

From Robert Toombs, speech, November 1860, in Frank Moore, ed., *The Rebellion Record, 1862–63* (Putnam Holt, 1864), Supplement to Vol. 1, pp. 367–368. This selection is also available in *Secession Debated: Georgia's Showdown in 1860,* William W. Freehling and Craig M. Simpson, eds. (Oxford University Press, 1992), pp. 48–49.

once losing your confidence. I am yet ready for the public service, when honor and duty call. I will serve you anywhere where it will not degrade and dishonor my country. Make my name infamous forever, if you will, but save Georgia. . . .

The Raleigh *North Carolina Standard* Weighs Honor and Secession, December 1860

. . . Disunion at this time will certainly occasion war. If a peaceful separation in the last resort could be effected, the two Confederacies, or any number of Confederacies *might* tread their respective paths without engaging in mortal conflict. They *might* at length re-unite in a new union on foundations more lasting than the present; but if any one State shall secede, with the expectation of drawing other States after her, and if blood shall be shed, the beginning, the middle, and the end will be civil war. The States thus forced out, though they will sympathize with the State which committed them to disunion against their will, and though they may stand by her and defend her in her extremity, yet they will dislike her and watch her as an evil star in the new constellation. A violent separation would, therefore, sow the seeds of discord in the new Confederacy. It would commence its career with growing antagonisms in its members. It would be a *forced* union which time would dissolve or passion fret to pieces.

There is only one evil greater than disunion, and that is the loss of honor and Constitutional right. *That evil the people of the South will never submit to.* Sooner than submit to it they would put their shoulders to the pillars, as Samson did, and tear down the temple, though they themselves should perish in the ruins. But our honor as a people is still untarnished—our Constitutional rights, so far as the federal government is concerned, are still untouched. If the federal government should *attempt* even to tarnish the one or to deprive us of the other, we for one would be ready to resist, and ready to dissolve the Union without regard to consequences. *But not now!*—the non-slaveholder says *not now!*—the slaveholder, whose property civil war would involve in imminent peril, says *not now!*—millions of our friends in the free States say *not now!* If we *must* dissolve the Union, let us do it as one people, and not by a bare majority. Let us wait until the people of the State are more united on the subject than they are now. Depend upon it our people are not submissionists. If their rights should be assailed they will defend them. But if they should not be assailed, and if we *can* preserve the government with safety and honor, to ourselves, in the name of all that is sacred let us do so.

E S S A Y S

Believing that no stone should be left unturned in determining whether war could have been avoided, historians have written extensively about the secession crisis and Lincoln's role in it. In the first essay, Kenneth M. Stampp of the University of California at Berkeley explains Lincoln's policy and outlines why it was justified. Bertram Wyatt-Brown of the University of Florida is the author of the second piece, which is an exploration of the role of honor in the South's growing alienation from the rest of the Union and in its final decision to secede.

From *North Carolina Standard,* editorial, December 5, 1860. This selection is also available in *North Carolina Civil War Documents,* W. Buck Yearns and John G. Barrett, eds. (University of North Carolina Press, 1980), pp. 9–10.

Lincoln and the Secession Crisis

KENNETH M. STAMPP

"Lincoln never poured out his soul to any mortal creature at any time. . . . He was the most secretive—reticent—shut-mouthed man that ever existed." This, the studied opinion of his former law partner, William H. Herndon, defined the perplexing quality in the character of Abraham Lincoln that caused both contemporaries and historians to view him as something of an enigma. This is why his acts frequently permit antithetical explanations; perhaps, too, why forthright motives sometimes appear devious. Because we tend to assume that "shut-mouthed" men are necessarily complex, his reticence always seemed to belie his self-professed simplicity.

As President-elect during the months of the secession crisis, Lincoln kept his own counsel even more rigidly than usual. The confessions of close associates such as Herndon and Judge David Davis that they knew nothing of his plans verified the remark of a newspaper correspondent that "Mr. Lincoln keeps all people, his friends included, in the dark. . . . Mr. Lincoln promises nothing, but only listens." This may help to explain why the available evidence has led some historians to conclude that Lincoln deliberately provoked hostilities at Fort Sumter, while others contended that the Sumter episode was precisely what he had hoped to avoid.

The debate over Lincoln's intentions began during the war itself, but Charles W. Ramsdell introduced it to modern scholarship in 1937 with an article that accused Lincoln of cynically maneuvering the Confederates into firing on Fort Sumter. His action, according to Ramsdell, resulted from a belief that a war was necessary to save not only the Union but his administration and the Republican party. Three years later, James G. Randall replied to Ramsdell in an article claiming that Lincoln's policy was at all times peaceful and that his Sumter strategy was designed to minimize the danger of war. David M. Potter, in a book-length study of the Republican party during the secession crisis, amplified Randall's thesis. Lincoln's policy, Potter argued, was based on a common northern belief that Unionism was still strong in the South and that a pro-Union reaction was bound to come. His aim, therefore, was to avoid further irritation of the South and thus to provide both time and the best possible conditions for southern Unionists to regain control. Potter, like Randall, believed that Lincoln was still trying to maintain the peace at the time of the crisis at Fort Sumter, that he considered evacuation under certain circumstances, and that ultimately he tried to relieve the fort in the manner least likely to provoke a hostile Confederate response. Therefore, Potter concluded, the Confederate attack on Sumter was a defeat, not a victory for Lincoln's policy. However, the same scanty evidence suggests still another possible interpretation.

Fortunately, the President-elect left the record unmistakably clear on two points. First, there can be no doubt that he was an intense nationalist and that he regarded the Union as indestructible. Lincoln was an old Whig, an admirer of Webster and Clay, and he repeatedly expressed pride in his political origins and scoffed at the dogmas of the state-rights school. In his first inaugural address, he took pains to prove that "the Union of these States is perpetual." While he added little to the classical nationalist argument, he showed that the thought of acquiescing in disunion never entered his mind:

It follows from these views that no State, upon its own mere motion, can lawfully get out of the Union,—that *resolves* and *ordinances* to that effect are legally void; and that acts of violence, within any State or States, against the authority of the United States, are insurrectionary or revolutionary, according to circumstances.

   I therefore consider that, in view of the Constitution and the laws, the Union is unbroken. . . .

Second, through private and confidential letters to political friends in Congress, Lincoln expressed firm opposition to any compromise on the issue of slavery expansion. His past speeches, he contended, provided sufficient evidence that he assumed no right to interfere with slavery in the states where it already existed, that he had no desire to menace the rights of the South, and that he would enforce the fugitive slave law. He would tolerate slavery in the District of Columbia and the interstate slave trade—"whatever springs of necessity from the fact that the institution is among us"—and he might even agree to the admission of New Mexico as a slave state. But he was "inflexible" on the territorial question, and he cautioned his friends to "hold firm as with a chain of steel."

   Any explanation of Lincoln's opposition to compromise must be speculative, for his words are sometimes ambiguous and subject to varying interpretations. He objected to the restoration of the Missouri Compromise line on the grounds that it would settle nothing, that it would simply stimulate "filibustering for all South of us, and making slave states of it. . . ." He also expressed a distaste for the personal humiliation involved in proposals to "buy or beg a peaceful inauguration" through concessions, thus indicating that considerations of prestige and "face-saving" were involved. He seemed to be no less concerned about the prestige of the federal government itself: "I should regard any concession in the face of menace the destruction of the government . . . and a consent on all hands that our system shall be brought down to a level with the disorganized state of affairs in Mexico." In addition, Lincoln apparently had decided that this was an appropriate time for a final settlement of the questions of secession and slavery expansion. If concessions were made, he warned, Southerners "will repeat the experiment upon us *ad libitum* [i.e., endlessly]. A year will not pass, till we shall have to take Cuba, as a condition upon which they will stay in the Union." Hence, he advised, "Stand firm. The tug has to come, and better now, than any time hereafter." Many Republican politicians and editors shared his determination to resolve the sectional crisis this time, whatever the cost. "If we must have civil war," wrote the conservative Edward Bates, "perhaps it is better now than at a future date." A western Republican paper asserted that "we are heartily tired of having this [secession] threat stare us in the face evermore. . . . We never have been better prepared for such a crisis than now. We most ardently desire that it may come." Throughout the secession crisis it is remarkable how often Lincoln shared, or merely reflected, popular Republican views.

   In his private advice against compromise the President-elect made some rather vague remarks to the effect that as soon as a compromise was adopted "they have us under again; all our labor is lost, and sooner or later must be done over." Compromise "would lose us everything we gained by the election," he wrote, adding that it would be "the end of us." These apprehensions might indicate deep concern for the well-being of the Republican party and a fear that compromise would spell its ruin. Most of Lincoln's political friends and advisers were acutely aware that concessions to the South would threaten their organization and that the radical wing might bolt the new administration. They remembered the fate of the Whig party, which, one Republican insisted, had "died of compromises." Thurlow Weed, on a visit to Washington, found the Republicans overwhelmed by this fear. Open the territories to slavery, warned one of the faithful, and "Republicanism is a 'dead dog.' "

Yet there was little in Lincoln's remarks on compromise to invalidate the possibility that, in opposing it, he was thinking less of party than of what he regarded as the best interests of the North, perhaps of the whole nation. More than likely the two concerns were fused in his mind. Politicians have a happy facility for identifying personal and party interests with broad national interests, and Lincoln may have believed sincerely that what was good for the Republican party was good for everyone.

Having flatly rejected both compromise and acquiescence in disunion, Lincoln could have hoped to deal with the secession crisis in only two other ways. Either he could encourage loyal Southerners to overthrow the secessionists, voluntarily renew their allegiance to the federal government, and thus achieve a peaceful reconstruction of the Union, or he could resort to whatever force might be necessary to collect federal revenues and to recover or maintain possession of federal property. To that extent, in other words, he could have coerced the secessionists, defining coercion broadly as any attempt to enforce federal laws against the wishes of state authorities or large bodies of disaffected citizens.

In all probability Lincoln regarded neither the device of peaceful reconstruction nor coercion as a basic policy. These were merely tactical alternatives to be used according to circumstances. From the traditional viewpoint of practical statesmanship the preservation of peace and the launching of war are never the supreme objects of policy. They are potential means to some desirable end; the more fundamental goal is to preserve, defend, or advance primary national interests. These interests are guarded by peaceful means when possible, but the use of force is never ruled out as a last resort. "National interest" is a loose concept easily abused, but it has ever been a prime concern of governments.

When Lincoln's problem is placed in this context, his words and acts during the secession crisis appear to be rational, realistic, and remarkably consistent. Because he opposed compromise and peaceful secession it does not follow that his basic purpose was to resort to force any more than it was to risk everything on a policy of peace. Rather, his chief concern was the maintenance of the Union, a national interest which he regarded as vital enough to take precedence over all other considerations. And the integrity of the Union continued to be his paramount objective throughout the ensuing conflict—even his Emancipation Proclamation was conceived and justified with that goal in mind. There is no reason to doubt that Lincoln would have accepted peaceful and voluntary reconstruction as a satisfactory solution within the time limits fixed by political realities, especially northern public opinion. But there is abundant evidence that the possible necessity of coercion entered his calculations as soon as he understood the seriousness of the crisis. Lincoln was not a pacifist, and as both a practical statesman and a mystical believer in an American mission to the world, he looked upon disunion as a sufficient threat to justify resistance by military force if necessary. . . .

The fact that Lincoln intimated the possible use of force does not necessarily imply that he visualized, as an inevitable consequence, a long civil war, or the need for any war at all. Like many others, he may have thought that "a little show of force," entailing a minimum of bloodshed, would suffice to crush the southern rebellion. Better still, a sufficient demonstration of federal power might result in the immediate collapse of the Confederacy without so much as a skirmish. However, the consequence of coercive measures was really out of the President's hands. It would depend upon the secessionists. And from this critical fact Lincoln formulated his basic strategy.

From the outset the new President, in dealing with the disunion crisis, had three clear advantages. First, the northern people, with few exceptions, agreed with him that the states did not have a constitutional right to secede. However many may have favored compromise and hoped to avoid the use of military force, the masses of Republicans and Democrats alike shared the belief that the Union was perpetual. It was not difficult, or even necessary, to convince them that the preservation of the Union was both a moral obligation and a vital national interest. Second, the burden of direct action rested upon the seceding states, which, after all, were seeking to disturb the political *status quo.* In order to make their independence a reality, they thought it essential to seize government forts and other property, and to destroy the symbols of federal authority. As a result, the Union government could easily claim that it would avoid aggressive action and merely assume a defensive posture. In other words, the exigencies of the situation would almost certainly suggest to a wise and practical political leader a strategy of defense—of throwing the initiative to the South.

This is where Lincoln's third important advantage made itself evident. Given the general northern belief that, in spite of southern ordinances of secession, the Union was not and could not be dissolved, the government was entitled to make a number of "defensive" moves. These presumably nonaggressive acts might include such things as collecting the revenues, holding federal property, perhaps even reinforcing the forts or recovering those that had been seized. Action of this kind, most Northerners believed, would be far different from marching a hostile army into the South to overawe and coerce it. "There is no form in which coercion . . . can be applied," wrote a northern editor. "The general government can do no more than see that its laws are carried out." Of course, secessionists, who regarded the dissolution of the Union as an accomplished fact, brushed aside these fine distinctions and branded any federal intervention in the South as coercion. Perhaps abstract logic was on their side, but to Lincoln that was irrelevant. Always holding the preservation of the Union above peace, he exploited his three strategic advantages in order to cast coercion in the mold of defense and to shift responsibility for any resulting violence to his "dissatisfied fellow-countrymen."

This defensive concept was in no sense an original idea of Lincoln's. Soon after the election of 1860 the Republican press began to propose the strategy with remarkable spontaneity. "The Republican policy," predicted the Springfield (Massachusetts) *Republican,* "will be to make no war upon the seceding states, to reject all propositions for secession, to hold them to the discharge of their constitutional duties, to collect the revenues as usual in southern ports, and calmly await the results. There can be no war unless the seceders make war upon the general government." The New York *Evening Post* suggested that if South Carolina should make it impossible to collect duties at Charleston, Congress could simply close it as a port of entry. "Here then we have a peaceful antidote for that 'peaceful remedy' which is called secession. It is no act of war, nor hostility, to revoke the permission given to any town to be opened as a port of entry; but when that permission is revoked it would be an act of hostility . . . to disregard the injunction." A northern clergyman summed up the strategy precisely in advising the South: "Secede on paper as much as you please. We will not make war upon you for that. But we will maintain the supremacy of the constitution and laws. If you make war on the Union, we will defend it at all costs, and the guilt of blood be on your heads." Thus the strategy, occasionally defined as one of "masterly inactivity," had been outlined in advance; Lincoln had only to read the newspapers to discover its value.

From the time the President-elect left Springfield in February until the firing on Fort Sumter, the central theme of his public utterances was the further development and clarification of a strategy of defense. Holding inflexibly to the conviction that his fundamental purpose must be the preservation of the Union, he chose his words carefully and shrewdly to protect himself from any charge of aggression. Appreciating the possibility that hostilities might ensue, Lincoln seemed preoccupied with an intense desire to leave the record clear, to make it evident to the northern people that war, if it came, would be started by the South. His words were not those of a man confused about the true situation, about what his policy should be, or about possible consequences. The coercive intimations were nearly always of a sort that would be perceived as such only by southern secessionists, seldom by northern Unionists.

During his first stop, at Indianapolis, Lincoln began at once to expound his defensive strategy. In a speech from the balcony of the Bates House he denied any intention to invade the South with a hostile army and made it clear that the government would only defend itself and its property. On February 21, he assured the New Jersey General Assembly that he would do everything possible to secure a peaceful settlement. "The man does not live who is more devoted to peace than I am." The next day, before the Pennsylvania legislature, he expressed regret "that a necessity may arise in this country for the use of the military arm. . . . I promise that, (in so far as I may have wisdom to direct,) if so painful a result shall in any wise be brought about, it shall be through no fault of mine." On the same day, in Philadelphia, Lincoln spoke with unusual clarity: "Now, in my view of the present aspect of affairs, there is no need of bloodshed and war. There is no necessity for it. I am not in favor of such a course, and I may say in advance, there will be no blood shed unless it is forced upon the Government. The Government will not use force unless force is used against it." . . .

Having already outlined his defensive strategy on several occasions, Lincoln's inaugural address contained no surprises on that score—only a final clear exposition of his nonaggressive intentions. Once more he insisted that in upholding the authority of the government "there needs be no bloodshed or violence; and there shall be none, unless it be forced upon the national authority." He would refrain from doing many things which he had a right to do, but which could be forgone without injury to the prestige of the government. However, though he desired a peaceful solution, the matter was beyond his control: "In *your* hands, my dissatisfied fellow-countrymen, and not in *mine,* is the momentous issue of civil war. The government will not assail *you.* You can have no conflict, without being yourselves the aggressors. *You* have no oath registered in Heaven to destroy the government, while *I* shall have the most solemn one to 'preserve, protect and defend it.' "

Thus, by the time of his inauguration, Lincoln had firmly established his intention to preserve the Union by measures that Unionists would accept as purely defensive. With consummate skill he had at once hamstrung the South, satisfied the great majority of Northerners that he contemplated no aggression, and yet conveyed his determination to defend the authority of the federal government. The Republican press glowed with appreciation. "No party can be formed against the administration on the issue presented by the inaugural," observed one friendly editor. Another noted that "the fiat of peace or war is in the hands of Mr. Davis rather than of Mr. Lincoln." Samuel Bowles of the

Springfield *Republican* believed that the inaugural had put "the secession conspirators manifestly in the wrong, and hedges them in so that they cannot take a single step without making treasonable war upon the government, which will only defend itself." By the fourth of March, Lincoln had already cornered the disunionists.

It should be evident, then, that Lincoln's reaction to the problem of supplying Fort Sumter, which confronted him immediately after his inauguration, was in perfect harmony with the strategy he had already conceived. His decision to sustain the Sumter garrison involved no change of plans—no reluctant abandonment of a policy of voluntary reunion, no sudden determination to provoke a war. It was a logical consequence of the President's fixed determination to defend the Union even at the risk of hostilities. Had the Sumter crisis not arisen, or had Lincoln been convinced ultimately that military necessity dictated evacuation, his strategy almost certainly would have led to a similar violent confrontation somewhere else. In fact, while he was exploring the possibility of sending supplies to Major Robert Anderson, he was also searching for other means of developing his defensive policy. For example, he instructed General Scott "to exercise all possible vigilance for the maintenance of all the places within the military department of the United States, and to promptly call upon all the departments of the government for the means necessary to that end." In addition, he offered the deposed Unionist governor of Texas, Sam Houston, military and naval support if Houston would put himself at the head of a Union party; and he considered the collection of duties from naval vessels off southern ports, or even a blockade of the Confederacy. . . .

Even before Lincoln's inauguration there were abundant signs that the general uncertainty was becoming intolerable. More and more it appeared that time was not on the side of the Union, that the secession movement was actually gaining in strength. After March 4, Republican leaders bombarded Lincoln with advice favoring decisive action, and with warnings that the people would not tolerate the abandonment of Sumter. Meanwhile, the differences between Union and Confederate tariff schedules frightened many conservative merchants into a mood for drastic remedies. By the end of March numerous businessmen had reached the point where they felt that anything—even war—was better than the existing indecision which was so fatal to trade. "It is a singular fact," wrote one observer, "that merchants who, two months ago, were fiercely shouting 'no coercion,' now ask for anything rather than *inaction*." Even anti-Republican and anti-coercion papers could bear the suspense no longer and urged that something be done. Lincoln might well have hoped for a little more time to organize his administration before dealing with the secessionists; but the general unrest in the North, as well as the Sumter crisis, forced his hand at once. The time for delay had passed.

Such was the atmosphere in which Lincoln dispatched a relief expedition to Fort Sumter. Every circumstance combined to make this a satisfactory culmination of his defensive strategy. Popular attention had long been focused on the small federal garrison in Charleston harbor. A southern attack was almost certain to consolidate northern opinion behind the new administration, while permitting the garrison to receive supplies would seriously damage Confederate prestige. Having authorized [Secretary of State William H.] Seward to promise the Confederate Commissioners in Washington that relief would not be sent without due notice, the President could be doubly sure that this step, one way or another, would be decisive. Equally important, the fact that he could force the issue merely by sending supplies served to underscore the defensive nature of his move. He instructed his messenger, Robert S. Chew, to notify Governor Francis W.

Pickens of South Carolina that "an attempt will be made to supply Fort Sumpter [*sic*] with provisions only; and that, if such attempt be not resisted, no effort to throw in men, arms, or ammunition, will be made, without further notice, or in case of an attack upon the Fort." After that, whether the Confederates attacked or submitted, Lincoln would triumph.

The President himself pointed to the Sumter expedition as the fulfillment of the policy he had outlined in the past. He did so first in his reply to Seward's memorandum of April 1, in which the Secretary of State proposed, for all practical purposes, Lincoln's own strategy, except that he favored the evacuation of Sumter. Professing surprise at this, Lincoln reminded Seward that his inaugural embraced "the exact domestic policy you now urge," except that he would not give up Fort Sumter. Even more emphatic was his response, on April 13, to a delegation sent by the Virginia convention to inquire about his policy. "Not having, as yet, seen occasion to change," he said, "it is now my purpose to pursue the course marked out in the inaugural address." He would hold federal property in the South. However, if it proved true that "an unprovoked assault" had been made on Sumter, he would feel free "to re-possess . . . like places which have been seized before the Government was devolved upon me." It was at this point, more clearly than ever before, that Lincoln expressed his unqualified decision in favor of coercion. Yet, he still insisted that his policy was altogether defensive, for he added that he would simply "repel force by force."

The Confederate attack upon Fort Sumter was, in effect, a striking victory for Lincoln's defensive strategy. Just as Republican editors had first suggested the formula, their appreciation of its success was immediate and spontaneous. In one great chorus they denounced the Confederates as the aggressors. "It was," wrote one, "an audacious and insulting aggression upon the authority of the Republic, without provocation or excuse." A Boston editor piously described the event as one furnishing "precisely the stimulus which . . . a good Providence sends to arouse the latent patriotism of the people." "*Let it be remembered,*" cried the Providence *Journal*, "*that the Southern government has put itself wholly in the wrong, and is the aggressor.* On its head must be the responsibility for the consequences." These were accurate expressions of the feelings of an indignant northern people. . . .

That Lincoln understood the probability of Confederate resistance at Charleston is beyond a reasonable doubt, for the messengers he sent there in March informed him of the state of opinion in South Carolina. During the period of preparation the President strove to organize the defenses of Washington and urged Governor Curtin of Pennsylvania to prepare for an emergency. Lincoln's secretaries, John G. Nicolay and John Hay, believed that it was "reasonably certain" that he expected hostilities to ensue, and they observed that when the news arrived of the attack upon Sumter he was neither surprised nor excited. Indeed, if he had believed that Sumter could be supplied peacefully, there was no reason why he should ever have considered evacuation as a possible military necessity. During the weeks when members of the Cabinet and military officers discussed the Sumter crisis, they simply took for granted that a federal relief expedition would result in a Confederate attack.

There is no evidence that Lincoln regarded the result of his strategy with anything but satisfaction. Having derived his policy from his determination to preserve the Union at all costs, he had reason to congratulate himself, for with a united North behind him he was likely to succeed. "You and I both anticipated," he wrote Captain Fox [Gustavus

Vasa Fox, who commanded the Sumter relief expedition], "that the cause of the country would be advanced by making the attempt to provision Fort-Sumpter [*sic*], even if it should fail; and it is no small consolation now to feel that our anticipation is justified by the result." A few months later, after Lincoln had gained greater perspective, he told Senator Orville H. Browning of Illinois that he had "conceived the idea" of sending supplies without reinforcements and of notifying the governor of South Carolina in advance. According to Browning, Lincoln added: "The plan succeeded. They attacked Sumter—it fell, and thus did more service than it otherwise could." . . .

The crucial point about the Sumter crisis was that, except for the important consideration of northern public opinion, it mattered little whether Lincoln attempted to supply Sumter in the least provocative or the most provocative way, because, as he had reason to know, *any* attempt was bound to open hostilities. Moreover, it is possible to argue that Lincoln's Sumter policy was not in fact the least provocative course he might have followed. For example, he might have done what he subsequently claimed that he had hoped to do—that is, evacuate Fort Sumter and reinforce Fort Pickens, as Seward suggested. The reinforcement of Pickens was accomplished with ease, and the federal position there was so strong that the fort was never lost to the Confederates. As to Sumter, before sending a relief expedition, Lincoln might have directed Major Anderson to try to obtain the needed supplies in Charleston. South Carolina authorities might well have refused such a request (though they permitted Anderson to purchase fresh meats and vegetables in the Charleston market), but the request was never made. Finally, although Lincoln assured the governor of South Carolina that the relief expedition would land provisions only, he also hinted that an attempt (with notice) to land "men, arms, or ammunition" might be made at some future time. A Sumter policy designed to minimize provocation would hardly have suggested such a possibility at that crucial juncture. Yet, it is not to accuse Lincoln of deliberately starting a war to conclude that the Confederate attack on Sumter was a triumph, not a defeat, for his policy.

With the fall of Sumter Lincoln's defensive policy had served its purpose, and instantly he changed his ground. In his proclamation of April 15, calling for 75,000 volunteers, he did not propose merely to "hold" or "possess" federal property and to collect the revenues. Instead, he summoned the militia to suppress an insurrection, "to re-possess the forts, places, and property which have been seized," "to cause the laws to be duly executed," to preserve the Union, and "to redress wrongs already long enough endured." A few days later, when addressing the Frontier Guard in Washington, Lincoln gave additional evidence that he had always preferred coercion to disunion. While professing peaceful intentions, he predicted that "if the alternative is presented, whether the Union is to be broken in fragments . . . or blood be shed, you will probably make the choice, with which I shall not be dissatisfied."

Although Lincoln accepted the possibility of war, which, in retrospect, was the almost certain consequence of his defensive strategy, the indictment—if such it be—can be softened considerably by surrounding circumstances. It was a burden that he shared with many others, for his standards of statesmanship and his concept of the national interest were those common to his age—and, for that matter, to ours as well. The Union was a thing worth fighting for! If Lincoln was no pacifist, neither were his contemporaries. The growing impatience in the North and the widespread demand for action no doubt helped to shape his final decision. And it is still a moot question whether politicians in a democracy are morally bound to yield to popular pressures or to resist them.

Moreover, without quibbling over who was guilty of the first act of aggression, the case would be distorted if one overlooked the fact that southern leaders shared with Lincoln the responsibility for a resort to force. . . .

It may well have been true, as [Charles W.] Ramsdell claimed, that the outbreak of war saved the Republican party from disintegration and that a practical politician such as Lincoln could not have ignored the political consequences of his action. But the Machiavellian implication of that hypothesis is based on sheer speculation. We cannot read Lincoln's mind and the available evidence makes equally valid the counter-hypothesis that he considered only the country's best interests. Or, again, he may have had a comprehensive understanding of what both the country and political expediency demanded. Perhaps it was simply Lincoln's good fortune that personal, party, and national interests could be served with such favorable coincidence as they were by his strategy of defense.

Honor and Secession

BERTRAM WYATT-BROWN

The reluctance of those with the most to lose was only one of several indications that more than just slavery was at work in the secessionist dynamic. Slavery was itself inseparable from other aspects of regional life, most especially from the southerners' sense of themselves as a people. That self-perception can be called the principle of honor. In modern times the term has so little meaning that it occupies, says sociologist Peter Berger, "about the same place in contemporary usage as chastity." Nevertheless, though sometimes seen as simply a "romance" to prettify the harsh reality of race control, it was a powerful force in the nineteenth-century South.

Honor may be described in a number of ways, both characterologic and social. It can be considered as general demeanor or gentlemanliness; virtue, that is, trustworthiness and honesty; entitlement; or class rank. Certainly southerners believed that dependability for truth-telling was a prime aspect of honorable character, but it was more than that and also more than a fascination with titles like Colonel and Judge, forms of address that southerners were notoriously prone to crave. Honor will be used here in two separate sociological and ethical senses: the southern mode, which might be called traditional honor, and the mid-nineteenth-century northern one. The latter represented, to use Berger's term, an "*embourgeoisement*" of the concept—diminishing its feudal and communal overtones and adding an institutional, impersonal, and middle-class element.

In regard to traditional honor, the concept involves process more than merely an idealization of conduct. First, honor is a sense of personal worth and it is invested in the whole person. Yet that whole covers more than the individual—it includes the identification of the individual with his blood relations, his community, his state, and whatever other associations the man of honor feels are important for establishing his claim for recognition. The close bonding of honor with an extended self, as it were, contrasts with the kind of honor that would place country before family, professional duty before other matters of importance. Second, honor as a dynamic connecting self and society requires that the individual make a claim for worthiness before the community. And third, it involves the acceptance of that self-evaluation in the public forum, a ratification that enables the claimant to know his place in society and his moral standing. "I am who I say I am" (or, more accurately, "I am who I seem to be"), says the man of traditional honor. We more likely might say, "I am who I am because of what I do." The timocratic community [a society governed by notions of honor] replies, "You are who you say you are." The exchange is completed with the registry of that reply upon the tablet of the individual's personality. He incorporates what is said and thought of him as part of his identity. Although honor can be directly internalized—to act *as if* a public were watching—it has few inner referents. Unlike the man of conscience, the individual dependent on honor must have respect from others as the prime means for respecting himself. Shifting fortunes, personal rivalries, worrisome doubts that one has been properly assessed make the ethical scheme an elusive, tense, and ultimately insecure method of self-acceptance. Western man has always known that traditional honor, being dependent upon public sanction, is a fickle mistress. Outward shows or honors—"place, riches, and favour, / Prizes of accident"—sometimes matter as much as or more than merit, to borrow from Shakespeare, the southerners' most admired playwright.

Ambiguities abound. On the one hand, moderation, prudence, coolness under duress, and self-restraint are admired and even idealized. The southern "Nestors" who urged calm deliberateness before entering on secession hoped to have these qualities approved in the public arena. On the other hand, the man of honor feels that defense of reputation and virility must come before all else. Otherwise, he is open to charges of effeminacy and fear. As Ulysses complains of his warrior colleagues:

> They tax our policy and call it cowardice,
> Count wisdom as no member of the war,
> Forestall prescience, and esteem no act
> But that of hand.

In political terms, honor was not at all confined to those at the top of the social order. It is the nature of the ethic that it must be recognized by those with less status; otherwise, there would be none to render honor to claimants. In the American South, common folk, though not given to gentlemanly manners, duels, and other signs of a superior élan, also believed in honor because they had access to the means for its assertion themselves—the possessing of slaves—and because all whites, nonslaveholders as well, held sway over all blacks. Southerners regardless of social position were united in the brotherhood of white-skinned honor—what George M. Fredrickson has called herrenvolk democracy [master-race democracy], though we might refer to it as people's timocracy.

It was upon this basis that John C. Calhoun and others came to admire the Periclean Greeks, devoted as the ancients were to *timē* (honor), democracy, republicanism, and small-community autonomy. In the Greek city-states "the passionate drive to show one's self in measuring up against others," said Hannah Arendt, was the actual basis for politics. To some extent, the same held true in the South. Politics was an arena in which peers—not necessarily the greatest magnates—were rivals for public acclaim and power. As a forum for self-presentation and public service, politics was a simple system to which elaborate bureaucracies, heavy taxes, statutory refinements, and other complexities were alien. Even the notion of party organization, as opposed to community consensus and unanimity on key principles, was suspect, at least among the firebrands for disunionism. In all societies where honor of this kind functions, the great distinction is drawn between the autonomy, freedom, and self-sufficiency of those in the body politic and the dependency, forced submissiveness, and powerlessness of all who are barred from political and social participation—that is, slaves or serfs. For the southern free white, dependency posed the threat of meaninglessness. Slaveholding ennobled, that is, enhanced one's status and independence because ownership provided the instruments for exercising power, not over the slave alone, but over those without that resource. By the same social perception, thralldom degraded and humbled. "The essence of honor," says one writer, "is personal autonomy" or freedom to do what one wishes, and its absence indicates powerlessness.

Under these circumstances, the reasons why the southerner felt so threatened by northern criticism should be clear. The dread of public humiliation, especially in the highly charged political setting, was a burden not to be casually dismissed. In general terms, whenever the public response to claims for respect is indifferent, disbelieving, hostile, or derisive, the claimant for honor feels as blasted, as degraded as if struck in the face or unceremoniously thrown to the ground. He is driven to a sense of shame—the very opposite of honor. The response is twofold: first, a denial that he, a persecuted innocent, seeks more than his due, and second, his outraged "honor" requires immediate vindication, by force of arms if need be. This was especially true for the antebellum southerner because he could hardly escape doubts that his section was perceived by the world as inferior, morally and materially. "Reputation is everything," said James Henry Hammond. "Everything with me depends upon the estimation in which I am held," confessed secessionist thinker Beverley Tucker. Personal reputation for character, valor, and integrity did not end there. Individual self-regard encompassed wider spheres. As a result, the southerner took as personal insult the criticisms leveled at slave society as a whole. . . .

Many examples might be used to illustrate the way in which honor and high-toned language pervaded local politics in the South. But only one will be offered here: a public letter sent to the early fire-eater John A. Quitman of Mississippi in 1851. The occasion was his release from trial over his violation of a federal neutrality act by aiding the ill-fated Cuba filibusterer, Narciso López. General Quitman, a hero of the Mexican War, had resigned the governor's chair after indictment, but now had the opportunity to regain the office sacrificed to save the state from association with his embarrassment. The committee used the formal language of deference in expressing gratitude for General Quitman's "chivalrous and patriotic defense not only of the rights of our common country but the rights of the South against the assaults of its enemies." Words such as *defamed* and *persecuted* referred to his injured innocence. The prosecutor's nolle prosequi was small vindication; only his return to the governorship could accomplish that. Preparatory to the upcoming campaign, the admiring suppliants offered to hold a barbecue in Quitman's honor, a distinctly informal affair compared to the style of the invitation. In reply, Quitman acknowledged that their celebration was "peculiarly gratifying." It demonstrated that they approved his conduct, and therefore he was "honored with their confidence and esteem." (He won nomination but later withdrew.) Although scarcely a major incident, the correspondence over the barbecue pointed toward a sectional distinction the significance of which might easily be dismissed. The late-nineteenth-century southern scholar William Garrott Brown once noted, "It is a superficial historical philosophy which dilates on the economic and institutional differences between the two sections, and ignores smaller divergences as appeared in the manners and speech of individuals."

The formality of language made all interchanges less threatening. Ritual words of praise and acceptance ensured a feeling of trust. Words, thoughts, and gestures that ordinary southerners and their leaders knew so well provided that sense of reliability. It was so necessary in the absence of those institutional safeguards which Stanley Elkins described as mediational devices for social and psychological security. Ritual speech softened the harsh world of personal rivalry, vengeance, threat, and hierarchy. It made the common white feel secure and it strengthened the confidence and persuasiveness of the leader. The discrepancy between language and deed, between barbecues and ragtag parades on the one hand and lofty and punctilious deferences on the other helped to ritualize honor. Often such use of language in the Old South is perceived as meaningless, but it was genuinely functional. By these means the planters and militia officers who organized the occasion, the ordinary citizens who attended it, and the former Mexican War general, John Quitman, running for the governor's seat reconfirmed shared attitudes. The exchange and celebration dedicated them all to the defense of the South against its enemies.

In still larger perspective, the employment of honor in its linguistic and political character helped immeasurably to reinforce the social order. The grandiloquent phrase, the references to manliness, bravery, nobility, and resolute action, for example, were scarcely reserved for politics alone, but political correspondence, public letters, editorials, and speeches all employed a tone that sounded bombastic and overblown to the unaccustomed ear. By and large, it was the rhetoric of gentlemen. Lesser folk often admired it. It sanctified the existing social system to lace speeches with Shakespearean and classical phrases, so long as they were familiar to the listeners. However exaggerated its character, the political vocabulary spoke to the most visceral feelings that southerners possessed.

Given the character of southern politics and its ethical framework, the road to secession does not seem so puzzling. In responding to northern criticism and self-assertiveness, the South's defenders had to emphasize vindication and vengeance. As a result, the purpose of so much southern rhetoric in the prewar period was to impugn the motives and policies of the abolitionists in and out of Congress. Any number of examples might be cited to show how southern anguish at criticism reflected the psychological processes of injured pride. Abolitionists like Garrison thought that their sermons against slavery would force the slaveholder to listen to his conscience, but the effort was futile. Instead, antislavery polemics evoked feelings, not of guilt, but of anger and indignation. As John S. Preston, a South Carolina proslavery advocate, declared, "There is not a Christian man, a slaveholder [in the South], who does not feel in his inmost heart as a Christian" that his fellow churchmen of the North have spilled "the last blood of sympathy [on the point of the] sword of the church. . . . They set the lamb of God between our seed and their seed."

Preston Brooks's assault on Charles Sumner in May, 1856, helps to illustrate the means for southern vindication. What outraged Brooks and his accomplice Lawrence Keitt, the South Carolina congressman, was the Massachusetts senator's tasteless vilification of Senator Andrew Pickens Butler, Brooks's kinsman, during the "Bleeding Kansas" speech. In addition, Sumner had dwelt upon the alleged ineffectuality, even cowardice, of South Carolina troops during the American Revolution. By the rules of honor, Brooks was under no obligation to call for a duel with Sumner because one fought on the field of honor only with one's social and moral peers. By southern standards, Sumner fell considerably below that status. In handling inferiors, a one-on-one horse-whipping was much more appropriate. The fire-eater Keitt explained the matter to the House after the event. By the ancient code, he said, "a churl was never touched with the knightly sword; his person was mulcted with the quarter-staff." This incident points to the sense of degradation that Yankees could feel when faced with southern aggression. "We all or *nearly* all felt," a Bostonian wrote the wounded Sumner, "that we had been personally maltreated & insulted." According to William Gienapp, the attack on Sumner, perhaps more than the troubles in Kansas, aroused northern opinion against the South. Even in conservative circles formerly hostile to the Massachusetts senator's course, concerns for northern self-respect and for free speech were evident.

For both sides, Brooks's violence heightened an awareness of honor's demands. But before such means of vengeance, there had been an escalation of verbal confrontations. The abolitionist rhetoric need not be described; our concentration is upon southern epithet and abuse. Southern spokesmen inflated antislavery denunciations to the level of treachery, betrayal, insurrection, and devilish anarchy. Antislavery attacks stained the reputation by which southern whites judged their place and power in the world. Such, for instance, was the reason why slaveholders insisted on the right to carry their property into the free territories at will. It was not solely a matter of expanding slavery's boundaries, though that was of course important. No less significant, however, was southern whites' resentment against any congressional measure which implied the moral inferiority of their region, labor system, or style of life. Such reflections on southern reputation were thought vile and humiliating. For example, in late 1846, Robert Toombs, senator from Georgia, took exception to the Wilmot Proviso, by which slaveholders would be barred from bringing slaves into lands seized from Mexico. Southern whites, he argued, "would be degraded, and unworthy of the name of American freemen, could they consent to remain, for a day or an hour, in a Union where they must stand on ground of inferiority, and be denied the rights and privileges which were extended to all others." Fear for personal losses from antislavery territorial laws did not matter half as much as the symbolism of such antisouthern measures: its signification of still more dire consequences to come. As Toombs remarked in Congress during the sectional crisis of 1850, the right to enter any territory with slaves involved "political equality, [a status] worth a thousand such Unions as we have, even if they each were a thousand times more valuable than this." This issue was no small matter, in his opinion. He elevated the question of slaveholder's territorial prerogatives to the level of a casus belli, at least to his own satisfaction. "Deprive us of this right," he warned the Senate, and it becomes "your government, not mine. Then I am its enemy, and I will then, if I can, bring my children and my constituents to the altar of liberty, and like Hamilcar, I would swear them eternal hostility to your foul domination."

The world of honor is Manichean—divided between Good and Evil; Right and Wrong; Justice and Injustice; Freedom and Slavery; Purity and Corruption. It was also apocalyptic—with the terms of reference being perfect peace or total war: stability or deference and affection toward the worthy, or servile rebellion, rapine, and slaughter of innocents. This style was scarcely incompatible with Protestant theology. But the primal character of the vision must be recognized, too. Dread of bloody revolt belonged to the world of honor, where few outsiders could be trusted. A telling example came from a speech of William L. Yancey at the Democratic convention in Charleston in which he vindicated the southern cause in these terms: "Ours is the property invaded; ours are the institutions which are at stake; ours is the peace that is to be destroyed; ours is the honor at stake—the honor of children, the honor of families, of the lives, perhaps, of all—all of which rests upon what your course may ultimately make a great heaving volcano of passion and crime." Harboring sentiments like these, southern leaders had no reason to question the use of violence as the best retort to obloquy. Thus, in 1858, Jefferson Davis roused a Democratic rally in New York City against Republican "higher law" politicians such as William H. Seward. The *"traitors* [to the Constitution], *these . . . preachers should be tarred and feathered, and whipped by those they have thus instigated."*

In societies where honor thrives, death in defense of community and principle is a path to glory and remembrance, whereas servile submission entails disgrace. So it had been in Revolutionary America, at least as South Carolina nullifier Issac Hayne portrayed the struggle for independence. The British imposition of "a three pence a pound tax upon Tea" had been just such a cause for revolution. With obvious reference to the current "tyranny" of unpopular tariff exactions, Hayne argued that the sums involved were not the issue at all. The Parliamentary tea tax would have driven no American into penury. But this and other British measures required patriots to accept meekly the statutory symbols of British imperialism, a surrender of liberty that was dishonorable and therefore unbearable. Nullifiers like Hayne, as well as secessionists later, often posed the splendors of honor against the degeneracy and cowardly temptation of peaceful capitulation. Robert Barnwell Rhett in 1828 assaulted the Unionist faction of South Carolina, stressing the dangers of lost self-confidence: "If you are doubtful of your selves . . . if you love life better than honor,—prefer ease to perilous liberty and glory, awake not! stir not!—Impotent resistance will add vengeance to ruin. Live in smiling peace with your insatiable oppressors, and die with the noble consolation, that your submissive patience will survive triumphant your beggary and despair." Dread of shameful subservience became a more pronounced southern theme after Lincoln's election. For instance, Alcibiade De Blanc of Saint Martin Parish introduced to the Louisiana secession convention a resolution that spoke to the southern fear of lost racial honor. The new president's party would force, he said, the southern people to accept an "equality [of blacks] with a superior race . . . to the irreparable ruin of this mighty Republic, the degradation of the American name, and the corruption of the American blood." . . .

Nearly every major sectional issue from Tallmadge's amendment to the Missouri enabling act to the Free-Soil Wilmot Proviso had brought out expressions from proslavery advocates that connected slaveholding with southern honor and fear of shame. According to William L. Yancey's "Alabama Platform," the Wilmot Proviso was a "discrimination as degrading as it is injurious to the slaveholding states." Words like degraded, shamed, demoralized, and humiliated all referred to the horrors of lost self-esteem. As northern contemporaries believed, southern polemics far exceeded the actual causes. Just how would the Wilmot Proviso affect the ordinary planter in South Carolina or Alabama? Surely his control over his work force was scarcely less secure than before the measure was introduced in Congress. Loss of honor was the great issue, though by no means disconnected from slavery's protection.

So far, this exposition may have helped to explain the ethical language of the two sections, but it does not illuminate how honor played a role in the process of disunionism itself. At once, a vexing problem appears: the failure of all southerners to reach the same conclusion about the crisis. If honor were as pervasive as claimed, one might argue, then why such curious divisions throughout the South? The answer is complex and can only be touched upon here. Honor, like any ethical scheme from Christianity to Confucianism, provides only *general* rules of behavior, from which variety one may readily choose according to personal temperament, experience, or reading of circumstance. (One might as well expect uniformity about the dispensing of worldly goods in Christian doctrine.)

Although traditional honor seemed the exclusive preserve of secessionists, the ethic could also be used to defend the status quo rather than revolutionary disunionism.

In ethical and strategic terms, the options were clearly drawn between the need for immediate vindication with a call to arms and the equally "honorable," Ciceronian course of moderation and coolness under provocation. Over the years, southern Unionists had roundly denounced and successfully turned aside the secessionist plea for hot-blooded action. Even at the close of the era, they did not believe that John Brown's raid or Lincoln's election required rebellious measures. Was there not a higher law of honor that demanded of the true-hearted southerner prudence after the results of the 1860 election were known? At the Alabama secession convention, delegate John Potter of Cherokee County, for instance, spoke to the issue. The secessionists tell us that "our honor must be vindicated," he observed. If that be the case, he said, then at least it was one powerful argument for disunion. But there is, Potter continued, "a morbid sense of honor" which often leads to extremes, and it "involves [men] in disgrace while they vainly seek to maintain their false view of true honor."

Potter and many others urged a policy of calculation and patience. The slave states should confer about their grievances and weigh the costs of resistance before plunging into the unknown, they begged. From the time of Cicero to the outbreak of the Civil War, gentlemen had often responded to the passions of the moment by appealing to the Stoic-Christian tradition of honor that repudiated recklessness and intemperate behavior. But the Unionists of the South—by and large, the more securely placed large-scale planters—well knew that their calls for calm deliberation could be impugned as coward-ice. For this reason among others, the Constitutional Unionists and those southerners who had voted for Douglas generally proclaimed themselves "conditional" Unionists. That position meant not only a readiness to negotiate or await the verdict of other slave-state allies but also a willingness to accept secession if that policy won overwhelm-ing popular support. It was a part of the honor code itself that community consensus forced dissenters to surrender to popular decision even if the dissenters thought the policy foolish. Otherwise, one ran the risk of communal disloyalty.

Because of the fears for slavery's future that Lincoln's election engendered, the advantages lay with those in the Lower South who insisted that the inaction of continued Unionism would mean disaster and disgrace. The secessionists largely relied upon two tactics, one negative and the other more moderate. The first involved outright intimida-tion, sometimes violence. Nowhere was community will to repress dissent more evident than in South Carolina upon news of the "Black Republican" victory. Venerable, wealthy, and Unionist, the state supreme court chief justice John Belton O'Neall found that his neighbors no longer shared his sentiments or accepted his leadership. At the Newberry County Courthouse, he urged repudiation of the autumn madness: "Freemen—descend-ents of the Patriots of '76—it is your duty to prevent such a disastrous [policy as secession]." In reply, the townsfolk pelted him with eggs.

In other states the pressure toward consensus for disunion grew as well. In Atlanta, the *Daily Intelligencer* labeled Unionists "Southern Abolitionists [who ought to be] strung up to the nearest live oak and permitted to dance on nothing." In Alabama, boasted the Hayneville *Chronicle,* "not a half dozen papers" had the temerity to challenge the inexorable will of the outraged populace. The Unionist John Hardy of the *Alabama State Sentinel* in Selma received an offer of $10,000 to shut down his press. When the bribe failed, Yancey and friends pursued him with a libel suit. After two so-called abolitionists were killed by lynch law in Fort Worth, Texas, the local Unionist editor had to sell his paper to secessionists or face a similar fate. An Arkansas mob seized from a steamboat a traveling newspaper distributor from Saint Louis and hanged him for the crime of carrying Horace Greeley's New York *Tribune*. Such activities as these did not at all belie southern claims as liberty-lovers. Southerners simply meant something different by the term. As historian Donald Robinson points out, secessionist editors justified such suppressions of a free press "on the ground that the South was fighting for its very life and could ill afford dissension among its people."

The power of popular coercion also intimidated the Unionist delegates to state secession conventions. At the Alabama meeting, for instance, Yancey darkly impugned the integrity of the Unionist opposition. He called them Tories no less subject to the laws of treason than the Loyalists of the American Revolution had been. At once Robert Jemison of Tuscaloosa leapt to his feet. "Will the gentleman go into those sections of the State and hang all those who are opposed to Secession? Will he hang them by families, by neighborhoods, by counties, by Congressional Districts? Who, sir, will give the bloody order? Is this the spirit of Southern chivalry?" Convinced that the South's material interests and even the safety of slavery lay in preservation of the Union, Jemison appealed to the higher laws of honor by which interpretation popular clamors should not deter the statesman from following the dictates of sound judgment. He put these concerns for public well-being and peaceful prosperity in terms of honor in order to meet secessionist objections that "principle" should overrule all other considerations, regardless of costs in blood, treasure, and risks to slavery itself. In like manner, Mississippi Unionists tried to show that genuine honor required a course quite different from the one secessionists proposed. A "fictitious chivalry," they said, offered only brave words but perversely claimed to be frightened of mannish Boston bluestockings and pious abolitionists. Honor, the Mississippi Unionists explained, demanded that the Gulf states do nothing precipitous: if they seceded at once, they would, in effect, leave their Upper South brethren in the clutches of hostile free-state majorities.

Nonetheless, the submissionists, as they were dubbed, generally received the worst of this line of reasoning. Albert Gallatin Brown of Mississippi gave them the lie in 1860: "If it should cost us the Union, our lives, let them go," he cried. Better that than meekly to "submit to a disgrace so deep and so damning" as abject submission to Black Republican rule. The message that he and others delivered was not casually thrust aside. James L. Alcorn, a Unionist politician and a Delta planter with vast holdings, confided to a friend that the belligerence of the secession majority at the state convention had become almost intolerable. "Should we fail to commit ourselves [to secession], it will be charged that we intend to desert the South. . . . The epithet of coward and submissionist will be everywhere applied to us. We shall be scouted by the masses!" He and his Unionist colleagues signed the secession ordinance under duress, but they naturally had to claim that their action was as honorable and manly as their previous opposition had been. Both positions, they insisted, served the interests of the community and the glory of their state. When a similar tide of secession enthusiasm swept North Carolina after Lincoln's mobilization order, former Whig Jonathan Worth sighed in resignation, "I think the South is committing suicide, but my lot is cast with the South and being unable to manage the ship, I intend to face the breakers manfully and go down with my companions." . . .

The contest over secession was not one that involved matters of conscience or the more legally serious problem of treason. Rather, nearly all politically active southerners assumed the right of secession; the question was the wisdom of the decision. The secessionists, though, had always insisted that advocacy of peace and patience was simply another name for cowardice. Historian John Barnwell points out that the secession extremists proudly accepted their critics' charge of being Hotspur [the nickname given to Harry Percy, the rival of Prince Hal, later Henry IV, in Shakespeare's play, *Henry IV,* Part I] whose fate served the South as an inspiring example to be followed—possibly into the grave. "Harry Percy failed," the hotheads retorted, not because of his rashness and arrogance but because his kinsmen and allies proved faithless. If southerners were equally untrustworthy, then by the rules of manly honor they deserved defeat and disgrace.

Like the Northumberland rebel [Harry Percy was the son of the Duke of Northumberland], most southern radicals throughout the antebellum years were likely to be men on the threshold of their careers, not well-established and aging property holders. Benjamin Perry, a South Carolina Unionist, noted that the upcountry secessionists in the 1850s were "a set of young enthusiasts inspired with notions of personal honor to be defended and individual glory, fame and military laurels to be acquired." Critics might object to their choler and recklessness, but these truculent southerners had an answer. Even if the South's break for freedom were crushed by northern might, they said, the chance for vindication had to be seized. James Jones, one of the South Carolina ultras, predicted, "If we fail, we have saved our honour *and lost nothing.*" The alternative was too demeaning to be considered: the slavery of "*Submission.*" The honor that Shakespeare's . . . [Harry] Percy represented could only save injured pride and animate a spirit of defiance. Perhaps it was fitting that the young should stand in the vanguard of secessionism. They were soon to be the first to meet enemy fire in the field. Whether that circumstance was just or not, the words of the victorious Prince Hal were, for many a fallen Confederate, soon and sadly to apply. He addressed Hotspur, slain and lying at his feet: "Thy ignominy sleep with thee in the grave, / But not rememb'red in thy epitaph."

FURTHER READING

William L. Barney, *The Secessionist Impulse: Alabama and Mississippi in 1860* (1974)
Gabor Boritt, ed., *And the Civil War Came* (1996)
Steven A. Channing, *Crisis of Fear: Secession in South Carolina* (1970)
Daniel W. Crofts, "Secession Winter: William Henry Seward and the Decision for War," *New York History* 65 (July 1984), 229–256.
——, *Reluctant Confederates: Upper South Unionists in the Secession Crisis* (1989)
Richard N. Current, "The Confederates and the First Shot," *Civil War History* 7 (1961), 357–369
——, *Lincoln and the First Shot* (1963)
Michael P. Johnson, *Toward a Patriarchal Republic: The Secession of Georgia* (1977)
George H. Knoles, ed., *The Crisis of the Union, 1860–1861* (1965)
Roy F. Nichols, *The Disruption of American Democracy* (1948)
Stephen B. Oates, *With Malice Toward None: The Life of Abraham Lincoln* (1977)
Phillip S. Paludan, "The Civil War as a Crisis of Law and Order," *American Historical Review* 77 (1972), 1013–1034
David M. Potter, *Lincoln and His Party in the Secession Crisis* (1942)
——, *The Impending Crisis, 1848–1861* (1976)
Charles W. Ramsdell, "Lincoln and Fort Sumter," *Journal of Southern History* 3 (1937), 259–288
Kenneth M. Stampp, *And the War Came: The North and the Secession Crisis, 1860–1861* (1950)
Eric H. Walther, *The Fire-eaters* (1992)

CHAPTER
4

Fighting the War:
The Generals

Did the North win the Civil War because its armies were better led? This is often said, and there is some truth in the claim. After all, the task of the Union armies was considerably more difficult. While the Confederacy was engaged in a struggle to maintain its independence and therefore had simply to defend its territory and repel Northern attacks, the Federals had to assume the offensive, move their troops great distances into the South, seize strategic locations, defeat enemy armies, and then occupy Confederate terrain and subjugate the population. Yet the Northern generals and their armies were ultimately victorious.

Offsetting these disadvantages, however, was the superiority of the North in the resources with which to wage a war, particularly one that lasted a long time. The Federal side could draw upon a greater reserve of manpower, since its population was three times the size of the South's if the slaves were excluded. Furthermore, the North had a preponderance of physical assets in the form of railroads and raw materials as well as a more diverse and self-sufficient economy. And, as the war dragged on, the North's superiority to the South actually increased.

It must also be acknowledged that it took the North a long time to develop a strategy that could win the war and to find generals capable of carrying it out. Lincoln may have understood what was necessary, but Generals George McClellan and Joseph Hooker and their subordinates proved stubborn and unadaptable. Meanwhile, Generals Robert E. Lee, T. J. ("Stonewall") Jackson, and Joseph E. Johnston managed to defend Confederate territory and keep the Federals at bay. Moreover, the Southerners were neither as unaware of the novel features of this war and its technology nor as incapable of adjusting to them as their numerous critics have maintained. Unfortunately, the Confederates did not have the opportunity to experiment with alternative strategies and objectives that their opponents had. Nevertheless, much of the evaluation of the Civil War generals has turned on this question of their relative ability to adapt and innovate.

By whatever standards the Civil War generals are judged, their capabilities and the decisions they made are of considerable interest to many people. "Civil War buffs," as they are called, number in the hundreds of thousands. And their primary interest is in the military history of the war—the battles and campaigns, the officers and the generals. Books on these subjects continue to roll off the presses. This fascination has continued building over the six years since this anthology first appeared, thanks to Ken

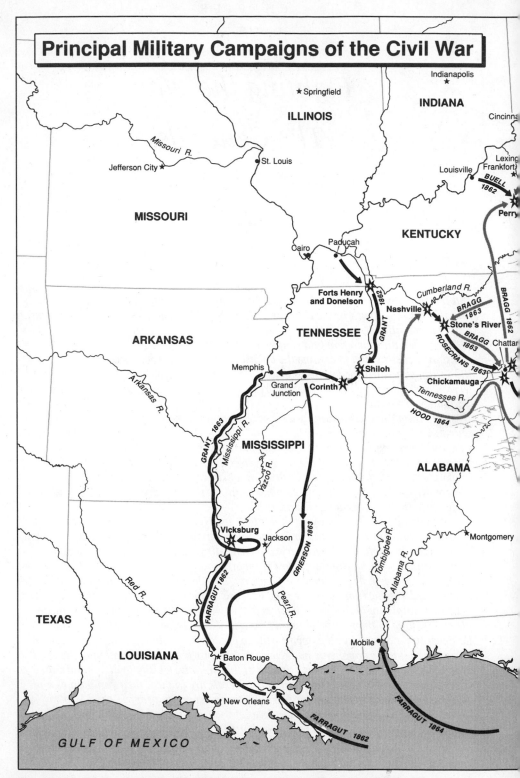

Principal Military Campaigns of the Civil War

From James McPherson, *Ordeal by Fire: The Civil War and Reconstruction.* Copyright © 1982.
Reprinted by permission of The McGraw-Hill Companies.

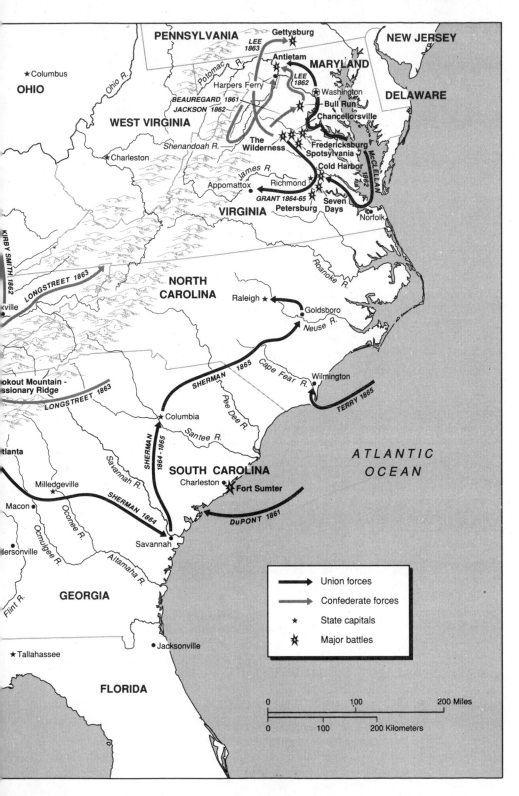

OHIO
★ Columbus

PENNSYLVANIA
Gettysburg
LEE 1863
Antietam
MARYLAND

NEW JERSEY

Potomac R.
Ohio R.
Harpers Ferry
LEE 1862

BEAUREGARD 1861
JACKSON 1862
WEST VIRGINIA
Washington
Bull Run
Chancellorsville
DELAWARE

Shenandoah R.
★ Charleston
The Wilderness
Fredericksburg
Spotsylvania
McCLELLAN 1862

James R.
Cold Harbor

Appomattox
Richmond
GRANT 1864-65
Petersburg
Seven Days
Norfolk
VIRGINIA

Roanoke R.

KIRBY SMITH 1862
LONGSTREET 1863

NORTH CAROLINA
Raleigh ★
Goldsboro
Neuse R.
xville

okout Mountain -
ssionary Ridge
LONGSTREET 1863

SHERMAN 1865
Cape Fear R.
Wilmington
TERRY 1865

tlanta

SHERMAN 1864-1865
Columbia
Santee R.
Pee Dee R.

ATLANTIC
OCEAN

Macon ●
Savannah R.
Oconee R.
SOUTH CAROLINA
Charleston ●
★ Fort Sumter

Milledgeville ★

ersonville
Ocmulgee R.
Altamaha R.
SHERMAN 1864
Savannah
DuPONT 1861

Flint R.
GEORGIA

● Jacksonville

★ Tallahassee

FLORIDA

	Union forces
	Confederate forces
★	State capitals
✳	Major battles

0   100   200 Miles

0   100   200 Kilometers

*Burns's documentary film on the Civil War and also to James McPherson's influential
and insightful volume on the war,* Battle Cry of Freedom *(1988). Both placed the
battlefield at the center of the conflict. For it is on the battlefield that decisions are made
and actions taken that can win or lose a war. The result has been a renewed emphasis,
among historians of the Civil War era, on the military aspect of the struggle as well as
a realization that individual military campaigns and battles, and the way they are conducted by each side, can be decisive in determining the outcome of the entire conflict.*

DOCUMENTS

Strategic thinking about the nature of the war and how to prosecute it is the subject matter of
the documents that follow. In the first, General George B. McClellan tells his commander-in-
chief what kind of war they are both involved in and how it should be conducted. This confidential letter of July 7, 1862, written during the Peninsula Campaign in Virginia and usually
referred to as "the Harrison's Landing letter," is an interesting discussion of grand strategy and
an excellent example of the general's overweening confidence. The second piece is General
Robert E. Lee's dispatch to President Davis of September 3, 1862, telling him, with similar per-
emptoriness, that he intends to embark on a risky, but in his view necessary, offensive into
Maryland, a dramatic example of the "offensive defense" advocated by both men. The next two
documents, the third and fourth in the set, are from General E. Porter Alexander, who was under Lee's command in the Maryland Campaign, which ended at the battle of Sharpsburg (Antietam). The extracts are from his memoirs, which have recently been discovered and published
by Gary W. Gallagher as *Fighting for the Confederacy.* They assess the rival generals, Lee and
McClellan, and also offer a broad critique of Confederate grand strategy.

The next three documents deal with the shift in the nature of the war in the spring and
summer of 1863. The fifth piece is a dispatch from the Union's commanding general, Henry W.
Halleck, to Ulysses Grant on the Mississippi, dated March 31, 1863, telling him how the war
has changed. The sixth document is an extract from Lieber's Code, the Union army's revision
of the rules of engagement, drawn up and issued in May 1863. The seventh document is General William T. Sherman's angry response to a request from the mayor and council of Atlanta
for leniency toward the civilian population. Dated September 13, 1864, Sherman's reply reflects his own understanding of how the war has changed. Finally, the eighth item is General
Grant's succinct explanation of how he conducted the operations of the Union armies as general-in-chief from spring 1864 until the surrender a year later.

General George B. McClellan Gives a Lesson in
Grand Strategy, July 1862

Head Quarters, Army of the Potomac
Camp near Harrison's Landing, Va. July 7th 1862

(*Confidential*)

Mr President

You have been fully informed, that the Rebel army is in our front, with the purpose
of overwhelming us by attacking our positions or reducing us by blocking our river

---

Letter, George B. McClellan to Abraham Lincoln, July 7, 1862, in *Official Records of the Rebellion,* Series 1,
Vol. 2, Pt. 2, pp. 73–74. This selection is also available in Stephen W. Sears, ed., *The Civil War Papers of
George B. McClellan: Selected Correspondence, 1860–1865* (Ticknor and Fields, 1989), pp. 344–345.

communications. I can not but regard our condition as critical and I earnestly desire, in view of possible contingencies, to lay before your Excellency, for your private consideration, my general views concerning the existing state of the rebellion; although they do not strictly relate to the situation of this Army or strictly come within the scope of my official duties. These views amount to convictions and are deeply impressed upon my mind and heart.

Our cause must never be abandoned; it is the cause of free institutions and self government. The Constitution and the Union must be preserved, whatever may be the cost in time, treasure and blood. If secession is successful, other dissolutions are clearly to be seen in the future. Let neither military disaster, political faction or foreign war shake your settled purpose to enforce the equal operation of the laws of the United States upon the people of every state.

The time has come when the Government must determine upon a civil and military policy, covering the whole ground of our national trouble. The responsibility of determining, declaring and supporting such civil and military policy and of directing the whole course of national affairs in regard to the rebellion, must now be assumed and exercised by you or our cause will be lost. The Constitution gives you power sufficient even for the present terrible exigency.

This rebellion has assumed the character of a War: as such it should be regarded; and it should be conducted upon the highest principles known to Christian Civilization. It should not be a War looking to the subjugation of the people of any state, in any event. It should not be, at all, a War upon population; but against armed forces and political organizations. Neither confiscation of property, political executions of persons, territorial organization of states or forcible abolition of slavery should be contemplated for a moment. In prosecuting the War, all private property and unarmed persons should be strictly protected; subject only to the necessities of military operations. All private property taken for military use should be paid or receipted for; pillage and waste should be treated as high crimes; all unnecessary trespass sternly prohibited; and offensive demeanor by the military towards citizens promptly rebuked. Military arrests should not be tolerated, except in places where active hostilities exist; and oaths not required by enactments—Constitutionally made—should be neither demanded nor received. Military government should be confined to the preservation of public order and the protection of political rights.

Military power should not be allowed to interfere with the relations of servitude, either by supporting or impairing the authority of the master; except for repressing disorder as in other cases. Slaves contraband under the Act of Congress, seeking military protection, should receive it. The right of the Government to appropriate permanently to its own service claims to slave labor should be asserted and the right of the owner to compensation therefore should be recognized. This principle might be extended upon grounds of military necessity and security to all the slaves within a particular state; thus working manumission in such state—and in Missouri, perhaps in Western Virginia also and possibly even in Maryland the expediency of such a military measure is only a question of time. A system of policy thus constitutional and conservative, and pervaded by the influences of Christianity and freedom, would receive the support of almost all truly loyal men, would deeply impress the rebel masses and all foreign nations, and it might be humbly hoped that it would commend itself to the favor of the Almighty. Unless the principles governing the further conduct of our struggle shall be made known and approved, the effort to obtain requisite forces will be almost hopeless.

A declaration of radical views, especially upon slavery, will rapidly disintegrate our present Armies.

The policy of the Government must be supported by concentrations of military power. The national forces should not be dispersed in expeditions, posts of occupation and numerous Armies; but should be mainly collected into masses and brought to bear upon the Armies of the Confederate States; those Armies thoroughly defeated, the political structure which they support would soon cease to exist.

In carrying out any system of policy which you may form, you will require a Commander in Chief of the Army; one who possesses your confidence, understands your views and who is competent to execute your orders by directing the military forces of the Nation to the accomplishment of the objects by you proposed. I do not ask that place for myself. I am willing to serve you in such position as you may assign me and I will do so as faithfully as ever subordinate served superior.

I may be on the brink of eternity and as I hope forgiveness from my maker I have written this letter with sincerity towards you and from love for my country.

Very respectfully your obdt svt

Geo B McClellan
Maj Genl Comdg

His Excellency A Lincoln
Presdt U.S.

General Robert E. Lee Takes the Offensive, September 1862

Headquarters, Alexandria & Leesburg Road
Near Dranesville, September 3, 1862

Mr. President:

The present seems to be the most propitious time since the commencement of the war for the Confederate Army to enter Maryland. The two grand armies of the United States that have been operating in Virginia, though now united, are much weakened and demoralized. Their new levies, of which I understand sixty thousand men have already been posted in Washington, are not yet organized, and will take some time to prepare for the field. If it is ever desired to give material aid to Maryland and afford her an opportunity of throwing off the oppression to which she is now subject, this would seem the most favorable. After the enemy had disappeared from the vicinity of Fairfax Court House and taken the road to Alexandria & Washington, I did not think it would be advantageous to follow him farther. I had no intention of attacking him in his fortifications, and am not prepared to invest them. If I possessed the necessary munitions, I should be unable to supply provisions for the troops. I therefore determined while threatening the approaches to Washington, to draw the troops into Loudoun, where forage and some provisions can be obtained, menace their possession of the Shenandoah Valley, and if found practicable, to cross into Maryland.

Letter, Robert E. Lee to Jefferson Davis, September 3, 1862, in *The Wartime Papers of R. E. Lee* (Boston, 1961), pp. 292–204.

The purpose, if discovered, will have the effect of carrying the enemy north of the Potomac, and if prevented, will not result in much evil. The army is not properly equipped for an invasion of an enemy's territory. It lacks much of the material of war, is feeble in transportation, the animals being much reduced, and the men are poorly provided with clothes, and in thousands of instances are destitute of shoes. Still we cannot afford to be idle, and though weaker than our opponents in men and military equipments, must endeavor to harass, if we cannot destroy them. I am aware that the movement is attended with much risk, yet I do not consider success impossible, and shall endeavor to guard it from loss. As long as the army of the enemy are employed on this frontier I have no fears for the safety of Richmond, yet I earnestly recommend that advantage be taken of this period of comparative safety to place its defence, both by land and water, in the most perfect condition. A respectable force can be collected to defend its approaches by land, and the steamer *Richmond* I hope is now ready to clear the river of hostile vessels. Should Genl [Braxton] Bragg find it impracticable to operate to advantage on his present frontier, his army, after leaving sufficient garrisons, could be advantageously employed in opposing the overwhelming numbers which it seems to be the intention of the enemy now to concentrate in Virginia. I have already been told by prisoners that some of [General Don Carlos] Buell's cavalry have been joined to Genl [John D.] Pope's army, and have reason to believe that the whole of McClellan's, the larger portions of [Ambrose E.] Burnside's & [Jacob D.] Cox's and a portion of [General David] Hunter's, are united to it. What occasions me most concern is the fear of getting out of ammunition. I beg you will instruct the Ordnance Department to spare no pains in manufacturing a sufficient amount of the best kind, & to be particular in preparing that for the artillery, to provide three times as much of the long range ammunition as of that for smooth bore or short range guns.

The points to which I desire the ammunition to be forwarded will be made known to the Department in time. If the Quartermaster Department can furnish any shoes, it would be the greatest relief.

We have entered upon September, and the nights are becoming cool.

I have the honor to be with high respect, your ob't
servant

R. E. Lee
Genl

General E. Porter Alexander, C.S.A., Assesses Lee and McClellan at Antietam, September 1862

... So that [September 15, 1862] our whole army was back on the Va. side of the Potomac except Longstreet's & Hill's divisions. These could have been easily retired across the river, & we would, indeed, have left Maryland without a great battle, but we would nevertheless have come off with good prestige & a very fair lot of prisoners & guns, & lucky on the whole to do this, considering the accident of the "lost order." And that seems to have been, perhaps at first, Gen. Lee's intention. For Jackson was first ordered to halt on the Va. side, but early on [the] 16th the orders were changed & he & every body else

From Edward Porter Alexander, *Fighting for the Confederacy,* Gary W. Gallagher, ed. (University of North Carolina Press, 1989), pp. 145–146, 153–154.

was ordered to come across the river to deliver battle. For the onus was on McClellan to attack. And this, I think, will be pronounced by military critics to be the greatest military blunder that Gen. Lee ever made. I have referred to it briefly once before, but I will give the reasons now more fully.

In the first place Lee's inferiority of force was too great to hope to do more than to fight a sort of drawn battle. Hard & incessant marching, & camp diseases aggravated by irregular diet, had greatly reduced his ranks, & I don't think he mustered much if any over 40,000 men. McClellan had over 87,000, with more & better guns & ammunition, &, besides that, fresh troops were coming to Washington & being organised & sent him almost every day. A drawn battle, such as we did actually fight, was the best *possible* outcome one could hope for. Even that we only accomplished by the Good Lord's putting it into McClellan's heart to keep Fitz John Porter's corps entirely out of the battle, & Franklin's nearly all out. I doubt whether many hearts but McClellan's would have accepted the suggestions, even from a Divine source. For Common Sense was just shouting, "Your adversary is backed against a river, with no bridge & only one ford, & that the worst one on the whole river. If you whip him now, you destroy him utterly, root & branch & bag & baggage. Not twice in a life time does such a chance come to any general. Lee for once has made a mistake, & given you a chance to ruin him if you can break his lines, & such game is worth great risks. Every man must fight & keep on fighting for all he is worth." . . .

When at last night put a welcome end to the bloody day [September 17] the Confederate army was worn & fought to a perfect frazzle. There had been no reserves all day. But on the Federal side Porter's corps had hardly pulled a trigger & Burnside's was comparatively fresh. In view of this, it seems strange that Gen. Lee did not take advantage of the night & recross the river into Virginia. For he knew too that McClellan had reinforcements coming to him & liable to arrive at any hour. But with sublime audacity the only question he debated with his generals, when they met at his headquarters after dark, was whether or not he should himself attack McClellan in the morning. Fortunately for somebody he decided to stand on the defensive. But surely military historians will say that McClellan again threw away a chance which no other Federal commander ever had, before or since. For he decided to wait for the considerable reinforcements now within a day's march. And when Lee appreciated his game he saw that there was nothing left to do but to return to Va. So all preparations were duly made & during the night of the 18th the whole army recrossed without accident, loss, or trouble. But I have always been proud of the fact that Gen. Lee did dare to stand & defy McClellan on the 18th. It not only showed his audacity as a commander, & his supreme confidence in his army; but it showed that in spite of distance from railroads, & of the excessive amount of fighting in the previous three weeks, his chief of ordnance still had plenty of ammunition at hand.

When McClellan found Lee gone he sent a force in pursuit which came near the river & opened with artillery upon everything in sight on our side. Now among the things in sight was my ordnance train under Maj. Duffey, & their first intimation of danger was the bursting of Federal shell among them. But they got up a very lively movement in very short order, & got away without any serious harm, though several of the vehicles got holes through unessential parts. To meet this fire old Gen. Pendleton, Gen. Lee's chief of artillery, deployed some reserve batteries he had had somewhere on the south side of the river & this artillery opened upon the enemy. But meanwhile the enemy sent two brigades of infantry across the river to capture these batteries, & they—having a very small infantry support—had to limber up & save themselves by flight, & Gen. P. with them, losing 4 guns. News of the affair reaching Gen. Lee he ordered A. P. Hill's division to turn back & meet the enemy. Hill did it most effectually, driving them into the river & shooting them down as they forded & swam so that their loss was quite severe. . . .

General Alexander Later Criticizes the Confederacy's Conduct of the War, c. 1900

We were now entering upon the third summer of the war [1863]. So far we had been able to hold the territory of the South practically intact. The enemy had lodgments upon our borders, but we still held the Mississippi River & all important railroads connecting Virginia with Georgia & the Gulf States. What we had lost to the enemy so far was only of outlying provinces which we could never have hoped to keep intact. But they were like wounds only skin deep & not affecting our power of resistance. Indeed, as the territory occupied by our principal armies became more compact, & the distances between these armies was diminished our power of resistance, according to all the rules & axioms of the great Game of War, was approaching its maximum.

And before taking up the history of the game, as we actually played it during this critical summer of 1863, I want to point out a variation which we might have played; & which Longstreet claims that he urged upon President Davis; & which, I think, must be pronounced by all military critics to have been much our safest play. Indeed, as will appear in due course of the narrative, we actually did make the play in September, after our return from Gettysburg, & with very fair success even then, although the circumstances were much less favorable than those prevailing in May.

No axiom of war is more obvious & of more frequent application than that pointing out the advantages possessed by the party occupying the *interior lines* or the center of the circle, against the adversary who operates around the circumference, or on the exterior lines. The principle is the same whether the question be one of a single battlefield, as is to be illustrated in the account of the field of Gettysburg; or of the whole territory occupied by opposing armies. The party having the interior lines can concentrate at any one point by shorter routes & consequently in less time than the party on the exterior. This offers opportunities to overwhelm portions of the exterior line, or isolated armies upon it, by sudden concentrations & attacks.

Our forces & resources were far inferior to those of the enemy upon the whole, but *the one single advantage* which we possessed was that of the interior lines. We could reasonably hope to transfer a large force from our Army of Northern Virginia to our Army of Tennessee, or vice-versa, much sooner than the enemy could discover & transfer an equivalent force to meet us. Such a manouvre, by the axioms of the game, was our best hold. And it was this manouvre which Gen. Longstreet states that he urged upon President Davis, as soon as he, Longstreet, then in Petersburg, with two divisions of his corps, knew that Gen. Lee with his reduced force had inflicted a demoralizing defeat upon Hooker's whole army at Chancellorsville. He states that he pointed out the fact that these divisions were not now needed with Lee, & were already well started on a trip to the

From Edward Porter Alexander, *Fighting for the Confederacy,* Gary W. Gallagher, ed. (University of North Carolina Press, 1989), pp. 219–220.

West. And he goes into some detail as to other troops which could have joined him and as to the opportunity of taking the enemy by surprise & striking him terrible blows in the West.

Unfortunately for the reception which this claim of Longstreet's has met among Confederate writers, his book, in several places, has given offence by alleged egotism & by seemingly harsh criticisms of Gen. Lee, & consequently much that he has had to say on this as well as on some other matters has been sneered or discredited in the Southern press. But looked at purely as a technical military question [of] which of the two plays in May 1863 was the most judicious for the Confederacy—to transfer as fast as possible heavy reinforcements to the West, or to invade Maryland & Pennsylvania—I must confess that the former seems to me so very much the best that I can excuse one who suggested it at the time for some warmth & earnestness in now pointing out its possibilities. Any rising enthusiasm, however, which my old personal Confederate sympathies may engender, over the things which apparently might so easily have been—either on this occasion or many others—does not long survive the reflection that had things been otherwise, I might not have been here to enjoy the experience of them. As the battles all went, I had the good luck to survive them, & the result has been a long life filled with happiness to myself & family. But who can say what would have been the result, to me & mine, even of a series of Confederate victories on different lines & in other places? So let us all gratefully accept things as they have happened & take up the narration of them without any more delay. . . .

General Henry W. Halleck, U.S.A., Acknowledges That the War Has Changed Course, March 1863

Headquarters of the Army,
Washington, March 31, 1863.

Maj. Gen. U. S. Grant,
                    Commanding Department of the Tennessee, near Vicksburg:

GENERAL: It is the policy of the Government to withdraw from the enemy as much productive labor as possible. So long as the rebels retain and employ their slaves in producing grains, &c., they can employ all the whites in the field. Every slave withdrawn from the enemy is equivalent to a white man put *hors de combat.*

Again, it is the policy of the Government to use the negroes of the South, as far as practicable, as a military force, for the defense of forts, depots, &c. If the experience of General Banks near New Orleans should be satisfactory, a much larger force will be organized during the coming summer; and if they can be used to hold points on the Mississippi during the sickly season, it will afford much relief to our armies. They certainly can be used with advantage as laborers, teamsters, cooks, &c., and it is the opinion of many who have examined the question without passion or prejudice, that they can also be used as a military force. It certainly is good policy to use them to the very best advantage we can. Like almost anything else, they may be made instruments of good or

Letter, Henry W. Halleck to Ulysses S. Grant, March 31, 1863, in *Official Records,* Series I, Vol. 24, Pt. 3, p. 157.

evil. In the hands of the enemy, they are used with much effect against us; in our hands, we must try to use them with the best possible effect against the rebels.

It has been reported to the Secretary of War that many of the officers of your command not only discourage the negroes from coming under our protection, but by ill-treatment force them to return to their masters. This is not only bad policy in itself, but is directly opposed to the policy adopted by the Government. Whatever may be the individual opinion of an officer in regard to the wisdom of measures adopted and announced by the Government, it is the duty of every one to cheerfully and honestly endeavor to carry out the measures so adopted. Their good or bad policy is a matter of opinion before they are tried; their real character can only be determined by a fair trial. When adopted by the Government, it is the duty of every officer to give them such a trial, and to do everything in his power to carry the orders of his Government into execution.

It is expected that you will use your official and personal influence to remove prejudices on this subject, and to fully and thoroughly carry out the policy now adopted and ordered by the Government. That policy is to withdraw from the use of the enemy all the slaves you can, and to employ those so withdrawn to the best possible advantage against the enemy.

The character of the war has very much changed within the last year. There is now no possible hope of reconciliation with the rebels. The Union party in the South is virtually destroyed. There can be no peace but that which is forced by the sword. We must conquer the rebels or be conquered by them. The North must conquer the slave oligarchy or become slaves themselves—the manufacturers mere "hewers of wood and drawers of water" to Southern aristocrats.

This is the phase which the rebellion has now assumed. We must take things as they are. The Government, looking at the subject in all its aspects, has adopted a policy, and we must cheerfully and faithfully carry out that policy.

I write you this unofficial letter simply as a personal friend and as a matter of friendly advice. From my position here, where I can survey the entire field, perhaps I may be better able to understand the tone of public opinion and the intentions of the Government than you can from merely consulting the officers of your own army.

Very respectfully, your obedient servant,

H. W. HALLECK.

The Union Army Redefines the Rules of War: Lieber's Code, May 1863

. . . 14. Military necessity, as understood by modern civilized nations, consists in the necessity of those measures which are indispensable for securing the ends of the war, and which are lawful according to the modern law and usages of war.

15. Military necessity admits of all direct destruction of life or limb of armed enemies, and of other persons whose destruction is incidentally unavoidable in the armed contests of the war; it allows of the capturing of every armed enemy, and every enemy of importance to the hostile government, or of peculiar danger to the captor; it allows of

From Lieber's Code, General Orders No. 100, April 24, 1863, in *Official Records,* Series III, Vol. 3, pp. 150–151.

all destruction of property, and obstruction of the ways and channels of traffic, travel, or communication, and of all withholding of sustenance or means of life from the enemy; of the appropriation of whatever an enemy's country affords necessary for the subsistence and safety of the Army, and of such deception as does not involve the breaking of good faith either positively pledged, regarding agreements entered into during the war, or supposed by the modern law of war to exist. Men who take up arms against one another in public war do not cease on this account to be moral beings, responsible to one another and to God.

16. Military necessity does not admit of cruelty—that is, the infliction of suffering for the sake of suffering or for revenge, nor of maiming or wounding except in fight, nor of torture to extort confessions. It does not admit of the use of poison in any way, nor of the wanton devastation of a district. It admits of deception, but disclaims acts of perfidy; and, in general, military necessity does not include any act of hostility which makes the return to peace unnecessarily difficult.

17. War is not carried on by arms alone. It is lawful to starve the hostile belligerent, armed or unarmed, so that it leads to the speedier subjection of the enemy.

18. When a commander of a besieged place expels the non-combatants, in order to lessen the number of those who consume his stock of provisions, it is lawful, through an extreme measure, to drive them back, so as to hasten on the surrender.

19. Commanders, whenever admissible, inform the enemy of their intention to bombard a place, so that the non-combatants, and especially the women and children, may be removed before the bombardment commences. But it is no infraction of the common law of war to omit thus to inform the enemy. Surprise may be a necessity.

20. Public war is a state of armed hostility between sovereign nations or governments. It is a law and requisite of civilized existence that men live in political, continuous societies, forming organized units, called states or nations, whose constituents bear, enjoy, and suffer, advance and retrograde together, in peace and in war.

21. The citizen or native of a hostile country is thus an enemy, as one of the constituents of the hostile state or nation, and as such as subjected to the hardships of the war.

22. Nevertheless, as civilization has advanced during the last centuries, so has likewise steadily advanced, especially in war on land, the distinction between the private individual belonging to a hostile country and the hostile country itself, with its men in arms. The principle has been more and more acknowledged that the unarmed citizen is to be spared in person, property, and honor as much as the exigencies of war will admit.

23. Private citizens are no longer murdered, enslaved, or carried off to distant parts, and the inoffensive individual is as little disturbed in his private relations as the commander of the hostile troops can afford to grant in the overruling demands of a vigorous war.

24. The almost universal rule in remote times was, and continues to be with barbarous armies, that the private individual of the hostile country is destined to suffer every privation of liberty and protection and every disruption of family ties. Protection was, and still is with uncivilized people, the exception.

25. In modern regular wars of the Europeans and their descendants in other portions of the globe, protection of the inoffensive citizen of the hostile country is the rule; privation and disturbance of private relations are the exceptions.

26. Commanding generals may cause the magistrates and civil officers of the hostile country to take the oath of temporary allegiance or an oath of fidelity to their own

victorious government or rulers, and they may expel every one who declines to do so. But whether they do so or not, the people and their civil officers owe strict obedience to them as long as they hold sway over the district or country, at the peril of their lives.

27. The law of war can no more wholly dispense with retaliation than can the law of nations, of which it is a branch. Yet civilized nations acknowledge retaliation as the sternest feature of war. A reckless enemy often leaves to his opponent no other means of securing himself against the repetition of barbarous outrage.

28. Retaliation will therefore never be restored to as a measure of mere revenge, but only as a means of protective retribution, and moreover cautiously and unavoidable— that is to say, retaliation shall only be resorted to after careful inquiry into the real occurrence and the character of the misdeeds that may demand retribution.

Unjust or inconsiderate retaliation removes the belligerents farther and farther from the mitigating rules of regular war, and by rapid steps leads them nearer to the internecine wars of savages.

29. Modern times are distinguished from earlier ages by the existence at one and the same time of many nations and great governments related to one another in close intercourse.

Peace is their normal condition; war is the exception. The ultimate object of all modern war is a renewed state of peace.

The more vigorously wars are pursued the better it is for humanity. Sharp wars are brief.

30. Ever since the formation and coexistence of modern nations, and ever since wars have become great national wars, war has come to be acknowledged not to be its own end, but the means to obtain great ends of state, or to consist in defense against wrong; and no conventional restriction of the modes adopted to injure the enemy is any longer admitted; but the law of war imposes many limitations and restrictions on principles of justice, faith, and honor. . . .

General William T. Sherman Explains How the War Has Changed, September 1864

Headquarters Military Division of the Mississippi, in the Field, Atlanta, Georgia, September 12, 1864.

JAMES M. CALHOUN, Mayor, E. E. RAWSON and S. C. WELLS, representing City Council of Atlanta.

Gentlemen: I have your letter of the 11th, in the nature of a petition to revoke my orders removing all the inhabitants from Atlanta. I have read it carefully, and give full credit to your statements of the distress that will be occasioned, and yet shall not revoke my orders, because they were not designed to meet the humanities of the case, but to prepare for the future struggles in which millions of good people outside of Atlanta have a deep interest. We must have peace, not only at Atlanta, but in all America. To secure this, we must stop the war that now desolates our once happy and favored country. To stop war, we must defeat the rebel armies which are arrayed against the laws and Constitution that all must respect and obey. To defeat those armies, we must prepare the

Letter, William T. Sherman to James M. Calhoun et al., September 12, 1864, in Sherman, *Memoirs of William T. Sherman* (Appleton and Co., 1875), Vol. 2, pp. 125–127.

way to reach them in their recesses, provided with the arms and instruments which enable us to accomplish our purpose. Now, I know the vindictive nature of our enemy, that we may have many years of military operations from this quarter; and, therefore, deem it wise and prudent to prepare in time. The use of Atlanta for warlike purposes is inconsistent with its character as a home for families. There will be no manufactures, commerce, or agriculture here, for the maintenance of families, and sooner or later want will compel the inhabitants to go. Why not go now, when all the arrangements are completed for the transfer, instead of waiting till the plunging shot of contending armies will renew the scenes of the past month? Of course, I do not apprehend any such thing at this moment, but you do not suppose this army will be here until the war is over. I cannot discuss this subject with you fairly, because I cannot impart to you what we propose to do, but I assert that our military plans make it necessary for the inhabitants to go away, and I can only renew my offer of services to make their exodus in any direction as easy and comfortable as possible.

You cannot qualify war in harsher terms than I will. War is cruelty, and you cannot refine it; and those who brought war into our country deserve all the curses and maledictions a people can pour out. I know I had no hand in making this war, and I know I will make more sacrifices to-day than any of you to secure peace. But you cannot have peace and a division of our country. If the United States submits to a division now, it will not stop, but will go on until we reap the fate of Mexico, which is eternal war. The United States does and must assert its authority, wherever it once had power; for, if it relaxes one bit to pressure, it is gone, and I believe that such is the national feeling. This feeling assumes various shapes, but always comes back to that of Union. Once admit the Union, once more acknowledge the authority of the national Govern-ment, and, instead of devoting your houses and streets and roads to the dread uses of war, I and this army become at once your protectors and supporters, shielding you from danger, let it come from what quarter it may. I know that a few individuals cannot resist a torrent of error and passion, such as swept the South into rebellion, but you can point out, so that we may know those who desire a government, and those who insist on war and its desolation.

You might as well appeal against the thunder-storm as against these terrible hard-ships of war. They are inevitable, and the only way the people of Atlanta can hope once more to live in peace and quiet at home, is to stop the war, which can only be done by admitting that it began in error and is perpetuated in pride.

We don't want your negroes, or your horses, or your houses, or your lands, or any thing you have, but we do want and will have a just obedience to the laws of the United States. That we will have, and, if it involves the destruction of your improvements, we cannot help it. . . .

But, my dear sirs, when peace does come, you may call on me for any thing. Then will I share with you the last cracker, and watch with you to shield your homes and families against danger from every quarter.

Now you must go, and take with you the old and feeble, feed and nurse them, and build for them, in more quiet places, proper habitations to shield them against the weather until the mad passions of men cool down, and allow the Union and peace once more to settle over your old homes at Atlanta. Yours in haste,

W. T. Sherman, *Major-General commanding.*

General Ulysses S. Grant Reports His Assignment Accomplished, July 1865

Report of Lieutenant-General U. S. Grant, of the United States Armies—1864–'65

Headquarters Armies of the United States,
Washington, D. C., July 22, 1865.

Hon. E. M. Stanton, Secretary of War.

Sir:—I have the honor to submit the following report of the operations of the Armies of the United States from the date of my appointment to command the same.

From an early period in the rebellion I had been impressed with the idea that active and continuous operations of all the troops that could be brought into the field, regardless of season and weather, were necessary to a speedy termination of the war. The resources of the enemy and his numerical strength were far inferior to ours; but as an offset to this, we had a vast territory, with a population hostile to the government, to garrison, and long lines of river and railroad communications to protect, to enable us to supply the operating armies.

The armies in the East and West acted independently and without concert, like a balky team, no two ever pulling together, enabling the enemy to use to great advantage his interior lines of communication for transporting troops from East to West, reinforcing the army most vigorously pressed, and to furlough large numbers, during seasons of inactivity on our part, to go to their homes and do the work of producing, for the support of their armies. It was a question whether our numerical strength and resources were not more than balanced by these disadvantages and the enemy's superior position.

From the first, I was firm in the conviction that no peace could be had that would be stable and conducive to the happiness of the people, both North and South, until the military power of the rebellion was entirely broken.

I therefore determined, first, to use the greatest number of troops practicable against the armed force of the enemy; preventing him from using the same force at different seasons against first one and then another of our armies, and the possibility of repose for refitting and producing necessary supplies for carrying on resistance. Second, to hammer continuously against the armed force of the enemy and his resources, until by mere attrition, if in no other way, there should be nothing left to him but an equal submission with the loyal section of our common country to the constitution and laws of the land.

These views have been kept constantly in mind, and orders given and campaigns made to carry them out. Whether they might have been better in conception and execution is for the people, who mourn the loss of friends fallen, and who have to pay the pecuniary cost, to say. All I can say is, that what I have done has been done conscientiously, to the best of my ability, and in what I conceived to be for the best interests of the whole country. . . .

From Ulysses S. Grant, *Personal Memoirs of Ulysses S. Grant* (Library of America, 1990), Appendix, pp. 781–782.

E S S A Y S

Two rather different perspectives on the way the military leaders fought the war are presented here. The first focuses on the critical campaign into Maryland that was undertaken by the Confederates in late summer 1862. Gary W. Gallagher of Pennsylvania State University examines how each side fought and what the outcome and effect of the entire operation were. Gallagher's contribution is taken from a volume of essays by military historians on the Maryland Campaign, one of a series of similar books on the major battles and campaigns of the Civil War that he is organizing and editing. The accompanying piece, by Mark Grimsley of Ohio State University, takes a topical approach to the war, stressing the policy toward civilians carried out by the Federal forces, rather than the more traditional focus on particular battles and the generals who fought them.

The Maryland Campaign in Perspective

GARY W. GALLAGHER

The broad consequences of the 1862 Maryland campaign exceeded those of any other operation of the American Civil War. The events of that autumn marked a watershed in the conflict. Soldiers and civilians alike strove to discover exactly what had been won and lost in a military sense. People behind the lines struggled to come to terms with hideous casualty lists. Photographic evidence from the battlefield at Antietam altered forever romantic conceptions of war. Abraham Lincoln took a momentous step toward emancipation, while European leaders recast their thinking about the likelihood of Confederate independence. Maryland remained firmly in the Union; Republicans breathed a bit more easily about the coming Northern elections. Complex in execution and impact, the Maryland campaign qualified as a pivotal event of the war.

In the area of military results, only the magnitude and horror of the fighting were beyond conflicting interpretation. A Pennsylvania soldier groping for the right words to describe the carnage stated simply, "No tongue can tell, no mind conceive, no pen portray the horrible sights I witnessed this morning." "Great God," wrote a Georgian to his wife the day after the battle, "what awful things I have to chronicle this morning! . . . One of the most awful battles that was ever fought was fought yesterday[.] [It] commenced at daylight and continued all day until dark. . . . This war will have to stop before long, as all the men will be killed off." Similar statements from other men appalled by the savagery of the battle abound in the literature on Antietam.

The overall military result of the campaign was more open to question. Almost from the moment the guns fell silent in the gathering dusk of September 17, 1862, people expressed contradictory reactions about what had transpired. Lee's official report and congratulatory order to his troops understandably emphasized the positive aspects of the expedition. The Confederate army had cleared Federals from northern Virginia, captured Harpers Ferry and its garrison, provisioned itself from western Maryland, and maintained a position near the south bank of the Potomac after its withdrawal. As for his soldiers' conduct in the battle, Lee told Davis with obvious pride that, "History records but few examples of a greater amount of labor and fighting than has been done by this army during the present campaign." To the Army of Northern Virginia, Lee expressed "admiration of the indomitable courage it has displayed in battle and its cheerful endurance of privation and hardship on the march." Absent was any hint of the straggling and desertion that had plagued Lee's movements; however, in a letter to Davis on September 25 Lee admitted that the army did not "exhibit its former temper and condition." James Longstreet, who doubtless was privy to Lee's thinking in the aftermath of the raid, recorded after the war that "General Lee was not satisfied with the result of the Maryland campaign."

Opinion from the Southern ranks generally spoke of success. Letters, diaries, and postwar accounts mentioned the prisoners and guns taken at Harpers Ferry, the steadfast courage of the men at Antietam, and McClellan's failure to drive the Army of Northern Virginia from the battlefield on September 18. "At night we lay down on our arms," remembered a Virginian of the night of September 17. "The next morning, expecting a renewal of the battle, we were up bright and early. But the enemy was badly whipped and did not make a demonstration during the day." Chaplain Nicholas A. Davis of Hood's Texas Brigade stated shortly after the campaign that "Harper's Ferry had fallen, and its rich prizes were ours." Davis emphasized that "our march to and across the river was undisturbed—This, of itself, will show to the world the nature of McClellan's victory. And if he had beaten and driven us, . . . why did he allow us to pass quietly away after holding the field a whole day and night?"

John Hampden Chamberlayne, a Virginia artillerist, cautioned his sister not "to suppose we were driven out of Maryland; no such thing; our campaign is almost unexampled for quickness & completeness of success." "We have done much more," Chamberlayne insisted, "than a sane man could have expected." In *The Lost Cause,* published in 1866, Edward A. Pollard suggested that the campaign had "few parallels in history for active operations and brilliant results." Pollard noted sarcastically that if "McClellan was under the impression that he had won a victory, he showed but little disposition to improve it, or to gather its fruits."

Confederate General Jubal A. Early ably enumerated the positive facets of the Maryland raid in his postwar autobiography. After forcing Union armies away from Richmond and out of northern Virginia, Lee "had crossed the Potomac, captured an important stronghold defended by a strong force, securing a large amount of artillery, small arms, and stores of all kinds. . . ." At Antietam he "fought a great battle with the newly reorganized and heavily reinforced and recruited army of the enemy, which later was so badly crippled that it was not able to resume the offensive for nearly two months." Lee then stood "defiantly on the banks of the Potomac, the extreme northern limit of the Confederacy," and from that position menaced Washington while at the same time freeing Richmond from direct threat. When the Federals finally moved into Virginia again, stated Early, Lee was in perfect position "to interpose his army, and inflict a new defeat on the enemy."

A few Confederates confessed doubts about their accomplishments in Maryland. Four days after Antietam, Walter H. Taylor of Lee's staff somewhat bitterly counseled his sister not to "let any of your friends sing 'My Maryland'—not 'my Western Maryland' anyhow." "We do not claim a victory . . . ," conceded Taylor, "It was not decisive enough for that." The young staff officer did add bravely that if either side had an edge at Antietam, "it certainly was with us." Brigadier General William Dorsey Pender informed his wife Fanny that he had heard but one feeling expressed about the raid into Maryland, "and that is a regret at our having gone there. Our Army has shown itself incapable of invasion and we had better stick to the defensive." A member of the Rockbridge Artillery made no effort to soften his blunt assessment: "The yankees slitely got the best of the fight in Maryland. You ought to have Seen us Skeedadling across the Potomac and the yankees close in our rear." South Carolinian Alexander Cheves Haskell praised the fighting qualities of the Confederates at Antietam, but stressed that huge numbers of their comrades had abandoned the army. "We are in far better condition in every respect," he affirmed from the Virginia side of the Potomac on September 28, "than when we first invaded the cold, treacherous soil of Maryland."

Voices on the Federal side also reflected mixed judgments about the military results of the campaign. Politics and personal loyalty colored many Northern attitudes—friends and supporters of the Democratic McClellan in one camp, Republicans and McClellan's enemies within the Union army arrayed against them. McClellan himself stood at one extreme, a pillar of unrelenting self-congratulation. He took pains to impress Mrs. McClellan with the magnitude of his achievement: "I feel some little pride in having, with a beaten and demoralized army, defeated Lee so utterly and saved the North so completely." "I have the satisfaction of knowing," he continued, "that God has, in His mercy, a second time made me the instrument for saving the nation." General-in-Chief Henry W. Halleck received, on September 19, McClellan's bombastic assurance that "our victory was complete. The enemy is driven back into Virginia. Maryland and Pennsylvania are now safe." Neither at the time nor in his postwar writings did McClellan grant that his conduct of the campaign had been anything less than brilliant.

For many Northerners, the fact of Lee's retreat signified a Union victory. Alpheus S. Williams, a divisional leader in the Federal Twelfth Corps, believed that "we punished the Rebels severely in the last battle. The number of dead they left on the field was enormous. In some places whole regiments seem to have fallen in their tracks." The Confederates sneaked back to Virginia, said Williams: "Their invasion of Maryland has been a sad business for them." George G. Meade, who as commander of the Army of the Potomac would repel a second Confederate raid nine months hence, pronounced Lee's Maryland adventure "the most lamentable failure." Although his unit did not fight at Antietam, Colonel Robert McAllister of the 11th New Jersey sent a letter to his family on September 21 that echoed McClellan's own estimate of the campaign: "McClellan has done well—gained a decided victory, saved Washington, Maryland, and Pennsylvania, and given the Rebels a hard stroke." " How splendidly his men fought under him, compared to what the troops did under Pope," McAllister added. Edward K. Wightman of the 9th New York arrived on the battlefield just after the Army of Northern Virginia had retreated. "The impression among our soliders," he found, "is that the war is finished. They think the battle of Wednesday the greatest of the war and decisive." A young officer from Massachusetts who heard the gunfire from Antietam but missed the battle recalled that it "was claimed as a victory by the Army of the Potomac because they held the field."

Some Federals sensed that McClellan had frittered away a splendid opportunity. Robert Goldthwaite Carter of Massachusetts and his three brothers, whose letters form a wonderful chronicle of the war in the East, considered Antietam at best a partial victory. One of the Carters had difficulty understanding why "McClellan did not let our corps finish up the 'rebs,' " and especially why the Federal commander allowed Lee to stand along Antietam Creek undisturbed throughout September 18 and then to cross the Potomac safely. Another brother also lamented the fact that the Confederates got away "to our shame, without much loss to their rear guard." "If McClellan had only attacked again early Thursday morning," observed disappointed Northern newspaper correspondent Albert D. Richardson two days after Antietam, "we could have driven them into the river or captured them. . . . It was one of the supreme moments when by daring something, the destiny of the nation might have been changed." Union First Corps chief Joseph Hooker agreed. An officer who visited the wounded general in Keedysville on September 19 recorded that he "talked a great deal about McClellan not renewing the attack yesterday."

No one in the North experienced deeper disappointment than Abraham Lincoln. He had considered Lee's movement into Maryland a wonderful opening for a Federal counterstroke. Far from home and tied to the fords on the Potomac, Lee was vulnerable to determined pressure. Antietam made a good start on the business of finishing Lee, but McClellan's inactivity on September 18 allowed the Confederate chieftain to extricate his army from a dangerous position. Lincoln prodded and implored McClellan to move, until finally, when seven weeks had passed and Lee remained ensconced in the northern frontier of Virginia, Lincoln removed Little Mac from command. A reading of Lincoln's correspondence with McClellan in that seven weeks conveys the depth of his disappointment and frustration. So too does Gideon Welles's entry in his diary for September 19, 1862: "Nothing from the army, except that, instead of following up the victory, attacking and capturing the Rebels, they, after a day's armistice, are rapidly escaping across the river." And then, in exasperation, the dour secretary of the navy went on, "McClellan says they are crossing, and that Pleasonton is after them. Oh dear!"

What is a fair reckoning of the military ledger sheet of the 1862 Maryland campaign? The Confederate side is a fascinating blend of accomplishment and useless loss, of brilliant leadership on the battlefield and questionable strategic decisions after September 15. Lee's movement north represented an effort to take the war out of Virginia, gather food and fodder, threaten Washington from the west, and prevent another Union incursion south of the Potomac before the onset of winter. He accomplished the first three of these, and managed also to postpone the next Federal drive toward Richmond until Ambrose E. Burnside's unusual winter campaign that ended ignominiously for the Union at Fredericksburg in mid-December. Mounting a raid rather than an invasion, Lee knew he would have to fall back to Virginia at some point, preferably in late fall. The battle of Antietam compelled him to withdraw sooner than he wished. But because McClellan allowed him to maintain a position immediately south of the Potomac, Lee was able to accomplish from northern Virginia what he had planned to do in western Maryland or southern Pennsylvania. The captures at Harpers Ferry constituted a bonus that Lee did not envision at the outset.

Against these positive results must be reckoned the loss of more than a quarter of the Army of Northern Virginia. The vast majority of those casualties came at Antietam, where Lee stood to gain not a single military advantage. After the fighting on South Mountain, Lee retained no viable offensive options. Harpers Ferry had fallen. No hope of surprise remained; an overwhelmingly more powerful foe was closing in from the east. The astute Porter Alexander subsequently observed that on September 15 "our whole army was back on the Va. side of the Potomac except Longstreet's & Hill's divisions. These could have been easily retired across the river, & we would, indeed, have left Maryland without a great battle, but we would nevertheless have come off with good prestige & a very fair lot of prisoners & guns, & lucky on the whole to do this, considering the accident of the 'lost order.' " Lee erred badly in choosing to give battle at Sharpsburg—it was, thought Alexander, his "greatest military blunder." His back was against the river, only Boteler's Ford invited escape should a crisis arise, and the disparity in numbers virtually guaranteed that the army would face a bitter contest.

Ironically, this battle that Lee should not have fought proved a showcase for the Confederate high command. Lee, Jackson, and Longstreet directed a tactical masterpiece, and their soldiers added heroic luster to a reputation already high. They also fell in such numbers that the Confederate government in Richmond hesitated to publish casualty lists for fear of the effect on the home front.

While fighting at Antietam was a mistake, Lee's decision to stay on the field another day and contemplate a counterattack amounted to sheer folly. The usual explanations are well known: Lee wanted the men to stand their ground lest morale drop; Lee knew the cautious McClellan would risk no further assaults; or, Lee felt confident of his army's ability to repulse the enemy. These rationalizations wither under even the slightest scrutiny. Lee realized all too well that morale already sagged among thousands of his soldiers. How would potentially catastrophic defeat along the river improve it? The second argument is equally flimsy. McClellan had attacked for twelve hours on September 17. How could Lee possibly know he would fail to resume those efforts on the eighteenth? As for the contention that Lee's army could repulse the enemy, the seventeenth had been a series of near disasters for Lee, and no factor had changed in his favor. Another round of similar assaults on September 18 almost certainly would break his army. In *R. E. Lee: A Biography,* Douglas Southall Freeman steps back in awe of Lee's resolute stand on the eighteenth: "What manner of man was he who would elect after that doubtful battle against vast odds to stand for another day with his back to the river?" The answer is that the R. E. Lee of September 18, 1862, was a man who irresponsibly placed at peril his entire army.

If Lee's gravest error was in striving to do too much with a limited force, McClellan's was in asking too little of a powerful one. High marks must be his for restoring confidence and discipline to a recently defeated army. He also forced Lee out of Maryland, a principal Federal goal in the campaign. In his mind that may have been enough. McClellan wanted a restoration of the old Union with the least possible cost in blood. He may have thought Antietam impressive enough to convince Southerners that independence was beyond their grasp, whereas a more decisive triumph might provide a springboard for Republicans to solidify their political grip on the nation and construct a new Union without slavery.

The salient feature of the entire Maryland campaign, however, was McClellan's opportunity to inflict a catastrophic defeat on Lee's army. No other commander on either side during the Civil War enjoyed a comparable situation. Following receipt of Lee's Special Orders No. 191, McClellan dawdled while the Army of Northern Virginia lay scattered across western Maryland. On September 15–16 he allowed Lee to concentrate his far-flung units near Sharpsburg. Porter Alexander's critique of McClellan at Antietam conveys a proper sense of disbelief: Lee managed a tactical draw on that day only "by the Good Lord's putting it into McClellan's heart to keep Fitz John Porter's corps entirely out to the battle, & Franklin's nearly all out." "I doubt whether many hearts but McClellan's would have accepted the suggestions, even from a Divine source," noted Alexander wryly. "For Common Sense was just shouting, 'Your adversary is backed against a river, with no bridge & only one ford, & that the worst one on the whole river. If you whip him now you destroy him utterly, root & branch & bag & baggage. . . . & such game is worth great risks. Every man must fight & keep on fighting for all he is worth.' " "No military genius," concluded Alexander, "but only the commonest kind of every day common sense, was necessary to appreciate that."

Priceless openings had come and gone over three crucial days, and Lee's decision to hold his lines on September 18 was McClellan's ultimate opportunity. Reinforced during the night, he outnumbered Lee nearly three to one. Thousands of his men were fresh, the enemy fatigued beyond telling. But once again McClellan lacked the fortitude to let his loyal soldiers seek complete victory. For all the talk of McClellan's love for his men, one fact stands out—he doubted their ability to defeat Lee's veterans. Their valor the day before on the rolling hills west of Antietam Creek fully matched that of the Confederate defenders. Their numbers should have told then; they would have told on September 18. They waited and watched through a long, tense day, and then it was over. The Army of Northern Virginia marched away that night to execute an undisputed crossing at Boteler's Ford. The Army of the Potomac possessed the requisite elements to deliver a fatal blow. Destruction of Lee's army would have uncovered Richmond and crippled Southern morale; it might have ended the war. Because McClellan chose not to force the issue, his military performance in Maryland must be judged harshly.

The absence of a clear-cut military decision in Maryland both bewildered and discouraged civilians in the North and South. Lee had hoped a successful raid would lead Northerners to examine the utility of continuing the war. But while his brief sojourn in Maryland prompted renewed scrutiny of Northern military leadership, it triggered no groundswell of support for a negotiated peace leading to Confederate independence. Many Northerners adopted an attitude similar to that of Republican war correspondent Whitelaw Reid, who pointed out that while the Confederates "certainly did not entirely succeed, if *we* claim the success, they can retort with force that never was victory more dear or barren." "Nor can any charity explain away that terrible, fateful delay after claiming a glorious victory," continued Reid. "It will not do to say our men were exhausted. If the vanquished and dispirited army had strength enough to gather up its fragments and retreat, the victorious army must have had strength enough to follow." "Let no weary patriot be deceived," Reid warned in summary. "We, indeed, took no steps backward at Antietam Creek, but we took very few forward."

Civilian sentiment south of the Potomac was generally pessimistic. Robert Garlick Hill Kean of the Confederate Bureau of War characterized Jefferson Davis in his diary as being "very low down after the battle of Sharpsburg." Davis confessed to Secretary of War George Wythe Randolph that the Confederacy's "maximum strength had been laid out, while the enemy was but beginning to put forth his." A young woman in Front Royal, Virginia, recorded with apprehension that "reports concerning the Sharpsburg battle are confirmed . . . our army are certainly recrossing the river. It looks rather gloomy for our prospects in Md. and I cannot possibly understand it all." The government did not at first disclose official figures for casualties—"a bad sign for us," thought Catherine Edmondston of Halifax County, North Carolina. "The possession of Harpers Ferry was claimed by us as worth the advance into Maryland," wrote Edmondston, "& yet we cannot hold it. God be with us! Turn not away Thy face, O God, but be with our army a help in time of need." Despite early stories in the *Richmond Enquirer* and elsewhere that Antietam was a stunning Confederate victory, few Southerners believed for long that the Maryland campaign had been more than a bloody standoff at best.

For Northerners, Antietam signaled a special turning point in the war. Photographers reached the battlefield before the dead had been buried—a first in American history. Their probing cameras captured the horrors along the Hagerstown Pike, east of the Dunker Church, and in the ghastly Sunken Road. In October 1862, Mathew Brady's New York gallery placed on exhibit a series of views entitled "The Dead at Antietam." Long lines of people passed through the gallery, including a reporter for the *New York Times* who described the experience in an article published on October 20. "Mr. Brady has done something to bring home to us the terrible reality and earnestness of war," he wrote. "If he has not brought the bodies and laid them in our door-yards and along the streets, he had done something very like it. . . ." *Harper's Weekly* and *Atlantic Monthly* also carried stories about the photographs, and *Harper's* included woodcuts of some of the death studies. Profoundly moved, those who saw the pictures would never again think of battle as carefully dressed ranks of brave men moving gallantly forward. Their understanding of war now included images of the twisted bodies of North Carolinians and Louisianians, of dead horses and broken equipment, and of a blasted landscape.

Apart from the debatable issue of military success, Lee's raid into Maryland was a profound failure. The most telling consequence came on September 22, 1862, when Lincoln told his cabinet that he would issue a preliminary proclamation of emancipation. Lincoln conceded that "the action of the army against the rebels has not been quite what I should have best liked. But they have been driven out of Maryland, and Pennsylvania is no longer in danger of invasion." That was victory enough to spare the proclamation any tinge of desperation. Should the states in rebellion refuse to return to the Union by January 1, 1863, said the president, their chattels "shall be then, thenceforward, and forever free." Vigorous and sometimes ugly debate ensued across the North, where millions of whites who hated or feared blacks resisted the notion of fighting in part to cast off the slaves' shackles. The South reacted with violent scorn, pointing out that Lincoln was freeing slaves only where he lacked the power to do so. What he really wanted, Southerners argued, was to precipitate a race war in the Confederacy. Lincoln's exemption of loyal Border States and all areas of the Confederacy under Federal control as of January 1, 1863, also led a few abolitionists in the North and Europe to charge hypocrisy. A number of twentieth-century historians have raised the same cry.

These critics displayed a poor grasp of the proclamation. Lincoln saw it as a war measure aimed at hastening Confederate defeat. Under the Constitution, he could seize material from the rebellious Confederacy; however, he lacked authority to take personal property from citizens residing in areas loyal to the United States government. He had done what was possible, and thereby helped open the way for nearly two hundred thousand black men to fight in Federal armies. The proclamation also foreclosed the option of reunion on the basis of the status quo ante bellum. The South's social and economic structure was doomed unless Confederate armies won independence on the battlefield. With issuance of the proclamation, the struggle became a total war for Union and freedom.

Lee's retreat from Maryland and the Emancipation Proclamation both influenced events in Europe. At flood tide in early September, Southern hopes for help from Europe receded quickly. Prime Minister Palmerston believed that "these last battles in Maryland have rather set the North up again." "The whole matter is full of difficulty," he thought, "and can only be cleared up by some more decided events between the contending armies." In a letter to Lord Russell on October 2, Palmerston suggested that "ten days or a fortnight more may throw a clearer light upon future prospects." William Gladstone and Russell continued their agitation for recognition through October. On the seventh of that month, Gladstone delivered his memorable paean to the Confederacy in a speech at Tyneside: "Jefferson Davis and other leaders of the South have made an army; they are making, it appears, a navy; and they have made what is more than either, they have made a nation."

The loud cheers that greeted those strident phrases were long forgotten when the British cabinet took up the question of recognition on October 28, 1862. With Palmerston made cautious by Antietam, the vote went against Russell and Gladstone. Shortly thereafter the cabinet also refused a French plan calling for Britain, France, and Russia to suggest a six-month armistice and suspension of the blockade. News of the Emancipation Proclamation further undercut friends of the South. American Minister to England Charles Francis Adams wrote happily that British antislavery sentiment was working to "annihilate all agitation for recognition." Adams undoubtedly overstated the impact of Lincoln's proclamation, for even some abolitionists in England continued to support the Confederacy. Neither Lee's withdrawal from Maryland nor the proclamation guaranteed that Europe would stay aloof, but together they helped persuade the British to wait until military developments favored the Confederates. Southern arms ultimately proved unequal to the daunting task of compiling enough victories to bring European intercession.

Lee's expectation of gathering recruits in Maryland came to little. Indeed, Southern illusions about pro-Confederate Marylanders waiting to break free of Union oppression disappeared even before the battle of Antietam. As early as September 7, Lee cautioned Davis that "notwithstanding individual expressions of kindness that have been given," he did not "anticipate any general rising of the people in our behalf." The next day, September 8, Lee issued a proclamation informing Marylanders that "our army has come among you, and is prepared to assist you with the power of its arms in regaining the rights of which you have been despoiled." No more than a few hundred Marylanders stepped forward to join the thin ranks of the Army of Northern Virginia.

The numerous Germans in western Maryland turned a distinctly cold shoulder to the intruders. The ragged clothing and gaunt frames of the Confederates, as well as their lice and pungent odor, put off even sympathetic civilians. In Frederick, citizens joyously welcomed McClellan's troops after the Army of Northern Virginia had moved on to the west. "Happy homelike faces beamed on us . . . ," wrote a Massachusetts soldier of his arrival in Frederick, "the people began to cook for us, bringing out as we passed, cake, pie and bread." A New Yorker related that "the place was alive with girls going around the streets in squads waving flags, singing songs & inviting the soldiers in for hot suppers."

As the Southern army crossed the Potomac into Virginia on the night of September 18, John H. Lewis of the 9th Virginia Infantry noted a changed attitude toward Maryland: "When going over the river the bays were singing 'Maryland, my Maryland.' But all was quiet on that point when we came back. Occasionally some fellow would strike that tune, and you would then hear the echo, 'Damn My Maryland.' All seemed to be disgusted with that part of Maryland."

Lee experienced a final failure relating to the Northern elections that fall. He had hoped to strengthen the peace interests, but the Army of Northern Virginia's two-week stay north of the Potomac supplied poor aid to those who opposed the Republican administration. If Union half-victories at Antietam and Perryville spawned little if any rejoicing in the North, they at least avoided the sort of dramatic defeat that might have sent Republican fortunes spinning downward. Ironically, the Emancipation Proclamation—made possible by Lee's retreat—did provoke angry reaction that helped the Democrats. Results of the canvass of 1862 showed only modest Democratic gains for an off-year election—thirty-four seats in the House of Representatives, gubernatorial victories in New York and New Jersey, and control of the Illinois and Indiana legislatures. The Republicans managed to gain five seats in the Senate and retain control of the House (their net loss in the House was the smallest in the last ten elections for the majority party). The war would continue under Republican direction.

The Maryland campaign holds a unique position in the galaxy of Civil War military operations. Its centerpiece was the surging maelstrom of Antietam, which stood out as the bloodiest single day of a conflict marked by great slaughter. The principal commanders offered a striking contrast in personality and style—Lee pressing his worn army to the edge of ruin in pursuit of beckoning opportunity; McClellan repeatedly shrinking from commitment of his proud host in circumstances favorable beyond the imaginings of most generals. Etched in grays rather than black and white, the military resolution invited debate. Lee went north and fought, avoided a series of lurking disasters, and found refuge in the end along the southern bank of the Potomac River. But the military events of mid-September 1862 bore bitter political and diplomatic fruit for the Confederacy. The nature of the conflict changed because of Lee's Maryland campaign. The South might have won the old war—seemed in the giddy season of late summer and fall 1862 to be doing so. But the new war would admit of no easy reconciliation because the stakes had been raised to encompass the entire social fabric of the South. The war after Antietam would demand a decisive resolution on the battlefield, and that the Confederacy could not achieve.

Gestures of Mercy, Pillars of Fire

MARK GRIMSLEY

Reading through the official reports of the Savannah Campaign, one is surprised by the brief treatment accorded the destruction that accompanied Sherman's great March to the Sea. Most of them sketch the foraging and burning in a few sentences or less, dwelling at length only on the odd skirmish with enemy militia and cavalry—or with the fairly extensive fighting required to capture Savannah itself and so reopen regular lines of supply. Finally a Pennsylvania officer, Colonel John Flynn, says outright what most of his colleagues implicitly suggest: "This campaign is, throughout its entire extent, void of interest to the soldier. . . ."

The comment is startling. *Void of interest to the soldier?* Here was the operation so often considered the dawn of twentieth century total war, the desolating march that revived war upon civilians as a normal military tactic, the prototype for strategic air bombardment against national economies. Colonel Flynn, however, clearly had no inkling that he and his men had just passed from one epoch to another. Instead he noted that by and large, "the army has not had occasion to form for battle; few bloody fields have been lost or won; no sieges have been commenced and ended, as the enemy has not in one instance made a stand of sufficient length to require the necessity of such measures." As far as the colonel was concerned, the chief element of significance—the clash of opposing armies decisively engaged—had been entirely lacking.

Tempting as it may be to believe that Colonel Flynn was just uncommonly short-sighted, a great deal of evidence suggests that the modern significance of Sherman's march, as well as other hard war measures, went substantially unrecognized by most contemporary observers. While Northern opinion hailed Sherman's marches as a form of divine retribution and also as a way to hit the South where it was most vulnerable, the arena of battle continued to exercise the decisive claim to attention. Sheridan's victories at the Battles of the Opequon, Fisher's Hill, and Cedar Creek, for example—which bracketed his devastation of the Shenandoah Valley—received far more press coverage than the devastation itself. The *Army and Navy Journal,* the voice of an emergent military professionalism, reported on Sherman's marches at length but emphasized the aspect of adroit maneuver far more than the attendant destruction. Similarly, although the post-war memoirs of Grant, Sherman, and Sheridan allude to the destruction of resources, they dwell far more heavily on the clash of armies, the conquest of cities and territory. None advocated economic warfare as one of the conflict's major lessons.

Yet the climactic raids of 1864–1865 at once became a staple of the American pageant, seared into the memory of everyone who experienced them and millions who only heard of them. The first book on Sherman's marches appeared in the same year Lee surrendered. By 1866, it had already been through twenty-six editions, and several other books had joined it. As the years went by, Union veterans told their children about the raids and white Southerners in the path of war told theirs. Grandmothers put pen to paper and reminisced for future generations about the coming of the Yankees. Everyone struggled to answer the same question: What did it mean?

The Dynamics of Escalation and Restraint

Although much changed between the innocent early days of the Civil War and its fiery conclusion, Union military policy toward Southern civilians had one important continuity. Federal officials instinctively understood what political scientist Thomas C. Schelling would one day argue. "The power to hurt," Schelling wrote, "is bargaining power. To exploit it is diplomacy—vicious diplomacy, but diplomacy." The Union army's policy toward Southern civilians was one long exercise in such diplomacy. The goals changed, the methods changed, but Federal officials always sought to coax or coerce white Southerners into desired behaviors.

Initially their effort primarily took the form of the conciliatory policy. Until recently, it was common among Civil War historians, especially military historians, to dismiss the policy as naive, an outgrowth of the picturebook-war delusions of the conflict's early months. In fact, proponents of the policy showed eminent good sense. Northern officials had every reason to suppose that political support for the fledgling Confederate government was shallow. The American South shared much in common with the North: the same language, the same heritage, the same republican ideals. Secessionists had tried for years to drag the South from the Union with signal lack of success. Their sudden triumph in 1860 seemed a ghastly fluke, the product, surely, of mutual misunderstanding or at worst a conspiracy hatched by an antidemocratic minority. Surely it did not express the considered will of the majority of white Southerners. Even after Lincoln's election and the defection of the Cotton South, Virginia, North Carolina, Arkansas, and Tennessee clung to the Union, seceding only when it became clear that the alternative was to make war upon their sister Southern states. And it was known that pockets of Unionism persisted in each.

The postwar myth of the solid South long obscured what historians have recently rediscovered: The assumptions of the proponents of conciliation were largely correct. The Confederate experiment was in trouble from the outset. White Southerners differed widely in their support for secession, the purposes they expected disunion to serve, and the means they were willing to countenance to preserve separate government. Paul Escott has described Jefferson Davis's unsuccessful bid to foster Confederate nationalism.

Richard E. Beringer, Herman Hattaway, Archer Jones, and William N. Still have argued vigorously that the divisions within the Confederacy fatally undermined its will to resist. From the perspective of the late twentieth century, it would seem to us an act of criminal folly if the North had *not* pursued a conciliatory strategy.

The policy proposed by Winfield Scott, George B. McClellan, and many others was brilliant in its simplicity. A federal judge in Missouri encapsulated it well in early 1862: "The exercise of power should be such as to leave no doubt of the ability to crush, yet there should be no crushing done." Confronted by the North's magisterial forbearance, white Southerners would quickly realize that the demons of tyranny and abolition were mere shadows trumped up by fire-eating politicians. Thus disabused, they would repudiate their deceivers and return to the Union fold.

Up to a point, the conciliatory strategy worked. The Union offensives during the first six months of 1862 gave Southerners a dismaying sense of their weakness. Mill Springs, Roanoke Island, Forts Henry and Donelson, Pea Ridge, Shiloh, Island No. Ten, New Orleans: The list of Confederate defeats ran on and on. The territory lost to Northern might numbered in the thousands of square miles. By June 1862, the North had given a powerful demonstration of its ability to crush. And the cordial reception sometimes received by Union soldiers, coupled with widespread carping at the secessionists, suggested that loyalty to the Confederate government was indeed weak. Respect and magnanimity might indeed produce a swift reunion. Just one more victory—at Richmond—and it would all be over.

Yet even as McClellan's scouts beheld the church spires of the Confederate capital, conciliation was also under enormous strain. To be successful, sending signals with force, like any other form of communication, requires the message to be clearly received. But from the outset, the conciliatory policy was often obscured or contradicted. Not all Northern officials embraced the policy. A tension soon emerged between those who basically thought the war a product of misplaced fears, and therefore emphasized a policy of general forbearance, and those who saw the origins of the war in a more sinister light and emphasized punishment for the guilty. Soldiers' depredations further undercut the message of conciliation, as did the necessary but sometimes draconian responses to guerrilla activity.

But perhaps the chief factor that obscured the message of conciliation was the North's unsettled policy toward slavery. The political scientist Richard Smoke, building on Schelling's work, has noted that belligerents generally signal a desire to limit their struggle by observing boundaries. A boundary may be geographical, like a river or a national border; qualitative, like the decision to employ a major weapon system previously forborne; or other things. The important criterion was that it must be understood by both sides and that its breaching should imply a change in the nature and intensity of the struggle. Once discovered and mutually recognized and observed, such boundaries become what Schelling called "salients," thresholds that define the scope and intensity of the fighting. The breaching of a salient represented escalation. In Smoke's formulation, it was an act that had "consequences and meaning for the overall pattern or nature of the ongoing war: its ground rules or limits."

If one applies this concept to the Civil War, the status of slavery in Union policy leaps to mind as the classic example of a salient. At the outset of the war, the Lincoln administration explicitly renounced any intention of interfering with slavery, and the doctrine of noninterference was a major hallmark of the conciliatory policy. Subsequently the administration reversed itself with an equally explicit Emancipation

Proclamation. Afterward, the conciliatory policy became a dead letter, and many observers saw the conflict as having become a "war of subjugation" or even "extermination."

In one sense, the slavery question formed a clearcut qualitative boundary or salient, and it is not difficult to argue that Federal policymakers intended their circumspection about slavery as a signal of the sort of war they intended to wage: They would fight Confederate armies in the field and destroy the military power of the rebel government, but they would not touch the basic social and economic fabric of Southern society. The decisiveness with which Lincoln resisted any attempt by Union commanders and policymakers to interfere with slavery is consistent with this interpretation. Even so, one must acknowledge that by the summer of 1862, slavery had also become what Smoke would describe as a "blurred saliency" because of many incremental intrusions upon it—the First and Second Confiscation Acts, the new article of war prohibiting Union forces from enforcing the Fugitive Slave Law, the liberally interpreted "contraband" doctrine, and the unauthorized but widespread attempts by Northern soldiers to encourage slaves to abandon their masters. Because of that, it is unlikely that the Southern people ever really understood the message of forbearance that Lincoln and other Northern moderates were trying to communicate.

McClellan's rebuff at the gates of Richmond ended whatever chance the conciliatory policy might have had to succeed. By giving the Confederacy a substantial victory at a time when one was desperately needed, it restored Southern morale and even set the stage for a major rebel counteroffensive in the summer of 1862. The ability of Federal armies to crush Confederate resistance was now repudiated. In the eyes of many Northerners, conciliation no longer communicated magnanimity, but weakness. Asked to comment on the policy, the prominent east Tennessee Unionist William G. "Parson" Brownlow offered a scathing assessment: "They [the rebels] attribute our forbearance toward them to cowardice and think that we are afraid of them."

The repudiation of the mild policy, however, was less the product of considered thought than of sheer frustration. Even before the Richmond failure, soldiers and civilians alike were becoming impatient with conciliation; as one man put it: "This administration seems terribly afraid of hurting somebody." Afterward, the military stalemate made conciliation impossible to endure. "The Union men want to see the Rebels made to suffer," a Missourian candidly informed a Lincoln cabinet official. Many in the North expressed rueful admiration for the uncompromising tenacity of the rebels. "A large amount of the success of our enemies has resulted from their boldness," Sherman wrote military governor Andrew Johnson. "They have no hair-splitting."

It was in such an environment that the Lincoln administration began to encourage military confiscation and moved toward emancipation. Some Confederates, mindful of the divisions within the South, actually welcomed such steps. "It is well," wrote J. B. Jones, a clerk in the Confederate War Department. "If the enemy had pursued a different course we should never have had the same unanimity. If they had made war only on men in arms, and spared private property, according to the usages of civilized nations, there would, at least, have been a *neutral* party in the South, and never the same energy and determination to contest the last inch of soil with the cruel invader."

Confederate President Jefferson Davis actively exploited these evidences of the North's "barbarity" in his effort to create an ideology to sustain the Confederate cause. Since only one white Southern family in four owned slaves, protection for slavery made a poor rallying cry. He tried to argue that the Confederacy actually embodied the values of the original American republic, but as the war ground on such an approach was increasingly inadequate. So by mid-1862, his speeches began instead to stress the "malignity" of the South's enemies, "who are daily becoming less mindful of the usages of war and the dictates of humanity."

Such pronouncements, of course, greatly distorted the actual nature of Federal policy. Even after Northern commanders repudiated conciliation and moved to a pragmatic policy instead, their measures remained well within the laws and usages of war applicable to international conflict. (Had they opted to apply the insurrectionary principle instead, the measures legitimately available to them were terrible to contemplate.) Still less did the Lincoln administration exploit the potentially explosive rage in the hearts of enslaved African Americans. In August 1863, the irrepressible General David Hunter suggested "a general arming of the negroes and a general destruction of the all the property of the slaveholders." In a letter to Edwin Stanton, he proposed to take an expeditionary force by sea, disembark on the Georgia coast, then march across the Deep South to New Orleans, "arming all the negroes and burning the house and other property of every slaveholder. A passage of this kind would create such a commotion among the negroes that they themselves could be left to do the rest of the work." This incendiary invitation was greeted with eloquent silence. The administration stood fast in its refusal to countenance the taking of slave vengeance.

In the war's eastern theater, both official policy and actual conduct changed little from the days of McClellan. In the west, armies greatly intensified their foraging activity but tried to distinguish between three varieties of Southern civilian—Unionists, neutrals, and active secessionists—and gave different treatment to each. The goal was to encourage loyal behavior, and although most commanders no longer expected to detach Southern whites en masse from their allegiance to the Confederacy, they still attempted to do so on a more limited scale.

In the lower Mississippi River valley, for example, Union policy makers pursued a program of "calculated magnanimity" whereby planters could reenter the lucrative cotton market if they would only take the oath of allegiance. As Major General Lorenzo Thomas archly put it, "[T]he prospect of a sale of two or three hundred bales of cotton, at the present high prices, is a powerful weight in the scale of loyalties." In the wake of the summer 1863 Vicksburg and Tullahoma campaigns, Grant and Rosecrans, respectively, issued orders that extended an olive branch to citizens in Mississippi and Tennessee. Grant believed Mississippi could be "more easily governed now than Kentucky or Missouri" if rebels from other states could be kept out.

Rampant guerrilla activity and the still-formidable rebel field armies, however, made effective wartime Reconstruction next to impossible, even on a limited basis. The Union military would have to break the strength of the Confederate armed forces, a task that by early 1864 seemed impossible to accomplish exclusively on the battlefield. Encouraged by the destructive expedition against Jackson, Mississippi, in July 1863, Grant expanded the scope of such operations into a strategy of raids that figured prominently in the Union campaigns of 1864–1865. With the advent of the hard war policy, civilian morale reemerged as a major strategic target.

The raids were intended to demonstrate two things to the Southern people—first, that they could be hurt, and second, that the Confederate government was powerless to protect them. Sherman said of his marches, "This may not be war but rather statesmanship," and Sheridan was grimly certain that white Southerners must experience firsthand the horrors of war. The civilians who waited at home "in peace and plenty," he wrote, knew little of its terrors. It was quite a different matter when "deprivation and suffering" were brought to their own doors. "Death," he continued implacably, "is popularly considered the maximum punishment in war, but it is not; reduction to poverty brings prayers for peace more surely and more quickly than does the destruction of human life, as the selfishness of man has demonstrated in more than one great conflict."

Yet the hard war policy was not born from a simple desire to hurt civilians. Its genesis was more complex. Although the shift from conciliation to pragmatism (or "war in earnest") reflected frustration, and emancipation helped establish the moral groundwork for hard war, the actual policy was spawned primarily by the tyranny of logistics. In that respect, it was not an anticipation of the terror bombing campaigns of the twentieth century, but rather a rediscovery of older forms of warfare.

The armies of early modern Europe had lacked systems of regularized supply. They depended on foraging to survive, particularly when in the field, and the constant need to live off the land often exerted near-dictatorial control over strategy. Foraging was an inherently unpleasant experience for the civilians whose crops and fodder disappeared into the maw of a hungry army. Theoretically a commander might intend simply to revictual his forces and mean no harm to the civilians from whom he took supplies. In practice, however, his soldiers would not be gentle about it, and would frequently contribute their own gratuitous thefts, rapes, and assaults.

The practice of living off the land had a negative corollary: If it made sense for an army to revictual itself from the regions through which it passed, it also made sense to deny that opportunity to the enemy. The result was "scorched earth" operations, sometimes inflicted as a defensive tactic on one's own territory, but at other times applied to enemy or even neutral territory as well. Such operations were usually much harder on civilians than simple foraging: Since time was frequently of the essence, and the denial of supplies muse be complete, the habitual recourse was to burn and destroy. When that occurred, the civilian population sometimes literally faced starvation, particularly in the early modern period when the peasantry generally lived at bare subsistence levels to begin with.

Foraging and area denial were in themselves so harsh that they had an intrinsic psychological effect. During the Middles Ages, peasants and townsmen, demoralized by repeated depredations, sometimes revolted against lords who proved impotent to protect them, as occurred during the *Jacquerie* of the Hundred Years War. Since extensive foraging and area denial operations could produce significant dislocations in the enemy camp, it made good sense—admittedly, reptilian good sense—to amplify the brutality as much as possible and so increase the psychological effect. The *chevauchées* [a French term for the large raiding expeditions carried out by the English in the Hundred Years' War] were one example; similar operations liberally punctuated the Dutch Revolt and the Thirty Years' War. Destructive expeditions took place even after the return to order that marked the period after the Treaty of Westphalia. The most famous episode was the Devastation of the Palatinate, but there were others. For example, in 1704, when the Duke of Marlborough's victory at Donauworth failed to persuade the Elector of Bavaria to capitulate, Marlborough conducted an eighteenth century *chevauchée* in an effort to "destroy the country and oblige the Elector on[e] way or other to a complyance." His troops razed some 400 villages to the ground.

The relevance of this earlier pattern to the American Civil War lies in two related points. First, the same logistical shortcomings that afflicted earlier European armies also affected the troops that fought the Civil War, eventually forcing them to adopt the age-old expedient of massive foraging. Second, the laws and usages of war, under which Civil

War commanders operated, reflected those same logistical imperatives. They were redolent in Vattel's *Law of Nations,* which remained a standard authority on the subject in 1861 and heavily influenced both Halleck's *International Law* and Lieber's Code.

Vattel and most other Enlightenment commentators sought to minimize the burdens of war on noncombatants. Nevertheless, their laws and usages of war did permit massive foraging, "scorched earth" operations, and draconian measures to put down civilian uprisings. The crucial requirement was, of course, "military necessity." But while that plea created a potentially gigantic breach in the whole edifice of noncombatant immunity, it was neither naive on the part of Vattel and others to acknowledge military necessity nor cynical on the part of commanders to exploit it. In contrast to present-day ethicists, who sometimes seem more interested in erecting an ethical system from which to critique military operations rather than one in which they can realistically be conducted, Vattel and his generation took seriously the idea that if they expected statesmen and field commanders to embrace their work, their prescriptions must be practical. Operating within this framework, Vattel and others were bound to incorporate actual European experience into their work, particularly the recognition of the logistical imperative that armies must find ways to supply themselves and by extension deny supplies to the enemy. It was this imperative, more than any other factor, that gave rise to the hard war measures of the Civil War.

That is one reason why Colonel John Flynn—and more to the point, Grant, Sherman and Sheridan—did not regard the hard war operations of 1864–1865 as innovations in any important sense of the term. They might have preferred at the outset to win the war with a minimum of damage to civilian property, but when military necessity prodded them to seize goods from Southern farmers and destroy Southern railroads and factories, they scarcely had to create a new paradigm of war. All they had to do was to invoke the letter of the established laws and customs of war—rules largely developed during the seventeenth and eighteenth centuries, and, on the whole, quite well-adapted to the demands of a mid-nineteenth century American civil war. . . .

The Mythology of Hard War

Since it is not at all difficult to show that Union forces exercised a directed severity during the *chevauchées* of 1861–1865, it is worth taking a moment to address the following (admittedly speculative) question: If the Union military effort against Southern property was indeed discriminate and roughly proportional to legitimate needs, why have so many interpretations insisted for so long that it was indiscriminate and all-annihilating? One likely reason such myth-making has been pervasive is that it has served a variety of agendas.

The idea that the Federals were conducting an immoral war in an immoral fashion goes back as far as the conflict itself. Fearful that "the hope of reconstruction was a latent sentiment in the bosom of the Southern community," Confederate nationalists portrayed the enemy as demons and blackguards in a bid to create an unbridgeable chasm to reunion. Jefferson Davis railed against "the savage ferocity" of Union military conduct. "The frontier of our country," he wrote in 1863, "bears witness to the alacrity and efficiency with which the general orders of the enemy have been executed in the devastation of farms, the destruction of the agricultural implements, the burning of the houses, and the plunder of everything movable."

Southerners continued to level such charges after the war had ended, snarling of Northern "atrocities" and "barbarism," of "soulless raiders" and their "hellish work." In the postwar South, the legend of Yankee ruffians waging campaigns of fire and vandalism was surely useful in several respects. First, it helped Redeemers convince their fellow white Southerners that a terrible wrong had been done them—a conviction that resonated well with the humiliations of military Reconstruction. Second, it played into the myth of a South beaten down by brute force, not defeated by military art and certainly not by internal divisions or a failure of national will. It also made it easier to overlook the Confederate government's tax-in-kind and impressment policies, as well as "scorched earth" practices carried out by the rebel army. When Grandpappy reminisced about how his team of prized horses had disappeared, he preferred to recall that Yankee vandals had done it—even if the real culprit had been a Confederate impressment agent.

Third, the myth of Yankee atrocities accounted for the economic disaster that gripped the South after 1865. As historians have since pointed out, the destruction of Southern crops, livestock, factories, railroads, and other infrastructure was anything but complete; much of the damage was repaired within a few years. The really serious economic losses can be traced to two things: the emancipation of slaves, which wiped out billions of dollars in Southern wealth, and the worthlessness of Confederate scrip, bonds, and promissory notes into which many Southerners had sunk most of their savings. Both, of course, could be better traced to the South's decision to secede—and so begin the war—than to anything that Union soldiers did. Thus the emphasis on hard war, as an explanation for the economic devastation of the South, may have diverted attention from Southern responsibilities in bringing on the war, and thus for the outcome. Even if Southerners conceded their responsibility for beginning the conflict, the myth of Yankee atrocities remained useful. Southerners could assert that they themselves had inaugurated a chivalrous struggle based on honor; the Yankees were responsible for the brutal, destructive war it eventually became.

The influence of this myth can hardly be exaggerated. Even educated Southerners, far removed in time from the conflict, accepted it uncritically, indeed passionately. When a fellow historian suggested that Woodrow Wilson tone down a passage about Sherman's "cruelty" in a manuscript he was writing, Wilson replied:

> I have modified it a little; but really there is no more deliberately considered phrase in the book. I am painfully familiar with the details of that awful march, and I really think that the words I used concerning it ought to stand as a piece of sober history. . . . As for the treatment of prisoners in the southern prisons, that was doubtless heartless upon occasion; but the heartlessness was not part of a system, as Sherman's was.

Eventually the murderous severity of the Union armies' attacks on civilian property became an article of faith. By the 1940s, one Southern historian could write, in a scholarly monograph, that "the invader did not limit himself to the property of people," but evidenced "considerable interest also in their persons, particularly the females, some of whom did not escape the fate worse than death"—without feeling the slightest need to document his lurid (and largely inaccurate) claim.

The myth of indiscriminate Union attacks on Southern civilians has served other agendas as well. For persons revolted by the slaughter on the Western Front, Sherman's marches and similar episodes aptly illustrated the brutalizing effects of war. Its utility in this respect has proven durable. Paradoxically, the image of a sweeping campaign of fire and sword also fits snugly into the "realist" image of war. The Union hard war measures resonate well with those who believe that in war one must do whatever is necessary to win. There is thus an admiring quality to some of the literature on William T. Sherman, the best known of the hard war advocates, whom Lloyd Lewis called a "fighting prophet." T. Harry Williams admired Grant's willingness to wage economic warfare, and called him the first of the great modern generals. Bruce Catton invariably discussed the Union war against Southern property as a case of "doing what has to be done to win."

Few of these characterizations did great violence to the facts. They simply emphasized certain facts at the expense of others. The Federal effort against Southern property was indeed widespread and quite destructive. But an effort was also made to direct destructive energies toward certain targets and away from others. Neither Southerners, "realists," nor those antipathetic toward war had any reason to emphasize the substantial restraint shown by Union forces in their operations against civilian property. For Southerners, to do so would have undercut their sense of righteousness and comparative lack of responsibility for the debacle that engulfed them. For realists, it would have qualified their belief that one must do whatever must be done to gain victory in war. For those repulsed by war, it would have seemed to mitigate the brutalizing effects that war assuredly has on both societies and individuals.

But perhaps the most pervasive reason for the emphasis on the destructiveness of Union military policy has been the way in which it seemed to anticipate the sweeping struggles of the twentieth century. Especially after the Second World War, the Civil War appeared a clear prototype of modern, total war. It had witnessed the early development and use of trench warfare, ironclad warships, rapid-fire weapons, and even airships and crude machine guns. Its soldiers had traveled to the battle front aboard railroad cars and steam-driven transports; its generals had communicated with one another via endless miles of telegraph wire. It was one of the first struggles in which manufacturing and mass politics significantly affected the fighting and the outcome. The conflict's most striking modern aspect, however, was the Union attacks on Southern civilians and property. What happened to them no longer seemed merely atrocious; it foreshadowed the strategic bombardment of civilians during the two world wars. . . .

The Persistence of Restraint

. . . [Historians] have illuminated the dynamic in a variety of ways, many of them quite insightful. But it is reasonable to note that historians have been mainly concerned with the extent and meaning of the destruction unleashed by Union armies. Mark E. Neely, Jr. observed precisely that in a provocative 1991 article entitled, "Was the Civil War a Total War?" Answering in the negative, he argued, "The *essential* aspect of any definition of total war asserts that it breaks down the distinction between soldiers and civilians, combatants and noncombatants, and this no one in the Civil War did systematically, including William T. Sherman."

The question remains, however: Why did such saving distinctions persist? Certainly what had gone before was far from benign. If the hallmark of modern total war is the erosion of the barrier between combatant and noncombatant, one must recognize that the barrier itself had acquired substance barely a century before the guns spoke at Fort Sumter. Until then, invading armies routinely considered the civilians in their path as enemies to be beaten, robbed, raped, or even killed. Europe had a tradition of brutal conduct going back hundreds of years. I have already noted that the Devastation of the

Palatinate in 1688–1689, to name but one incident, offered an example of systematic destruction that made Sheridan's razing of the Shenandoah Valley seem comparatively restrained. The measures used to throttle insurgencies were even worse. An English participant wrote of a sixteenth century punitive expedition against the Irish:

> We have killed, burnt and spoiled all along the lough [Lough Neagh] within four miles of Dungannon, . . . in which journeys we have killed above one hundred people of all sorts, besides such as were burnt, how many I know not. We spare none of what quality or sex soever, and it has bred much terror in the people, who heard not a drum nor saw not a fire there for a long time.

Philip II of Spain advocated a similar policy for quelling the Dutch Revolt. Even the "age of limited war" in the eighteenth century can be exaggerated. When one acknowledges the gusto with which colonists annihilated whole tribes of American Indians, to say nothing of the ease with which the western Allies as well as totalitarian regimes embraced area bombing against population centers, the restraint of Union armies in the Civil War acquires fresh salience.

Any explanation must begin with the fact that official policy intended restraint to be exercised. The Federal government deliberately chose to conduct the war largely as a contest between two nations, despite the fact that it explicitly denied the Confederacy's right to exist. It applied the insurrectionary principle sparingly. Had it done so broadly and consistently, captured Confederate soldiers and civilians who gave aid and comfort to the Confederate regime might well have faced execution. Instead the Federal government threw its moral and legal authority squarely behind the preservation of distinctions between combatants and noncombatants.

Field commanders too reinforced the distinction through an endless stream of general orders that forbade pillaging and wanton destruction. Critics who cite the orders as evidence of continued depredations miss the crucial point. In war, nothing undercuts the claims of personal conscience faster than the demands of public authority. The syllogism, "If his cause be wrong, our obedience to the king wipes the crime of it out of us," has a long and melancholy history. Many soldiers, decent in themselves, have willingly performed the most sickening tasks in the name of duty. By insisting on proper conduct toward civilians, Union generals encouraged rather than corroded the better angels of their soldiers' nature.

The persistence of morality among the soldiers forms a second part of the explanation. In their correspondence, both official and personal, justice is a frequent theme, a concern occasionally robust enough to balk at expedients urged by higher authority. Many soldiers would have understood the sentiments of a Union colonel in West Virginia. Faced with much guerrilla activity in his district and an order from Major General David Hunter to burn houses near the sites where bushwhacking occurred, he demurred nevertheless. "To men who have taken the oath, unless charges could be made and sustained, I do not feel authorized to apply General Hunter's order. . . . I would not hesitate, but it is an important and serious matter, and should not be done hastily, or in the wrong place. . . . I would rather spare two secesh than burn up one Union man's property."

A third explanatory feature was the similarity of white Southerners to their Northern counterparts. The claims of morality are stronger when one can recognize the enemy's human face. Despite regional idiosyncracies, Union soldiers and Southern civilians shared the same language, the same heritage, and much the same culture. The comments of Federal soldiers on white Southerners often noted oddities and differences, but it is misleading to suggest that these indicate a depersonalization of the enemy. Far from depicting an alien people, the soldiers' descriptions often brought enemy civilians vividly to life. Sergeant Rufus Mead, for instance, enjoyed talking to a secessionist woman: "[S]he would talk like a steamboat." Many soldiers empathized with the plight of Southern civilians even when they approved of the stern measures against them. Of Sherman's evacuation order, an Ohio army surgeon wrote his wife, "It seems very hard but serves them right for most of the *women* of the south are generally stronger secess [sic] than the men." Such sentiments did not prevent him from asking in the next sentence, "How would you like to be made to leave Marietta [Ohio] with your family and have to find a new home?"

The Southern whites who least resembled Northern men were the poor, and the soldiers' comments concerning them are most unflattering. But the condition of the poor whites reflected less an alien breed than the degenerative effects of slavery, which focused attention back on the slaveholding aristocracy. A Pennsylvania cavalryman serving in northern Virginia opined that the South contained only two kinds of residence: "The one are the mansions of the wealthy and are generally fine and elegant and the other are the huts of the poorer classes and the slaves which are wretched houses. The neat little home of the northern laborer is nowhere to be found in the south." Another soldier wrote, "The poor class are all loyal or would be if they dared, but they are really more enslaved than the negroes. . . ."

Such observations introduce the final component that helps explain the persistence of restraint: the Union soldiers' political sensitivity. As Lincoln maintained, they were "thinking bayonets," the product of universal white male suffrage, stump speeches, torchlight political rallies, and unabashedly partisan newspapers—in short, members of one of the most politically aware societies on earth. They debated politics around the campfire and in their letters home. Not content with that, a considerable number bombarded local newspapers with epistles on the conduct of the war. They rejected conciliation because it did not accord with their opinion of what was really required to end the rebellion. But by and large they observed the distinctions, not only between combatants and noncombatants but also between Unionist, passive, and secessionist civilians, because such distinctions made political as well as moral sense to them.

When considering the evolution of Federal policy toward Southern civilians and property, several points stand out. First, although the North began the war committed to an informal policy of conciliation, that policy represented a deliberate restriction of effort. It was not merely the result of a view that saw war exclusively in terms of a clash between rival armies, though dominant conceptions of war lent credibility to the hope that the rebellion could be suppressed in this manner. Second, when attacks on Southern property did emerge, the continuities of Federal practice with previous European experience were more striking than the contrasts—in contradiction to the view that this brand of warfare represented something novel and modern. Finally, if the Union's hard war effort displayed a novel element, it lay primarily in the linkage with a democratic society. That made it possible to blame Southerners for the outbreak and continuation of the war, and so justify the destruction. But it also made possible a politically and morally aware citizen-soldiery capable of discrimination and restraint as well as destruction. The Union volunteer who marched under Grant, Sherman, and Sheridan was a very different instrument than the *ancien régime* soldier under Turenne, Marlborough, or Frederick the Great; for that matter, a different instrument even than contemporary European soldiers.

It was the peculiar nature of the Federal citizen-soldier—his civic-mindedness, his continued sense of connection with community and public morality—that made possible the "directed severity." The Federal rank-and-file were neither barbarians, brutalized by war, nor "realists" unleashing indiscriminate violence. Their example thus holds out hope that the effective conduct of war need not extinguish the light of moral reason.

FURTHER READING

Michael C. Adams, *Our Masters the Rebels: A Speculation on Union Military Failure in the East, 1861–1865* (1978)

Richard E. Beringer, Herman Hattaway, Archer Jones, and William N. Still, Jr., *Why the South Lost the Civil War* (1986)

Gabor S. Boritt, ed., *Why the Confederacy Lost* (1992)

Albert Castel, *Decision in the West: The Atlanta Campaign of 1864* (1992)

Bruce Catton, *Army of the Potomac,* 3 vols. (1951–1953)

———, *U. S. Grant and the American Military Tradition* (1954)

———, *The Centennial History of the Civil War,* 3 vols. (1961–1965)

Thomas L. Connelly, "R. E. Lee and the Western Confederacy," *Civil War History,* 15 (1969), 116–132

——— and Archer Jones, *The Politics of Command: Factions and Ideas in Confederate Strategy* (1973)

David Donald, ed., *Why the North Won the Civil War* (1960)

Michael Fellman, *Inside War: The Guerrilla Conflict in Missouri during the Civil War* (1989)

Douglas S. Freeman, *Lee's Lieutenants: A Study in Command,* 3 vols. (1942–1944)

Edward Hagerman, *The American Civil War and the Origins of Modern Warfare* (1988)

Herman Hattaway and Archer Jones, *How the North Won: A Military History of the Civil War* (1983)

Archer Jones, *Civil War Command and Strategy* (1992)

John F. Marszalek, *Sherman: A Soldier's Passion for Order* (1993)

William S. McFeely, *Grant: A Biography* (1981)

Richard McMurry, *Two Great Rebel Armies: An Essay in Confederate Military History* (1989)

James M. McPherson, *Battle Cry of Freedom: The Civil War Era* (1988)

Grady McWhiney, "Who Whipped Whom? Confederate Defeat Reexamined," *Civil War History* 11 (1965), 5–26

——— and Perry D. Jamieson, *Attack and Die: Civil War Military Tactics and the Southern Heritage* (1982)

Allan Nevins, *The War for the Union,* 4 vols. (1959–1971)

Alan T. Nolan, *Lee Considered* (1991)

James I. Robertson, *Stonewall Jackson* (1997)

Charles Royster, *The Destructive War: William Tecumseh Sherman, Stonewall Jackson, and the Americans* (1991)

Stephen W. Sears, *George B. McClellan: The Young Napoleon* (1988)

———, *Landscape Turned Red: The Battle of Antietam* (1983)

Brooks D. Simpson, *America's Civil War* (1996)

Emory Thomas, *Robert E. Lee: A Biography* (1995)

Russell Weigley, *The American Way of War: A History of United States Military Strategy and Policy* (1973), chapters on Grant and Lee

T. Harry Williams, *Lincoln and His Generals* (1952)

———, *The History of American Wars from 1745 lo 1918* (1981)

Steven Woodworth, *Jefferson Davis and His Generals: The Failure of Confederate Command in the West* (1990)

CHAPTER 5

Fighting the War:

The Soldiers

⌐┐

In recent years, the field of history has been transformed by a growing awareness of and concern about the doings of ordinary people. Military history has also been affected by this interest in the masses—"history from the bottom up" instead of "from the top down." Beginning perhaps with John Keegan, in his Face of Battle (1976), which explored the experience of combat by British soldiers in three major battles—Agincourt in 1415, Waterloo in 1815, and the Somme in 1916—many military historians have become social historians of battles and wars. This kind of attention is also being directed toward American military history, especially the Civil War. Studies of how battles were fought from the ground up are appearing, as are analyses of the combat experience of the rank and file.

The sources for this kind of account and analysis for the American Civil War are particularly rich, because the participants left an immense array of memoirs and recollections, a large number of which were published. This unusual outpouring of accounts by ordinary soldiers occurred for several reasons, besides the high level of literacy among the combatants. First, there was a great deal of interest among the civilian populations in a war that was fought on their own soil rather than in a foreign land. And second, those who fought were greeted with respect, even awe, when they returned home, since both sides regarded the struggle as worthy and heroic. So there was an audience eager to read the reminiscences of Civil War soldiers.

Besides these more formal accounts written by soldiers, there are the private letters sent home and the personal diaries and logs composed during service in the field. Over the years, these firsthand accounts have surfaced sporadically and have then been published. But, in the six years since the first edition of this anthology appeared, the discovery and publication of the correspondence and diaries of Civil War soldiers has become a flood. What is more, these new additions have consisted, not of random and occasional letters, but frequently of voluminous correspondence lasting many years and discussing many aspects and episodes of the war. The impact of these sources on *historians' understanding of what it was like to be a soldier and what the soldiers thought about it all is likely to be far-reaching.*

Already, some surprising trends seem to be emerging from these new documents. The memoirs that were published by the combatants soon after the war tended to emphasize the adventure and bravery involved in the experience or else to narrate what happened in great detail, without revealing their own feelings and emotions while under fire or in the hospitals and camps. By contrast, the letters home and the diaries were not written for publication. Not only might they be more revealing, but they might also be expected to stress the grisly and seamy side of the war, and to be full of complaints and frustration. Historians who have examined and probed these newly available materials seem to be finding something rather different, however. Amid the horror and drudgery of the war, a humanity and decency, even high-mindedness, seems to have been present among the soldiers of both sides. The length and grimness of the conflict seem not to have overwhelmed them. At all events, the history of the rank and file in the Civil War—its social history—is proving to be a novel and revealing area of investigation.

DOCUMENTS

The experience and attitudes of the soldiers themselves are the topics of the documents for this chapter. But they are not merely personal and narrow in scope; they discuss larger issues and aspects of the war. The first and second documents deal with soldiers' encounters with combat. Eugene Blackford of the 5th Alabama Infantry wrote to his father on July 22, 1861, telling him about his first battlefield experience, while John Dooley, an Irish infantryman in the Army of Northern Virginia who went into battle on many occasions, explained how he usually felt during combat.

The next four documents are from letters sent home, and they mainly offer reactions to battles and observations about the conduct of the war and morale. The third piece is from Charles Harvey Brewster to his mother, written in camp, near Harrison's Landing, on the Virginia Peninsula, July 12, 1862. Brewster talks mainly about the Union army's lack of progress in moving on Richmond and about the failure of young men from his town of Northampton, Massachusetts, to volunteer and how well those who did join up are acquitting themselves. The fourth item is Robert Gould Shaw's discussion of the Preliminary Emancipation Proclamation (he would later become a captain of the famous 54th Massachusetts, an African American regiment) and of the battle of Antietam and its aftermath. This letter to his mother was written on September 25, 1862.

The fifth extract was written by Wilbur Fisk of Montpelier, Vermont, who sent dispatches from the front to his hometown newspaper. His numerous articles have now been published; the one cited here was written while Fisk was on the Virginia Peninsula a year after Brewster. Dated April 19, 1863, it discusses the soldiers' morale and their feelings about the opposition to the war at home. A letter from Tally Simpson, from Pendleton, South Carolina, is the sixth item. He writes to his cousin Carrie about the impact of the Confederate defeat at Gettysburg in July 1863. The last item is the famous observation by Walt Whitman speculating about how the war will be written up by the historians. He assumed that the actions of the ordinary soldiers would be overlooked. Whitman himself participated in the war in a minor and unobtrusive way, as a nurse in New York military hospitals. His comment appeared in a collection called *Specimen Days,* published in 1882–83.

Eugene Blackford, C.S.A., Describes His First Experience with Combat, July 1861

Bivouac Camp of the Advanced Guard,
on the railroad near Union Mills
Above Manassas

22nd July, 1861

My Dear Father:

We are very much fatigued and jaded by our late movements. I must relieve your anxiety by letting you know that I am alive and well. I was in the great battle of yesterday, tho our regt. arrived too late to take any considerable part in the action. But I will go back and let you know what I have been doing since this day a week.

Last Monday the enemy advanced their lines considerably and caused our pickets to fall back some two miles. We were up all Tuesday night expecting to march down to the battery to defend it. At 8 o'clock Wednesday, the advance guard of the enemy appeared, and we went out to give battle. We all took our positions behind our entrenchments, and remained there some time while parties of our men were skirmishing in front.

At last they were driven in, and the firing commenced upon our line. The enemy, having minie muskets, could fire upon us long before we could think of returning the compliment, and so we had to take it coolly. No wound was sustained by our men (in my company) except one pretty badly wounded. The balls make a very loud singing noise when they pass near you, and at first caused me to duck my head, but I soon became used to it. I never expected to be alarmed or excited in battle, but really it is a very different affair from what I thought it. I never was cooler in my life, and have ever since been very much pleased therefore, as I shall have no trouble hereafter.

Just as we were about to make our fire general, news was brought that the [Illinois] had retreated from Fairfax Court House and thus had exposed our flank. Of course there was nothing to be done but to retreat. This we barely had time to do, the enemy was almost in sight of the crossroads when we passed at double quick. Had we been twenty minutes later, we would have been cut off utterly. As I said before, we marched quick time for twenty miles to this place, my company being deployed as skirmishers on the side next to the enemy. The part was one of honor and implied trust, but it was at a great cost, as the country was awfully rough, and we suffered very much. . . .

We then came right about and set off to reinforce our men in the great battle (not yet named) about ten miles from us. This distance we marched at double time and came on the field about five o'clock, too late as I said to do much service, but early enough to smell a little gunpowder and receive a little of the enemy's fire. We went over the battlefield several miles in extent. T'was truly awful, an immense cloud of smoke and dust hung over the whole country, and the flashing of the artillery was incessant tho none of the balls struck my company. One bomb burst a little above me, and killed and wounded several. This was our only loss. Had we been an hour earlier, many would not have lived to tell of it.

Letter, Eugene Blackford to his father, July 22, 1861, in *The Brothers' War: Civil War Letters to Their Loved Ones from the Blue and the Gray,* Annette Tapert, ed. (Time Books, 1988), pp. 8–11.

I shan't attempt to describe the appearance of the field, literally covered with bodies, and for five miles before reaching it I saw men limping off, more or less wounded. We met wagon loads of bodies coming off to Manassas, where they are now piled in heaps. While we were looking over the field, an order came for us to go back to our batteries ten miles off, and defend them from the enemy who were advancing upon them, so we had to go back, tired as we were, to our holes, where we arrived half dead at twelve o'clock last night, having marched twenty-six miles heavily loaded. We have no protection against the rain, which has been falling all day. I have no blanket, not having seen my baggage since leaving Fairfax; I never was so dirty before in my life and besides I have scurvy in my mouth, not having anything but hard bread and intensely salty meat to eat, and not enough of that.

I do not however complain, nor do my men, tho I never thought that such hardships were to be endured. We have our meat in the blaze, and eat it on our bread. A continual firing is now going on around us.

Your affectionate son,
Eugene Blackford

John Dooley, C.S.A., Acknowledges the Persistence of Fear (Undated)

The Psychology of Soldiers' Fear

We know how straight into the very jaws of destruction and death leads this road of Gettysburg; and none of us are yet aware that a battle is before us; still there pervades our ranks a solemn feeling, as if some unforeseen danger was ever dropping darksome shadows over the road we unshrinkingly tread.

For myself, I must confess that the terrors of the battlefield grew not less as we advanced in the war, for I felt far less fear in the second battle of Manassas than at South Mountain or even at Fredericksburg; and I believe that soldiers generally do not fear death less because of their repeated escape from its jaws. For, in every battle they see so many new forms of death, see so many frightful and novel kinds of mutilation, see such varying fortunes in the tide of strife, and appreciate so highly their deliverance from destruction, that their dread of incurring the like fearful perils unnerves them for each succeeding conflict, quite as much as their confidence in their oft tried courage sustains them and stimulates them to gain new laurels at the cannon's mouth.

Charles Harvey Brewster, U.S.A., Assesses the Contribution of His Family and Community to the War, July 1862

... Meanwhile we lie here and rest and recoup, and gather strength for the next attempt, and little Mac has been through the lines and says "we give them one more turn boys,

---

From John Dooley, "The Psychology of Soldiers' Fear," in Dooley, *John Dooley, Confederate Soldier: His War Journal,* Joseph T. Durkin, ed. (University of Notre Dame Press, 1963), p. 99.

Letter, Charles Harvey Brewster to "Dear Mother," July 12, 1862, in *When This Cruel War Is Over: The Civil War Letters of Charles Harvey Brewster,* David W. Blight, ed. (University of Massachusetts Press, 1992), pp. 167–168.

and that will be the end of it". I wonder if it will though it will be the end of it, for many of us, no doubt of that, and so we wait and wonder, and go up to the breastworks and peer off over the fields and into the deep shades of the woods, and wonder what next? and when? Ah well it will come sooner or later, soon enough for some. I see it all the march in the noontide sun, the watchful anxious vigils of the nights, the hunger, the thirst, then the crack of one musket, two! quicker! faster! the war the smoke, the whistling bullet, the screeching shell, the shouts and cheers and then the silence, and the survivors gather together and relate the wonderous tales, the narrow escapes, with a pitying word and lowering voice, for the missing companion, then the shovel and spade, and hasty burial and the survivors move on.

It has all to be gone through with again. Three long months, Thousands upon Thousands of lives Millions of Treasure gone, lost and to what end. As far, yes farther from Richmond than at the beginning.

Somebody most certainly has blundered, but nobody is to blame. Why in Thunder don't they go to drafting? Where are all the brave ones who were "coming after us, when they were actually needed"? there were thousands of them when we came away. why don't they come on? Don't they think they are needed yet? I can tell them that if this is not the time they never will see it, but enough of this they cannot be expected to come. it is not half so pleasant to be out here in the woods and swamps as tis to stay at home so I don't wonder at them much only there were so many coming "when they were *really needed*" that I almost wonder that the fifteen thousand from Mass are not on the way already. perhaps they have not heard that they are needed.

Well we have finally heard from Cal as I suppose you have before. he is in Washington in the General Hospital Judiciary Square. he writes in pretty good spirits, but says he would rather be here than there. I think it mean enough outrageous, that they don't let such cases go to thier own houses. I would not like to say it before the men, but under the same circumstances I should be strongly tempted to start for home, leave or no leave, noble Cal how I wish I could shake his hand. It was good for the eyes, of an "*East Ender*" of the old race, to look at him in the battle the other day, so cool, so brave, and so intent upon the business in hand. he was just what I knew Bill would be, and as I watched that day I thought of Bill a hundred times. Poor Johnnie Cook was not in this fight, but he kept the reputation of the old neighborhood good in the others we have been in and his trials were worse than ours sick and weak riding in a wagon, that would kill a well man to ride in. (I always prefer to walk rather than to ride in one of them) He has been sent to the Hospital and at the Landing to day where he will be more comfortable, and where I have no doubt he will be sent north, and once in the land of civilization he will get all right again, but I don't think Johnnie is strong enough for a soldier. I have this morning made out papers for his discharge and hope to get them through. Poor fellow, I asked him if he wanted his discharge, but he would not say yes. To much pluck left for that, but I could see the longing look and I thought it best, and we shall try hard to get them through and shall punch the Dr up all I can. All I could get Johnnie to say when I asked him if he wanted it was "you know how I have been this spring" brave fellow he would not ask for it himself. I am proud of the old neighborhood it has furnished no cowards for this army unless its me. I can answer for myself, but no others that I can swear to.

I can tell a different story of some Northampton boy's. Fred Clark for instance has been lining some for a month trying to get a discharge and playing sick, but he is all together to healthy to lie still long enough to make any kind of a show of sickness in fact there is not a tougher healthier man in the Army of the Potomac and now I see he ranks as wounded in the late battle he was not wounded in the battle one of our wounded wanted to speak to him as he lay behind the company the next thing he was gone. he did not wait to see the end of the battle. he was seen the next day all right and the next thing he sent word that he was accidentally wounded in the hand by a revolver. nobody doubts that he shot himself. I don't want you to say anything about this for I do not want it to come from me, but he is small loss he was a trembling little coward anyway. . . .

Robert Gould Shaw, U.S.A., Describes His Reaction to Antietam and to Possible Emancipation, September 1862

. . . So the "Proclamation of Emancipation" has come at last, or rather, its forerunner. I suppose you are all very much excited about it. For my part, I can't see what *practical* good it can do now. Wherever our army has been, there remain no slaves, and the Proclamation will not free them where we don't go. Jeff Davis will soon issue a proclamation threatening to hang every prisoner they take, and will make this a war of extermination. I would give anything to have had Harry free before Lincoln issued that; I am so afraid it will go hard with him. The condition of the slaves will not be ameliorated certainly, if they are suspected of plotting insurrection, or trying to run away; I don't mean to say that it is not the right thing to do, but that, as a war measure, the evil will overbalance the good for the *present*. Of course, after we have subdued them, it will be a great thing. . . .

I have just got a letter from Effie of 14th inst. She walks into McClellan for not following up the Rebels; but I don't sympathize with her a bit. If he is not a very great general, he is the best we have, I fully believe, and the same men who didn't behave well at Manassas, fought without faltering, the other day, under him. The men place the most implicit faith in him, and he never appears without being received with cheers.

Those who talk of rapid pursuit, don't know that there were, and are, about five thousand stragglers between here and Alexandria; a march made by easy stages. In my opinion, the individuals to be walked into are our rulers, who, after fifteen months' experience, continue a military system by which it is impossible to form a well-disciplined army, and on account of which thousands and thousands of lives have been thrown away. They not only continue the old system, but they neglect to fill up old regiments who have been through a long campaign, and have some *esprit de corps* and desire to distinguish themselves, and send out new ones which are perfectly unmanage-able and useless. You can't find an old regiment with more than five hundred in it, and very few have more than three hundred and fifty; it is folly to say the new are as good as the old; I, myself, saw a regiment of two hundred and fifty stand under a sharp fire until ordered to retreat, when a new one of nine hundred men had broken ranks by its side, and left it alone. Marching is as important as fighting, but, if the sun is a little hot or we don't halt before dark, our new brethren in arms take matters into their own hands,

Letter, Robert Gould Shaw to his mother, September 25, 1862, in *Blue-Eyed Child of Fortune: The Civil War Letters of Robert Gould Shaw,* Russell Duncan, ed. (University of Georgia Press, 1992), pp. 245–247.

halt at a convenient place, and go to housekeeping. I don't say they are not just as brave men, and I know they are physically far superior to the first levies, but there is no discipline, and without it a soldier is not a soldier. There is little enough of it in the old regiments, but they are inured to hardship, and accustomed to the sound of battle. Then they have learnt, in a great measure, that safety and honour depend on obedience to orders, and many come to it from their natural good sense. Recruits mixed in with old men do well; that's our experience. . . .

Wilbur Fisk, U.S.A., Discusses Morale among the Soldiers, April 1863

. . . There are but very few men in this regiment that desire peace on any terms short of entire submission on the part of the enemy. There may be some, there always is in every regiment some who care but little whether the North or South whips so long as they can have a jolly, easy time. A few days' hard marching with short allowances of hard tack and meat, is very apt to convert such soldiers into violent copperheads. But they are not the rule, they are exceptions, and there is hardly enough of them to make a decent exception. I wish these peace politicians could come into the old Second Regiment just for the experiment, and pick out their worshippers, and have on the other hand the unconditional Union men select out those who will stand by them at whatever hazard, and let the moral and intellectual capacities, and all that go to make up a *man,* of each, be put into a balance and see which way the scale would tip. It would be as between a pile of froth and a wedge of gold. If the copperheads would not be ashamed of his party here, then there could hardly be found anything outside of the infernal regions that would shame them. I do not say that it is absolutely impossible for a man strictly conscientious to desire peace through disunion and compromise. Paul consented to the martyrdom of Stephen, and afterwards claimed to have lived "in all good conscience" to that day. So a man may consent to see our Government martyred, and if he don't know any better, charity may reluctantly admit, perhaps, that he is sincere and honest; but if a man is endowed with conscientiousness, bravery and wisdom altogether, he will hardly fail to feel a personal sacrifice or personal risk. Turn this regiment loose, and I know the boys would hardly brook to hear the treasonable talk about peace that is sometimes echoed from home. They would consider that it tarnished their honor and robbed them of the praise and glory that would justly belong to them as benefactors of the country. It is as much as our patience can bear to hear the secesh, that live about here, continually twit us of our inability to conquer the rebels, and the folly of our trying to do so. But we expect this of them. We don't expect friends at home will imitate them, however. It is really remarkable how exactly similar the arguments of the rebels here and the rebels at home are. The points most prominent in both are always "abolition" or "nigger," "Lincoln's tyranny" "State rights" etc., blaming the North and excusing the South. If our friends at home join hands with the citizen rebels here and advocate their cause, they will expect to receive the same regard from the soldiers that we give these; and that is just what we are obliged to give them and no more.

Letter, Wilbur Fisk to newspaper in Montpelier Vermont, April 19, 1863, in *Hard Marching Every Day: The Civil War Letters of Private Wilbur Fisk, 1861–1865,* Emil and Ruth Rosenblatt, eds. (University Press of Kansas, 1992), pp. 68–70.

All the way up the Peninsula, these citizen rebels, male and female, told us of our certain defeat and probable destruction. We laughed them to scorn, and marched proudly and confidently on. By lack of management on the part of our leaders, and through no fault of ours, as these leaders are willing to testify, their prophesies proved true, and we were obliged to accept their bitter taunts, and skedaddle for our lives. A vast change then came over the feelings and spirits of the boys. From being bold and confident, proudly conscious of our strength and prowess, we were humbled in a great measure, and seriously distrusted our ability to cope with the enemy. We respected our enemies more and ourselves less. Demoralization was the certain consequence, desertions frequent. But defeats are not the only means to demoralize our army. Preach to them the justice of the rebel course, dwell largely on their grievances, speak of the injustice and corruption of our own Government, and if soldiers will believe you, you have done more to demoralize the army than the enemy could by a thorough victory of their arms. The numerous desertions which has so marred the reputation of this army, were caused as much by copperhead ideas—I don't know what else to call them—as by any reverses they had suffered. They thought it useless to struggle any longer. The South must in the end succeed, and after all, they were not so much to blame for seceding. The North were the oppressors, and their government was very corrupt. In short, the sentiments of almost every one that deserted would almost exactly square with those of Fernando Wood [Democratic Mayor of New York City and a critic of the war effort] as expressed in some of the recent political meetings in Connecticut. If the honorable gentleman himself was in the army, I don't believe but that he would try every means to get out of it, though I do not doubt but that he is as courageous as a lion.

There has been a great change for the better, in the minds of the men of this regiment during the last few months respecting the war, and no doubt the whole army are improved in the same way. A while ago it was no uncommon thing to hear men answer to their names "Here, but it is the last time," and often they made true their statement. Officers as well as men spoke frequently of their determination to desert, and not help carry on an "abolition war." It is very materially changed now. Good discipline is effectually restored. Confidence in the Government, and respect for it, is reestablished. Many a time have I heard boys, with more perverseness than good sense, remark that they would never carry a gun against the enemy again. There is but little of this disposition manifested now, and it is becoming decidedly unpopular. As the soldiers see more fully the depths of principle involved in this controversy, and the wisdom of the policy the Government is adopting to bring it to an issue that God must forever approve, the more determined and anxious are they to carry the war out successfully. Whatever tends to weaken the faith cannot be born of patriotism. But I owe the reader an apology for presuming upon his patience so long. We soldiers have a personal feeling in this matter of fighting or surrendering, and it may sometimes be that we are almost oversensitive in regard to it. Having taken up the subject I hardly knew when to drop it.

Tally Simpson, C.S.A., Reports on the Aftermath of Gettysburg, July 1863

Bunker's Hill Va
Saturday, July 18th /63

My dear Carrie

It had been a very long time since I received a letter from you when your last arrived, and I'll assure you it afforded me much pleasure.

Ere this reaches its destination you will have heard of the terrible battle of Gettysburg and the fate of a portion of our noble Army. I am a good deal of Pa's nature—extremely hopeful. But I must confess that this is a gloomy period for the Confederacy. One month ago our prospects were as bright as could well be conceived. Gallant Vicksburg, the Gibraltar of the West and the pride of the South, has fallen the victim to a merciless foe. Port Hudson has surrendered unconditionally, and it is now reduced to a fact that cannot be disputed that the Mississippi is already or must very soon be in the possession of the Yankees from its source to its mouth. And what good will the Trans Mississippi be to the Confederacy thus cut off?

A few weeks ago Genl Lee had the finest Army that ever was raised in ancient or modern times—and commanded by as patriotic and heroic officers as ever drew a sword in defence of liberty. But in an unfortunate hour and under disadvantageous circumstances, he attacked the enemy, and tho he gained the advantage and held possession of the battle-field and even destroyed more of the foe than he lost himself, still the Army of the Potomac [earlier name for Army of Northern Virginia] lost heavily and is now in a poor condition for offensive operations. I venture to assert that one third of the men are bare-footed or almost destitute of necessary clothing. There is one company in this regt which has fifteen men entirely without shoes and consequently unfit for duty. This is at least half of the company alluded to. The night we recrossed the river into Virginia, Harry's shoes gave out, and he suffered a great deal marching over rough turnpikes. But when he reached Martinsburg, he purchased a pair of old ones and did very well afterwards.

Tis estimated by some that this Army has been reduced to at least one fifth its original strength. Charleston is closely beset, and I think must surely fall sooner or later. The fall of Vicksburg has caused me to lose confidence in something or somebody, I can't say exactly which. And now that the gunboats from the Mississippi can be transferred to Charleston and that a portion of Morris Island has been taken and can be used to advantage by the enemy, I fear greatly the result of the attack. I trust however, if it does fall, its gallant defenders will raze it to the ground that the enemy cannot find a single spot to pitch a tent upon the site where so magnificent a city once raised, so excitingly, its towering head. Savannah will follow, and then Mobile, and finally Richmond.

These cities will be a loss to the Confederacy. But their fall is no reason why we should despair. It is certainly calculated to cast a gloom over our entire land. But we profess to be a Christian people, and we should put our trust in God. He holds the destiny of our nation, as it were, in the palm of his hand. He it is that directs the counsel of our leaders, both civil and military, and if we place implicit confidence in Him and go to

Letter, Tally Simpson to Carrie, June 18, 1863, in *Far, far from home; The Wartime Letters of Dick and Tally Simpson, 3rd. South Carolina Volunteers,* Guy R. Everson and Edward H. Simpson, Jr., eds. (Oxford University Press, 1994), pp. 256–259.

work in good earnest, never for a moment losing sight of Heaven's goodness and protection, it is my firm belief that we shall be victorious in the end. Let the South lose what it
may at present, God's hand is certainly in this contest, and He is working for the accomplishment of some grand result, and so soon as it is accomplished, He will roll the
sun of peace up the skies and cause its rays to shine over our whole land. We were a wicked,
proud, ambitious nation, and God has brought upon us this war to crush and humble our
pride and make us a better people generally. And the sooner this happens the better for us.

Carrie, I feel satisfied that this kind of chat does not suit you, and before you reach
this point in my letter you will pout that sweet, rosylip pout and say, "Well I'll declare,
Bud Tallie certainly has got the blues, and I despise to hear him talk so." You may censure
me, but I can't help it. . . .

Walt Whitman Speculates That "The Real War Will Never Get in the Books," 1882–83

And so good-by to the war. I know not how it may have been, or may be, to others—to
me the main interest I found, (and still, on recollection, find,) in the rank and file of
the armies, both sides, and in those specimens amid the hospitals, and even the dead on
the field. To me the points illustrating the latent personal character and eligibilities of these
States, in the two or three millions of American young and middle-aged men, North and
South, embodied in those armies—and especially the one-third or one-fourth of their
number, stricken by wounds or disease at some time in the course of the contest—were
of more significance even than the political interests involved. (As so much of a race
depends on how it faces death, and how it stands personal anguish and sickness. As, in
the glints of emotions under emergencies, and the indirect trait and asides in Plutarch,
we get far profounder clues to the antique world than all its more formal history.)

Future years will never know the seething hell and the black infernal background
of countless minor scenes and interiors, (not the official surface-courteousness of the
Generals, not the few great battles) of the Secession War; and it is best they should
not—the real war will never get in the books. In the mushy influences of current times,
too, the fervid atmosphere and typical events of those years are in danger of being totally
forgotten. I have at night watch'd by the side of a sick man in the hospital, one who could
not live many hours. I have seen his eyes flash and burn as he raised himself and recurr'd
to the cruelties on his surrender'd brother, and mutilations of the corpse afterward. (See,
in the preceding pages, the incident at Upperville—the seventeen kill'd as in the
description, were left there on the ground. After they dropt dead, no one touch'd
them—all were made sure of, however. The carcasses were left for the citizens to bury
or not, as they chose.)

Such was the war. It was not a quadrille in a ballroom. Its interior history will not
only never be written—its practicality, minutiæ of deeds and passions will never be even
suggested. The actual soldier of 1862–'65, North and South, with all his ways, his
incredible dauntlessness, habits, practices, tastes, language, his fierce friendship, his
appetite, rankness, his superb strength and animality, lawless gait, and a hundred
unnamed lights and shades of camp, I say, will never be written—perhaps must not and
should not be.

Walt Whitman text from *Specimen Days,* from *The Viking Portable Library: Walt Whitman,* Mark Van Doren, ed., 1945, pp. 557, 586–588.

The preceding notes may furnish a few stray glimpses into that life, and into those lurid interiors, never to be fully convey'd to the future. The hospital part of the drama from '61 to '65, deserves indeed to be recorded. Of that many-threaded drama, with its sudden and strange surprises, its confounding of prophecies, its moments of despair, the dread of foreign interference, the interminable campaigns, the bloody battles, the mighty and cumbrous and green armies, the drafts and bounties—the immense money expenditure, like a heavy-pouring constant rain—with, over the whole land, the last three years of the struggle an unending, universal mourning-wail of women, parents, orphans—the marrow of the tragedy concentrated in those army hospitals—(it seem'd sometimes as if the whole interest of the land, North and South, was one vast central hospital, and all the rest of the affair but flanges—those forming the untold and unwritten history of the war—infinitely greater (like life's) than the few scraps and distortions that are ever told or written. Think how much, and of importance, will be—how much, civic and military, has already been—buried in the grave in eternal darkness.

☞ E S S A Y S

The essays reprinted here reflect the emerging scholarship on the social history of the military experience. The first covers the Civil War career of Charles Harvey Brewster, a volunteer from Massachusetts who served for three years and experienced the war in a myriad of ways. David W. Blight of Amherst College, who has edited Brewster's rich and lengthy correspondence, is the author. The companion piece is by Reid Mitchell of the University of Maryland, Baltimore County, who discusses several aspects of the process whereby a raw recruit was shaped into a soldier. Since most soldiers in both armies were volunteers, this same sequence was experienced widely.

A Union Soldier's Experience

DAVID W. BLIGHT

With the First World War as his model, Paul Fussell wrote that "every war is ironic because every war is worse than expected." As national calamity and as individual experience, certainly this was the case with the American Civil War. That slavery could only be abolished by such wholesale slaughter, that new definitions of freedom could only be affirmed in the world's first total war, and that national unity could be preserved only through such fratricidal conflict provide some of the most tragic ironies of American history. Epic destruction of life and treasure led to epic possibilities in a new and redefined American republic in the 1860s. The freedom of the slaves and the liberties of the free were achieved or preserved at horrifying costs. The Civil War was ironic because it both violated and affirmed the nineteenth-century doctrine of progress; it would become the source of America's shame as well as its pride; and it would haunt as well as inspire the national imagination. For many Americans, the whole affair would become humankind's madness somehow converted to God's purposes. On a grand scale, such ironies are easily summarized, but as Fussell observes, all "great" wars consist of thousands of "smaller constituent" stories, which are themselves full of "ironic actions." The thousands of individuals, North and South, who brought the values and aspirations of

Reprinted from *When This Cruel War Is Over: The Civil War Letters of Charles Harvey Brewster,* edited with an introduction by David W. Blight (Amherst: University of Massachusetts Press, 1992). Copyright © 1992 by Historic Northampton.

their communities to so many campgrounds, battlefields, and hospitals provide the constituent stories of this American epic. One of those stories is recorded in the remarkable Civil War letters of Charles Harvey Brewster of Northampton, Massachusetts. When viewed through the lens of social history, letters like Brewster's reveal the experience of an ordinary American man caught up not only in the sweeping events of the Civil War, but also in the values of his age and the struggle of his own self-development.

In a 1989 article historian Maris Vinovskis asserted that American "social historians have lost sight of the centrality of the Civil War." In recent years, responding to this and other challenges, a new social history of the Civil War era has begun to emerge, and nowhere is this more apparent than in new studies of the common soldier's experience. The questions, assumptions, and subjects of social historians have tended to make them de-emphasize, if not ignore, major political, military, or diplomatic *events*. Social historians are typically concerned with the values and life cycles of ordinary people, with social structures, community dynamics, demography, family patterns, and change as *process*. Conversely, too many Civil War historians have treated the war as almost exclusively an affair of presidents and generals, of leadership in unprecedented crises. But there is now good reason to believe that these two approaches to the Civil War era can find common ground. The magnitude of casualties suffered in the war, the social and psychological dislocation experienced by so many soldiers, women, and children, the economic growth or stagnation caused by unprecedented war production and destruction, and the emancipation of more than four million slaves demonstrate that the Civil War was an event in which profound social changes occurred. More than three million Americans, including 189,000 blacks in the Union forces, served in the armies and navies. At the end of the war, one of every six white males and one of every five blacks who served were dead. A larger proportion of the American population died in the Civil War than the British population in the First World War. Many towns and farming communities sent large percentages of their male citizenry to the war to have them replaced only by monuments on their town greens and commons in years to come. White northern widows would ultimately benefit from a pension system, but white southern widows and African-American widows in both sections would make do on their own. Some social historians now consider broad social structure, the lives of ordinary people, racial, gender, and class values, and the impact of such transforming events as the Civil War on an equal footing. That major *events* may be returning to the agenda of social historians is, indeed, a welcome occurrence.

A close reading of the Brewster letters affords an intriguing window into most of the categories of inquiry mentioned above. The letters will be of interest to military historians and readers; they are an excellent source for the study of men experiencing war. But as Bell Wiley first observed in the 1940s and 1950s, the letters of Civil War soldiers are an extraordinary source for the social history of nineteenth-century America, and Brewster's letters from the front are an especially illuminating example of this phenomenon. The emotions and ideas represented in these letters range from naïveté to mature realism, from romantic idealism to sheer terror, and from self-pity to enduring devotion. Most of all, Brewster seems honest with his correspondents; there are very few simple pieties in his writing and he was boldly descriptive about the immense tragedy he witnessed. His homesickness and despair, as well as his ambition and sense of accomplishment, are quite palpable.

Born and raised in Northampton, Brewster was a relatively unsuccessful, twenty-seven-year-old store clerk and a member of the local militia when he enlisted in Company

C of the Tenth Massachusetts Volunteers in April 1861. Companies of the Tenth Massachusetts were formed from towns all over the western section of the state: Springfield, Holyoke, Great Barrington, Westfield, Pittsfield, Shelburne Falls, Greenfield, and Northampton. The citizens of Northampton were infected by the war fever that swept the land in the spring and summer of 1861. On April 18, only three days after the surrender of Fort Sumter, the first meeting of the Company C militia (an old unit chartered in 1801) turned into a large public rally where forty new men enlisted. By April 24, seventy-five Northampton women rallied and committed their labor to sew the uniforms of the local company. As the cloth arrived, some women worked at home and others sewed in the town hall. Local poets came to the armory to recite patriotic verses to the drilling, would-be soldiers. Yesterday farmers, clerks, and mechanics; today they were the local heroes who would "whip secesh." On May 9 Company C marched some seven miles to an overnight encampment in Haydenville, passing through the towns of Florence and Leeds on the way. In each village, a brass band, an outdoor feast, and a large crowd cheered them. War was still a local festival in this first spring of the conflict. By June 10 the seventy or so members of the company attended a farewell ball, and four days later they strode down Main Street through a throng so large that a corridor could hardly be formed. Flags waved everywhere, several brass bands competed, and Brewster and his comrades joined two other companies of the Tenth on a train for Springfield. En route the soldiers continued the joyous fervor of the day by singing "patriotic airs" to the accompaniment of a lone accordion. Like most of his comrades, Brewster had enlisted for three years, never believing the war would last that long. . . .

The Tenth Massachusetts spent the rest of 1861 and the winter of 1862 in Camp Brightwood, on the edge of the District of Columbia. There they joined the Seventh Massachusetts, the Thirty-sixth New York, and the Second Rhode Island as part of "Couch's Brigade." For three years, Brewster shared the same brigade and battle experiences as Second Rhode Island private, ultimately colonel, Elisha Hunt Rhodes, whose diary became famous as part of a 1990 PBS television documentary on the Civil War. The Tenth participated in almost every major battle fought by the Army of the Potomac, beginning with the Peninsula campaign through Antietam and Fredericksburg in 1862, Chancellorsville, Gettysburg, Bristow Station, and Rappahannock Station in 1863, and the Wilderness, Spotsylvania, and Cold Harbor in 1864. When the survivors of the Tenth were mustered out at the end of their three-year enlistment and returned to Springfield in June 1864, only 220 of the nearly one thousand in the original regiment were still on active duty. They had witnessed their summer outing transform into the bloodiest war in history, seen thousands die of disease, practiced war upon civilians and the southern landscape, loyally served the cause as variously defined, and tried their best to fulfill their communities' expectations. They returned, in the words of their last commander, Col. Joseph B. Parsons, a "shattered remnant" of "mourners." Brewster would probably have agreed with Parsons's characterization of the survivors; as the adjutant of the regiment it had been his duty to record constantly that shattering in casualty reports and death notices. But Brewster's letters to the women in his family record not only the ugliness and futility of war—and there is plenty of that—but also the myriad social attitudes, values, and self-perceptions of a relatively ordinary and reflective mid-nineteenth-century white American male. . . .

Letters were a soldier's means of expressing and understanding the absurdity of war, as well as a way of reaffirming commitment to the enterprise. But nothing threw this paradox into greater relief than letters to and from dead men. There are two examples of this in Brewster's letters. In the immediate aftermath of the battle of Gettysburg, Brewster lifted three letters from "a dead Rebels cartridge box, written to his mother and sisters." He sent them to his sister Mary as a souvenir. "Poor fellow," Brewster remarked, "he lay upon the field with his entrails scattered all about by a cannon shot, I cannot help pity him although as you see he expresses no very kindly intentions towards poor us. . . ." Backhandedly, Brewster expressed a sense of kinship with his dead enemy. "The mother & sisters will look in vain in the far off Florida for his return," wrote the New Englander, "or even his grave among the green hills of Penn. where his body probably lies in a pit with lots of his comrades. . . ." Brewster maintained a certain emotional distance from his unnamed foe in an unmarked grave. But the symbol of the confiscated letters to "mother & sisters" could only have made him and his family back home wonder in what "pit" beneath which "green hills" Brewster might soon find oblivion. Moreover, during the worst of the Wilderness-Spotsylvania campaign of 1864 he expressed the great "joy" with which the regiment received two large grain bags of mail. Brewster saw to the sorting of the letters, "but alas," he declared, "there was terrible sorrow connected with it which was the many letters for our dead and wounded comrades. I think I found as many as a dozen letters for poor Lt Bartlett who was killed only the day before." Letters represented the continuity of life, even when they were to or from the dead.

One of the principal themes of Brewster's letters was his quest for and pride in a commission. Readers will find very little abstract discussion of patriotism here, but a great deal about Brewster's desire for a "chance" to "better" himself, for the respect of his fellow soldiers, for the symbols and authority of rank, and for increased wages so that he could send money back home. To a significant degree Brewster's war was one man's lonely effort to compensate for prior failure and to imagine a new career within the rigid and unpredictable strictures of the army. Brewster was disappointed that he had to enter the service as a noncommissioned first sergeant and he spent the first summer and autumn of the war pining for the status a commission would bring. Put simply, Brewster had a chip on his shoulder about the hand that life had dealt him. He frequently referred to a prewar pattern of bad luck as he gossiped about those who got promotions, resented perceived slights, desperately relished compliments about his performance, and moaned to his mother that it was "hope deferred that maketh the heart sick." Brewster constantly measured himself against his fellow soldiers and calculated his chances of promotion against their character and health. He could not hide his increased hope in November 1861 when he reported that the "Adjutant is very sick and to day the Doctors report that he cannot live." "Consequently," Brewster concluded, "they will have to promote a 1st Lieutenant to his place, so I am quite certain that I shall have a chance." But his desires are noteworthy for their commonality, not their venality; his relations with his comrades were a typical combination of male bonding and competition. Brewster also had a workingman's sense of practical self-interest. "A fellow can sleep very warm even in the woods," he told his mother in December 1861, "with a commission in his pocket."

Brewster received his much-coveted commission and promotion to second lieutenant in December 1861. In one of the most revealing letters in the collection, he sent a detailed description of the sword, sash, belt, and cap which were purchased for him as gifts at considerable cost by members of his company. The letter reads like a description of an impending graduation or a wedding night. "My heart is full to overflowing tonight," Brewster informed his sister. All pettiness and resentment vanished as he realize the "evidence of my standing in the affections of the men." His comrades pooled more than fifty dollars to buy the officer's accoutrements, and Brewster confessed to feeling "wicked" over his good fortune while his comrades in the ranks honored him. The army in winter quarters had become a society of men living together, developing their own rituals and conventions of domestic relations. On the eve of a ceremony that would recognize his new rank, Brewster prepared for a rite of passage and new living arrangements. "I am writing in *my* tent," he told his sister. "I have not slept in it yet but am going to tonight. Lieut. Weatherill and myself have been arranging things all day." There were "new bunks" in his "future home" and he informed Mary that he would be ready to entertain her when she visited. Brewster made the most of this milestone in his life, and a certain tenderness crept into his language as he marveled at the "spontaneous outbreak of feeling" among the men.

Brewster learned what war has often taught us: that men frequently find love and respect for each other more readily in warlike activities than in civilian pursuits. After first wearing his "new uniform," Brewster declared that he felt "quite like a free man once more, now that I am a commissioned Officer. it is wonderful what a difference two little straps on the shoulders make. . . ." Once again, he recognized his own aims as practical and personal. "Before I had lots of work and very little pay," he wrote, "and now I have very little work and lots of pay." In other words, to Brewster promotion meant increased wages, status, and independence in controlling his own labor. But Brewster's new status also represented some ideals in the relations among men that only the army seemed to provide: loyalty, respect, and the opportunity to experience the burdens and joys of leadership. Brewster would have been deeply heartened by a September 1861 letter written by Henry W. Parsons, a twenty-two-year-old private in his company. "In reguard to Charley Brewster," Parsons wrote to his aunt, "he improves every day he is the best officer in the company that we have had with us yet you will find a large heart beneth his coat." Within a month of writing this tribute to his favorite officer, Parsons would die of disease at Camp Brightwood, but not before informing his aunt that Brewster was "a gentleman to all and will do all for the men that lays in his power—his friends may feel proud of him . . . let me tell you Aunt that this is the place to find out mens disposition one can soon tell a man from a knave or coward. . . ." Deeply affected by the loss of such a friend so early in their service, Brewster told his mother that he could not "get over Henry Parsons' death. it came so sudden and he was a particular friend of mine, and he and myself had many a confidential talk together. . . ." The quest for status, the love and respect of friends, and the sheer struggle for physical survival all became part of a young officer's daily existence.

As soldiers like Brewster developed their military identities, their letters revealed what historian Reid Mitchell has called the "immense distance that grew up between the worlds of civilian and soldier." Soldiers who find themselves in a "community of the front," as Eric Leed has aptly described it, or those who experience extreme alienation because of the violence and degradation of soldiering, become acutely aware of how different they are from civilians. Frequent letter writers like Brewster were readily reminded of the radical disjuncture between their precarious existence and that of the community left behind. "How I wish some of the stay at homes could enjoy one winter campaign with us," Brewster complained in 1862, "I fancy we should hear less of 'onward to Richmond.' " Once a soldier was fully initiated to war and to its psychological shocks, his misery found expression in his contempt for civilians. "People at the north do not realize at all what a soldier's life is . . . ," Brewster wrote in 1863, "a soldier has more misery in one day than occurs in a lifetime of a civilian ordinarily and their greatest comforts would be miseries to people at home." Brewster left a veteran volunteer's classic statement of the increasing estrangement of soldiers from civilians in a prolonged war. "It is the general feeling among the old regiments, the real *Volunteers*," he said, "that the generality of the citizens loathe and hate them." Well into his third year of campaigning, the end of the war nowhere in sight, and about to face another winter at the front, Brewster retreated to personal and unit pride—to comradeship and fatalism—in order to give meaning to his experience.

By 1864 Brewster felt estranged from his hometown and homesick at the same time. Conscription laws exacerbated such ambivalence, creating greater distance between the original volunteers—who by 1863–64 had constructed a self-image as suffering victims—and the draftees from their hometowns. As Northampton strained to fill a draft quota in February 1864, Brewster declared that he did not "believe in drafted patriotism." "I do not love the people of that delightful village as a whole," he informed his sister Martha, "and as I owe them ooo I would not lift my little finger to get a man for them." The otherness of his military experience also made him genuinely fearful of his chance of making a living in the civilian world and would prompt him, eventually, to reenlist. War defined a man's future as well as his days, and Brewster worried about what would become of him once his war was over. "This Military is a hard worrying and at the same time lazy miserable business," he wrote in April 1864, "but it pays better than anything else so I think I had better stick to it as long as I can." In words representative of Everyman's lament, Brewster declared that he had done his "share of campaigning but somebody must campaign and somebody else must have all the easy money making places and as the harder lot was always mine in civil life I suppose I must expect the same in Military."

Brewster's sentiments toward civilians, as well as his fears of making a living after the war, will remind many readers of dilemmas faced by veterans of other American wars. "I don't know what I am to do for a living when I come home," Brewster wrote in his last letter from the front in June 1864. "As the end of my service grows near," he said, "I cannot but feel rather bad to leave it for all its hardships and horrors & dangers it is a fascinating kind of life, and much freer from slander jealousy & unkindness than civil life which I almost dread to come back to." Brewster groped to explain why the joy of going home should be so tarnished by fear of civilian livelihood. Suddenly, the army seemed an island of clarity, honesty, and genuineness in a laissez-faire sea of treachery. "The Veterans," he said, "wear rather long faces." He spoke for the veterans in warning that "those who will welcome them with such apparent joy," will be "ready to do them any injury for the sake of a dollar." Brewster had learned much about the terrible irony of war, about its capacity to pervert values and make organized violence seem like an ordered and strangely attractive alternative to the disorder of society. Even while still in the trenches of Virginia with one week remaining in his term of service, Brewster had begun to think like a veteran of a bygone war. His fears of civilian life and nostalgia for the comradeship of the army already made him a candidate for the cycles of selective memory that would both plague and inspire Civil War veterans. Brewster's wartime letters presaged what historian Gerald Linderman has called the "militarization of thought and the purification of memory" in postwar American society.

Brewster, like most men of his generation, was deeply imbued with the Victorian American values of "manhood" and "courage." He perceived war as the test of his courage, and he constantly sought reassurance that he could meet the challenge. He aspired to the individualized and exemplary conception of bravery, by which officers especially had to exhibit their courage to the rank and file. "Courage was the cement of armies," writes Linderman, in the best study of this concept among Civil War soldiers. Especially in the early stages of the war, there is no question that fear of personal dishonor, so rooted in social constructions of masculinity and in American culture, provided the motivation and much of the discipline of Civil War armies.

But the social expectations of manliness in the face of modern war and the degradation of disease almost overwhelmed Brewster, though he only guardedly admitted it. He was both a victim and a perpetrator of these values. His letters are full of observations about the endless struggle between courage and cowardice, his own and that of his comrades. Like most young men who went to war in the nineteenth century (and in our own more violent century as well), Brewster followed a destructive quest for manhood, fashioned a heroic self-image at every opportunity, and marveled at the capacity of war to subdue the environment. He also wrote of camp life and war itself as places strictly separating men from women, all the while imagining their scenes and horrors for his female correspondents. Such sentiments, of course, are not merely stored away in the nineteenth century, to be unpackaged for modern boyhood fantasies or for the mythic uses of the vast Civil War literature. Readers of great memoirs from recent wars, like William Manchester's *Goodbye Darkness: A Memoir of the Pacific War,* may find certain echoes in Brewster's letters. When Manchester, the son and grandson of soldiers, writes of his withdrawal from Massachusetts State College and enlistment in the marines in 1942, "guided by the compass that had been built into me," he represents a male tradition deeply ingrained in American society—one that common and less literary men like Brewster had helped to cultivate. Brewster's own manly compass sent him irresistibly off to war, however unprepared or ill-equipped for what it would do to his body or his imagination.

In May 1862, just before the battle of Fair Oaks, Brewster wrote almost daily for a week. His letters are dramatic accounts of the impending battle, but even more they are chronicles of his desperate struggle with dysentery and "terrible exposure" while sleeping nightly in the mud. At one point he declares himself so sick that he will have to resign and go home, but to fall back then to some makeshift hospital, he believed, would surely mean a hideous and ignoble death. He declared himself eager for battle, because it represented movement, and compared to sickness and exposure it meant a welcome "chance to live." Courage in this instance, Brewster learned, merely meant endurance and a few strokes of good luck. He could "give up" and seek a furlough, he reasoned, but he feared that the "brave ones that staid at home would call me a coward and all that so I must stay here until after the fight at any rate." In a despairing letter two months later Brewster described "burying comrads who die of disease" as the "saddest thing in the service. . . ." Wondering what he would write to a dead comrade's parents, he took heart at how well the man had performed in battle: "thank the lord I can tell them he was brave."

Unable to walk and humiliated by his chronic diarrhea, Brewster spent the battle of Fredericksburg (December 1862), five miles behind the lines where he could only hear that desperate engagement. "I never felt so mean in my life . . . ," he wrote. "I lie here like a skulking coward and hear the din of battle but cannot get there it is too bad." The situation is reminiscent of the scene in Stephen Crane's *The Red Badge of Courage,* where Henry Fleming, tormented by the sounds of battle—"the crackling shots which were to him like voices"—feels "frustrated by hateful circumstances." Henry and Brewster had different burdens to bear; the latter had not run from battle. But in a letter a week later Brewster demonstrated his ambivalence about the vexing concept of courage. He hoped that the sickness would not seize him again "when there is a battle in prospect, for it lays me open to the imputation of cowardice, which I do not relish at all, although I don't claim to be very brave." This final touch of honesty is an interesting contrast with all the times Brewster complained about "cowards" in his letters. In the boredom, frustration, and danger of three years at the front, sometimes Brewster could manage to assert his own manhood only by attacking that of others. But with time he became a realist about the meaning of courage. On the eve of the Wilderness campaign in April 1864, he hoped that his corps would be held in reserve in the impending fight. "I suppose you will call that a cowardly wish," he told Mary, "but although we see a great many in print, we see very few in reality, of such desperate heroes that they had rather go into the heat of battle than not, when they can do thier duty just as well by staying out. . . ." A veteran's hard-won sense of self-preservation prevailed over these sentiments, and it may help explain why Brewster survived what his regiment was about to endure. Having just lived through the worst combat of the war in late May 1864, he could write about courage without pretension. "You are mistaken about thier being nothing cowardly about me," Brewster informed Martha. "I am scared most to death every battle we have, but I don't think you need be afraid of my sneaking away unhurt." When introspection overtook the need for camaraderie and bravado, as it frequently did in the last months of his service, Brewster found the moral courage to speak honestly about physical courage.

On the experience of battle Brewster's letters are often dramatic and revealing. Readers will find much of interest in his accounts of the Peninsula campaign of 1862, the Chancellorsville and Gettysburg campaigns of 1863, and the Wilderness-Spotsylvania-Cold Harbor battles of 1864. In these letters one can follow a young man's romantic anticipation of battle through to his experience of pitilessly realistic warfare. After landing on the Virginia peninsula in April 1862, active now in the great mobilization of McClellan's army and describing his first image of the "horrible" destruction of a town (Hampton, Va.), Brewster contrasted the "sounds of drums," the "neighing of horses," and the "hum of voices" among the multitude of troops with the quietude of a "Mass fast day" back home. Torturing his mother's emotions, he concluded the letter with the story that he had been awakened from a dream the night before by a "tremendous Thunder shower" that he mistook for the "firing of cannon."

Brewster kept his women correspondents informed but probably full of tension as he encountered real war. Upon seeing the aftermath of a battlefield for the first time at Williamsburg, he described it as a "fearful, fearful sight." "The ground was strew [strewn] with dead men in every direction . . . ," he told his mother. "But language fails me and I cannot attempt to describe the scene. if ever I come home I can perhaps tell you but I cannot write it." Brewster would see much worse yet, and he would continue to write it into and out of his memory. But he was caught in that dilemma of literate soldiers in all modern wars: the gruesomeness of battlefields seemed, as Fussell put it, "an all-but-incommunicable reality" to the folks back home. Brewster's letters seem to have anticipated what Alexander Aitken wrote about his own rendering of the battle of the Somme in 1916: "I leave it to the sensitive imagination; I once wrote it all down, only to discover that horror, truthfully described, weakens to the merely clinical." Brewster had a sensitive imagination, and he did try to write it all down; one wonders, though, if after the war, looking back at his letters, he might not have felt the same way Aitken did.

In its own historical moment the obscenity of war, it seems, begs description; whereas, in retrospect, it often must be repressed in memory as people confront the tasks of living.

During Brewster's first major battle campaign (the Peninsula and the Seven Days, April–July 1862), he wrote a stunning series of letters where he expressed virtually every reaction or emotion that battle could evoke. At the battle of Fair Oaks, Brewster's regiment lost one of every four men engaged (killed, wounded, or missing) and, with good reason, the young officer wondered why he was still alive. He tried to describe the sounds and the stench of the battlefield, and the excitement and pulse of the fighting. He also began to demonize the enemy at every turn. In surviving such madness Brewster felt both manly exhilaration and dehumanization. The "life" the soldiers sustained, he said, "would kill wild beasts"; and the farmers of Northampton, he maintained, "would call it cruelty to animals to keep their hogs in as bad a place as we have to live and sleep...." Most of all Brewster coped with fear and loaded up on opium to command his bowels. Anticipating the great battle for Richmond, he said he could only "dread it," as he had already "seen all I want to of battle and blood." But he had two more years of this to endure; his demeanor and his language would both harden and expand with the experience.

While squatting in a field or brooding in a trench, Brewster sketched battle and its aftermath from a soldier's interior perspective, rather than from the sanitized vantage point of headquarters. References to generals and grand strategy are relatively scarce in these letters; they provide an example, as John Keegan put it, of how very different the "face of battle" is from the "face of war." Although he had no serious literary pretensions, Brewster's horror-struck depictions of battle scenes will remind some readers of the agonizing ironies and relentless realism of Ambrose Bierce's short stories. After Gettysburg Brewster described the countless corpses of dead men and horses as if they were macabre monuments. At Spotsylvania in 1864 the "terrors" he witnessed had become so common that he sometimes worried about his own lack of "feeling," and other times just lost himself in grim details. Describing one trench with dead and wounded Confederates piled "3 or 4 deep," he saw "one completely trodded in the mud so as to look like part of it and yet he was breathing and gasping." In the next letter came the vision of "the most terrible sight I ever saw," a breastwork fought over for twenty-four hours with the dead "piled in heaps upon heaps...." As Brewster gazed over the parapet at dawn, "there was one Rebel sat up praying at the top of his voice and others were gibbering in insanity others were groaning and whining at the greatest rate...." Steeling his nerves, preparing himself to continue this "terrible business," and ever the partisan, Brewster took an awkward solace that he had not, he claimed, heard any wounded Union soldiers "make any fuss." ...

After the Tenth returned home Brewster, anxious about civilian life, reenlisted under the auspices of the state of Massachusetts to be a recruiter of black troops in Norfolk, Virginia. From late July [1864] to early November he worked as a recruiter, and during this final stage of his service, he wrote some of his most interesting letters. Away from the front, living in a boardinghouse, Brewster could observe the war and society from a new perspective. He was merely one among a horde of recruiters who descended upon eastern Virginia and other parts of the upper South in 1864. Brewster quipped in frustration that "there are two agents to every man who will enlist." He frequently denigrated the very blacks he sought to recruit, commenting on their alleged propensity to "lie and steal" and their "shiftless" attitude toward work. But he seemed delighted at the presence of a black cavalry regiment that made the local "secesh" furious, and, after holding back judgment, he finally praised the black troops who had "fought nobly" and filled the local hospitals with "their wounded and mangled bodies." For Brewster, as for most white Americans, a full recognition of the manhood of blacks only came with their battlefield sacrifices.

Unhappy and shiftless in his own way, feeling as though he were "living among strangers," and deeply ambivalent about what to do with the rest of his life, Brewster went about his business with an element of greed and very little zeal. He continually took stock of himself, as well as of the ironies and absurdities of war that surrounded him. He boarded with a southern woman named Mrs. Mitchell who had just taken the oath of allegiance to the Union. Her husband and one brother were in the Confederate army, while a second brother served in the Union navy. All the servants at the house, of course, were black and now "free." When Brewster, the Yankee conqueror and occupying officer, was not trying to find and spirit black men into the army, he spent time playing with Mrs. Mitchell's three small children, or going to the market with his landlady's mother and a "darky girl." Such bizarre domestic tranquility in the midst of this catastrophic civil war makes an unforgettable image. Moreover, images of death and maiming frequently appear in Brewster's last letters from the war. He writes compassionately of the family of a dead New Hampshire soldier who had lived at the boardinghouse, of a former sergeant in the Tenth Massachusetts who returned from the hospital hobbling on a cane and insisting that he wanted reappointment at the front rather than in the Invalid Corps, and of street "murders" committed in Norfolk, which he contrasts with the killing in war. His only use of the concept of "courage" in these final letters was applied either to black troops or to the surgeons who volunteered to go fight a "raging" yellow fever epidemic in North Carolina. Living among a subdued enemy, and quietly observing the revolution that Confederate defeat and black emancipation might bring, Brewster sat in a recruiting office reading and writing "love letters" for black women to and from their husbands at the front. This is what remained of his job and his war, and it was a remarkable vantage point. Still patronizing toward the freedpeople, he nevertheless acknowledged their humanity and their influence. "We have to read thier letters from and write letters to thier husbands and friends at the front daily," Brewster observed, "so that I expect I shall be adept in writing love letters, when I have occasion to do so on my own account, they invariably commence (the married ones) with 'my dear loving husband,' and end with 'your ever loving wife until death.' " If we can imagine Brewster sitting at a table with a lonely freedwoman, swallowing his prejudices toward blacks and women, and repeatedly writing or reciting the phrases "give my love to . . ." and "you Husband untall Death" we can glimpse in this tiny corner of the war the enormous potential of the human transformations at work in 1864. Thousands of such quiet ironies—the Northampton store clerk turned soldier, recruiter, and clerical conduit for the abiding love among black folks that slavery could not destroy—helped produce what Lincoln referred to in his Second Inaugural Address as "the result so fundamental and astounding."

Brewster left the war for good in November 1864, and for a while he returned to working in a store. By 1868, he must have written some love letters of his own, for he married Anna P. Williams, the sister of one of his friends in the Tenth, Sidney Williams. Charles and Anna would eventually have six children, some of whom achieved local prominence in western Massachusetts. By the mid-1870s Brewster had reversed his prewar failures and was the owner of a steady sash, door, and paint business. By 1880, he had bought one of the most prominent houses in Northampton, built three greenhouses, and opened a successful year-round florist business. Local friends remembered him as a man "of great independence of character"; he remained an active Republican until the election of 1884 when, for reasons unknown, he supported the Democrat Grover Cleveland rather than James G. Blaine. Brewster became a financially successful, Gilded Age businessman and a prominent citizen. The disdainful, insecure, ambitious soldier of the war letters became the old veteran and family man who grew flowers, speculated in land and other property, made a comfortable living, and actively participated in the G.A.R. (the Grand Army of the Republic, the Union veterans organization). The soldier of 1864 who so feared civilian life had married well and prospered after all. His sister Mary remembered that she had always looked upon her garden for signs of Charlie's "interest in and love for us." Brewster's story seems prosaically American, chronicling as it does the ups and downs of a white middle-class life and generational mobility, and that of an entrepreneur who, through pluck and luck, seems to have beaten the boom-and-bust cycles of the Gilded Age.

But the war, and those remarkable letters, became part of Brewster family lore. By the 1880s, like most veterans, Brewster was ready for reconciliation with Confederate veterans and willing to suspend competitive prospecting in favor of a misty retrospection. He seemed to love regimental reunions and other G.A.R. activities. In October 1886 he attended Blue-Gray reunions at Gettysburg and Fredericksburg, writing to his children that "papa has had the grandest time he ever had in his life." Of the Confederate veterans, he could only marvel at how they "seem as glad to see us as though we were brothers or cousins at least." The landscape of Virginia, like Brewster's own memory, was still scarred from the war. The veteran wrote that the tour of the Gettysburg battlefield "brings the fearful old days so fresh." He was reminded of all the "old miseries," but was also full of a survivor's awe and pride. The visit to the slopes where he had endured the battle of Chancellorsville was the "most glorious time," he reported, marred only by the regret that he did not get to see the "old long breastwork" at Spotsylvania. Partly as tourists, partly as icons of a refurbished martial ideal, partly just as old men searching for their more active and noble youth, and partly as "symbols of changelessness" in a rapidly industrializing age, veterans like Brewster discovered a heroic nostalgia in these reunions. The former soldier who had so fervently sought a sense of community and status in the army could now truly belong in a society building monuments and rapidly forgetting the reality of combat and the deep racial and ideological roots of the war. . . .

From Volunteer to Soldier: The Psychology of Service

REID MITCHELL

One thing that helped a soldier bear the hardships of his life was the respect of his fellow citizens. Men who had made considerable sacrifices and who were risking their lives expected a certain amount of adulation from those who had not joined them in service. If army life degraded him, acclaim could exalt the soldier to the status of a hero. The dehumanization of military service could be offset by the gratitude of one's country. Respect provided a salutory context for soldiering—a means to resist degradation.

Early in the war their fellow citizens willingly gave the soldiers the respect they demanded. The passage of volunteers through a town was a cause of celebration. Just as their hometowns had sent the troops to war with lavish public ceremony, other communities welcomed their patriotic defenders. For example, the Oglethorpe Light Infantry received the warmest greetings as they proceeded from Savannah to the Virginia war front. They marched through the streets of Petersburg to the tunes of brass bands, with the eyes of lovely women on them, and banners waving over their heads. The ladies called them the "company of bachelors"—the soldiers were sixteen to twenty-five, without a married man among them. ". . . indeed, we looked like boys," one wrote his mother, "with our handsome blue uniforms & smooth faces." They were great favorites everywhere they went.

Occasionally civilian response was overenthusiastic. When the 5th New Jersey passed through Philadelphia in August 1861, citizens came to the train station to see them off. Young ladies freely distributed cigars, tobacco, handkerchiefs, and flowers to the soldiers. The train left the station "amid the crack of firearms and the cheers from thousands of throats." One soldier of the 5th New Jersey was shot in the arm during this patriotic demonstration, and later discharged from service.

Such accidents aside, these receptions cheered the volunteers—who felt they deserved them. The public placed the value on the soldier that military life threatened to deny them. As the war continued, however, the sight of a soldier became commonplace. Civilians no longer thronged to meet the soldiers. In fact, as civilians went about their daily pursuits, they did not simply take soldiers for granted—they looked down on them. Or so the soldiers came to feel.

Soldiers began to hear stories of civilian disdain; they began to complain of their treatment on their furloughs home. Cpl. Rudolphe Rey of the 102nd New York Volunteers received a discouraging letter from a fellow soldier who had lost a leg. Upon his return home, the crippled soldier reported that all his friends acted as if they could not remember him; he swore he would be able to support himself without their aid. He warned Rey that if he wore his uniform home while on leave, he could travel with a railroad car to himself. Another New York soldier said much the same thing: at home, "Soldiers and dogs go together."

It might be thought that indifference toward soldiers was characteristic of a money-grubbing, unchivalrous North and not the militaristic South. As early as 1862, however, a Virginia Confederate observed that "six months ago a soldier was the greatest thing in the world but now they are worse than the devil not countenanced by nobody at all but the soldiers." Confederate soldiers, campaigning near Jackson, Mississippi, in June 1863, heard rumors that "The City Council in compliance with the solicitations of many citizens attempted some time since to pass an ordinance forbidding *soldiers the use of the pavement* and *sidewalks* and forcing them to walk in the middle of the streets. The motion was defeated by a majority of *only Three* votes." When the soldiers marched through the city, they would cry out, "Boys, don't get on the sidewalk!" and "Corporal of the Guard, here's a soldier on the sidewalk!" and the citizens nervously assured them, "Yes, you *can* walk on the sidewalks." "The Boys would frequently ask them 'where the Yankees walked while they were here'? They would cry out good-humoredly while passing a crowd of Ladies and Gentlemen, 'Here's the boys that cant walk on the pavements.' *We* can fight for you though.' " Whether the proposed civic ordinance existed or not, it is significant that the soldiers so readily believed that it did.

Whatever the indifference or contempt of the civilian population at large, soldiers felt a particularly acute grievance when it seemed that the members of their own local communities did not respect their efforts. It violated the very notion that the soldier who had gone to war was an extension of that community. As the war went on, soldiers found it difficult not to see themselves as distinct from the folks back home. Instead of representing his community he began to feel alienated from it—another way in which the volunteer became a soldier.

One source of discontent was the soldiers' feeling that the people did not understand how difficult their job was. Both sides went to war expecting a quick victory; both sides were quickly, but not thoroughly, disillusioned. Soldiers who were themselves reluctant to admit that the war would not end with the next big battle were likely to be sensitive to accusations that victory could easily be achieved with different strategy, different commanders, and different armies. Even though all soldiers reserved the right to grumble about the mistakes of their superior officers, most resented it when home folks judged the operations of the army in the field unfavorably. In part, of course, such judgments were felt to reflect not only on the commanders but on the men as well. Furthermore, the soldier felt that civilian judgments were made in ignorance. The folks at home had no concept of the difficulties experienced by the soldiers in the field. A Pennsylvania lieutenant wrote home testily, when civilians were complaining that McClellan allowed Lee to escape after Antietam, that if men there "think the Rebble army can be Bagged let them come & bagg them. . . . Bagging an army is easy to talk about." The men who remained at home had forfeited their right to criticize those who had marched away to war.

A Confederate wrote his cousin on the subject of civilian military expertise thus: "I saw a gentleman who left DeSoto Parish about two weeks since. He says the old men at home are all generals now—gather in groups in the little towns over there and talk about the war and discuss the abilities of our Generals—Know more than any of them—Except General Lee only—They admit him to be a great man, but all the others do wrong all the time. Our soldiers have all come to the conclusion that they have no friends out of the army except the ladies." And Lee himself, admitting that "the movements of our armies cannot keep pace with the expectations of the editors of papers," said he would like to see them exercise their abilities in the field.

Another, more onerous grievance was the difference between the economic positions of the soldier and the civilian. Many civilians did well during the war, particularly in the North. Soldiers and their families, conversely, often suffered. With furloughs home and the surprisingly frequent exchange of mail between the front and home, soldiers were perfectly well informed as to the economic success of those they had left behind.

A particular problem arose when the soldier thought that the people at home were not fair to his family or were grasping and picayune in money matters while he risked his life for the cause. John Pierson, a Union officer, reacted angrily when he learned that one of his creditors in Pontiac, Michigan, dunned his wife. "Those left at home in the quiet pursuit of their business," he told his daughter, "can well aford to wait. The business I am engaged in is a game of heads and I may loose mine and his is in no danger unless they chose to get up a war at home. . . .

When the man continued to hound his wife, Pierson wrote her "any man that is so avaricious as to dun a woman for a small demand he may have against her Husband while he is in the Army helping to Suppress this Montrous Rebelion is mean enough to make a false bill and ought to lose and honest one." He assured her, "If I get home Pontiac will not suffer much on my account if I get killed they may come where I am and collect. . . ."

The issue was not simply one of personal debts. It was also one of forgone opportunities for profit in the wartime economy. Henry Seys, the Union abolitionist, summed up the soldiers' fears and pride well when he wrote his wife from Chattanooga: "True I sometimes think why should *I* care so much of what is my duty to my country? Why not do as others, stay at home and fatten in purse on the blood of the land?" In ten years, he predicted, "the parvenu, made rich by lucky speculation, or some swindling contract" would "elbow from place the soldier broken down or maimed, by long exposure or ghastly wound received on some battle field or lonely picket post. . . ." But he answered his question by saying that he served because his childhood education and his concern for the respect of his own children made him patriotic both "in *deed* as well as word." He asked his wife to teach their children that, "their duty to the land of their birth is next to their duty to God."

Those soldiers who believed that their immediate family had become indifferent to them probably felt the most wretched sense of abandonment. In May 1862 an officer in the Army of the Potomac, then located near Richmond, complained, "I am tired of soldiering and were it not for us being just where we are, I would not stay a day longer not careing whether you wanted me home or not I cannot understand why you deserve [desire?] me to stay I see other letters to young men from their parents, begging and imploring of them to come home this makes me feel sad and sometimes I think I am not wanted at home by my parents[.]" He was killed not long after, at the battle of Seven Pines.

Civilian disdain was as potent a source of degradation as military life. Still, the soldiers' resentment of civilian contempt and indifference was not always unambiguous. Sometimes they feared it was deserved. Soldiers knew that military life might indeed transform men into beasts and this could inform a soldier's reactions to civilians. For example, in the fall of 1862 a Union soldier in Illinois suffered from the usual camp diseases and decided to treat himself with "some fresh air and a good bed to sleep in. . . ." He went to a farm near camp to request a place to stay for the night; the "old lady" was obviously suspicious and reluctant to shelter him but the soldier persuaded her to relent. When he wrote his parents, he explained, "The people here are suspicious of soldiers just as Ma is of pedlars and dont like to put them into their beds and I cannot blame them either some of the soldiers have not pride enough to keep themselves halfway decent. Some of them seem to think that being a soldier is a license for a man to make a brute of himself."

In 1863 a Mississippi Confederate heard that a military hospital was planned for his hometown. The idea depressed him. "It seems to me that wherever soldiery predominate decay and scarcity follow, and a certain appearance of cheerlessness (as far as the inhabitants are concerned) seems to exist in proportion as the number of soldiers (locusts) increase." Charity compelled him to add, "Anyway, as they are stationed upon you, you do the best you can for poor fellows! they have a hard time even when not sick."

So while men sometimes prided themselves on their patriotism and soldierly qualities, they also worried about the changes military service had made in their fellows when they compared the men around them to their families back home. The psychological transformation caused by war sometimes upset men more than anything else. Lyman C. Holford, a Wisconsin soldier, wrote in his diary entry, "a little after dark I saw something which was a little the worst of any thing I have yet seen in the army. Some of the boys of the 24th Mich (a new Regt lately attached to our Brigade) found a cow which had been dead for several days and being a little meat hungry they went to work and cut meat from the cow and carried it to camp and ate it." It was not just the spectacle of dead animals and rotten meat that disgusted Holford; as a veteran of battle he had seen far worse. What disgusted Holford was seeing men reduce themselves to hyenas. Somehow the dehumanization implicit in that selfish and sickening act was greater than that of killing and wounding in battle, for it showed men turned into beasts.

Dehumanizing treatment was inflicted from outside; it might be resisted. Psychological transformation was more insidious. The changes that soldiering made in men might be impossible to eradicate. The Assistant Surgeon of the 12th Michigan observed, "Soldiering is certainly not beneficial to the mind, and the large lists of sick do not look as if it improved the bodily health much. I think it certainly engenders laziness." He attributed this laziness to "the alternation of very hard work, which is compulsory, and nothing at all to do, with very few resources for amusement." Laziness, unfortunately, might become a permanent part of the volunteer's personality. The Surgeon feared, "When the war is over if that happy time ever comes, I believe the greater part of them will join the regular service, from sheer unfittness for anything else."

The Union surgeon was echoed by Confederate soldiers. Henry Greer wrote his mother from the lines near Petersburg, "If I stay much longer in service I fear that I will never be fit for anything but the army." Richard Webb, a regimental chaplain, may have been more worried about the changes he detected in himself. "This is a very demoralized kind of life. So hardening to human feelings. I can now walk over a battlefield and see the ground strewed with dead bodies, or see a man's lim amputated without any of that tendency of fainting that the sight of blood used to cause." The irony was that serving as chaplain hardened Webb's feelings at a time when a chaplain was particularly valued by other frightened men for his sensitivity.

In some cases, men were surprised by the direction of the moral transformation engendered by war. One Confederate soon learned that "War is a strange scale for measuring men." He described a fellow soldier, from whom nobody expected very much, who "made as good a soldier as there was in the Regiment. Cool and brave in battle and always on hand and never shirking duty in camp." This man proved a far better soldier than "others who occupied honorable positions in society." A New York regiment enlisted one of its soldiers after finding him sleeping drunkenly in a lumberyard. "He was dirty filthy and covered with vermin." They exchanged his rags for a new uniform. John Fleming remembered that "Strange as it may appear, that man became very steady, and one of the cleanest men and best soldiers we had." While such improvements in character were no doubt welcome, they also served to reinforce the distance felt between civilian life and the life of the soldier. These reformations were only extreme examples of how little one's peacetime identity seemed to relate to one's soldiering.

The families back home shared the fears that the Civil War experience would change men beyond recognition. Soldiers frequently reassured wives and parents in their letters that they would not change or that their love was constant, apparently responding to the distressed queries of their loved one. Such fears found their expression whether those they possessed wanted to admit them or not. A dream about her husband terrified one Georgia woman. She dreamed he had gone mad and had to be brought home. "I thought you would not speak to me. I thought all you wanted to do was to fill up the roads with logs and brush so that Lincoln's Army could not pass through the country. it pestered me worse than any dream I ever dreamed before but I hope there is nothing of it." Such a dream revealed the fear on the woman's part that the war, which ironically was often cast as a defense of the home, would alienate husbands and fathers from their families.

In most cases the transformation experienced by Civil War soldiers was not as dramatic or as clear-cut as that from drunkard to model soldier, devoted husband to madman, or man to beast. Men found that the war called forth a broad array of emotional responses. One of the most perceptive analysts of the psychology of soldiering was a Union soldier, James T. Miller. While Miller's letters home reveal him to be a man particularly concerned with the ways war was influencing his character, his observations probably applied to men less articulate and introspective.

The battle of Chancellorsville sparked Miller's self-scrutiny. In May 1863 he wrote home, "i can hardly make it seem possible that three short weeks ago that i was rite in the thickest of a terrible battle but such is a soldiers life. . . ." Miller confessed that such a life had its appeal "for a brave reckless man who has no family even in war times it has a good many charms and i think i can begin to understand something of the love an old sailor has for his ship and dangers of the Ocean." The appeal, in part, may have been aesthetic. A month after Chancellorsville, Miller explained to his parents, "steadyness under fire is the great beauty of a soldier[.]" One is reminded that Robert E. Lee, watching the advance of Burnside's troops at Fredericksburg, said, "It is well that war is so terrible; we should grow too fond of it."

Miller analyzed at length the emotions experienced by the soldier. He admitted the danger inherent in war, but explained "in regard to the danger I have passed through that part is very pleasent[.]" Soldiers amused themselves after battle by sitting around campfires and laughing over stories of "hairbreadth escapes" told in a "gay reckless carless way." An observer "would be very apt to think that we were the happiest set of men" he had ever seen.

"But if you should go with us to the battle filed and see those that are so gay thier faces pale and thier nervs tremblings and see an ankziety on every countenance almost bordering on fear," Miller said, "you would be very apt to think we were all a set of cowardly poltrouns[.]" The soldiers should be imagined this way "just before the fight begins and the enemy is in sight and the dul ominous silence that generaly takes places before the battle begins[.]" The soldier does not fear the dangers he has been through already, but he fears those that are to come.

Once skirmishers had been deployed, and the firing of cannons and small arms had begun, Miller observed that the soldiers' expressions changed remarkably. They could now "see the solid columns of the foe advance in plain sight every man seeming to step as proudly and steadily as if on parad and even while the artilery tears large gaps in thier line still on they come hardly faltiring for a moment[.]" This spectacle of war left the men still pale, "but see the firm compressed lips the eye fixed and [persevering?] and blood shot and the muscels rigid and the veins corugated and knoted and looking more like fiends than men[.]" When the order to charge came, "away we in to the very jaws of death and never for one moment faltering but yeling like devils up to the mouths of the Canon and then to hear the wild triumphant cheer[.]" Yet in a few hours these men who had resembled devils would be ministering to the wounded left on the field, both friends and enemies, "with the kindness and tenderness of a woman[.]" Miller concluded that, "by the time you have seen this you will begin to think that a soldier has as many carackters as a cat is said to have lives[.]"

Miller's description points to the fact that a soldier could not be well-defined in simple terms—either as patriotic hero or as savage beast. The war demanded a full range of responses from men. Miller understood that "a soldiers life is a sucession of extreems, first a long period of inactivity folowed by a time when all his energies both mental and phsical are taxed to the utmost[.]" The rapid and extreme changes that men underwent increased the anxiety created by the war. No one "character" would serve for a man in such an environment.

This was true in other ways. The Massachusetts college student, Samuel Storrow, wrote home about the various physical tasks in which military life required proficiency. "When I get home I shall be qualified for any position, either that of a boot black, a cleaner of brasses, a washer—(wo)man, cook, chambermaid, hewer of wood & drawer of water, or, failing in all these I can turn beggar & go from door to door asking for 'broken vittles'. In all these I should feel prefectly at home by long practise therein." Storrow was middle class and was perhaps more amused—or chagrined—by his new roles than most soldiers were. But the occupations he lists were all notable for their lack of dignity. Most of them were associated with servants and other dependents; beggars commanded even less respect; and "hewer of wood & drawer of water" was a Biblical phrase that usually denoted a slave. These demeaning roles were unwelcome additions to one's image as a soldier and hero; they were ways in which military life broke down civilian ideas of status and identity.

Another contradiction experienced by the soldier was that between his image of the volunteer as the preeminently virtuous patriot and the reality of the men with whom he shared army life. Where he had expected to find paragons, he found mortal men. Both the Union and Confederate armies had their share of petty thieves, drunkards, slackers, and other lowlife.

The camp was simultaneously immoral and virtuous, full of temptation and full of piety. Christopher Keller of the 124th Illinois was shocked by the temptations to vice open to men when they first went into camp after his regiment was raised in the fall of 1862. Apparently the other men of his company were shocked as well, for they soon voted to have their captain teach a regular Bible class. Shortly after their arrival Keller wrote a description of his camp that caught the two contrary impulses displayed there. "My bunkmate is reading his bible and in the bunk below they are having a prayer meeting on a small scale while others are cutting up, some swearing, some laughing, some writing, and others reading." He concluded that camp was "the place to see human nature in all its different varieties."

Luther C. Furst, who volunteered early in the war, noted that "The history of the four kings" was the most popular book in camp. His discouragement with the immorality of the camp was deepened by his belief that the war was brought on by national wickedness. And a soldier in the 140th New York observed that the only reason many men in camp knew when it was Sunday was that stores were closed that day and they could buy no liquor.

One Confederate pronounced camp "the last place for me or any other sivil man." The noise and misconduct of his fellow volunteers appalled him. And another deplored the absence of religion in camp. "I haven't heard a sermon in I can't tell when. You hear no more talk about religion here than if there was no such thing. The army is more demoralizing than I ever dreamed of. Three-fourths I recon, of the officers and men in this Regiment are profane swearers and card players."

The contradiction between image and reality, the excitement and fear of combat, the psychological exhaustion caused by the extremes in a soldier's life, the dehumanization of the army, even the risk of bestialization—the volunteer had to suffer all these to fight for his cause. It is not surprising that he sometimes felt resentful of those who had remained at home and that he acquired a new identity as a soldier. It is not even surprising that some soldiers did act like the beasts that most soldiers feared they might become.

After the surrender of Confederate Gen. Joseph E. Johnston's army, Union Gen. W. T. Sherman marched his victorious soldiers north from Bennett Place, North Carolina, to Washington, D.C. Along the way they stopped to visit the battlefields of the east, where the Army of the Potomac had long struggled with Robert E. Lee's forces. Robert Strong's company passed through the Wilderness, where one of the greatest battles of the war had been fought. "Right in the line of breastworks stood a lone house," Strong remembered. "When we passed the house it was occupied only by women, not a single living man. They were surrounded by the bones of thousands of dead men."

The women in the house came to the door to watch the Union soldiers march by. One of Strong's fellow soldiers had picked up a skull from the battlefield. He greeted the women and asked them, "Did you have any friends in this fight?"

One of them replied her brother had been killed in the battle.

"Here is his head," the soldier said, and "tossed the skull in among them."

The soldiers of the Civil War did not escape the psychological terror most associated with war: the full shock of the horrors of combat. A surgeon with the Army of the Ohio expressed both the romanticism that led some men willingly to war and the reality ultimately encountered. Joshua Taylor Bradford felt "the attraction of war and *fascination* of its *pomp* and *glitter*" as the army marched in February 1862, "with banners flying and music filling the air with melody." The army passed crowds of spectators, cheering it on. Nine days later, as Buell's columns left behind sick men who had fallen out, the surgeon commented on the pathos of war. And in March, when he visited military hospitals in Nashville and saw "hundreds, yea, thousands, in their narrow *bunks,* some dead Some dying, and many tossing the 'wild and fevered limbs in delerious forebodings,' " he found the sight "a sermon preached to the understanding, more potent than words." He called it "a humiliating evidence of war." A month later he participated in the battle of Shiloh.

Eric Leed, in *No Man's Land,* a study of World War I soldiers, suggests that the changes produced in soldiers by exposure to the realities of war are more than psychological. He argues that they are also cultural stereotypes—that the disillusioned soldier is just as much a cultural artifact as the innocent volunteer. The classic point at which disillusionment occurs, whether in fiction or in the experience of the Civil War soldier, is battle—the soldier's initiation into large-scale horror.

Many soldiers awaited their first battle impatiently; they felt eager to prove their courage and to defeat the enemy. One Confederate wrote a friend, "I want to be in one Battle, just for the curiosity of the thing." An Illinois soldier fretted that the war might be over before he had a chance to fight in battle. "I sometimes feel as if the war was to end now I would never dare to say I had been a soldier. I do not feel as if I had earned it." He explained his desire to participate in a battle by saying, "I hope we will have something to do not because I *want* to get into a fight but if there is fighting to do I am willing to bear my share so as to have this war over as soon as possible so I if alive can return home. . . ."

The disillusionment that followed such eagerness is predictable. One Union soldier had complained when he was promoted to Ordnance Sergeant as it diminished his chance of fighting; "when I think of you & the babies I am almost glad for what would you do if I should be kiled but that is not what I came for I came to fight & kill and come back[.]" A year and a half later he wrote his wife, "it makes me laugh to see the papers talk about this regiment and that and that the men ar eager for a chanc to get at the enemy all in your eyes, thare is none that wants to fight or will if they can keep clear of it."

The actual experience of battle horrified some men. One Confederate wrote home after his first battle, "I have bin in one battle and that satisfied me with war and I would beg to be excused next time for I tell you that there cannons and the shot and shell flying as thick as hail and the grape and cannister flying between the shot and shells." The battle had been furious; "there was a [patch] of woods behind the gun that we was at work at and to look back through the woods and it looked like the trees were falling faster than a hundred men could cut them down with axes and the ground was torn all to peaces holes large enough to bury a horse and so thick that I did not see how a man escaped for it looked like there was not room any where for a man to stand up nor lay down without being hit by a shot or shell[.]" A Union soldier who survived the inferno at Cold Harbor simply noted, "God has spared me this time I pray he will spare me to return to you alive & well. I shan't reinlist."

Shiloh was the first great battle in which many western soldiers participated. One Confederate, who told of seeing the branches of springs all colored with blood, wrote a correspondent, "you could never form an idea of the horrors of actual war unless you saw the battlefields while the conflict is progressing." He explained that "Death in every awful form, if it really be death, is a pleasant sight in comparision to the fearfully and mortally wounded. Some crying, oh, my wife, my children, others, my Mother, my sisters, my brother, etc. any and all of these you will hear while some pray to God to have mercy and others die cursing the 'Yankee sons of b————s.' "

One Union soldier wrote after Shiloh, "I have seen since I have been here what I never saw before and what I never want to witness again." George W. Crosley, an Iowan, admitted he could not describe the battle, but tried to evoke the quality of the corpse-strewn field after the fighting had ceased by telling his correspondent to "call to mind all the horrible scenes of which you ever saw or heard. then put them all together and you can form some faint conception of the scene I witnessed in passing over this bloody Battlefield of Pittsburgh Landing."

Yet horror did not entirely overwhelm men during their first battle; they responded in other ways as well. Crosley recalled that during the battle of Shiloh he did not fear death because he knew "I was in the performance of the noblest duty—except the worship of God that a man is ever permitted to perform here upon earth." And one thing that kept him from fear was the image of the woman he loved: "My dear Edna I have thought of you a hundred times while engaged in Battle. Your image would rise before me in the heat of conflict. . . ."

Many men felt bolstered by such images. Shepherd Pryor, a Confederate, admitted to his wife that he thought of her and their children all through his first battle. A devout man, he thanked God he "had the nerve to stand it," but confessed, "I felt bad thinking I might be shot dead every moment[.]" The association of family with the bloodshed of battle might seem incongruous. But the men of the Civil War era quite sincerely regarded their participation in the war as an extension of their duty to protect their family. It was appropriate then that when that defense reached its moment of greatest stress, in battle, men should remember their sweethearts, wives, and children. Of course the duty for which these remembrances steadied men was that of killing.

Both Crosley and Pryor also received consolation from their religious faith while they were in battle. This was not uncommon among Civil War soldiers. American Christians were particularly prone to attribute escape from death in battle to providential intervention, the result of prayer and devotion. "I have not Received as much as a scratch," R. F. Eppes wrote after the Seven Days Battles. "Surely God has been with mee hee has kept me in the hollow of his hand Surely he has heard theese heart pleadings of those near and dear ones at home for the Fervent Effectual Prairs of the Writious availeth much." Just as men might think of their loved ones to strengthen them in battle, they might also think of God.

Other men found themselves caught up in the compulsions of battle from the first. One Confederate ran across a field with his company under Union fire in his first engagement; he positioned himself behind a tree where the soldier next to him was wounded. While they crossed the field, he "expected to get shot every step." But once he had gotten into a place he could return fire in relative safety, he "did not think of any thing but shooting yankees." Joseph Cotten was grateful for having been at Bull Run, even though Providence had prevented him from actually firing his gun. He described the battle as "sublime." Looking forward to at least "one more great struggle," he thought that it would suffice to win Confederate independence.

Adjusting to battle meant more than facing and overcoming fear. As long as the soldier concentrated on the possibility—often probability, occasionally near-inevitability—of death, he could think of himself as a suffering patriot or a victim of war. Soldiers could not, however, free themselves from the moral burden of killing other men, for that was the nature of war. Despite the cruelty of the foe, some soldiers had trouble reconciling themselves to the idea that going to war for liberty meant killing their fellowmen. One expected savages, dupes, and mercenaries to murder without thought—the enemy was far more bloodthirsty than the legitimate ends of war demanded. But to embrace killing personally was to give way to impulses that society had long demanded be kept under strict self-restraint. Needless to say, different men felt very differently about the bloodshed of the Civil War.

When his company was first issued ammunition, Confederate Edmund DeWitt Patterson meditated, "These are the first 'Cartridges' that I have ever seen, and is it possible that we are actually to *kill men? Human beings?* . . . Yes, this is war and how hardened men must become." Richard M. Campbell made a diary entry as he hid in the bush watching for Union soldiers while on picket near Williamsburg: "My gun lies near at hand & my orders are to shoot whoever of my fellow man shows himself in front of the line. Such are the ways of war. It is a terrible scourge to any nation." The tension of the wait and of holding still wearied Campbell as if he "had been taking active exercise all day."

In May 1863 Hugh Roden confessed that his fellow Union soldiers admired the late Stonewall Jackson a great deal. He explained, "there was something so daring a[nd] Noble in his way of fighting that made his enemys love him." Nonetheless, he said, "those men that praise him and his daring would not hesitate a moment if they had the Chance to send a Ball through his *heart*." The soldiers welcomed Jackson's death as they would the death of any rebel. "A soldier praised Bravery no mater where found a soldier will shake hands with the enemy one moment and shoot him the next—Such is war."

Roden recognized this mixture of respect and cold-blooded killing as only one of the psychological strains combat placed upon the soldier. War's "sickening sights" saddened men, yet its excitement made them "unconscious of danger." In battle "everything *home life* everything that is dear" was forgotten and a man changed into "a Blood thirsty Being." "all his Better feelings forsake him" He reached the condition where he not only could kill his fellow men, men whose bravery he respected, but where he rejoiced in their deaths.

Other soldiers showed more hesitation in embracing their role of killers. Numa Barned, who had fraternized with rebels against orders, said, "I don't know that I ever shot any one or dont want to know." He had shot at many Confederates but in battle his policy was "as long as I can see a man head in front of me I will shoot and never look at the consequences." If he knew he had shot a man he would not admit it; "I do not want any man's blood on my hands." Having volunteered to be a soldier, Barned seemed to think he could kill and not be a killer if he only remained ignorant of the deaths he caused. During the battle of Arkansas Post, Henry C. Bear thought of his wife's Dunkard convictions against war, but shot at the Confederates as much as anyone else did. But when the battle was over, and he and the rebel prisoners had shaken hands and shared a meal of bread and meat, he wrote his wife, "I hope I did not hit any person if they are Rebles."

Hatred was one way soldiers reconciled themselves to killing. A Southern soldier wrote in 1863 that he hoped they could drive the Yankees from Virginia "without having to kill them, but if it is impossible to move them, I hope that we may slay them like wheat before the sythe in harvest time." He had some Christian scruples about his animosity toward the Northerners, but confessed, "if it is a sin to hate them, then I am guilty of the unpardonable one." After his first battle, Michael Donlon was no longer "afraid of the Rebel guns, for i have had one trial of them and I shot 4 men." He told his brother that he must not judge him a murderer for these killings, "for it wer my duty to Shoot as many of the Devils as I could and so i did."

Sometimes the eagerness with which men approached battle surprised even themselves; it could represent a strange reversal of emotion. A Union soldier remembered a counterattack he participated in during the battle of Gettysburg: "Charge we did drove the foe like chaff before the wind. Strange it does seem to be these men that a few moments before was driving our Men Now threw Down their arms & begged for mercy at our hands they said they could not stand our fire Strange too, our men that A Short time before seemed to be almost Dead was now as full of life and vigor as men could be As for myself, I never felt better then I did when making that grand charge"

Other men felt no such excitement while in battle. William Nugent, a Confederate, wrote, "You have frequently heard of the wild excitement of battle. I experience no such feelings. There is a sense of depression continually working away at my heart, caused by a knowledge of the great suffering in store for large numbers of my fellow men, that is entirely antagonistic to any other emotions. It is doubtless true that I feel exhilarated when the enemy is driven back and our troops are cheering and advancing. Still I cannot be happy as some men are in a fight. I believe the whole machinery of war is indefensible on moral grounds, as a general proposition, and nothing but a sense of duty and the sacredness of our cause, could at all buoy me."

Nonetheless, a soldier's lack of enthusiasm for battle made little difference so long as his loyalty remained constant. Duty and patriotism were as successful as hatred and bloodlust in motivating men to fight. The soldier who did not relish combat continued to fight—out of "a sense of duty"; because of "the sacredness of our cause." John Frederic Holahan, a Union soldier, explained that he belonged "to Uncle Sam, mentally, morally, and physically." Part of his obedience lay in fighting. He belonged to Uncle Sam "*Morally*—for my virtues and vices must correspond to that of my fellows; I must *lie* to rebels, *steal* from rebels and *kill* rebels;—Uncle Sam making vicarious atonement for these sins." Both the Confederate Nugent and the Federal Holahan resigned their moral sense to the greater cause, trusting that that would absolve them of any moral blame. And they continued to fight. Thus they reconciled their Christian morality with their patriotism and tried to soldier without becoming a soldier. Thus they resisted the final transformation from citizen to killer. Perhaps those men who embraced the warrior's role had an easier time of it.

Before the battle of Agincourt, in Shakespeare's *Henry V,* John Bates, a common English soldier, explains to the disguised Henry that if the cause for which they fight is wrong, "our obedience to the king wipes the crime out of us." But Michael Williams, another soldier, adds, "But if the cause be not good, the king himself hath a heavy reckoning to make when all those legs and arms and heads, chopped off in a battle, shall join themselves in the latter day and cry all, 'We died at such a place,' some swearing, some crying for a surgeon, some upon their wives left poor behind them, some upon the debts they owe, some upon their children rawly left."

Perhaps there is less difference than is immediately apparent between the attitude of Bates and Williams and that of Union veteran Oliver Wendell Holmes when he praised the faith of the soldier. "But in the midst of doubt, in the collapse of creeds, there is one thing I do not doubt, that no man who lives in the same world with most of us can doubt, and that is the faith is true and adorable which leads a soldier to throw away his life in obedience to a blindly accepted duty, in a cause he little understands, in a plan of campaign of which he has no notion, under tactics of which he does not see the use." But where the Shakespearian soldiers at least hope that the cause they fight for blindly is just, the modern man is reduced, in relativist fashion, to justifying the cause because of the soldier's faith.

The Civil War volunteer, however, was certain that his cause was just. It was not simply the cause of the king or of Uncle Sam. In a democratic society the volunteer had helped make the decision to go to war. The cause of the Union or of the South was bound up with one's community, one's home and family, and one's God. That is what allowed men like Nugent and Holahan to fight when they feared fighting was immoral, and that was why the Civil War volunteer not only submitted to his transformation into a soldier, but took pride in it. Ultimately, the worth of the cause was the worth of the soldier. . . .

✎ *F U R T H E R   R E A D I N G*

Michael Barton, *Goodmen: The Character of Civil War Soldiers* (1981)

Bruce Catton, "Hayfoot-Strawfoot!" *American Heritage* 8 (1957), 30–37

Henry Steele Commager, ed., *The Blue and the Gray,* 2 vols. (1950)

David Donald, "The Confederate as a Fighting Man," *Journal of Southern History* 25 (1959), 178–193

Drew Gilpin Faust, "Christian Soldiers: The Meaning of Revivalism in the Confederate Army," *Journal of Southern History* 53 (1987), 63–90

Joseph T. Glatthaar, *The March to the Sea and Beyond: Sherman's Troops in the Savannah and Carolina Campaigns* (1985)

———, *Forged in Battle: The Civil War Alliance of Black Soldiers and White Officers* (1990)

Lee Kennett, *Marching through Georgia: The Story of Soldiers and Civilians during Sherman's Campaign* (1994)

Gerald Linderman, *Embattled Courage: The Experience of Combat in the American Civil War* (1987)

James M. McPherson, *What They Fought For, 1861–1865* (1994)

———, *For Cause and Comrades: Why Men Fought in the Civil War* (1997)

Reid Mitchell, *The Vacant Chair: The Northern Soldier Leaves Home* (1993)

Eugene C. Murdock, *One Million Men: The Civil War Draft in the North* (1971)

James I. Robertson, *Soldiers, Blue and Gray* (1988)

Paul E. Steiner, *Disease in the Civil War* (1968)

Bell I. Wiley, *The Life of Johnny Reb* (1943)

———, *The Life of Billy Yank* (1952)

Abraham Lincoln As Political and Military Leader

In America's Civil War, one person stands above all others, supreme and indispensable: Abraham Lincoln. As president of the United States, he was head of the victorious government; as commander-in-chief, he was instrumental in the defeat of the armies of its enemy, the Southern Confederacy. Furthermore, in both his civil and his military capacities, he committed the United States to ending slavery. These achievements by themselves would be enough to ensure his historical reputation. But Lincoln had one more contribution to make. His words, enunciated in his formal addresses and messages, gave to the conflict the meaning it has held in American public memory ever since.

Small wonder, then, that, in the polls conducted among historians of the United States, Lincoln is generally voted the greatest president. Being the widely acknowledged "greatest president" justifies giving him considerable attention in any book on the Civil War. But, in an anthology that is about "major problems," this nearly universal approbation of Lincoln would perhaps disqualify him on the grounds that there is nothing problematic about him at all. Yet his success and the subsequent veneration of him do give rise to a set of questions that should not be ignored.

Just because he prevailed, along with the nation he headed, does not mean that their success was certain, since very little, if anything, is inevitable. So why did Lincoln and his side win? Furthermore, to what degree was Northern victory attributable to Lincoln's own decisions and actions? Was his leadership, in fact, vital? Alternatively, the question could be posed quite differently: Did Lincoln do anything to delay, or perhaps jeopardize, the victory of the United States? Maybe Union victory was likely, no matter what Lincoln did. In other words, Lincoln's claim to greatness cannot be based solely on his involvement with the success of the Union. Only if he made a decisive contribution, played a vital and essential role, can his reputation be justified. So what exactly did he do to win the war? What characteristics and what actions of his were crucial to Northern success?

Of course, Lincoln has had his detractors as well. Some have questioned his abilities as a military strategist and have reprimanded him for his willingness to put up with poor generals. Others have berated him for his racial prejudice and doubted his sincerity about emancipation. Still others have criticized him for his conservative political instincts and his apparent caution, even indecisiveness in some instances.

But these specific strictures have never amounted to a full-scale assault on his reputation and record overall. Rather, they have been merely critical observations of the sort that one would expect to be directed at any public figure. Lincoln, after all, was a mere

mortal; indeed, he was very human, and that is the feature that makes him so fascinat-
ing and so appealing. Despite his great renown and achievement, his humanity, even
his ordinariness, is undeniable. And that means that he is not, in some way, above his-
tory and beyond criticism. Instead, his particular role and contribution need to be un-
derstood and assessed, regardless of his high standing in historians' polls and in the
national pantheon.

D O C U M E N T S

The primary sources for this chapter show first, how Lincoln approached the issue of slavery and equal rights and second, how he functioned as commander-in-chief. The opening document is the president's famous reply to the query from Horace Greeley, the editor of the *New York Tribune,* asking when Lincoln would proceed against slavery. It is dated August 22, 1862, exactly a month before Lincoln decided to announce his Preliminary Proclamation of Emancipation, after the battle of Antietam. The second item is the account by the secretary of the treasury, Salmon P. Chase, of President Lincoln's presentation to the cabinet of that very same proposal on September 22. The third piece is the Gettysburg Address of November 19, 1863; in this brief and justly celebrated statement, the president explains the meaning of the conflict as not simply the fulfillment of the nation's commitment to equal rights, but the expansion of those rights. The fourth document is Lincoln's explanation of how he moved toward his position on emancipation and how, in doing so, he was always operating within the mandate of the Constitution.

The next two documents deal with military matters. In differing ways, they illustrate how Lincoln functioned as a military leader. The fifth item is a dispatch to General Don Carlos Buell at the beginning of the war, on January 13, 1862, that shows how quickly the inexperienced Lincoln developed a good sense of military strategy, often more astute than that of most of the generals he had to deal with. Lincoln's communication with his general-in-chief, Henry W. Halleck, on September 19, 1863 is the sixth document in the series, and it illustrates his ability to expose errors in the assumptions often made by his military commanders.

A final set of two documents contains attacks on Lincoln's conduct of the war from left and right. The first is the speech of August 1, 1862, at a meeting in Abington, Massachusetts, by the prominent abolitionist Wendell Phillips, assailing the administration for its caution. Paired with Phillips' onslaught is the vitriolic speech in the House of Representatives on January 14, 1863 by the leading Copperhead Democrat, Clement L. Vallandigham of Ohio, calling for a cessation of the war and denouncing Lincoln for his incompetence. These are the seventh and eighth documents on the topic.

Lincoln Explains His "Paramount Object" of Saving the Union, August 1862

Executive Mansion,
Washington, August 22, 1862.

Hon. Horace Greely.

DEAR SIR

I have just read yours of the 19th. addressed to myself through the New-York Tribune. If there be in it any statements, or assumptions of fact, which I may know to be

---

Letter, Abraham Lincoln to Horace Greeley, August 22, 1862, in *The Political Thought of Abraham Lincoln,* Richard N. Current, ed. (Bobbs-Merrill, 1967), pp. 214–215.

erroneous, I do not, now and here, controvert them. If there be in it any inferences which I may believe to be falsely drawn, I do not now and here, argue against them. If there be perceptable in it an impatient and dictatorial tone, I waive it in deference to an old friend, whose heart I have always supposed to be right.

As to the policy I "seem to be pursuing" as you say, I have not meant to leave any one in doubt.

I would save the Union. I would save it the shortest way under the Constitution. The sooner the national authority can be restored; the nearer the Union will be "the Union as it was." If there be those who would not save the Union, unless they could at the same time *save* slavery, I do not agree with them. If there be those who would not save the Union unless they could at the same time *destroy* slavery, I do not agree with them. My paramount object in this struggle *is* to save the Union, and is *not* either to save or to destroy slavery. If I could save the Union without freeing *any* slave I would do it, and if I could save it by freeing *all* the slaves I would do it; and if I could save it by freeing some and leaving others alone I would also do that. What I do about slavery and the colored race, I do because I believe it helps to save the Union; and what I forbear, I forbear because I do *not* believe it would help to save the Union. I shall do *less* whenever I shall believe what I am doing hurts the cause, and I shall do *more* whenever I shall believe doing more will help the cause. I shall try to correct errors when shown to be errors; and I shall adopt new views so fast as they shall appear to be true views.

I have here stated my purpose according to my view of *official* duty; and I intend no modification of my oft-expressed *personal* wish that all men every where could be free. Yours,

A. Lincoln

Salmon P. Chase Reports Lincoln's Decision on Emancipation, September 1862

September 22, 1862

To department about nine. State Department messenger came with notices to heads of departments to meet at twelve. Received sundry callers. Went to the White House. All the members of the cabinet were in attendance. There was some general talk, and the President mentioned that Artemus Ward had sent him his book. Proposed to read a chapter which he thought very funny. Read it and seemed to enjoy it very much; the heads also (except Stanton). The chapter was "High-Handed Outrage at Utica."

The President then took a graver tone and said: "Gentlemen, I have, as you are aware, thought a great deal about the relation of this war to slavery, and you all remember that, several weeks ago, I read to you an order I had prepared upon the subject, which, on account of objections made by some of you, was not issued. Ever since then my mind has been much occupied with this subject, and I have thought all along that the time for acting on it might probably come. I think the time has come now. I wish it was a better time. I wish that we were in a better condition. The action of the army against the rebels has not been quite what I should have liked best. But they have been driven out of

From Salmon P. Chase on the cabinet meeting of December 22, 1862, in *Inside Lincoln's Cabinet: The Civil War Diaries of Salmon P. Chase,* David Donald, ed. (Longman's, 1954), pp. 149–151.

Maryland, and Pennsylvania is no longer in danger of invasion. When the rebel army was at Frederick I determined, as soon as it should be driven out of Maryland, to issue a proclamation of emancipation such as I thought most likely to be useful. I said nothing to any one, but I made a promise to myself and (hesitating a little) to my Maker. The rebel army is now driven out, and I am going to fulfill that promise. I have got you together to hear what I have written down. I do not wish your advice about the main matter, for that I have determined for myself. This I say without intending anything but respect for any one of you. But I already know the views of each on this question. They have been heretofore expressed, and I have considered them as thoroughly and carefully as I can. What I have written is that which my reflections have determined me to say. If there is anything in the expressions I use or in any minor matter which any one of you thinks had best be changed, I shall be glad to receive your suggestions. One other observation I will make. I know very well that many others might, in this matter as in others, do better than I can; and if I was satisfied that the public confidence was more fully possessed by any one of them than by me, and knew of any constitutional way in which he could be put in my place, he should have it. I would gladly yield it to him. But though I believe that I have not so much of the confidence of the people as I had some time since, I do not know that, all things considered, any other person has more; and however this may be, there is no way in which I can have any other man put where I am. I am here. I must do the best I can and bear the responsibility of taking the course which I feel I ought to take."

The President then proceeded to read his Emancipation Proclamation, making remarks on the several parts as he went on, and showing that he had fully considered the subject in all the lights under which it had been presented to him. . . .

Lincoln Proclaims the Meaning of the Conflict, The Gettysburg Address, November 1863

November 19, 1863.

Four score and seven years ago our fathers brought forth on this continent, a new nation, conceived in Liberty, and dedicated to the proposition that all men are created equal.

Now we are engaged in a great civil war, testing whether that nation, or any nation so conceived and so dedicated, can long endure. We are met on a great battle-field of that war. We have come to dedicate a portion of that field, as a final resting place for those who here gave their lives that that nation might live. It is altogether fitting and proper that we should do this.

But, in a larger sense, we can not dedicate—we can not consecrate—we can not hallow—this ground. The brave men, living and dead, who struggled here, have consecrated it, far above our poor power to add or detract. The world will little note, nor long remember what we say here, but it can never forget what they did here. It is for us the living, rather, to be dedicated here to the unfinished work which they who fought here have thus far so nobly advanced. It is rather for us to be here dedicated to the great task remaining before us—that from these honored dead we take increased devotion to that cause for which they gave the last full measure of devotion—that we here highly resolve

The Gettysburg Address, in *The Political Thought of Abraham Lincoln,* Richard N. Current, ed. (Bobbs Merrill, 1967), pp. 284–285.

that these dead shall not have died in vain—that this nation, under God, shall have a new birth of freedom—and that government of the people, by the people, for the people, shall not perish from the earth.

Lincoln Recounts How He Proceeded toward Emancipation, April 1864

A. G. Hodges, Esq   Executive Mansion,
Frankfort, Ky.   Washington, April 4, 1864.

My dear Sir: You ask me to put in writing the substance of what I verbally said the other day, in your presence, to Governor Bramlette and Senator Dixon. It was about as follows:

"I am naturally anti-slavery. If slavery is not wrong, nothing is wrong. I can not remember when I did not so think, and feel. And yet I have never understood that the Presidency conferred upon me an unrestricted right to act officially upon this judgment and feeling. It was in the oath I took that I would, to the best of my ability, preserve, protect, and defend the Constitution of the United States. I could not take the office without taking the oath. Nor was it my view that I might take an oath to get power, and break the oath in using the power. I understood, too, that in ordinary civil administration this oath even forbade me to practically indulge my primary abstract judgment on the moral question of slavery. I had publicly declared this many times, and in many ways. And I aver that, to this day, I have done no official act in mere deference to my abstract judgment and feeling on slavery. I did understand however, that my oath to preserve the constitution to the best of my ability, imposed upon me the duty of preserving, by every indispensable means, that government—that nation—of which that constitution was the organic law. Was it possible to lose the nation, and yet preserve the constitution? By general law life *and* limb must be protected; yet often a limb must be amputated to save a life; but a life is never wisely given to save a limb. I felt that measures, otherwise unconstitutional, might become lawful, by becoming indispensable to the preservation of the constitution, through the preservation of the nation. Right or wrong, I assumed this ground, and now avow it. I could not feel that, to the best of my ability, I had even tried to preserve the constitution, if, to save slavery, or any minor matter, I should permit the wreck of government, country, and Constitution all together. When, early in the war, Gen. Fremont attempted military emancipation, I forbade it, because I did not then think it an indispensable necessity. When a little later. Gen. Cameron, then Secretary of War, suggested the arming of the blacks, I objected, because I did not yet think it an indispensable necessity. When, still later, Gen. Hunter attempted military emancipation, I again forbade it, because I did not yet think the indispensable necessity had come. When, in March, and May, and July 1862 I made earnest, and successive appeals to the border states to favor compensated emancipation, I believed the indispensable necessity for military emancipation, and arming the blacks would come, unless averted by that measure. They declined the proposition; and I was, in my best judgment, driven to the alternative of either surrendering the Union, and with it, the Constitution, or of laying strong hand upon the colored element. I chose the latter. In choosing it, I hoped for greater

Letter, Abraham Lincoln to A. G. Hodges, April 4, 1864, in *The Political Thought of Abraham Lincoln*, Richard N. Current, ed. (Bobbs-Merrill, 1967), pp. 297–300.

gain than loss; but of this, I was not entirely confident. More than a year of trial now shows no loss by it in our foreign relations, none in our home popular sentiment, none in our white military force,—no loss by it any how or any where. On the contrary, it shows a gain of quite a hundred and thirty thousand soldiers, seamen, and laborers. These are palpable facts, about which, as facts, there can be no cavilling. We have the men; and we could not have had them without the measure.

["]And now let any Union man who complains of the measure, test himself by writing down in one line that he is for subduing the rebellion by force of arms; and in the next, that he is for taking these hundred and thirty thousand men from the Union side, and placing them where they would be but for the measure he condemns. If he can not face his case so stated, it is only because he can not face the truth. ["]

I add a word which was not in the verbal conversation. In telling this tale I attempt no compliment to my own sagacity. I claim not to have controlled events, but confess plainly that events have controlled me. Now, at the end of three years struggle the nation's condition is not what either party, or any man devised, or expected. God alone can claim it. Whither it is tending seems plain. If God now wills the removal of a great wrong, and wills also that we of the North as well as you of the South, shall pay fairly for our complicity in that wrong, impartial history will find therein new cause to attest and revere the justice and goodness of God. Yours truly

A. LINCOLN

Lincoln Reveals an Early Grasp of Military Strategy, January 1862

Executive Mansion,

Washington, Jan. 13, 1862.

Brig. Genl. Buell.

My dear Sir:

Your despatch of yesterday is received, in which you say "I have received your letter and Gen. McClellan's; and will, at once, devote all my efforts to your views, and his." In the midst of my many cares, I have not seen, or asked to see, Gen. McClellan's letter to you. For my own views, I have not offered, and do not now offer them as orders; and while I am glad to have them respectfully considered, I would blame you to follow them contrary to your own clear judgment—unless I should put them in the form of orders. As to Gen. McClellan's views, you understand your duty in regard to them better than I do. With this preliminary, I state my general idea of this war to be that we have the *greater* numbers, and the enemy has the *greater* facility of concentrating forces upon points of collision; that we must fail, unless we can find some way of making *our* advantage an overmatch for *his;* and that this can only be done by menacing him with superior forces at *different* points, at the *same* time; so that we can safely attack, one, or both, if he makes no change; and if he *weakens* one to *strengthen* the other, forbear to attack the strength-ened one, but seize, and hold the weakened one, gaining so much. To illustrate, suppose

Letter, Lincoln to Gen. Don Carlos Buell, January 13, 1862, in *Abraham Lincoln: Selected Speeches, Messages, and Letters,* T. Harry Williams, ed. (Holt, Rinehart, 1957), pp. 174–175.

last summer, when Winchester ran away to re-inforce Manassas, we had forborne to attack Manassas, but had seized and held Winchester. I mention this to illustrate, and not to criticise. I did not lose confidence in [General] McDowell, and I think less harshly of [General] Patterson than some others seem to. In application of the general rule I am suggesting, every particular case will have its modifying circumstances, among which the most constantly present, and most difficult to meet, will be the want of perfect knowledge of the enemies' movements. This had it's part in the Bull-Run case; but worse, in that case, was the expiration of the terms of the three months men. Applying the principle to your case, my idea is that Halleck shall menace Columbus, and "down river" generally; while you menace Bowling-Green, and East Tennessee. If the enemy shall concentrate at Bowling-Green, do not retire from his front; yet do not fight him there, either, but seize Columbus and East Tennessee, one or both, left exposed by the concentration at Bowling Green. It is a matter of no small anxiety to me and one which I am sure you will not over-look, that the East Tennessee line, is so long, and over so bad a road.

Yours very truly

A. Lincoln

Lincoln Advises against Engaging Lee's Army after Gettysburg, September 1863

Executive Mansion,
Washington, Sepbr. 19, 1863.

Major General Halleck:

By Gen Meade's despatch to you of yesterday, it appears that he desires your views, and those of the Government, as to whether he shall advance upon the enemy. I am not prepared to order, or even advise an advance in this case, wherein I know so little of particulars, and wherein he, in the field, thinks the risk is so great and the promise of advantage so small. And yet the case presents matter for very serious consideration in another aspect. These two armies confront each other across a small river, substantially midway between the two Capitals, each defending its own Capital, and menacing the other. Gen. Meade estimates the enemy's infantry in front of him at not less than forty thousand. Suppose we add fifty per cent. to this for cavalry, artillery, and extra-duty men stretching as far as Richmond, making the whole force of the enemy sixty thousand, Gen. Meade, as shown by the returns, has with him, and between him and Washington, of the same classes of well men, over ninety thousand. Neither can bring the whole of his men into a battle, but each can bring as large a per centage in as the other. For a battle, then, Gen Meade has three men to Gen. Lee's two. Yet, it having been determined that choosing ground and standing on the defensive gives so great advantage that the three cannot safely attack the two, the three are left simply standing on the defensive also. If the enemy's sixty thousand are sufficient to keep our ninety thousand away from Richmond, why, by the same rule, may not forty thousand of ours keep their sixty thousand away from

Letter, Abraham Lincoln to Gen. Henry W. Halleck, September 19, 1863, in *The Collected Works of Abraham Lincoln*, Roy P. Basler, ed. (Rutgers University Press, 1953), Vol. 6, pp. 466–467.

Washington, leaving us fifty thousand to put to some other use? Having practically come to the mere defensive, it seems to be no economy at all to employ twice as many men for that object as are needed. With no object, certainly, to mislead myself, I can perceive no fault in this statement, unless we admit we are not the equal of the enemy, man for man. I hope you will consider it.

To avoid misunderstanding, let me say that to attempt to fight the enemy slowly back into his entrenchments at Richmond, and there to capture him, is an idea I have been trying to repudiate for quite a year. My judgment is so clear against it, that I would scarcely allow the attempt to be made, if the General in command should desire to make it. My last attempt upon Richmond was to get McClellan, when he was nearer there than the enemy was, to run in ahead of him. Since then I have constantly desired the Army of the Potomac to make Lee's army, and not Richmond, its objective point. If our army cannot fall upon the enemy and hurt him where he is, it is plain to me it can gain nothing by attempting to follow him over a succession of intrenched lines into a fortified city.

Yours truly,
A. Lincoln

Wendell Phillips Criticizes Lincoln's War Policy, August 1862

I quite agree with the view which my friend (Rev. M. D. Conway [another abolitionist who criticized the administration for its caution on slavery]) takes of the present situation of the country, and of our future. I have no hope, as he has not, that the intelligent purpose of our government will ever find us a way out of this war. I think, if we find any way out of it, we are to stumble out of it by the gradual education of the people, making their own way on, a great mass, without leaders. I do not think that anything which we can call the *government* has any *purpose* to get rid of slavery. On the contrary, I think the present purpose of the government, so far as it has now a purpose, is to end the war and save slavery. I believe Mr. Lincoln is conducting this war, at present, with the purpose of saving slavery. That is his present line of policy, so far as trustworthy indications of any policy reach us. The Abolitionists are charged with a desire to make this a political war. All civil wars are necessarily political wars,—they can hardly be anything else. Mr. Lincoln is intentionally waging a *political* war. He knows as well as we do at this moment, as well as every man this side of a lunatic hospital knows, that, if he wants to save lives and money, the way to end this war is to strike at slavery. I do not believe that McClellan himself is mad or idiotic enough to have avoided that idea, even if he has tried to do so. But General McClellan is waging a political war; so is Mr. Lincoln. . . . When Mr. Lincoln, by an equivocal declaration, nullifies General Hunter [who ordered all slaves in his department to be considered free, May 1862], he does not do it because he doubts either the justice or the efficiency of Hunter's proclamation; he does it because he is afraid of [slaveholders of] Kentucky on the right hand, and the Daily Advertiser [a conservative Republican paper published in Boston] on the left. [*Laughter.*] He has not taken one step since he entered the Presidency that has been a purely military step, and he could not. A civil war can hardly be anything but a political war. That is, all civil wars

From Wendell Phillips, "The Cabinet," August 1, in *Wendell Phillips: Speeches, Lectures, and Letters* (Lee and Shepherd, 1870), pp. 448–449, 457.

are a struggle between opposite ideas, and armies are but the tools. If Mr. Lincoln believed in the North and in Liberty, he would let our army act on the principles of Liberty. He does not. . . .

If we go to the bottom, it will be because we have, in the providence of God, richly deserved it. It is the pro-slavery North that is her own greatest enemy. Lincoln would act, if he believed the North wanted him to. The North, by an overwhelming majority, is ready to have him act, will endorse and support anything he does, yes, hopes he will go forward. True, it is not yet ripe enough to demand; but it is fully willing, indeed waits, for action. With chronic Whig distrust and ignorance of the people, Lincoln halts and fears. . . . He is not a genius; he is not a man like [John C.] Fremont, to stamp the lava mass of the nation with an idea; he is not a man like Hunter, to coin his experience into ideas. I will tell you what he is. He is a first-rate *second-rate* man. [*Laughter.*] He is one of the best specimens of a second-rate man, and he is honestly waiting, like any other servant, for the people to come and send him on any errand they wish. In ordinary times, when the seas are calm, you can sail without a pilot,—almost any one can avoid a sunken ledge that the sun shows him on his right hand, and the reef that juts out on his left; but it is when the waves smite heaven, and the thunder-cloud makes the waters ink, that you need a pilot; and to-day the nation's bark scuds, under the tempest, lee-shore and maelstrom on each side, needing no holiday captain, but a pilot, to weather the storm. . . . Democracy is poisoning its fangs. It is making its way among the ballot-boxes of the nation. I doubt whether our next Congress will be as good as the last. That is not saying much. . . .

Congressman Clement L. Vallandigham
Condemns the Northern War Effort,
January 1863

. . . Money and credit, then, you have had in prodigal profusion. And were men wanted? More than a million rushed to arms! Seventy-five thousand first, (and the country stood aghast at the multitude,) then eight-three thousand more were demanded; and three hundred and ten thousand responded to the call. The President next asked for four hundred thousand, and Congress, in their generous confidence, gave him five hundred thousand; and, not to be outdone, he took six hundred and thirty-seven thousand. Half of these melted away in their first campaign; and the President demanded three hundred thousand more for the war, and then drafted yet another three hundred thousand for nine months. The fabled hosts of Xerxes have been out-numbered. And yet victory, strangely, follows the standard of the foe. From Great Bethel to Vicksburg, the battle has not been to the strong. Yet every disaster, except the last, has been followed by a call for more troops, and every time, so far, they have been promptly furnished. From the beginning the war has been conducted like a political campaign, and it has been the folly of the party in power that they have assumed, that numbers alone would win the field in a contest not with ballots but with musket and sword. But numbers, you have had almost without number—the largest, best appointed, best armed, fed, and clad host of brave men, well organized and well disciplined, ever marshaled. A Navy, too, not the most

From Clement L. Vallandigham, "The Great Civil War in America," speech in the U.S. House, January 14, 1863, *Congressional Globe,* Vol. 33, Pt. 2, Appendix, pp. 54–55.

formidable perhaps, but the most numerous and gallant, and the costliest in the world, and against a foe, almost without a navy at all. Thus, with twenty millions of people, and every element of strength and force at command—power, patronage, influence, unanimity, enthusiasm, confidence, credit, money, men, an Army and a Navy the largest and the noblest ever set in the field, or afloat upon the sea; with the support, almost servile, of every State, county, and municipality in the North and West, with a Congress swift to do the bidding of the Executive; without opposition anywhere at home; and with an arbitrary power which neither the Czar of Russia, nor the Emperor of Austria dare exercise; yet after nearly two years of more vigorous prosecution of war than ever recorded in history; after more skirmishes, combats and battles than Alexander, Cæsar, or the first Napoleon ever fought in any five years of their military career, you have utterly, signally, disastrously—I will not say ignominiously—failed to subdue ten millions of "rebels," whom you had taught the people of the North and West not only to hate, but to despise. Rebels, did I say? Yes, your fathers were rebels, or your grandfathers. He, who now before me on canvas looks down so sadly upon us, the false, degenerate, and imbecile guardians of the great Republic which he founded, was a rebel. And yet we, cradled ourselves in rebellion, and who have fostered and fraternized with every insurrection in the nineteenth century everywhere throughout the globe, would now, forsooth, make the word "rebel" a reproach. Rebels certainly they are; but all the persistent and stupendous efforts of the most gigantic warfare of modern times have, through your incompetency and folly, availed nothing to crush them out, cut off though they have been, by your blockade, from all the world, and dependent only upon their own courage and resources. And yet, they were to be utterly conquered and subdued in six weeks, or three months! Sir, my judgment was made up, and expressed from the first. I learned it from [William Pitt the Elder, Earl of] Chatham: "My lords, you can not conquer America." And you have not conquered the South. You never will. It is not in the nature of things possible; much less under your auspices. But money you have expended without limit, and blood poured out like water. Defeat, debt, taxation, sepulchers, these are your trophies. In vain, the people gave you treasure; and the soldier yielded up his life. "Fight, tax, emancipate, let these," said the gentleman from Maine, [Mr. Pike,] at the last session, "be the trinity of our salvation." Sir, they have become the trinity of your deep damnation. The war for the Union is, in your hands, a most bloody and costly failure. The President confessed it on the 22d of September [with the promulgation of the Preliminary Emancipation Proclamation], solemnly, officially, and under the broad seal of the United States. And he has now repeated the confession. The priests and rabbis of abolition taught him that God would not prosper such a cause. War for the Union was abandoned; war for the negro openly begun, and with stronger battalions than before. With what success? Let the dead at Fredericksburg and Vicksburg answer. . . .

But ought this war to continue? I answer, no—not a day, not an hour.

ESSAYS

The first essay, by Phillip Shaw Paludan of the University of Kansas, is an abbreviated version of the interpretation of Lincoln that he developed in his recent book on Lincoln's presidency. He argued that Lincoln was an institutional conservative who saw emancipation as compatible with the political system and its values, rather than at odds with them. Thus, he claims, the ending of slavery was achieved through the Constitution, not despite it. The accompanying piece is by James M. McPherson of Princeton University who has become the preeminent authority on the Civil War as a result of his *Battle Cry of Freedom* (1988) and a series of recent books and essays on aspects of the conflict. Noting the strange paucity of studies of Lincoln as a military leader, he offers here a succinct assessment of his performance as commander-in-chief.

Emancipating the Republic: Lincoln and the Means and Ends of Antislavery

PHILLIP SHAW PALUDAN

It is one of the commonplaces of Lincoln scholarship that each generation seeks to "get right with Lincoln." David Donald, Don Fehrenbacher, Mark Neely, Gabor Boritt, and most thoroughly now Merrill Peterson, have all demonstrated the ways in which Americans have turned to Lincoln over the years to support their political positions or to anoint and exemplify their hopes and dreams.

Yet this ongoing struggle for Lincoln's blessing has often resulted in a series of alternate Lincolns, either/or Lincolns. This may simply be a result of the fact that emphases change over time; and one aspect of Lincoln seems more relevant or more appealing at any one time. But too often one finds publicists, politicians and scholars not just revealing one of many sides of a complex man, rather one finds them insisting that they have the true Lincoln which others distort or ignore. Lincoln is found, rather than sought. He becomes part of a polemic rather than an inquiry. When that happens, I believe, this very complex and admirable man becomes part of the problem, rather than part of the solution. Instead of providing, out [of] the rich and subtle complexity of thought that he generated, new ways of seeing and solving problems, he helps adversaries dig in and reinforce their positions.

In such an environment, when factions use the nation's most subtle thinkers to reinforce their polemics, societies can get stuck. They get stuck because they are unable to think clearly about how to achieve their best hopes. Their ideas and institutions have been captured by ways of thinking that do not allow new paths and saving directions. William Butler Yeats knew such a time when "the falcon cannot hear the falconer" when "the best lack all conviction while the worst are full of passionate intensity." Voices rise and the politics of fear replaces the politics of hope. Lacking positive and protean visions we know the weakness of every alternative. The cacophony rises "liberals are liars"; "conservatives are extremists"; vote against this, vote against that. It is a familiar song. It is at such times, as E. J. Dionne has noted, that Americans hate politics and politicians. They also fear and distrust lawyers as standing for the worst of the nation's values.

Lincoln lived in a time somewhat like this, and he was a politician and a lawyer. His nation was stuck on the issue of slavery. Lincoln's task was to get it unstuck—to find a way for the nation to think about its hopes, ideals, and institutions in better ways. We might say new and better ways, but I think he might have said older and better ways. He looked for ways that fulfilled the nation's promises. He would have to show the nation that law and politics—what I call the political constitutional system—could work to fulfill the best hopes of this land. Being the kind of man he was, he had no alternative

---

but to embrace the political constitutional system to achieve the ideal of equality and thus kill slavery.

I think that Harry Jaffa understood this Lincoln best. Speaking of the Emancipation Proclamation, he observes, "In a sense it is true that Lincoln never intended to emancipate the Negro: what he intended was to emancipate the American republic from the curse of slavery, a curse which lay upon both races, and which in different ways enslaved them both."

Jaffa is clearly right about Lincoln's actions during the war, but the insight applies equally well to Lincoln's efforts before Sumter. It was then that he developed a way of thinking about the nation and about slavery that would ultimately free the Republic. To understand that emancipation, it is necessary to understand the powerful and wide-ranging impact of slavery. The power of slavery consisted of more than the immediate force that whites could use upon blacks, more than whips and guns and shackles and threats to separate families. The power was sustained by "a lock with a hundred keys," as Lincoln said. And the keys were held throughout the nation in the form of ideas that whites held that protected slavery. Racism was the most potent of these ideas, yet equally potent was the belief, in North and South, that the rule of law, and hence the Constitution itself, somehow protected slavery. Reinforcing that belief were the arguments, by Stephen Douglas especially, that democracy was compatible with slavery. Two ideas and institutions that whites treasured, that were part of their daily experience and enduring self-image, had thus been almost captured by slavery. Unless slavery could be separated from them, it might endure forever. It was Lincoln's prewar task to emancipate whites from these ideas.

Before the conflict began, Lincoln had begun the process of emancipating the Republic. What he did before the war made it possible to free the slaves during the war and connect emancipation with the other goals of the war, saving the Union and preserving the Constitution. But connecting Lincoln to both equal liberty and the rule of law, especially in the prewar years, is not an easy task because there is a powerful Lincoln who stands in the way. Lincoln's words and deeds make him compelling, and we not only want to get right with Lincoln, but we also want him to guide us as we face our problems.

There is no more compelling contemporary problem than defining and securing equality. And because he was the great emancipator, nothing seems more natural than to turn to Lincoln on the topic, as historians and the general public have done so passionately. Historians and the public have created and admired a man whose foremost contribution was freeing the slaves, overcoming constitutional obstacles and transcending the conservative impulses of mere Union-saving as he did so.

In Garry Wills's view, he is the idealist for equality whose "words . . . remade America" by changing the way Americans think about the meaning of the nation and the Constitution. Wills believes that Lincoln thought that the "Declaration somehow escaped the constraints that bound the Constitution. It was free to state an ideal that transcended its age, one that serves as a touchstone for later strivings." Wills sees Lincoln as a twentieth-century egalitarian, a champion who could master modern states' rights advocates, from Wilmore Kendall in 1963 to Robert Bork, Edward Meese, and Ronald Reagan in the 1980s, who denied that equality was a national commitment. Wills argues that the Gettysburg Address made advancing equality a federal responsibility. The instrument of that advance was the use of the "Declaration . . . as a way of correcting the Constitution itself." The flawed Constitution must be redeemed by a glorified Declaration that would advance the modern struggle for equality. The rule of law must be rescued by an appeal to something nobler.

Understandably, Lincoln the egalitarian, not the constitutionalist, is compelling in the age of the Second Reconstruction. Americans in the last third of the twentieth century live in a world of 'Freedom Now.' Equality's greatest modern hero, Martin Luther King, Jr., spoke for a higher law and met often bloody opposition from those who wrapped themselves in the constitutional rhetoric of states' rights and interposition. When the specific words of segregation were stricken from constitutional law, "institutional racism" remained, perhaps even more insidious than its blatant, ugly, brutal parent. In 1987, as the nation celebrated the bicentennial of the Constitution, the contrast between constitutionalism and a commitment to equality may have reached its most respectable peak. Thurgood Marshall, who was the first black justice of the Supreme Court and who had fought racism from within the legal system for decades, publicly doubted that blacks should rejoice: "Commemorating the Wrong Document?" he asked. Here was a disturbing and forceful contrast between constitutional order and equality.

Historians contributed to the contrast. They had been engaged in discussions that split Lincoln the constitutionalist from Lincoln the liberator. They debated whether Lincoln was devoted to the Declaration of Independence *or* to the Constitution. The two documents stand at the foundation of what the country is and define the terms and possibilities for the polity. The Constitution is admired for the machinery that established national supremacy and preserved a Union, the Declaration for proclaiming the ideal that "all men are created equal" and resting legitimate government on that ideal. Reflecting the modern egalitarian consensus, the authoritative *Abraham Lincoln Encyclopedia* says, "As an antislavery man, Lincoln had a natural affinity not for the Constitution (with its compromising protections of the slave interest) but for the Declaration of Independence." The powerful Lincoln that stands in our way is Lincoln the egalitarian, the defender of the Declaration rather than the Constitution.

I think this view of Lincoln is wrong. And I think that if we accept it without qualification we weaken our faith in the ability of political-constitutional institutions to achieve our egalitarian ideals. When we lose that faith, we have seriously crippled our ability to reach such ideals at all. Ironically, if Lincoln the emancipator overcomes Lincoln the constitutionalist, the possibility for securing equality will be weakened.

The point to remember, if we wish to understand the past and enhance Lincoln's relevance to modern times, is this: He was equally committed to the political constitutional system and to the ideal of equality. Both mattered profoundly to him, and he believed that one could not be achieved without the other. He fashioned a connection between them, not during the war years, but before.

Before the war, the nation witnessed a great debate about the viability of its institutions, a discussion provoked by the presence of slavery in a nation that proclaimed equality. Of course, the debates between Lincoln and Douglas are well known, but during the late 1850s the nation experienced a three-cornered debate. Lincoln faced Douglas, but Douglas introduced a third party—Roger Taney and the Supreme Court's Dred Scott decision. Douglas and Taney represented two ideas. Douglas represented himself as the spokesman for democracy. He argued that the people of a territory or state could decide for themselves whether they wanted slavery. The great principle of self-government, of democracy in action, was the sovereignty of the people. He called it "popular sovereignty." Democracy, Douglas said, could legitimately endorse slavery. And, turning the proposition around, if someone attacked the people's decision about slavery, that someone—Lincoln, for example—would be challenging democratic self-government.

Then Douglas injected Roger Taney into the debate, and Taney, as chief justice of the U.S. Supreme Court, represented the voice of the Constitution. Douglas pointed out that the nation's highest tribunal in the Dred Scott decision had protected slavery in the territories. According to the Dred Scott decision, the Framers of the Constitution believed in slavery and endorsed its expansion. Again turning the proposition around, if someone—Lincoln, for example—attacked slavery, he attacked the Constitution.

Faced with the propositions that democratic self-government and the Constitution protected slavery, some turned against this debased rule of law. Demanding the equality of all people as promised in the Declaration of Independence, abolitionists such as William Lloyd Garrison said, "To Hell with the Constitution." Garrison burned copies of the Constitution in public, and some of the era's best and brightest agreed that law-breaking was necessary to attack slavery. Harriet Beecher Stowe indicted lawyers along with politicians and market-driven flesh peddlers as responsible for slavery. Emerson called the fugitive slave law a "filthy enactment," and vowed, "I will not obey it by God!" Thoreau wrote *Civil Disobedience* to insist that breaking the law was the only recourse in a society in which respecting the law meant protecting slavery.

The ideas were noble, but dangerous in a society that respected law so passionately. The Constitution, almost since its creation, has been the nation's "uncrowned king." Americans overwhelmingly have debated alternatives in constitutional terms. To call a law unconstitutional has either ended the debate or inspired a countercharge also made in constitutional terms. Few people in the nation's history have ever successfully answered the argument that a position is constitutional by saying, "Big deal!" or "So what?" Burning the Constitution, whether literally or figuratively, is like burning the flag. It burns people up. Respect for the Constitution and the processes it establishes are basic to being an American. However divided we may be by race, class, gender, or ethnicity, the one thing that unites and defines Americans is the political-constitutional process. As Senator Christopher Dodd, among others, has said, "Our means *are* our ends." There is, therefore, a great deal at stake in the process of getting right with the Constitution and the rule of law.

Lincoln faced the formidable challenge of proving Taney and Douglas wrong. He had to show that the Constitution and the democratic process supported his position and that of his party, that "all men are created equal" included, to some degree or other, black people as well as whites. The alternative to slavery did not have to be law-breaking or anarchy. Douglas and the Democratic party he represented insisted at almost every opportunity that Lincoln and the Republican party were abolitionists who threatened the established order and endangered the constitutional process. Lincoln's job was to refute that assertion and show how order and justice, the Constitution and the Declaration's faith in equal liberty, could be reconciled.

Although the dominant modern writing about Lincoln has emphasized his egalitarian ideas, a truer Lincoln is found by revealing his more dominant side. That does not mean that we must substitute Lincoln the lawyer for Lincoln the emancipator. It does mean that we must respect the fact that this very complex man was both, and one depended on the other. Lincoln's commitment to the existing order shaped the way he integrated the Declaration's ideals into the system of order at the core of his personality and beliefs. It is a story of evolution.

In the early days of his life, Lincoln paid minimal attention to the Declaration's ideals. He was working his way into, and then shaping, the institutions that defined the status quo. He was part of the establishment in at least two critical senses. Economically, he was a successful lawyer whom the major business in the state, the Illinois Central Railroad, hired to defend its interests. More viscerally, Lincoln had worked his way up to this position from the bottom. Starting as a landless, uneducated laborer separated by choice from his father's support and backing, such as it was, he advanced in the system whose major myths eulogized just such a rise. His personal experience both validated and personified that myth.

Lincoln built his economic security on the two occupations most entwined with the system: He was a lawyer and he was a politician. His law practice required that he know the rules and procedures that settled disputes and distributed resources. For years of his life he traveled the circuit in Illinois, without the respite of home for many weeks at a time, absorbed in the camaraderie and the contests of argument and negotiation, and he learned to link fellowship and vocation. Because he was the most admired and welcomed of his colleagues in this arena, he could hardly escape believing that things went well there. The law and the environment of lawyering, of making the system work, were integral to Lincoln's life.

And, as Herndon said, "Politics were his life." He spent seven formative years in the Illinois state legislature, one term in Congress, and maneuvered and manipulated the political system throughout his mature years, working out political bargains in which ambitious men might take turns holding public office. His papers are interwoven with lists and evaluations of vote totals as well as letters discussing which candidates would get the most votes where and why. And he reveled in it. There, in the public sphere, doing the public's business, Lincoln replicated his legal career—admired and enjoyed by colleagues, forming coalitions, logrolling, forging majorities, compromising, and cajoling. He had seen and shaped politics with considerable pleasure and frequent success.

Lincoln's private and personal values strongly emphasized order. The climb out of rural poverty had shown him the need for the mind to overcome a life controlled by nature and circumstance. His experiences showed the terror of the loss of reason. He had been present, and only sixteen, when young Matthew Gentry, a companion in Indiana, suddenly went insane. The memory haunted him for years. He did not drink alcohol because it made him feel "flabby and undone." He studied the six books of Euclid's *Geometry* in order to train himself to think carefully and keenly, a regimen that paralleled his reading of the law. Thus the utopia he envisioned was of a "happy day when all appetites controlled, all passions subdued, all matters subjected, *mind,* all conquering *mind* shall live and move." If ever a man had reason for devotion to the system, the establishment in all of its manifestations, it was Abraham Lincoln.

The public political environment in which he matured also inspired commitment to order. As Jacksonian democracy rose it was accompanied by mob rule and by vigilante attacks on abolitionists, bank officers, gamblers and blacks. Jackson inspired establishment leaders to fear that things were not going their way; one in fact called Jackson "a concentrated mob." In this environment Alexis de Tocqueville worried about "the tyranny of the majority" and lauded local self-government institutions as a remedy. Anti-Jackson politicians formed the Whig party, built on challenges to Jackson's "mobocracy" as well as in support of government aid for economic development. Although President Jackson had said, "Never for a moment believe that the great body of the citizens . . . can deliberately intend to do wrong," Lincoln was dubious. His view of "the people" consistently was cast within discussions of government, laws, and the need for restraint. He was so little committed to Jackson's shibboleth that although he

analyzed other political concepts at length he gave posterity a thirty-three-*word* definition of democracy. Lincoln was no democrat as the word was understood in his century.
It is not surprising that he left the Democratic party his father had supported and joined
the Whigs. This anti-Jacksonian frame of mind positioned Lincoln to not be disarmed
by Douglas's incantations about popular sovereignty.

Thus young Lawyer Lincoln cast the balance between the accomplishments of 1776
and those of 1787 by arguing that the Constitution and the institutions it established were fundamental. Speaking in early 1838 at the Young Men's Lyceum of Springfield on "the
perpetuation of our political institutions," he noted that with Jefferson and the other
Framers dead a new generation had to achieve their ideals by respecting the institutions
the Founders had made, not simply by proclaiming their principles. With the men of the
Revolution gone, succeeding generations could fulfill their mission by making reverence
for the Constitution and the laws "the political religion of the nation. . . . as the patriots of
seventy six did to support the Declaration of Independence. . . . so to the support of the Constitution and the Laws, let every American pledge his life, his property and his sacred honor."

The Constitution was thus the means to the Declaration's ends. But how? At first
Lincoln was not very clear about that. He was not even very clear about what the ends
of the Declaration might be with respect to equality. During the 1840s and early 1850s
he was essentially satisfied with the course of events, too busy building a career to attend
to the issue seriously.

Clearly, Lincoln hated slavery in principle. "If slavery is not wrong, nothing is
wrong," he told a correspondent in 1864. "I cannot remember when I did not so think,
and feel." He cared about the suffering of the slaves, but his sympathy was held in check
by other commitments. Until the institution reached out to trouble and threaten the overall
operation of the polity, he was content to stick to his law business, and even within that
business to defend at least one slave-chaser's right to his chattel.

He understood, but would not join, abolitionist organizations that attacked the
personal and human horrors of the institution. Lincoln first spoke publicly against slavery
in 1837. He joined another Springfield lawyer and Whig to protest against resolutions
that attacked abolition societies and defended states' rights to property in slaves. Lincoln
called slavery unjust and bad policy but asserted that abolition societies "tend[ed] rather
to increase than to abate its evils." In July 1848 he supported the Wilmot Proviso and
challenged the expansion of slavery into the territories. But his challenges to that
expansion came while defending the Whig party's overall program against charges that
the Free-Soil party was a better choice than his own. The existing party system was
adequate to deal with all the evils of society. In 1852 Lincoln was still defending the
established polity, emphasizing that devotion to the rule of law would somehow keep
alive the Declaration's principles. In his eulogy to Henry Clay he applauded his "beau
ideal of a statesman" for both opposing slavery and maintaining respect for the Union
and the laws. In the campaign of that year Lincoln again linked his opposition to slavery
with respect for the political-constitutional system. Arguing that the Whig party would
oppose slavery more faithfully than the Democrats, he still disavowed opposition
outside existing institutional channels. Noting that Democrats were trying to use Seward's inflated rhetoric to discredit the Whigs, Lincoln embraced order. He said that if
Seward's "higher law" speech "may attempt to foment a disobedience to the constitution
or to the constitutional laws of the country, it has my unqualified condemnation." Lincoln
did hate slavery, but he was aroused to passionate opposition only when it threatened the
constitutional-political system.

Until 1854 Lincoln saw little threat. It was enough to decry democratic excesses, to deflate occasional overenthusiastic bombast, to temper abolitionist zeal with rather standard admonitions about respecting order, and to deplore slavery but basically to let the issue alone. It is likely that Lincoln believed that the processes begun in 1787 were quietly and inevitably keeping the promises of 1776.

But on May 22, 1854, everything changed. The House of Representatives passed the Kansas-Nebraska bill, repealed the Missouri Compromise, and opened a million square miles of territory to slavery. More than that, it proclaimed loudly that the constitutional system no longer incorporated promises of equal liberty. Stephen Douglas had found that popular sovereignty justified repealing the Missouri Compromise. The Illinois senator argued that the people of a territory could do whatever they chose about slavery there. The law of the land was now neutral on equal rights. Popular government meant that some men could deny equal liberty to others because of the color of their skin. The Declaration's idea that "all men are created equal" had been banished from its constitutional context.

Lincoln's task was to put it back into that context, to retain the ties between declaring ideals and constituting a political-constitutional culture to realize them. Throughout the 1850s he began to think more deeply about the interrelationships between the documents and principles of 1776 and 1787. The result would be an even greater interconnection between constitutional process and egalitarian promises. But creating that interconnection would have a consequence. It would require that Lincoln change the nature of Jefferson's 1776 promise.

Lincoln's reconciliation of the Constitution and the Declaration rested on both logic and history. In the first place, he simply equated self-government with equality. Challenging the Kansas-Nebraska bill, he wrote, "At the foundation of the sense of justice there is in me" is the "proposition that each man should do precisely what he pleases with all that is exclusively his own." That was at the core of self-government. "No man is good enough to govern another man, *without that other's consent.*" And this principle, "the sheet anchor of American republicanism," rested on the ideals of the Declaration that "all men are created equal," which meant that governments had to rest on the consent of those men. "Allow all the governed an equal voice in the government, and that, and that only is self government." The ideal of equality was manifested in acts of self-government. Ideal depended on process. Expanding slavery imperiled process and ideal.

Lincoln also used history to integrate ideals and institutions. Douglas had employed history to show that the Framers wanted to leave slavery alone and hence had no moral objection to it. Chief Justice Taney in the Dred Scott case had used history (Harold Hyman calls it "twistory") to argue that the Declaration of Independence revealed the proslavery ideals of the Framers. Both Taney and Douglas thus created a proslavery founding and a proslavery Constitution.

When Lincoln turned historian, the past that he found and fashioned revealed freedom's Constitution, not slavery's. The angle of vision he adopted was to look into the founding years and see not two founding events but one founding age. The age of the Founders that Lincoln found turned the writing of the Declaration in 1776 and the writing of the Constitution in 1787 into one event. Eleven years passed between the two gatherings in Independence Hall, and only six men who signed the Declaration signed the Constitution. For Lincoln, however, they were essentially one meeting, bonded in the act of founding the country. In the entire corpus of his writing he never separated the two events.

And he insisted that the egalitarian principles that animated the Declaration abided in the writers of the Constitution. Speaking against the Kansas-Nebraska bill in October 1854, he noted that the writers of the Constitution thought that slavery violated basic principles, and so they never mentioned slavery in the document. And "the earliest Congress, under the constitution, took the same view of slavery. They hedged and hemmed it in to the narrowest limits of necessity." In his February 1860 Cooper Union Address, he researched the history of the Framers' world extensively to prove that they had wanted to place slavery in the course of ultimate extinction. Because almost all the Framers thought slavery was an evil that contradicted the ideal of equality, they voted frequently and consistently throughout the 1780s and 1790s, Lincoln said, to prohibit slavery in the territories. At Gettysburg he would envision a nation born in 1776 and dedicated to equality, but it was "*government* of the people by the people and for the people" that would bring to life the "equality proposition." The government he had in mind was that created by the Constitution in 1787.

Lincoln stepped over the constitutional fences of the Taney Court; he moved beyond guidelines proclaimed by his Democratic opponents. And they indicted him as an enemy of the Constitution. But this was an accusation, not a legitimate verdict. Lincoln operated within the constitutional possibilities of the founding years. For him, achieving the ideals of the Declaration meant preserving the government brought forth in 1787. He referred to the idea of "Liberty to all" in the Declaration as an "apple of gold," and to the "Union and the Constitution" as "the picture of silver." Although asserting that the picture was made for the apple and not vice-versa, he also said, "Let us act, that neither picture, or apple shall ever be bruised or broken."

Lincoln insisted on his devotion to the Declaration's basic ideal that all men are created equal. "I have never had a feeling politically," he said, "that did not spring from the sentiments embodied in the Declaration of Independence." His strongest charge against the expansion of slavery was that it showed how far the nation had fallen from its founding ideals. "Near eighty years ago we began by declaring that all men are created equal," he observed, "but now from that beginning we have run down to the other declaration, that for SOME men to enslave others is 'a sacred right of self government.'" Thus the rise of proslavery sentiment revealed a decline of the nation from a purer past in which the constitutional system had put slavery on a course to ultimate extinction.

But if the basic ideal abided, Lincoln's political environment required changes in what the Framers meant by that ideal. These changes would highlight constitutional process. Illinois in Lincoln's time was hardly committed to racial equality; a state law of 1853 kept blacks out. The Illinois legal code forbade interracial marriage, kept blacks off juries and out of the state militia, banned black testimony against whites, denied blacks the vote, and made no provision for black schools. Racism, especially in the southern half of Illinois, predominantly settled from slave-holding states, was a powerful and practically unchallengeable notion.

Thus when Lincoln challenged the expansion of slavery by proclaiming that all men were created equal, Douglas and other Democrats played the race card. They howled miscegenation and named Republicans "Black Republicans." To counter the charge Lincoln had to reassure constituents, first in Illinois, then in the Midwest and beyond as his political horizons expanded, that he did not favor Negroes voting, performing jury service, or holding office. He did believe that the Declaration's promise of equality extended to life, liberty, and the pursuit of happiness. To Lincoln in the prewar years that meant that blacks had "the right to eat the bread, without leave of anybody else, which his own hand earns." And he mocked Douglas's charges by noting that treating blacks as human beings, with rights to keep the fruits of their own labor, hardly required intermarriage. But he also knew the dangers of advocating full equality and so was pushed to temporize by speaking of an equality to come. It was clearly a more respectable position than slavery forever and the assertion that blacks were inalterably inferior in everything, but it pandered. Political prejudice on race thus played its role in moving Lincoln to a new, or at least more well-defined, position not only on what equality might mean but also on how and when it would be achieved.

So did the charges that Republicans were disunionists. At times Lincoln fed those allegations—his House Divided speech spoke of the nation split in two and suggested the threat in that division by noting that *either* freedom or slavery must triumph. But the future president was quick to deny this accusation. What was at stake, he claimed, was a struggle for the minds of men over the question of whether slavery or freedom controlled the territories and hence the future. It was a debate that would be resolved not with invasion or threat, but through political discourse that would create a return to idealism. This reassurance actually only promised Dixie a slow death for slavery if people like Lincoln won office. But it also suggested how a healthy political-constitutional process could bring the Declaration's egalitarian promise to life. This too pushed Lincoln toward redefining the meaning of 1776.

Lincoln built another element of his evolving constitutional egalitarianism thanks to Chief Justice Roger Taney. When the Supreme Court issued its Dred Scott decision Lincoln again was forced to ponder new directions. Less than a year earlier he had spoken of trusting the Court to decide the constitutional question of the exclusion of slavery from the territories. But when the decision was handed down, Lincoln enlarged his ground and expanded the arena of constitutional discussion. He flanked the decision on two sides. First, Lincoln adopted Andrew Jackson's argument that the Court did not stand alone as interpreter of the Constitution. "The Congress, the executive and the court, must each for itself be guided by its own opinion of the Constitution." Congressmen and chief executive now joined judges in the constitutional debate. The meaning of the Constitution was too important to be left to judges. Second, Lincoln posited a discussion expanded in time as well as numbers. An important judicial decision would be binding, Lincoln said, only after a long process of discussion and litigation had taken place. What legitimized such a decision was "the steady practice of the departments throughout our history," arguments in previous courts in which the decision "had been affirmed and reaffirmed though a course of years." This process of determining what the Constitution meant also involved electing to office men who would reflect public opinion on such questions. The people would join the debate to instruct their leaders and to maintain their own authority as ultimate sovereigns. The electoral process set up by the Constitution would, in time, overcome the flawed constitutional vision of the Supreme Court.

Having formulated a vigorous and involved political-constitutional debate that responded to the political imperatives of his age, Lincoln was now ready to evoke a new Declaration, one demanded by the system he envisioned and the world he occupied. He did not change his commitment to equality. But where the Founders had declared all men are created equal to be a "self-evident truth" Lincoln envisioned it as a "proposition"— the word would wait until Gettysburg, the idea was present in 1857. Equality was a "standard maxim for a free society, which should be familiar to all and revered by all;

constantly looked to, constantly labored for, and even though never perfectly attained, constantly approximated, and constantly spreading and deepening its influence, and augmenting the happiness and value of life to all people of all colors everywhere." And the only way for that process to occur was for constitutional government to endure. Equal liberty and the order of law were thus intertwined and interdependent.

"A house divided against itself cannot stand" Lincoln had said. Yet equally destructive were conflicting national ideals: democracy and the rule of law set against equality. But Lincoln had integrated these widespread and deeply felt ideals by showing that equality could only be achieved within their institutions of self-government. The beloved Constitution was not the property of Taney and the slave owners for whom he spoke any more than the democratic self-government that Douglas endorsed required implacable racism. Lincoln had helped the nation to become "unstuck"; he had provided a way of thinking about the sectional crisis that united the nation's best and most inescapable qualities in the struggle to free the nation from slavery.

Lincoln so interwove the ideals of the Declaration with the Constitution, with the processes of self-government, that attempts to unravel the threads dissolve his thought. And such efforts also obscure the meaning of his presidency. Saving the Union and ending slavery and defending the right of the people to change governments by ballots not bullets, and thus show the world that self-government worked, were interrelated parts of what Lincoln wanted to do. And as he assumed office he took "the most solemn oath" to preserve protect and defend a Constitution that in his view embodied all of those parts.

There was irony in the fact that Lincoln in the White House had more power to preserve the Declaration's ideal than any other person in the country and had made a clearer promise to do so than almost any other public official. His attacks on slavery were eloquent enough to rally an electoral majority behind him. He had gained their support in perhaps the only way that the age permitted, by appealing to their faith that the system would work for the best of their ideals. If Taney or Breckenridge or Bell or even Stephen Douglas had his way, freedom moved to a future so distant as to be unimaginable and unacceptable to most whites and blacks. Lincoln countered that. But his process-based egalitarianism made only long-term promises. If he would have his way, he said in August 1858, "The crisis would be past and the institution might be let alone for a hundred years, if it should live so long, in the States where it exists, yet it would be gone out of existence in the way best for both the black and the white races." Somehow, the process would work for the ideal; somehow, the Constitution would implement the Declaration. The North now had the vision to believe that, but achieving it would be a complex and agonizing process for the people and the president who assumed power in 1861.

Yet at least Lincoln's thought—and his education of the public in that thought—had laid the foundation for making a struggle for the Union simultaneously a struggle for the ideal of equality. The people of the North were passionate in their commitment to self-government and devoted to the Constitution as they understood it. Lincoln made it possible for that devotion to incorporate the promises of 1776 within the processes of 1787. He had begun the process of emancipating the Republic from slavery. He had suggested how the best might regain their conviction that their most admirable hopes could be achieved within the system of order they were devoted to. War might accelerate this union of equality with the rule of law even as Lincoln and the North fought to save the Union.

Tried by War: Lincoln As Self-Taught Strategist

JAMES M. McPHERSON

Abraham Lincoln is revered as the Great Emancipator. He is remembered most for the Gettysburg Address, the Emancipation Proclamation, and the closing lines of his second inaugural address, which urged the binding up of the nation's wounds with malice toward none and charity for all. Biographies focus on his rise from humble birth in a frontier log cabin, his political career, and his attitude toward slavery.

Far less vivid is our image of Lincoln as commander in chief of the largest army, in proportion to population, ever sent into the field by the United States. Scholarship on Lincoln's military leadership is much thinner than on other aspects of his career. The best reference work, Mark E. Neely's *Abraham Lincoln Encyclopedia* (1982), devotes less than five percent of its space to military matters. Of the 17 essays on Lincoln published in 1987 by Don E. Fehrenbacher, one of the foremost Lincoln scholars of our time, not one deals with the president as a military leader. On the 175th anniversary of Lincoln's birth, Gettysburg College hosted a conference on recent Lincoln scholarship. There were three sessions on psychobiography, two on the assassination, two on Lincoln's image in photographs and popular prints, one each on his economic ideas, religion, humor, Indian policy, and slavery. But there were no sessions on Lincoln as commander in chief—a remarkable irony for a conference held on the site of the largest battle in the history of the Western Hemisphere.

Merrill D. Peterson's splendid study *Lincoln in American Memory* (1994) has chapters on Lincoln and the South, religion, politics, Reconstruction, civil rights, and several other themes, but no chapter on Lincoln and the army. The most recent biography, by David Herbert Donald (1995), and the most recent study of Lincoln's presidency, by Phillip Shaw Paludan (1994), give less attention to Lincoln as commander in chief than to politics, slavery, and emancipation. It is almost as if historians take at face value Lincoln's self-mocking reference, in a congressional speech of 1848, to his earlier militia service in the 1832 Black Hawk War: "Did you know I am a military hero? . . . I fought, bled, and came away" after "charges upon the wild onions" and "a good many bloody struggles with the mosquitoes."

Whatever his role in the Black Hawk War, Lincoln's task as commander in chief during the Civil War was deadly serious. We must not forget that he was a *war president*. His entire tenure in office was bounded by war—from the crisis of impending war that landed on his desk the day after his March 1861 inauguration, to the Confederate partisan's bullet that took his life in April 1865. As Lincoln himself expressed it in his second inaugural address: on "the progress of our arms . . . all else chiefly depends."

That was why military matters required more of Lincoln's attention than did anything else during his presidency. He spent more time in the War Department telegraph office than anywhere except the White House. During crucial military operations he sometimes stayed all night at the telegraph office, reading and sending dispatches and snatching a few hours of sleep on a cot. He probably wrote the first draft of the Emancipation Proclamation in that office while awaiting news from the armies. That was quite appropriate, for the legal justification of the proclamation was Lincoln's war power to seize enemy property—slave labor—being used to wage war against the United States.

Lincoln was painfully aware that his Confederate counterpart in Richmond was better qualified than he as a military leader. Jefferson Davis had graduated from West Point, commanded a regiment in the Mexican War, and served four years (1853–1857) as an outstanding U.S. secretary of war. To remedy his deficiencies, Lincoln borrowed books on military strategy from the Library of Congress and burned the midnight oil reading them. His experience as a self-taught lawyer and his analytical mind (for mental exercise he had mastered Euclidean geometry on his own) stood him in good stead. By 1862 his orders and dispatches demonstrated a sound grasp of strategic principles.

Lincoln was intuitively aware of the concept that Prussian military theorist Karl von Clausewitz, in his classic treatise *On War* (1833), had defined as the essence of war: the continuation of politics by other means. He would also have recognized the distinction that modern military theorists make between two kinds of strategy: *national* strategy, or the shaping and defining of a nation's political goals in time of war, and *military* (or operational) strategy, the use of armed forces to achieve those goals. As president, Lincoln shared the power to determine national strategy with Congress and his cabinet. As commander in chief he could delegate power to his top generals to shape military strategy.

In both capacities, however, Lincoln believed himself ultimately responsible, and he jealously guarded his prerogatives, especially with respect to national strategy. Secretary of State William H. Seward initially aspired to be "premier" of Lincoln's administration. In his notorious memorandum of April 1, 1861, Seward proposed to abandon Union-held Fort Sumter in South Carolina's Charleston Harbor and pick a quarrel with European nations as a way to defuse passions in the South and reunite the country against a foreign foe. "Whatever policy we adopt," wrote Seward, "it must be somebody's business to pursue and direct it." He left little doubt as to whom he had mind. Lincoln ignored Seward's advice about provoking a foreign incident, stated that he intended to resupply Fort Sumter, and concluded firmly that whatever was done, "I must do it." Later that year, when Major General John Frémont issued a military order emancipating the slaves of Confederate supporters in Missouri, Lincoln rescinded it. He did so because his national strategy of keeping the border slave states—Delaware, Maryland, Kentucky, and Missouri—in the Union was then balanced on a knife edge. He feared that those states would join the Confederacy if Frémont's order stood. Eight months later, in May 1862, Major General David Hunter issued a similar emancipation edict in his military district embracing Union-occupied regions along the southern Atlantic coast. Stating angrily that "no commanding general shall do such a thing upon my responsibility, without consulting me," Lincoln rescinded Hunter's order. But he also warned that, as a matter of national strategy, he might soon find it necessary to exercise his war powers to declare the slaves in Confederate states free. Several months later, of course, he did so. When a Senate leader protested Lincoln's denial of Congress's constitutional power to legislate emancipation while simultaneously asserting his own power as commander in chief to proclaim it, Lincoln responded coolly: "I conceive that I may in an emergency do things on military grounds which cannot be done constitutionally by Congress."

These examples concern matters of national strategy: On questions of military strategy, Lincoln at first deferred to the professionals. The consummate professional in

1861 was General in Chief Winfield Scott, who formulated what the press derisively termed the "Anaconda Plan." A Virginian, Scott wanted to defeat the Confederacy at the lowest possible cost in lives and property. He proposed to "envelop" the South with a blockade by sea and a fleet of gunboats supported by soldiers moving down the Mississippi River to seal off the Confederacy from the outside world and "bring them to terms with less bloodshed than by any other plan."

Lincoln supported this military strategy. It was consistent with his initial national strategy of a limited war to *restore* the Union as it had existed before 1861. That national strategy in turn was grounded on the belief that a silent majority of the Southern people was Unionist at heart, but had been swept into the Confederacy by the passions of the moment. In his first Message to Congress, on July 4, 1861, Lincoln questioned "whether there is, to-day, a majority of the legally qualified voters of any State, except perhaps South Carolina, in favor of disunion." Once the Federal government demonstrated its firmness and determination by sealing off the Confederacy, those presumed legions of Unionists would regain control of their states and resume their normal place in the Union. That is why, in his initial call for militia on April 15, 1861, Lincoln defined the conflict not as a war but as a domestic insurrection—"combinations too powerful to be suppressed by the ordinary course of judicial proceedings"—and declared that in suppressing this insurrection the federalized militia would avoid "any devastation, any destruction of, or interference with, property, or any disturbance of peaceful citizens."

The Anaconda Plan would eventually achieve considerable success. The blockade slowly strangled the Confederacy, and the Mississippi was sealed off from Confederate use by July 1863. In the meantime, however, both national and military strategy evolved a long way from the limited war of 1861.

The first step in that evolution occurred at Bull Run, Virginia. This was a battle that Scott, distrustful of his 90-day militia, had not wanted to fight. But Northern opinion clamored for a push "Forward to Richmond!" Lincoln concurred with Quartermaster General Montgomery Meigs that "we would never end the war without beating the rebels" in a battle. Such a battle was consistent with a limited-war national strategy, for a Union victory would embolden the silent majority of Southern Unionists. When field commander Brigadier General Irvin McDowell protested that he needed more time to train his raw troops, Lincoln said, "You are green, it is true, but they are green, also; you are all green alike."

Defeat at Bull Run on July 21 sobered Lincoln. But it did not change his purpose or determination. The next day, he signed a bill for the enlistment of 500,000 three-year men. Three days later he signed a second bill authorizing another 500,000. He called Major General George B. McClellan, who had won minor victories in western Virginia, to become commander of the Army of the Potomac. He sat down and wrote a memorandum outlining a proposal for simultaneous advances in Virginia (Manassas and the rail junction of Strasburg) and in Tennessee (its eastern region and Memphis) once the new three-year men were trained. And he initially granted McClellan's pleas for plenty of time to train them. "All [I] wanted," Lincoln was later quoted as saying, "was some one who would take the responsibility and act. . . . [I] had never professed to be a military man or to know how campaigns should be conducted and never wanted to interfere with them." Even after McClellan replaced the aged and infirm Scott as general in chief on November 1, 1861, and began treating with disdain Lincoln's desire to be kept informed,

Lincoln had only this to say: "I will hold McClellan's horse if he will only bring us success."

Lincoln's faith in the silent majority of Southern Unionists began to wear thin after Bull Run. His military strategy focused increasingly on seizing crucial Confederate transport hubs and territory. He urged McClellan to move forward, and relayed similar wishes to Brigadier General Don Carlos Buell and Major General Henry W. Halleck in the West during the winter of 1861–1862.

By this time Lincoln's study of military strategy had begun to pay off. He grasped, sooner than many of his generals, the strategic concept that modern military theorists define as "concentration in time." Because their overall strategy was one of defending a territory that lay behind their front the Confederates had the advantage of "interior lines." That enabled them to shift reinforcements from inactive to active fronts—concentration in *space*—unless the Union used its superior numbers to attack on several fronts at once—concentration in *time*. On January 13, 1862, Lincoln wrote to Buell: "I state my general idea of this war to be that we have *greater* numbers, and the enemy has *greater* facility of concentrating forces upon points of collision; that we must fail, unless we can find some way of making our advantage an overmatch for *his;* and that this can only be done by menacing with superior forces at *different* points, at the same time; so that we can safely attack, one, or both, if he makes no change; and he weakens one to strengthen the other, forbear to attack the strengthened one, but seize, and hold the weakened one, gaining so much."

Napoleon could scarcely have expressed it better. But not for more than two long years would Lincoln have a general in chief who understood this idea. From Buell, Halleck, and McClellan came only a list of excuses for not moving forward. Almost in desperation, Lincoln tried on January 27, 1862, to prod his commanders into action. His General Order No. 1 instructed them to move forward on February 22, George Washington's birthday.

The order availed nothing. But before February 22, Brigadier General Ulysses S. Grant, the general who would earn Lincoln's greatest confidence, had captured Forts Henry and Donelson in Tennessee, along with 13,000 Confederate soldiers, and opened the Tennessee and Cumberland Rivers into the Confederacy's heartland. These successes started a ring of remarkable Union victories several locations in the winter and spring of 1862: Roanoke Island and New Bern in North Carolina; Pea Ridge, Arkansas; Shiloh, Tennessee; Corinth, Mississippi; and the whole Mississippi River—including New Orleans, Island No. 10, and Memphis—except (after July) the stretch between Vicksburg, Mississippi, and Fort Hudson, Louisiana. Even McClellan got off the mark and moved the Army of the Potomac up the Virginia Peninsula to within hearing distance of Richmond's church bells by May. The Confederate capital seemed doomed, and the Union military strategy of capturing important *places* seemed a brilliant success.

But then the Union war machine went into reverse. By September 1862 Confederate counteroffensives in Virginia, Tennessee, and Kentucky took Southern armies from the verge of defeat all the way across the Potomac River into Maryland and north almost to the Ohio River. This inversion stunned Northerners and caused home front morale to plummet. But Lincoln did not falter. He issued a new call for volunteers and declared that "I expect to maintain this contest until successful, or till I die, or am conquered, or my term expires, or Congress or the country forsakes me."

The period of spring and summer in 1862—that muddle of Union victories and defeats—was also the time when Lincoln had the most hands-on control over military strategy. When the dilatory McClellan had finally lurched the Army of the Potomac into motion in March, Lincoln had demoted him from general in chief and had, in effect, taken over that post himself. When Confederate Major General Thomas J. "Stonewall" Jackson carried out his offensive in Virginia's Shenandoah Valley in May, Lincoln stayed in the War Department telegraph room almost around the clock and fired off 50 telegrams to a half-dozen generals in an effort to get them to trap and destroy Jackson's army north of Winchester. But Jackson moved too fast and Union commanders moved too slowly, to Lincoln's disgust. Jackson slipped through the trap to wreak more havoc. A month later Lincoln again haunted the telegraph office, wiring repeated dispatches lo McClellan during the Seven Days' Campaign, in which General Robert E. Lee's Army of Northern Virginia drove the Yankees away from Richmond.

These experiences convinced Lincoln that he needed a military professional to take the burden of day-to-day operations from his shoulders. From the West he called Halleck, who had taken credit for successes in that theater. He also brought John Pope east, promoted him to major general, and gave him command of the newly created Army of Virginia. Lincoln supported Halleck's decision to withdraw the Army of the Potomac from the Virginia Peninsula to reinforce Pope's drive southward from Manassas. But McClellan dragged his feet, Pope put his headquarters where his hindquarters should have been, and in August 1862 the patched-together Union army lost the Second Battle of Bull Run.

Halleck almost broke down under the strain of this campaign and the simultaneous Confederate invasion of Kentucky. In this and subsequent crises Lincoln tried to get him to analyze problems and make decisions. "If in such a difficulty as this you do not help, you fail me precisely in the point for which I sought your assistance," Lincoln wrote to him. "Your military skill is useless to me, if you will not do this." Although Halleck remained in his position, Lincoln in effect had to take over his decision-making responsibilities, subsequently remarking that Halleck was little more than "a first-rate clerk"—useful in his way, but not in the way the president had hoped.

Against the advice of a majority of his cabinet, Lincoln put McClellan back in command of the merged Army of Virginia and Army of the Potomac after the Second Battle of Bull Run. Lincoln believed McClellan had "acted badly" in his slowness to reinforce Pope, but that he "has the Army with him. . . . We must use the tools we have. There is no man in the Army who can lick these troops into shape half as well as he. . . . If he can't fight himself, he excels in making others ready to fight."

McClellan did lick the army into shape and led it a victory, of sorts, in the September 17 Battle of Antietam, Maryland. But he let Lee get away to Virginia without further punishment, to Lincoln's despair. In the following weeks Lincoln alternately goaded and coaxed McClellan to attack Lee. "Cross the Potomac and give battle," read a telegram from Washington to McClellan. "Your army must move now while the roads are good." Lincoln went personally to talk with McClellan at the front—for the third time. After returning to the White House, he sat down and wrote McClellan a fatherly letter. "You remember my speaking to you of what I called your over-cautiousness. Are you not over-cautious when you assume that you can not do what the enemy is constantly doing?" McClellan had argued that his men could not march and fight until fully re-equipped. Yet the Confederates marched and fought with fewer supplies than McClellan already had. To wait for a full supply pipeline, Lincoln said, "ignores the question of *time*." If McClellan crossed the Potomac quickly and got between the enemy and Richmond he could force Lee into a fight to the finish. "We should not operate as to merely drive him away. If we can not beat the enemy where he now is [west of Harpers Ferry, in western Virginia], we never can. . . . If we never try, we shall never succeed."

But McClellan continued to sit tight. Meanwhile Buell's Army of the Ohio stopped the Confederate invasion of Kentucky at Perryville in October. Like McClellan, however, Buell proved sluggish in pursuit of the retreating Rebels, blaming supply shortages and bad roads. Lincoln grew exasperated. He could not "understand why we cannot march as the enemy marches, live as he lives, fight as he fights." To McClellan's complaints about broken-down horses, Lincoln fired back a sarcastic telegram: "Will you pardon me for asking what the horses or your army have done since the battle of Antietam that fatigues anything?" Lincoln's patience finally snapped. When Buell allowed the Confederates to get safely back to Tennessee, Lincoln removed him from command on October 24 and replaced him with Major General William S. Rosecrans. Two weeks later he finally sacked McClellan and replaced him with Major General Ambrose E. Burnside. Lincoln was tired, he told one of McClellan's supporters, of trying "to bore with an augur too dull to take hold."

Burnside got the message. He moved quickly, but was delayed in December by the failure of pontoons to arrive in time to form a bridge across the Rappahannock River at Fredericksburg. Lee got to Fredericksburg first, and dug in on heights above the town. Burnside attacked anyway, with disastrous results. A month later he tried a flanking movement, but was defeated by the elements when heavy rains bogged down his army in the notorious "Mud March." Army morale sank to an all-time low. Soldiers deserted by the hundreds, generals squabbled, and corps commander Major General Joseph Hooker said the country needed a dictator. Burnside clearly had to go. So Lincoln removed him from command, shifted several other malcontent generals to other theaters, resisted pressures to bring back McClellan—and put Hooker in command. Lincoln sent Hooker a letter: "I have heard, in such a way as to believe it, of your recently saying that both the Army and the Government needed a Dictator. Of course it was not *for* this, but in spite of it, that I have given you the command. Only those generals who gain successes, can set up dictators. What I ask of you now is military success, and I will risk the dictatorship."

Hooker started well, revived morale, reorganized his cavalry into a potent striking force, executed a superb flanking move that brought him onto Lee's rear at Chancellorsville, Virginia—and then froze, yielded the initiative to Lee, and lost the ensuing battle. Lee pressed his advantage and invaded Pennsylvania. He hoped to climax his year of extraordinary successes with one more victory—this time on Northern soil—that would force Lincoln to negotiate a peace that recognized Confederate independence. Hooker moved north, tracking Lee and complaining petulantly, like McClellan, that the administration was failing to support him. Lincoln took this as a bad sign, and on June 28, 1863, replaced Hooker with Major General George Gordon Meade, the sixth (if one counts McDowell and Pope) and, as it turned out, last commander of the Army of the Potomac.

While Lincoln tried one commander after another in the East, he stuck with his commander of the Army of the Tennessee in the West despite enormous pressures to get rid of him. After its meteoric rise at Fort Donelson, Ulysses S. Grant's star wavered and fell during the subsequent year. Barely snatching victory from the jaws of defeat at

Shiloh, he endured slights from Hallock, rumors of excessive drinking, and the failure of his first campaign against Vicksburg in December 1862. Through it all, Lincoln saw qualities in Grant that others failed to see. "*I can't spare this man; he fights,*" Lincoln said to those who criticized Grant as incompetent, a drunk, and a political liability to the administration. During the first three months of 1863, Grant's army seemed to be floundering aimlessly in swamps and bayous in its second attempt to get at Vicksburg. A rising crescendo of criticism demanded Grant's removal. Lincoln retained his faith in the general and parried these demands. "I think Grant has hardly a friend left, except myself," Lincoln said. But "what I want . . . is generals who will fight battles and win victories. Grant has done this, and I propose to stand by him." The next three months, April through June 1863, vindicated Lincoln's faith. When Confederate Lieutenant General John C. Pemberton surrendered Vicksburg and 30,000 soldiers to Grant on the Fourth of July, Lincoln declared: "Grant is my man and I am his the rest of the war."

One reason why Lincoln supported Grant was that the two men had come to share the conviction that the war could be won only by destroying enemy armies. Earlier, both had subscribed to conventional wisdom that capturing territory and important points such as ports, railroad junctions, and cities would bring the Confederacy to its knees. Union forces did all these things in the spring of 1862, driving the Confederates out of 50,000 square miles of their own territory. But then, in April, the Southerners counterpunched Grant at Shiloh so hard that they almost knocked him out. From June 1862 to June 1863 Confederate armies regained part of the territory they had lost, inflicted punishing defeats on Union forces, and invaded the North. Clearly, conquest and occupation of enemy territory would not win the war so long as enemy armies remained capable of reconquering it.

By May 1862 Grant had already changed his thinking; he considered the Union capture of Corinth a defeat because General P. G. T. Beauregard's Confederate army got away. In September, Lincoln regarded Lee's invasion of Maryland a blessing in disguise because it gave the Army of the Potomac an opportunity to cut off and trap the invaders. "Destroy the rebel army," Lincoln had instructed McClellan as he restored him to command. McClellan's failure to do so was the principal reason for his dismissal. In a strategy memorandum for Hooker before the Battle of Chancellorsville, Lincoln wrote that "our prime object is the enemies' army in front of us and is not with, or about Richmond." When Lee began to move north after the battle, Hooker proposed to cut in behind him to take Richmond. "*Lee's* Army, and not *Richmond,* is your true objective point," Lincoln wired back. As the Army of Northern Virginia moved into Pennsylvania, Lincoln told Hooker that this invasion "gives you back the chance that I thought McClellan lost last fall" to cripple the enemy far from his base. Three months later, Lincoln declared in frustration that "to attempt to fight the enemy slowly back to his intrenchments in Richmond . . . is an idea I have been trying to repudiate for quite a year. . . . If our army can not fall upon the enemy and hurt him where he is, it is plain to me that it can gain nothing by attempting to follow him over a succession of intrenched lines into a fortified city."

Lincoln believed that the July 1863 victory at Gettysburg presented the best chance of the war to destroy Lee. "If General Meade can complete his work, so gloriously prosecuted thus far, by the literal or substantial destruction of Lee's army, the rebellion will be over," Lincoln wrote when, almost simultaneously, he heard news of success at both Gettysburg and Vicksburg. When Meade let Lee get away without further damage,

Lincoln became angry and depressed: "Our Army held the war in the hollow of their hand & they would not close it." When Meade spoke of "driving the invader from our soil," Lincoln lost his temper. "Great God! . . . This is a dreadful reminiscence of McClellan. The same spirit moved McC. to claim a great victory because Pennsylvania and Maryland were safe. . . . Will our Generals never get that idea out of their heads? The whole country is our soil!" Lincoln sat down to write Meade a letter, which concluded: "My dear general, I do not believe you appreciate the magnitude of the misfortune involved in Lee's escape. He was within your easy grasp, and to have closed on him would, in connection with our other late successes, have ended the war. . . . Your golden opportunity is gone, and I am distressed immeasurably because of it." Upon reflection, Lincoln did not send this letter, which would surely have prompted Meade's resignation.

By 1863 Lincoln's conception of what it would take to win the war had evolved to a third stage. Because the conquest of territory and the destruction or crippling of enemy armies had both proved insufficient, Lincoln, like Major General William T. Sherman, became convinced that it was necessary to destroy Confederate resources used to wage war. This was a conviction that had begun to take root in his mind when Confederate counteroffensives in the summer of 1862 knocked Union forces back on their heels. It was the conviction that underlay the Emancipation Proclamation. "We must free the slaves or be ourselves subdued," Lincoln told his cabinet in July 1862. "The slaves were undeniably an element of strength to those who had their service, and we must decide whether that element should be with us or against us. . . . Decisive and extensive measures must be adopted. . . . We wanted the army to strike more vigorous blows. The Administration must set an example, and strike at the heart of the rebellion"—slavery.

The same logic fueled the orders that Pope issued in July 1862, with Lincoln's approval, when he took command of the Army of Virginia. Pope authorized his officers to seize Confederate property without compensation, to execute captured guerrillas who fired on Union troops behind the lines, and to expel civilians who sheltered guerrillas. In August 1862 Halleck sent orders to Grant in Tennessee, also with Lincoln's approval: "Take up all active [Rebel] sympathizers, and either hold them as prisoners or put them beyond our lines. Handle that class without gloves, and take their property for public use. . . . It is time that they should begin to feel the presence of the war."

Inevitably, Northern conservatives and purported Southern Unionists protested these policies. Lincoln had lost faith in those professed Unionists and the strategy of limited war that he had pursued in 1861 to avoid alienating them. Did they expect, he now asked sarcastically, him to fight this war "with elder-stalk squirts, charged with rose water? . . . This government cannot much longer play a game in which it stakes all, and its enemies stake nothing. Those enemies must understand that they cannot experiment for ten years trying to destroy the government, and if they fail still come back into the Union unhurt."

Sherman carried this logic to its ultimate conclusion. He left smoldering ruins in his tracks from Vicksburg to Meridian, Mississippi; from Atlanta to Savannah, Georgia; and from Savannah to Goldsboro, North Carolina. To Confederates who called him a barbarian, Sherman responded that they were lucky to get off so lightly. A commander "may take your house, your fields, your everything, and turn you all out, helpless, to starve. It may be wrong, but that don't alter the case. . . . Our duty is not to build up; it is rather to destroy both the rebel army and whatever of wealth and property it has founded its boasted strength upon." Lincoln never reproved Sherman for his scorched-earth strategy. On the contrary, after the destructive March to the Sea, Lincoln sent Sherman's army his "grateful acknowledgements." And to Major General Philip Sheridan, who cut a similar swath of destruction through the Shenandoah Valley, Lincoln conveyed the "thanks of the Nation, and my own personal admiration and gratitude."

When Grant came east in March 1864 to become general in chief and to make his headquarters with the Army of the Potomac, Lincoln finally had a commander who saw eye to eye with him on military strategy. Grant said that in the past the Union armies on various fronts had "acted independently and without concert, like a balky team, no two ever pulling together." This had enabled the Confederates to shift troops from one point to another to meet the most pressing danger of the moment—as they had done by sending Lieutenant General James Longstreet with two divisions from Virginia to Chickamauga, Georgia, in September 1863. Grant planned a campaign in 1864 for five Union armies stretched over a front of a thousand miles to undertake coordinated offensives. The two principal armies were those commanded by Meade in Virginia and Sherman in Georgia. "Lee's Army will be your objective point," Grant told Meade. "Wherever Lee goes, where you will go also." There was no mention of capturing Richmond. To Sherman Grant sent orders "to move against Johnston's army, to break it up and to get into the interior of the enemy's country as far as you can, inflicting all the damage you can against their war resources."

Lincoln was impressed. He told his secretary Grant was carrying out his "old suggestion so constantly made and as constantly neglected, to Buell & Halleck, *et al,* to move at once upon the enemy's whole line so as to bring into action our advantage our great superiority of numbers"—in other words, *concentration in time* to counteract the Confederacy's use of interior lines to *concentrate in space.* The smaller Union armies, even if they did not successfully attack the Confederates in their front, could at least pin them down and prevent reinforcements from being sent to Lee and General Joseph E. Johnston. As Lincoln put it, "Those not skinning can hold a leg." As matters turned out, the leg-holders (Major Generals Nathaniel P. Banks, Benjamin F. Butler, and Franz Sigel) did not do their job, enabling the Confederacy to hold out for another year. But in the end the skinners—Grant, Sherman, Sheridan, and Major General George H. Thomas—took off the South's hide.

With this military team in place, Lincoln could give more attention to the larger questions of *national,* rather than *operational* strategy—chiefly the conditions under which the war would end. On this matter Lincoln never wavered; his policy was unconditional surrender. In 1861 and 1862 this had meant return to the Union; by 1863 it meant a new birth of freedom as well. Through the flurry of peace feelers in the summer of 1864, when the war seemed to be going badly for the North, to the Hampton Roads peace conference in Virginia in February 1865, when it was going well, Union and emancipation were Lincoln's terms. Just as adamantly, Jefferson Davis insisted on Confederate independence. As Lincoln put it in December 1864, Davis "does not attempt to deceive us. He affords us no excuse to deceive ourselves. He cannot voluntarily reaccept the Union; we cannot voluntarily yield it. Between him and us the issue is distinct, simple, and inflexible. It is an issue which can only be tried by war, and decided by victory."

Four months after he wrote these words, Lincoln was struck down by an assassin's bullet at the moment of victory.

☞ *FURTHER READING*

Gabor S. Boritt, *Lincoln and the Economics of the American Dream* (1978)

——, ed., *Lincoln the War President* (1992)

——, ed., *Lincoln's Generals* (1994)

Richard Current, *The Lincoln Nobody Knows* (1958)

William C. Davis, *Jefferson Davis: The Man and His Hour* (1991)

David Herbert Donald, "Abraham Lincoln, Whig in the White House," in Donald, *Lincoln Reconsidered* (1961)

——, *Lincoln* (1995)

Don E. Fehrenbacher, *Prelude to Greatness: Lincoln in the 1850s* (1962)

——, *Lincoln in Text and Context: Collected Essays* (1987)

George M. Fredrickson, "A Man but Not a Brother," *Journal of Southern History* 41 (February 1975), pages 39–58

Herman Hattaway and Archer Jones, "Lincoln as Military Strategist," *Civil War History* 26 (1980), 293–303.

Ludwell H. Johnson, "Abraham Lincoln and Jefferson Davis as War Presidents: Nothing Succeeds Like Success," *Civil War History* 27 (1981), 49–63

James M. McPherson, *Abraham Lincoln and the Second American Revolution* (1991)

——, ed., *"We Cannot Escape History": Lincoln and the Last Best Hope of Earth* (1995)

Grady McWhiney, "Jefferson Davis as Military Strategist," *Civil War History* 21 (1975), 101–112

Mark E. Neely, Jr., *The Fate of Liberty: Abraham Lincoln and Civil Liberties* (1991)

——, *The Last Best Hope of Earth: Abraham Lincoln and the Promise of America* (1993)

Phillip Shaw Paludan, *The Presidency of Abraham Lincoln* (1994)

T. Harry Williams, *Lincoln and His Generals* (1952)

Garry Wills, *Lincoln at Gettysburg: The Words that Remade America* (1992)

Steven Woodworth, *Jefferson Davis and His Generals: The Failure of Confederate Command in the West* (1990)

CHAPTER
7

The Northern Home Front

Histories of wars concentrate on the movements and engagements of armies and on the actions of generals and soldiers. This is, after all, to be expected. In the case of the American Civil War, the preservation of its battlefields as parks and museums and the continuing fascination with its generals and battles mean that the actual fighting of the war will remain at the center of most people's interest in and awareness of this dramatic episode in the nation's history.

Yet armies, and the soldiers who fight in them, do not operate in a void. Their weapons, their food, and their uniforms are supplied by the economy of the society they are fighting for. In addition, the encouragement to persevere and the directives about the aims of the war and how they are to be achieved come from the civilians and government of that society. So the course of a war conducted by rival societies or states cannot be explained adequately without giving due consideration to the home front.

It is often and compellingly argued that the Union won the war because of the abundance of its resources, rather than the superiority of its generals and armies. With a considerably larger population and a more diversified and adaptable economy, the North had the material advantage. As the war progressed, this lead actually became more pronounced. Northern victory has also been attributed to the North's more effective system of government and political leadership. Both of these explanations direct attention away from the battlefield and toward the civilian world of the home front. As a result, there has been extensive study of the northern economy and how its resources were mobilized to sustain the war effort, as well as of the way the federal government raised troops and taxes and galvanized the states into cooperation rather than obstruction.

In recent years, historians' interest in the home front has changed direction. Instead of examining how the civilian economy and society contributed to the war, they have reversed the sequence and wondered how the war affected the citizenry. In other words, what was it like to live in the Northern states during the Civil War? What impact did the war have on communities when their young men left for the battle zone and pressure was placed by the demands of war on local facilities and resources? How were ordinary people affected by the war? These questions deemphasize the war and stress instead society during wartime. Even when the draft or other institutions created by the needs of war are studied, the emphasis is not so much on how they aided the war effort, as on who was involved, what those involved did in this particular situation or organization, and what changes in their own lives and in society at large re-

sulted. What emerges from this approach is the social history of the North during the war years.

As a result of this new perspective, the home front has taken center stage. But so too, ironically, has the battlefield, though in a different way from before. This resurgence of interest in both of these aspects of the war does not involve a contradiction, because it arises, to a large extent, from a common source. The people who have become the focus of attention on the home front are very similar to those who have piqued the curiosity of historians of combat. For both groups consist of the ordinary folk who lived in the towns and communities of the North. Some of them stayed at home, and others went off to war. Both civilians and soldiers were citizens of the same society, and their attitudes and experiences during those years when they participated in what Lincoln once called "a people's contest" are now being scrutinized and narrated afresh.

D O C U M E N T S

In this chapter on the Northern home front, both achievements and sacrifices are represented. The opening three documents illustrate the work of the United States Sanitary Commission. The first is extracted from an article written by Henry W. Bellows, the president of the Commission, in the *North American Review* of January 1864, explaining the commission's aims and operation. The speech Lincoln gave at the Philadelphia Central Fair on June 16, 1864 is the second item. And the third piece is Mary A. Livermore's account of how she and other women of the Northwestern branch of the commission took the initiative in the spring of 1863 to organize the first Sanitary Fair; the piece is extracted from her book, *My Story of the War* (1889).

The next group of documents deals with working people and their reaction to the war's impact. The fourth selection is a report to Secretary of State Seward concerning the feeling toward the new draft policy among workers in New Jersey; it comes from Martin Ryerson of Newton and was dated July 18, 1863. The fifth selection is the call by a group of trade union members, headed by S. Gilchrist of Louisville, Kentucky, for a meeting to form a North American assembly coordinating all the trades in the United States and Canada. Issued on August 13, 1864, this was one of the first attempts to coordinate the fledgling trade unions. The contemporaneous National Labor Union (NLU) was another, and more successful. The sixth item is a petition by seamstresses from Cincinnati, Ohio, who were employed to produce military uniforms. Their demand of February 20, 1865 was for better wages.

Henry W. Bellows Explains the Work and Goals of the Sanitary Commission, January 1864

. . . We have expended all this space and time upon the early struggles of the Sanitary Commission, not merely for the purpose of exhibiting the resolution with which it forced itself into a real existence, and became a power in the nation, but more especially to show how sturdily it held on to its original principle,—the root of whatever good it has accomplished; namely, that the government is, or ought to be, the soldier's best friend, the only friend in a situation to give him constant and efficient protection; and that the main service any outside allies can afford him must consist in arousing the government

From Henry W. Bellows, "The Sanitary Commission," *North American Review,* January 1864, pp. 178–179, 183–184.

to its duties to the soldier, and accustoming the soldier to recognize, respect, and lean upon the government care. Whatever struggles with the Medical Department the Sanitary Commission has at any time had, have always been, not in the way of obtaining rights, privileges, or opportunities for itself,—of making itself more active, important, and influential,—but, on the contrary, always in the way of stirring up the Department to a larger sense of its own duty, a more complete occupation of its own sphere, and such a successful administration of its affairs as would tend to render the Sanitary Commission, and all other outside organizations of beneficence to the army, unnecessary. . . .

. . . The objections to the Sanitary Commission have been precisely the objections that led to the rebellion, and to the war that made this Commission necessary,—objections to a Federal consolidation, a strong general government, a nationality and not a confederacy. State and local powers were claimed to be, not only more effective in their home and immediate spheres, but more effective out of their spheres, and in the promotion of ends that are universal. As South Carolina said she could take better care of her own commerce and her own forensic interests than the United States government, so Iowa and Missouri and Connecticut and Ohio insisted that they could each take better care of their own soldiers, after they were merged in the general Union army, than could any central or federal or United States commission, whatever its resources or its organization. Narrow political ambition, State sensibilities, executive conceit, and the pecuniary interests of agents, produced the same secessional heresies in regard to the national Sanitary Commission, that they either actually created, or have vainly tended to create, in regard to the general government itself.

Yet it can truly be said, that, while these tendencies have sometimes pulled with a fierce current against the Commission, they have never dragged it from its own moorings. They have borne away from it vast quantities of needed supplies upon most uncertain errands; they have greatly diminished the resources which should have poured into the reservoirs of the Sanitary Commission. But the wonder is, that, in spite of them, there should have been so prodigious a triumph of the Federal principle in the humane work of ministering to the army. Local, personal, and religious prejudices have all yielded, more or less slowly, but steadily, to the self-vindicating claims of the Sanitary Commission. At this moment, the only region in the loyal States that is definitely out of the circle is Missouri. The rest of our loyal territory is all embraced within one ring of method and federality. This is chiefly due to the wonderful spirit of nationality that beats in the breasts of American women. They, even more than the men of the country, from their utter withdrawal from partisan strifes and local politics, have felt the assault upon the life of the nation in its true national import. They are infinitely less *State-ish,* and more national in their pride and in their sympathies. They see the war in its broad, impersonal outlines; and while their particular and special affections are keener than men's, their general humanity and tender sensibility for unseen and distant sufferings is stronger and more constant. The women of the country, who ar the actual creators, by the labor of their fingers, of the chief supplies and comforts needed by the soldiers, have been the first to understand, appreciate, and co-operate with the Sanitary Commission. It is due to the sagacity and seal with which they have entered into the work, that the system of supplies, organized by the extraordinary genius of Mr. [Frederick Law] Olmsted, has become so broadly and nationally extended, and that, with Milwaukee, Chicago, Cleveland, Cincinnati, Louisville, Pittsburg, Philadelphia, New York, Brooklyn, New Haven, Hartford, Providence, Boston, Portland, and Concord for centres, there should be at least fifteen thousand Soldiers' Aid Societies, all under the control of women, combined, and united in a common work,—of supplying, through the United States Sanitary Commission, the wants of the sick and wounded in the great Federal army.

President Lincoln Addresses the Philadelphia Central Fair, June 1864

I suppose that this toast was intended to open the way for me to say something.

War, at the best, is terrible, and this war of ours, in its magnitude and in its duration, is one of the most terrible. It has deranged business, totally in many localities, and partially in all localities. It has destroyed property and ruined homes; it has produced a national debt and taxation unprecedented, at least in this country; it has carried mourning to almost every home, until it can almost be said that the "heavens are hung in black."

Yet the war continues, and several relieving coincidents have accompanied it from the very beginning which have not been known, as I understand, or have any knowledge of, in any former wars in the history of the world. The Sanitary Commission, with all its benevolent labors; the Christian Commission, with all its Christian and benevolent labors; and the various places, arrangements, so to speak, and institutions, have contributed to the comfort and relief of the soldiers. You have two of these places in this city—the Cooper Shop and Union Volunteer Refreshment Saloons. And lastly, these fairs, which, I believe, began only last August, if I mistake not, in Chicago, then at Boston, at Cincinnati, Brooklyn, New York, and Baltimore, and those at present held at St. Louis, Pittsburgh, and Philadelphia. The motive and object that lie at the bottom of all these are most worthy; for, say what you will, after all, the most is due to the soldier who takes his life in his hands and goes to fight the battles of his country. In what is contributed to his comfort when he passes to and fro, and in what is contributed to him when he is sick and wounded, in whatever shape it comes, whether from the fair and tender hand of woman, or from any other source, it is much, very much. But I think that there is still that which is of as much value to him in the continual reminders he sees in the newspapers that while he is absent he is yet remembered by the loved ones at home. Another view of these various institutions, if I may so call them, is worthy of consideration, I think. They are voluntary contributions, given zealously and earnestly, on top of all the disturbances of business, of all the disorders, of all the taxation, and of all the burdens that the war has imposed upon us, giving proof that the national resources are not at all exhausted, and that the national spirit of patriotism is even firmer and stronger than at the commencement of the war.

It is a pertinent question, often asked in the mind privately, and from one to the other, when is the war to end. Surely I feel as deep an interest in this question as any other can; but I do not wish to name a day, a month, or a year, when it is to end. I do not wish to run any risk of seeing the time come without our being ready for the end, for fear of disappointment because the time had come and not the end. We accepted this war for an object, a worthy object, and the war will end when that object is attained. Under God, I hope it never will end until that time. Speaking of the present campaign, General Grant is reported to have said, "I am going through on this line if it takes all summer." This war has taken three years; it was begun or accepted upon the line of restoring the national

From Abraham Lincoln, "Address at the Philadelphia Sanitary Fair," June 16, 1864, in *Abraham Lincoln: His Speeches and Writings,* pp. 751–753.

authority over the whole national domain, and for the American people, as far as my knowledge enables me to speak, I say we are going through on this line if it takes three years more.

My friends, I did not know but that I might be called upon to say a few words before I got away from here, but I did not know it was coming just here. I have never been in the habit of making predictions in regard to the war, but I am almost tempted to make one. If I were to hazard it, it is this: That Grant is this evening, with General Meade and General Hancock, and the brave officers and soldiers with him, in a position from whence he will never be dislodged until Richmond is taken; and I have but one single proposition to put now, and perhaps I can best put it in the form of an interrogative. If I shall discover that General Grant and the noble officers and men under him can be greatly facilitated in their work by a sudden pouring forward of men and assistance, will you give them to me? Are you ready to march? [Cries of "Yes".] Then I say, Stand ready, for I am watching for the chance. I thank you, gentlemen.

Mary Livermore Recounts How She Organized the Northwestern Sanitary Fair in 1864, 1889

The continued need of money for the purchase of comforts and necessaries for the sick and wounded of our army, had suggested to the loyal women of the Northwest many and various devices for the raising of funds. Every city, town, and village had had its fair, festival, party, picnic, excursion, concert, and regular subscription fund, which had netted more or less for the cause of hospital relief, according to the population, and the amount of energy and patriotism awakened. But the need of money for this sacred purpose still continued. Our brave men were still wrestling with the Southern rebellion, which, though oft-times checked, was not conquered. The hospitals whose wards were vacated by death, or recovery of their patients, were speedily refilled by new faces which disease had rendered pallid, and new forms shattered by cannon-shot or sabre-stroke. It was necessary to continue to pour down sanitary supplies for the comfort and care of the suffering soldiers, whose well-being, at that time, lay so near the hearts of all loyal men and women. Since the most valuable sanitary supplies could only be obtained with money, the ingenuity of women was taxed to the utmost to raise funds.

The expenses of the Northwestern Sanitary Commission had been very heavy through the summer of 1863, and every means of raising money had seemed to be exhausted. At last, Mrs. Hoge and myself proposed a great Northwestern Fair. We had been to the front of the army ourselves, and had beheld the practical working of the Sanitary Commission, with which we were associated. We knew its activity, its methods, its ubiquity, is harmony with military rules and customs, and we knew that it could be relied on with certainty when other means of relief failed. We saw that an immense amount of supplies was necessary for the comfort and healing of the army of brave invalids, and wounded men, that filled our military hospitals, and our hearts sank as we realized the depleted condition of the treasury of the Commission.

We were sure that a grand fair, in which the whole Northwest would unite, would replenish the treasury of the Commission, which, from the beginning, had sent to battle-fields and hospitals thirty thousand boxes of sanitary stores, worth, in the aggregate, a million and a half dollars. We knew, also, that it would develop a grateful

Mary A. Livermore, *My Story of the War* (Hartford: A. D. Worthington & Co., 1889), pp. 409–413.

demonstration of the loyalty of the Northwest to our beloved but struggling country. That it would encourage the worn veterans of many a hard-fought field, and strengthen them in their defence of our native land. That it would reveal the worth, and enforce the claims of the Sanitary Commission, upon those hitherto indifferent to them. That it would quicken the sacred workers into new life.

Accordingly, we consulted the gentlemen of the Commission, who languidly approved our plan, but laughed incredulously at our proposition to raise twenty-five thousand dollars for its treasury. By private correspondence, we were made certain of the support and co-operation of our affiliated Aid Societies, and our next step was to issue a printed circular, embodying a call for a woman's convention, to be held in Chicago on the 1st of September, 1863. Every Aid Society, every Union League, and every Lodge of Good Templars in the Northwest, were invited to be present, by representatives. Some ten thousand of these circulars were scattered through the Northwest. A copy was sent to the editor of every Northwestern paper, with the request that it might appear in his columns—a request generally granted—and clergymen were very generally invited by letter to interest their parishioners in the project.

Pursuant to this call, a convention of women delegates from the Northwestern states was held in Chicago on the 1st and 2d of September, at Bryan Hall. The convention was harmonious and enthusiastic. The fair was formally resolved on. The time and place for holding it were fixed. The delegates came instructed to pledge their respective towns for donations of every variety, and help to the utmost. The women delegates were remarkably efficient and earnest; for each society had sent its most energetic and executive members. This convention placed the success of the fair beyond a doubt, and Mrs. Hoge and myself saw clearly that it would surpass in interest and pecuniary profit all other fairs ever held in the country. . . .

This first Sanitary fair, it must be remembered, was an experiment, and was pre-eminently an enterprise of women, receiving no assistance from men in its early beginnings. The city of Chicago regarded it with indifference, and the gentlemen members of the Commission barely tolerated it. The first did not understand it, and the latter were doubtful of its success. The great fairs that followed this were the work of men as well as of women, from their very incipiency—but this fair was the work of women. Another circular was now issued, and this enumerated and classified the articles that were desired. It was a new experience to the Northwest, and advice and plans were necessary in every step taken. . . .

Martin Ryerson Reports How Workers Are Reacting to the Draft, July 1863

NEWTON, N.J., *July* 18, 1863.

Hon. WM. H. SEWARD,
        Secretary of State:

Dear Sir: I have learned this week much in relation to the state of affairs in New Jersey concerning the draft, which I deem it my duty to communicate through you to the Government, to the end that we may be spared the horrors of the New York riots.

Letter, Martin Ryerson to Secretary of State William Seward, Newton, N.J., July 18, 1863, *Official Records,* Series I, Vol. 27, Pt. 2, pp. 935–936.

On Monday last I went with my family to visit some friends in Trenton; returned yesterday, spending two days in Trenton; also visiting Elizabeth City, Newark, and Orange, seeing intelligent persons from other parts of the State, and have had abundant opportunities to learn facts, which I beg leave to lay before you.

In many parts of the State, especially in the cities and towns along the railroads and in the mining districts, there are large numbers of Irish, and I am convinced that they are organized in every part of the State to resist the draft, many of them armed, and the arming for this purpose has not been confined to them. I get my information from so many independent sources of information that I cannot doubt it. I know that in this town, and in other parts of this county and the adjacent county of Morris, among the iron and zinc mines, they are organized and armed. In this town several loyal citizens, both Democrats and Republicans, have been threatened with personal violence, and the destruction of their houses and stores. To produce this state of things, our Copperhead leaders have been engaged in holding meetings, beginning last March in Trenton, and extending to every part of the State, addressed by such men as Wall, Chauncey Burr, Tharin, Fernando Wood, and others of the same stamp, inflaming in every possible way the prejudices and passions of the people, and preparing their minds for an uprising at the concerted signal. We have had at least twelve such meetings in this county, one large one in this town, attended certainly by over 1,500, and the others at night in the different townships. We have also in the State some of the worst papers in the country; the two worst here and at Newark.

The minds of the poor, even of Republicans, are terribly inflamed by the $300 clause in the enrolling act, the objections to which certainly have much force. A rich man, who without this might have had to pay $1,000 or $2,000, or more, for a substitute, can now get off for $300, and the poor, and those in middling circumstances, say they ought to have been left to make their own bargains, for they could have procured substitutes for less than $300. You can readily perceive how demagogues use this to inflame the poorer and ignorant classes. The clause was well meant, but in my judgment is an unfortunate mistake.

Should the attempt be made at this juncture to enforce the draft in New Jersey, you may be sure it will be met by a widespread and organized resistance. The police force of the State is of very little account, and we have but few organized regiments or companies of militia, and some of them are mainly composed of Copperheads. And, what is worse, while our Governor means right, and I believe earnestly desires the suppression of the rebellion, yet he lacks the nerve and decision necessary for such a crisis, and is so hampered by party ties and associations that he could not be relied on to do his whole duty. I am satisfied of this from a conversation with him last Wednesday, at Trenton. I am convinced that in this country we cannot now enforce the draft, and the attempt would result in sad scenes of havoc and bloodshed, and am persuaded that the same is true of many other counties.

I forgot to mention one of the most mischievous clamors raised by demagogues— that the Government has never officially announced the whole number to be drafted nor the quota of the different States and districts, and that the officers give no public notice of the time and place of the drawing, which gives demagogues an opportunity to say that the whole thing is managed in a secret Star Chamber way; that men are purposely kept in ignorance till they receive notice of being drafted, and that the quotas are unfairly apportioned, so as to favor Republican districts.

Cannot these last objections be removed, and deprive the malignants of some of their weapons?

I earnestly desire the enforcement of the draft, as well for its present absolute necessity to crush speedily the rebellion as to settle for all time that we have a Government capable of defending itself, and in March last spent a good deal of time in writing for the New York Observer and papers of New Jersey to sustain the constitutionality of the law, and enforce the duty of obeying that and all other laws till properly adjudged to be unconstitutional, one of which articles, I believe that in the Observer, I sent you; but in view of the present state of affairs, I would respectfully but most earnestly solicit that for the present the draft be suspended in New Jersey until it is first thoroughly enforced in New York.

Trade Union Members Call for an International Industrial Assembly of North America, August 1864

To the Officers and Members of the Trades' Assemblies that are now organized on the Continent of America, or that may be organized before the twenty-first of September.

GENTLEMEN: As our notice, which has been inserted in *Fincher's Trades' Review* for the last three months, has failed to elicit a correspondence from all the Trades' Assemblies that are now organized, we are forced to adopt this method of communicating with you in regard to calling an international convention of the trades' assemblies of the United States and Canada.

We think great results would be produced by organizing ourselves into an international body. Are not capitalists and employers of almost every city organizing themselves into unions, and is it not patent to every one that their object is the overthrow of our organizations? Are we to shrink with fear when we behold this spectacle? We answer, no; but it should stimulate us to powerful exertion; we ought to work with renewed energy and labor zealously to organize the mechanics of every branch, and if necessary, laboring men into protective unions, and draw these unions into international bodies, the same as the molders, machinists and blacksmiths, printers, etc. In a word, the trades' assemblies ought to be the agents through which the mechanics of the different branches will be organized into local unions, and from local unions to international unions.

Suppose that we should be successful in organizing the mechanics of America as above stated: according to our views, the result would be this, viz: should the employers by combination attempt to overthrow any one branch of the trades, the other branches or organizations of mechanics would make the cause of the trade or branch struck at, their cause, and would lend their aid and sympathy to the trade; for if one branch was overthrown, we as a body would be weakened by it, knowing that the next blow struck might be at our branch, hence we are bound to protect each other.

There are many other benefits to be derived by combinations, but we have not the time nor space to mention but one more, and we think that it is sufficient of itself to stir you to action; it is this, combination will do away with strikes, for by combination we will become so powerful that the capitalists or employers will cease to refuse us our just demands, and will, if we make any unreasonable demands, condescend to come down on a level with us, and by argument and positive proof, show to us that our demands are

From International Industrial Assembly, call, in *Fincher's Trades' Review,* August 13, 1864. This selection is also available in *A Documentary History of American Industrial Society,* John R. Commons and John B. Andrews, eds. (1958), Vol. 9, pp. 118–120.

unjust; but this would have to be explained to the satisfaction of the trades' assembly of the city in which the demand was made.

We believe there are over two hundred thousand mechanics now represented in protective unions in the United States and Canada, and that they could be brought under the jurisdiction of the International Trades' Assembly in less than six months.

Gentlemen, we exhort you to send delegates to the convention, it will not cost much, and if you do not think that you will be benefited by it, you can instruct your delegates to withdraw.

We would suggest that Wednesday, the twenty-first of September, be named as the day of assembling, and that Louisville be the place; we name Louisville for the reason that if we have to correspond with each other, for the purpose of selecting a place, it would take six months to come to an understanding.

We expect that the first convention will adjourn to meet about the first of May, 1865, by this date we expect to see a trades' assembly in nearly every city of the United States and Canada.

Hoping that you will take immediate action on the subject, and that you will proceed to elect one or two delegates to represent you, and immediately notify us of your determination, we remain, fraternally yours,

R. GILCHRIST, Pres.

Alex. Burleigh, of Evansville, Indiana; William Bailey, St. Louis, Missouri; Thomas C. Knowles, Buffalo, New York; Richard Trevellick, M. Sintzenich, Detroit, Michigan; Robert Gilchrist, C. M. Talmage, Louisville, Kentucky; S. S. Whittier, Boston, Massachusetts; W. H. Gudgeon, E. F. Bigler, Cincinnati, Ohio; J. W. Lafflin, Trades' Union League, St. Louis; John Blake, Chicago.

Cincinnati Sewing Women Protest Their Wartime Wages, February 1865

Cincinnati, O., Feb. 20, 1865.

TO HIS EXCELLENCY, ABRAHAM LINCOLN, President of the United States: The undersigned, wives, widows, sisters, and friends of the soldiers in the army of the United States, depending upon our own labor for bread, sympathizing with the Government of the United States, and loyal to it, beg leave to call the attention of the Government, through his Excellency the President, to the following statement of facts:

1. We are willing and anxious to do the work required by the Government for clothing and equipping the armies of the United States, at the prices paid by the Government.

2. We are unable to sustain life for the price offered by contractors, who fatten on their contracts by grinding immense profits out of the labor of their operatives. As an example, the contractors are paid one dollar and seventy-five cents per dozen for making gray woolen shirts, and they require us to make them for one dollar per dozen. This is a sample of the justice meted out to us, the willing laborers, without whom the armies could not be promptly clothed and equipped.

Letter, Cincinnati Sewing Women to Abraham Lincoln, February 20, 1865, in *Fincher's Trades Review,* March 18, 1865. This selection is also available in *A Documentary History of American Industrial Society,* Vol. 9, pp. 72–73.

We most respectfully request that the Government, through the proper officers of the Quartermaster's Department, issue the work required directly to us, we giving ample security for the prompt and faithful execution of the work and return of the same at the time required, and in good order.

We are in no way actuated by a spirit of faction, but desirous of aiding the best government on earth, and at the same time securing justice to the humble laborer.

The manufacture of pants, blouses, coats, drawers, tents, tarpaulins, etc., exhibits the same irregularity and injustice to the operative. Under the system of direct employment of the operative by the Government, we had no difficulty, and the Government, we think, was served equally well.

We hope that the Government, in whose justice we have all confidence, will at once hear us and heed our humble prayer, and we will ever pray, etc.

E S S A Y S

The two essays on the Northern home front are examples of the current focus on the social, rather than the military and political, history of the war years. The first is by J. Matthew Gallman of Loyola College, Maryland, who discusses volunteer work in support of the war, using the Great Central Fair (usually called Sanitary Fairs elsewhere) in Philadelphia in June 1864 as a specific case. This essay offers a summary of one aspect of his book on the social history of Philadelphia during the war, *Mastering Wartime* (1990). The companion piece, by Phillip Shaw Paludan of the University of Kansas, is a chapter from his pioneering study of the wartime society and economy of the North, *A People's Contest* (1988). The chapter assesses the impact of the war on the working people of the Northern states, the class probably most hurt and certainly the most vocal about its suffering.

Voluntarism in Wartime:
Philadelphia's Great Central Fair

J. MATTHEW GALLMAN

In September 1864 Philadelphian John J. Thompson penned a lengthy description of America's "fearful ordeal" to a cousin overseas. Although there had been "gloomy and discouraging periods," as the conflict came to a close the iron manufacturer found cause for pride:

> The progress of our war has of course worked great changes in military and naval matters— but it has also developed an amount of sympathy, active, earnest and working, with suffering sick & wounded soldiers, such as has no parallel in the history of the world—The amount of volunteer labor on the battle fields, and in the Hospitals, has been extraordinary and the voluntary contributions by our citizens through the Sanitary Commissions amount to many millions of dollars in money & hundreds of tons in merchandize etc!

This enthusiasm for Civil War voluntarism was especially marked in Philadelphia. Soldiers passing through the City of Brotherly Love repeatedly paid tribute to its particularly benevolent citizenry. As one French traveler reported, "Philadelphia has not lost her religious character; she remains equally faithful to her philanthropic traditions."

Civil War Voluntarism

Thousands of Philadelphians took part in the "peoples' contest" from behind the lines by working at sewing circles, visiting hospitals, staffing refreshment saloons, or raising money for one of the score of local and national soldiers' aid organizations. Philadelphia supported its own array of voluntary groups, but two national organizations—the United States Sanitary Commission (USSC) and the United States Christian Commission (USCC)—dominated the national scene. In the war's first months a New York group, led by Unitarian minister Henry W. Bellows, organized the USSC to improve health conditions for Union soldiers. Although military authorities initially disapproved of civilians on the battlefield, the Sanitary Commission soon gained official recognition and blossomed into an enormous national organization, bringing clothing and medical supplies to Union field hospitals. While the USSC was strongly conservative and militantly secular, the YMCA–sponsored Christian Commission, launched in November 1861, dispensed Bibles and evangelical enthusiasm with their blankets and bandages.

Despite their differences, the two national commissions shared a common structure: Each had a central executive committee, regional branches based in major cities, and hundreds of local affiliates. At the local level, both bodies were dominated by female volunteers. As he closed the first of his four-volume *War for the Union,* Allen Nevins considered Northern society after a year of war and observed that "[a]ll over the map . . . voluntary effort had exhibited a vision and strength which shamed inertia and self- seeking. It was already clear that women could write a lustrous page in public affairs . . . and [the Sanitary Commission's] success was to show that a new era of national organization was opening." Three volumes later Nevins concluded that "[p]robably the greatest single change in American civilization in the war period . . . was the replacement of an organized nation by a highly organized society—organized, that is, on a national scale."

These two interpretive threads—that the Civil War accelerated America's evolution toward "a highly organized society" and that the experience of women in the war's voluntary organizations helped thrust them into "public affairs"—are woven, usually independently, through much of the scholarship on American social history. In his analysis of the Sanitary Commission, George Fredrickson argued that "[i]ts success and the public acceptance of its policies . . . symbolized this new willingness of Americans to work in large, impersonal organizations." Anne Firor Scott has suggested that women's "long apprenticeship in [antebellum] voluntary associations" left them better prepared to orchestrate affairs on the home front than their male counterparts were to fight on the battlefield. This wartime experience, in turn, she claims, aided women in the "process of inventing a public role" in the postwar decades. Nancy Hewitt, in her study of women's activism in Rochester, New York, found that their voluntary experiences "led wartime workers into wider public service when the [Soldier's Aid Society] disbanded."

The Great Central Fair

Organization.   Between June 7 and June 28, 1864, Philadelphia held its Great Central Fair, which raised over $1 million to replenish the Sanitary Commission's dwindling funds. This grand event was the product of months of labor by thousands of Philadelphians. Its organization and character are an excellent lens through which to view life on the Philadelphia home front. Moreover, the fair offers an opportunity to examine the centralizing forces underlying wartime voluntarism and to investigate the role of women within the newly fashioned patriotic organizations.

The Sanitary Commission's "fair movement" began in Chicago in late 1863 with a ten-day fund-raising fair for its Northwestern Branch. This event earned nearly $80,000, a figure that was almost doubled one month later in Boston. Soon Cincinnati, Cleveland, Albany, Brooklyn, and St. Louis followed suit. New York's Metropolitan Fair, which cleared $1,183,505 in April 1864, was the most successful of these ventures, topping Philadelphia's total by about $150,000. By the end of the war, roughly thirty "sanitary fairs" had been held, earning about $4.4 million. Some raised money for regional branches of the USSC; others collected funds for supplies to be sent to the home troops through Sanitary Commission channels. Over 80 percent of the $2.7 million funneled directly into the USSC's coffers came from the New York and Philadelphia fairs.

The Great Central Fair extended established practices. Antebellum Americans had often turned to fund-raising fairs to support civic charities, and as the Civil War progressed Philadelphians learned to rely on festive affairs to stir the patriotic sentiments of a war-weary citizenry. But the sanitary fairs melded entertainment and benevolence in events that eclipsed anything in America's experience, in both scope and design. Like London's Great Exhibition of 1851, these fairs enticed their visitors with a wide array of manufacturing and artistic exhibits displaying local accomplishments and foreign curiosities. But whereas Prince Albert conceived of the Crystal Palace to showcase the marvels of industrial progress, the sanitary fairs' organizers devoted their ingenuity to creating diverse methods for extracting money from their guests' pockets.

The initial impetus for Philadelphia's fair came from the highly patriotic Union League, which passed a resolution on January 11, 1864, asking the Philadelphia associates of the Sanitary Commission to join the nationwide fair movement. Two weeks later the USSC's local branch voted to put on a fair, under the supervision of an executive committee headed by prominent merchant John Welsh. On February 20 the committee announced the coming fair in the city's newspapers. Its open letter set the tone for the ensuing months:

> We call on every workshop, factory, and mill for a specimen of the best thing it can turn out; on every artist, great and small, for one of his creations; on all loyal women for the exercise of their taste and industry; on farmers, for the products of their fields and dairies. The miner, the naturalist, the man of science, the traveler, can each send something that can at the very least be converted into a blanket that will warm, and may save from death, some one soldier who the government supplies have failed to reach.

The organizers sought to touch everyone by emphasizing that no gift would be too small.

The Philadelphia fair's organizational structure was enormously complex, with over 3,000 volunteers in nearly 100 different committees, ranging from the 5-member Committee on Gas Fixtures to the roughly 330-strong Committee on Schools. Most committees were organized around a particular craft or branch of manufacturing. A member visited each of the city's establishments in search of donations of cash or goods to be sold at the fair. Other committees solicited flowers, fruit, handmade items, or "Relics, Curiosities, and Autographs." Tea merchant L. Montgomery Bond's Committee on Labor, Income, and Revenue adopted a massive advertising campaign encouraging all Philadelphians to donate the proceeds of a day's work to the fair.

Volunteers. One of the first orders of business for the executive committee was to recruit people to chair the various committees. The burden of chairing a committee was large, and more than 40 nominees refused to serve. Nevertheless, the executive committee enlisted many of Philadelphia's business leaders. J. B. Lippincott headed up the Committee on Book Publishers, Booksellers, and Bookbinders; David S. Brown, one of the region's largest textile manufacturers, chaired the Wholesale Dry Goods Committee; William J. Horstmann, the proprietor of the city's foremost military uniform and regalia establishment, led the Committee on Military Goods.

It was up to the chairs to form their own committees; once formed, individual groups adopted quite different structures. The members of the Ladies' Committee on Boots, Shoes and Leather visited stores individually, only meeting periodically to report their progress and to discuss plans for decorating their display. The official list includes 26 women on the committee, but the minutes show that only 3 came to all six meetings, one-half came to four or more, and 2 never attended. The minutes of the Women's Committee of the Children's Department of Toys and Small Wares reveal a far more complex infrastructure. Initially, this group of 33 women split into six subcommittees to visit local dealers. Later they formed seven topical subcommittees, which met separately (each keeping its own minutes) for the next month. The all-male Wholesale Dry Goods Committee also had poor attendance at committee meetings, with most of the serious work being accomplished in smaller subcommittees.

As with many peacetime organizations, the fair's committee structure divided men and women into separate but parallel bodies. Although the women's committees enjoyed substantial autonomy, their tasks often reflected different concerns and circumscribed gender roles. The Wholesale Dry Goods Committee voted to leave the designing of a suitable badge to their ladies' committee; the women's committee of the Children's Department of Toys and Small Wares left the construction of a Maypole to their male affiliates. The women's committees generally devoted special attention to determining the appropriate apparel for committee members to wear at the fair.

Despite its enormous scale, the Great Central Fair was a notably decentralized, individualized event. At each level citizens sought to mold the fair to their own desires. Much of recording secretary H. H. Furness's time was devoted to sorting out squabbles among committee heads. These battles reflected the difficulties inherent in forcing independent-minded volunteers into a large cooperative structure. . . .

Like other wartime relief organizations, the fair relied on donations of money and goods. In some cases the gift entailed only a small sacrifice, but in other instances the offering was—to the giver—quite significant. Individuals flooded the Receiving Department with all manner of heirlooms, trinkets, handicrafts, and farm products. One Union League member donated a deed to a downtown plot of land valued at $500; another man offered to share the proceeds from a holding in Iowa worth $1,500. A Wilmington inventor wanted to raffle off his patent for coal-oil burners (splitting the profits with the Sanitary Commission), and a second inventor hoped to display his new gas stove. If these latter gifts appeared partly self-serving, the same could not be said for the man who sent pieces of wood he had collected at Gettysburg or the New Yorker who contributed 5 gallons of water from the Amazon River.

Perhaps the most interesting assortment of gifts came to the Department of Singing Birds and Pet Animals. One poor woman wrote that since her husband would not give her any money she was sending six kittens. The offerings from the countryside included a pet donkey that purportedly had served in the War of 1812 and two white mice from China. One 10-year-old boy had only his black terrier to offer; the committee chairwoman gratefully accepted the donation, bought it herself, and returned it to its young owner. Finally, the chairwoman reported, there were "thirty-six parrots, well accustomed to low company," with vocabularies befitting their background.

Numerous organizations and labor groups sent contributions to the fair. The employees of John Bromley's carpet factory gave $41.50; the city's policemen donated over $1,000 in wages; the men aboard the steamer *Ladona* offered a day's pay; members of Philadelphia's Anderson Troop collected items in the field; and the officers and crew of the ship of war *Constellation* sent $842.75 all the way from Italy. The fair also enjoyed one day's profits from an all-star baseball game; a traveling circus; the Chestnut Street Theater; several local railways; and Bird's Billiard Saloon. Small businesspeople, such as dressmaker Mrs. E. C. Tilton and grocer Joshua Wright, offered part of their revenues; the Great Valley Association for the Detection of Horse Thieves sent $30. The range of donations was limited only by the reach of citizens' imaginations. The Carpenters and Bricklayers helped construct the Logan Square buildings, and representatives of various fire departments agreed to cooperate to protect the fair from fire.

Many businesses used the festivities for publicity. Newspapers reported on a fierce competition between sewing-machine companies, each seeking the title of most generous establishment in the city. The Singer Sewing Machine Company donated $300; three days later the Florence Sewing Machine Company matched that figure. The American Button Hole Machine Company gave two of its machines (valued at $650) and $50 in cash, which the *Bulletin* acknowledged as "the largest contribution of any sewing machine company so far." . . .

[**Participation**].   Over 250,000 people bought tickets to the fair. There were roughly 608,000 Philadelphians in 1864. Even allowing for thousands of visitors from out of town, the fair attracted a large proportion of the city's population. Most accounts of the Great Central Fair stress that all segments of Philadelphia society combined to make it a success. Two months before the fair began George Fahnestock wrote, "Everybody is working for it, talking about it, begging for it. The newspapers are full of it—advertising columns and all—and everybody in town, male and female, is on some committee—self appointed or otherwise." The *North American and United States Gazette* marveled at "how thoroughly this Great Fair has worked into the popular sympathy," and the *Bulletin* noted the "thousands of men, women and children" who worked for its success and the further "thousands who contributed money, labor, time, gifts or loans." *Forney's War Press* made the case even more directly: "There is not one man, woman, or child out of a hundred within the limits of the city, who is not directly interested in the Great Central Fair, who has not given it at least one day's labor, and a month's sympathy and earnest aid." . . .

Appeals for contributions usually stressed the twin pulls of patriotism and benevolence. In an editorial on a benefit opera for the fair, the *Ledger* observed that "Patriotism dictates a general attendance." The *Press* argued that "our only tribute to the fallen must be our care for the living." *Our Daily Fare* continually emphasized the good works of the Sanitary Commission and saw the fair as the latest expression of the war's "ongoing tide of benevolence." After the first day, the *Bulletin* concluded that "this scene of wonderful beauty has arisen at the call of the noblest instincts of the human heart—patriotism and humanity."

Beneath the surface patriotism there were other motivations. The committee chairs often used the profit motive to their advantage, reminding businessmen of the goodwill a donation could purchase. A circular aimed at the oil refiners of western Pennsylvania argued that by providing the fair with a good display, "contributors whilst aiding the soldiers of the Union, will at the same time, advertise their respective establishments." The Committee on Labor, Income and Revenue appealed to the pride of the city's shoemakers by announcing that it "had full confidence that the contributions from that branch will be in proportion as liberal as from any source from which it applies." Bond's committee ensured that no benevolent light would be hidden under a bushel by taking out regular newspaper advertisements listing all the latest donations.

Beyond the profits it brought to the Sanitary Commission, the Great Central Fair temporarily freed Philadelphia from the gloom of war. One writer in *Our Daily Fare* argued that even if the fair earned no money at all, it would perform a useful function by spurring the local economy and taking people's minds off the conflict. The fair made Philadelphians proud of themselves and of their city. Much of the pre-fair boosterism challenged the local citizenry to top New York's effort. The *Bulletin* predicted that Philadelphia would outdo New York in size, variety, artwork, and proceeds. This, it said, "affords additional proof that the cause of patriotism is more liberally sustained in money as well as men in the City of Brotherly Love than in any other city in the Union."

The Significance of the Great Central Fair

. . . What can Philadelphia's Great Central Fair tell us about the role of wartime benevolence in social change? We began this account by identifying two common themes: (1) that transition from "the improvised war" to "the organized war" saw an increased centralization of activity; (2) that the wartime experience of female volunteers helped launch women into the public sphere in the postwar years. The fair would seem a logical place to find evidence of each phenomenon.

In his study of Northern intellectuals during the Civil War, George M. Fredrickson argues that the Sanitary Commission's founders embraced a "conservative, basically nonhumanitarian philosophy." These men sought to impose order and discipline in American society by centralizing philanthropy and by ridding it of the sentimental and individualistic aspects that had characterized antebellum charities. The commissioners succeeded in their task in that they directed a large share of the North's benevolent funds toward "suitable" activities. But Philadelphia's experience suggests that these representatives of the nation's elite did not meet their larger goals. Numerous other local and national charities provided the humanitarianism and individualism that the Sanitary Commission rejected. Rather than a highly centralized structure, wartime benevolence took a chaotic form reminiscent of antebellum America.

Moreover, the Sanitary Commission's own fair movement reveals the superficial nature of this centralized control. The impetus for Philadelphia's fair came not from the national commissioners, or even from the local Philadelphia associates, but from a resolution by the independent Union League. The fair was exclusively a local event; moreover, it was essentially a grass-roots effort. Although the executive committee watched over the activities, most of the important work was performed in small subcommittees or by individual volunteers. As we have seen, the papers of the recording secretary are full of letters from interested citizens offering unsolicited counsel on all aspects of the fair's organization, and local diarists repeatedly referred to the fair with a fierce local pride. Such evidence reinforces the conclusion that this was clearly "the people's fair."

What of the wartime experiences of Philadelphia's women? Thousands of local women served in patriotic organizations, thus giving them valuable experience in organizing. Moreover, these sacrifices did not go unnoticed. Contemporary observers frequently noted the activities of female volunteers, and in the postwar years several publications heralded their contributions to the cause. But what were these contributions, and how were they recognized?

Although women numerically dominated many of the Great Central Fair's committees, the executive committee was entirely male, and where men and women formed parallel subcommittees the men consistently received top billing. In fact, the fair's organizers seemed particularly proud of this structure. As the event came to a close, *Our Daily Fare* looked back on the successful venture and concluded that "[o]ne of the distinguished features of this fair is that its management is more under the control of the gentlemen than any one which had preceded it."

When the doors opened, the relationship between male and female volunteers seemed reminiscent of the gender roles within the Union Benevolent Association. Whereas in the peacetime organization men "managed" and women "visited," during the fair the men managed and the women attended to the selling. Certainly these efforts earned Philadelphia's women substantial notice. *Forney's War Press* applauded the efforts of women, who, "forbidden to fight or to vote for the Union," took this opportunity to aid the cause. "There is scarcely a department of the Fair," the editorial continued, "[to] which the hand of woman has not added a charm."

But generally such accolades revealed unflattering gender stereotypes. As opening day approached, the *Press* reported that "[t]he ladies are in a state of excitement about all the little details of the great display." A male committee member wrote, "[W]e have agreed with every female member of our committees on every suggestion that they have made, and when you consider the variety of the suggestions, and their utter inconsistency . . . you may imagine the mental strain upon us." *Our Daily Fare* consistently spoke condescendingly of female volunteers, who were "sending palpitations to the masculine heart" while selling their wares, and predicted "extra orders for wedding-cake and white stain, 'when this cruel fare is over.' " One observer described how enthusiastic committeewomen ignored all the "formalities of social intercourse" and, on occasion, bullied men like "accomplished overseer[s]." And in response to those who questioned the fair's utility, *Our Daily Fare* pointed out that it had improved young ladies' skills in darning socks, sewing buttons, and writing with a graceful hand.

In private some men appeared even less complimentary. One Philadelphian insisted on turning over his gift to a man, because "[a] woman is a woman" and should not be trusted with "property." L. Montgomery Bond endorsed a proposed mock presidential election for women as an "amusing scheme" that would delight local women by given [sic] them "an opportunity for once in their lives to be heard on the great question of the Presidency" while also pleasing "the 'womens rights' people."

As a large, citywide event designed to support a national patriotic organization, Philadelphia's Great Central Fair is a reasonable place to look for evidence of the Civil War's centralizing impulses. The widely recognized role of women in ensuring its success also makes the fair a logical starting point in a search for a widening role for women in the public sphere. But in both cases the signs of change seem outweighed by the evidence of persistent localism and gender divisions. A glance into the following decade emphasizes the point.

The Centennial City

. . . In 1876 Philadelphia hosted the nation's Centennial Exhibition. The exhibition's planning and organization followed some of the patterns set by the 1864 sanitary fair. But the two events were different, suggesting how circumstances had changed in the postwar decade.

In 1870, Philadelphia's Select Council officially resolved to hold an international exhibition to mark the centennial of the Declaration of Independence, and soon afterward the state legislature voted its support of the proposal. In the following year, Congress passed a bill naming Philadelphia the official site of the Centennial Exhibition and providing for the selection of exhibition commissioners from each state. In 1872 Congress authorized the creation of a Centennial Board of Finance to sell stock in the exhibition.

The Board of Finance, which was dominated by the same core of Philadelphia elites who had orchestrated the sanitary fair and Philadelphia's other wartime activities, had to raise $10 million to ensure the exhibition's success. In early 1873, the City Council appropriated $500,000 to the fund; eventually the city donated a total of $1.5 million. The state legislature added $1 million to finance the construction of a permanent Memorial Hall on the exhibition site. Philadelphians held numerous fund-raising mass meetings; the city's coal, railroad, and lumber companies made large donations, as did local publishers, fraternal societies, and various other economic and social organizations. But by mid-1874, only $1.5 million in stock had been sold. The federal government resisted requests that it provide financial support for the project, until finally, as the exhibitions opening day approached, Congress lent the Board of Finance $1.5 million to guarantee that the celebration would open.

The Centennial Exhibition, modeled on the world's fairs held in London (1851), Paris (1855 and 1867), New York (1853), and Vienna (1873), featured displays of industrial progress from across the globe, filling more than two hundred buildings that covered 450 acres of Fairmount Park. Between May and November more than 10 million visitors came to Philadelphia to share in the celebration.

How did the 1876 exhibition compare with the Great Central Fair of 1864? The exhibition's physical design was much like that of its wartime predecessor but on a grander scale. Both fairs featured special horticultural, art, and manufacturing displays. Each had a section reserved for guns and military regalia. Both boasted elaborate restaurants and oddities from around the world. For the visitor, the biggest difference was that the 1876 exhibition was much more ambitious than the earlier fair and included many more international displays. And while the sanitary fair was completely dismantled after a few weeks, the exhibition lasted for half a year, and some of its buildings remained as permanent structures.

Apart from its scale and international aspect, one display in particular set the Centennial Exhibition apart from the wartime fair. In 1876 the Citizens' Centennial Finance Committee formed a women's committee headed by 13 prominent Philadelphia women. This body carried out a grass-roots fund-raising campaign that quickly collected $40,000. When it became evident that the Centennial Exhibition's male organizers had made no plans to display women's work, the women's committee collected an additional $30,000 to finance the construction of a women's building. The Women's Pavilion housed an eclectic assortment of displays, ranging from a 6-horse-power engine to a head carved out of butter, all produced by women. In a fair that heralded the nation's progress, this exhibit—unlike those of its wartime predecessor—explicitly acknowledged women's role in that development.

A further difference between the two fairs was in their organization. Whereas the executive committee of Philadelphia's sanitary fair acted independently of the national Sanitary Commission and without any government aid, the 1876 exhibition received large donations from the city, state, and federal governments as well as financial support from foreign nations. Still, both fairs relied on the direction of a handful of Philadelphia elites, the voluntary efforts of hundreds of local men and women, and the financial support of the city's businesses, fraternal societies, and private citizens.

In 1879 the formation of the Philadelphia Society for Organizing Charitable Relief and Repressing Mendicancy (PSOCR) marked a major milestone in the city's benevolent history. The organization, which had been formed to eliminate the evils of overlapping philanthropies, gave Philadelphia charities the centralized agency that the war years had lacked. The PSOCR's complicated structure included a wide array of subcommittees and an entirely male board of directors, which supervised the activities of affiliated organizations in each ward.

The PSOCR and its ward associations introduced greater efficiency and organization into Philadelphia's benevolent world and also reflected an increased recognition of the role of Philadelphia's charitable women. The original plan followed tradition by placing women in circumscribed roles, attending to visitation and the like, while men served in the highest offices and controlled the funds. But the *2nd Annual Report* included a call for increased "Cooperation of Men and Women Workers" and even indicated that "in some wards women had been placed on the Board of Directors." By 1884 the Eighth Ward Association had 5 male and 5 female directors; in 1888 the combined Thirteenth and Fourteenth Wards Association reported an evenly balanced board of directors and a woman superintendent.

By the end of the 1870s Philadelphia's charities were increasingly centralized and efficient, as well as more open to putting women in positions of authority. Those changes emerged in the postwar years, however. The city that set out to stage a three-week fund-raising fair in 1864 relied on traditional practices rather than recasting familiar ways.

Industrial Workers and the Costs of War

PHILLIP SHAW PALUDAN

There were more than 9 million workers in the North. Almost 3,500,000 of them, farmers and farm laborers, directly benefited from the boom in agriculture. Another 5,600,000 workers found employment off the farms or engaged in professional or domestic service, trade, transportation, manufacturing, mining, and mechanical industries. These were domestic servants, laborers, teachers, clerks, railroad workers, middlemen, blacksmiths,

From Phillip Shaw Paludan, "Industrial Workers and the Cost of War," in *A People's Contest: The Union and the Civil War, 1861–1865.* Copyright © 1988. Reprinted by permission of Philip Paludan.

boot and shoemakers, carpenters, cotton mill workers, miners, tailors. Those linked to the farm economy experienced good times, too. But a growing proportion of Northern workers lived in the growing industrial world, gathering together in increasing numbers in shops and factories and on work gangs. In this population about a million people were self-employed and/or company officials, but the majority worked for someone else. These were the workers who forecast the future structure of the economy. They were also the workers whose fate had caused so much prewar attention.

Although their work experience forecast a modern industrial society, that society was not yet in place in the war years. Older localistic contexts endured side by side with a burgeoning industrial environment. Workers experienced this new world in that older context. While nationalizing forces moved in the land, local communities were dominant in the lives of almost everyone. Few workers were organized. A reasonable estimate puts the number at approximately 300,000, less than 10 percent of all industrial workers in the 1860s belonging to local or regional organizations. As of 1860 there were only five national unions: the Printers, the Stonecutters, the Hat Finishers, the Iron Molders, and the Machinists. When workers sought protection or progress they formed local mixed trade assemblies—uniting delegates from workingmen's clubs, trade unions, and general reform societies that were interested in workingmen's problems. Such assemblies usually sought political power, but occasionally they supported boycotts and strikes by member organizations or acted as bargainers in settlements. . . .

On the eve of conflict the workers of the North lived in a world of conflicting and contrasting experiences, of local community attachments, with an economy predominantly rural but one where industrialization was a force of growing size and potential danger. Class consciousness was a fact in some places but mitigated in many others by hopes, by strategies, by options kept open, by lack of experience with the evils that called it forth. There was widespread concern about the shape of things to come, but that concern focused inevitably on the controversy over slavery, which symbolized so well the anxieties they felt.

The secession crisis found labor divided in its sympathies, though more inclined to peace. German laborers in the Midwest offered their staunch support to Lincoln as he traveled to Washington. Troy, New York, workers pledged loyalty. Milwaukee workers resolved that if the crisis were not solved peacefully, "revolutionary" means would be justified since the South was responsible for the crisis. In Cincinnati Lincoln was told that

> we, the German free working men of Cincinnati, avail ourselves of this opportunity to assure you . . . of our sincere and heartfelt regard. . . . Our vanquished opponents have in recent times made frequent use of the term workingmen and workingmen's meetings in order to create the impression that the mass of workingmen were in favor of compromise between the interests of free labor and slave labor. . . . We firmly adhere to the principle which directed our votes to your favor.

But if some labor organizations supported Lincoln at this time, signs of opposition were more frequent. Just recovering from the impact of the mid-1850s depression, many workers feared that disunion would bring economic disaster. They also knew that they would be the ones on the battlefields of any war. Pro-Southern factory owners had helped foster opposition by closing their factories. Other businessmen had nurtured fears by retracting activity in the face of the crisis. Workers in all parts of the nation thus joined large antiwar rallies. Meetings in the East, in Philadelphia, Newark, and Boston, were balanced with Western gatherings in Reading, St. Louis, and Louisville. Sylvis of the Iron Molders was in Louisville and then in Philadelphia publishing a call that brought five thousand worker representatives to that city to demand compromise. The future founder of the Knights of Labor, Ira Stewart, joined in attacking the extremists who had spawned the crisis. The Louisville meeting damned "disorganizing traitors" and "congressional extremists" and insisted that both were disloyal and enemies to labor.

But wishes for peace could not withstand the Confederate attack on Fort Sumter. Workers throughout the North surged forward to crush an attack on the nation and to punish the slave power. Industrial conflicts were quickly submerged in the rush to arms. The ironworkers of Troy were organizing a strike when the news from Sumter came in. Large numbers of the membership enlisted. The weakened union lost more ground when management used the opportunity to hire nonunion workers, required that these workers not join any union, and brought charges against the union for conspiracy. By early fall 1861 Troy ironworkers were largely disbanded, meeting only three times in five months. One Philadelphia local ended its 1861 meeting in this way: "It having been resolved to enlist with Uncle Sam for the War, this union stands adjourned until either the union is safe or we are whipped." Throughout the North the story was the same. Workers of all sections and all ethnic groups flocked to the army. In proportion to their percentage of the population, more industrial workers served in the Union army than any other group except for professionals. Looking at military service after the war, statistician Benjamin Gould noted that for every 1,000 soldiers there were likely to be 487 farmers or farm workers, 421 mechanics and laborers, 35 workers involved in commerce, 16 professionals, and 41 from a range of other occupations.

But if the workers were willing to fight for their country, the war also gave them the chance to fight for their own interests as well. The ideology of the conflict had a strong impact on them. Lincoln's description of the war as a people's contest, a struggle to remove burdens from the backs of labor and give to everyone an equal chance in the race of life, spoke directly to their feelings. Furthermore, the president made clear on several occasions a sympathy for the workers. As early as his speech at Cooper Union he applauded a system where workers could strike. In the aftermath of the great Lynn [Massachusetts] strike, when a delegation of machinists and blacksmiths came to see him at the White House, he allegedly told them that "I know in almost every case of strike the men have just cause for complaint." He told another delegation, "I know the trials and woes of workingmen. I have always felt for them." A believer in the labor theory of value, Lincoln commented that labor "deserves much higher consideration" than capital. "I myself was a hired laborer," he reminded several audiences. Such words suggested that the war might directly benefit workers. From being a single group contesting others for support, the cause of labor became linked to the cause of all loyal Northerners.

And yet this same phenomenon also might undercut labor's advancement. Workers' special needs and aspirations might be absorbed into the general, ill-defined free labor cause. With the North united under this banner all classes could lay claim to the patriotic ideals of the Union, and worker protest might lose its strength. More tellingly, the workers themselves fell prey to this patriotic homogenizing. Many began to identify their cause with that of the Republican party. They thus fell into bed with the very businessmen that they had been challenging. Lynn offers an example of this phenomenon at work in the most striking way. The Workingmen's party had won city elections in 1860 and 1861, but by 1863 the Republican party was in control, and by 1864 no votes at all were cast for anyone but the Republican candidate. Small towns growing into cities, like Spring-field, Massachusetts, were often Republican strongholds, and workers in most of the major Northern cities throughout the war voted Republican.

Experienced Republican party politicians with reputations as friends of the workers, such as Henry Wilson, argued that his party was the free labor party. "We have made labor honorable," Wilson declared, "even in the rice swamps of the Carolinas and Georgia; we have taken the brand of dishonor from the brow of labor throughout the country and in so doing that grand work we have done more for labor, for the honor and dignity of laboring men, than was ever achieved by all the parties that arose in this country from the time the Pilgrims put their feet upon Plymouth Rock up to the year 1860." Such appeals were frequently persuasive even to working-class leaders. Samuel Gompers cast the first vote of his life in 1872 for Grant in the belief that the Republican struggle against slavery showed party dedication to the cause of free labor. But Democrats also tried to collect labor votes by a similar appeal to the general and widely popular idea that the end of slavery was a victory for the working classes. In early 1865 the party published a pamphlet, "America for Free Working Men!" collecting material from the *New York Evening Post* to show how Democrats fought slavery for years, thus earning the support of free workers of the North.

The credo of the war offered both promise and problems for the workers of the North. The actual experience of life behind the lines was similarly mixed. The war expanded the number of jobs available, providing work for the unemployed. The large number of enlistments in the army opened up jobs, and workers were there to fill them. Unskilled workers filled in for skilled enlistees, and that justified some pay reductions, but workers were glad to get whatever jobs were available. Employers began to complain that they could not fill all the openings they had.

Similarly, workers' families benefited from the bounties and wages paid to soldiers. Lacking opportunities to spend their pay, the young men sent millions of dollars home; as much as $400,000 might be shipped north in a single payday. The national government paid approximately $300 million in bounties for enlistment; state and local authorities paid an additional $285 million. These funds went into the hands of hundreds of thousands of working-class families. But they hardly brought the families a life of ease. Practically every community in the North had its organization to care for the families of soldiers.

The economic suffering of the war years was only partly the product of inflation and men being away at war. When war broke out the United States was experiencing a period of growing economic inequality. This phenomenon had begun somewhere around the 1820s, just as industrialism made its presence felt. By 1860 the top 10 percent of the Northern population held an estimated 68 percent of the total wealth, an increase of nearly 15 percent from 1774. Nearly 95 percent of the wealth of the nation was held by 30 percent of the population—a figure applicable to both North and South individually. When the war began, inequality of wealth distribution may have been at an all-time high.

Wages reflected inequality, too. Skilled workers' pay rose much faster than that of unskilled workers. Between 1840 and 1850 the wages of New York bricklayers rose 18 percent faster than did the pay of common laborers. Carpenters and joiners gained increases that were 37 percent better than those gained by unskilled men. Machinists in New York City achieved the same improvement, while Massachusetts iron molders gained 13 percent more in the decade than did common laborers. These differences remained constant with only slight variations from 1820 to 1880.

In some minor respects the war reduced the gap between the standard of living of the lower and upper classes. While gains in overall wealth in that period are not easily measured, the cost of living seems to have gone up less for lower- than for upper-class people. This was because expensive items rose more in price than did common goods. Increasing fuel, light, rent, and food costs hurt the lower classes, but prices of clothing, house furnishings, and other nonessentials were higher.

But war helped the comfortable more than it did average folk. Increased profits in the wartime boom, the protection provided by the tariff, the tax system in which excise taxes carried most of the freight, all assisted people at the top. Newspapers carried frequent editorials on the ostentations and vulgar display that the wartime boom called forth. William Cullen Bryant echoed many:

> Extravagance, luxury, these are the signs of the times; are they not evidence of a state of things unhealthy and feverish, threatening to the honest simplicity of our political life; and threatening not less evil to the ideas and principles of which that life has hitherto been a fair exponent? What business have Americans at any time with such vain show, with such useless magnificence? But especially how can they justify it to themselves in this time of war? Some men have gained great fortunes during the past two or three years, but that does not excuse their extravagance. . . .

Suffering a decline in their already precarious living standard, and angered at the ostentation of war-made millionaires, workers were further threatened by hundreds of thousands of immigrants who surged into the country during the war. While many became soldiers, most went looking for jobs, competing with native laborers and driving wages down. When the Congress passed and Lincoln signed the 1864 Emigrant Aid Act permitting private businesses to bring immigrants to the United States, workers were bitter. [The labor activist William H.] Sylvis called the American Emigrant Company "the most infamous in America," and even the mayor of New York protested: "At a time when nearly 50,000 operatives in this city alone are contending against the oppression of capital, and the wages paid are inadequate for their support is it just to them or to the European laborers to bring the latter into conflict for existence with the former, for the benefit of employers, through the agency of societies called into existence by this act of Congress?"

Some protests were misdirected. Despite the hostility that they faced, the wartime immigrants quickly integrated themselves into the mainstream labor movement, increasing its numbers. English immigrants often became leading figures in American unions. Irish and, to a lesser extent, Germans joined existing unions or more frequently formed their own local organizations. These groups provided the same social support for members that native locals did. They worked for the same economic goals of higher wages, shorter hours, less competition from machines, union control over apprenticeships, and occasionally even restriction of immigration. Most important, foreign-born regiments augmented the Union army and shared the deadly cost of conflict. Such behavior helped diffuse the nativism that had often marred relations between foreign and domestic workers.

But the other target of workers' wartime hostility could do little or nothing to escape hatred. The black contribution to the Union army was minimized by workers who were frightened by the specter of cheap labor competition and afflicted with racial hatred. Encouraged by a Democratic party press, urban workers again and again took out their frustrations on Negroes. As early as 1862 New York City Irish longshoremen attacked black strikebreakers, and the police had to be called in. In August between two thousand and three thousand people from a predominantly Irish neighborhood in Brooklyn threatened to burn down the factories of a local firm unless the black women and children employees quit or were fired. In early 1863 the docks of that city again witnessed clashes between black and white workers. Such fights mirrored similar ones in Buffalo, Chicago, Cincinnati, and other cities in the North.

Most wartime workers saw their standard of living decline. While skilled workers stayed a short step ahead of inflation, the larger number of unskilled workers saw a steady decline in real wages. While their wages increased by perhaps 50 to 60 percent, prices went up by almost 100 percent. Eggs rose from 15¢ per dozen in 1861 to 25¢ in late 1863; potatoes rose from $1.50 per bushel to $2.25 per bushel in the same period. Bread prices almost doubled, and rents and fuel also increased markedly. A New York newspaper in July 1864 estimated that a family of six in the city needed $16 per week for necessities and that the average wage in the city was just at the $16 figure. This left no money for clothing, medicine and doctors, transportation to and from work, or luxuries of any kind. The next month the paper observed that the cost of these same necessities stood at $18.50.

The wages of men workers at least kept commodities within their extended reach, but women workers, who did about one-fourth of the manufacturing work in the country, suffered even more. On the average, their wages increased by less than half that of men. In some businesses their pay actually went down as costs skyrocketed. Seamstresses in New York saw wages go from 17.5¢ per shirt in 1861 to 8¢ per shirt in 1864. Women who worked a fourteen-hour day at this job received on the average $1.54 per week. "The sewing women in Cincinnati" wrote to President Lincoln in March 1865: "We are unable to sustain life for the prices offered by contractors, who fatten on their contracts by grinding immense profits out of the labor of their operatives." Women umbrella makers in New York worked from 6:00 A.M. to midnight and received 6–8¢ for each umbrella they made. They could earn from 72 to 94¢ a day. In the fall of 1863 they struck, and won the concession from owners of 2¢ more per umbrella. . . .

As the war dragged on, the initial patriotic enthusiasm of workers began to diminish. Soldiers' letters home, newspaper reports, revealed war's horrors. Labor spokesmen began to question the alleged unity of labor and capital in the war against slavery. Speaking to the National Iron Molders meeting in January 1864, Sylvis catalogued the suffering of workers and declared that "nothing can be more absurd" than to believe in the natural unity of labor and capital. While capital was "selfish, haughty, proud, insolent," wallowing in the luxury of wartime prosperity, labor was "reduced to the lowest possible condition of wretchedness." In New York City thirty thousand sewing women worked day and night to earn between one and three dollars a week to sustain not only themselves but children and parents. Thirty thousand people lived in Manhattan cellars "literally buried alive, huddled together like cattle in a pen," wrapped in a "mental and moral darkness" that would make "angels weep."

In cotton mills it required "the combined labor of . . . husband, wife, and every child old enough to walk to the factory, [working] from twelve to fifteen hours a day to earn sufficient to keep body and soul together." "Anyone who will take the trouble to investigate and study" the conditions of the nation's industrial workers would "find thousands sunk to a degree of mental, moral and physical wretchedness horrible to contemplate, whose very soul are crushed within their living bodies." And the capitalists, "the worst enemies of our race, . . . make commerce of the blood and tears of helpless women and merchandize [*sic*] of soul. In the poverty, wretchedness and utter ruin of their helpless victims they see nothing but an accumulating [pile] of gold. In the weeping and *wailing of the distressed* they hear nothing but a 'metallic ring.' "

Feelings like these, the greater activity of the economy, and the needs of the war helped to create hundreds of new labor organizations. In 1863 the leading labor newspaper, *Fincher's Trades Review,* listed 79 local unions. Within a year the list had grown to 270. By March of 1864 *Fincher's* had reported on strikes around New York City by "Slate and Metal Roofers," "Segar makers," "Long shoremen," "Jewellers," "Bricklayers," "House Carpenters," "Printers," "Dry dock practical painters," "Plumbers," "Blue Stone Cutters and Flaggers," "Piano Forte makers," "Iron Moulders," "Cabinet-makers and Tailors," "Carvers," "Shipwrights," "Brush makers," "Wheelwrights and Blacksmiths," "Coopers," "Coach painters and coach trimmers."

The number of tradewide strikes in New York City alone continued to rise from thirteen in 1862 to twenty-nine in 1863 and hit a high of forty-two by 1864. During this last year there were also forty-six single-shop strikes. For the most part, workers struck for higher wages, as when seven thousand machinists went out in the winter of 1863. But sometimes workers protested the use of machines to do the work of men. In June 1862 the surge of wartime orders led the owners of port facilities in New York City to use grain-unloading machines. Five thousand workers struck at this time, but lost their protest. Shop, factory, and mine workers throughout the North struck during 1863 and 1864 when work stoppages reached their peak. Most of these strikes were successful, since war needs and profits encouraged owners to give in. But, after mid-1864, as ultimate victory seemed assured, management became more determined to prepare for projected postwar retrenchments and workers backed away from militance. By the end of the war labor leaders were urging members to consider strikes as a last resort and speaking more often of mutual interests between capital and labor. . . .

The feelings of the working class were often complex and contradictory. They included a powerful patriotism, shown in the overwhelming response to the Sumter attack, and continuing throughout the war with strong enlistments and reenlistments and large Republican majorities in many elections. But there was also unrest and anxiety and, in many places, growing anger as the war continued. As workers' enlistments had been extraordinary given their percentage of the population, so were their casualties. They were experiencing the most heartrending of the costs of war in proportions larger than almost any group in the population. At the Battle of Fredericksburg, Meagher's New York Irish Brigade lost all but 280 of its 1,200 men. The 116th Pennsylvania Regiment suffered bitterly at Fredericksburg and Gettysburg. Similarly, large Irish losses in other battles alienated many at home and in the field. Some believed that commanders intentionally risked Irish lives in dangerous situations.

War losses combined with economic suffering, racial hostilities, and cultural antagonism to the modernizing forces of industrial society all combined to fuel an explosion by workers in New York City in the summer of 1863. Still mourning Fredericksburg, the Irish community of New York, overwhelmingly the largest group of New York City workers, were infuriated over the Conscription Act passed by Congress on March 3. Declining enlistments had provoked legislators into passing this major bill, but its provisions demanded far more of poor than of wealthy Americans. The requirement that all men between twenty and forty-five be enrolled for potential conscription portended an intrusion by government into the daily lives of citizens, but it could be understood as a war necessity. The provision for calling up single men from twenty to twenty-five and married men from twenty to thirty-five before calling older married men seemed more debatable. Older married men were likely to be better off and their children more capable of caring for themselves, but at least some attention was paid to family needs. But the provision allowing draftees to hire a substitute or to buy their way out of service with a $300 commutation provoked outrage.

Three hundred dollars was at least half a year's wages, and substitutes would hardly be available for anything less. "A rich man's war and a poor man's fight" was the cry that rose up against the draft law. The *New York Copperhead* parodied a popular recruiting song with the words "We're coming Father Abraham three hundred thousand more. / We leave our homes and firesides with bleeding hearts and sore, / Since poverty has been our crime, we bow to the decree; / We are the poor who have no wealth to purchase liberty." Another paper offered a simpler parody: "We are coming Father Abraham, 300 dollars more." Labor spokesman Fincher urged that the $300 fee be repealed so that "rich men" could fight their own war. Opposition to such injustice was not disloyalty to the government, he argued, it was loyalty to the working class.

Protests against the inequities of the draft and the economic suffering of workers broke out into violence in New York City on three sweltering days, July 13–15, 1863, just after the Gettysburg and Vicksburg victories. Encouraged by the protests of Democratic newspapers in the city, and to some extent by a speech given by Governor Horatio Seymour, tensions exploded when the names of draftees were drawn. Early controlled protest by union artisans was replaced by mobs of unskilled workers, including women and boys, who surged through the city attacking draft officials and policemen, turning on soldiers set against them. They burned draft offices, pro-administration newspapers, and the homes of known abolitionists (including the composer of the recruiting song "We Are Coming Father Abraham"), beat up well-dressed gentlemen whom they called "$300 men," and sometimes turned their fury on street sweeping machines or mechanical grain elevators.

But their greatest hatred focused on the city's Negroes. Rioters burned a Negro orphanage to the ground, and black men and women were hunted in the streets and murdered when caught. At the height of the rioting economic activity almost completely stopped in the city, and fears grew that the mob might rule the city. When order was finally restored an estimated 119 people were found to have been killed and over 300 to have been wounded or injured, making these riots the largest civil disturbance in the nation's history to that time.

The composition of the mob at the peak of its fury showed the frustrations of the poor. The rioters were overwhelmingly Irish and predominantly unskilled workers. While a few criminals took advantage of the disorder, the large majority of the rioters had no previous criminal record. Of the over 350 later identified, 92 were not themselves eligible to be drafted. These were the people at the bottom of New York City's society, angered by their suffering, fearful of further inroads on their lives, resentful of both those above them, whose money protected them, and those below them, who seemed potential beneficiaries of the war now that emancipation was a goal. Sufferings, envy, hatred, all served to spark the uprising.

The draft riots advanced the rioters' cause after the violence was crushed. Blacks fled New York City in large numbers, reducing labor competition. Those who stayed suffered even after the riots were over when private charity ran out. The city council voted $2 million to buy substitutes or pay commutation money for any policeman, fireman, or member of the militia who might be drafted. And any other poor New Yorker who could prove that induction would impoverish his family received the same benefits. Furthermore, few of the rioters were ever punished. Grand juries refused to indict them, and under neighborhood pressures, few victims chose to press charges.

New York City was not the only place where workers reacted to war and the pressures of industrialization with antidraft violence. The Tenth Congressional District of Pennsylvania also saw bitter resistance. Irish-American miners there experienced conditions that reminded them of English oppression at home. They had to rent their homes from company officials, buy provisions at company stores, and work under the supervision of the more highly skilled English and Welsh miners. Targets of nativism in the mid-1850s suspicious and bitter over Republican puritanism, they forged their community ties all the more strongly for self-protection and identity. When the draft began, their anger crystallized, and almost three hundred miners gathered to stop the process. Troops came to help the government and for a time kept the lid on. But when the troops left, a well-known mine owner who had given a lavish party for the soldiers was murdered, and community pressure blocked prosecution of the killers. In the meantime opposition to the draft had become so bitter that Pennsylvania governor Curtin feared using more troops to enforce the law. Lincoln told him that the law either had to be executed or at least appear to have been executed. Curtin took the latter course. The quota of draftees from the miners' district was filled by crediting previous enlistees who had once lived there to the district.

Parts of the country as urban as Chicago and as rural as Vermont also showed the hostility of foreign-born communities to the imposition of the draft. Chicago's Third Ward was called "the Patch" by Republican newspapers, the home of "the very lowest, most ignorant, depraved and besotted rabble that can be found in the city" (a typical description of immigrant communities by outsiders). Here a mob of between three thousand and four thousand men, women, and children first obstructed draft procedures with mass protests, then attacked the police when they tried to arrest protesters. Bricks, stones, and bottles rained down upon the authorities, and ultimately the police had to release their captives. Vermont's approximately one thousand protesters were Irish workers in marble quarries in Rutland. Their protests were answered by the local provost marshals calling in soldiers to teach them a lesson. Counterforces from the quarry met the soldiers with stones and clubs, and order was restored only with great difficulty. Similar opposition, varying in intensity, took place in every section of the country from Boston to Portsmouth, New Hampshire, to Troy, New York, to Milwaukee, Wisconsin, to St. Paul, Minnesota.

Worker protest against the draft was not just economic in nature. Workers were attacking an economic environment that had limited their chances for success, indeed that threatened them with at least military service and possibly with death because of their poverty. Men with $300 could stay home, those without it had to serve. But beyond the obvious economic elements of their condition workers were also protesting the transformations of a society that intruded on their community life. They were fighting the long reach of the registration and draft official whose loyalties were to a vague national ideal and who reported to officials of the distant national government. Local upper-class elites often enforced national draft laws. Workers protested not only with violence against the draft, but with evasion by running away to Canada or the West, or simply vanishing into their local communities. At the beginning of the war the over 160,000 men who dodged the draft tended to be poor immigrant Catholic Democrats from the cities. Other portions of the population followed their lead, especially border state men with family and cultural ties to Dixie. Protest against conscription marked another example of the cultural divisions that characterized the political environment of the North, divisions that often found antagonists to Republican-generated economic modernization seeking to protect traditional cultural life-styles.

Official reactions to this protest moderated federal policy. In the aftermath of the draft riots many New York cities wrote and adopted ordinances to pay commutation for any drafted man. While the *New York Times* charged that this was a "scheme for propitiating the mob," towns like Utica, Brooklyn, Albany, Troy, Syracuse, and Auburn passed such measures in the summer of 1863. Other states didn't follow this method, but they did increase the bounties to volunteers. . . .

While the antidraft rioting captured the headlines and did reveal serious suffering among the working class, the majority remained loyal to the Union cause. The Sixty-ninth New York Regiment, an all-Irish unit, marched from the battlefield at Gettysburg and helped to crush the mobs in New York streets. Labor leaders like Sylvis and Fincher damned the riots, even as they demanded a repeal of the major inequities of the draft law. Most of the rioters were unskilled workers, and organized labor in New York City was almost unanimous in condemning the riots. Most of the fire companies, composed of lower-class workers, courageously stood up to bricks and stones and fought the city's fires. Trade unions in the city organized the Democratic-Republican Workers Association to demonstrate their loyalty by propagandizing for the war effort.

Workers continued to vote for the Republican party in most places. In 1864 Lincoln carried twelve of the largest urban centers, while McClellan carried only seven. And just before the draft riots, as Lee invaded Pennsylvania, the coal workers of Philadelphia organized six companies to repel his invasion. New York City and Brooklyn stayed Democratic, but even in the metropolis Tammany Hall, led by prowar factions, was gathering power and dominated the antiwar Mozart Hall faction.

The increasing number of strikes and of unions produced a reaction by employers. They, too, began to organize associations to advance their cause. Usually meeting in secret to avoid charges of monopoly, these associations protested, as the Ohio Founders and Machine Builders Association put it, against "every combination which has for its object the regulation of wages. . . . We desire the utmost individual liberty both for employers and employees. The demand for and the supply of labor, the merits of each individual workman, and the cost of living, are the natural causes which should regulate wages." To be sure that "natural causes" worked, these organizations often set maximum rates of pay, worked to blacklist any allegedly dangerous worker, lobbied for anti-union legislation in state capitals. Several states responded by passing "anti-intimidation laws" that proscribed efforts to prevent someone from working.

Other laws that the associations successfully urged challenged union activities as conspiracies, and allowed companies to evict strikers and their families from company-owned housing. Operating in the iron industry, building trades, shipbuilding, and railroads, these organizations gave businessmen the opportunities to get to know each other better and to thus further the integration of the economy. Of course, the competitive business spirit still remained vital, and members of the associations sometimes refused to be bound by the rules of the organization, but the associations gave industry experience with the benefits of organization and combination that they would later use to advantage.

Labor newspapers and organizations kept a sharp eye on the employers' organizations. Their own nationalizing efforts were further stimulated by such employer enterprise. War experience would find use in some postwar labor organizing. But in wartime workers could do little but protest in response to the military support of employers when strikes seemed to affect the war effort. When workers struck an ammunitions factory in Cold Spring, New York, the army was called in and the strike leaders were first thrown in jail without a trial and then driven out of town. Striking dock workers in Brooklyn were locked in the yards and had their pay taken away. Troops ran the Reading Railroad when engineers struck. The strikers gave in and went back to work. Workers at a government arsenal in Nashville went out when promises of overtime pay were broken. The army marched them back to work at bayonet point and gave the workers half pay. Commanding General George Thomas exiled two hundred of these men as "untrustworthy." In St. Louis in April 1864 union workers striking against nonunion labor met the wrath of General William Rosecrans. The general outlawed strikes, provided the names of the strikers to army officials, and threatened a military tribunal for transgressors. This "attack upon the private rights and the military power of the nation by organizations led by bad men," Rosecrans declared, would be stopped. The next month General Burbridge in Louisville copied this order and also used bayonets to drive the strikers back to work. All in all, worker protests against soldiers' intimidating workers in a struggle for free labor had no effect. Lincoln did intercede indirectly by telling officials at the Brooklyn navy yard to return workers' pay. The president may also have been responsible for telling army leaders not to "interfere with the legitimate demands of labor." But usually military necessity overrode labor protests. The general public and even some labor leaders supported the hierarchy that put military success first, labor advancement second.

In sum, during the war the urban working classes on the whole suffered greatly from inflation and from military support used to crush strikes. They provided an enormous number of soldiers for the Union army, given their percentage of the population, and this patriotism served to seriously weaken the power of nativism in the nation. The war also provoked an outburst of organizing of local and national unions and workingmen's associations, although by far the greatest activity took place on the local level. Ideologically the war gave support to the ideals of free labor and demonstrated the utility of organizing resources to achieve its goals.

But a major element in the ideology of the North also served to diffuse the claim of workers for special attention. Since all of society was linked in the free labor struggle, owners, industrialists, capitalists, might equally assert their devotion to free labor goals, thus weakening the special force of labor's claim to the idea. In a society not yet clearly industrialized, a society just beginning to develop the clear divisions between wage earners and independent owners, it was, in fact, easy to deny the permanence of the growing gap. By its emphasis on unity and loyalty the war helped hide this distinction. On the other hand, the war, with the economic costs it exacted from labor and the organization it stimulated, with the contrasts between free labor ideology and wage slavery reality, provoked many labor leaders to greater efforts. These would have their impact in fostering a stronger labor movement after the conflict. One of the reasons for the endurance of the labor movement and its growth after the war was the fact that the war did very little, if anything, to decrease the actual economic inequality in the nation. Possibly Northern labor made minimal gains overall, but the gap between rich and poor and between wage earner, hired laborer, and the owners of shops, factories, and farms narrowed hardly at all. The war taught labor the need and efficacy of organizing to achieve its goals. It did little to bring those goals much closer.

F U R T H E R   R E A D I N G

Richard Franklin Bensel, *Yankee Leviathan: The Origins of Central State Authority in America, 1859–1877* (1990)

Iver Bernstein, *The New York City Draft Riots* (1990)

George M. Fredrickson, *The Inner Civil War: Northern Intellectuals and the Crisis of the Union* (1965)

J. Matthew Gallman, *Mastering Wartime: A Social History of Philadelphia during the Civil War* (1990)

———, *The North Fights the Civil War: The Home Front* (1994)

James W. Geary, *We Need Men: The Union Draft in the Civil War* (1991)

Harold M. Hyman, *A More Perfect Union: The Impact of the Civil War on the Constitution* (1973)

Frank W. Klement, *The Limits of Dissent: Clement L. Vallandigham and the Civil War* (1970)

William Q. Maxwell, *Lincoln's Fifth Wheel: The Political History of the United States Sanitary Commission* (1956)

Eric L. McKitrick, "Party Politics and the Union and Confederate War Efforts," in William Nisbet Chambers and Walter Dean Burnham, eds., *The American Party Systems* (1967)

Grace Palladino, *Another Civil War: Labor, Capital, and the State in the Anthracite Regions of Pennsylvania, 1840–68* (1990)

Anne C. Rose, *Victorian America and the Civil War* (1992)

Joel Silbey, *A Respectable Minority: The Democratic Party in the Civil War Era* (1977)

Maris A. Vinovskis, ed., *Toward a Social History of the American Civil War: Exploratory Essays* (1990)

CHAPTER
8

The Southern Home Front

Over the years, the South's home front has been examined thoroughly and intensively by historians. The reason for this is the widespread assumption that the explanation for Confederate defeat lay behind the lines, in the civilian sector. The Confederate armies and their leaders have generally been excused from blame for the failure of the South's bid for independence. Even though the performance of the western command was lackluster or worse, the view has grown up that military forces led by the likes of Lee, Jackson, and the two Johnstons could not have been the major weakness of the Confederacy.

Accordingly, historians have most often stressed deficiencies intrinsic to the Confederacy, such as its uninspiring and unattractive cause, the protection and perpetuation of slavery; the thinness of the communal and nationalistic sentiment undergirding its drive to create a separate nation-state; and the brittleness of its governmental institutions when subjected to the pressure of war's demands. Over and above these difficulties, there was the sheer magnitude of the task of establishing a government and creating armies from scratch at a moment's notice, something the Union was never confronted with. In effect, historians have considered the Confederacy's problems so fundamental that battlefield victories could not possibly have offset them, but could only delay the final reckoning.

All the same, the Confederacy did have some advantages initially. Militarily, its armies had only to repel the enemy's forces, whereas the Union had to invade and conquer its adversary. Also, the South had been battling to defend its way of life for over a generation before the war broke out, and so perhaps its people had developed a greater sense of their region's interests and destiny. And finally, the Confederacy came under military attack soon after its secession, and so its inhabitants quickly had a cause—the protection of their homes and neighborhoods from an external but very real and imminent threat—that was far more compelling and immediate than anything the Union could offer its citizenry.

Because a large number of Southerners, as opposed to very few Northerners, encountered the war at first hand, the experience of civilians was considerably different in the Confederacy. Those living in the border states of Tennessee, North Carolina, and Virginia had to endure Union armies marching through the districts where they lived, commandeering—and sometimes destroying—provisions and property, and ultimately occupying large tracts of their homeland. As the war went on, more and more Confederate territory was occupied and brought under Union control. In recent years, historians have begun to investigate this phenomenon and have produced studies of particular communities and localities where occupation, or even the troop movements of the South's own armies, resulted in social disturbance and disorder. Indeed, most of the social history of the Confederacy that is now emerging tends to depict the disruption and distress that was the experience of Southern civilians far more than of their Northern counterparts. For the impact of the war was considerably more unsettling and dislocating within the Confederacy. The draft and taxation were imposed on both societies and caused similar reactions. But the citizens of the Confederacy had to endure, in addition, an embargo on cotton sales, a Union naval blockade, impressment of foodstuffs, alarming inflation, and a growing scarcity of food and goods—and, on top of all this, invasion and a war waged increasingly against the civilian population. So the story of the Confederate home front, despite the similarities of wartime restrictions and hardships, became qualitatively different from that of the North as time went on. Thus, the history of Southern society during the Civil War is characterized by dissent and resistance, social strain and disorder. The war affected civilians in the North, often quite personally and directly. But the war came into the South even more forcefully. It was fought there, and, increasingly, civilians found themselves in its path, becoming not just its victims but its prey.

DOCUMENTS

The documents for this chapter focus on the political dissent and social strain that the war generated within the Confederacy. All but one come from the states of North Carolina and Georgia, which are also the areas of the Confederacy covered by the two essays.

The first item is from a speech by President Jefferson Davis to the Mississippi legislature on December 26, 1862, explaining the aims and objectives of the Confederate struggle. In the second document, a letter of September 1, 1862, Governor Joseph E. Brown of Georgia tells his friend Alexander H. Stephens, the Confederate vice president, why the Confederate government has to be kept in check. The third piece is a plaintive petition, dated February 18, 1863, from a group of barely literate citizens of Bladen County, North Carolina, to Governor Zebulon B. Vance, describing the severe hardship they are suffering.

The fourth document is a letter of January 22, 1864, from Alexander H. Stephens to Jefferson Davis showing how fundamentally the two men differed over how best to run the war. The fifth selection is a formal protest from the North Carolina legislature on May 28, 1864, against the Confederate government's most recent draft provisions and its suspension of the writ of habeas corpus.

By 1864, a peace party had begun to emerge in North Carolina. In the sixth document, the main newspaper of this movement, the Raleigh *Standard,* calls on voters in the upcoming state election to vote against the "Destructives" led by Governor Vance; the editorial appeared on July 13, 1864. And the seventh, and last, selection is a letter from Confederate Congressman Warren Akin of Georgia to a friend, Nathan Land, on October 13, 1864, discussing political prospects and complaining about the slaveholders' unwillingness to sacrifice for a cause in which they had a greater stake than most.

President Davis Explains the Confederate Cause, December 1862

... The issue before us is one of no ordinary character. We are not engaged in a conflict for conquest or for aggrandizement, or for the settlement of a point of international law. The question for you to decide is: "Will you be slaves or will you be independent?" Will you transmit to your children the freedom and equality which your fathers transmitted to you, or will you bow down in adoration before an idol baser than ever was worshipped by Eastern idolators? Nothing more is necessary than the mere statement of this issue. Whatever may be the personal sacrifices involved, I am surprised that you will shrink from them whenever the question comes before you. Those men who now assail us, who have been associated with us in a common union, who have inherited a government which they claim to be the best the world ever saw—these men, when left to themselves, have shown that they are incapable of preserving their own personal liberty. They have destroyed the freedom of the press; they have seized upon and imprisoned members of State Legislatures and of municipal councils, who were suspected of sympathy with the South; men have been carried off into captivity in distant States without indictment, without a knowledge of the accusations brought against them, in utter defiance of all rights guaranteed by the institutions under which they live. These people, when separated from the South and left entirely to themselves, have, in six months, demonstrated their utter incapacity for self-government. And yet, these are the people who claim to be your masters. These are the people who have determined to divide out the South among their Federal troops. Mississippi they have devoted to the direst vengeance of all. "But vengeance is the Lord's," and beneath his banner you will meet and hurl back these worse than vandal hordes.

The great end and aim of the government is to make our struggle successful. The men who stand highest in this contest would fall the first sacrifice to the vengeance of the enemy in case we should be unsuccessful. You may rest assured, then, for that reason, if for no other, that whatever capacity they possess will be devoted to securing the independence of the country. Our government is not like the monarchies of the Old World, resting for support upon armies and navies. It sprang from the people, and the confidence of the people is necessary for its success. When misrepresentations of the government have been circulated, when accusations have been brought against it of weakness and inefficiency, often have I felt in my heart the struggle between the desire for justice and the duty not to give information to the enemy—because at such time the correction of error would have been injurious to the safety of the cause. Thus, that great and good man, General A. S. Johnston, was contented to rest beneath contumely and to be pointed at by the finger of scorn, because he did not advance from Bowling Green with the little army under his command. But month after month he maintained his post, keeping the enemy ignorant of the paucity of his numbers, and thus holding the invaders in check. I take this case as one instance; it is not the only one by far.

The issue then being: will you be slaves; will you consent to be robbed of your property; will you renounce the exercise of those rights with which you were born and which were transmitted to you by your fathers? I feel that in addressing Mississippians

---

From Jefferson Davis, Speech to the Mississippi Legislature, December 26, 1862, in *The Rebellion Record, 1862–63,* Frank Moore, ed. (1863), Vol. 6, pp. 298–299.

the answer will be that their interests, even life itself, should be willingly laid down upon the altar of their country. . . .

Governor Joseph E. Brown of Georgia Denounces Confederate Policy, September 1862

(Private.)

Canton, [Ga.], Sept. 1st, 1862.

Dear Sir: I have the pleasure to acknowledge the receipt of your letter of the 26th ult. and am gratified that you take the view which you have expressed about the action of Genl. Bragg in his declaration of martial law over Atlanta and his appoint[ment], as the newspapers say, of a civil governor with aids, etc.

I have viewed this proceeding as I have others of our military authorities of late with painful apprehensiveness for the future. It seems military men are assuming the whole powers of government to themselves and setting at defiance constitutions, laws, state rights, state sovereignty, and every other principle of civil liberty, and that our people engrossed in the struggle with the enemy are disposed to submit to these bold usurpations tending to military despotism without murmur, much less resistance. I should have called this proceeding into question before this time but I was hopeful from the indications which I had noted that Congress would take such action as would check these dangerous usurpations of power, and for the further reasons that I have already come almost into conflict with the Confederate authorities in vindication of what I have considered the rights of the State and people of Georgia, and I was fearful, as no other governor seems to raise these questions, that I might be considered by good and true men in and out of Congress too refractory for the times. I had therefore concluded to take no notice of this matter till the meeting of the legislature when I expect to ask the representatives of the people to define the bounds to which they desire the Governor to go in the defense of the rights and sovereignty of the state. I confess I have apprehensions that our present General Assembly does not properly reflect the sentiments of our people upon this great question, but if the Executive goes beyond the bounds where he is sustained by the representatives of the people he exposes himself to censure without the moral power to do service to the great principles involved. I fear we have much more to apprehend from military despotism than from subjugation by the enemy. I trust our generals will improve well their time while we have the advantage and the enemy are organizing another army. Hoping that your health is good and begging that you will write me when your important duties are not too pressing to permit it, I am very truly your friend.

Letter, Joseph E. Brown to Alexander H. Stephens, September 1, 1862, in U. B. Phillips, "Correspondence of Toombs, Stephens and Cobb," *Report of the American Historical Association for 1911* (1913), Vol. 2, pp. 605–606.

Plain Folk Protest the Burden of the War, February 1863

february The 18th 1863

M. Z. vance Govener of NC

Sir we take the privilege of writing you a fiew lines to inform you of a fiew things that is mooving at this time in the State of N C the time has come that we the common people has to hav bread or blood & we are bound boath men & women to hav it or die in the attempt some of us has bin travling for the last month with the money in our pockets to buy corn & tryed men that had a plenty & has been unable to buy a bushel holding on for a better price we are willing to gave & obligate two Dollars a bushel but no more for the idea is that the slave oner has the plantations & the hands to rais the brad stufs & the common people is drove of in the ware to fight for the big mans negro & he at home making nearly all the corn that is made & then becaus he has the play in his own fingers he puts the price on his corn so as to take all the solders wages for a fiew bushels & then them that has worked hard & was in living circumstances with perhaps a good little homestid & other thing convenient for there well being perhaps will be credited until the debt will about take there land & every thing they hav & then they will stop all & if not they will hav to Rent there lands of there lords sir we hoos sons brothers & husbands is now fighting for the big mans negros are determd to have bredd out of these barns & that at a price that we can pay or we will slaughter as we go—if this is the way we common people is to be treated in the confedercy we hope that you & your friends will be as smart as govener Elis & his friends was take us out with out the voice of the people & let us try to maniage & defend our own State we hope sir that you will duly consider the a bove mentioned items & if it is in your power to Remedy the present evils do it speedly it is not our desiar to organise and commence operations for if the precedent is laid it will be unanimous but if ther is not steps taken soon nessesity will drive us into measurs that may prove awful we dont ask meet on fair terms for we can live on bread perhaps it would be better for you to isue your proclamation that no man should sell in the State at more than $2 pr bushel you no best &c if you cant remedy Extosan on the staff of life we will & we as your subjects will make Examples of all who Refuse to open there barn Doors & appoint other men over there farms who per haps will hav better Harts we no that this is unlawful at a common time but we are shut up we cant trade with no body only Just those in the confedersy & they can perish all those that has not and it seems that all harts is turned to gizards—Sir consider this matter over & pleas send us a privat letter of instruction direct it to bryant Swamp post office Bladen county N C & to R.L. as our company will be called Regulators

[no signatures]

From unsigned petition to Governor Vance, February 18, 1863, in Governor's Papers, Zebulon B. Vance, N. C. Department of Archives and History, Raleigh. This selection is also available in *North Carolina Civil War Documentary*, W. Buck Yearns and John G. Barrett, eds. (University of North Carolina Press, 1980), pp. 218–219.

Vice President Alexander H. Stephens
Recommends an Alternative Confederate Strategy,
January 1864

Crawfordville, Ga

22 Jan 1864

Private

His Excellency Jefferson Davis

Dear Sir

. . . I feel great interest in what is doing in Congress and shall go on as soon as I feel able—One thing I would say to you. Great apprehension is beginning to be felt amongst the people here that Congress will pass an act suspending the writ of habeas corpus and putting the country under Martial Law. Such an act would in my judgment be exceedingly unwise & impolitic as well as unconstitutional—and I trust if it should pass it will never receive the Executive approval. I am aware of the difficulties and embarrassments on all sides. But there is nothing more important than preserving the entire confidence and cordial support of the great mass of the people in their Government. They have looked upon it from the beginning as a struggle for Constitutional liberty—and as long as this view is kept before them they will give an enthusiastic support of the cause under the greatest trials deprivations and sacrifices. Our greatest, surest last hope is in the willing hearts of the people. This should never be lost sight of. I do not take the same view of our present situation that many do. There is in it really nothing to discourage if prudent & wise counsels prevail. Our strength does not lie in an attempt to match the enemy in the size of our armies—or number of men in the field. This we can not do—and by an attempt to approximate this equality of force we only weaken ourselves. No people can put and keep all its arms bearing population in the field for a long time. A large portion of them must be retained to supply subsistence, munitions of war etc. My opinion respectfully submitted is that we should not attempt to increase our present force in the field. We have got as many as we can maintain in view of the probable continuance of the war. The enemy doubtless looks forward to the coming summer campaign as a decisive one. With this view they will put forth their greatest efforts. Should these premeditated blows be parried or avoided or repelled by energy and skill on our part as they may be, quite a different aspect will rest upon the state of affairs next fall. Their armies may penetrate farther in the interior of the country than they have ever yet done but this will not bring the war any nearer to a conclusion than it was at the beginning if the hearts of our people are kept right. There is such a thing in wars, long wars especially, as whipping the fight without fighting it. In the great inequality of numbers existing between us & our enemy we must rely upon and use our advantages. We must preserve and keep our essential resources active. We must not collapse for want of subsistence. On this point great care prudence and system—real business system—is necessary . . . [there follows a calculation of the provisions now available to the Confederacy].

My opinion is with proper system & management the Govt has nearly enough food to support the army this year without purchasing any more except meat—And how much

---

Letter, Alexander H. Stephens to Jefferson Davis, Crawfordsville, Ga., January 22, 1864, *Alexander H. Stephens Papers,* Duke University Library.

of this will have to be bought would be very soon ascertained. I call your attention to this because over here when tythes [taxes in kind on farm produce] are lying ready to be sent off, officers are going through the country buying & impressing—this is all wrong & for the want of a proper system and business management. In this connection I will also state that I deem it *essential* that the producing capacity & energy of the country should not be weakened this year. To keep them at the point they were last year two things are essential. First plantations must not be deprived of overseers and managers—and secondly—fair market prices—or in other words just compensation for all articles of subsistence the Govt shall be compelled to buy. The greatest stimulant to production is gain or the hope of it—It is an unalterable law of nature. Please excuse this rambling letter. I am too weak & feeble to continue it. . . .

The North Carolina Legislature Protests the Confederate Draft and Martial Law, May 1864

Resolved, That while the people of North-Carolina have ever been and still are anxious to strengthen the administration of the Confederate government in every legitimate way, and to promote the success of the common cause in order that we may have a speedy and honorable peace, they view with deep concern and alarm every infraction of the Constitution by the Congress of the Confederate States, and this General Assembly doth, in their name, protest against such infractions as of pernicious example and fatal tendency.

Resolved, That the act of the late Congress, entitled "An act to suspend the privilege of the writ of *habeas corpus* in certain cases," violates the fundamental maxim of republican government which requires a separation of the departments of power, clothes the Executive with judicial functions which Congress cannot constitutionally confer even on the judiciary itself, and sets at naught the most emphatic and solemn guarantees of the Constitution.

Resolved, That this General Assembly, representing the people of North Carolina, doth not consent to the sacrifice of the vital principles of free government in a war carried on solely to secure and perpetuate them, and doth declare that "no conditions of public danger," present or prospective, probable or possible, can render the liberties of the people incompatible with the public safety.

Resolved, That the act of the same Congress, entitled "An act to organize forces to serve during the war," declaring all white men, residents of the Confederate States, between the ages of seventeen and fifty, to be in the military service, embracing in its provisions every State officer in all the departments, executive, legislative and judicial, and subjecting all the industrial pursuits of the country to military supervision and control, reduces the State government to mere provincial administrations, dependent on the grace and favor of Congress and the Executive, is destructive of state sovereignty, and imports an assertion of the power on the part of Congress to convert the Confederate government into a consolidated military despotism.

Resolved, That this General Assembly doth therefore request our Senators and Representatives in Congress to use their best endeavors to procure a repeal of the first

From *Public Laws of North Carolina Passed by the General Assembly in the Adjourned Session of 1864,* pp. 23–25, in *North Carolina Civil War Documents,* W. Buck Yearns and John G. Barrett, eds. (University of North Carolina Press, 1980), pp. 279–280.

mentioned act, and such modifications of the second as shall secure the rights and preserve the integrity of the States of the Confederacy. . . .

The Raleigh *North Carolina Standard* Urges Voters to Endorse a Negotiated Peace, July 1864

We appeal to our friends to be at the election ground early in the day, and to work for the true Conservatives and against the Destructives and their associates, until sunset, with the utmost determination and zeal. The issue is *War* or *Peace,* and *Liberty* against *Despotism.* Gov. Vance and his supporters are not only in favor of the war going on, and on, and on, and not only opposed to negotiations for peace unless they can be brought about in *their* way, which is the way pointed out by President Davis; but they are *Davis* men—endorsers of his administration, and *with* him in every essential particular. To vote for Gov. Vance is to endorse President Davis, and at the same time to encourage the continuance of the war with all its horrors, with no earnest or determined efforts to stop it by negotiations.

We are known to be in favor of peace, and also to be in favor of civil liberty and the rights of our State. We do not fear to trust the people with their own affairs, whether in Convention or otherwise; and we would regard any treaty of peace that might be made as honorable, which, after having been submitted to the people at the ballot-box, should receive their approval. If rejected by them, it would be dishonorable. The people of North-Carolina will never agree to any peace that is not honorable. One of the best plans thus far presented . . . will be found in the resolutions introduced in the last House of Representatives by the Hon. J. T. Leach, of the 3d District from this State. . . . Gov. Vance is *opposed* to the peace plan contained in these resolutions, as is conclusively proved by his speeches and the course of his subsidized organs.

Remember that Gov. Vance is the Destructive candidate for Governor; that the Destructives expect to use him for their own purposes, and thus destroy the Conservative party; that if elected by their aid he will be bound to carry out their views; that if elected it will be understood that the war is to go on until *the South subjugates* the North, or the North subjugates the South; and that if defeated, *a great moral influence will at once go out in favor of negotiations and an honorable peace.* Mark the fact . . . that the Destructives are his most active supporters. "A man is known by the company he keeps." . . . Let every true Conservative *work* to prevent this result. . . .

Congressman Warren Aiken of Georgia Contemplates the Fate of Slavery, October 1864

. . . As to calling out the negro men and placing them in the army, with the promise that they shall be free at the end of the war, I can only say it is a question of fearful magnitude. Can we prevent subjugation, confiscation, degradation and slavery without it[?] If not, will our condition or that of the negro, be any worse by calling them into service[?]

From Raleigh *Standard,* editorial, July 13, 1864. This selection is also available in *North Carolina Civil War Documentary,* W. Buck Yearns and John G. Barrett, eds. (University of North Carolina Press, 1980), p. 318.

Letter, Warren Aiken to Nathan Land, October 13, 1864, in *Letters of Warren Aiken: Confederate Congressman,* Bell I. Wiley, ed. (University of Georgia Press, 1959), pp. 32–33.

On the other hand: Can we feed our soldiers and their families if the negro men are taken from the plantations? Will our soldiers submit to having our negroes along side them in the ditches, or in line of battle? When the negro is taught the use of arms and the art of war, can we live in safety with them afterwards? Or if it be contemplated to send them off to another country, when peace is made, will it be right to force them to a new, distant and strange land, after they have fought for and won the independence of this? Would they go without having another war? Involving, perhaps a general insurrection of all the negroes? To call forth the negroes into the army, with the promise of freedom, will it not be giving up the great question involved by doing the very thing Lincoln is now doing? The Confederate States may take private property for public use, by paying for it; but can we ever pay for 300,000 negro men at present prices, in addition to our other indebtedness? The Confederate Government may buy the private negro property of the Citizens, but can it set them free among us, to corrupt our slaves, and place in peril our existence? These are some of the thoughts that have passed th[r]ough my mind on the subject. But I can not say that I have a definite and fixed opinion. If I were convinced that we will be subjugated, with the long train of horrors that will follow it, unless the negroes be placed in the army, I would not hesitate to enrol our slaves and put them to fighting. Subjugation will give us free negroes in abundance—enemies at that—while white slaves will be more numerous than free negroes. We and our children will be slaves, while our freed negroes will lord it over us. It is impossible for the evils resulting from placing our slaves in the army to be greater than those that will follow subjugation. We may (if necessary) put our slaves in the army, win our independence, and have liberty and homes for ourselves and children. But subjugation will deprive us of our homes, houses, property, liberty, honor, and every thing worth living for, leaving for us and our posterity only the chains of slavery, tenfold more galling and degrading than that now felt by our negroes. But I will not enlarge, I have made suggestions merely for your reflection.

Have you ever noticed the strange conduct of our people during this war? They give up their sons, husbands, brothers & friends, and often without murmuring, to the army; but let one of their negroes be taken, and what a houl you will hear. The love of money has been the greatest difficulty in our way to independence,—it is now our chief obstacle. "For the love of money is the root of all evil; which while some coveted after they have erred from the faith, and pierced themselves through with many sorrows." What a fearful realizing of this truth many will feel after this war. Their hearts will be "pierced through with many sorrows." . . .

E S S A Y S

The two essays on the Southern home front deal with different aspects of the problems faced by the Confederacy as the war progressed. The first, by Marc W. Kruman of Wayne State University, examines the vigorous disagreement that arose within the Confederacy over the central government's conduct of the war. In some states like North Carolina, this dissent became particularly vehement, and the author offers an explanation for the severity of the reaction in the South compared with that in the North. The accompanying piece, by J. William Harris of the University of New Hampshire, is a study of the impact of the war on a particular region of the Confederacy—the area around Augusta, Georgia, on the state's northeastern border with South Carolina, where the adjacent counties are Richmond in Georgia and Edgefield in South Carolina. Although both essays deal with the effect of the Confederate war effort, one focuses on the political aspect and the other on the social.

Dissent in the Confederacy: The North Carolina Experience

MARC W. KRUMAN

Since 1925, when Frank L. Owsley published his seminal book, *State Rights in the Confederacy,* historians have been aware that white southerners during the Civil War were not a united people fighting selflessly to preserve a way of life. Owsley identified substantial opposition to the Confederate government among state rights advocates. He believed that in order for the Confederacy to mount a successful war effort, it needed to centralize decision-making. But the insistence of southern politicians that their cherished theories of state rights be implemented caused constant bickering between the Confederate and state governments and ultimately paralyzed the Confederate war effort. In the end, Owsley concluded, the Confederate States of America "died of state rights."

Other historians have emphasized different reasons for popular hostility to the Confederate government. Albert Burton Moore, for example, pointed to the disaffection that grew out of the enactment of the conscription laws. Georgia Lee Tatum catalogued a number of causes of disloyalty in the Confederacy: persistent unionism, the conscription laws, impressment, the tax-in-kind, the suspension of the writ of habeas corpus, and the economic suffering caused by the war. Bell I. Wiley suggested that class legislation, like the exemption from the draft of a man to oversee twenty or more slaves, generated discontent among "plain folk."

Such interpretations dwell upon the symptoms of dissent in the Confederacy but overlook the underlying causes. They virtually ignore the one cause of opposition to the Confederate government that preoccupied contemporaries. Antagonists of the Confederate government feared that it was becoming a "central military despotism," intent upon robbing the people of their liberty. One might dismiss these fears as political propaganda, but they were repeated too frequently in private correspondence to be regarded as such. It is also tempting to slight such anxieties as mere rhetorical devices designed to cover up more practical objections to individual policies of the Confederate government. To be sure, conscription aroused opposition among those men who did not want to fight, and the tax-in-kind antagonized farmers who hated heavy taxes. But those measures and others also generated deeper fears for the survival of popular liberty.

Those fears reflected the inheritance of more than a century of English and American political belief. Eighteenth-century Americans feared that liberty, their liberty, would be crushed by power, usually the power of government. They portrayed liberty as fragile and passive, power as aggressive and unrelenting. Liberty was always under siege, always threatened. Citizens of the early republic sought the preservation of liberty in the constitutional republican governments of the states and nation. If the republic survived and remained strong, freedom would be protected. But they were also aware that past republics had been relatively short-lived. Hence, Americans remained sensitive to threats to republican government and the liberty it protected. Historians have identified the

From Mark W. Kruman, "Dissent in the Confederacy: The North Carolina Experience," *Civil War History,* Volume 27, #4, 1981, pp. 293–303, 306–313. Copyright © 1981. Reprinted by permission of The Kent State University Press.

expression of those fears in the political struggles of the 1790s, in the decision to declare war in 1812, and in the nullification crisis.

During the 1820s and 1830s, the equality of white men became inextricably linked to the concept of liberty. Men, they believed, who were not the equals of other citizens were not truly free. This ideological commitment to the preservation of republican government and white liberty and equality shaped the contours of political debate in the decades before the Civil War. All of the major parties—Democratic, Whig, American, and Republican—portrayed themselves as the best defenders of freedom. Only by electing us, they each contended, can despotism be averted. Thus, on the eve of the Civil War, the threat that power posed to liberty remained as real to Americans as it had to their fathers and grandfathers. It is in this historical context that popular fears for the survival of liberty developed in the Confederacy. But the nature of those fears, how and why they grew, and how they were expressed and ultimately resolved still require explanation. North Carolina, with a deserved reputation as a state hostile to the Confederate central government, offers an excellent case study of the rise of opposition among white southerners to that government. An examination of the ideological foundations of North Carolinians' hostility toward the central government and of the political context in which it developed reveals why the government aroused such widespread fear and anger among its loyal citizens.

In the winter of 1860–61, after Abraham Lincoln had been elected president and the seven states of the deep South had seceded from the Union and formed the Confederate States of America, North Carolinians remained firmly attached to the Union. On February 28, 1861, a slight majority of North Carolina voters defeated a referendum calling for a convention to consider secession. At the same time they elected an overwhelming majority of unionists to the proposed convention.

However, public opinion shifted dramatically from strong unionism to almost unanimous support for secession after April 15, the day that Lincoln called for troops to suppress the rebellion in the lower South. North Carolina unionists and secessionists had long opposed any attempt to "coerce" the seceded states. They warned the North that any attempt to compel the return of those states to the Union would cause North Carolina's secession. North Carolinians rejected coercion by the North primarily because they perceived it as an attempt to subjugate the South, to suppress the liberties of free men, to deny men the right to govern themselves. If the federal government could force a restoration of the Union, could it not compel North Carolinians to accede to other kinds of demands? As one secessionist put it, coercion changed "the issue . . . from the Negro to that of a question of popular liberty."

As news of Lincoln's proclamation spread, steadfast unionists became secessionists. W. N. H. Smith, a Whig member of Congress and a strong unionist, wrote to his colleague Zebulon Vance: "The Union feeling *was strong* up to the recent proclamation. This War Manifest Extinguishes it, and resistance is now on every mans lips and throbs in every bosom. . . . Union men are now such no longer." Several weeks after Lincoln called for troops, Josiah Cowles, a Yadkin county Whig politician and a slaveholder, explained to his son why his views had changed: "I was as strong a union man as any in the state up to the time of Lincolns proclamation calling for 75000 volunteers. I then saw that the south had either to submit to abject vassallage or assert her rights at the point of the Sword." Cowles reminded his son that he had opposed coercion, "believing it to be virtually a distruction to liberty." The transformation of Josiah Cowles's attitude toward the Union reflected the changes of thousands of other North Carolinians. The press and politicians proclaimed that the incipient war would be fought in the name of popular liberty. On May 20, 1861, delegates to a state convention unanimously adopted an ordinance of secession and ratified the Provisional Constitution of the Confederate States of America.

North Carolinians entered a war that they expected to win quickly, and they assumed that such a war would leave intact their traditionally aloof relationship with the central government. But as it became apparent that the war would last more than a few months, some southerners came to appreciate the need to centralize the war effort and to strengthen the central government enough to curb disloyalty. Would North Carolinians now accept a stronger, more centralized government, one that would almost inevitably infringe on popular liberties? Should they surrender some cherished liberties, they asked themselves, in order to obtain independence from the northern despots? And if they gave up some of their liberties for the duration of the war, would they be able to regain them afterward? The answers North Carolinians gave to these questions played a significant role in the development of their attitudes toward the Confederate government.

The attitudes of North Carolinians toward the centralization of governmental authority and the subsequent infringements on individual liberty can be traced by examining the views of the major political group in the state the Conservative party. The Conservatives, composed mostly of former members of the Whig party and of persons who had been unionists up to Lincoln's proclamation, began to act publicly as a political party in late 1861 and won massive victories over the Democratic party, which had dominated the state's politics for more than a decade, in the gubernatorial and legislative elections of 1862. Though seriously rent by factionalism after 1862, the party captured nine of the state's ten congressional seats in 1863 and provided both gubernatorial candidates in 1864. Loyal to the Confederacy, the Conservatives nevertheless attacked many Confederate policies. Their attitudes toward the preservation of liberty and toward various measures of the Confederate government mirrored the attitudes of most North Carolinians and revealed how opposition to the Confederate government grew in North Carolina.

Conservatives, adhering to the ideas of their revolutionary ancestors and of antebellum politics, defined liberty to mean freedom from an arbitrary government. Governments had to act within the limits set by freedom's "chosen instruments—the constitution and the laws." A free man was the equal of all other free men, protected from arbitrary arrest and imprisonment and from unduly heavy taxation. Within the bounds of law, he was able to express himself freely and to own property unmolested.

A man who was not free was a slave. Slavery meant more to white North Carolinians than a system of forced labor for blacks; it was a social and political concept indicating a person's submission to the arbitrary will of another. They believed that a white man deprived of his liberties was just as much a slave as the black bondsman. Black slavery was only the most extreme example of slavery. But the presence of black slaves was important because it constantly reminded white North Carolinians just what it meant to be enslaved. Black slavery also reinforced a belief in the fragility of their own liberty. Unless they protected liberty constantly and carefully, it would be destroyed. "We must retain our self-possession, and our liberties, too, in the progress of this war," wrote one Conservative, "or we will look in vain for them at its close."

Conservative sensitivity to threats to popular liberty reflected not only a response to actions of the Confederate government, but also a persistence of antebellum beliefs. Antebellum political dialogue revolved around the promotion and protection of the freedom and equality of North Carolina white men. The major political issue in the state from 1848 until the mid-1850s was the Democratic party's advocacy of the elimination of the fifty acre requirement for senatorial electors, a measure the party called "equal suffrage." In response to the Democratic proposal, Whigs from the underrepresented western part of the state argued that only increased western representation in the state legislature, through the adoption of the "white basis," would make white North Carolinians truly free and equal. Later the entire Whig party claimed that the same benefits could be derived from taxing slaves on an ad valorem basis. The promotion of white equality and freedom was also the goal of politicians in both parties when they defended the right of southerners to settle with their slaves in federal territories. And politicians based their defense of slavery on the grounds that the debasement of black people promoted equality and freedom among whites. On such issues, politicians spoke to the white North Carolinian's fear of having his equality and freedom abridged. In our hands, partisans declared, white liberty and equality are safe.

The threat to liberty and equality and to the republican government which was their guardian came from the aggressive, expansive power of government officials. "All encroachments [on liberty]," warned one Conservative editor, "are sure to begin with and eminate from our rulers." If checks were not placed on the power of rulers, they would concentrate power in their hands and use it to destroy the liberties of the people. Therefore, the people needed specific safeguards for their liberties. First, they demanded that civil power always be supreme over military power. This axiom of English political thought had particular relevance to southerners at war. Because the strength of the military necessarily increased during wartime, it seemed possible that the military power would become supreme. Therefore, Conservatives argued that it was "necessary to hold in check that propensity which war is always likely to bring fourth—a military rule to override the civil power." For this reason, Conservatives were especially sensitive to any encroachments of the military on the civil power.

A strong state government was the second safeguard of the people's liberties. It could serve as a buffer between the people and the arbitrary will of the central government. Because they considered the state as the major defender of their freedom, North Carolinians were acutely aware of all the central government's infringements on the power and rights of the states.

Jefferson Davis first raised the specter of a strong military government in March 1862, when he asked Congress to enact a law permitting the conscription of white men between the ages of eighteen and thirty-five. Since most soldiers in the Confederate army had volunteered for one year, their enlistment would end that April. Davis argued that conscription was needed to prevent the army's collapse and to maintain some continuity in its membership. Although the bill passed easily in the Confederate Congress, men of all political persuasions in North Carolina were reluctant to accept the need for conscription. Their state had provided more than its quota of soldiers. Why, North Carolinians asked, should they have to contribute more men when other states were not meeting their requirements? If many more men were drafted, the few remaining men in nonslaveholding areas of the state would be unable to cultivate sufficient crops to feed the people.

More important than those complaints was the fear that conscription represented the first step toward military despotism. If the central government and the military alone decided when and how many troops were needed and then took sole responsibility for recruiting them, it would be but a small step for the military thus to attain complete ascendancy in the South. Upon hearing of Davis's request for a conscription law,

Congressman Thomas S. Ashe wrote to a friend: "It is said by [its] friends . . . to be the only means of saving the country, but I must confess I fear [it] will be the inauguration of a strong military government."

By assuming complete control over recruitment, the Confederate government apparently infringed on the powers of the states. Richard Puryear, who had been a member of the Confederate Provisional Congress, worried that the doctrine of state rights "is repudiated and trodden under foot and germs of consolidation is already springing up on its ruins. Consolidation leads to despotism—and further than this I would not lift the veil." Because conscription strengthened the military and weakened the state government, Puryear continued, it threatened the people's liberty. "The people are jealous of their rights and many begin to fear that their rulers have designs upon their liberty. Amidst the difficulties which surround us and the dangers which threaten us nothing should be done to increase their fears and apprehensions. And what is better calculated to do this than this conscription?" Despite Conservative apprehension over the loss of civil liberty, as the need for the conscription law became evident, they grudgingly acquiesced to it. But they warned that "we are in the very midst of perils, no not only from the common enemy, but also from those whom we have delegated to transact our public business."

Similar fears were aroused by the suspension of the writ of habeas corpus. The Confederate Congress first authorized the president to suspend the writ from February 27 to October 13, 1862, and then extended authorization to February 13, 1863. Davis used that authority in Salisbury, North Carolina, site of a Confederate prison. Those actions excited fears of arbitrary arrests by military authorities. Conservative Governor Zebulon B. Vance, in his message to the General Assembly in November 1862, feared that once the writ was suspended "no man is safe from the power of one individual. He could at pleasure seize any citizen of the State, with or without excuse, throw him into prison, and permit him to languish there without relief—a power that I am unwilling to see intrusted to any living man." The possibility of arbitrary arrests became a reality in the fall of 1862, when Confederate authorities arrested the Reverend R. J. Graves on grounds of disloyalty and removed him to Richmond's Confederate prison, Castle Thunder. Upon learning of his case, the General Assembly passed a resolution instructing the governor to demand Graves's release. Although Vance obtained the prisoner's freedom, Graves's arrest had frightened persons like the editor of the Raleigh *Standard,* who worried that it "is a gross violation of the Constitution and Bill of Rights of this State, and of the first principles of liberty." The military arrests of men like Graves impelled Tod R. Caldwell, attorney and Conservative party leader, to write that "no man, even tho he is clothed with a little brief military authority should be allowed to trample the laws under his feet and set himself up as superior to law & the law making power." He warned that "if something is not done to crush out this tyranny, we had as well confess ourselves slaves, for we are truly no better than slaves."

The suspension of the writ and the subsequent arrests of North Carolina citizens also excited apprehension about the independence of the state's judiciary. Conservatives regarded an independent judiciary as critical to the protection of liberty. Only judges neither bound to the authorities nor indebted to them for favors could check governmental encroachments on liberty. Such independence seemed threatened in mid-1863 when Secretary of War James A. Seddon attempted to obstruct the judicial process. Seddon blamed the desertion of North Carolina troops on the general belief that the state courts had declared the conscription law unconstitutional and asked the governor to use his influence to restrain the judges. Vance, who considered an independent judiciary "the only hope of freedom in times of passion & of violence," indignantly refused. "An upright judge," he wrote, "must deliver the law as he conceives it to be, whether it should happen to comport with the received notions of the military authorities or not. I must therefore most respectfully decline to use my influence in restraining or controlling that co-ordinate branch of the government which [is] . . . in great danger of being overlapped and destroyed by the tendency of the times."

The controversies surrounding several cases before the state supreme court in the spring and summer of 1863 confirmed fears of central government subversion of the judiciary's independence. In October 1862, Congress had passed a second conscription act, which extended the eligibility of white males to age forty-five. Under the first act, John W. Irwin had hired as a substitute a man between the ages of thirty-five and forty-five. The War Department determined that Irwin's substitute could now be conscripted, leaving Irwin without a representative in the army and therefore liable to conscription himself. Military authorities arrested Irwin for draft evasion. Upon Irwin's request, state supreme court Chief Justice Richmond Pearson, who maintained that the second law did not pertain to substitutes, granted a writ of habeas corpus and ordered Irwin freed.

Believing Pearson's decision erroneous, Secretary Seddon refused to release the prisoner. This action led to a heated exchange of letters between the secretary and the governor and eventually to Vance's order that the state militia prevent Confederate authorities from rearresting men released on writs of habeas corpus. In the interest of military efficiency, Vance and Seddon eventually reached a compromise regarding such men, but the conflict itself indicated to North Carolinians that the Confederate authorities were undermining judicial independence. In August 1863, the chief justice cautioned Vance "that the independence of the judiciary cannot be maintained, unless all encroachments are met with firmness."

By mid-1863, the threats to the state's judiciary, the arbitrary arrests, the suspension of the writ of habeas corpus, and the conscription laws had convinced many North Carolinians that the Confederate government was becoming what Congressman Burgess S. Gaither called "a consolidated military despotism." Their fears were increased by the apparently arbitrary impressment of goods by the army and by the implementation of a ten percent tax-in-kind for farmers, many of whom were just barely subsisting on their harvests. The appointment of a nonresident to administer the tax-in-kind seemed further evidence of the central government's intentions.

North Carolinians expressed their discontent at almost one hundred meetings held in all parts of the state in July and August of 1863. At these meetings they urged North Carolinians to unite to "declare whether they shall be freemen or slaves." They complained of the central government's unfair treatment of North Carolina. They also praised the independence of the state's judiciary and Vance's defense of it. Judicial decisions, said the participants at one meeting, "will be disrespected by none but oligarchs, tyrants, despots, and haters of republican liberty." The meetings also lauded the state's soldiers for their sacrifices and bravery. "But," they added, "if the civil law is not maintained, and if civil liberty is not to be the great result of this contest, then will these services have been offered in vain." They also called for the initiation of peace negotiations with the North. With the congressional elections only a few months off, the participants at most meetings either nominated candidates or proclaimed their refusal to support anyone not committed to the commencement of peace negotiations.

After an appeal from Governor Vance on September 7, no additional protest meetings were held, but the discontent persisted and deepened. In the November congressional elections, voters elected nine conservatives. During the months following the elections, it appeared to more and more North Carolinians that, through a new conscription act, another suspension of the writ of habeas corpus, and a renewed attack on the judiciary, the Davis administration sought to fasten the chains of a military despotism on the people. . . .

By early 1864, the future of liberty seemed bleak. In late February, Augustus Merrimon reported from Asheville "that the people are really alarmed, greatly alarmed for the safety of their liberties under our forms of government. They are indeed alarmed, and I confess there is cause for the alarm, and believe me when I tell you, this very alarm, but too well founded, is going far towards precipitating the South upon a fearful doom." In January, Congressman James T. Leach asked Senator William Graham: "What shall we do to stay the hand of a military despotism more to be dreaded than death itself; is not the priceless gem of civil and religious liberty worth the risk of rescueing it from the hands of the wicked dynasty that is now shaping our ruin?" In April 1864, the president of the Council of State, Fenner B. Satterthwaite, urged the governor to speak out against the suspension of the writ of habeas corpus. "It may," he wrote, "be instrumental in saving civil liberty, for I confess that I am alarmed myself at the rapid strides which have been made towards a Military Despotism."

Some alarmed Conservatives argued that North Carolina should take formal steps to protect herself and her citizens from that threat. They determined that the legislature should call a state convention, so that the state could act in her sovereign capacity to defend herself. According to Conservative editor William W. Holden, such a convention would seek an armistice with the North and, at the same time, would "protect the State against the encroachment of arbitrary power. It would see to it that the proud head of the State was bowed to no despot. It would insist that the civil law should prevail in all cases." A convention would also "demand that the Congress and the military shall respect that civil law and the inalienable rights of our people." Petitioners throughout the state pleaded with Governor Vance to convene the legislature so that it could call a convention, because they viewed "with indignation & alarm the encroachments of Congress & the executive on the Sovereignty of the State & the constitutional rights of the citizens, which neither plighted faith, the sanctity of contracts nor the gauranties of the constitution serve to restrain. . . . The inevitable tendency . . . unless speedily checked is the overthrow of civil liberty, & the establishment of a military despotism." . . .

Historians who have examined the purposes of the convention movement, agreeing with the assessment of Governor Vance, have seen it an effort to achieve a reconstruction of the Union. It is true that reconstructionists supported the proposal and that if a convention had been called to defend the rights of the state and its people, it may have found no defense against the encroachments of the Confederate government except through reunion with the North. But because reconstruction was a logical culmination of the convention movement does not mean that it was the goal of convention advocates. On the contrary, the evidence cited above suggests that many Conservatives were trying to extricate themselves from an almost inextricable situation. They wanted to protect their freedom and seek an honorable peace, but in the Confederacy. State Treasurer Jonathan Worth advised Vance not to attack convention supporters as reconstructionists "*intending* to withdraw the State from the Confederacy. I presume very few favor a convention for this purpose." Other convention supporters declared that a convention would be able to seek an honorable peace. If those efforts failed, "it can in no case injure, but would greatly strengthen the cause, for in that event, we would fall back united, upon the Cannon & the sword with redoubled courage & energey, as the last & only alternative." . . .

The split in the Conservative party over the convention question broadened into open political warfare in March 1864, when William Holden announced himself as a candidate opposed to the reelection of Governor Vance. Holden argued that Vance had inadequately protected popular liberty in North Carolina and, indeed, had only a lukewarm commitment to its protection. Only a state convention, Holden argued, could protect the state and its citizens from the overweening power of the Confederate government. He denied that the culling of a convention would lead to reconstruction. Hence, Vance's opposition to the convention was, in Holden's eyes, opposition to the establishment of safeguards for the threatened liberty of the people. While the candidates spent much of the campaign discussing the merits of the convention, each devoted substantial time to proving that he was the better defender of civil liberty. The campaigners expressed the fears of North Carolinians that they were losing their freedom, and, by so doing, they simultaneously reinforced those fears.

Vance began his reelection campaign in February 1864 with a speech to the citizens of Wilkesboro, in the mountainous northwest corner of the state. He vigorously defended the righteousness of the southern cause and attacked the proposal for a convention. He also upset his Conservative supporters by what seemed to them to be an apologia for the suspension of the writ of habeas corpus. John H. Haughton, one of the governor's political confidants, advised him to answer the serious charge that he had endorsed "that justly odious law suspending the great writ of Habeas Corpus." Council President Satterthwaite informed Vance that "the *only* ground of complaint against you is the *fear* of some of your friends that . . . you are yielding two much to the Richmond administration, and have not taken that *decided* opposition to the serious encroachments, which has been made upon the *rights* and *liberties* of the people. That is the ground upon which Mr. Holden and his friends assale you." He suggested that Vance "take the very highest ground in favour of 'Constitutional liberty'. Express your opinion boldly upon the policy of the suspension of the writ of habeas corpus." Satterthwaite assured Vance that "it would remove every ground of suspicion and Complaint against you! it would take 'all the wind out [of] Mr. Holden sale' and he would be compelled to withdraw, and give you his support or be so badly beaten in the race as never to raise his head again."

Accepting the advice of Haughton, Satterthwaite, and others, Vance "boldly" defended the sacred writ of habeas corpus in a major speech delivered before three thousand people in Fayetteville on April 22, in his message to the General Assembly on May 17, and thereafter on the stump. In his message, which occupied four and one-half columns of the Fayetteville *Observer,* Vance's denunciation of the suspension of the writ of habeas corpus covered two full columns. His new tactic succeeded. The Reverend A. W. Cummings reported to Vance that while traveling his circuit in the mountains he had talked with many people about the election. "Two weeks ago Holden would have received a majority of votes within my bounds." In one precinct he had found all but one man supporting Holden. "I am from that country to day," he wrote in early May. "I am happy to find a great change going on among the people all in your favor. It arises from what they learn to be your opinions and action upon the Habeas Corpus, and the continuance of the war." After Vance's message was delivered to the General Assembly, Jonathan Worth, who sympathized with Holden, declared: "I see no cause to H[olden] for continuing in the field, and I think V[ance]'s friends who were becoming alienated have generally expressed their satisfaction."

While Vance portrayed himself as a friend of liberty and of peace, he argued that the convention would produce neither. A state convention, he declared, could do nothing that the legislature could not, except take the state out of the Confederacy. That would lead North Carolina into a war with the Confederacy and ultimately back into the Union. A return to the Union would not mean a restoration of freedom, Vance declared but rather "the destruction of *everything*." A vote for Holden, Vance and his supporters argued, was a vote for continued war and for a return to northern despotism.

Underlying Vance's attack on Holden was the charge that Holden was disloyal to the Confederacy. Only a month before the election, Vance Conservatives discovered the existence of a secret unionist organization, the Heroes of America. The organization existed, as did unionism in parts of the state, but the exposure of the organization just weeks before the election was surely no coincidence. Vance's supporters widely publicized the existence of the Heroes during July, the month before the election, and though most did not charge Holden with being a member of the organization, they did try to associate him with it and with unionist sentiment in the state.

Vance ran a masterful campaign. Between February and May he changed the issues of debate in the campaign. In February, he had been on the defensive because of his apparently lukewarm defense of the liberties of North Carolinians. Vance eliminated that issue by coming out vigorously in defense of the writ of habeas corpus. By early summer, the issue had become the loyalty of William Holden and the aims of the convention movement. By the end of July, Holden spent much of his time denying that he was a member of the Heroes of America or that he wanted North Carolina to make a separate peace with the Lincoln administration. Vance, in effect, gave the electorate what it desired. He defended the liberties of the state's citizens while demanding that southerners continue their armed struggle for independence. And he contended that the convention would do nothing to protect liberty or promote peace but, instead, would lead to a bloody war with the other Confederate states and to submission to the despotic North.

Soldiers and civilians came to the polls and gave Vance a massive victory. He won 80 percent of the total vote, 87.9 percent of the soldier vote, and 77.2 percent of the civilian vote. Holden obtained a majority in only three of the state's counties. In twenty of the counties unoccupied by the Union army, Holden obtained less than fifty votes. Vance's victory represented a popular commitment to a position that ultimately proved untenable. The intense opposition to conscription, the suspension of the writ of habeas corpus and other acts indicated the unwillingness of North Carolinians to accept the centralization of governmental operations necessary for an effective war effort or to allow any incursions on their rights. But they rejected the alternative of returning to the old Union, where the Lincoln administration had snuffed out liberty. In the end, they could only assume a negative stance and fight to preserve civil liberty in the South.

The fears for liberty excited by the Confederate government among North Carolinians and other white southerners rested upon a firm historical foundation. Inheriting many of the political beliefs and fears of the American revolutionaries, southerners were prepared to divine the worst of motives in the government's actions. Those fears were exacerbated further because the war brought a central government in contact with most people for the first time. Before the war, the vast majority dealt with the federal government only through the postmaster. The war brought conscription, arbitrary arrests of civilians, the central government's apparent subversion of the judiciary, the impressment of private property, heavy taxes, and the suspension of the writ of habeas corpus. Southerners viewed those drastic actions with horror and asked whether the government had designs on their liberty.

The anxieties of North Carolinians and other white southerners were paralleled in the North, yet the contours of dissent in the two regions differed. A comparison of the Union and the Confederacy reveals why dissent assumed distinctive forms and why North Carolinians were especially sensitive to threats to their liberty. Recent historians have argued that northern popular discontent with the Lincoln administration was limited by the existence of a two-party system there. The partisan desire to defeat the Democratic party helped to unite even discontented Republicans behind Lincoln's policies. And the existence of a strong Republican organization, ready to denounce even a hint of Democratic disloyalty, moderated Democratic actions.

The Democratic party played an additional role in shaping and moderating dissent in the North. Just as North Carolina Conservatives attacked and distrusted the apparently despotic Davis administration, so too did northern Democrats fear the Lincoln administration. But the Democrats, with an effective national organization, could hope to oust Lincoln in 1864. They offered northerners the traditional means by which Americans protected their liberty, voting for the opposition party. Voters in North Carolina and other Confederate states were offered no such alternative. Because North Carolina Conservatives had ties with no national party, they could not hope to neutralize Davis, and because he was serving one six-year term, they could not remove him. Conservatives saw no way to rid themselves of the threat of despotism through the ballot box. North Carolina Conservatives were thus left with two unsatisfying choices. A small portion moved unwittingly in the direction of disloyalty to the Confederacy and reconstruction of the Union; the larger portion was left to complain bitterly and impotently of the threat to their freedom.

The absence of a national two-party system shaped the attitudes of North Carolinians toward the Confederate government; so too did the presence of a statewide two-party system. While North Carolinians had evinced much anxiety about the exercise of power by the Confederate government, they had accepted the exercise of considerable power by the state government. Under Governor Vance, for example, the state engaged in blockade running, clothed its troops, and effectively enforced the conscription laws. The acceptance of state power derived less from an ideological commitment to state rights than from the state's party system. The party system provided an effective mechanism for removing from power those rulers who threatened popular liberty. After all, the voters had overwhelmingly elected Conservative Zebulon Vance in 1862 and thereby rebuked the Democratic party, which had controlled the state government since 1850 and which was associated with the Davis administration.

While the Democratic party remained an effective opponent, it moderated the positions assumed by the Conservatives; but when it declined in strength in 1863, the need to preserve Conservative unity also declined. That trend culminated in the gubernatorial campaign of 1864, in which the two Conservative adversaries sought to outdo each other in their attacks on the Davis administration and in their defense of freedom. The moderation of 1862 was gone. Therefore, North Carolinians may have reaffirmed their loyalty to the cause of southern independence by voting for Vance, as Vance himself believed, but the election campaign exacerbated the hostility which North Carolinians felt toward the Confederate government.

While the structure of politics shaped the way in which North Carolinians responded to the Confederate government, that response was also influenced by a nonpolitical factor, the state's geographic location. Although the enemy occupied part of the state's coastline and threatened the mountain counties on the Tennessee border, North Carolina was one of the southern states most isolated from military action. As an interior state, North Carolina was more susceptible to the demands of the Confederate government than other states. For example, North Carolina and two other states paid about two-thirds of the total produce collected under the tax-in-kind, conscription, and the suspension of the writ of habeas corpus were not readily apparent to North Carolinians because the enemy posed no immediate threat. Thus, North Carolinians were called upon to make more sacrifices than were people in other states at a time when they least perceived the need for such an effort.

Those geographic and political factors combined to make North Carolinians especially alert to any incursions on their liberty. By 1864, most had come to feel that the Confederate government was seeking to establish a military despotism and rob them of their liberty. They agreed with merchant Leander S. Gash when he wrote to Governor Vance: "Gradually the last vestige of freedom is departing from us. We all feel it. None of us feel that we have the manhood we once had. It is humiliating yet it is so."

During times of crisis, societies often reveal the inner fears and tensions that are less evident in peaceful, stable times. The crisis of war laid bare the American fear, northern and southern, that their freedom was in jeopardy. While the political structure of the states and nations and the location of the states influenced the way people responded to the behavior of the central governments, the fear for liberty remained central to the thinking of Americans. The North Carolina experience may have been extreme in the extent to which those fears were developed and expressed, but in its extremity it revealed most fully the fears of the American people.

Strains of War

J. WILLIAM HARRIS

The forebodings of a few were drowned out after the outbreak of hostilities at Fort Sumter in April 1861. By then, most dissidents, including Alexander H. Stephens, had pledged full support for their states and section, even if they had opposed secession. Indeed, Stephens had, in February 1861, been chosen vice president of the new Confederacy, as southern political leaders sought to demonstrate that they were now fully united and determined to establish the South's independence.

This new-found unity seemed to be reflected in every local community near Augusta [located in northeast Georgia on the border with South Carolina]. The attack on Sumter and Abraham Lincoln's call for troops to suppress the Confederacy created an outburst of enthusiasm among the vast majority of whites in Augusta's hinterlands. Divisions over the wisdom of secession were apparently forgotten, as men everywhere rushed to volunteer. Wealthy men and ambitious men of lesser means competed to form their own companies, battalions, and regiments. Indeed, one Hart county correspondent of Governor Joseph E. Brown of Georgia complained of the "derangement" of men who were so

From J. William Harris, "Strains of War," pp. 140–159 from *Plain Folk and Gentry in a Slave Society: White Liberty and Black Slavery in Augusta's Highland.* © 1985 by J. William Harris, Wesleyan University Press by permission of University Press of New England.

anxious to join the army that they threatened to leave no one behind to take care of the women and children and get in the crops.

No doubt, part of the enthusiasm was based on a conviction that the war would be glorious, short, and, of course, successful. In January 1861, the editor of the Augusta *Constitutionalist* predicted that if the northern armies were foolish enough to invade, southern volunteers would drive them out "as easily as the whirlwind sweeps the chaff before it." The [Augusta] *Chronicle*'s editor echoed a standard argument that the North was "filled with festering corruption, the venality, the luxurious effeminacy" that presaged total decay and made that section obviously unfit to prevail in war with the South. James Henry Hammond confidently predicted that southern men would "mow down" Lincoln's "foreign" troops "like sheep. Our trouble will be the fatigue of slaughtering." Many volunteers feared the war might end before they got a chance to fight in it.

In every county and district near Augusta, companies were quickly organized with the support of all segments of the white population. Some companies, especially in South Carolina, were prepared to volunteer at the outset of hostilities. Typically, a large community ceremony, heavy with symbols of unity, sent each company off to battle. In Hamburg, for example, on April 24, the "ladies of Hamburg" presented Captain Spires's company with a flag, and Spires replied with an elaborate speech of acceptance, repeating the rhetoric of southern rights. The Stars and Stripes, Spires said, had been dishonored by the North, which had tried so hard to deprive southerners of their "rights and equality in the Union" and had aimed "a death blow to our institutions." To submit would have cost the South its wealth and honor and would have reduced "our mothers, our sisters, our wives, and our daughters to shame" and our progeny to equality with creatures fit by the Almighty only as "slaves for man."

Public meetings in Georgia counties spurred volunteering and contributions to equip local companies. In May, "the ladies of Hancock" presented a banner to Captain Arnold and his company; in July, two more companies left Hancock after speeches by Alexander H. Stephens and by a Methodist bishop. At this ceremony, a reporter assured the *Chronicle*'s readers, the soldiers vowed to abandon "the sin of profanity"; the spirit of self-sacrifice must have seemed boundless that day. On July 11 in Gibson, the Glascock Independent Guards received their flag, the presentation preceded by a joint march with companies from neighboring Jefferson and Warren counties, which went through "some elegant evolutions." A Miss Cheeley, daughter of one of Glascock's richest planters, presented the flag, with an address that "evinced high female acquirements in rhetoric, logic and grace, bidding the soldiers to go forward, . . . [and] demonstrating very clearly that the ladies fully understand and appreciate the government of the Confederate States." After long and "deafening" applause, the crowd of 2,500 listened to a sermon, and concluded the day with a public barbecue.

These ceremonies dramatized and cemented community support for the fight. It seemed that slaveowners and poor men would stand shoulder to shoulder in defense of their homes and their new nation. In an 1861 sample of Confederate volunteers from the area, forty-two were heads of or sons from slaveowning families, and forty-eight were from nonslaveowning families.

Those who could not be soldiers volunteered in other ways. Women formed aid societies to make uniforms and blankets. George W. Ray, of Warrenton, wrote to Stephens to volunteer as a nurse, since he was too old to serve as a soldier. Older and also wealthier men contributed thousands of dollars to buy arms and uniforms. Hammond gave $100 to a company in Greenville, in the South Carolina upcountry. Tillman Watson of Edgefield promised to equip the company raised by Martin W. Gary. Public meetings in Taliaferro, Hancock, and other counties brought in contributions. By the summer of 1862, almost 200 people in Hancock had contributed to outfit volunteers. In some areas, meetings resulted in plans to levy "voluntary" contributions on everyone in certain neighborhoods. In the Mt. Willing neighborhood of Edgefield district, a public meeting voted to assess an extra "tax" to furnish volunteers, and formed a committee to collect the assessments. Other meetings urged county governments to borrow money immediately to equip local volunteers and to support the families of poor soldiers. In August, one of Stephens's correspondents assured him that "the people in this section grow in their patriotism. Surely such a people cannot be subjugated." Another wrote him that there had never "been a time when the People has more confidence in the Government, both civil and military—never was a time, when the officers of government were more beloved, by the people."

Even in the midst of this enthusiasm, however, were portents of troubles to come. Many opponents of secession had been converted into strong Confederates, but others had simply fallen silent. In July, D. F. Bardon wrote to Stephens to urge a negotiated peace to avoid an invasion, and he worried that "a spirit of insubordination is rife all over this land."

More significantly, problems that would come to plague the Confederate war effort appeared almost as soon as the army began to form. Secession was justified in terms of the ideals of the white community—centered on liberty, autonomy, and independence—but free, autonomous, and independent men and communities were not necessarily the best material for a long and massive war. Class strains that had been carefully contained by means both subtle and overt began to break out into the open almost at once. On May 1 in Hancock county, a fight erupted between members of the local infantry company and Eppes Sykes of the cavalry company. Sykes and most of the other men in the cavalry company were relatively wealthy and could afford fine horses; for them, the cavalry was a symbol of social prestige. On the contrary, according to Linton Stephens, in the infantry company, "a good many of the men" were poor. The company had accepted donations from local planters to buy uniforms and equipment. The fight began when Sykes made "some jeering remark" about these donations, and Sykes and two others were wounded. Poor men would accept support from the community's elite, but not at the expense of condescension from those whose right to own slaves they were going off to defend.

The touchy individualism of southern white men permeated every level of the army and was exacerbated by the popular democracy that characterized the army as much as it did the local community. At the beginning of the war, most officers up to and including colonels were elected by their men. One obvious way to become an officer was to recruit a company or a regiment, and the skills of recruiting were much the same as those required for electioneering in general, from courting neighbors to building coalitions. So, not surprisingly, officers tended to be wealthier, and more often owned slaves, than the privates who formed most of the army. Privates in a sample of soldiers from three counties came from families that owned an average of two slaves and $2,809 in property; families of those who were elected officers (from corporal to captain) averaged twice those figures. And altogether, those from slaveowning families were twice as likely as those from nonslaveowning families to enter service at a rank above private.

The competition in recruiting perhaps helped to swell the army's rolls at early stages, but it also created conflicts. David C. Barrow helped recruit five companies for the service, but G. B. Harben, a prospective colonel, complained that Barrow had enticed two Elbert county companies away from his own regiment and into Barrow's battalion.

The Confederate army, in short, reflected the southern political community, with its strengths and weaknesses. The rather brief military career of Thomas W. Thomas, of Elbert county, epitomizes much of both. Thomas, a politician and a man of considerable wealth, was a friend of Alexander and Linton Stephens. During late spring and early summer of 1861, he exercised his political skills to form his new regiment. He began with men from his own county, and sought alliances with companies in other counties. He had the ear of Governor Brown, and was thus in a strong position to bargain with companies already formed and eager to get accepted into the service. His letters to Brown reveal local politics at work. On July 1, he wrote of his concern that "outside influence hostile to" its captain might break up one Lincoln county company. He asked Brown to accept one Hancock company that was not quite filled because that company was crucial to keeping a second Hancock company "so connected" to it that if the first were left out, the second might fall apart. As in civilian politics, connections sometimes competed with one another. Thomas, for example, refused to appoint a Hancock man as quartermaster of the regiment because he had already chosen his own brother for the job; he would, he assured Linton Stephens, "gratify the Hancock men" in almost any other request, "reasonable or unreasonable."

Thomas succeeded in becoming Colonel Thomas. By August, he was in Virginia. The life of an army camp, however, proved most uncongenial to this high-spirited political soldier. He was bored with inactivity, chafed under discipline, and, by October, was writing letters critical of Jefferson Davis and the administration of the army. "Matters are managed very badly here, without sense, system, or policy," he wrote to Alexander Stephens, and "there also exist partiality and corruption in high quarters. . . . The troops widely feel the unjust oppression and partial hand that is laid upon them, and in my opinion the spirit of the army is dying. I have seen some things that made my blood boil; and that makes one unconsciously begin to debate with himself whether the assassin's knife be justifiable."

Shortly afterward, Thomas wrote that "we have to bear things here that no freeman ought to bear, and perhaps outraged nature may speak out in me and bring me into trouble"; indeed, he predicted, only half in jest, that he might be court-martialed within sixty days. At the end of the year, he visited his family back in Elberton, and wrote that the people were "dispirited, uneasy, and apprehensive." He blamed it all on Jefferson Davis and the "peculiar people he trusts," who had given "sufficient cause to every gentleman in the army to mutiny." People in Elbert county "are whining and complaining and probably thinking of a compromise by going back." Thomas himself was full of "an indignation" verging "on hate," and we may doubt his claim that he was covering this up to avoid damaging public opinion any further. By the spring of 1862, Thomas was trying to resign his commission and was bitterly protesting the treatment he received from his commanding officer; when his health deteriorated, his resignation was accepted.

Many shared Thomas's reaction to army discipline. Robert Toombs, a former United States senator from Georgia, went through a similar trial of pride and independence. Toombs, from Wilkes county, was made Secretary of State in the Confederacy, but resigned in July 1861 to become a brigadier general in one of Georgia's new brigades then serving in Virginia. His letters, like those of Thomas, were filled with complaints about the army. General Joseph E. Johnston, in command, was a "poor devil, small, arbitrary and inefficient," who undertook everything merely out of a fondness for power;

he "harasses and obstructs but cannot govern the army." The army, he predicted, would have as its epitaph, "*died of West Point.*" Toombs ultimately was court-martialed, although charges were dropped; he, too, finally resigned his commission and returned home to complain about the conduct of the war.

Intense localism as well as individualism confronted the Confederate high command. In June 1861, Governor Brown was engaged in several disputes with companies that had received arms from the state. He claimed that these arms were to be used to defend Georgia from invasion, and forbade their export to Virginia without his express permission. He ordered one Newton county company to surrender its arms or to pledge in writing that it would not leave the state with them. In commenting on these disputes, the Augusta *Constitutionalist*'s editor confidently remarked that "the old vexed question, as to the relative claims of the State and Federal Government upon the allegiance of the citizen, can never again arise at the South," that the first allegiance of citizens must be to the state. This dispute was only a hint of many more to come, and attachments to states, rather than to the central government in Richmond, were only one aspect of a pervasive localism in Augusta's hinterlands that also characterized other regions of the South.

In May 1861, for example, an Edgefield, South Carolina, company was split when some of its members were recruited to enter a regiment being sent to Richmond from the South Carolina coast. Defending those who had not gone to Virginia, one officer explained that they wanted to defend South Carolina first. That fall, the Edgefield *Advertiser*'s editor recommended that the state not call more upcountry men to defend Charleston, now threatened by the Union army at Port Royal, because Edgefield already had contributed more volunteers to the cause than had Charleston itself. In April 1862, one South Carolina regiment was accused of mass desertion, and a defender explained that many members had joined on the assumption that they were liable for duty only in South Carolina; they had stopped off to visit their families when called out of the state.

Similar disputes cropped up among Georgia's troops. An Augusta artillery company complained bitterly in a letter published in May 1862 that General Braxton Bragg had disallowed their election of a new captain and had given the captaincy to a man from Alabama. "We enlisted in this war as representatives from Georgia," the letter claimed, and now other states might get praise for the successes of Georgia troops. The editor of the Augusta *Constitutionalist,* in which the letter appeared, agreed that the appointment of the Alabama captain was an "injustice which should not be tolerated" and that the members of the company were quite naturally "jealous of the rights of our citizens, and of the honor of our city and state."

As the war stretched on, the Confederate government had to interfere in the lives of its citizens in countless ways, and that interference provoked resistance from many who regarded it as an unjustified assault on the independence and autonomy of states, local communities, and individuals.

In the spring of 1861, almost all southerners assumed that the war could be fought much as had others in the past, that the South would rely essentially on the voluntary efforts of public-spirited citizens and the cooperative efforts of local communities and state governments. Most obviously, volunteers would man the ranks. By the spring of 1862, it had become clear that volunteering would not suffice to supply the army. Many volunteers were sure to return home when their twelve-month terms expired.

In April 1862, the Confederate congress, at Jefferson Davis's behest, responded to the shortage of manpower by establishing the first national conscription system in U.S.

history. From the beginning, public leaders in the Augusta area were divided on the wisdom and justice of conscription. The editors of both the Augusta *Constitutionalist* and the Edgefield *Advertiser* supported a draft. As early as February 1862, the *Advertiser* argued that one salutary effect of a draft would be to force into the army some of those who wanted only to see "how much money they can make out of the war." The *Constitutionalist* agreed that expediency required a draft, since volunteering had almost "run its course." Others, however, denounced the draft as a violation of individual liberty and states' rights. "J. W. J.," a correspondent of the Augusta *Chronicle,* argued that conscription would turn the South into a military despotism. Another correspondent raised a crucial issue when he argued that a draft would discriminate against the poor, who could not afford to hire substitutes, as allowed by the new law.

Governor Joseph E. Brown of Georgia was one of the South's best known and most consistent opponents of conscription. His primary objection, he claimed, turned on the obscure point that the Confederate constitution, he maintained, allowed the central government to choose officers only for volunteer forces. Drafts had to depend on state militias and had to be called through the states, and therefore only the states (meaning, in Georgia, Brown himself) should have charge of appointing officers for conscripted troops. This precious reasoning was shared by many influential leaders, including Alexander and Linton Stephens and the editor of the *Chronicle,* who called the conscription act a "most deadly" blow to the rights of states. Historians have attributed the opposition of the Stephens brothers and of Brown to selfish political motives or to sheer spite, and perhaps these were significant. There can be no doubt, however, that they were sincere in their strenuous objections to conscription. Their private correspondence is filled with their denunciations of conscription and other "unconstitutional" acts of the Confederate congress. In August 1862, for example, Linton Stephens was lamenting the apparent acquiescence to conscription in the population at large. "Our public mind is unfit for the boon of constitutional liberty," he declared. "It is surprising and painful to see how utterly indifferent our people are to the observance of constitutional limitations upon the power of our rulers." In December, he wrote a private, twenty-two-page letter to his brother outlining his objections to the draft. Not only was it patently unconstitutional to prevent soldiers from electing their own officers, but also the effect of the act would be "to mould the army into a fit instrument for despotism, and to *unfit* them for a return to the duties of citizens." An army in war is "essentially a despotism, and a *school* where despotism is learned"; the tendency of Davis's policies was "to destroy liberty." Stephens was turning the old devotion to republican liberty against the Confederacy itself.

Defenders of the draft were content to point to its practical consequences and to the decisions of state courts, including the Georgia Supreme Court, which confirmed the constitutionality of the conscription act. Despite briefly wavering on the question of constitutionality, the Augusta *Constitutionalist* by the end of 1862 was giving strong editorial support to the draft. In November, the editor deplored Brown's attack on conscription, arguing that publicizing his dissent might "greatly embarrass" the Confederate government. If the draft "fills up our armies . . . with good and reliable soldiers," he continued, "why should any patriot refuse to acquiesce in its enforcement?" It was necessary, its editor later claimed, to satisfy those already in the army that the people at home supported their fight.

Enforcement of conscription compounded the Confederacy's problems. It required the imposition of a new centralized bureaucracy on a population with hardly any experience in dealing with such an institution. No doubt, the bureaucrats were not always very good at their jobs; accusations of favoritism, interference with necessary work, and plain meddling abounded. More important, because more damaging to the Confederacy's cause, the draft inevitably bore more heavily on the poor than on the wealthy, and hence seriously widened class divisions among whites.

Poor men and women, for obvious reasons, saw the issue of conscription in a different light from that of the rich. While one argument for a draft was that it would spread the sacrifices of war more equally among all citizens, it was bound to affect the families of slaveless farmers much more than those who still had someone to plow and harvest. Letters of woe poured into the governor's offices and also to Alexander Stephens, who presumably had special influence as vice president of the Confederacy. From Hart county came a request for a discharge for Milton Grubbs, "son of a destitute widow"; from Sandersville, a plea for a discharge for a youngest son, for "i am left in a dredful Condision i am lo in health and unable to help myself. . . . i have no protection for all my boys wear gon in service but William . . . an he now gon too an lef me alone to shift for my self." From Martha Denny, place unidentified, came this appeal: "I pray you may favour me as the pour all lays in your hans." Two of her sons had been killed; another had been drafted and had left her with his three small motherless children. Now "they" wanted her youngest son; "I think I have done a nof for they army for you to let me have my younges child. . . . pleas let me have my baby." From Taliaferro county came a request to have a son discharged; "he left home without my knowledge or consent he was not 16 years old when he left he is verry much distressed he rote to me for God sake to get him home. . . . you know I am verry poor hardly able at this to walk about." From Warrenton was a petition to be detailed to home to provide support for a family, including a daughter and two daughters-in-law whose husbands were already in the army, and all indigent, supported only by "the scanty allowance made by the State, their own exertions, and the efforts I can make by my own labor."

The poor petitioned also to exclude their doctors and the teachers of their children from service. Greene county parents asked for an exemption for a teacher of thirty-six children, whose parents could not afford to send them elsewhere. In the same county, the petition noted, Penfield University had four exempted professors, even though "their parents are able to send them [the students] anywhere to school." From Lincoln county came a petition to exempt Dr. B. F. Bently, who had given his word "to *many* of the volunteers" that he would "attend to their families," without charge if necessary.

Such people complained bitterly when wealthy men were exempted for no obvious reasons. Particularly galling was the policy of exempting one man, owner or overseer, on plantations of twenty or more slaves. As a poor Mississippi woman explained to Alexander Stephens, "our Army is making a great to do at the Exemption Law It does look hard to exempt a man because he has 20 Negroes they say it is a Rich mans war and a poor mans fight." When Governor Brown called up the Georgia militia to aid the defense of Atlanta in the summer of 1864, one Crawfordville man wrote to Alexander Stephens that many of the local men would refuse to go. "A great deal of dissatisfaction exists among some at the course of others. I have heard some men argue & complain that they being poor must go but that Ben Reid and George Whitehall who have money are & will be permitted to remain." At about the same time, a Wilkes county man wrote to Brown that one miller who had been exempted from service not only "does not see his mill once a month," but also bragged that "you nor any other man could put him in service . . . and brags that he has made a fortune by the war."

Wealthy planters did try to bend the rules of conscription to their favor, whether out of selfish or of patriotic motives. Connections, money, and the sophistication to deal with new bureaucracies all helped give the wealthy considerable advantage, quite aside from the "twenty Negro" law. Linton Stephens, for example, wrote his brother that he would be stuck at home "till I get my overseer [who had a bad leg] through the conscription gin." David C. Barrow expended considerable energy attempting to keep his overseers out of the draft, arguing that they were needed to police the slaves and raise corn. At one point, Barrow convinced some of his neighbors to give an affidavit that his overseer Baker Daniel "does a great deal for the poor soldiers families in his neighborhood, and there are a good many of them around him."

James Henry Hammond wanted, quite simply, to keep his sons out of danger. When they insisted on volunteering, he managed to have them assigned to staff positions, away from the front lines. He rejoiced when his son Paul finally agreed to hire a substitute. And he was incensed when the Davis administration planned to do away with substitutes, partly because of complaints that the substitute policy discriminated against the poor. Hammond agreed about the discrimination, but denounced the change. "The poor hate the rich," he wrote to James L. Orr, "& make war on them every where & here especially with universal suffrage & therefore they demand that rich men shall not put in substitutes. The war is based on the principle and *fact* of the inequality of mankind—for policy we say *races,* in reality, as all history shows it as the *truth* is *classes.*" More circumspectly, he wrote to Orr that substitutes were necessary to protect the planting interest so that the army could be supplied with provisions. The editor of the Augusta *Constitutionalist,* who supported the draft, agreed with Hammond on exemptions. He noted that exemptions of overseers from the draft produced dissatisfaction about "an unjust and injurious distinction between rich and poor." Overseers, he thought, performed a vital police service, and "we have no patience with the miserable cant about rich and poor. The inequality of mankind, as regards wealth, can not be remedied by human laws." When exemption of overseers was severely limited in the spring of 1863, the *Constitutionalist*'s editor complained that the new law discriminated against the rich because it did not specifically exempt owners of slaves as well as some overseers.

For whatever reasons, the rich in Augusta's hinterlands did manage to avoid Confederate service more often than did the poor. When men of the same age and family status (such as household head, son, or boarder) are compared, those who did not serve in the army were wealthier, and owned more slaves, than those who did serve. . . . And as the war continued, the disparity increased. Each year's new soldiers came from poorer families than did those who had joined the year before.

The discontent of the poor was, therefore, based on reality. And Governor Brown undoubtedly sharpened this discontent with his polemical attacks on the draft. The operation of the Conscription Act, he told the Georgia General Assembly, "has been grossly unjust and unequal between the two classes." While thousands of nonslaveholders were on the battlefield, "a large proportion of the wealthy class of people have avoided the fevers of the camp and the dangers of the battlefield, and have remained at home in comparative ease and comfort."

Conscription filled the armies at the cost of alienating both rich and poor southerners. Simultaneously, the central government was failing disastrously to cope with financing the war. Richmond, capital of the Confederacy, at first refused to authorize significant direct taxation and hoped to rely on state support and borrowing. In fact, the war effort was financed primarily by printing money. When that was combined with the shortages inevitable during any large war, but especially in a country blockaded by a superior naval power, the result was first a steady and then an explosive inflation. Burgeoning prices made it difficult either to supply the army or to care for the poor, including the families of poor soldiers. To supply the army, the Confederate government turned to impressment, and thus further alienated farmers and planters, who also were expected to carry the burden of supporting the poor with voluntary contributions or state and local taxes. This expectation, too, fell victim to the size of the war. Impressment and poverty, no less than conscription, raised vexing questions about liberty and equality in the Confederacy, questions that split white society many ways.

From the beginning of the war, southerners had realized that special provision would have to be made for the families of poor soldiers if they were to be successfully recruited. In October 1861, for example, Elisha Cain of Hancock county had raised a new company of volunteers, but he wanted to wait until November 20 for the company to be accepted into the service, since "many of my men are farmers and poor men. . . . By that time my men can all make their arrangements gather their crops etc and be ready to leave home for the winter . . . otherwise my company will be disbanded." By the beginning of 1862, little Glascock county was supporting the families of at least eight soldiers; by the end of that year, Edgefield, South Carolina, was supporting 500 families, or almost one-sixth of all families in the district. Ultimately, Georgia and South Carolina together raised millions of dollars to provide relief for the poor during the war. Georgia's 1864 property-tax rates, for example, were fifteen times the 1860 rate, and the state also enacted a progressive income tax. More than half these taxes, by far the highest in Georgia's history, went directly to civilian welfare spending.

These efforts were supplemented by a large expansion of the traditional support of neighbors by wealthier slaveowners. James Henry Hammond sold salt (to preserve meat) at bargain prices to needy neighbors and sold corn at below-market prices to several families. In 1862, John Hollingsworth of Edgefield donated 500 bushels of corn to indigent soldiers' families. In 1863, Dr. Thomas Janes of Greene county gave away or sold at low prices more than 3,000 bushels of wheat. In 1862, Turner Clanton of Columbia county offered corn for sale to poor families of Augusta (in neighboring Richmond county) at half the prevailing market price. David C. Barrow supplied corn to people who lived near all his plantations during the war.

Yet these efforts could not prevent privation and destitution, especially as the war went on and prices soared. A Washington county woman complained to Governor Joseph E. Brown that women with two children "onley got 40 dollais for tha year and this year we hant got but 40 dollais and we cant get nothing but what we have to give government price." Local planters and farmers, she added, "has got so hardhearted tha wont let us have it without tha ful price." An Oglethorpe county war widow wrote to Alexander H. Stephens that the county inferior court "gives me nothing from some cause I [know] not. . . . I am in greatt need I have no money." The Edgefield "Vigilant Association," which pledged to support the poor in their neighborhood, was breaking down by the end of 1861, and little money was being contributed. A notice in the *Advertiser* asked nonattending members, "Will you leave it for a few to bear the burthens in which all are interested?" In the spring of 1862, the *Advertiser*'s editor noted that the $16,000 tax raised in Edgefield for the year to support the poor would fall far short of the need; as it turned out, the tax provided only $16 per person during the year, about enough to buy ten bushels of corn at Augusta wholesale prices. In November 1862, the relief board, in charge of spending Edgefield's relief funds, received a petition signed by "ten suffering women of Edgefield" who alluded to "their privations in the pitiable terms of unaffected distress." All their husbands were in the army. (The editor of the *Advertiser* decided not to print the letter, although he did mention it in his columns.) By August 1862, Hammond was not sure he could "keep up my poor neighbors another year."

Inflation itself gave rise to almost universal complaints of "speculation" and "extortion." At first, in the autumn of 1861, these complaints were directed mainly against merchants and other middlemen. As early as September in a Charleston newspaper, "Phyllis" denounced merchants for raising their prices, and her letter was reprinted in Edgefield. Cotton planters began to realize that their 1861 crop would have no market, and anxiously wondered "what is the prospect of getting money for our cotton"; people began to worry that their property would be "sacrificed to the advantage of a few whom the War makes fat." Merchants replied, with some justice, that they simply passed on high prices for goods they bought. In any case, attachment to free-market principles created a strong prejudice against any attempt to control prices directly. For example, when the price of salt rose precipitously in late 1861, Governor Brown ordered his agents to seize all salt being sold for more than $5 a sack, paying that amount in compensation. The Augusta *Chronicle* editorialized that his action showed a danger that the South would lose its liberty to an internal tyranny. James Thomas, who had written the summer before about the great patriotism evident everywhere in Hancock county, thought by February 1862 that "we are wanting in patriotism, we hate the Yankees, but I fear we have no love of country. . . . I fear and believe we have started on our new government with all the corrupting influences we had." High prices were his chief evidence of corruption. If he were in power, he wrote, he would "hang without law ½ Doz. speculators & extortioners in this County."

One response to the rise in prices and the prospects of a long war was the movement to replace cotton with corn in the fields. Even in 1861, some had seen the war as an opportunity to put into practice the old dream of a diversified agriculture, to get southern farmers off "the same old beaten track, planting each year all the cotton they can cultivate, and just enough corn and small grain to make out with." Early in 1862, the necessity for a large grain crop was obvious; as the *Southern Cultivator* of Augusta put it, farmers must make an "OVERWHELMING AND SUPER-ABUNDANT CROP OF PROVISIONS." The Edgefield *Advertiser* argued that "the poor soldier has a right . . . to expect that in pitching their crops, the aim should not be to keep corn and meat at extortionate prices, but to make them abundant and cheap. . . . He has a right to expect that the fortunate owners of lands and negroes will patriotically bend all their energies and resources to fill the land with plenty, and make its defence a cheap and cheerful task." Planters in every neighborhood met to vow they would restrict the cotton crop. Warren county planters resolved that "no true and enlightened patriot will plant a full crop of cotton." Hancock county planters resolved to "devote their whole resources to the production of provisions." Greene county planters resolved to plant cotton for home production only, and that anyone who planted more would "give aid and comfort to the enemy, and make war upon his neighbors, his country, and his own prosperity."

Even this common-sense plan was resisted by many farmers who wanted no direction from any quarter, including public opinion. The reporter of the Hancock meeting mentioned that "a very few, have refused to PLEDGE, not, however, because of opposition to the policy, but because they are opposed to SIGNING written pledges." Many planters and farmers found it difficult to give up the king of crops. Dolly Burge, in March 1862, noted in her diary that "everybody says we must plant little or no cotton. I hardly know what to do about it." In May, she was planting corn, but "dislike[d] doing it, however." In a notorious incident, Robert Toombs himself defied local sentiment in the southwest Georgia county where he owned an absentee plantation. Apparently just to assert his prerogatives and demonstrate his personal independence, he ordered his overseer to plant a cotton crop even larger than usual. The local "Committee of Safety" denounced his "avarice" with "unqualified indignation" and resolved that Toombs should destroy his crop in the field and turn over his slaves to the committee to labor on river fortifications. Such attitudes led to state laws restricting cotton production in both Georgia and South Carolina. In Georgia, for example, cotton planting was restricted to a maximum of three acres per hand. Governor Brown, indeed, urged a further restriction to a maximum of one-quarter acre per hand. Slaveholders, Brown argued, "are dependent upon our white laborers in the field of battle, for the protection of their property, and in turn this army of white laborers and their families are dependent upon the slaveowner for a support." The cotton restriction, Brown argued, would help keep food prices within reach of the poor. The legislature, however, left the three-acre restriction in place. In any case, the restriction was one policy that was helped by the market, at least at first; as Dolly Burge noted, the cotton market was too uncertain during the war. Most planters finally turned almost wholly to grain crops. The tax assessments of Stephens and of Barrow, for example, show that they were planting almost no cotton by 1864.

Still, the vast increase in the availability of grain crops did not ease prices, nor make life much easier for the poor. As the war continued, it became obvious that what critics called the "spirit of extortion" had invaded almost every household. Farmers, like everybody else, waited until the price was right. In September 1862, the Edgefield *Advertiser* mentioned in its weekly letter to soldiers that wheat "is said to have stampeded and left the premises, *en masse,* to the tune of four, five and latterly, even *six dollars* per bushel. The temptation was irresistible, and the wheat market is closed." In October, the Hancock county grand jury condemned the "spirit of extortion manifested by a considerable portion of the citizens of these states and spreading with greatest rapidity, to every branch of trade." "Front Face," in a letter to the Augusta *Chronicle,* declared that "landholders and slaveholders" were often as guilty of extortion as were merchants. He argued that large slaveholders should sell "superfluous" land and slaves to "their less fortunate neighbors for moderate prices," a policy not likely to be of help to truly poor families. In November 1862, Reverend John H. Cornish of Aiken, South Carolina, spent an entire day "in quest of food," but was only partially successful, since "the country people" were bringing in little produce. "They seem to have caught the spirit of extortion." Four months later, Cornish seems to have caught some of it himself. He traded some tea, which had cost him $48, for 200 yards of cloth and $75 in cash. He then sold the cloth in Augusta for another $218, thus realizing, in the space of ten days, a profit of some 500 percent.

Inflation led to various official attempts to control or regulate markets and prices. In addition to restrictions on cotton production, South Carolina and Georgia sharply limited distilling. Both states passed laws against extortion, and there were at least some convictions under the laws. Governor Bonham of South Carolina forbade the export of corn into Augusta, presumably the home of the worst speculators. Hart county even forbade corn to be taken beyond county lines, and set a maximum price (in May 1863) of $2 a bushel. "Justice," in a letter to the Edgefield *Advertiser* in early 1863, urged the state legislature to regulate prices more generally. These efforts came largely to nothing, partly because such economic regulation was anathema in this free-market economy. The Augusta *Chronicle*'s editor denounced vigilance committees that tried to regulate corn markets, on the grounds that the interference would destroy the markets altogether. The *Constitutionalist* made the reasonable argument that financial policies and shortages, rather than speculation and extortion, were at the bottom of price rises; it also made the less reasonable argument that seizing salt or other goods to distribute among the poor was a sign of "despotism." When Kate Rowland of Augusta paid $30 for a pair of shoes, she wrote in her diary that she was "sure we shall never have peace so long as this spirit of extortion pervades the country." Yet in the same diary entry, she branded the government's seizure of salt for less than market prices as "a perfect species of *swindling* . . . I think a person perfectly justified in hiding it from the government." Hammond was helpful to his poor neighbors when he could be, but he also casually assumed that "Negroes & poor people . . . must learn to do without bacon & the rich eat it sparingly, & all meat pretty much the same." Meanwhile, Hammond's brother and son were "involved in speculations—against my protest."

So people were left with laments and jeremiads. "Peter the Hermit," in the Edgefield *Advertiser,* exhorted "The Farmers of South Carolina" to "*arise from the worship of your golden calves*" and save the country from the "*despotism—slavery*" brought on by speculators. The Augusta *Constitutionalist* printed a "Sermon Suited to the Times" on the text "He that withholdeth corn, the people shall curse him; but blessings shall be upon the head of him that selleth it." The *Chronicle*'s editor noted with regret "the spirit of selfishness and sordidness which has long prevailed among certain classes of our people." The Morgan county grand jury denounced extortion, but did not single out any individuals because the practice was so extensive that "we know not where to begin, and if we begin where to end. . . . It is beyond human power to suppress it."

FURTHER READING

Stephen V. Ash, *Middle Tennessee Society Transformed, 1860–1870: War and Peace in the Upper South* (1988)
———, *When the Yankees Came: Conflict and Chaos in the Occupied South* (1995)
Richard E. Beringer, Herman Hattaway, et al., *Why the South Lost the Civil War* (1986)
Gabor Boritt, ed., *Why the Confederacy Lost* (1992)
David Donald, ed., *Why the North Won the Civil War* (1960)
Wayne K. Durrill, *War of Another Kind: A Southern Community in the Great Rebellion* (1990)
Paul Escott, *After Secession: Jefferson Davis and the Failure of Southern Nationalism* (1978)
———, "Southern Yeomen and the Confederacy," *South Atlantic Quarterly* 77 (1978), 146–158
Drew Gilpin Faust, *The Creation of Confederate Nationalism* (1988)
Harry P. Owens and James J. Clarke, eds., *The Old South in the Crucible of War* (1983)
George C. Rable, *The Confederate Republic: A Revolution against Politics* (1994)
Kenneth M. Stampp, "The Road to Appomattox: The Problem of Morale in the Confederacy," in Stampp, *The Imperiled Union* (1980)
Daniel E. Sutherland, *Seasons of War: The Ordeal of a Confederate Community, 1861–1865* (1995)
Emory M. Thomas, *The Confederacy as a Revolutionary Experience* (1971)
———, *The Confederate Nation, 1861–1865* (1979)
Bell I. Wiley, *The Plain People of the Confederacy* (1943)

CHAPTER
9

Women in Wartime

♫

In both North and South, the home front was the place where women were to be found, while their husbands and sons went off to war. But there were exceptions. Many women worked as nurses in facilities close to the battlefield. A few women, determined to serve in the military, disguised themselves as male soldiers and engaged in combat. Others became spies. The war had a significant impact on the lives of countless women on both sides. Equally, women influenced the war in a variety of ways.

Although the secondary historical literature on women during the war is still quite meager, it is growing steadily. A lot more is known now about women in the context of the war and about the extent to which they affected its course. This interest in women's roles and activities in the Civil War arises from the developing field of women's history. But it is complemented by the renewed attention being paid to the civilian side of the conflict, with its focus on how the people at home thought and lived regardless of whether they contributed to the war effort or not (i.e., the social history of civilians).

Women, it is clear, acted as vital intermediaries between the home front and the war zone through their links with and influence on their menfolk—often "boyfolk," in fact—who went away to war. They encouraged their sons or husbands to enlist and, once they were in the army, sustained their morale with letters and parcels of food and clothing. If the war began to seem less worthy of their support in comparison to the needs of the family at home, women were also capable of urging desertion, as quite possibly happened on a large scale in the last year of the Confederacy. Also vital was women's ability to assume new and burdensome responsibilities as breadwinners and heads of household, even taking on the task of running the family farm. When women did this—and millions did, on both sides—they were stepping outside the "woman's sphere" to which nineteenth-century men had consigned them. Others broke out of this confining status in a more public fashion. Some, for example, became involved in the local activities of the U.S. Sanitary Commission, which raised funds and organized fairs to provide medical supplies, food, and clothing for Union soldiers. At the same time, a number of women volunteered as nurses in the army hospitals at home and in the field.

Nursing was an interesting phenomenon in the Civil War. On the one hand, it was consistent with the nurturing, domestic role designated for women of that era. On the other, it required these women not only to leave home, but also to enter a world of men and be exposed to scenes that were both gruesome and indelicate. Furthermore, the doctors and surgeons resented their presence, and so the women had to fight them in order to be able to carry out their tasks. Although American women were not the first to work as army nurses—Florence Nightingale and her aides had served in the

Crimea a few years earlier—their action was nevertheless so unusual that it sparked controversy about gender roles. Since women on both sides became nurses, it might be possible to make comparisons between the sections if women fared differently in the respective hospital settings or if there were contrasts in how their later lives were affected by their nursing experience.

Because of wartime pressures that led women to think and act in ways that were previously unacceptable or unimagined, it is quite possible that, in many areas of life in both sections, notions about gender and the behavior appropriate to it were shaken for a brief time, or even altered permanently. On the other hand, since soldiering is a manly activity, the heightened masculinity of the war years might have served as a counterweight to women's changing perceptions of their role. At all events, the war and its aftermath was almost certainly a time of tension and shift in relations between the sexes, though the nature and extent of this is only now being uncovered and assessed.

DOCUMENTS

Like the soldiers who went to war, many women who served in the military hospitals as nurses wrote about their experiences. In the first document in this chapter, Hannah Ropes confides to her diary in October 1862 her frustration at how things are being run and how she is being treated at Union Hospital in Washington, D.C. The second piece is a complaint by Kate Cumming, a Confederate nurse, who wrote in her journal on September 3, 1862 of her annoyance that so many Southern women were unwilling to serve as nurses like herself. In the third extract, by contrast, Phoebe Yates Pember, a nurse in Richmond, Virginia, congratulates Southern women on their service to the cause as nurses. The fourth document consists of two brief items from Susie King Taylor's *Reminiscences of Life in Camp* (1902) with the 33rd Colored Troops on the Sea Islands off South Carolina in 1864.

The remaining items deal with other aspects of women's activities during the war. The fifth extract is an account, by Mary Livermore of Chicago, of the central role of women in the provision of medical supplies and care packages (called "comfort bags" in those days) for the soldiers; it is from her memoir, *My Story of the War* (1889). Her explanations of the central role of women in organizing the first sanitary fair (see Chapter 7, document 3) should also be consulted. The sixth extract is from the diary of Ella Gertrude Clanton Thomas of Augusta, Georgia, in November 1864, expressing worry and frustration about the prospects for the Confederacy. In the seventh selection, Catherine Ann Devereux Edmondston, a North Carolina planter's wife, writes a diary entry on January 9, 1865 that reflects a mixture of gloom and hope about the future of the Confederacy and also comments on what the war has forced her to learn to do within the household. The eighth is from the diary of Cornelia Peake McDonald of Winchester, Virginia, a few months later, in March 1865, when things looked even worse, causing her to reflect on desertion and conscription.

Hannah Ropes Expresses the Frustration of a Union Nurse, October 1862

October [1–9], 1862.

New days bring new trials to combat; and, while we are cheered with the prospective recovery of most of those brought in after the battles in which General Pope's command was engaged, we turn away with saddened eyes from the long list of those whose last

From Hannah Ropes, diary entries October 1–9, 1862, in *Civil War Nurse: The Diary and Letters of Hannah Ropes*, John R. Brumgardt, ed. (University of Tennessee Press, 1980), pp. 71–73.

sleep has fallen upon them in this hospital. Fifteen have died within the month just ended, some of them so worn out with fatigue and fasting as to be wholly unable to rally, others kept along with wounded limbs until too exhausted to bear amputation, and thus died. It would be folly to say they all might have lived with more prompt attention; it is also unjust to a true conviction not to say they have lost their only chance through a lack of earnest interest in the superior surgeon. Apothecary and medicine chest might be dispensed with if an equal amount of genuine sympathy could be brought home to our stricken men and the rations be converted into more delicate food. Not more than eight cents per day is the cost actually dealt out by the steward! Our men have been saved only by the best of nurses and the kind and constant help from friends at home; and to those good people we turn our eyes, as the fainting mariner throws his glance across the dreary distance of ocean towards some approaching sail.

This steward I think will prove the climax of unfaithful servants. Indeed they are a strange race of mortals, so far as I have watched them; and, as we have had four during our hospital life of three months, perhaps I am as well prepared to judge them as others. Our first was a *Jew*—round faced, beady eyes, black hair and short of stature. He would talk so sweet to me, and rob me of a bottle of wine, a shirt or pretty pocket handkerchief at the very moment I was looking at him to reply! It was the kind will of providence that this spawn of the reptile species should be sent to the Peninsula, after ushering into his place a gentle, well disposed Pennsylvanian, who knew about as much of the world and society as his neighboring Dutch farmers, of the present President. He soon grew tired of the annoyances of his position and was transferred. Number 3 was from Virginia, young, compact, becoming his uniform remarkably well; but his features all turned up and his manner suggested to me the nature of a porcupine.

He thrust his quills at everybody and the waters of our earnest but harmonious life were terribly troubled. I kept out of his way till he came to my premises. Then we had a pitched battle over the rights of the soldiers, lasting a good hour. At the close, he hauled down his colors, took a cup of hot tea from my hand, and we laid some plans for bettering the diet of the patients.

In a few days he was transferred to another hospital. When he came to tell me I told him I was *really sorry,* for I had become reconciled to him, and took him to be honest at heart, and not to blame for being born under the influence of slavery. We parted friends, and in kindness. Our next and last, a French Canadian, came in with the doubtful, dreary sphere of a raven or a bat. Dressed in his dark blue suit of pants and close fitting jacket, with a wide, bright green stripe down the side, and making a cuff to the sleeve above the elbow, a stiff linen collar up under his ears, and both hands thrust down into his pockets, we felt that this man was the opener of a new epoch.

The head surgeon was also a new man, tall, stiff, thin, light hair, whity blue eyes, and whity yellow complexion, glasses on eyes, and a way of looking out at the end of his glasses at you, surreptitiously, if I may use so big a word. He was young and I took to him. He was ignorant of hospital routine; ignorant of life outside of the practice in a country town, in an interior state, a weak man with good intentions, but puffed up with the gilding on his shoulder straps. If he had not been weak, and it had been my style to make a joke at the expense of others, there was a fine chance here; but he was safe at my hands, for he *was* weak, and I am strong in the knowledge at least which comes with age. And it is likely that in some way even this man, made giddy with an epaulette, will learn that God has made the private and officer of one equality, so far as the moral treatment of each other is concerned.

Kate Cumming Criticizes Southern Women,
September 1863

. . . There is one very important item which I have left out in this "Alabama woman's" letter. She says, let the women go into the hospitals. Now she comes to what is woman's true sphere: in war, the men to fight, and the women to nurse the wounded and sick, are words I have already quoted. I have no patience with women whom I hear telling what wonders they would do if they were only men, when I see so much of their own legitimate work left undone. Ladies can be of service in the hospitals, and of great service. I have heard more than one surgeon say, if he could get the right kind, he would have them in almost every department. I could name many things they could do, without ever once going into a ward.

All have not the gift of nursing, but they can do the housekeeping, and there is much of that in a hospital.

I know many will say the surgeons will not have them, nor can I blame the surgeons if the stories are true which I have heard about the ladies interfering with them. I have been nearly two years in the hospital service, and I have never spent one day without seeing women's work left undone, and I have had no time to do the surgeons'.

The sick in a hospital are as much under the care of the surgeon and assistant surgeons as men in the field are under the control of their officers. And would we not think a woman out of her senses were she to say that because she had made the clothes the soldiers wore, and attended to their wants otherwise, she had a right to command them; or that she would do nothing for them because that right was not given her, even if she had a better knowledge of Hardee's tactics than some of our officers. The surgeons are alone responsible for the sick under their control, and have the right to direct what should be done for them.

Are the women of the South going into the hospitals? I am afraid candor will compel me to say they are not! It is not respectable, and requires too constant attention, and a hospital has none of the comforts of home! About the first excuse I have already said much; but will here add, from my experience since last writing on that subject, that a lady's respectability must be at a low ebb when it can be endangered by going into a hospital.

I have attended to the soldiers of our army in hospitals and out of them, and in all sincerity I can say that, so far as their bearing toward ladies is concerned, I have never heard one word spoken or seen one act at which the most fastidious and refined woman could take exception.

This was more than I looked for; I knew that our army was composed of the lowest as well as the highest, and I did expect to find some among them void of delicacy.

I can not tell whether our army is an exception to the rule or not; but about it I can say that, as regards real native refinement, that which all the Chesterfields in the world can not give, a more perfect army of gentlemen could not be than they are. I do not know what they are in camp, but speak of what I have seen in other places.

To the next two excuses—that is, to constant work, and hospitals not being like home—I wonder if soldier's work is just such as they wish, and if the camp is any thing like home?—I think there is no need of giving the answers; they are obvious. . . .

From Kate Cumming, extract, September 1863, in *Kate: The Journal of a Confederate Nurse,* Richard B. Harwell, ed. (Louisiana State University Press, 1959), pp. 135–136.

Phoebe Yates Pember Commends Southern Women (Undated)

. . . The women of the South had been openly and violently rebellious from the moment they thought their states' rights touched. They incited the men to struggle in support of their views, and whether right or wrong, sustained them nobly to the end. They were the first to rebel—the last to succumb. Taking an active part in all that came within their sphere, and often compelled to go beyond this when the field demanded as many soldiers as could be raised; feeling a passion of interest in every man in the gray uniform of the Confederate service; they were doubly anxious to give comfort and assistance to the sick and wounded. In the course of a long and harassing war, with ports blockaded and harvests burnt, rail tracks constantly torn up, so that supplies of food were cut off, and sold always at exorbitant prices, no appeal was ever made to the women of the South, individually or collectively, that did not meet with a ready response. There was no parade of generosity; no published lists of donations, inspected by public eyes. What was contributed was given unostentatiously, whether a barrel of coffee or the only half bottle of wine in the giver's possession.

About this time one of these large hospitals was to be opened, and the wife of George W. Randolph, Secretary of War, offered me the superintendence—rather a startling proposition to a woman used to all the comforts of luxurious life. Foremost among the Virginia women, she had given her resources of mind and means to the sick, and her graphic and earnest representations of the benefit a good and determined woman's rule could effect in such a position settled the result in my mind. The natural idea that such a life would be injurious to the delicacy and refinement of a lady—that her nature would become deteriorated and her sensibilities blunted, was rather appalling. But the first step only costs, and that was soon taken.

A preliminary interview with the surgeon-in-chief gave necessary confidence. He was energetic—capable—skillful. A man with ready oil to pour upon troubled waters. Difficulties melted away beneath the warmth of his ready interest, and mountains sank into mole-hills when his quick comprehension had surmounted and leveled them. However troublesome daily increasing annoyances became, if they could not be removed, his few and ready words sent applicants and grumblers home satisfied to do the best they could. Wisely he decided to have an educated and efficient woman at the head of his hospital, and having succeeded, never allowed himself to forget that fact.

The day after my decision was made found me at "headquarters," the only two-story building on hospital ground, then occupied by the chief surgeon and his clerks. He had not yet made his appearance that morning, and while awaiting him, many of his corps, who had expected in horror the advent of female supervision, walked in and out, evidently inspecting me. There was at that time a general ignorance on all sides, except among the hospital officials, of the decided objection on the part of the latter to the carrying out of a law which they prognosticated would entail "petticoat government"; but there was no mistaking the stage-whisper which reached my ears from the open door of the office that morning, as the little contract surgeon passed out and informed a friend he met, in a tone of ill-concealed disgust, that *"one of them had come."*

From Phoebe Yates Pember, extract, in *A Southern Woman's Story: Life in Confederate Richmond,* Bell I. Wiley, ed. (Ballantine Books, 1959), pp. 16–17.

Susie King Taylor Describes Her Role in
Union Army Camps, 1864

. . . I taught a great many of the comrades in Company E to read and write, when they were off duty. Nearly all were anxious to learn. My husband taught some also when it was convenient for him. I was very happy to know my efforts were successful in camp, and also felt grateful for the appreciation of my services. I gave my services willingly for four years and three months without receiving a dollar. I was glad, however, to be allowed to go with the regiment, to care for the sick and afflicted comrades.

. . . About four o'clock, July 2, [1864], the charge was made [on Fort Gregg, James Island, S.C.]. The firing could be plainly heard in camp. I hastened down to the landing and remained there until eight o'clock that morning. When the wounded arrived, or rather began to arrive, the first one brought in was Samuel Anderson of our company. He was badly wounded. Then others of our boys, some with their legs off, arm gone, foot off, and wounds of all kinds imaginable. They had to wade through creeks and marshes, as they were discovered by the enemy and shelled very badly. A number of the men were lost, some got fastened in the mud and had to cut off the legs of their pants, to free themselves. The 103d New York suffered the most, as their men were very badly wounded.

My work now began. I gave my assistance to try to alleviate their sufferings. I asked the doctor at the hospital what I could get for them to eat. They wanted soup, but that I could not get; but I had a few cans of condensed milk and some turtle eggs, so I thought I would try to make some custard. I had doubts as to my success, for cooking with turtle eggs was something new to me, but the adage has it, "Nothing ventured, nothing done," so I made a venture and the result was a very delicious custard. This I carried to the men, who enjoyed it very much. My services were given at all times for the comfort of these men. I was on hand to assist whenever needed. I was enrolled as company laundress, but I did very little of it, because I was always busy doing other things through camp, and was employed all the time doing something for the officers and comrades.

Mary Livermore Explains the Role of Women in
the Union War Effort, 1889

Organizations of women for the relief of sick and wounded soldiers, and for the care of soldiers' families, were formed with great spontaneity at the very beginning of the war. There were a dozen or more of them in Chicago, in less than a month after Cairo was occupied by Northern troops. They raised money, prepared and forwarded supplies of whatever was demanded, every shipment being accompanied by some one who was held responsible for the proper disbursement of the stores. Sometimes these local societies affiliated with, or became parts of, more comprehensive organizations. Most of them worked independently during the first year of the war, the Sanitary Commission of Chicago being only one of the relief agencies. But the Commission gradually grew in public confidence, and gained in scope and power; and all the local societies were

From Susie King Taylor, extract, in *Reminiscences of My Life in Camp* (Arno Press, 1968), pp. 21, 34–35.

From Mary A. Livermore, *My Story of the War* (Hartford: A. D. Worthington & Co., 1889), pp. 135–137, 139–140.

eventually merged in it, or became auxiliary to it. As in Chicago, so throughout the country. The Sanitary Commission became the great channel, through which the patriotic beneficence of the nation flowed to the army.

When the local aid society of which I was president, merged its existence in that of the Sanitary Commission, I also became identified with it. Thenceforth, until the bells rang in the joyful news of peace, my time and energy were given to its varied work. In its busy rooms I was occupied most of the time when not in the hospitals, or engaged with some of the Northwestern soldiers' aid societies.

Here, day after day, the drayman left boxes of supplies sent from aid societies in Iowa, Minnesota, Wisconsin, Michigan, Illinois, and Indiana. Every box contained an assortment of articles, a list of which was tacked on the inside of the lid. These were taken out, stamped in indelible ink with the name of the "CHICAGO SANITARY COMMISSION," the stamp as broad as your hand, and the letters so large as to be easily read across a room. For the convenience of the hospitals they were repacked,—shirts by themselves, drawers by themselves, and so on. Then they awaited orders from the hospitals.

One day I went into the packing-room to learn the secrets of these boxes,—every one an argosy of love,—and took notes during the unpacking. A capacious box, filled with beautifully made shirts, drawers, towels, socks, and handkerchiefs, with "comfort-bags" containing combs, pins, needles, court-plaster, and black sewing-cotton, and with a quantity of carefully dried berries and peaches, contained the following unsealed note, lying on top:—

> DEAR SOLDIERS,—The little girls of —— send this box to you. They hear that thirteen thousand of you are sick, and have been wounded in battle. They are very sorry, and want to do something for you. They cannot do much, for they are all small; but they have bought with their own money, and made what is in here. They hope it will do some good, and that you will all get well and come home. We all pray to God for you night and morning.

The box was carefully unpacked, each article stamped with the mark of the Commission, as a preventive to theft, and then carefully repacked just as it was received. That sacred offering of childhood was sent intact to the hospital. . . .

Rarely was a box opened that did not contain notes to soldiers, accompanying the goods. In the pocket of one dressing-gown, a baby's tin rattle was found—in another, a small china doll, tastefully dressed—in another, a baby's photograph—in yet another, a comic almanac. In every box was a good supply of stoutly made "comfort-bags." A "comfort-bag" usually contained a small needle-book, with a dozen stout needles in it, a well-filled pin-ball, black and white thread, buttons, etc. These "little usefuls," as the boys called them, were invaluable to the handy fellows, who very often became skillful extempore tailors.

As whittling and wood-carving were among the prime amusements of the hospital, a jack-knife was added, and generally a pair of scissors. Sometimes a square piece of tobacco was included among the miscellanies, nor was the "comfort-bag" considered less valuable in consequence. Often a small Testament increased the value of the little bag, with the name and residence of the donor on the fly-leaf.

And if the comfort-bag contained no letter, with a stamped envelope, and blank sheet of paper added, its recipient was a little crestfallen. The stationery was rarely forgotten. Folded in the sleeves of shirts, tucked in pockets, wrapped in handkerchiefs, and rolled in socks, were envelopes with stamps affixed, containing blank sheets of note paper, and usually a pencil was added. The soldiers expressed their need of stationery in almost every letter they wrote. Most of the letters sent to the army contained stamped envelopes, and paper, for the men were without money so much of the time, that when the sutlers had stationery for sale at exorbitant prices, the soldiers were unable to buy it. . . .

Gertrude Thomas Finds Confederate Prospects Gloomy, November 1864

Augusta, November 17, 1864   Three weeks since writing last, my frequent letters to Mr Thomas forming a record of the time since I have moved into town, but I am in trouble and instinctively I turn to my journal. Today I dined with Ma having been out in the morning with Aunty Cousin Emma and Cora. As I entered the house a telagram was handed Mamie who opened it and found that it was intended for me. I read it and then with the foolish remark "I believe I am going to do as I did when the cow ran after me, I am going to cry," I burst into tears. The telagram, dated Macon contained these words "Wheeler Dragoons & self—all well."

This is a dark hour in our country's history. Lincoln has been elected by 300,000 majority and Northern papers say that Sherman is preparing for a winter campaign through the cotton states with five corps, leaving a sufficient force to hold Chattanooga and look after Hood. Sherman some years ago was stationed at the arsenal at the Sand Hills and has been the recipient of hospitality from numerous citizens of this place. President Davis in his message says that we are better off than we were this time last year, but when President Davis advocates the training of Negroes to aid us in fighting— promising them, as an inducement to do so, *their freedom,* and in the same message intimates that rather than yield we would place every Negro in the Army—he so clearly betrays the weakness of our force that I candidly confess I am disheartened. I take a woman's view of the subject but it does seem strangely inconsistent, the idea of our offering to a Negro the rich boon—the priceless reward of freedom to aid us in keeping in bondage a large portion of his brethren, when by joining the Yankees he will instantly gain the very reward which Mr Davis offers to him after a certain amount of labor rendered and danger incurred. Mr Davis to the contrary, the Negro has had a great deal to do with this war and if—but I fear I grow toryish in my sentiments—

Monday, November 21, 1864   Oh God will this war never cease? Will we ever settle quietly in our old peaceful domestic relations? How strange it all seems. Even now I can scarcely realize the state of suspense in which we have all been placed during the past few days. I don't believe I have felt so gloomy at anytime tho as I did Saturday afternoon. During the morning I rode out (Friday), and just as I was leaving the house I received a letter from Mr Thomas written the Sunday previous—Said he "Ah you can form no idea how much I miss you—good bye to you and all my little ones." . . .

Short as the time has been since Thursday, I can scarcely collect the link of events sufficiently to tell how the time has been spent. Oh I remember now that Mr Scales spent Friday night with us. He was taking a gloomy view of our prospects, but he talked just this way I remember one year ago. Then I confess I felt more determined "to do and dare and die" than I do now. Saturday we were busy hauling wood from the depot, Mr Selkirk the agent having been good enough to let me have two car loads brought up. It was

From Ella Gertrude Clanton Thomas, *The Secret Eye: The Journal of Ella Gertrude Clanton Thomas, 1848–1889,* Virginia Ingraham Burr, ed. (University of North Carolina Press, 1990), pp. 243–244.

fortunate I received it when I did as the trains are occupied now in removing government stores to the exclusion of everything else. It was, as yesterday and today have been, dull gloomy days. The whole heavens overcast with clouds—All nature appearing to mourn over the wretched degeneracy of her children and weeping to see brothers arrayed in hatred against each other. "Man, the noblest work of God." Verily, when I witness and read of the track of desolation which Sherman's army leaves behind them, I am constrained to think that the work reflects little credit upon the creator. I know that sounds irreverent but I sigh for the memory of those days when man's noblest, better nature was displayed, when the brute "the cloven foot," was concealed and I could dream and believe that ours was the very best land—ruled by the very best men under the sun!! . . .

Catherine Edmondston of North Carolina Discusses Matters Public and Domestic, January 1865

"Out of the abundance of the heart the mouth speaketh," but the hand writeth not. Never were we more absorbed in outward matters, never have we looked on them so anxiously as now, & yet it is days since I have written aught of them. This negro question, this vexed negro question, will if much longer discussed do us more injury than the loss of a battle. Gen Lee advises the Conscription & ultimate Emancipation of 200,000 Slaves to be used as soldiers. One or two rabid partizan papers, Democratic, I might almost say Agrarian to the core, seize on the proposal, hold it up to the people, to the army, in the most attractive lights. They promise the white soldier that if the negro is put in the army, for every negro soldier fifteen white ones will be allowed to return home. They use it as an engine to inflame the passions of one class against another, tell the poor man that the War is but for his rich neighbor's slaves, that his blood is poured out to secure additional riches to the rich, etc., etc., nay one paper, to its shame be it said, the Richmond Enquirer, openly advocates a general Emancipation! as the price for fancied benefits to be obtained by an alliance with England & France. Actually it offers to sell the birthright of the South, not for a mess of pottage, but only for the hope of obtaining one. The Traitor, recreant to principle, lost to every sense of national honour, & blind to what constitutes a true national prosperity—the wonder is that he finds anyone either to read or think seriously of his monstrous proposition. But so it is. Coming as it does on the evacuation of Savannah when we are almost ready to sink under the accumulation of Yankee lies & Yankee bragg, over their boasted Victory over Hood, our money depreciated & depreciating daily more & more, deafened on one side by loud mouthed politicians who advocate "Reconstruction to save Annihilation," "Reconstruction as a choice of Evils," & on the other by the opponents of the Government who expatiate with alass too much truth upon the mismanagement, the waste, the oppression which, cast our eyes which way we will we see around us, threatened again with a new suspension of Habeas Corpus, the Constitution daily trampled under foot by Impressment Laws & Government Schedules, what wonder that many unthinking people catch at this straw as at hope of salvation & delivery from present misery without pausing to ask themselves what will be their condition when they have accepted it. But sounder & better councils will prevail. This

From Catherine Edmondston, *Journal of a Secesh Lady,* Ben G. Crabtree and James W. Patton, eds. (Raleigh: N. C. Department of Archives and History, 1979), pp. 652–654.

beaten and crushed Abolitionist, the Enquirer, will find that the body of the people are against him, that the foxes who have lost their tails are too few in number to govern those who still retain theirs. Slaveholders on principle, & those who hope one day to become slaveholders in their time, will not tacitly yeild their property & their hopes & allow a degraded race to be placed at one stroke on a level with them. But these discussions & these thoughts have occupied us for the past fortnight & such a deluge of gloomy forebodings have been penned out upon us that I almost hailed the frequent mail failures as a blessing. . . .

As for ourselves, since the negroes holiday at Christmas, for Christmas shone no holiday to any but them, we have been engaged with our year's supply of meat. Frying up Lard, squeezing out cracklins, & all the, to me, disagreeable et ceteras of "a hog killing" are I beleive a perfect happiness to Cuffee! The excitement & interest over the weight of their favorites, the feasting on chitterlings & haslets, the dabbling in grease, seems to constitute a negro paradise, whilst the possession of a "bladder to blow" or better still a hog tail is all a negro child needs of earth's enjoyments. Well we "killed Hogs" here, then we went to Hascosea [the Edmondstons' summer home] & did the same thing there.

As usual we were weatherbound & detained 24 hours longer than we intended to remain. Mr E ordered a large box of books, principally farming periodicals (which we had bound the winter before the commencement of the war & which came home whilst we were in great excitement about Ft Sumter & which we have since refrained from opening on account of our unsettled state & the determination we from time to time take to pack up all our books) to be opened, & we passed the time most pleasantly & profitable, rubbing up our old knoledge, forming new plans, agricultural, horticultural, & domestic which this spring & summer we hope to put in execution. I lent an especial eye to the Poultry yard—am armed with several infalible receipts to cure & to prevent "the gapes," all of which I shall try on my spring chickens. In Vinegar receipts too I have come home quite learned & I now sigh for a peice of genuine Vinegar plant! I have some very fine Vinegar made from the skimmings of last year's Sorghhum, but alas, it is too little for my many uses. I used to be famous for Pickles, but my cunning has departed, as the price of whisky and Apple Brandy has risen, for on them did I rely to give my Vinegar body. I am now making yeast by the pailful and even contemplate malting some corn to supply the deficiency. This war is teaching us many things. Dying, spinning, and weaving are no longer unknown mysteries to me. I think of making a compilation of all my practical knoledge on the subject and I intend for the future Peace or war to let *homespun* be my ordinary dress. The object of my ambition is to have a black watered silk trimmed with black thread lace. Think of it! How shall I feel when I pull off my russet yarn spun & woven on the Plantation & bedeck myself in that style! It seems so long since I wore a silk dress that I begin to doubt if I ever owned one. . . .

Cornelia Peake McDonald Comments on Class and Conscription, March 1865

March came in gloomy and melancholy, and brought with it a dreadful certainty of disaster and defeat. One thing that almost quenched the last hope in me, was seeing the

From Cornelia Peake McDonald, *A Woman's Civil War,* Minrose C. Gwin, ed. (University of Wisconsin Press, 1992), pp. 224–226.

men coming home; every day they passed, in squads, in couples, or singly, all leaving the army. What must have been the anguish of Lee's great heart when he saw himself being deserted by his men when pressed so sorely by the enemy. Many stopped at my house asking for food. I gave them a share of such as I had, though I felt a scorn for giving up when defeat was near, instead of remaining to the end. It is hard to call them deserters, but such they were, and they knew it, for each one would tell of how hard Lee was beset, and how impossible it was for him to hold out any longer, as if to excuse his own delinquency. After all though, when I thought of it afterwards, I could not wonder that they did desert. The conscription had forced many unwilling ones to go to the army, leaving unprotected wives and children in lonely mountain huts to abide their fate whatever it might be, freezing or starvation. Though the conscription was made necessary by the exigency of the times, it was nevertheless a dreadful tyranny; and though I have never said so, I have often thought that no greater despotism could be than that government was in the last months of its existence. To those whose education and habits of life made them enthusiastic, or whose pride acted as an incentive for them to endure and suffer, as was the case with the higher classes, it wore no such aspect, but to those who had but their poor homes and little pieces of ground by which they managed to provide very little more than bread for their families, who knew that they would be as well off under one government as another, it was oppression to be forced into the army, and not ever to be free from the apprehension that their families were suffering.

One man told me that he had remained in the trenches till a conscript who had lately arrived from his neighborhood told him that his family was starving. All the winter hordes of deserters had been gathering in the mountains, and entrenching themselves; had resisted all attempts to arrest them. Indeed they sometimes captured officers and soldiers of the Confederate army and detained them.

One night Col. Richard Henry Lee was retiring from a fight in which he had been separated from his command, and was captured by them and held for several days. Those men had resisted the conscription, though they would not desert to the enemy, and were ready if attacked or pursued to defend themselves.

They proved rather formidable neighbors to the dwellers near their mountain dens, for they often descended upon helpless people and took all their grain and cattle.

No one was to be blamed for such a state of things, but the cruel circumstances in which we were placed compelled it. If the brave, the well born and the chivalrous could have done all the fighting there would have been no shrinking, no desertion; but alas! their boys lay buried on every battlefield in Virginia; a whole generation nearly, of young men of good birth and breeding had been swept away, and as many others who, though of plainer people, had true soldierly hearts, and bore themselves bravely in the shock of battle, and patiently and unmurmuringly in the long march or the weary watch. There was no house, high or low in the length and breadth of Virginia, that had not to mourn some lost boy.

One evening I went to a house where I was having some weaving done, and saw there an old woman who talked a great deal about the war, but did not seem to understand very clearly what it all meant. She spoke of having lost her only son in some battle in the valley near Winchester. She did not know the name of the place. "I never knowed where it was," she said, "but they told me he was killed about there though I did not know he was killed for certain for more than a year after." I found out afterward that it was the battle of Kernstown.

One sad instance of the kind of tyranny that seemed a necessity in those hard times, made me feel very sorrowful. A butcher by the name of Hite lived in a nice little cottage at the lower end of the town. He had a wife and two small children. I often went there to get meat when he had it, which was not at all times now. He was conscribed and marched off. What became of him I never heard but in mid-winter (he was taken off in November), his wife finding it impossible to provide for her children where she was, sold her furniture and got a horse and wagon with which she set out with her children to try to make her way into the Federal lines to join her people who lived in Pennsylvania. When two days on her journey she was stopped by some lawless people who questioned her about where she was going, and when she said she was going to Pennsylvania, they said she was a traitor and enemy, and that her wagon and horse were confiscated. So they set her down by the roadside and took her property.

That was of course done by no authority, but it served to show how little law there was that was effectual in anything but filling up the ranks of the army. Now, however, it failed even in that, for men deserted faster than the conscripts were brought in. . . .

✏ ESSAYS

Aspects of the experience of women in both sections are treated in the essays that follow. In the first, Elizabeth D. Leonard of Colby College shows how Northern nurses fared and how they reacted to the war and to their circumstances through an examination of one particular nurse, Rebecca Usher, a middle-aged, well-to-do woman from Maine. In contrast to this case-study approach, Drew Gilpin Faust of the University of Pennsylvania generalizes across the entire region in her examination of Confederate women. The selection presented here consists of two parts, the first a short extract about nursing in the Confederacy and the second an entire chapter dealing with war weariness among the women of the Confederacy's upper class and how this affected the course of the war.

Civil War Nurse, Civil War Nursing:
Rebecca Usher of Maine

ELIZABETH D. LEONARD

Rebecca Usher was born in 1821 to Hannah Lane and Ellis Baker Usher. Ellis Usher was a wealthy mill owner and lumberman who also served at different times as a delegate to Maine's state constitutional convention, as town clerk for Hollis, and as state senator for his district. Rebecca seems to have received a good basic education as a young girl, probably at a local girls' seminary. By sixteen she had left Hollis for an Ursuline Convent at Three Rivers in Canada, where she remained for four years studying and then teaching French. At age twenty she returned to Maine and her family, perhaps responding to her sister Martha's deep longing for her presence. "You must come home with Pa," wrote Martha, in December 1840. "We shan't consent to your remaining any longer, but shall indeed give up if you dont come home this month." We then lose sight of Usher's path again until the outbreak of the Civil War, although we do know that she did not marry

From Elizabeth Leonard, "Civil War Nurse, Civil War Nursing: Rebecca Usher of Maine," *Civil War History,* Volume 41, #3, 1995, pp. 190–207. Copyright © 1995. Reprinted by permission of The Kent State University Press.

during this time (or for the rest of her life, for that matter). Instead, she most likely supported herself as a teacher and continued to live at home or with relatives.

It was in the aftermath of Antietam, in the fall of 1862, that female nurse recruitment in the North got underway in a serious manner. In October Rebecca Usher received a letter from one A. F. Quinby indicating that a nursing position under the authority of the Union army's superintendent of women nurses, Dorothea Dix, was available. "No particular qualifications or specifications are required . . . a common experience in nursing, & plain, sensible clothing. Our travelling expenses are paid, & we are allowed [paid] 40 cts per day." Around the same time that Quinby was writing to Usher, Surgeon General William Hammond was in the process of appointing Adaline Tyler of Boston matron of the Union army's General Hospital at Chester. Independent of Dix's authority by virtue of her appointment directly by the surgeon general, Tyler called for volunteer, unpaid nurses to work with her. It was her call rather than Dix's that caught Usher's attention. "[Eight] ladies responded," Usher later recalled. "Mrs Duquindre of Michigan, Miss Ellis of Mass, Bishop Southgate's daughter of New York, Miss Sarah Tucker, Miss Dupee, Miss Louise Titcomb and myself, from Portland Maine and vicinity." . . .

By the end of the first week in December—about two weeks after her arrival—Usher was in charge of her own ward. "I am in ward E no 2," she wrote excitedly to Martha. "Louise is in the same ward no 1, so that my room opens out of hers. I shall now soon get acquainted with my men & will write you about them." The assignment to a ward had come just in the nick of time, from Usher's perspective, as matron Tyler was also considering giving Usher the position of superintendent of the laundry. "She said she thought Louise or I could fill the place," Usher wrote, noting that Tyler was not satisfied with the woman currently engaged to do so. "But I should not be willing to take it & I could not recommend it to any one. The superintendent [*sic*] is not expected to wash any of the clothes," she confessed, "but she has about 20 women under her, & is obliged to be there in the steam all the time to arrange the work & see that it goes on well. They [the washerwomen] wash & iron there every day but Sunday." Better to be tending to the soldiers, Usher believed firmly, than doing even supervisory duty over such grueling, menial labor (although she did admit to helping the "chamber woman" on occasion "in cleaning the [soldiers'] stockings" when her regular activities permitted).

What *were* Usher's, and the other women nurses', "regular activities"? According to Frank Moore [compiler of *Women of the War,* 1866], the daily work of the women nurses at Chester did *not* include the "immediate and constant nursing" of the soldiers, which was instead performed by convalescent "soldiers detailed for the purpose." Linus Brockett and Mary Vaughan, like Moore, commemorators of Northern women's work in the Civil War, agreed that the basic duties of the female nurses at Chester consisted not so much of medical assistance but rather, as they described it, of the "dispensing of the extra and low diet [specially prepared foods for the most ill] to the patients; the charge of their clothing; watching with, and attending personally to the wants of those patients whose condition was most critical; writing for and reading to such of the sick or wounded as needed or desired these services, and attending to innumerable details for their cheer and comfort." Indeed, Usher's letters from her months at Chester do not indicate any involvement (or any desire for involvement) in gritty medical procedures performed on the often severely wounded or desperately ill soldiers, or even in activities such as wound dressing or bathing or the dispensing of medicines. Rather, Usher's days were fully taken up with the more broadly defined "caretaking" of the soldiers in her ward, which included seeing to their meals (although rarely cooking for them). In a letter to Martha, Usher described the process by which meals were generally served. The bulk of the soldiers ate in the central dining rooms, not attended by the female nurses; only those too ill to leave the wards had their food—prepared in Matron Tyler's special kitchen—brought to them. Although Usher spoke of "serving" the men in her ward, in fact female nurses acted more as supervisors of the serving process at mealtimes. . . .

In addition to supervising soldiers' meals, nurses expended considerable energy distributing to them precious stores from the homefront, including clothing. On more than one occasion Usher wrote home with gratitude for receiving a box of supplies. She wrote to Ellen [her sister],

> You can hardly imagine what an exquisite pleasure it is to open a box at a hospital. No miser ever counted his gold with half the zest, with which we handle & count the nice warm clothing & delicate comforts sent to the soldiers. Tears of gratitude rise to all our eyes, & exclamations of delight burst from our lips, as we bring up from the depth of the box, the many things which we scarcely dared hope for, in this our country's time of need. . . . Two of the flannel shirts I gave to Louise & two I kept to dispense myself; one of these I gave to my dyptheria patient, whom they had stripped as soon as he arrived here & sent all his clothes to the wash-house; & replaced his two shirts with only a cotton one.

Elsewhere she noted, "we are bending all our efforts towards giving [the soldiers] a change of stockings once a fortnight[.] We do not like to have our men wear their shirts a month, & their stockings three weeks without washing, but we know that in other places there are many that have neither stockings nor shirts to wear, & so we make the best of it."

And then there was tobacco, a highly prized treat among the sick and wounded soldiers at Chester, as no doubt elsewhere. Usher's letters home repeatedly request and give thanks for donations of tobacco for the soldiers' use. The following letter to Ellen in December 1862 is typical:

> I was very glad to receive your letter containing $5.00 for tobacco[;] I have it still on hand, as I had a present of quite a large package of tobacco last week, & I am very economical with it & try to make it last as long as possible, giving it out in small parcels to the men. I am indebted to Mr. Newhall of Germantown Penn for it. He is a cousin of Susan [Newhall, another nurse at Chester] & came to call upon her, when without intending to beg I mentioned our need of tobacco . . . & the next week he came again bringing his wife & baby & Mr Barclay of Philadelphia & a large package of tobacco to be devided [*sic*] between Miss Newhall Louise & myself.

Usher's kindly concern for the soldiers' tobacco supply contrasted sharply with her own personal opinion of tobacco, revealed in a diary entry toward the end of the war: "This tobacco chewing is a great national misfortune & disgrace. Our public buildings are made filthy by it & even at the President's Levee [which she had attended some weeks before], the officer who stood at the entrance of the Green-room every now & then turned & expectorated on the carpet."

What seems to have given Usher the greatest pleasure in her work, and occupied the bulk of her time, was simply becoming acquainted with and providing sisterly (or maternal) companionship to the men who surrounded her; chatting with the soldiers; listening to their stories; keeping them company; easing their homesickness, war-weariness, and despair; writing letters for them; and otherwise helping to maintain their connections with loved ones on the homefront. "[We nurses] care little for our rooms," she wrote, "our whole interest is with the soldiers." In her letters home she described various individuals and their particular circumstances. "We have a Rebel Lieut[enant] from North Carolina," she wrote on one occasion. "He was shot through the right shoulder and his right arm is lashed to his side. He is very feeble and the Surgeon thought he should be obliged to amputate his arm; but his wound is doing better. . . . He is a young man about 22 or 3—is very patient & we all feel a good deal of sympathy for him. We do not see in him a Rebel, but only a wounded soldier." Elsewhere she wrote, "Last Saturday a . . . soldier in Miss Newhall's ward died from amputation. He was so low that he did not recover from the effects of the ether. . . . He told [Miss Newhall] that he did not think he should live through the operation. He said he should be willing to die if he was sure he was prepared: that he had never spoken but one profane word, & then he got angry with a boy at school, & it had always haunted him;—that he had always endeavored to do his duty through life, but he was afraid he was not a christian." Usher took special note of those soldiers whose ethnic origins were distinct from her own, specifically the Irish. She wrote to Ellen, "I am very much interested in my ward. I have several Irishmen in it. Pretty rough looking men some of them, but they are gentle as lambs to me." And in another letter she wrote, "[An] Irishman about 70 years old who had taken a little too much whiskey came to me one evening & insisted on shaking hands with me. I was afraid he might do or say some absurd thing & tried to withdraw, but I could not get rid of him; he shook me by the hand & then patted me on the shoulder, telling me not to be afraid of him much to the amusement of the other men. So you see I've got on the right side of the Paddies as usual." Overall, Usher admitted in a letter to a niece, "I get so much interested in many of my men that I feel sorry to part with them when they are discharged or sent to their regiments."

Yet all Usher's intense interest in "her men" remained purely in the realm of the platonic, although she frequently hinted at the possible romantic overtones of her close contact with so many soldiers. Indeed, early on in her tenure at Chester it seems to have been somewhat difficult for this forty-ish single woman to get used to being around so many men at once. "I rose this morning at quarter before seven & went down to Mrs Tyler's kitchen," she wrote to Martha. "I usually go down through the courts in the morning, as the men in the wards are not always ready to receive visitors so early in the morning, & when they are, it is some what embarrassing, to march down alone through a quarter of a mile of men." "But," she added, "one soon becomes accustomed to it, so that it is rather pleasant than otherwise, & you soon find yourself talking with one another as you pass along." . . .

It is perhaps tempting to feel sorry for Usher in reading these words, or even these, written to Jeannie several weeks later: "I am really sorry to disappoint you, Jenny, but I haven't had an offer since I came to the hospital! I cannot say so much for Louise however, as I have more than once gone into her little ward-room & found a young man pressing his suit." And yet various factors combine to diminish one's pity for Usher's hypothetical loneliness and yearning, not the least of which is her own lack of self-pity and the general attitude of joy that she displayed repeatedly in her letters and that seems to have steadily characterized her time at the Chester hospital. Undoubtedly the soldiers' thankfulness for the nurses' presence contributed significantly to Usher's pleasure. "I have never seen anything like the gratitude of the soldiers for the smallest favor & the most common attention," Usher wrote in February 1863. Her attitude was also influenced by the soldiers' own fortitude, described vividly in a letter written by Usher's colleague at Chester, Louise Titcomb. "You may think it strange," Titcomb wrote to her correspondent, "that our contact with suffering, does not impress us differently. It does give us anxious hours, but the men themselves are so indifferent to pain, they joke so about their amputations, and their crippled condition, the idea of death impresses them so lightly, that one's sympathies are not kept alive, as they would be under any other circumstances." Furthermore, the generally smooth interrelations among the nurses, between the nurses and the matron, and between the nurses and the male medical staff can only have made life at Chester more felicitous. Of matron Tyler, Usher wrote, "I certainly never saw a woman so well adapted to her position as matron of a Hospital or one I would like so well to work under." Of her closest male colleague in the hospital she wrote, "I have a nice little ward master. To be sure he isn't a 'six footer,' not more than five feet four, but he's a handsome gentlemanly fellow & I like him very much." Usher described her ward surgeon as a "good Surgeon & very kind & attentive to his men," and the hospital's surgeons as a whole she claimed would "compare favorably with the same number anywhere." Of the convalescent male soldiers detailed to her ward she wrote, "Three of my four nurses are everything I could wish, so I am very fortunate . . . & we all move on most harmoniously." The other female nurses she described as "very pleasant" and happy with their work. "I think Louise was never so well contented in her life," Usher wrote to Jeannie.

Of course, Usher's awareness of her personal contribution to the Union's cause only heightened her delight in the labor she had taken up. "[N]othing can dishearten me," she informed Jeannie in January 1863. "I am sure of our cause. The sacrafice [*sic*] of human life, of most noble and precious human lives, is fearful: But I know there is compensation in the future, and that our country and the human race will move more rapidly and more securely in the pathway of true greatness. . . . I only wish I was worth half a million [dollars], that I might in the meantime succor the suffering soldiers, and send help to their destitute families." Overall, Usher found her work at Chester rewarding, exciting, fulfilling. "I am perfectly well & enjoy my work," she wrote to Ellen. "We enjoy our work here very much," she wrote to Jeannie. To Martha she commented reassuringly, "the Hospital has its sunny side." Far more graphically she added, "I am delighted with hospital life[,] feel like a bird in the air or a fish in the sea, as if I had found my native element." . . .

On the basis of her racial and socioeconomic status, was Usher a "typical" candidate for work as a Civil War nurse in the North? The answer is yes, but this is a more complicated answer than one might initially expect. What makes the answer complex is this: according to Jane Schultz, "virtually all of the 5,600 women listed in the Union hospital . . . records as 'nurse' were white and middle class." However, a total of not 5,600, but approximately 20,000 women worked in Union military hospitals during the Civil War, and among this number, approximately two-thirds were working-class black and white women (including many former slaves), about whose personal experience of Civil War hospital work we have only the most limited evidence. In other words, female Civil War hospital workers fell into several categories: matrons, nurses, cooks, and laundresses, with each classification carrying its own race and class implications. Significantly, the classification of "nurse" (Usher's classification) "carried with it the ethos of Christian duty and feminine self-sacrifice, whereas 'cook' and 'laundress' were classifications devoid of sacred cultural associations. . . . Hospital administrators and their female deputies made explicit the link between social status and the perceived value of work by assigning black and working-class women to jobs that required contact with the bodily functions of strangers."

Usher's regular daily work of caring for the soldiers shielded her from such contact. Even if she had been assigned superintendent to the laundry, as early on she feared she might be, by her own admission she would not have been "expected to wash any of the clothes" but rather would have had "about 20 [washer]women [presumably black and white working-class women] under her" for whom she would have only to "arrange the work & see that it goes on well." But Usher made it clear that this was not the kind of work she had come to do; she had not come to the war to stand "in the steam [of a laundry room] all the time," nor had she come to be a chambermaid (although she might assist that woman on occasion). She had come as a female "nurse," with all that title implied about her class status, her subsequent status among female hospital employees, and her particular responsibilities toward the soldiers. In short, Usher's socio-economic background did indeed make her a typical nurse candidate, but not a typical candidate for female hospital work of just any sort. Civil War hospitals were as stratified in terms of class and race as was the society within which they functioned.

What of her marital status? It seems clear that a sizable proportion of the women who traveled to the front as nurses for the Union army were unmarried, sometimes widows but often never-married women such as Usher. Certainly it was easier for an independent woman with limited (if any) immediate family responsibilities to commit to Civil War service away from home. Interestingly, however, the combination of youth and singlehood tended to pose particular obstacles for middle-class women who struggled to find nursing positions in the first place. Quite simply, their "virtue" was, in the eyes of many, more "at risk" than the "virtue" of married women who followed their enlisted husbands into the military as regimental nurses, for example, or of older widows and "spinsters" whose maturity (and presumed sexlessness) guarded them against accusations of impropriety. Many questioned whether young, single women would be able to resist the advances of lonely men far from home and the social constraints of community. And after all, military hospitals were teeming with young men, as Usher's description of her solitary walk "through a quarter of a mile of men" indicated. Hospitals also generally afforded women little privacy, sometimes providing "only the length of an unpainted board for the partition walls between wards, halls, nurses' quarters, and all other officers." Thus one finds that young, single female nurses frequently wrote home to assure family and friends that their "virtue" was safe. "No soldier," wrote Cornelia Hancock of Pennsylvania in 1864, "would be allowed to come into my house without knocking even in the daytime, and at night they could not get in without sawing out the logs."

When the middle-aged, unmarried reformer Dorothea Dix, named superintendent of women nurses for the Union army in June 1861, compiled her list of regulations for nurse candidates, she did not insist that they be married but did specify that they fall between the ages of thirty-five and fifty and that they be of strong health and "matronly" appearance. In an environment of popular opinion that was dubious about the idea of middle-class women at the front in the first place, Dix clearly was hoping to build a team of nurses whose "virtue" was beyond reproach. That Rebecca Usher met Dix's requirements no doubt explains both her ready welcome into the service by Dix (recall that her first offer of a position came from a woman who was informing her of a position under Dix's authority) and the level of comfort that she quickly established in the highly masculinized context of the military hospital. Indeed, one assumes that it accounts, as well, for the jocular attitude she took in discussing with family members her romantic possibilities (or lack thereof) at Chester. Being single was not unusual for Civil War nurses. But in combination with being young, and especially being perceived as attractive, it instantly raised to new heights the specter of rampant immorality in a dangerously sexualized hospital setting. . . .

Usher's silence on the matter of paid versus unpaid labor might lead one to wonder . . . whether or not Usher herself was terribly concerned with the relative merits of paid versus unpaid labor for middle-class women in Civil War hospitals. . . . In fact many women nurses believed that there was—for better or worse—a very sharp difference between middle-class women nurses working for free and working for pay, and the issue was a contested one throughout the war and beyond.

Some people, of course, thought it made perfect sense for middle-class women nurses to receive pay for their labor. Sophronia Bucklin, who served under Dix for three years during the Civil War, throughout the war earned Dix's stipulated pay of forty cents per day, or twelve dollars per month. (Just by way of comparison, white private soldiers in the Union army earned thirteen dollars per month, just one dollar more than the nurses.) In her memoir, *In Hospital and Camp* (1869), Bucklin—an unmarried, independent seamstress from Auburn, New York—displayed no compunction about taking wages for her labor. The unidentified (but probably male) author of the memoir's introduction, however, took the question on in such a way as to make it clear that he knew popular opinion on the issue was sharply divided. "*Pay and rations!*" he wrote, establishing a clear comparison between female nurses and male soldiers: "Who says, because they were *paid,* the sacrifice which [the soldiers] laid on their country's smoking altar was not a voluntary blood offering?"

Indeed, some like Dorothea Dix (though she took no wages herself) believed that the only way successfully to continue to recruit female nurses over the war's long haul was to offer them more than the satisfaction of a grateful soldier's smile—it was, in fact, to pay them. After all, even women of the middle class—single and widowed women especially—needed to survive financially somehow. In the case of married women, especially women whose husbands had gone off to war, any form of additional income might be crucial to keep the family afloat, or simply to keep it from slipping into poverty.

But many, including many women nurses, believed that to pay individual middle-class women for such work was to degrade their patriotism in response to the sectional crisis and was as well to act in crude defiance of what it meant to *be* a middle-class woman in Victorian America. Mary Newcomb, herself a middle-class nurse for the Union, claimed proudly in her memoir that she had never been "after money," as she put it, but had only desired to "be where the men were, and where I could do the most good."

Apparently, Newcomb believed it improper for a decent woman of her status to take money for work that was rightfully and morally hers to perform, and indeed she never directly drew wages herself. However, it is worth noting that in her later life even Newcomb gladly accepted a government pension on the basis of having been a Civil War nurse. Moreover, her pension file indicates that after the early-1862 death of her husband, Hiram A. W. Newcomb, a sergeant with the 11th Illinois, she began to draw his $8.00-per-month pension, which certainly helped to subsidize her "voluntary" services as a nurse.

As for Rebecca Usher, she chose a position as a volunteer nurse, no doubt to some extent because her own and her family's financial stability meant that she could choose such a position. Usher did not openly dwell on the respective merits of paid versus unpaid labor. Nevertheless the issue was a burning one for observers of (and participants in) middle-class women's Civil War nursing. It was a burning issue because, like the issue of precisely the sort of work middle-class women should be expected to perform in the context of the Civil War hospital, it was an issue profoundly wrapped up in prevailing notions of Victorian womanhood. . . .

Which brings us to a final issue—the issue of what the war, and the work of Civil War nursing, meant to women such as Rebecca Usher. What long-term impact did it have on their lives, their goals, their social status in American culture? The Civil War was in many ways a watershed for middle-class American women because it provided them with opportunities for work in the public sphere that took them out of their homes, required them to demonstrate skills they did not even know they possessed, in many cases remunerated them in the form of wages and titles and so gave them a new sense of their own (potential) professionalism. Moreover, according to some scholars, middle-class American women's Civil War work provided them for the first time with a sense of their own citizenship in a national polity, undoubtedly raising their hopes for such manifestations of their new stature as suffrage.

To argue, as a late-twentieth-century historian, that the Civil War was a significant milestone for middle-class American women in their journey toward social equality is not to assert, however, that postwar historians perceived these women's Civil War service in the same way. Indeed, one could argue that Frank Moore and others—precisely because they recognized the possibility of a change in these women's lives, goals, and social status as a result of their contributions to the Civil War effort—fought such a possibility with every form of ammunition in their arsenal. One recalls Moore's promise to Usher that she would receive "no more prominence" in his account than she might desire. Might this not be interpreted as an indication to Usher that the door back into the private sphere, from which she might have strayed, remained open?

In any case, the Civil War did not leave middle-class women entirely unchanged, nor did it leave them untouched by questions of long-term meaning and significance for their gender. Louise Titcomb, Usher's friend and colleague at Chester General Hospital, wrote to her later in the war in words that beautifully capture the sentiment of many women who participated actively in the war and who knew that their lives—and their futures—had been fundamentally altered by the experience. "It will surely take years," Titcomb wrote, "to talk over our experience. What a life . . . to ripen and darken one[']s years, and yet such light dawns on every revolution of the wheel, blood-stained as it is, that one feels a kind of growth of the spirit that defies age or care." One wonders whether Usher felt such a sense of deep transformation as a result of the experience of being a Civil War nurse. Sadly, this question cannot be answered with certainty, if only because Usher's papers do not include any indication of the direction her life took after the war. There are no postwar letters reflecting on the meaning of the war for her life; there is no memoir; there are no political treatises, no explicit, recorded postwar demands for a permanently larger sphere of action. We cannot make much of her continued singlehood, as she was by Victorian standards quite past her marrying prime even before she went to war, and in any case a decision not to marry might have been based on any number of factors.

But there is a tidbit of evidence on which one can speculate about how Usher may have responded to what could be called the "postwar reordering of Victorian gender arrangements" as a result of women's active participation in the war, their proven abilities, and their increased demands. This evidence takes us back to Usher's days at the Ursuline Convent in Three Rivers, where as a young woman of sixteen she wrote at least one essay that merits our attention.

In the essay, entitled "Ought Women to be allowed Political Rights," written more than a decade before the first women's rights convention at Seneca Falls, Usher articulates a vision of "woman" that strongly suggests that for her, and for a variety of reasons, Civil War work in the public sphere would have a powerful personal and political impact. It is true, she noted in her 1837 essay, that women have traditionally been considered unfit for political activity by virtue of their mental and physical weakness. But, she continued, these weaknesses are "circumstantial, and not natural." Both are a consequence of social conditioning. "Vanity and false ideas of beauty," she wrote,

> have done much, and her habits of life more[,] to make woman weak and sickly, confined a great part of the time to her needle, and her mind not fixed on any particular object, and not sufficiently cultivated to possess a mine of treasures within itself. . . . [Y]ou [men] say you are better able to exercise our rights for us than we for ourselves. . . . [But] are you not an interested party, and therefore not an impartial judge? This remains yet to be proved, and can only be done by giving woman a fair trial of her powers.

Certainly Usher and thousands of women like her saw in the adventure of Civil War nursing an opportunity for middle-class women to receive a "fair trial of their powers," both physically and mentally. Even if their work was not of the most grueling sort, it was work different than, and in significantly different context than[,] they had ever known— work, therefore, that proved to them a great deal about their own strengths and endurance in highly unfamiliar and often physically hazardous circumstances. If Usher saw the Civil War as an opportunity for a "fair trial of her powers," can we believe that she would have expected anything less than a just verdict from those who constituted the popular jury determining Victorian women's political and social fate?

Patriotism, Sacrifice, and Self-Interest

DREW GILPIN FAUST

I. Nursing in the Confederacy

However rewarding, hospital work posed intimidating demands and real dangers. [Ada] Bacot [of South Carolina] contracted jaundice; numbers of other nurses were afflicted with typhoid. When Miss Wight from a Virginia hospital died from the disease, one of her fellow nurses justly observed that "she saved life at the sacrifice of her own." Juliet Opie Hopkins of Alabama herself became a casualty when she broke her leg while lifting a wounded officer on the battlefield at Seven Pines. She limped for the rest of her life. Curiously, public discussion of nursing's dangers ignored these physical threats to women's well-being, concentrating instead on the cultural and social perils inherent in its challenges to morality and propriety.

Whether southern women feared losing their respectability, their lives, or simply the comforts of home, they did not volunteer for hospital work in the numbers needed in the face of mounting casualties. Advertisements seeking female nurses continued to appear in southern newspapers throughout most of the war, and the makeshift arrangement of much of Confederate hospital care persisted, despite efforts by the government to centralize and standardize military medicine.

In some sense these continuing irregularities gave women more varied opportunities, perpetuating hospital roles outside the multitiered system of surgeons, matrons, assistant matrons, ward matrons, and nurses established by Confederate legislation. Even in the most carefully administered institutions, the neat bureaucratic prescriptions of the law poorly described day-to-day reality. Wives, mothers, and sisters arrived to nurse their own kin. On one of Phoebe Pember's wards such a visitor even appropriated her husband's cot to deliver a baby during the course of her lengthy stay. Volunteers wandered through the wards with Bibles, eatables, or words of cheer. Many facilities depended on contributions from women of the surrounding community to meet basic needs for food and supplies, and thus "feeding departments" attracted significant female energy. These official hospitals comprised only a part of the South's effort to care for its fallen soldiers. There were simply never enough government hospitals to deal with the thousands of wounded who appeared in the aftermath of bloody battles. Whole communities near the sites of costly encounters found themselves abruptly transformed, as almost every citizen, regardless of inclination, experience, or considerations of propriety would be called upon to aid in the crisis. In Winchester after Antietam, for example, Laura Lee described twenty-four hospitals set up in almost every available public space—schools, churches, banks, and town hall—in addition to the countless private homes that took in small numbers of injured Confederates. The town, she noted, had become a giant hospital, and all its remaining inhabitants—overwhelmingly female—hospital workers. Those unwilling to confront the carnage fled to become refugees.

But in spite of the variety of opportunities for hospital work and the sometimes all but irresistible demands for their labor, most elite women served intermittently or not at all. The government's effort to enlist substantial numbers of Confederate women for the hospitals was doomed to fail. Unlike military conscription, the Confederacy's manpower and mobilization policies for women rested on persuasion rather than coercion. Confronted with a choice, most white southern women avoided the hospital's hardships and dangers. After her initial difficulties, Mary Chesnut ultimately volunteered in a wayside hospital, where patients were generally convalescent rather than critical or moribund, and other women, like her, took advantage of the continuing variety of options to temper their involvement and to avoid the most trying medical environments. For many women who worried about performing their Christian duty, it often seemed enough to send provisions, visit wards to read the Bible, or serve meals to soldiers passing through by train—to make occasional contributions rather than any commitment to full-time or long-term duties.

What were the salient factors shaping women's decisions? Why did so many women disappoint Kate Cumming, Phoebe Pember, and Susan Smith by not embracing this opportunity for female service and patriotism? Why, as Cumming asked, was woman's "sacred duty . . . left undone"? Why, in Smith's words, did "more ladies not lend a helping hand . . . when there was such a wide field for every indispensable usefulness before them"? What were the special attributes or motivations that distinguished those who did defy convention to undertake these essential roles?

Many young ladies were clearly unable to overcome the fears for what Emma Crutcher called "the dignity which belongs to my sex and position." The notion of ladyhood—with its dimensions of both class and gender identity—comported poorly

with much of hospital work. But numbers of women struggled to balance such considerations against their compelling urge to be useful by performing services that, like
Crutcher's, were carefully delimited by dictates of propriety. Emma Crutcher almost
perfectly embodied the tension between the attractions of nursing as exciting, patriotic,
and meaningful work and its repulsions as sordid and demeaning. At one juncture Emma
sought to resolve her ambivalence by reminding her absent husband that he could exert
his authority and forbid her further involvement at the hospital. Like Crutcher, other
women seemingly escaped their own inner conflict by inviting or invoking male pressure
as justification for avoiding hospital duties they acknowledged as both appealing and
important. Even after she had gone to Virginia as a nurse, Ada Bacot was . . . relieved to
have a physician friend make the decision about whether she should take on a hospital
matronship. Augusta Jane Evans, a best-selling author in her late twenties, explained that
her plans to serve as a nurse had initially been vetoed by her brothers, and so she had
dutifully submitted—"reluctantly and with great disappointment." Sarah Morgan cited
the force of similar opposition. "If I was independent, if I could work my own will
without causing others to suffer for my deeds, I would not be poring over this stupid
page, I would not be idly reading or sewing. I would put aside woman's trash, and take
up woman's duty, and I would stand by some forsaken man and bid him God speed as
he closes his dying eyes. That is Woman's mission! and not Preaching and Politics. . . .
If I could help these dying men! Yet it is as impossible as though I was a chained bear[,]
. . . coward, helpless woman that I am! If I was free," she pondered. Yet as Morgan at
once excused and berated herself, it seems almost as if she was relieved not to confront
the responsibilities of freedom.

Women who served in permanent, quasi-professional hospital positions did tend to
be, as Morgan suggested, "independent." Pember and Bacot, for example, were widows,
and Cumming was an unmarried lady of sufficient maturity to be considered a spinster.
Many of the South's most active volunteers—Louisa McCord and Mary Lee, for
example—were widows as well. It was women outside the structures of direct patriarchal
control and domestic obligation who found it easiest to devote themselves to public
responsibility. As one aspiring nurse explained in her letter of application to Juliet Opie
Hopkins, she was "without any incumbrance."

Serious, committed, long-term hospital work remained the domain of these exceptional women. It was not the experience of the overwhelming majority of the South's
ladies, "only a few, a very few" of whom, in Pember's words, became matrons or nurses.
Women's contributions as nurses in the Civil War have often been hailed as a landmark
in their progress toward equality and toward an expanding sense of achievement and
self-worth. Civil War nursing itself has been regarded as the beginning of women's entry
into the health professions. For the South, neither of these celebratory characterizations
is accurate. Although training schools for nurses were established in the North after the
war and although leaders of wartime nursing such as Clara Barton exerted significant
influence on health policy and women's roles in the postwar years, no such developments
occurred in the southern states. The Cummings, Pembers, and Newsoms of the South
wrote their memoirs and faded away.

Taken as a whole, the hospital work of white southern women was not calculated to
foster new confidence about themselves and their abilities. As many of the South's most
dedicated nurses made clear, women's overall record was one of failure, not success.
They had not come forward in the numbers requested and, in the eyes of Kate Cumming,

would bear much of the liability for the South's ultimate defeat. "I have said many a time that, if we did not succeed, the women of the South would be responsible. . . . Not for one moment," she continued, "would I say that there are no women in the South who have nobly done their duty, although there was an adverse current, strong enough to carry all with it."

II. "Sick and Tired of This Horrid War"

For all their efforts to cling to accustomed privileges and familiar identities, women of the South's master class found themselves buffeted by change and tried by adversity. As years passed with no end to war in sight, emotional and material deprivation took their inescapable psychological toll. A rising sense of personal desperation, an eroding confidence in those on whom they had relied for protection, and an emerging doubt about their own ability to endure prompted women to reconsider the most fundamental assumptions about their world. As females they had long been socialized to think first of others. But faced with the unrelenting hardships of war and the escalating difficulty of simple self-preservation, they had begun inevitably to think about themselves. The ideology and practice of self-sacrifice and the persistence of self-denial demanded by the dictates of patriotism seemed increasingly to threaten individual survival. By the end of the war, suffering and loss had produced a profound transformation in women's understanding of the relationship between self and society; pain brought forth a new conception of themselves as individuals with needs, interests, and even rights, not just duties and obligations. Beginning as personal and psychological, this change ultimately involved significant implications for society and politics in the late Civil War South.

So Much Rests upon the Mind   In the aftermath of Vietnam we have seen with new clarity and force the psychological impact of war on its participants. But our heightened awareness of these deep and lingering scars has focused almost exclusively on combatants, perhaps because American casualties and victims were overwhelmingly military personnel. For an invaded rather than an invading nation, however, suffering is more widely distributed, with civilians sometimes enduring even greater depredations and brutalities than uniformed troops. The people of Vietnam, like those of the Confederate South, understood this dimension of war all too well. The traumatic stress reactions that have been identified among so many Vietnam veterans would have had their Civil War counterpart, not just among soldiers but among southern civilians and, in particular, southern women, who faced significant terror, destruction, and loss.

Women themselves recognized the challenge long years of war posed to their emotional stability. Mary Jane Cook Chadick of Alabama began her diary entries for 1865 with anticipations of difficult months ahead. Listing the "trying circumstances" she confronted—a seemingly endless separation from her husband, responsibility for the "care of a large family," and the gloomiest economic and political prospects—she noted that she was "just recovering from another one of my nervous attacks, which are becoming more frequent of late." In Tennessee, Virginia French seemed to suffer a similar fate: increasingly severe and frequent "nervous attacks." "I fear," she confessed, "that I am giving way at last under this long, long pressure of anxiety and tension upon the nerves." Emma Dobson of Virginia admitted she was "out of my mind at times[.] I candidly confess that from distress I sometimes have violent attacks of histeria." Complaining of her destitution and despair, Annie Upshur of Lynchburg declared herself "almost upon the borders of crazziness."

The intrepid Mary Lee, who had passed most of the war on the front lines in the contested town of Winchester, felt that by 1865 she was coming "completely unhinged." She noted the admission to Virginia's Insane Asylum at Staunton of a number of new patients "made insane by the War—all women." But, she reflected, "I do not wonder at it." By June 1865, with the Confederate experiment in ruins, Mary Lee declared herself "completely broken down mentally." Catherine Cooper of Tennessee feared a similar loss of balance, which her circumstances made hardly surprising. Living in an area ravaged by both Union and Confederate forces, Cooper had given ten sons and five grandsons to the army. Five of her sons died and four returned wounded. News of the illness of a tenth, she reported, "almost derainged me. I think sometimes my trials are greater than I can bear." In the last months of the war Emily Harris of North Carolina repeatedly worried that she was going insane. From early in the conflict she had seen it her duty to "shut up my griefs in my own breast" in order to protect her young children. "Truly," she remarked, "I have no time to grieve." But this denial took its toll. By 1864 she had begun to question the purpose of her efforts. "Life is not desirable for life's sake," she remarked, "but for the sake of those who need my services." She began to fear the loss of her reason as well. "I have felt crazy," she wrote. "I could almost feel the wrinkles coming on my face and the hair turn gray on my head."

Many women understood the relationship between their physical condition and their mental state. For some, material deprivation wielded a significant psychological impact. Cornelia McDonald of Winchester struggled to provide for her nine children; she herself often went without food in order to relieve their hunger. "Growing thin and emaciated," she found herself becoming "faint hearted" as well. "My feelings were beyond control. . . . I had lost the power of resistance and all my self command." Her depression was so intense she felt she "could willingly say 'good night' to the world and all in it." But physical debilitation was as often the result as the cause of mental strain. Women described worry so consuming that it rendered them unable to eat or sleep. "Every one is kept in such anxiety of mind by this dreadful war," Mary Legg wrote her friend Hattie Palmer in South Carolina, "that it is not strange when we see the body sometimes give way when so much rests upon the mind."

Unremitting stress drove some women into the protection of an emotional numbness. Abbie Brooks of Georgia wrote just a few days before Appomattox that her "sufferings and trials" had "petrified" her, turned her to stone and deadened her feelings. "I care very little for anybody or any thing. I enjoy nothing, am neither sorry nor glad." Grief had, one Virginia woman remarked, "stunned and stupefied" many of her acquaintances, and Sara Pryor of Virginia observed that "everyone who has suffered a overwhelming misfortune must be conscious of a strange deadening of feeling." *Callous* was a word that many women chose to describe their changed outlook. "I have sometimes felt," Lizzie Neblett wrote her husband, Will, "like my heart was *seared*, incapable of feeling as it once did."

Repression of feeling often encompassed depression of spirits and a sense of futility that arose both from the burden of suffering and its apparent uselessness in the face of mounting Confederate military losses. "For what am I living?" Belle Edmondson demanded. "Why is it that I am spared, from day to day with no happiness myself[?]" "Why have I lived to see this?" another woman angrily demanded. Under war's pressures, "I am wearing a way." The sense of threatened health and sanity gradually redirected women's attention away from nation and community, even sometimes from husbands and families, toward themselves and their own survival. "In my present frame of mind and state of health," Virginia French wrote after Union troops consolidated their hold over most of Tennessee, "I must confess I feel *unpatriotic* enough not to care a continental about it any way if I could only be well." She was, she admitted, "so low" that she persuaded herself she did not "care one jot for the Confederacy or anybody in it." "The Confederacy!" wrote Emily Harris, "I almost hate the word."

You *Must* Come Home   The patriotism women had so enthusiastically embraced in 1861 began to erode before seemingly endless—and increasingly purposeless—demands for sacrifice. After the defeats of the summer of 1863 Julia Davidson exclaimed to her husband, John, "Oh how I do pray this war was at an end. If the Yankees are going to whip us I wish they would hurry about it." Gertrude Thomas expressed a similar "impatience to have it over." As a New Orleans woman wrote her soldier son, "je ne vois que des sacrifices, des victimes, la ruine, la misère, rien de gagné." By 1864 the war's battles seemed no longer glorious but "massacres sans résultat." Women's willingness to be selfless, to embrace the needs of the nation as prior to their own, had begun to disappear. Their initial dedication to the Cause proved to be conditional, dependent on their own capacities to endure war's hardships and on a hope for the Confederacy's future that was rapidly evaporating. On a tour of the battlefield at Seven Pines in search of her wounded cousin, Constance Cary reported seeing men "in every stage of mutilation" and proclaimed herself "permanently convinced that nothing is worth war!" Margaret Junkin Preston greeted news of the death of her stepson and several of his friends by protesting, "Who thinks or cares for victory now!" Sarah Jane Sams proclaimed herself "sick and tired of trying to endure these privations to which we are all subjected," and as early as 1862 Julia Le Grand had come to believe that "nothing is worth such sacrifice."

A practical pacifism born of exhaustion and despair was replacing the mood of romantic militarism that had earlier gripped elite women. One of the most striking and curious expressions of this new outlook appeared in Marinda Branson Moore's *Dixie Speller,* published in Raleigh in 1864. During the war Moore produced a series of primers, readers, and spellers for Confederate youth. The 1864 speller was the last of these, and its lesson 22 contained sentiments very unlike the exuberant patriotic exercises that had filled the earlier volumes. In words of one syllable, Moore offered Confederate children a sharply dissenting voice, protesting not so much the South's political values but the cost of these commitments in human suffering.

> This sad war is a bad thing.
> My pa-pa went, and died in the army.
> My big broth-er went too and got shot. A bomb shell took off his head.
> My aunt had three sons, and all have died in the army. Now she and the girls have to work for bread.
> I will work for my ma and my sis-ters.
> I hope we will have peace by the time [I] am old enough to go to war.
> If I were a man, and had to make laws, I would not have any war, if I could help it.
> If little boys fight old folks whip them for it; but when men fight, they say "how brave!"

Moore's textbook offered the sentiments of a Confederate woman in the language of a small southern boy. To twentieth-century ears, though, it echoes the irony, the distance, and the detachment we have come to associate with writing from the Great War [World War I] and the world that followed in its aftermath.

As Confederate women discussed the war, they increasingly employed words such as *worth* and *gain,* scrutinizing their circumstances with a new attention to costs and benefits and with a new sense of self-interest born of what was for most elite southerners the novelty of privation and loss. Commitment to the Cause was not unbounded but had to be calculated in a balance sheet on which the burden of further hardship and the growing likelihood of ultimate defeat figured large. An elderly Virginia lady confessed her growing doubt about the whole Confederate experiment as she experienced the escalating trials of war. "I cannot help being unpatriotic—to feel a little selfish some-times—and," she continued significantly, "regret our peace and comfort in the old Union." In October 1864 Sal Mabry of North Carolina asked her husband Robert, "what do you think of going back into the Union[?] dont you think it would be better than to have all our men killed[?] . . . I often think if I could make peace how soon I would have you and all my loved ones with me."

By the last years of the conflict, war with its hardships and shortages had begun to nurture not nobility and sacrifice so much as a new selfishness, a novel awareness of individual needs and desires, of requirements for minimal personal survival, even if not happiness. In the Confederacy at large an emerging venality was evident in widespread speculation and extortion, problems that consumed considerable public attention, prompted state and national legislation, and won religious notice as the besetting sin of the South. Women were most often victims rather than perpetrators of these economic and moral crimes, however, for they participated in the market chiefly as consumers.

Women instead displayed their new self-absorption and self-interest in a growing reluctance to continue to yield their loved ones to the Confederate army. At the outset of the war, women had urged husbands and brothers into service, but by the later years of conflict quite a different attitude became evident. Even at the expiration of men's first terms of enlistment, as early as 1862 or 1863, many wives insisted that their husbands had already given enough to the Cause. As Mary Bell of North Carolina bluntly proclaimed to Alfred in July 1862, "I think you have done your share in this war." An initial romantic fascination with military heroism had quickly given way to a sobering recognition of war's dangers. Louisa Rice of Georgia wrote her husband, Zachariah, at the end of 1862 urging him to leave the army for a post that would shield him from conscription. "You have served long enough," she declared, "to rest awhile." Mary Williams Pugh, a refugee in Texas in the fall of 1862, warned her husband that both she and her slaves required his return. Not only had he "done enough now to satisfy yourself & everyone else," but she had borne his absence so "patiently and cheerfully," she calculated, "that surely now I deserve some reward." Pugh urged him either to hire a substitute or to take advantage of the October 1862 law exempting slave supervisors. "My good behavior now is all put on & will soon disappear unless I see something brighter ahead." The expectation of his imminent return, moreover, was the only cause of his slaves' "good behavior," she warned. "The truth is . . . you *must* come home." In Florida during the same year, Octavia Stephens urged her husband, Winston, to "give up now while you have life." In her view it was foolish to "talk of the defense of your home & country for you can not defend them, they are too far gone now so give up before it is too late." Losing the war and keeping her husband seemed to Tivie Stephens a far better bargain than losing both, but Winston would fight for another two years before fulfilling Octavia's worst fears.

Mounting draft calls prompted first reluctance then resistance from mothers, wives, and sisters. "We felt like clinging to Walter and holding him back," a Virginia woman explained. "I for one had lost my nerve. I was sick of war, sick of the butchery, the anguish . . . the fear." Emily Harris declared that she felt as much like fighting the men who kept her husband in uniform as she did the Yankees. In South Carolina, Margaret Easterling balanced the dictates of patriotism against her own desires and decided firmly in favor of the latter. With two sons in the army, she wrote Jefferson Davis, "I need not tell you of my devotion to my country, of the sacrifices I have made, and of the many more I am willing to make. . . . But I want my oldest boy at home." Facing the conscription of her last son, Mary Scales wrote movingly and revealingly to the Confederate secretary of war. "I know my country needs all her children and I had thought I could submit to her requisitions. I have given her cause my prayers, my time, my means and my children but now the last lamb of the fold is to be taken, the mother and helpless woman triumph over the patriot."

Mary Scales sought to retreat from the public sphere of patriotic duty and to reassert the primacy of the domestic, the private, and the dependent in female lives. Scales hoped to reinstate the moral economy of gender in which women traded "helplessness" and subservience for care and protection; she sought a return to a world in which the needs of her heart, her family, and her household could take precedence over necessities of state. Writing to her son in a northern military prison, Mary Chichester expressed a similar desire. "I hope," she confessed, "when you do get exchanged, you will think, the time past has sufficed for *public* service, & that your own family require yr protection & help—as others are deciding." Gertrude Thomas saw the conflict of loyalties and its resolution clearly. "Am I willing to give my husband to gain Atlanta for the Confederacy? No, No, No, a thousand times No!"

In one sense the erosion of women's patriotism simply represented a reversion to conventional female concerns, an almost reactionary reassertion of the private and domestic and a rejection of the more public and political burdens women had been urged to assume. But at the same time, women's new perspectives involved an articulation of individual right and identity, of self-interest, that was strikingly modern in its implications. Their retreat from the public realm was fueled in considerable part by their recognition that in the Confederacy the public interest did not encompass their own, for it threatened to kill their loved ones, deprive them of life's basic necessities, and require them to manage recalcitrant, rebellious, and often frightening slaves. A nation that had acknowledged no legitimate female political voice had in crisis failed adequately to consider women's needs.

Before the war, women of the southern elite had regarded themselves as dependents within an organic social order in which female subordination was accepted in return for protection and support. Yet white men's wartime failure to provide women with either physical safety or basic subsistence cast this world and its social assumptions into question. Relationships of unchallenged status, of assumed superiority and inferiority, were transformed into what political theorists would call social relations of contract. Women came to regard their sacrifice and subordination as no longer inevitable but contingent on men's fulfillment of certain expectations. The notions of "virtual" political representation—which argued that women's interests would be protected by their men—had proved hollow indeed. Women began to acknowledge and defend their own interests apart from those of their families and their nation and to regard themselves as individuals possessing rights and legitimate desires, not just duties and obligations.

This warborn evolution in female self-perception parallels a much broader transformation in American political life, one that many scholars have designated as a shift during the early and middle years of the nineteenth century from republican to liberal political forms and values, as a replacement of virtue and community by faction and self-interest. The changing outlook of southern women in the course of the Civil War helps remind us of the psychological foundations of such a transformation, for women's shifting understanding of their larger social place arose from a newfound ability to perceive themselves as more than simply appendages to other, more important social actors.

In their recognition of individual needs and desires amidst all but unbearable emotional and even material deprivation, Confederate women discovered both new self-interest and new selves. It was not, however, as so many discussions of women and war would have it, that new achievements and new accomplishments—as nurses or teachers or plantation managers—yielded the basis for enhanced self-esteem; this new sense of self was based not in the experience of success but in desperation, in the fundamental need simply to survive. "Necessity," as Confederate women so often intoned, was in this sense truly "the mother of invention"; only "necessity," as Julia Davidson wrote her husband, John, could "make a different woman of me."

By the last months of the war many women, especially those of the middling and lower orders, were not just holding husbands and brothers back from service but were actively urging them to desert. The risk of execution and the shame of flight now seemed acceptable in the face of almost certain and almost certainly useless injury or death at the front. Confederate leaders recognized the power that women exerted in persuading soldiers to abandon their posts. One military officer even went so far as to urge the secretary of war to begin to censor the mails, for, he insisted, "the source of all the present evils of Toryism & desertion in our country is letter writing to . . . the army." As a Confederate official in North Carolina bluntly proclaimed, "Desertion takes place because desertion is encouraged. . . . And though the ladies may not be willing to concede the fact, they are nevertheless responsible . . . for the desertion in the army and the dissipation in the country." At every level of the social order women were making their particular contributions to Confederate military failure.

Public lamentations about women's shortcomings as patriots became standard fare in the Confederate press. An 1864 correspondent to the *Montgomery Daily Advertiser* deplored eroding female commitment to the Cause. At first, wrote the pseudonymous Micare, "women were rivalling the other sex in patriotic devotion. . . . But a change, and such a change, has come over the spirit of their dream. The Aid societies have died away; they are a name and nothing more. The self-sacrifice has vanished; wives and maidens now labor only to exempt husbands and lovers from the perils of service." Beginning with a discussion of women's interference with military recruitment and retention, Micare moved to a second, widely articulated indictment of women's wartime failures. "Never," Micare continued, "were parties more numerous. . . . Never were the theatres and places of public amusement so resorted to. . . . The love of dress, the display of jewelry and costly attire, the extravagance and folly are all the greater for the brief abstinence which has been observed."

Mirth and Reckless Revelry   Late in 1864 Augusta Jane Evans published in the *Mobile Register* a similarly scathing attack on her countrywomen. "Can mirth and reckless revelry hold high carnival in social circles," she demanded, "while every passing breeze chants the requiem of dying heroes? . . . Are Southern women so completely oblivious of the claims of patriotism and humanity, that in this season of direst extremity, they tread the airy mazes of the dance, while the matchless champions of freedom are shivering in bloody trenches or lying stark on frozen fields of glory?" Evans invoked "spectral bands" of Confederate dead to join her in lamenting women's betrayal, in crying, "Shame! Shame upon your degeneracy."

Evans was hardly unique in criticizing the frivolity that seized elite Confederate society in 1864 and 1865. Women's growing sense of self-interest shaded into self-indulgence; sacrifice was replaced by its polar opposite, excess. Even a council of Presbyterian elders in Alabama felt compelled in 1865 to reprimand their usually sober congregants and to "deplore the presence, and we fear, the growing prevalence, of a spirit of gaity, especially among the female members of some of our congregations." Sara Pryor of Virginia found this "disposition to revel in times of danger and suffering" to be "passing strange," but Grace Elmore of South Carolina understood that "utter abandonment to the pleasure of the present" offered the possibility of "shutting out for the moment the horrors that surround us." As hardships mounted, escape seemed all the more desirable. Gertrude Thomas tried to explain the gaiety in her Georgia town by suggesting that long years of war had to some degree hardened southerners' feelings and had left them insensitive to others' sufferings. James Chesnut certainly feared such a lack of sympathy in his wife, Mary, and declared her "dissipated" for her refusal to abandon constant parties and frivolity. Yet Chesnut was but one of dozens of Richmond hostesses contributing to the "whirl" of sociability that gripped the capital city in the last months of war. Preeminent was Mrs. Robert Stannard, who was reputed to have spent more than $30,000 on entertainment during a winter that saw Confederate troops camped in nearby counties suffering for bare subsistence.

In February 1864 the *Richmond Enquirer* expressed its hope that the arrival of Lent would bring an end to the "season of reckless frivolity that has made Richmond during this winter, a carnival of unhallowed pleasure." Incessant parties and balls in the capital represented, in the paper's judgment, "shameful displays of indifference to national calamity . . . a mockery of the misery and desolation that covers the land." At the opposite end of the Confederacy, in Texas, "ladies of Galveston" planned a midwinter ball for the officer corps stationed in the port city. But the anticipated "revelry and carousal" so offended underpaid and underfed enlisted men that they plotted a raid against the tables of delicacies. When word of the soldiers' intentions reached Confederate officers, they ordered cavalry to stand ready to act against rebellious privates. The cavalry indicated its unwillingness to serve in such a capacity, however, and called for the cancellation of the ladies' entertainment.

The frivolity that attracted such widespread attention and remark in the last months of the Confederacy represented an assertion of class privilege in the face—and in defiance—of its rapid erosion. The women indulging in much-criticized revelry were not those of the lower orders who lacked the means for such excess. Poorer women were more likely to express their dissent from the ideology of sacrifice and the reality of deprivation in the bread riots that swept across the South in the late years of the war. In

Savannah, Mobile, High Point, Petersburg, Milledgeville, Columbia, and even in the capital city of Richmond itself, crowds of desperate females joined together to claim provisions they believed their due, and in more rural locations bands of female marauders swept into plantation areas to seize food crops ready for harvest in the fields. These seemingly unrelated phenomena—upper-class women's frivolity and lower-class women's violence—both represented responses to the Confederacy's violation of white women's expectations within the South's paternalistic social order. Bread riots and reckless revelry both embodied a new level of female self-assertiveness. Both represented forceful statements of women's desires, and both explicitly rejected the ideology of sacrifice.

Differing economic and class realities and differing understandings of life's possibilities shaped emerging dissent to produce quite different behavior among women of the elite and women of the lower orders. Despite a common sense of deprivation and anger, these groups of females harbored little mutual sympathy; each regarded the actions of the other as depraved. Poor women accused elite families of abandoning their responsibilities to the less fortunate, even while "the rich livs as well as ever tha did"; respectable middle- and upper-class females were both frightened and appalled by rioters' abandonment of deference and propriety, even when they felt pity for their desperate plight. "The time appears rapidly approaching," Gertrude Thomas worried, "when we have almost as much to dread from our own demoralized mob as from the public enemy." Self-interest had undermined noblesse oblige just as it had eroded patriotism. As a poor woman complaining of starvation in Spotsylvania County, Virginia, wrote to the president, "it is folly for a poor mother to call on the rich people about here[.] there [sic] hearts are of steel[.] they would sooner th[r]ow what they have to spare to their dogs than give it to a starving child."

War had called white women across the South to make many similar sacrifices. The gendering of the army as male and of the homefront as overwhelmingly female and the high rates of military enrollment—and military casualties—among men of all classes constituted important commonalities in white southern women's wartime experience. Yet class differences separated even as gender united Confederate females. At the end of the conflict Cornelia McDonald reflected on the comparative impact of the war on rich and poor. "I have often thought," she mused,

> that no greater despotism could be than that government was in the last months of its existence. To those whose education and habits of life made them enthusiastic, or whose pride acted as an incentive for them to endure and suffer, as was the case with the higher classes, it wore no such aspect, but to those who had but their poor homes and little pieces of ground by which they managed to provide little more than bread for their families, who knew that they would be as well off under one government as another, it was oppression to be forced into the army, and not ever to be free from the apprehension that their families were suffering.

Put simply, upper-class southerners had a greater investment than their poorer countrywomen and -men in the system that had given them their superior status. For all their disillusionment with slavery, with Confederate leadership, and with their individual men, elite southern women clung to—even reasserted—lingering elements of privilege. Even when patriotism had been exhausted by war and even when the Confederacy had died, elite white women of the South held fast to the traditional hierarchical social and racial order that had defined their importance. Indeed, their disillusionment with the Confederacy arose chiefly from its failure to protect and preserve that privilege, to serve white female self-interest.

In ladyhood southern women accepted gender subordination in exchange for continuing class and racial superiority. Yet their understanding of that bargain had changed profoundly in the course of the war. Their expectations for male protection had all but disappeared; their new sense of themselves, born in necessity rather than opportunity, made them sharply aware of both the dangers of dependence and the daunting demands of autonomy. Filled with doubts about both themselves and their men, elite southern women faced the postwar world with a new realism, a deep-seated bitterness, and a frightening sense of isolation. The social order they were determined to preserve offered them only the best of a bad bargain; the ideal of male strength and competence that had justified the paternalistic southern world had been proven mythical, and women had discovered little foundation in their own competence or effectiveness for trying to replace male power and authority with their own. In the face of the frightening reality of black emancipation, however, white women came to regard the rehabilitation of patriarchy as a bargain they were compelled to accept. The postwar commemoration of male courage and wartime achievement by the Daughters of the Confederacy, the Confederate Memorial Society, and other female celebrants of the Lost Cause represented women's effort to make what they regarded as necessary seem once again legitimate. If white men were once again to run the world, southern ladies would struggle to demonstrate the confidence in male superiority that would convince both themselves and others that such a social order was both natural and desirable.

F U R T H E R   R E A D I N G

Michael Chesson, "Harlots or Heroines? A New Look at the Richmond Bread Riot," *Virginia Magazine of History and Biography* 92 (1984) 131–175

Catherine Clinton and Nina Silber, eds., *Divided Houses: Gender and the Civil War* (1992)

Ellen DuBois, *Feminism and Suffrage: The Emergence of an Independent Women's Movement in America, 1848–1869* (1978)

Ann Douglas, "The War Within a War: Women Nurses in the Union Army," *Civil War History* 18 (September 1972), 197–212

Drew Gilpin Faust, "Altars of Sacrifice: Confederate Women and the Narratives of War," *Journal of American History* #76 (March 1990), 1200–1228

——, *Southern Stories: Slaveholders in Peace and War* (1992)

Elizabeth D. Leonard, *Yankee Women: Gender Battles in the Civil War* (1994)

Mary Elizabeth Massey, *Bonnet Brigades: American Women and the Civil War* (1966)

Stephen B. Oates, *Woman of Valor: Clara Barton and the Civil War* (1994)

George C. Rable, *Civil Wars: Women and the Crisis of Southern Nationalism* (1989)

Ruth Scarborough, *Belle Boyd: Siren of the South* (1983)

Wendy Hammond Venet, *Neither Ballots Nor Bullets: Women Abolitionists and the Civil War* (1991)

Lee Ann Whites, *The Civil War As a Crisis in Gender—Augusta, Georgia, 1860–1890* (1995)

Bell I. Wiley, *Confederate Women* (1975)

CHAPTER
10

Emancipation

As the war began, Frederick Douglass lamented that, since the North was antislavery but opposed to abolition, the outcome of the contest was of little concern to the slaves themselves. Whichever side won, they would still remain in slavery. Nevertheless, pressure to widen the scope of the conflict to include abolition as a war aim was constantly brought to bear on the Lincoln administration.

This pressure arose from two sources. The first came from the abolitionists—who had agitated against and denounced slavery throughout the quarter-century before war broke out—as well as from their political allies within the radical wing of the Republican party. They both demanded confiscation of rebel property, which, they hoped, might include the slaves. And they also insisted that the aims of the war be broadened beyond just putting down the rebellion, to encompass the undermining, if not the ending, of slavery.

The second source of pressure for emancipation was the slaves themselves. Whenever Union troops moved into Southern territory, initially through a series of beachheads along the Atlantic coast and the Mississippi River, slaves left their owners and the plantations where they worked to seek refuge and ultimately liberation inside Union lines. Their growing numbers confronted the Union army with the options of returning them to their owners and therefore to continued enslavement, or giving them a different status, though what that might be was not apparent. In numerous other ways, slaves acted as a fifth column inside the Confederacy, aiding and encouraging Northern troops as they advanced into the South, offering to join the Union army, and causing slowdowns and disruption on the plantations. It soon became evident to Northern commanders in the field and to military and civil officials back in Washington that the future of the slaves was inseparable from victory in the war.

Initially, President Lincoln resisted these demands. He feared that any advocacy of emancipation would stiffen Confederate resistance and, quite probably, scare slaveholders in Union areas like Missouri and Kentucky into carrying their states over to the Confederacy. Besides giving comfort to the enemy, sympathy for abolition would certainly frighten Northern whites, who widely feared the consequences of slave liberation and would hesitate to support or fight in a war to free millions of blacks.

By midsummer 1862, after the border states had rejected his offer of financial compensation in return for gradual abolition, President Lincoln was compelled to move against slavery more forcefully. In September he announced his intention of proclaiming emancipation on January 1, 1863. This was a courageous and radical step. It made the destruction of slavery a certain consequence of Northern victory, and it also *confronted the nation with the disturbing prospect of eventually assimilating a vast population of black people. In the meantime, slaves within the Union lines could be conscripted into the Union army and, with guns in their hands, fight to secure their own freedom. Other aspects of Lincoln's initiative were less bold, however. The proclamation applied only to the slaves currently located inside the Confederacy, and so in practice it freed no slaves at all. Moreover, emancipation would not be officially achieved until 1865, when the Thirteenth Amendment was ratified. Also, the tenor of Lincoln's announcement was rather grudging. He did not grandly proclaim liberation. Rather, he indicated that he was embarking upon it primarily out of military necessity.*

The revolutionary implications of the decision for emancipation were, in effect, tempered by the cautious manner of its execution. Similarly mixed was the experience of emancipation by the slaves themselves. After the exhilaration of the first months of liberation, the former slaves soon discovered that their freedom was to be severely limited. Gains were made, but frequently these turned out to be more fleeting and insubstantial than had been hoped. The freedmen must therefore have wondered, as have historians ever since, how radical and transforming emancipation really was.

D O C U M E N T S

Emancipation was both a question of policy at the highest levels of the federal government and a matter of action and practical experience for the slaves. The documents in this chapter reflect both of these aspects. Some of the selections in Chapter 6 on Lincoln's approach to emancipation are also relevant.

The first item illustrates the dilemma that Union commanders in the field encountered once the war entered the South and slaves left their owners and crossed into the Union lines. In this famous dispatch of July 30, 1861, General Benjamin F. Butler asks what he should do about the fleeing slaves he refers to as "contraband of war." The second piece is a brief extract from the report of the Freedmen's Inquiry Commission of June 30, 1863; it reveals the way the sympathetic commission members approached the question of what the freed blacks' status in society should be. In the third document, President Lincoln explains his policy on emancipation to a friend in Illinois. Because Lincoln could not attend a meeting of Union men arranged by his correspondent, he wrote this letter instead, expecting it to be made public. It is dated August 26, 1863.

The fourth selection is a report from the United States Adjutant General, Lorenzo Thomas, on August 23, 1863. He was writing from Cairo, Illinois, where he was responsible for the slaves who were fleeing from the plantations within Confederate lines as the Union forces moved down the Mississippi. In the fifth document, a Union soldier who was an African American explains the bad treatment he and his family had experienced at the hands of the U.S. Army. His complaint was made before a hearing board of two officers, and the sworn affidavit that resulted was dated November 26, 1864. The sixth selection is an account of racial discrimination in the grim Battle of the Crater, outside Petersburg. The allegation is made in a letter of James H. Payne, a quartermaster sergeant in the 27th U.S. Colored Infantry, that racial bias on July 30 had a decisive effect on the military outcome of the engagement. As the war concluded, Frederick Douglass took the opportunity, in an address to the Massachusetts Anti-Slavery Society in April 1865, to indicate the approach that the federal government should take toward the freedmen in the South. This is the seventh document. The eighth and final piece is the lament of a Georgia slaveowner, Gertrude Thomas, that her slaves were leaving. Her feelings were confided to her diary on May 29 and June 12, 1865.

General Benjamin F. Butler Discovers the "Contrabands," July 1861

Headquarters Department of Virginia
Fortress Monroe, July 30, 1861.

Hon. Simon Cameron, Secretary of War:—

. . . This ordering away the troops from this department, while it weakened the posts at Newport News, necessitated the withdrawal of the troops from Hampton, where I was then throwing up intrenched works to enable me to hold the town with a small force, while I advanced up the York or James River. In the village of Hampton there were a large number of negroes, composed in a great measure of women and children of the men who had fled thither within my lines for protection, who had escaped from maurauding parties of rebels who had been gathering up able-bodied blacks to aid them in constructing their batteries on the James and York Rivers. I had employed the men in Hampton in throwing up intrenchments, and they were working zealously and efficiently at that duty, saving our soldiers from that labor under the gleam of the mid-day sun. The women were earning substantially their own subsistence in washing, marketing, and taking care of the clothes of the soldiers, and rations were being served out to the men who worked for the support of the children. But by the evacuation of Hampton, rendered necessary by the withdrawal of troops, leaving me scarcely 5,000 men outside the Fort, including the force at Newport News, all these black people were obliged to break up their homes at Hampton, fleeing across the creek within my lines for protection and support. Indeed it was a most distressing sight to see these poor creatures, who had trusted to the protection of the arms of the United States, and who aided the troops of the United States in their enterprise, to be thus obliged to flee from their homes, and the homes of their masters who had deserted them, and become fugitives from fear of the return of the rebel soldiery, who had threatened to shoot the men who had wrought for us, and to carry off the women who had served us, to a worse than Egyptian bondage. I have, therefore, now within the Peninsula, this side of Hampton Creek, 900 negroes, 300 of whom are able-bodied men, 30 of whom are men substantially past hard labor, 175 women[,] 225 children under the age of 10 years, and 170 between 10 and 18 years, and many more coming in. The questions which this state of facts presents are very embarrassing.

First, What shall be done with them? and, *Second,* What is their state and condition?

Upon these questions I desire the instructions of the Department.

The first question, however, may perhaps be answered by considering the last. Are these men, women, and children, slaves? Are they free? Is their condition that of men, women, and children, or of property, or is it a mixed relation? What their *status* was under the Constitution and laws, we all know. What has been the effect of rebellion and a state of war upon that *status*? When I adopted the theory of treating the able-bodied negro fit to work in the trenches as property liable to be used in aid of rebellion, and so contraband of war, that condition of things was in so far met, as I then and still believe, on a legal and constitutional basis. But now a new series of questions arises. Passing by women, the children, certainly, cannot be treated on that basis; if property, they must be

Letter, Gen. Benjamin F. Butler to Secretary of War, July 30, 1861, in *The Rebellion Record,* 1860–61, Frank Moore, ed. (G. P. Putnam, 1862), Vol. 2 (1862), pp. 437–438.

considered the incumbrance rather than the auxiliary of an army, and, of course, in no possible legal relation could be treated as contraband. Are they property? If they were so, they have been left by their masters and owners, deserted, thrown away, abandoned, like the wrecked vessel upon the ocean. Their former possessors and owners have causelessly, traitorously, rebelliously, and to carry out the figure, practically abandoned them to be swallowed up by the winter storm of starvation. If property, do they not become the property of the salvors? but we, their salvors, do not need and will not hold such property, and will assume no such ownership: has not, therefore, all proprietary relation ceased? Have they not become, thereupon, men, women, and children? No longer under ownership of any kind, the fearful relics of fugitive masters, have they not be their masters' acts, and the state of war, assumed the condition, which we hold to be the normal one, of those made in God's image. Is not every constitutional, legal, and moral requirement, as well to the runaway master as their relinquished slaves, thus answered? I confess that my own mind is compelled by this reasoning to look upon them as men and women. If not free born, yet free, manumitted, sent forth from the hand that held them never to be reclaimed. . . .

Pardon me for addressing the Secretary of War directly upon this question, as it involves some political considerations as well as propriety of military action. I am, sir, your obedient servant,

BENJAMIN F. BUTLER.

The Freedmen's Inquiry Commission Considers Policy toward the Ex-Slaves, June 1863

. . . The commission here desire to record their profound conviction, that upon the judicious selection of department superintendents and of superintendent general of freedmen will mainly depend the successful practical workings of the . . . plan of organization. The African race, accustomed to shield itself by cunning and evasion, and by shirking of work, whenever it can be safely shirked, against the oppression which has been its lot for generations, is yet of genial nature, alive to gratitude, open to impressions of kindness, and more readily influenced and led by those who treat it well and gain its confidence than our race, or perhaps than any other. The wishes and recommendations of government, if they are not harshly enforced, but quietly communicated by those who understand and sympathize with the African nature, will be received and obeyed as commands in almost every instance. It is highly important, therefore, that those who have in charge the interests of these freedmen shall be men not only of administrative ability, but also of comprehensive benevolence and humanitarian views.

On the other hand, it is equally desirable that these refugees, as readily spoiled as children, should not be treated with weak and injurious indulgence. Evenhanded justice, not special favor, is what they need. Mild firmness is the proper spirit in which to control them. They should find themselves treated, not as children of preference, fostered by charity, dependent for a living on government or on benevolent associations, but as men from whom, in their new character of freedmen, self-reliance and self-support are demanded. . . .

From Freedmen's Inquiry Commission, Preliminary Report, June 30, 1863, *Official Record,* Series III, Vol. 3, pp. 430–454. This selection is also available in *The Radical Republicans and Reconstruction, 1861–1870,* Harold M. Hyman, ed. (Bobbs Merrill, 1967), pp. 122–123.

President Lincoln Defends Emancipation, August 1863

Executive Mansion,
Washington, August 26, 1863.

Hon. James C. Conkling

My Dear Sir:

. . . To be plain, you are dissatisfied with me about the negro. Quite likely there is a difference of opinion between you and myself upon that subject. I certainly wish that all men could be free, while I suppose you do not. Yet I have neither adopted, nor proposed any measure, which is not consistent with even your view, provided you are for the Union. I suggested compensated emancipation; to which you replied you wished not to be taxed to buy negroes. But I had not asked you to be taxed to buy negroes, except in such way, as to save you from greater taxation to save the Union exclusively by other means.

You dislike the emancipation proclamation; and, perhaps, would have it retracted. You say it is unconstitutional—I think differently. I think the constitution invests its commander-in-chief, with the law of war, in time of war. The most that can be said, if so much, is, that slaves are property. Is there—has there ever been—any question that by the law of war, property, both of enemies and friends, may be taken when needed? And is it not needed whenever taking it, helps us, or hurts the enemy? Armies, the world over, destroy enemies' property when they cannot use it; and even destroy their own to keep it from the enemy. Civilized belligerents do all in their power to help themselves, or hurt the enemy, except a few things regarded as barbarous or cruel. Among the exceptions are the massacre of vanquished foes, and non-combatants, male and female.

But the proclamation, as law, either is valid, or is not valid. If it is not valid, it needs no retraction. If it is valid, it cannot be retracted, any more than the dead can be brought to life. Some of you profess to think its retraction would operate favorably for the Union. Why better *after* the retraction, than *before* the issue? There was more than a year and a half of trial to suppress the rebellion before the proclamation issued, the last one hundred days of which passed under an explicit notice that it was coming, unless averted by those in revolt, returning to their allegiance. The war has certainly progressed as favorably for us, since the issue of the proclamation as before. I know as fully as one can know the opinions of others, that some of the commanders of our armies in the field who have given us our most important successes, believe the emancipation policy, and the use of colored troops, constitute the heaviest blow yet dealt to the rebellion; and that, at least one of those important successes, could not have been achieved when it was, but for the aid of black soldiers. Among the commanders holding these views are some who have never had any affinity with what is called abolitionism, or with republican party politics; but who hold them purely as military opinions. I submit these opinions as being entitled to some weight against the objections, often urged, that emancipation, and arming the blacks, are unwise as military measures, and were not adopted, as such, in good faith.

You say you will not fight to free negroes. Some of them seem willing to fight for you; but, no matter. Fight you, then, exclusively to save the Union. I issued the

---

Letter, Lincoln to James C. Conkling, August 26, 1863, in *The Political Thought of Abraham Lincoln* (Bobbs-Merrill, 1967), Richard Current, ed., pp. 268–271.

proclamation on purpose to aid you in saving the Union. Whenever you shall have conquered all resistance to the Union, if I shall urge you to continue fighting, it will be an apt time, then, for you to declare you will not fight to free negroes.

I thought that in your struggle for the Union, to whatever extent the negroes should cease helping the enemy, to that extent it weakened the enemy in his resistance to you. Do you think differently? I thought that whatever negroes can be got to do as soldiers, leaves just so much less for white soldiers to do, in saving the Union. Does it appear otherwise to you? But negroes, like other people, act upon motives. Why should they do any thing for us, if we will do nothing for them? If they stake their lives for us, they must be prompted by the strongest motive—even the promise of freedom. And the promise being made, must be kept. . . .

Peace does not appear so distant as it did. I hope it will come soon, and come to stay; and so come as to be worth the keeping in all future time. It will then have been proved that, among free men, there can be no successful appeal from the ballot to the bullet; and that they who take such appeal are sure to lose their case, and pay the cost. And then, there will be some black men who can remember that, with silent tongue, and clenched teeth, and steady eye, and well-poised bayonet, they have helped mankind on to this great consummation; while, I fear, there will be some white ones, unable to forget that, with malignant heart, and deceitful speech, they have strove to hinder it.

Still let us not be over-sanguine of a speedy final triumph. Let us be quite sober. Let us diligently apply the means, never doubting that a just God, in his own good time, will give us the rightful result. Yours very truly,

A. Lincoln

The U.S. Adjutant General Describes the Condition of Fleeing Slaves, August 1863

Adjutant General of the Army to the Secretary of War

Cairo, Illinois, Aug' 23. 1863.

Sir, I arrived at this place this morning with General Grant, and shall return with him to-day or tomorrow to Vicksburg.

I have delayed making a report of the condition of affairs until I visited the several positions on the river. I was disappointed at finding but few negroes at Vicksburg, as they had been either absorbed by the several Departments as laborers, or taken to fill up the regiments previously organized. Of these regiments I get good accounts and some of them are in a high state of discipline. I visited Natchez, which at the present time is the best place for obtaining negroes, and gave orders for the immediate organization of two regiments, one as heavy Artillery to garrison Vicksburg, and also a Cavalry regiment to be mounted on mules. These animals can be obtained in great abundance.

I was fortunate in arriving at Memphis before General Steele left Helena for the interior of Arkansas as I was enabled to have him instructed to bring back all the blacks he could possibly gather, and sent recruiting officers with him. This expedition must give

From *Freedom: A Documentary History of Emancipation, 1861–1867—The Destruction of Slavery* (Cambridge University Press, 1985), pp. 308–309.

me a large number of men. A force also goes up Red River, and another from Goodrich's Landing back to bayou Macon, and their commanders are also instructed to collect the able bodied men, and in future such will be the standing orders. All the surplus blacks employed by the troops, or hovering round the Camps will be gathered up, General Grant having at my request issued such an order. He gives me every assistance in my work.

On arriving at Lake Providence on my way to Vicksburg, I found upwards of a thousand negroes, nearly all women and children, on the banks of the river, in a most helpless condition, who had left the plantations in consequence of the withdrawal of the troops on account of sickness. They had successfully sustained one attack of guerillas, aided by a gunboat, but expected another attack. I took them all to Goodrich's Landing where there is a garrison of negro troops. The number of this helpless class in the various camps is very large and daily increasing, and altho' everything is done for their well being, I find that sickness prevails to an alarming extent, and the bills of mortality are very high. This results from their change of life and habits, from daily work to comparative idleness, and also from being congregated in large numbers in camps, which is a matter of necessity. Besides, they will not take care of themselves much less of those who are sick. I have therefore after much reflection and consultation with officers, come to the conclusion that the old men, women and children should be advised to remain on the plantations, especially on those within our lines where we can have an oversight of them. Besides, it is important that the crops on the plantations within our lines should be gathered. A number of those now in our camps express a desire to return to their old homes, and indeed many have already done so. All such will be encouraged to do so, in cases where we are satisfied their former masters will not run them off or sell them. I have conversed with a number of planters, several strong union men at Natchez especially, and they all express the opinion that slavery has received its death blow, and cannot again exist in regions passed over by our armies. They are perfectly willing to hire the negroes and adopt any policy the Government may dictate. Many citizens of Mississippi, Louisiana and Arkansas are desirous that their States should resume their position in the Union with laws providing for the emancipation of slaves in a limited number of years. This feeling is constantly increasing, even among those who were strong advocates of secession. They now see it is vain to resist our arms, and only see utter ruin to themselves as the war goes on.

It is important that woodyards should be established on the river, and General Grant is encouraging the measure. I will permit persons duly authorized to cut wood for steamboats, to hire wood-choppers from those who are unfit for military service, including the women. It will be far more for their benefit to support themselves than to sit in idleness in camps depending on the Government for subsistence.

I have issued an order for general distribution in the armies of Generals Grant and Rosencrans [*sic*] setting forth some of the above points, a copy of which is enclosed—special Order No 45.—

I should be pleased to receive your instructions if my action is in any respect not in accordance with your views. The subject is now assuming vast proportions, and while I will do every thing in my power to carry out the policy of the administration and support the Government, I feel that my responsibilities are great and need the advice of my superiors. . . .

L.[orenzo] Thomas

Joseph Miller, U.S.A., Protests the Mistreatment of His Family by the U.S. Army, November 1864

Camp Nelson   Ky   November 26, 1864

Personally appered before me E. B. W. Restieaux Capt. and Asst. Quartermaster Joseph Miller a man of color who being duly sworn upon oath says

I was a slave of George Miller of Lincoln County Ky. I have always resided in Kentucky and am now a Soldier in the service of the United States. I belong to Company I 124 U.S.C. Inft now Stationed at Camp Nelson Ky. When I came to Camp for the purpose of enlisting about the middle of October 1864 my wife and children came with me because my master said that if I enlisted he would not maintain them and I knew they would be abused by him when I left. I had then four children ages respectively ten nine seven and four years. On my presenting myself as a recruit I was told by the Lieut. in command to take my family into a tent within the limits of the Camp. My wife and family occupied this tent by the express permission of the aforementioned Officer and never received any notice to leave until Tuesday November 22 when a mounted guard gave my wife notice that she and her children must leave Camp before early morning. This was about six O'clock at night. My little boy about seven years of age had been very sick and was slowly recovering My wife had no place to go and so remained until morning. About eight Oclock Wednesday morning November 23 a mounted guard came to my tent and ordered my wife and children out of Camp The morning was bitter cold. It was freezing hard. I was certain that it would kill my sick child to take him out in the cold. I told the man in charge of the guard that it would be the death of my boy I told him that my wife and children had no place to go and I told him that I was a soldier of the United States. He told me that it did not make any difference. he had orders to take all out of Camp. He told my wife and family that if they did not get up into the wagon which he had he would shoot the last one of them. On being thus threatened my wife and children went into the wagon My wife carried her sick child in her arms. When they left the tent the wind was blowing hard and cold and having had to leave much of our clothing when we left our master, my wife with her little one was poorly clad. I followed them as far as the lines. I had no Knowledge where they were taking them. At night I went in search of my family. I found them at Nicholasville about six miles from Camp. They were in an old meeting house belonging to the colored people. The building was very cold having only one fire. My wife and children could not get near the fire, because of the number of colored people huddled together by the soldiers. I found my wife and children shivering with cold and famished with hunger They had not recieved a morsel of food during the whole day. My boy was dead. He died directly after getting down from the wagon. I Know he was Killed by exposure to the inclement weather I had to return to camp that night so I left my family in the meeting house and walked back. I had walked there. I travelled in all twelve miles Next morning I walked to Nicholasville. I dug a grave myself and buried my own child. I left my family in the Meeting house—where they still remain And further this deponent saith not

his

(Signed) Joseph   Miller

mark

From Ira Berlin et al., eds., *Freedom: A Documentary History of Emancipation, 1861–1867,* Vol. 4, *The Black Military Experience* (Cambridge University Press, 1982), pp. 269–271.

James H. Payne, U.S.A., Complains of
Racial Discrimination on the Battlefield,
August 1864

. . . I will now give you a brief and concise account of the battle of the 30th of July, in which I called the members of our regiment together, and delivered an exhortation and held a prayer meeting. Indeed, it was a solemn and interesting time among us. Many professors [of religion] appeared to be greatly stirred up; while sinners seemed to be deeply touched and aroused to a sense of their danger and duty. Our prayer meeting was short but not without good and lasting impressions being made upon the hearts and minds of many. About 12 o'clock that same night, orders came to march. Our brave boys, as on all such occasions, were soon ready to move off. The direction soon proved to them that they were going to contest the strength of the enemy; it was the first time, too. Did they flinch or hang back? No; they went forward with undaunted bravery! About 4 o'clock, on Saturday morning the 30th, one of the enemy's forts in which the garrison were reposing in pleasant slumber, dreaming of no danger, nor apprehending any, was blown up destroying nearly all who were in it at the time. At this moment, the Union line for a mile opened upon the enemy with their batteries, and the most terrific cannonading continued until 10 o'clock A.M. But about 9 o'clock our brave boys, the colored troops belonging to the Fourth Division, Ninth Army Corps, made one of the most daring charges ever made since the commencement of the rebellion. The First Brigade, consisting of four regiments, namely, the Forty-third [U.S. Colored Infantry] Pennsylvania, Twenty-seventh [USCI] Ohio, and Thirtieth and Thirty-ninth [USCI] Maryland, led in the charge. The first two named regiments drove the enemy from their breastworks, and took possession of the blown up fort; but while they did, all the white soldiers lay in their pits and did nothing to support our men in the struggle; they lay as if there was nothing for them to do for one hour after the explosion took place. The rebels deserted all their forts fearing that some more of their works were about to be blown up.

How easily Petersburg could have been taken on the 30th of July, had the white soldiers and their commanders done their duty! But prejudice against colored troops prevented them. Instead of a general effort being made, as was contemplated, only a few men were taken in to be slaughtered and taken prisoner, which is the equivalent to death, for no mercy is shown to them when captured, although some still plead that the rebels are treating the colored prisoners very well; but before I can be convinced that this is so, I wish to hear one of the prisoners tell the story.

After our men had driven the enemy and taken possession of a portion of their works, I cannot conceive of a plausible reason why it was that reinforcements were not sent to them. This neglect was the cause of their being repulsed with such heavy loss. I can only conclude that our men fell unnecessarily in the battle of the 30th. In their retreat, they received the cross-fire of the enemy, and no small number were killed by our own artillery.

Such was the terrible fate of the day. Time will tell who was in the fault, and who made the great blunder in the battle of the 30th of July. . . .

Letter in *A Grand Army of Black Men: Letters from African-American Soldiers in the Union Army, 1861–1865,* Ewin S. Redkey, ed. (Cambridge University Press, 1992), pp. 113–114.

Frederick Douglass States the Freedmen's
Demands, April 1865

. . . I have had but one idea for the last three years to present to the American people, and the phraseology in which I clothe it is the old abolition phraseology. I am for the "immediate, unconditional, and universal" enfranchisement of the black man, in every State in the Union. Without this, his liberty is a mockery; without this, you might as well almost retain the old name of slavery for his condition; for in fact, if he is not the slave of the individual master, he is the slave of society, and holds his liberty as a privilege, not as a right. He is at the mercy of the mob, and has no means of protecting himself. . . .

It may be asked, "Why do you want it. Some men have got along very well without it. Women have not this right." Shall we justify one wrong by another? This is a sufficient answer. Shall we at this moment justify the deprivation of the Negro of the right to vote, because some one else is deprived of that privilege? I hold that women, as well as men, have the right to vote, and my heart and my voice go with the movement to extend suffrage to women; but that question rests upon another basis than that on which our right rests. We may be asked, I say, why we want it. I will tell you why we want it. We want it because it is our *right,* first of all. No class of men can, without insulting their own nature, be content with any deprivation of their rights. We want it again, as a means for educating our race. Men are so constituted that they derive their conviction of their own possibilities largely from the estimate formed of them by others. If nothing is expected of a people, that people will find it difficult to contradict that expectation. By depriving us of suffrage, you affirm our incapacity to form an intelligent judgment respecting public men and public measures; you declare before the world that we are unfit to exercise the elective franchise, and by this means lead us to undervalue ourselves, to put a low estimate upon ourselves, and to feel that we have no possibilities like other men. Again, I want the elective franchise, for one, as a colored man, because ours is a peculiar government, based upon a peculiar idea, and that idea is universal suffrage. If I were in a monarchial government, or an autocratic or aristocratic government, where the few bore rule and the many were subject, there would be no special stigma resting upon me, because I did not exercise the elective franchise. It would do me no great violence. Mingling with the mass I should partake of the strength of the mass; I should be supported by the mass, and I should have the same incentives to endeavor with the mass of my fellow-men; it would be no particular burden, no particular deprivation; but here where universal suffrage is the rule, where that is the fundamental idea of the Government, to rule us out is to make us an exception, to brand us with the stigma of inferiority, and to invite to our heads the missiles of those about us; therefore, I want the franchise for the black man. . . .

. . . Let me not be misunderstood here. I am not asking for sympathy at the hands of abolitionists, sympathy at the hands of any. I think the American people are disposed often to be generous rather than just. I look over this country at the present time, and I see Educational Societies, Sanitary Commissions, Freedmen's Associations, and the like,—all very good: but in regard to the colored people there is always more that is benevolent, I perceive, than just, manifested towards us. What I ask for the Negro is not

From Frederick Douglass, Address to the Massachusetts Antislavery Society, April 1865, in *Negro Social and Political Thought: Representative Texts, 1850–1920,* Howard Brotz, ed. (Basic Books, 1966), pp. 278–279, 282–283.

benevolence, not pity, not sympathy, but simply *justice.* The American people have always been anxious to know what they shall do with us. Gen. Banks [the federal commander in Louisiana, 1863–1864] was distressed with solicitude as to what he should do with the Negro. Everybody has asked the question, and they learned to ask it early of the abolitionists, "What shall we do with the Negro?" I have had but one answer from the beginning. Do nothing with us! Your doing with us has already played the mischief with us. Do nothing with us! If the apples will not remain on the tree of their own strength, if they are wormeaten at the core, if they are early ripe and disposed to fall, let them fall! I am not for tying or fastening them on the tree in any way, except by nature's plan, and if they will not stay there, let them fall. And if the Negro cannot stand on his own legs, let him fall also. All I ask is, give him a chance to stand on his own legs! Let him alone! If you see him on his way to school, let him alone, don't disturb him! If you see him going to the dinner-table at a hotel, let him go! If you see him going to the ballot-box, let him alone, don't disturb him! If you see him going into a work-shop, just let him alone,—your interference is doing him a positive injury. . . .

Gertrude Thomas Is Upset that Her Slaves Are Leaving, May 1865

Monday, May 29, 1865   Out of all our old house servants not one remains except Patsey and a little boy Frank. We have one of our servants Uncle Jim to take Daniel's place as driver and butler and a much more efficient person he proves to be. Nancy has been cooking since Tamah left. On last Wednesday I hired a woman to do the washing. Thursday I expected Nancy to iron but she was sick. In the same way she was sick the week before when there was ironing to do. I said nothing but told Patsey to get breakfast. After it was over I assisted her in wiping the breakfast dishes, a thing I never remember to have done more than once or twice in my life. I then thoroughly cleaned up the sitting room and parlour. . . . In the afternoon I went in the ironing room and in to see Nancy. The clothes were all piled upon a table, the flies swarming over them. The room looking as if it had not been cleaned up in several weeks. Nancy's room was in just the same state. I asked her "if she was not well enough to sprinkle some of the clothes." "No" she replied "she was not well enough to do anything." Said I, "Nancy do you expect I can afford to pay you wages in your situation, support your two children and then have you sick as much as you are?" She made no reply and I came in.

The next morning after Patsey had milked the cow & had fire made in the kitchen, she [Nancy] volunteered to cook breakfast—Immediately after breakfast as I was writing by the window Turner directed my attention to Nancy with her two children, Hannah and Jessy, going out of the gate. I told him to enquire "where she was going." She had expected to leave with flying colours but was compelled to tell a falsehood for she replied "I will be back directly." I knew at once that she was taking "french leave" and was not surprised when I went into her room sometime afterwards to find that all her things had been removed. I was again engaged in housework most of the morning. . . .

Susan, Kate's nurse, Ma's most trusty servant, her advisor, right hand woman and best liked house servant has left her. I am under too many obligations to Susan to have harsh feelings toward her. During six confinements Susan has been with me, the best of

From Ella Gertrude Clanton Thomas, *A Secret Eye: The Journal of E.G.C.T.,* Virginia Ingraham Burr, ed. (University of North Carolina Press, 1990), pp. 272–275.

servants, rendering the most efficient help. To Ma she has always been invaluable and in case of sickness there was no one like Susan. Her husband Anthony was one of the first to leave the Cumming Plantation and incited others to do the same. I expect he influenced Susan, altho I have often heard Pa say that in case of a revolt among Negroes he thought that Susan would prove a ringleader. Aunt Vilet the cook a very excellent one at that left Sunday night. She was a plantation servant during her young days and another favorite of Ma's. Palmer the driver left the same morning with Susan, remained longer than anyone expected that he would. He is quite a Beau Brummell as he gallants a coloured demoiselle or walks up the street with his cigar in his mouth. . . . Yesterday numbers of the negro women some of them quite black were promenading up the streets with black lace veil shading them from the embrowning rays of a sun under whose influence they had worked all their life. . . . On Thursday Rev Dr Finch of the Federal Army addressed the citizens on the subject of their late slaves and Saturday addressed the Negroes at the parade ground on *their* duty. I think now they have the Negroes free they don't know what to do with them—

Belmont, Monday, June 12, 1865   I must confess to you my journal that I do most heartily dispise Yankees, Negroes and everything connected with them. The theme has been sung in my hearing until it is a perfect abomination—I positively instinctively shut my ears when I hear the hated subject mentioned and right gladly would I be willing never to place my eyes upon another as long as I live. Everything is entirely reversed. I feel no interest in them whatever and hope I never will—

✐ E S S A Y S

In recent years, the phrase *self-emancipation* has emerged among historians to convey the active role the slaves themselves played in bringing pressure to bear on the military in the South, and thereby also on the authorities in Washington, to concede emancipation. In the first essay, Ira Berlin of the University of Maryland at College Park discusses this notion and weighs its accuracy and utility. The companion piece is by Joseph T. Glatthaar of the University of Houston, who describes and analyzes the role of African American soldiers in the Union army and their contribution to the success of the Union war effort. Because of their active involvement, black soldiers made it very difficult for the North to break the promise offered in the Emancipation Proclamation, and thus they guaranteed—in fact, won—their own freedom.

Who Freed the Slaves?
Emancipation and Its Meaning

IRA BERLIN

. . . The debate over the origins of Civil War emancipation in the American South can be parsed in such a way as to divide historians into two camps: those who understand emancipation primarily as the product of the slaves' struggle to free themselves, and those who see the Great Emancipator's hand at work. James McPherson has made precisely such a division. While acknowledging the role of the slaves in their own liberation, he came down heavily on the side of Lincoln's authorship of emancipation,

From Ira Berlin, "Who Freed the Slaves? Emancipation and Its Meaning," in *Union and Emancipation: Essays on Politics and Race in the Civil War Era*, edited by David W. Blight and Brooks R. Simpson. Copyright © 1997 by The Kent State University Press. Reprinted by permission of The Kent State University Press.

a fact he maintained most ordinary Americans grasped intuitively but one that eluded some scholars whose taste for the complex, the nuanced, and the ironic had blinded them to the obvious. McPherson characterized the critics of Lincoln's preeminence—advocates of what he called the "self-emancipation thesis"—as scholarly populists whose stock in trade was a celebration of the "so-called 'non-elite.'" Such scholars, McPherson implied, denied the historical role of "white males," and perhaps all regularly constituted authority, in a misguided celebration of the masses.

McPherson singled out Vincent Harding as the high priest of the self-emancipationists, declaring Harding's *There Is A River: The Black Struggle for Freedom in America* "almost a Bible" for the revisionists. But there were other culprits, among them Robert F. Engs and myself and my colleagues on the Freedmen and Southern Society Project at the University of Maryland, whose multivolume documentary history, *Freedom,* he termed "the largest scholarly enterprise on the history of emancipation." He gave special attention to Barbara Jeanne Fields, a member of the project who had articulated many of *Freedom*'s themes on Ken Burns's TV documentary "The Civil War." Together, these historians were responsible for elevating the "self-emancipation thesis" into what McPherson called "a new orthodoxy." . . .

Lincoln's proclamation of January 1, 1863, as its critics have noted, freed not a single slave who was not already entitled to freedom under legislation passed by Congress the previous year. It applied only to the slaves in territories then beyond the reach of Federal authority. It specifically exempted Tennessee and Union-occupied portions of Louisiana and Virginia, and it left slavery in the loyal border states—Delaware, Maryland, Kentucky, and Missouri—untouched. Indeed, in a strict sense, the Proclamation went no further than the Second Confiscation Act of July 1862, which freed all slaves who entered Union lines professing that their owners were disloyal, as well as those slaves who fell under Federal control as Union troops occupied Confederate territory. Moreover, at its fullest, the Emancipation Proclamation rested upon the President's wartime power as commander in chief and was subject to constitutional challenge. Lincoln recognized the limitations of his ill-defined wartime authority, and, as his commitment to emancipation grew firmer in 1863 and 1864, he pressed for passage of a constitutional amendment to affirm slavery's destruction.

What then was the point of the Proclamation? It spoke in muffled tones that heralded not the dawn of universal liberty but the compromised and piecemeal arrival of an undefined freedom. Indeed, the Proclamation's flat prose, ridiculed by the late Richard Hofstadter as having "all the moral grandeur of a bill of lading," suggests that the true authorship of African American freedom lies elsewhere—not at the top of American society but at its base. McPherson and others are correct in noting that the editors of the Freedmen and Southern Society Project and other revisionists built upon this insight.

From the first guns at Fort Sumter, the strongest advocates of emancipation were the slaves themselves. Lacking political standing or a public voice, forbidden access to the weapons of war, slaves nevertheless tossed aside the grand pronouncements of Lincoln and other Union leaders that the sectional conflict was only a war for national unity. Instead, they moved directly to put their own freedom—and that of their posterity—atop the national agenda. Steadily, as opportunities arose, slaves risked their all for freedom. By abandoning their owners, coming uninvited into Union lines, and offering their lives and labor in the Federal cause, slaves forced Federal soldiers at the lowest level to recognize their importance to the Union's success. That understanding traveled quickly up the chain of command. In time, it became evident to even the most obtuse

Federal commanders that every slave who crossed into Union lines was a double gain: one subtracted from the Confederacy and one added to the Union. The slaves' resolute determination to secure their liberty converted many white Northern Americans—soldiers and civilians alike—to the view that the security of the Union depended upon the destruction of slavery. Eventually, this belief tipped the balance in favor of freedom, even among Yankees who displayed little interest in the question of slavery and no affection for black people.

Slaves were not without allies. Abolitionists, black and white, dismissed the Republican doctrine that slavery should be respected and given constitutional protection where it existed. Instead, abolitionists, like the slaves, saw the war as an opportunity to assault a system they believed was immoral and pressed for its extradition. Rather than condemn slavery from the comfort of their drawing rooms, some radical opponents of slavery volunteered to fight slavery on its own terrain, strapped on their haversacks, and marched south as part of the Union army. But soldiering was young men's work, and sex, age, condition, and circumstance barred many radicals from the Federal army. Most abolitionists could only fume against slavery in petitions, editorials, and sermons. Although their campaign on behalf of emancipation laid the foundation for congressional and then presidential action against slavery, the majority of abolitionists had but slender means to attack slavery directly. Only slaves had both the commitment and the opportunity to initiate the assault on slavery.

Some slaves did not even wait for the war to begin. In March 1861, before the first shots at Fort Sumter, eight runaways presented themselves at Fort Pickens, a federal installation in Florida, "entertaining the idea"—in the words of the fort's commander—that Federal forces "were placed here to protect them and grant them their freedom." The commander believed otherwise and delivered the slaves to the local sheriff, who returned them to their owner. Although their mission failed, these eight runaways were only the first to evince publicly a conviction that eventually became widespread throughout the slave community.

In making the connection between the war and freedom, slaves also understood that a Union victory was imperative. They did what they could to secure it, throwing their full weight behind the Federal cause, volunteering their services as teamsters, stable hands, and boatmen; butchers, bakers, and cooks; nurses, orderlies, and laundresses; blacksmiths, coopers, and carpenters; and, by the tens of thousands, as common laborers. Slaves "tabooed" those few in their ranks who shunned the effort. Hundreds of thousands of black men and women would work for the Union army, and more than 135,000 slave men became Union soldiers. Even deep within the Confederacy, where escape to Federal lines was impossible, slaves did what they could to undermine the Confederacy and strengthen the Union—from aiding escaped Northern prisoners of war to praying for Northern military success. With their loyalty, their labor, and their lives, slaves provided crucial muscle and blood in support of the Federal war effort. No one was more responsible for smashing the shackles of slavery than the slaves.

Still, slaves could not free themselves. Nowhere in the four volumes of *Freedom* do the editors of the Freedmen and Southern Society Project claim they did. Nowhere in the four volumes of *Freedom* is the term *self-emancipation* employed. As far as I can discern, Harding, Litwack, and Engs do not use the term *self-emancipation*. Slaves could—and they did—put the issue of freedom on the wartime agenda; they could—and they did—make certain that the question of their liberation did not disappear in the complex welter of the war; they could—and they did—ensure that there was no retreat from the commitment to emancipation once the issue was drawn. In short, they did what was in their power to do with the weapons they had. They could not vote, pass laws, issue field orders, or promulgate great proclamations. That was the realm of citizens, legislators, military officers, and the president. However, the actions of the slaves made it possible and necessary for citizens, legislators, military officers, and the president to act. Slaves were the prime movers in the emancipation drama, not the sole movers. Slaves set others in motion, including many who would never have moved if left to their own devices. How they did so is nothing less than the story of emancipation.

Among the slaves' first students were Union soldiers of the lowest rank. Arriving in the South with little direct knowledge of slavery and often contemptuous of black people, Federal soldiers encountered slaves who were eager to test their owners' fulminations against Yankee abolitionists and black Republicans. Union soldiers soon found their camps inundated with slaves, often breathless, tattered, and bearing marks of abuse who were seeking sanctuary and offering to assist them in any way possible. In so doing, slaves took a considerable risk. They not only faced sure punishment if captured, but Union soldiers often turned upon them violently.

Still, some gained entry into Federal lines, where they found work aplenty. Sometimes the slaves' labor cut to the heart of the soldiers' military mission, as slaves understood that the enemy of their enemy was their friend and were pleased to impart information about Confederate troop movements, assist in the construction of Federal fortifications, and guide Union troops through a strange countryside. But just as often, slaves ingratiated themselves with Federal troops in ways that had no particular military significance. They foraged for firewood, cooked food, cleaned camps, and did dozens of onerous jobs that otherwise would have fallen to the soldiers themselves.

Northern soldiers did not have to be Free-Soilers, abolitionists, or even radical egalitarians to appreciate these valuable services. Thus, soldiers were dismayed to discover that they had violated orders by harboring the fugitives. They were more upset when the men and women who cleaned their camps and cooked their food were dragged off to certain punishment by angry masters or mistresses. Indeed, even those soldiers who stoutly maintained that they fought only for Union bitterly resented being implicated in the punishment of men and women who had done nothing more than do them a good turn in exchange for a blanket and a few morsels of food. "I don't care a damn for the darkies," declared one midwestern volunteer in March 1862, "but I couldn't help to send a runaway nigger back. I'm blamed if I could." The "blame" many Union soldiers felt at being implicated in slavery was compounded by their outrage when they discovered that the very same men and women they had returned to bondage were being mobilized by the Confederate enemy against them. To Union soldiers, the folly of denying themselves the resources that their enemy used freely—indeed, assisting their enemy in maintaining those resources—seemed senseless to the point of absurdity.

These same lessons were also learned by Federal officers. The protection and employment offered to fugitive slaves by individual Northern soldiers created numerous conflicts between slaveholders and the Union army, embroiling officers in disagreeable contests whose resolution required considerable time and effort. Slaveholders, many of them brandishing Unionist credentials, demanded that Northern troops return fugitives who had taken refuge within their encampments. If regimental officers could not or would not comply, they blustered about connections that reached the highest level in Washington. Generally, the bluster was just that. But often enough, the officers soon felt the weight of high authority upon them. Officers of the middle ranks not only bore the brunt of the soldier's frustrations with Federal policy but also the sting of official rebuke. Made apologists for policies that they too believed contradicted experience and good sense, many field officers found themselves in the uncomfortable position of having to enforce that which they disdained. They objected particularly to being compelled to do the slave master's dirty work, and they intensely disliked being demeaned before their men. The high-handed demands of slave owners turned many Federal officers into the slaves' champion. When Federal policy toward fugitive slaves finally changed in the summer of 1862, one could hear an almost-audible sigh of relief from the Union officer corps. "This thing of guarding rebels property has about 'played out.' . . . We have guarded their homes and property long enough. . . . The only way to put down this rebellion is to hurt the instigators and abettors of it. Slavery must be cleaned out."

Faced with conflicting demands—the need for labor versus the requirements of Federal policy, the desire to protect hapless fugitives versus the demands of Unionist owners—many Union soldiers and officers searched for ways to stand clear of the entire business, to be, in the idiom of the day, neither slave catcher nor slave stealer. Union policy toward slaves beginning in the fall of 1861 through the spring of 1862 was designed to eliminate the "devilish nigger question," as one Maryland official called it, by excluding fugitive slaves from Union lines. But slaves refused to surrender their belief that the Federal army was a refuge from slavery; they would not allow Federal soldiers to evade the central reality of the war.

Slaves continued to press themselves on soldiers, bringing gifts of food, information, and of course labor. There always seemed to be a few Yankee soldiers who, for whatever reason, sheltered runaways, and a handful who encouraged slave flight. But even when the fugitives were denied entry to Federal lines, they camped outside, just far enough away to avoid expulsion by Union commanders, just close enough to avoid capture by Confederate soldiers. Meanwhile, alert for ways to turn the military conflict to their own advantage, slaves continued to search the seams of Federal policy looking for an opening: the ascent of a sympathetic commander or a crisis that might inflate the value of their knowledge or their muscle. Many learned the letter of the law so that they could seemingly recite from memory passages from the House Resolution of 1861, the additional Article of War of March 1862, the First Confiscation Act of August 1861, or the Second Confiscation Act of July 1862. Time and time again, slaves forced Federal soldiers and officers to make the choice, a choice that became easier as the Union army's need for labor grew. Change did not come at once, but it came.

The lessons slaves taught soldiers and soldiers taught officers slowly ascended the Union chain of command and in November 1861 reached Lincoln's cabinet for the first time. Secretary of War Simon Cameron publicly endorsed a proposal to arm slaves to fight for the Union and freedom. Lincoln quieted Cameron and packed him off to Russia as minister, but the slaves continued undeterred to press their case.

The slow shift in Federal policy gained momentum as the Union army penetrated deeper into the Confederacy, where slaveholders were not reluctant Unionists but outright rebels. In these circumstances, some field commanders became quick learners. Their respect for the old order yielded to a willingness to challenge the rights of the master and finally to a firm determination to extirpate slavery. Others learned slowly, imperfectly, or not at all. However, before long, the most obdurate generals began to disappear from places of high command, and the quick studies rose to the top.

The broad outline of the story was always the same. Slaves forced the issue: what should be done with them? Deciding the matter was always difficult, for it required a choice between the contradictory interests of the master and of the slave. At first slaveholders held the upper hand, but in time the advantage slipped to the slaves. When the slaves' loyalty became more valuable than the masters' in the eyes of Federal authorities, the Federal army became the slaves' willing partner rather than [their] reluctant enemy. The process by which the Union army became an army of liberation was in its essence political and reveals how black people had been incorporated into American politics long before they had the vote, the right to petition, or independent standing at law.

But if the story was always the same, it was also always different. Individuals made a difference. A few generals—John C. Frémont, David Hunter, John W. Phelps—openly advertised their Free-Soil and abolitionist convictions; some generals, especially in the border states, were themselves slaveholders or sympathizers, and others were tied to the Democratic party; many, like William Tecumseh Sherman, would have preferred to avoid the "negro problem," although Sherman had his own understanding of the relationship of slavery to the war.

But the beliefs of individual field commanders and their willingness to act on them only partially accounted for differences in the evolution of Federal policy; the story also differed from place to place and changed over time. Acceptance of the slaves' truth generally came quickest in the Confederate heartland. Marching through Alabama in May 1862, Gen. Ormsby M. Mitchel considered that the "negroes are our only friends," an insight he quickly shared with Secretary of War Edwin M. Stanton, whose own evolution to an advocate of emancipation was proceeding apace in the spring and summer of 1862. Doubtless the greatest change came with the enlistment of black soldiers and later news of their battlefield valor at Fort Wagner, Port Hudson, and Milliken's Bend.

The slaves' lesson, moreover, did not travel merely within the military chain of command. As news of the war filtered northward, it moved outside of military lines entirely. In their letters home, citizen-soldiers not only informed the Northern public; they formed Northern opinion. At a time when rumor competed with gossip and hopes with wishes, perhaps nothing carried as much weight as the opinion of a husband, father, or son battling the enemy. Thus, the lesson slaves had taught soldiers reverberated in general-store gossip, newspaper editorials, and sermons throughout the North. It seemed particularly compelling to wives who wanted their husbands home and to parents who were fearful for their sons. It appealed to Northerners who were tired of the war and fearful of the Federal government's seemingly insatiable appetite for young men. Many white Northerners enlisted in the slaves' cause even though they feared and despised black people. In August 1862, Governor Samuel J. Kirkwood of Iowa, no friend of abolition, put the matter bluntly in commenting on the possible employment of slave laborers. "When this war is over & we have summed up the entire loss of life it has imposed on the country I shall not have regrets if it is found that a part of the dead are *niggers* and *all* are not white men."

The lesson that slaves taught common soldiers, that common soldiers taught officers, that officers taught field commanders, that field commanders taught their desk-bound superiors in Washington, and that resonated in the North was not wasted on Abraham Lincoln. In many ways, Lincoln was a slow learner, but he learned.

Lincoln was no friend of slavery. He believed, as he said many times, that "if slavery is not wrong, nothing is wrong." But, as president, Lincoln also believed he had a constitutional obligation not to interfere with slavery where it existed. Shortly before his inauguration, he offered to support a proposed constitutional amendment that would have prohibited any subsequent amendment authorizing Congress "to abolish or interfere . . . with the domestic institutions" of any state, including slavery. As wartime leader, he feared the disaffection of the loyal slave states, which he understood to be critical to the success of the Union. He crafted much of his wartime policy respecting slavery to avoid alienating loyal slaveholders, especially in Kentucky, Missouri, and Maryland. "I think to lose Kentucky is nearly the same as to lose the whole game," Lincoln wrote to Orville H. Browning, the senator from Illinois, in the fall of 1861. "Kentucky gone, we can not hold Missouri, nor, as I think, Maryland. These all against us, and the job on our hands is too large for us." Lincoln needed the border states, and even courted slaveholders in tiny Delaware, where fewer than two thousand black people remained in slavery.

But Lincoln's solicitude for the concerns of slaveholders, particularly Whiggish ones, went beyond the strategic importance of the border states and the fear that if they opted for secession, or refused to furnish soldiers to the Federal cause, the Union would be indefensible. Throughout the war, Lincoln held tight to the notion that Whiggish slaveholders retained a residual loyalty to the Union and could be weaned away from the Confederacy. Much of his policy in wartime Louisiana was crafted precisely toward this end, and this premise would shape his plans for postwar Reconstruction.

Lincoln also doubted whether white and black could live as equals in American society and thought it best for black people to remove themselves physically from the United States. Like many white Americans from Thomas Jefferson to Henry Clay, Lincoln favored the colonization of former slaves in Africa or elsewhere. At his insistence, the congressional legislation providing for the emancipation of slaves in the District of Columbia in April 1862 included a $100,000 appropriation to aid the removal of liberated slaves who wished to leave the United States. The Second Confiscation Act added another half million dollars to the funds for the same purpose. Through the end of 1862, Lincoln continually connected emancipation in the border states to the idea of colonizing slaves somewhere beyond the boundaries of the United States. Lincoln clung to the policy of expatriating black people long after most had abandoned it as a reasonable strategy to gain acceptance for emancipation or as a practical policy to address the consequences of emancipation.

Where others led on emancipation, Lincoln followed. Lincoln responded slowly to demands for emancipation as they rose through the military chain of command and as they echoed on the Northern home front. Even as pressure for emancipation grew in the spring of 1862, Lincoln continued to urge gradual, compensated emancipation. The compensation would be to slaveholders for property lost, not to slaves for labor stolen. In late September 1862, even while announcing that he would proclaim emancipation on January 1 if the rebellious states did not return to the Union, he again called for gradual, compensated emancipation in the border states and compensation for loyal slaveholders elsewhere. The preliminary emancipation proclamation also reiterated his support for colonizing freed slaves "upon this continent or elsewhere." While some pressed for the enlistment of black soldiers, Lincoln doubted the capacity of black men for military service, fearing that former slaves would simply turn their guns over to their old masters.

As black laborers became essential to the Union war effort and as demands to enlist black men in the Federal army mounted, the pressure for emancipation became inexorable. By the summer of 1862, Lincoln understood the importance of the sable arm as well as any. On July 12, making yet another plea for gradual, compensated emancipation in the Union's own slave states, Lincoln bluntly warned border-state congressmen that slavery was doomed "by mere friction and abrasion—by the mere incidents of the war," and that it would be impossible to restore the Union with slavery in place. Ignored once again, Lincoln acted on his own advice. In late July 1862, five days after signing the Second Confiscation and the Militia acts, he issued an executive order translating the new legislation into instructions for the Union army and navy. He authorized military commanders operating in the seceded states to "seize and use any property, real or personal, which may be necessary or convenient for . . . military purposes," and he instructed them to "employ as laborers . . . so many persons of African descent as can be advantageously used for military and naval purposes." Although he also reiterated the customary injunctions against wanton or malicious destruction of private property, there was no mistaking the import of Lincoln's order.

Lincoln had decided to act. On July 22, he informed the cabinet of his intention to issue a proclamation of general emancipation. The slaves' determination had indeed made every policy short of emancipation untenable. To those who might raise a voice in opposition, Lincoln declared that he could not fight "with elder-stalk squirts, charged with rose water. . . ." "This government," he added on the last of July 1862, "cannot much longer play a game in which it stakes all, and its enemies stake nothing."

On January 1, 1863, Lincoln fulfilled his promise to free all slaves in the states still in rebellion. Had another Republican been in Lincoln's place, that person doubtless would have done the same. Without question, some would have acted more expeditiously and with greater bravado. Without question, some would have acted more cautiously and with lesser resolve. In the end, Lincoln did what needed to be done. Others might be left behind; Lincoln would not. It does no disservice to Lincoln—or to anyone else—to say that his claim to greatness rests upon his willingness to act when the moment was right.

When Lincoln finally acted, he moved with confidence and determination. He stripped the final Emancipation Proclamation of any reference to compensation for former slaveholders or colonization for former slaves. He added provisions that allowed for the service of black men in the Union army and navy. The Proclamation opened the door to the eventual enlistment of more than 179,000 black men, most of them former slaves. More than anything else, the enlistment of black men, slave as well as free, transformed the Federal army into an army of liberation. At war's end, the number of black men in Federal uniform was larger than the number of soldiers in Lee's Army of Northern Virginia. Military enlistment became the surest solvent of slavery, extending to places the Emancipation Proclamation did not reach, especially the loyal slave states. Once slave men entered the Union army, they were free and they made it clear that they expected their families to be free as well. In March 1865, Congress confirmed this understanding and provided for the freedom of the immediate families of all black soldiers. Lincoln's actions, however tardy, gave force to all that the slaves had risked. The Emancipation Proclamation transformed the war in ways only the president could. After January 1, 1863, the Union army marched for freedom, and Lincoln was its commander.

Lincoln understood the importance of his role, both politically and morally—just as the slaves had understood theirs. Having determined to free the slaves, Lincoln declared he would not take back the Emancipation Proclamation even when military failure and political reversals threatened that policy. He repudiated his misgivings about the military abilities of black soldiers and became one of their great supporters. Lincoln praised the role of black soldiers in preserving the Union and ending chattel bondage and vowed not to "betray" them. The growing presence of black men in the Union army deepened Lincoln's commitment to emancipation. "There have been men who proposed to me to return to slavery the black warriors of Port Hudson & Olustee to . . . conciliate the South," Lincoln reflected in August 1864. "I should be damned in time & in eternity for doing so." Lincoln later suggested that black soldiers might have the vote, perhaps his greatest concession to racial equality. To secure the freedom that his proclamation had promised, Lincoln pressed for the final liquidation of slavery in the Union's own slave states where diehards obstructed and delayed. To that end and to write freedom into the nation's highest charter, Lincoln promoted passage of the Thirteenth Amendment, although he did not live to see its ratification.

The Emancipation Proclamation's place in the drama of emancipation is thus secure—as is Lincoln's. To deny it is to ignore the intense struggle by which freedom arrived. It is to ignore the Union soldiers who sheltered slaves, the abolitionists who stumped for emancipation, and the thousands of men and women who, like Lincoln, changed their minds as slaves made the case for universal liberty. Reducing the Emancipation Proclamation to a nullity and Lincoln to a cipher denies human agency just as personifying emancipation in a larger-than-life Great Emancipator denies the agency of the slaves and many others, and trivializes the process by which the slaves were freed. And, as in many other cases, process is critical.

Both Lincoln and the slaves played their parts in the drama of emancipation. Denying their complementary roles limits understanding of the complex interaction of human agency and events that resulted in slavery's demise. The editors of *Freedom,* who have sought to make the slaves central to the study of emancipation, have tried to expand the terrain of historical understanding, documenting the *process* by which freedom arrived. They have maintained that the slaves were the prime movers of emancipation; they do not believe they were the only movers, and nowhere do they deny Lincoln's importance to the events that culminated in universal freedom. In fact, rather than single out slaves or exclude Lincoln (as the term *self-emancipation* implies), the editors argue for the significance of others as well: white Union soldiers—few of them racial egalitarians—who saw firsthand how slavery weakened the Union cause; their families and friends in the North, eager for Federal victory, who learned from these soldiers the strength the Confederate regime drew from bonded labor; the Northern men and women, most of whom had no connection with the abolition movement, who acted upon such news to petition Congress; and the congressmen and senators who eventually moved in favor of freedom. This roster, of course, does not include all those involved in the social and political process that ended slavery in the American South. It omits the slaveholders, no bit players in the drama. Taken as a whole, however, the new understanding of emancipation does suggest something of the complexity of the process by which freedom arrived and the limitation of seeing slavery's end as the product of any one individual—or element—in the social order.

Emphasizing that emancipation was not the work of one hand underscores the force of contingency, the crooked course by which universal freedom arrived. It captures the ebb and flow of events which, at times, placed Lincoln among the opponents of emancipation and then propelled him to the forefront of freedom's friends. It emphasizes the clash of wills that is the essence of politics, whether it involves enfranchised legislators or voteless slaves. Politics, perforce, necessitates an on-the-ground struggle among different interests, not the unfolding of a single idea or perspective, whether that of an individual or an age. Lincoln, no less than the meanest slave, acted upon changing possibilities as he understood them. The very same events—secession and war—that gave the slaves' actions new meaning also gave Lincoln's actions new meaning. To think that Lincoln could have anticipated these changes—or, more strangely still, somehow embodied them—imbues him with a power over the course of events that no human being has ever enjoyed. Lincoln was part of history, not above it. Whatever he believed about slavery in 1861, Lincoln did not see the war as an instrument of emancipation. The slaves did. Lincoln's commitment to emancipation changed with time because it had to. The slaves' commitment to universal freedom never wavered because it could not.

Complexity—contrary to McPherson—is not ambivalence or ambiguity. To tell the whole story, to follow that crooked course, does not diminish the clarity of an argument or mystify it into a maze of "nuance, paradox, or irony." Telling the entire tale is not a form of obfuscation. If done right, it clarifies precisely because it consolidates the mass of competing claims under a single head. Elegance or simplicity of argument is useful only when it encompasses all of the evidence, not when it excludes or narrows it.

In the perennial tests in which constituted authority searches for the voice of the people and when the people are testing the measure of their leaders, it is well to recall the relationship of both to securing freedom's greatest victory. In this sense, slaves were right in celebrating January 1, 1863, as the Day of Jubilee. As Loretta Hanes noted 130 years later, "It meant so much to people because it was a ray of light, the hope of a new day coming. And it gave them courage." Indeed, the Emancipation Proclamation reminds all—both those viewing its faded pages and those studying it—that real change derives both from the actions of the people and from the imprimatur of constituted authority. It teaches that "social" history is no less political than "political" history, for it too rests upon the bending of wills, which is the essence of politics, and that no political process is determined by a single individual. If the Emancipation Proclamation speaks to the central role of constituted authority—in the person of Abraham Lincoln—in making history, it speaks no less loudly to the role of ordinary men and women, seizing the moment to make the world according to their own understanding of justice and human decency. The connection between the two should not be forgotten.

Black Glory: The African American Role in Union Victory

JOSEPH T. GLATTHAAR

During the final year of the war, Lt. Gen. Ulysses S. Grant employed his overwhelming superiority in manpower to defeat the Confederacy. Simply stated, Grant's plan was to mobilize every available man, apply pressure on all fronts, and stretch the Confederacy to enable forces under Maj. Gen. William Tecumseh Sherman to break up one of the two primary Confederate commands, the Army of Tennessee. Then, with all other forces maintaining the same stranglehold, Sherman's army was to devastate the Confederate military infrastructure—its railroads, its factories, its agriculture, and its labor supply—thus bringing the Confederacy to its knees.

There were, however, numerous drawbacks to this strategy of 1864. Grant's scheme required that regiments remain filled, that states achieve their manpower quotas, and that commanders position the maximum number of soldiers at the front. This compelled states to raise more troops, an unpopular and even dangerous policy, particularly in the wake of draft riots the previous summer. As Federal armies launched campaigns in all theaters, losses surpassed those of earlier years. Such a strategy exacerbated existing hardships for soldiers and their families and created an entirely new class of war widows, orphans, and mourners. Finally, to work, Grant's strategy needed time, one of the few commodities in very short supply for the Lincoln administration. After nearly three years of bloody fighting, and hundreds of thousands of casualties, the last thing the northern population had was patience. The Union was war-weary.

In retrospect, it seems that Grant adopted an appropriate strategy for the situation, one that, if he and his subordinates saw through to its conclusion, was most likely to result in a Federal victory. But at the time the outcome was far from certain. The Union party, an amalgamation of Republicans and War Democrats, could claim little more than limited progress after three years of combat, and 1864 was a presidential election year. Some Unionists plotted to dump Lincoln from the head of the ticket, and for a time that spring and summer Lincoln seriously doubted he would win re-election. The highly touted offensives of Grant in the East and Sherman in the West soon bogged down. Grant locked into a siege at Petersburg, while Confederates apparently stalemated Sherman's forces outside Atlanta. Meanwhile, Union losses were staggering, some 60,000 in barely a month in Grant's campaign alone. To the northern public, a successful conclusion to the war appeared dim. Indeed, these were dark days for Lincoln and the advocates of reunion.

The president wisely stuck with Grant and his strategy, and when Sherman cracked the tough Confederate nut called the Army of Tennessee and seized Atlanta, Lincoln's re-election was virtually assured. But suppose in the spring of 1864 his administration had to muster out of service one of its two primary commands, the Army of the Potomac or Sherman's Army of the West. How would that have affected the outcome of the war? Could Grant have even adopted this strategy without those 100,000 men? How would the campaigns of 1864–65 have transpired?

Such conjecture helps to elucidate, in just one area, the critical contributions of blacks to the defeat of the Confederacy. During those key months in the late spring and summer, when the picture for the Lincoln administration looked bleakest and the Union desperately struggled to maintain its uniformed strength, more than 100,000 blacks were serving in the Union army and thousands more were in the Federal navy. In fact, there were more blacks in Union blue than either Grant commanded outside Petersburg or Sherman directed around Atlanta. Their absence would have foiled Grant's strategy and quite possibly doomed efforts at reunion; their presence enabled Grant to embark on a course that promised the greatest hope of Federal victory.

At the outbreak of the war, leadership on neither side envisioned the varied and dramatic contributions that blacks would make to Confederate defeat. Nearly 180,000 served in the Union uniform with muskets in hand. As newfound laborers for the Federal war effort, blacks grew cotton and foodstuffs and aided in all sorts of construction and logistical endeavors, and as lost laborers for a fledgling wartime nation that so depended on its slaves for food production and other essentials, blacks caused shortages, hardships, and disillusionment among soldiers and civilians alike. Slaves who could not run away to northern lines supported the Union war effort through work sabotage, general unruliness that created insecurity among white southerners, and assistance to Federal troops who escaped from Confederate prison camps. Blacks alone did not win the war, but timely and extensive support from them contributed significantly and may have made the difference between a Union victory and stalemate or defeat. Lincoln himself admitted this in late 1864, when he wrote:

> Any different policy in regard to the colored man, deprives us of his help, and this is more than we can bear. We can not spare the hundred and forty or fifty thousand now serving us as soldiers, seamen, and laborers. This is not a question of sentiment or taste, but one of physical force which may be measured and estimated as horse-power and Steam-power are measured and estimated. Keep it and you can save the Union. Throw it away, and the Union goes with it.

Free and slave, they tipped the delicate balance of power squarely in favor of the North.

Blacks were at the very heart of the Civil War. Although most southerners seceded and went to war first to preserve their "rights" and then to protect their homes, the issue of slavery was always central. Secessionists sought protection of individual and state rights from Federal interference, specifically, the right to own property (read slaves) and take that property anywhere without fear of loss or seizure; the right to retrieve stolen or runaway property anywhere; and the right to live peaceably, without attempts by outsiders to subvert the existing state of order, an order with slavery as its cornerstone. The ferocious aspersions that the Rebels cast toward "Black" Republicans and abolitionists suggested the central role of slavery. In the minds of most Confederate soldiers, these northerners were the arch-villains, the group that provoked this wholly unnecessary crisis and shattered the greatest government in the world through its anti-slavery activities.

Even more obscure but no less essential among northerners was the role of slavery. While there was considerable disapproval of the institution, racial prejudices were widely held, and few of the early enlistees sought the destruction of the slave system. Instead, in most cases, Federals marched off to war for the restoration of the Union. It took Lincoln's keen mind, with his uncanny ability to cut to the root of problems, to recognize that the status of blacks was the core issue of the war, something which few outside the black race grasped. Lincoln realized that had northerners not found slavery morally reprehensible, and the institution incompatible with the new economic, political, and social directions of the country, war never would have happened.

Nevertheless, whites on both sides wanted to keep blacks on the periphery. The Lincoln administration resisted pleas from blacks "to allow us the poor priverlige of fighting and (if need be dieing) to suport those in office who are our own choise." There were more white volunteers than the government could accept into uniform, and black military service was highly controversial, especially in the border states where Lincoln had to struggle to maintain Unionist ascendancy.

In the Confederacy, several states permitted free blacks to join the militia, but President Jefferson Davis had no intention of opening the Confederate ranks to blacks, either free or slave. The entire premise of such service was incongruous with the concept of slavery, as Georgia governor Joseph E. Brown argued: "Whenever we establish the fact that they are a military race, we destroy our whole theory that they are unfit to be free."

Instead, the Confederacy employed blacks as southerners had done for two hundred years, as laborers. Slaves continued to plow the earth, hoe the fields, and harvest the crops, producing foodstuffs to feed the huge Confederate armies and the civilian population, and cotton with which to purchase the tools of war. They also dug trenches, erected fortifications, maintained railroads, mined essential minerals, manufactured war matériel, and performed sundry tasks that benefited Confederate troops. No doubt, in the early stages of the war, and to a lesser degree to the end, black labor was an important asset to the Confederacy.

Since whites refused to thrust slavery into the forefront, blacks forced the issue. It all began on a quiet May night in 1861 near Fort Monroe in Virginia. Three slaves, hired out as laborers on a Confederate fortifications project, slipped away from quarters, commandeered a canoe, and paddled into Union lines. The following morning, a Confederate officer approached the fort under a flag of truce. He came, he stated, to claim the runaways based on the fugitive slave law. The Federal commander Brig. Gen. Benjamin Butler refused to hand over the slaves. A shrewd courtroom lawyer and prominent politician before the war, Butler insisted that since Virginia had seceded from the Union, the fugitive slave law was inapplicable. Furthermore, since the Confederates had used these men for strictly military purposes, they were contraband of war and therefore subject to confiscation. Then, without much thought, Butler hired them for pay to construct a bakery for Federal soldiers. In one eventful day, Butler had, in effect, freed three slaves and then employed them to work for the Union army. The secretary of war promptly endorsed Butler's rationale, and two months later Congress passed the First Confiscation Act, which converted policy into law.

Together these three slaves and Benjamin Butler had struck a monstrous blow for freedom and the Federal war effort. They carved out the first path for wartime emancipation and set a precedent for military employment. Once the Federal government granted tacit freedom to runaways hired to labor for the Confederate military, it opened the door for all sorts of other cases and set the Lincoln administration on the rocky trail toward emancipation. And once the War Department began hiring blacks for wages, the practice initiated the breakdown of opposition to the use of blacks in other military capacities. First it was the construction of a bakery, then the erection of fortifications, and later labor as teamsters and cargo handlers. In each instance, blacks filled jobs traditionally performed by soldiers, which enabled military authorities to place more troops in combat commands as early as 1861.

As Federal armies penetrated deeper into the Confederacy, blacks flocked to Union lines for sanctuary from slavery. At first, Federal troops returned runaways who were not employed on Confederate military projects to their masters. This should not be, as Maj. Gen. George B. McClellan lectured Lincoln, a war to destroy slavery; rather, the object of the war was to save the Union. But for many northerners in and out of uniform, the situation was not that simple. Some soldiers abhorred the notion of returning anyone to slavery, while others found the practice of assisting masters in retrieval of slaves a nuisance that took away from their ability to wage war. It was also galling to civilians and soldiers alike that the Federal government was aiding individuals who had cast their lot with secessionists. By early 1862 the War Department prohibited the use of Federal troops in the retrieval of runaway slaves, and four months later, Congress went even further. In the Second Confiscation Act, it freed all escaped slaves of Rebel masters upon their entering Union lines.

Precisely how many slaves found refuge with Union forces is unknown. The best estimates range between 500,000 and 700,000 during the course of the war. While some slaves traveled great distances and undertook enormous risks to reach Union sanctuary, most had to await the arrival of Lincoln's soldiers. Personal and family hardships en route, a lack of specific information on the whereabouts of Union and Confederate forces, and the real fear of capture all acted as powerful deterrents to flight. Many slaves, therefore, had no choice but to let the Union army cut the freedom trail for them.

Such was the case for slaves on the family plantations of the crusty old fire-eater Edmund Ruffin. Situated outside Richmond, the Ruffin farms were marvels of innovation and experimentation. As Federal troops pushed up the Peninsula toward Richmond in May 1862, discipline and loyalty among slaves for their masters began to erode. First a dozen fled to Union lines, while the remainder at one plantation enforced a work stoppage, despite entreaties from Ruffin's son-in-law to return to the fields. Over the next few weeks, more and more slaves slipped off to the Federals, sometimes in dribbles, other times in droves, so that by the end of June there were not enough slaves left to care for the crops and animals. Cutting losses, Ruffin's son sold much of his share of slaves and livestock and relocated his remaining bondsmen to the south near Petersburg. His father attempted to salvage what was left of his property, but the haunting question remained: Why this rash of runaways, when "no where were they better cared for, or better managed & treated, according to their condition of slavery?"

With a slave population in the Confederate States of approximately three and one-half million, perhaps 15 or 20 percent reached safety with the Federals. Yet their impact was so much greater than their numbers. The war demanded a major alteration in the Confederate economy. Not only did the Confederacy have the same number of mouths to feed and bodies to clothe as before the war, but the loss of men to military service diminished the labor force significantly. In addition, the war machine consumed all sorts of material in tremendous quantities, some of which southerners had not produced before 1861. At the same time, the Federal blockade reduced the available amount of imported war necessities. The Confederacy had somehow to furnish these essentials itself, and that placed even greater demands on the laboring force. White women partially offset the manpower loss, but southerners were counting on black labor to take up the slack. Without it, workers were at a premium, commodities were scarcer, and demand significantly aided a spiraling inflation that wreaked havoc on society, driving prices up by 1865 to ninety-two times their prewar level. Thus, the Confederacy simply could not afford the loss of hundreds of thousands of black producers.

In areas such as Virginia, for example, where Federal forces campaigned frequently, the dearth of slave laborers proved critical. Soldiers on both sides, few of them well disciplined, scoured the countryside for eatables, dismantled fences for firewood, trampled fields, pilfered livestock, scattered the inhabitants, and generally wrecked agricultural output in one of the Confederacy's most productive states. Over time, Lee needed to draw more and more food and fodder for his army via railroad from the fertile Shenandoah Valley, which, remarkably, had managed to avoid the serious devastation. But the principal line, the Virginia Central Railroad, was in such serious need of repair by early 1863 that the superintendent informed Jefferson Davis its "efficiency is *most seriously impaired.*" Despite a reduction of freight loads by 25 percent, the line still suffered four derailments in five days that winter due to faulty track, and this at an average rate of speed of only eight miles per hour. Repairs were impossible because laborers were unavailable. Many white workers were in the army, the superintendent complained, and black workers ran off with the Federal troops, as had nearly all the local slaves. Essentials like railroad ties, in ample supply before the war, were unobtainable, even at triple their prewar price, because there were no workers to chop down trees and make them. As a result, over the final two years of the war, Lee had to look toward the Carolinas and occasionally Georgia for more and more supplies, at greater expense to the Confederacy over railroads heavily burdened and suffering increasingly from disrepair. Nor was this problem unique to Lee's army. Overused, inadequately maintained railroads burdened other Confederate commands as well—and the southern economy as a whole.

Runaways, moreover, undercut the sense of stability in society. The thought of desperate slaves, beyond the control of whites, roaming the countryside, hiding by day and traveling at night in search of Union lines, and seeking succor from fellow blacks was deeply disturbing. It also challenged perceptions of social order. Slaves whom they had known, cared for, and looked after for years, slaves in whom they had placed trust, were now abandoning them in these perilous times in search of freedom. For Edmund Ruffin and thousands of others, steeped in the delusion of the contented slave, the situation challenged their core beliefs.

Nor were runaways the only bondsmen who aided the Union war effort. Slaves who lacked opportunity to escape nonetheless found ways of contributing to Confederate defeat. At great peril to themselves, some slaves concealed, fed, and directed runaways or escaped Federal prisoners of war on the journey to freedom. Others sabotaged farm and labor equipment or assumed an uncooperative attitude with owners and overseers, to slow down work and promote widespread insecurity among whites at home. In time such deeds paid great dividends, as Confederate troops deserted ranks to look after the welfare of loved ones at home.

Slave protests also fueled another potent weapon against southern whites, fear of servile insurrection. Revolts would have been self-destructive to blacks, particularly in the heightened military state of the Confederacy, and resulted only in brutal reprisals. But the fear of revolts brought deep worry to both military personnel and white civilians in the South. Confederate soldiers, always looking rearward, wondered whether the rumors of some massive slave rebellion this time came true. Their relatives and friends at home in turn lived uneasily, hearing similar tales and knowing they could some day become reality.

These acts—obstruction, unrest, and flight to sanctuary behind Union lines—alerted northerners to the changing conditions of the war and to the potential value of blacks toward Union victory. Through their behavior, slaves compelled Federal authorities to adapt their policies to match the increasing magnitude of the war. Originally, the objective of the war was simply to preserve the Union. Then, Federals as a war measure confiscated slaves employed on Confederate military projects, and later any slaves of Rebel masters. "So long as the rebels retain and employ their slaves in producing grains &c.[etc.]," explained General in Chief Henry W. Halleck to Grant, "they can employ all the whites in the field. Every slave withdrawn from the enemy is equivalent to a white man put *hors de combat* [out of action]."

The next logical step was to remove slaves from Confederate hands and to direct their labor on behalf of the Union. Starting in 1862 federal officials placed women, children, and elderly and unfit males on abandoned plantations to cultivate cotton and other valuable commodities. The men served in all sorts of capacities with the army, from teamsters and cooks to stevedores and laborers, taking over the more disagreeable duties of soldiers and freeing up more bluecoats for combat. Whether northern whites wished it or not, the circumstances of war were moving the nation in the direction of black military service.

Among the small black population in the North, the desire to serve in Union blue was widespread. A group from Boston, expressing its commitment to the Union cause, vowed "there was not a man who would not leap for his knapsack and they would make it intolerable hot for old Virginia." Leaders, such as Frederick Douglass, chided the Lincoln administration for failing to utilize its resources to the fullest: "this is no time to fight with one hand, when both are needed; that this is no time to fight only with your white hand, and allow your black hand to remain tied." The war offered a rare opportunity to strike a mighty blow at slavery, dispel prejudice, and demonstrate to all that blacks could contribute in real and significant ways to the nation in times of crisis, and therefore merited full and equal rights. The best means of accomplishing those goals was through military service.

Blacks had already gained admission to the United States Navy. Perhaps as many as one in every ten or twelve men in the navy, or nearly 10,000, were black. They manned ships in the blockade and fought on numerous occasions in river operations. Although none appear to have received commissions as officers, blacks served in every enlisted capacity, including gunners, with distinction. Four black sailors earned Medals of Honor, and Robert Smalls, who stole a vessel and piloted it out of Charleston harbor to safety, was a national hero.

But this was primarily a ground war, and it was in the army that blacks had to make their mark. "Once let the black man get upon his person the brass letters, U.S., let him get an eagle on his button, and a musket on his shoulder and bullets in his pocket," Douglass predicted, "and there is no power on earth which can deny that he has earned the right to citizenship in the United States."

Unfortunately, in the eyes of many northern whites there was a giant gulf between blacks as military laborers and as soldiers in the United States Army. In the early stages of the war whites neither wanted black troops nor believed they had the capacity to withstand the rigors of soldiering. A Pennsylvanian who opposed black military service justified his opinion by saying, "God never intended a nigger to put white people Down," while a Connecticut infantryman insisted that black troops would be less valuable than hogs: "I think a drove of hogs would do better brought down here for we could eat them and the nigers we can't."

Yet as the war dragged on from months to a year and more and initial enthusiasm waned, a transformation in the minds of many soldiers, politicians, and even some civilians occurred. "The character of the war has very much changed within the last year," noted Halleck in early 1863. "There is now no possible hope of reconciliation with the rebels. The Union party in the South is virtually destroyed. There can be no peace but that which is forced by the sword. We must conquer the rebels or be conquered by them." The harsh realities of military life, the staggering and wholly unanticipated loss of life, and the lack of satisfactory success forced Unionists to recommit themselves to their cause and reexamine their approach to the war. A gradual escalation of the war followed. The Yankees learned to view the Confederate nation, its soldiers and civilians, as the enemy and were far less respectful of their needs and property. Northerners also concluded that the demands of the war, particularly in the area of manpower, outweighed certain traditional values and beliefs. It was in this atmosphere that Lincoln was able to garner support for emancipation and black enlistment outside abolitionist circles.

An opponent of slavery since his youth, the president had subordinated his personal views to the welfare of the country. But when hostilities reached such a scale and Union losses were so great that a peaceful reconciliation was no longer possible, he decided to issue the Emancipation Proclamation. Lincoln reasoned that slavery had been the major divisive issue between the North and South. A restored Union had to move beyond the slavery controversy, and the best way to do that was to place the peculiar institution on the road to extinction. Slavery, moreover, had enormous military value. Emancipation would strike a terrific blow at the Rebel war effort by depriving it of invaluable laborers.

At home and in military service, emancipation provided an ideological boost to the war effort. Understandably, opponents of slavery rejoiced. Lincoln had launched a powerful attack on America's great evil and resolved for all abolitionists a moral problem of fighting for the Union and the Constitution that protected a reprehensible institution. Despite some initial reluctance to endorse the new policy, supporters of the Union, too, recognized its worth. Even many of those who grumbled over the proclamation, especially soldiers, acquiesced in time. They could not help but notice that Lincoln demonstrated a willingness to employ any weapon to aid them in their struggle against the Confederacy.

In the international arena, the Emancipation Proclamation pulled the rug from beneath Confederate efforts to gain recognition from Great Britain and France. For some time the British and French governments had debated whether to recognize the Confederacy as an independent nation and to offer services as mediators. Although recognition and mediation would not necessarily have led to military intervention, many benefits would have accrued to the Rebels. While the French, with dreams of an overseas empire in Mexico, urged a strong, united position for mediation, the British hesitated. The Confederacy had by no means won in the summer of 1862, and large portions of British society opposed slavery under any circumstances. As Lee drove the Federals out of Virginia and then penetrated into Maryland in August and September, the movement for recognition gained momentum in the British Parliament. But just as quickly, fortunes reversed. Lee's army fell back from Maryland after the Battle of Antietam, and Lincoln issued the Emancipation Proclamation, seizing the high moral ground for the North. By early January 1863, British antislavery forces had gained ascendancy. As Union Ambassador to Great Britain, Charles Francis Adams noted with satisfaction that "this development of sentiment is to annihilate all agitation for recognition."

Still, emancipation was only part of Lincoln's policy. Its consummation was his decision to accept blacks into the army. As Douglass had explained nearly two years earlier, blacks were the largest untapped resource available to the Union. Enlistments had slowed to a trickle and Congress, hoping to avoid wholesale conscription, passed the Militia Act of July 17, 1862, that authorized the president to organize blacks and use them "for any military or naval service for which they may be found competent." Lincoln, interpreting the loose phraseology to his advantage, viewed the act as congressional justification for black enlistment.

It was a bold military stroke. In one swoop he deprived the Confederacy of a great resource and converted it into one for the Federals. Not only would the Union take slaves, it would arm and train them to fight for the Confederacy's defeat.

In an unusual twist, the Federal government actually began accepting blacks into the army before Lincoln issued the Emancipation Proclamation. He decided on emancipation and black enlistment around the same time, but due to the state of military affairs, he delayed the announcement of the Emancipation Proclamation until after the next significant Union victory, which did not occur until September. Otherwise, the Proclamation would have looked like the desperate act of a nation in defeat. With the repulse of Lee's raid into Maryland, Lincoln's pronouncement came from a position of greater strength.

Because the Lincoln administration was sensitive to the controversial nature of black enlistment, it implemented the program with caution. Less than three years earlier John Brown had attempted to seize the arsenal at Harper's Ferry, Virginia, in an effort to arm slaves, to the horror of northerners as well as southerners. To be sure, the war had altered public attitudes, and the circumstances were quite different, but racism remained powerful and opposition to the black soldier was strong. Lincoln rejected one endeavor to raise black troops on the South Carolina Sea Islands in the spring of 1862, and stalled on another in Kansas, opting to await better circumstances.

He found them in distant Louisiana, where Maj. Gen. Benjamin Butler needed manpower immediately. After the Federal occupation of New Orleans, local black militiamen had tendered their services to Butler, who respectfully declined. Several months later, however, he suddenly reversed himself and swore the men into national service, spurred on no doubt by an official suggestion he had received from Secretary of the Treasury Salmon P. Chase. The New Orleans volunteers were mostly free blacks, many of them well-to-do, with a tradition of military service dating back to the War of 1812. Strangely enough, they were militiamen who in 1861 had volunteered their services to the Confederate state government of Louisiana. Now they entered the Union army with dozens of black captains and lieutenants and even a black major.

Once the Lincoln administration broke the color barrier of the army, blacks stepped forward in large numbers. Service in the army offered to blacks the opportunity to strike a decisive blow for freedom, and recognition by whites that blacks could contribute in vital ways during this national crisis. "This was the biggest thing that ever happened in my life," asserted one former slave. "I felt like a man with a uniform on and a gun in my hand." While standing there during his first roll call, another freedman proudly recalled, "I felt freedom in my bones."

In order to make black military service more palatable to northern whites, and also to serve the prejudices of policy makers, nearly all officers in black units were white. The two Louisiana regiments with their seventy-five black officers comprised approximately two-thirds of all black officers in the war. With a few exceptions in 1865, the only other black officers held posts as chaplains and surgeons. Even Butler's Louisiana officers did not last. His successor squeezed them out by 1864 under the guise of their incompetence.

The basic premise for an exclusively white officer corps was that blacks lacked the qualities to become good soldiers. Many whites believed that blacks by nature were bad material, that they did not possess the requisite character, discipline, and courage to stand up to the rigors of combat. They were lazy, irresponsible, and childlike, with a strain of latent savagery—the quality that caused southerners to fear slave revolts—none of which were well suited to the development of controlled, disciplined, effective troops. The assumption was that only the best white officers could convert them into passable soldiers.

The decision for a white officer corps proved to be a mixed blessing. Unquestionably, the policy stifled opportunities for talented blacks, and even though the whites who commanded black soldiers did so voluntarily, they were men of their time and almost always held some degree of racial prejudice. But nearly all the white officers were experienced soldiers, far superior as a whole to their counterparts in white volunteer units. They had to furnish letters of testimonial vouching for their character, and had to pass an examination on a wide range of subjects, from history to general military knowledge, and from arithmetic to tactics.

Unlike officers of white volunteers, these men knew their business from study and personal experience before they took command, and black soldiers were the true beneficiaries. Early in their service, blacks performed under the microscopic eye of northern whites, many of whom keenly hoped for the failure of this great experiment. If the Lincoln administration wanted to expand the role of blacks in military service, the first units had to perform well. Worse yet, while they were new to soldiering, their Confederate adversaries were seasoned veterans. It was especially important, then, that black troops had talented, experienced officers who could prepare them for battle.

In their initial combat experiences, black soldiers demonstrated a willingness to fight. At Port Hudson, Louisiana, two black regiments, one of them with nearly all black officers, launched several gallant rushes against an almost impregnable Confederate defense. In failure, however, they earned glory and, more importantly, respect. "The men, white or black, who will not flinch from that will flinch from nothing," penned a *New York Times* correspondent on the scene. "It is no longer possible to doubt the bravery and steadiness of the colored race, when rightly led." Fortunately for the black enlistment movement, neither the northern government nor public learned that the black attackers inflicted no casualties on the Confederate defenders.

Less than two weeks later, wholly untested and virtually untrained black troops repelled a vigorous Confederate assault at Milliken's Bend on the Mississippi River, when the white Union defenders fled the scene. Although their marksmanship was poor (many had only been in uniform for a week or two), these blacks fought desperately, at times hand-to-hand, against the Rebel attackers. One black regiment had almost 45 percent of its men killed or mortally wounded, and even the Confederate commander had to concede that the black troops resisted with "considerable obstinacy." The performance of blacks at Milliken's Bend and elsewhere during the Vicksburg campaign convinced Grant that emancipation, in conjunction with black enlistment, "is the heavyest blow yet given the Confederacy."

In mid-July 1863, black soldiers had their most important early test, the assault on Fort Wagner. The fort protected a battery that defended a portion of Charleston harbor. That alone made it an important target, but the regiment assigned to lead the charge, the 54th Massachusetts (Colored) Infantry, aroused the attention of the northern public beyond the engagement's significance. Raised with considerable fanfare throughout the North, the 54th Massachusetts had a host of sons of important abolitionists, including its commander, Colonel Robert Gould Shaw. At sunset, with northern journalists observing, the 54th Massachusetts stormed the works, succeeded by several waves of white regiments. None could wrest control of Fort Wagner from the Rebel defenders.

Yet in failure, black soldiers emerged victors. Witnesses acknowledged the gallantry of the 54th Massachusetts, which suffered the greatest casualties, over 40 percent of its men. Among its dead was Shaw, who became a martyr throughout the North when Confederates attempted to insult white sensibilities by burying him "with his niggers."

The bravery of the men in the 54th Massachusetts, and the extensive publicity they received, ensured the continuation and expansion of what the Federal government now called the United States Colored Troops.

In spite of their fine conduct on three battlefields, considerable prejudice remained. Blacks had to fight Confederates in the front and discrimination in the rear. Riding on the combat successes, the War Department accelerated its program to create black units, and at the same time meekly accepted an opinion from its chief civilian attorney, the solicitor general, that black troops should receive inferior pay to whites. Although individual black soldiers demonstrated their leadership capacity in battle, the War Department was loath to award any of them commissions as lieutenants or captains in combat units.

High-ranking officers, too, relegated black troops to subservient roles. Many generals refused to believe that blacks could fight as well as whites and instead employed blacks in peripheral assignments, such as fatigue labor and occupation duty, where disease, rather than Confederate bullets, sapped their strength. Since some had no intention of sending their black troops into combat, they had no qualms about issuing them the worst weapons and designating very little training time. As these generals learned, however, battles occur in the most unpredictable locations, and when shooting begins, a commander wants every available soldier, black or white, on the front lines or in the designated reserve.

Of the almost 37,000 black soldiers who lost their lives, fewer than 3,000 died in combat, far below the percentage of whites killed in action. That, however, represented the length of their military service and the number of major battles in which they participated and bore little relationship to their effectiveness on the battlefield. Black soldiers fought aggressively, compensating for their lack of training and experience with inspiration and dash. The knowledge that this was the "War for Freedom," as one woman termed it, provided them with an added incentive. "Boys, it may be slavery or Death to some of you today," announced an officer, just before an advance. A black soldier calmly replied, "Lieutenant, I am ready to die for Liberty," and just minutes later a ball pierced his heart. Like white troops, they gained confidence in themselves as soldiers through extensive service and ultimately left their mark on dozens of battlefields.

With experience and achievement in combat, too, came respect from white Union volunteers. Nothing neutralized the distrust and disdain that whites held for blacks like success on the battlefield. "I never believed in niggers before," exclaimed a surprised Irish soldier, "but by Jasus, they are hell for fighting." After black troops fought gallantly to repulse an assault by Confederate cavalryman Nathan Bedford Forrest, the Union commander admitted to a similar change of heart: "I have been one of those men, who never had much confidence in colored troops fighting, but these doubts are now all removed, for they fought as bravely as any troops in the Fort." Whether it was three hearty cheers that men in the 14th U.S. Colored Infantry received from whites for their defense of Decatur, Alabama, or the cries of "Bully for you" white cavalrymen bestowed on three black regiments after a successful assault near Petersburg, whites were admitting that black soldiers were making genuine and important contributions to the war effort. Perhaps the greatest tribute white volunteers paid to black soldiers came after that same Petersburg attack, when veterans from Hancock's Corps, arguably the best in the Army of the Potomac, congratulated the men and treated them with dignity and respect. "A few more fights like that," noted an officer of black soldiers, "and our Col*d* [Colored] boys will have established their manhood if not their Brotherhood to the satisfaction of even the most prejudiced."

In a peculiar way, Confederates helped to legitimize and enhance the reputation of blacks within the Union Army. Rebels attempted to undermine the effectiveness of black units by singling them out for especially heavy fire, declining to exchange black prisoners of war, or capturing and executing black soldiers and their white officers on the spot. Such practices, however, backfired. They not only bonded black soldiers and their white officers closer, for both faced the same fate, but elevated the standing of the United States Colored Troops in the Union army. White volunteers could not help but notice that officers and men in black units incurred greater risks.

The unwillingness of Confederate officials to include black troops in prisoner exchanges also contributed in an unforeseen way. This discriminatory policy alerted Grant to the unequal nature of one-for-one exchanges. The Confederacy, with severe manpower limitations late in the war, benefited more from exchanges than the Union, and Grant halted the practice.

By the end of the war, black soldiers had fought in over forty major engagements and 449 lesser firefights. Like white troops, they acquitted themselves well under good officers with satisfactory training and poorly under incompetent ones with insufficient drilling. Over all, they measured up to white troops. Lincoln himself noted in 1864: "So far as tested, it is difficult to say they are not as good soldiers as any." The sixteen Medals of Honor earned by black soldiers in the war is but small testimony to their valor.

In the final year of the war, when their ranks eventually swelled above 120,000, black soldiers proved indispensable to the Union war effort. With Grant around Petersburg, thirty-three regiments were black, or approximately one in every eight soldiers. Along with the infamous Battle of the Crater, the United States Colored Troops fought in many of the significant if little known battles, including Second Petersburg, First Hatcher's Run, Second Deep Bottom, Chaffin's Farm, Second Darbytown Road, Second Fair Oaks, and Third Watkins Farm.

Sherman preferred to use his black soldiers for guard and occupation duty and logistical support. Such service, while not nearly as glamorous or exciting as combat, was critical to success, especially during the Atlanta campaign, and it freed up others to serve in the front lines.

After Sherman and his army drove toward Savannah, black soldiers saw extensive action. During the Battle of Nashville in December 1864, two black brigades charged with such force that they concealed the major point of attack, the opposite flank, which resulted in a rout of Rebel forces. The next day, blacks and whites together stormed the Confederate works and contributed substantially to the decisive victory. Walking over the ground where hundreds of lifeless black and white soldiers lay mingled, an officer noticed that "the blood of the white and black man has flowed freely together for the great cause which is to give freedom, unity, manhood and peace to all men, whatever birth or complexion." Several months later, blacks led the assault on Fort Blakely, near Mobile. Due to miscommunication, black troops attacked prematurely but nonetheless shattered the Confederate lines just as other Federals launched their attack.

Nearly 180,000 blacks joined the Union army, and adding the estimated 10,000 in the navy, close to 190,000 servicemen were black. They made good soldiers and sailors, on the whole no better nor worse than whites. They came in large numbers when the Union needed them most, in the final two years of the war. In addition to their military service, and their important work as laborers for the North, they helped destabilize the southern home front through their disloyalty to the Confederate cause. Thus blacks played a major role in its defeat.

Perhaps the most telling statement of black wartime contributions came from the Confederates. By early 1864, Maj. Gen. Patrick Cleburne, one of the best division commanders in the war, led a group of officers who insisted "slavery has become a military weakness." The institution turned foreign powers against the Confederacy and supplied the Union with "an army from our granaries." Its breakdown had so shaken southern whites that "the fear of their slaves is continually haunting them, and from silence and apprehension many of these soon learn to wish the war stopped on any terms." Cleburne and his subordinates called for emancipation and black enlistment in the Confederate army. They hoped that such a move would "at one blow strip the enemy of foreign sympathy and assistance," undercut the northern crusade for abolition, and expand the Rebel ranks with black troops, who would earn freedom for themselves and their families in defense of their homes. While the Davis administration quashed the proposal, southerners continued to bandy about the idea, and by early 1865 Lee publicly endorsed the enlistment of blacks. He believed they could make "efficient soldiers." He added: "I think we could at least do as well with them as the enemy, and he attaches great importance to their assistance." With Lee's support, the Confederate Congress authorized the recruitment of black soldiers in March 1865. Although this was too little, too late for the Confederacy, the legislation acknowledged the vital wartime role of black people.

After the war, when black leaders tried to point out the contributions of their race to Union victory, whites began to close ranks. They claimed that blacks entered the war at the eleventh hour, and that blacks did not fight in appreciable numbers in the critical Virginia Theater until well after Gettysburg, which experts widely acknowledged as the turning point. But the arguments neglected two major considerations. Whites failed to recognize the devastating effect runaways and disruptive slaves had on the Confederacy. They also did not realize that the turning point thesis is predicated on Union success in 1864 and 1865. Whether one takes Gettysburg, Vicksburg, or even Antietam as the turning point, it becomes so only because of Union successes afterward. Those victories came, at least in part, because of blacks' efforts.

In 1861 few foresaw the pivotal position of blacks in the American balance of power. Through their actions as slaves and free men and women, blacks helped to force supporters of the Union to re-examine their approach to war. Unionists had to fight a war against the Rebels and adopt more vigorous methods of prosecution, such as the destruction of property and the use of blacks in the armed forces. For the Confederacy, they were a crucial workforce, providing food and essential labor for a wide range of civilian and military projects. Their steady loss to the Federals caused supply shortages, various hardships, and escalating inflation, all of which took a terrible toll on Confederate fighting men and civilians. Then, by converting blacks into soldiers, the Union not only deprived the Confederacy of a great resource, but employed it against the foe. As Lincoln explained to Grant in 1863, "I believe it is a resource which, if vigorously applied now, will soon close the contest. It works doubly, weakening the enemy and strengthening us." In time he proved right.

The impact of blacks on the Civil War is comparable to the American experience in the First World War. To insist that blacks defeated the Confederacy, like assertions that the Americans defeated Germany, dismisses the efforts of all those others who had fought long and hard during the war. But like the doughboys in World War I, blacks helped to make the difference between victory and stalemate or defeat. They arrived in great numbers at the critical moment, and their contributions on and off the battlefield, in conjunction with those of whites, were enough to force the enemy to capitulate.

Shortly after Appomattox, Major Martin Delany told a black crowd: "Do you know that if it was not for the black men this war never would have been brought to a close with success to the Union, and the liberty of your race if it had not been for the Negro?" At the time it sounded audacious, even militant; now, it sounds plausible.

FURTHER READING

Herman Belz, *A New Birth of Freedom: The Republican Party and Freedmen's Rights, 1861–1866* (1976)

George R. Bentley, *A History of the Freedmen's Bureau* (1965)

Ira Berlin, et al., eds., *Freedom: A Documentary History of Emancipation,* 4 vols., 1984–1993

——, Barbara J. Fields, et al., *Slaves No More: Three Essays on Emancipation and the Civil War* (1992)

David W. Blight, *Frederick Douglass, Civil War: Keeping Faith in Jubilee* (1989)

Dudley T. Cornish, *The Sable Arm: Negro Troops in the Union Army* (1956)

LaWanda Cox, *Lincoln and Black Freedom* (1981)

Eric Foner, *Nothing but Freedom: Emancipation and Its Legacy* (1983)

John Hope Franklin, *The Emancipation Proclamation* (1963)

Louis S. Gerteis, *From Contraband to Freedman: Federal Policy toward Southern Blacks, 1861–1865* (1973)

——, "Salmon P. Chase, Radicalism and the Politics of Emancipation, 1861–1864," *Journal of American History* 60 (1973), 42–62

Thomas Holt, "'An Empire over the Mind': Emancipation, Race and Ideology in the British West Indies and the American South," in J. Morgan Kousser and James M. McPherson, eds., *Region, Race, and Reconstruction* (1982), 283–314

James M. McPherson, "Who Freed the Slaves?" in McPherson, *Drawn by the Sword: Reflections on the American Civil War* (1996)

Clarence L. Mohr, *On the Threshold of Freedom: Masters and Slaves in Civil War Georgia* (1986)

Donald G. Nieman, *To Set the Law in Motion: The Freedmen's Bureau and Legal Rights for Blacks, 1865–1869* (1979)

Benjamin Quarles, *The Negro in the Civil War* (1953)

Roger Ransom and Richard Sutch, *One Kind of Freedom: The Economic Consequences of Emancipation* (1977)

James L. Roark, *Masters Without Slaves: Southern Planters in the Civil War and Reconstruction* (1977)

Armstead L. Robinson, "'Worser Dan Jeff Davis': The Coming of Free Labor During the Civil War, 1861–1865," in Thavolia Glymph and John J. Kusma, eds., *Essays on the Postbellum Southern Economy* (1985)

Willie Lee Rose, *Rehearsal for Reconstruction: The Port Royal Experiment* (1964)

V. Jacque Voegeli, *Free But Not Equal: The Midwest and the Negro during the Civil War* (1967)

Bell I. Wiley, *Southern Negroes, 1861–1865* (1938)

Forrest Wood, *Black Scare: The Racist Response to the Civil War and Reconstruction* (1968)

C. Van Woodward, "The Price of Freedom," in David Sansing, ed. *What Was Freedom's Price?* (1978)

CHAPTER 11

Congress's Terms for the

Defeated South

Reconstruction was, in a real sense, what the war was all about. After putting down the Southerners' attempted secession and liberating their slaves in the process, the federal government now had to decide what kind of society should emerge in the South. Simply ending slavery and terminating hostilities were not enough. The freed slaves had to be protected and given the opportunity to enjoy and solidify their new status. This meant guaranteeing their legal rights and economic security, perhaps even giving them the vote or land. At the same time, the leaders of the rebellion had to be punished and their political influence curbed, if not eliminated altogether. Since most of these men were also slaveholders, their economic power had been reduced, and would be reduced further if some of their land was to be made available to the former slaves. All of these elements had to be considered as part of a final settlement of the issues and problems raised by the sectional conflict and the war that had ensued.

In the seven months between Andrew Johnson's sudden accession to the presidency in April 1865 and the convening of the Thirty-ninth Congress in December of that year, the president's approach to Reconstruction was to impose minimal demands on the South. He required only minor concessions from the former Confederates before allowing them to resume their political rights and retain their lands. As for the freedmen, he seemed to think that they needed no further protection beyond the fact of their emancipation. The Republican-dominated Congress disagreed, however. The terms for Southern readmission were, in its view, to be determined by the legislative branch—a position that had already brought Congress into a confrontation with Lincoln over the Wade-Davis bill and his veto of it in 1864. The Republican majority in Congress also rejected the specifics of Johnson's terms as far too conciliatory.

But exactly what alternative did the party have in mind? Some Republicans recognized that the former Confederates needed firmer restrictions and the freedmen greater protection, but they were concerned about causing further disruption in Southern society and politics and about involving the federal government in the internal affairs of states now that the war was over. Other Republicans, however, saw the moment of Southern defeat as a vital opportunity to reorganize the region's politics and economy, and move it in a new, more democratic and egalitarian direction.

From early 1866 until March 1867, the congressional Republicans struggled to establish a policy to replace that of the president. After their first proposal, the Four-

teenth Amendment, met with resistance from both Johnson, who vetoed it, and the South, which rejected it, the Republicans proposed a plan to reorganize the Southern state governments and enfranchise the freedmen. This measure was called the Recon- struction Act, and its terms were mandatory.

This lengthy and difficult struggle revealed the dimensions of Republican thought on the problem of reunion and Reconstruction. What was the general thrust of the party's thinking and policymaking? Was the party radical and innovative in its ap- proach, or was it, in reality, rather cautious? Historians have debated this question al- most as vigorously as the Republicans in Congress debated Reconstruction policy.

☞ D O C U M E N T S

The testimony about Congress's Reconstruction policy in the documents that follow comes from Republican congressmen who were involved in the formulation and passage of the legisla- tion or from others who were affiliated with the party. The first document contains extracts from the "Grasp of War" speech given in Boston on June 21, 1865, by Richard Henry Dana, Jr., a prominent Republican lawyer, in which he outlined an important constitutional theory about Reconstruction, a theory that is later discussed in one of the essays in this chapter. In the sec- ond selection, Senator Lyman Trumbull's view of the scope of his Civil Rights bill is presented. His remarks are from two speeches in the Senate—the first on January 29, 1866, when the bill was initially introduced, and the second on April 4, 1866, when the Senate was about to over- ride President Johnson's veto of it.

The remaining documents relate to the Reconstruction Act of 1867, which embodied the Republican-dominated Congress's final terms for Southern readmission. The third selection is from a speech of January 3, 1867, by Representative Thaddeus Stevens on an early version of the bill; in this speech, Stevens stated his radical views about Reconstruction. The specifics of a radical approach to Reconstruction are enumerated in the fourth extract, which is from a speech of January 28, 1867 called "Regeneration before Reconstruction" by George W. Julian, a radi- cal Republican congressman from Indiana. The position of a more conservative Republican is presented in the fifth document where Senator John Sherman of Ohio raises objections to some of the proscriptive terms of the bill in a Senate speech on February 19, 1867. The sixth selec- tion contains the text of the Reconstruction Act of March 2, 1867, and of the Fourteenth Amendment, which the South had already rejected in the fall of 1866 but which was now part of the terms required for readmission under the Reconstruction Act. The seventh and last selec- tion is from the 1879 novel, *A Fool's Errand,* by Albion W. Tourgee, an Ohioan who had been a leading figure in the Republican party of North Carolina during Reconstruction but who re- garded the provisions of the Reconstruction Act as quite inadequate for the task at hand.

Richard H. Dana, Jr., Presents His "Grasp of War" Theory, June 1865

. . . A war is over when its purpose is secured. It is a fatal mistake to hold that this war is over, because the fighting has ceased. [Applause.] This war is not over. We are in the attitude and in the *status* of war to-day. There is the solution of this question. Why, suppose a man has attacked your life, my friend, in the highway, at night, armed, and after a death-struggle, you get him down—what then? When he says he has done fighting,

---

From Richard Henry Dana Jr., "Grasp of War" speech, June 1865, in Richard Henry Dana, Jr., *Speeches in Stirring Times.* Richard Henry Dana III, ed. (Houghton Mifflin, 1910), pp. 246–247, 250, 257, 258–259.

are you obliged to release him? Can you not hold him until you have got some security against his weapons? [Applause.] Can you not hold him until you have searched him, and taken his weapons from him? Are you obliged to let him up to begin a new fight for your life? The same principle governs war between nations. When one nation has conquered another, in a war, the victorious nation does not retreat from the country and give up possession of it, because the fighting has ceased. No; it holds the conquered enemy in the grasp of war until it has secured whatever it has a right to require. [Applause.] I put that proposition fearlessly—*The conquering party may hold the other in the grasp of war until it has secured whatever it has a right to require.*

But what have we a right to require? We have no right to require our conquered foe to adopt all our notions, our opinions, our systems, however much we may be attached to them, however good we may think them; but we have a right to require whatever the public safety and public faith make necessary. [Applause.] That is the proposition. Then, we come to this: *We have a right to hold the rebels in the grasp of war until we have obtained whatever the public safety and the public faith require.* [Applause, and cries of "good."] Is not that a solid foundation to stand upon! Will it not bear examination? and are we not upon it to-day? . . .

We have a right to require, my friends, that the freedmen of the South shall have the right to hold land. [Applause.] Have we not? We have a right to require that they shall be allowed to testify in the state courts. [Applause.] Have we not? We have a right to demand that they shall bear arms as soldiers in the militia. [Applause.] Have we not? We have a right to demand that there shall be an impartial ballot. [Great applause.] . . .

When a man accepts a challenge to a duel, what does he put at stake? He puts his life at stake, does he not? And is it not childish, after the fatal shot is fired, to exclaim, "Oh, death and widowhood and orphanage are fearful things!" They were all involved in that accepted challenge. When a nation allows itself to be at war, or when a people make war, they put at stake their national existence. [Applause.] That result seldom follows, because the nation that is getting the worst of the contest makes its peace in time; because the conquering nation does not always desire to incorporate hostile subjects in its dominions; because neutral nations intervene. The conqueror must choose between two courses—to permit the political institutions, the body politic, to go on, and treat with it, or obliterate it. We have destroyed and obliterated their central government. Its existence was treason. As to their states, we mean to adhere to the first course. We mean to say the states shall remain, with new constitutions, new systems. We do not mean to exercise sovereign civil jurisdiction over them in our Congress. Fellow citizens, it is not merely out of tenderness to them; it would be the most dangerous possible course for us. Our system is a planetary system; each planet revolving round its orbit, and all round a common sun. This system is held together by a balance of powers—centripetal and centrifugal forces. We have established a wise balance of forces. Let not that balance be destroyed. If we should undertake to exercise sovereign civil jurisdiction over those states, it would be as great a peril to our system as it would be a hardship upon them. We must not, we will not undertake it, except as the last resort of the thinking and the good—as the ultimate final remedy, when all others have failed.

I know, fellow citizens, it is much more popular to stir up the feelings of a public audience by violent language than it is to repress them; but on this subject we must think wisely. We have never been willing to try the experiment of a consolidated democratic republic. Our system is a system of states, with central power; and in that system is our safety. [Applause.] State rights, I maintain; State sovereignty we have destroyed. [Applause.] Therefore, although I say that, if we are driven to the last resort, we may adopt this final remedy; yet wisdom, humanity, regard for democratic principles, common discretion, require that we should follow the course we are now following. Let the states make their own constitutions, but the constitutions must be satisfactory to the Republic [applause], and—ending as I began—by a power which I think is beyond question, the Republic holds them in the grasp of war until they have made such constitutions. [Loud applause.]

Senator Lyman Trumbull of Illinois Explains His Civil Rights Bill, January and April 1866

I. January 29, 1866

. . . With this bill passed into a law and efficiently executed we shall have secured freedom in fact and equality in civil rights to all persons in the United States. There will be no objection to this bill that it undertakes to confer judicial powers upon some other authority than the courts. It may be assailed as drawing to the Federal Government powers that properly belong to "States"; but I apprehend, rightly considered, it is not obnoxious to that objection. It will have no operation in any State where the laws are equal, where all persons have the same civil rights without regard to color or race. It will have no operation in the State of Kentucky when her slave code and all her laws discriminating between persons on account of race or color shall be abolished. . . .

II. April 4, 1866

. . . This bill in no manner interferes with the municipal regulations of any State which protects all alike in their rights of person and property. It could have no operation in Massachusetts, New York, Illinois, or most of the States of the Union. How preposterous, then, to charge that unless some State can have and exercise the right to punish somebody, or to deny somebody a civil right on account of his color, its rights as a State will be destroyed. It is manifest that unless this bill can be passed, nothing can be done to protect the freedmen in their liberty and their rights.

Whatever may have been the opinion of the President at one time as to "good faith requiring the security of the freedmen in their liberty and their property" it is now manifest from the character of his objections to this bill that he will approve no measure that will accomplish the object. That the second clause of the constitutional amendment [the Thirteenth, abolishing slavery] gives this power there can be no question. Some have contended that it gives the power even to confer the right of suffrage. I have not thought so, because I have never thought suffrage any more necessary to the liberty of a freedman than of a non-voting white, whether child or female. But his liberty under the Constitution he is entitled to, and whatever is necessary to secure it to him he is entitled to have, be it the ballot or the bayonet. If the bill now before us, and which goes no further than to secure civil rights to the freedman, cannot be passed, then the constitutional amendment proclaiming freedom to all the inhabitants of the land is a cheat and a delusion. . . .

From Lyman Trumbull, small extracts from speeches in the Senate, January 29, 1866, *Congressional Globe,* 39 Cong., 1 Sess., Vol. 36, pt. 1, p. 476, and April 4, 1866, *Congressional Globe,* 39 Cong., 1 Sess., Vol. 36, pt. 2, p. 1761.

Representative Thaddeus Stevens of Pennsylvania
States His Terms, January 1867

. . . It is to be regretted that inconsiderate and incautious Republicans should ever have supposed that the slight amendments [embodied in the pending Fourteenth Amendment] already proposed to the Constitution, even when incorporated into that instrument, would satisfy the reforms necessary for the security of the Government. Unless the rebel States, before admission, should be made republican in spirit, and placed under the guardianship of loyal men, all our blood and treasure will have been spent in vain. I waive now the question of punishment which, if we are wise, will still be inflicted by moderate confiscations, both as a reproof and example. Having these States, as we all agree, entirely within the power of Congress, it is our duty to take care that no injustice shall remain in their organic laws. Holding them "like clay in the hands of the potter," we must see that no vessel is made for destruction. Having now no governments, they must have enabling acts. The law of last session with regard to Territories settled the principles of such acts. Impartial suffrage, both in electing the delegates and ratifying their proceedings, is now the fixed rule. There is more reason why colored voters should be admitted in the rebel States than in the Territories. In the States they form the great mass of the loyal men. Possibly with their aid loyal governments may be established in most of those States. Without it all are sure to be ruled by traitors; and loyal men, black and white, will be oppressed, exiled, or murdered. There are several good reasons for the passage of this bill. In the first place, it is just. I am now confining my argument to negro suffrage in the rebel States. Have not loyal blacks quite as good a right to choose rulers and make laws as rebel whites? In the second place, it is a necessity in order to protect the loyal white men in the seceded States. The white Union men are in a great minority in each of those States. With them the blacks would act in a body; and it is believed that in each of said States, except one, the two united would form a majority, control the States, and protect themselves. Now they are the victims of daily murder. They must suffer constant persecution or be exiled. The convention of southern loyalists, lately held in Philadelphia, almost unanimously agreed to such a bill as an absolute necessity.

Another good reason is, it would insure the ascendency of the Union party. Do you avow the party purpose? exclaims some horror-stricken demagogue. I do. For I believe, on my conscience, that on the continued ascendency of that party depends the safety of this great nation. If impartial suffrage is excluded in rebel States then every one of them is sure to send a solid rebel representative delegation to Congress, and cast a solid rebel electoral vote. They, with their kindred Copperheads of the North, would always elect the President and control Congress. While slavery sat upon her defiant throne, and insulted and intimidated the trembling North, the South frequently divided on questions of policy between Whigs and Democrats, and gave victory alternately to the sections. Now, you must divide them between loyalists, without regard to color, and disloyalists, or you will be the perpetual vassals of the free-trade, irritated, revengeful South. For these, among other reasons, I am for negro suffrage in every rebel State. If it be just, it should not be denied; if it be necessary, it should be adopted; if it be a punishment to traitors, they deserve it.

From Thaddeus Stevens, speech in House, January 3, 1867, *Congressional Globe,* 39 Cong., 2 Sess., Vol. 37, pt. 1, pp. 251–253. This selection is also available in *Radical Republicans and Reconstruction,* Harold M. Hyman, ed. (Bobbs-Merrill, 1967), pp. 373–375.

But it will be said, as it has been said, "This is negro equality!" What is negro equality, about which so much is said by knaves, and some of which is believed by men who are not fools? It means, as understood by honest Republicans, just this much, and no more: every man, no matter what his race or color; every earthly being who has an immortal soul, has an equal right to justice, honesty, and fair play with every other man; and the law should secure him those rights. The same law which condemns or acquits an African should condemn or acquit a white man. The same law which gives a verdict in a white man's favor should give a verdict in a black man's favor on the same state of facts. Such is the law of God and such ought to be the law of man. This doctrine does not mean that a negro shall sit on the same seat or eat at the same table with a white man. That is a matter of taste which every man must decide for himself. The law has nothing to do with it. . . .

Representative George W. Julian of Indiana Outlines the Scope of Reconstruction, January 1867

. . . Mr. Speaker, I further object to the measure [the proposed Reconstruction bill] before us that it is a mere enabling act, looking to the early restoration of the rebellious districts to their former places in the Union, instead of a well-considered frame of government contemplating such restoration at some indefinite future time, and designed to fit them to receive it. They are not ready for reconstruction as independent States, on any terms or conditions which Congress might impose; and I believe the time has come for us to say so. We owe this much to their misguided people, whose false and feverish hopes have been kept alive by the course of the Executive and the hesitating policy of Congress. I think I am safe in saying that if these districts were to-day admitted as States, with the precise political and social elements which we know to exist in them, even with their rebel population disfranchised and the ballot placed in the hands of radical Union men only, irrespective of color, the experiment would be ruinous to the best interests of their loyal people and calamitous to the nation. The withdrawal of federal intervention and the unchecked operation of local supremacy would as fatally hedge up the way of justice and equality as the rebel ascendency which now prevails. Why? Simply because no theory of government, no forms of administration, can be trusted, unless adequately supported by public opinion. The power of the great landed aristocracy in these regions, if unrestrained by power from without, would inevitably assert itself. Its political chemistry, obeying its own laws, would very soon crystallize itself into the same forms of treason and lawlessness which to-day hold their undisturbed empire over the existing loyal element. What these regions need, above all things, is not an easy and quick return to their forfeited rights in the Union, but *government,* the strong arm of power, outstretched from the central authority here in Washington, making it safe for the freedmen of the South, safe for her loyal white men, safe for emigrants from the Old World and from the Northern States to go and dwell there; safe for Northern capital and labor, Northern energy and enterprise, and Northern ideas to set up their habitation in peace, and thus found a Christian civilization and a living democracy amid the ruins of the past. That, sir, is what the country demands and the rebel power needs. To talk about suddenly building up independent States where the material for such structures is fatally wanting,

From George W. Julian, "Regeneration Before Reconstruction," January 28, 1867, in George W. Julian *Speeches on Political Questions* (Negro Universities Press, 1970 [1872]), pp. 352–353.

is nonsense. States must *grow,* and to that end their growth must be fostered and protected. The political and social regeneration of the country made desolate by treason is the prime necessity of the hour, and is preliminary to any reconstruction of States. Years of careful pupilage under the authority of the nation may be found necessary, and Congress alone must decide when and upon what conditions the tie rudely broken by treason shall be restored. Congress, moreover, is as solemnly bound to deny to disloyal communities admission into our great sisterhood of States as it is to deny the rights of citizenship to those who have forfeited such rights by treason. . . .

Senator John Sherman of Ohio Urges Caution and Moderation, February 1867

. . . We sweep from our legislation all tests for voting except such as each State may prescribe. We build reconstruction upon the broadest humanity and invite all men to take part in the work. So far as voting is concerned we proclaim universal amnesty in exchange for universal suffrage, and yet the Senator [Sumner] is not satisfied. What more did he ask a year ago? Nothing. If we exclude from voting the rebels of the South, who compose nearly all the former voting population, what becomes of the republican doctrine that all governments must be founded on the consent of the governed? I invoke constitutional liberty against such a proposition. Beware, sir, lest in guarding against rebels you destroy the foundation of republican institutions. I like rebels no better than the Senator from Massachusetts; but, sir, I will not supersede one form of oligarchy in which the blacks were slaves by another in which the whites are disfranchised outcasts. Let us introduce no such horrid deformity into the American Union. Our path has been toward enfranchisement and liberty. Let us not turn backward in our course, but after providing all necessary safeguards for white and black, let us reconstruct society in the rebel States upon the broad basis of universal suffrage.

This [Reconstruction] bill does not proclaim universal amnesty except as to voting. On the contrary, it requires these States to adopt a constitutional amendment [the Fourteenth] by which the leading men disable themselves from holding office. Six thousand or perhaps ten thousand of the leading men of the South are embraced in the restriction of the constitutional amendment, and are forever excluded from holding office until two thirds of both Houses of Congress relieve them from that restriction. Is not that enough? Is it not enough that they are humiliated, conquered, their pride broken, their property lost, hundreds and thousands of their best and bravest buried under their soil, their institutions gone, they themselves deprived of the right to hold office, and placed in political power on the same footing with their former slaves? Is not that enough? I say it is, and a generous people will not demand more.

But, sir, when the attempt is made to defeat a measure of this kind, which yields all that the Senator has ever openly demanded in the Senate, all that has ever been demanded by any popular community in this great country, all that has been demanded by any Legislature, more than we claimed at the last election, I have the right to characterize this opposition as unusual and unnatural. Sir, let us issue this call to the people of the southern States. We have given here our deliberate judgment on a legal proposition: we say that the State governments organized by the President of the United States [Andrew

From John Sherman, speech in Senate, February 19, 1867, *Congressional Globe,* 39 Cong., 2 Sess., Vol. 37, pt. 3, p. 1564.

Johnson in 1865] were without authority of law, because they were without the sanction of Congress. We therefore sweep them away, not for all purposes, but for all State purposes. We deny their validity as State governments. They only have the same force and effect as the local Mexican law had in California after we conquered California, the same effect that the local law of Maryland would have if the British should overrun the whole of Maryland; no more, no less. The State communities are swept out of existence, and the people are required to proceed in their own way to form State governments. What objection can there be to this? . . .

Congress's Terms for Readmission and Reconstruction, June 1866 and March 1867

I. 14th Constitutional Amendment

Joint Resolution proposing an Amendment to the Constitution of the United States.

Be it resolved by the Senate and House of Representatives of the United States of America, in Congress assembled, (two-thirds of both Houses concurring,) That the following article be proposed to the Legislatures of the several States as an amendment to the Constitution of the United States, which, when ratified by three-fourths of said Legislatures, shall be valid as part of the Constitution, namely:

Article XIV.

Section 1.   All persons born or naturalized in the United States, and subject to the jurisdiction thereof, are citizens of the United States and of the State wherein they reside. No State shall make or enforce any law which shall abridge the privileges or immunities of citizens of the United States; nor shall any State deprive any person of life, liberty, or property, without due process of law, nor deny to any person within its jurisdiction the equal protection of the laws.

Sec. 2.   Representatives shall be apportioned among the several States according to their respective numbers, counting the whole number of persons in each State, excluding Indians not taxed. But when the right to vote at any election for the choice of electors for President and Vice President of the United States, representatives in Congress, the executive and judicial officers of a State, or the members of the Legislature thereof, is denied to any of the male inhabitants of such State, being twenty-one years of age, and citizens of the United States, or in any way abridged, except for participation in rebellion or other crime, the basis of representation therein shall be reduced in the proportion which the number of such male citizens shall bear to the whole number of male citizens twenty-one years of age in such State.

Sec. 3.   No person shall be a Senator or Representative in Congress, or elector of President and Vice President, or hold any office, civil or military, under the United States, or under any State, who, having previously taken an oath as a member of Congress, or as an officer of the United States, or as a member of any State Legislature, or as an executive or judicial officer of any State, to support the Constitution of the United States,

The Fourteenth Amendment and the Reconstruction Act, in Edward McPherson, *The Political History of the U.S. During the Period of Reconstruction* (Negro Universities Press, 1969 [1875]), pp. 191–192.

shall have engaged in insurrection or rebellion against the same, or given aid or comfort to the enemies thereof. But Congress may, by a vote of two thirds of each House, remove such disability.

Sec. 4.   The validity of the public debt of the United States, authorized by law, including debts incurred for payment of pensions and bounties for services in suppressing insurrection or rebellion, shall not be questioned. But neither the United States nor any State shall assume or pay any debt or obligation incurred in aid of insurrection or rebellion against the United States, or any claim for the loss or emancipation of any slave; but all such debts, obligations, and claims shall be held illegal and void.

Sec. 5.   That Congress shall have power to enforce, by appropriate legislation, the provisions of this article.
Passed June 13, 1866.

II. Reconstruction Act of Thirty-Ninth Congress

An act to provide for the more efficient government of the rebel States.

Whereas no legal State governments or adequate protection for life or property now exists in the rebel States of Virginia, North Carolina, South Carolina, Georgia, Mississippi, Alabama, Louisiana, Florida, Texas, and Arkansas; and whereas it is necessary that peace and good order should be enforced in said States until loyal and republican State governments can be legally established: Therefore

Be it enacted, &c., That said rebel States shall be divided into military districts and made subject to the military authority of the United States, as hereinafter prescribed, and for that purpose Virginia shall constitute the first district; North Carolina and South Carolina the second district; Georgia, Alabama, and Florida the third district; Mississippi and Arkansas the fourth district; and Louisiana and Texas the fifth district.

Sec. 2.   That it shall be the duty of the President to assign to the command of each of said districts an officer of the army, not below the rank of brigadier general, and to detail a sufficient military force to enable such officer to perform his duties and enforce his authority within the district to which he is assigned.

Sec. 3.   That it shall be the duty of each officer assigned as aforesaid to protect all persons in their rights of person and property, to suppress insurrection, disorder, and violence, and to punish, or cause to be punished, all disturbers of the public peace and criminals, and to this end he may allow local civil tribunals to take jurisdiction of and to try offenders, or, when in his judgment it may be necessary for the trial of offenders, he shall have power to organize military commissions or tribunals for that purpose; and all interference under color of State authority with the exercise of military authority under this act shall be null and void.

Sec. 4.   That all persons put under military arrest by virtue of this act shall be tried without unnecessary delay, and no cruel or unusual punishment shall be inflicted; and no sentence of any military commission or tribunal hereby authorized, affecting the life or liberty of any person, shall be executed until it is approved by the officer in command of the district, and the laws and regulations for the government of the army shall not be affected by this act, except in so far as they conflict with its provisions: *Provided,* That no sentence of death under the provisions of this act shall be carried into effect without the approval of the President.

Sec. 5.   That when the people of any one of said rebel States shall have formed a constitution of government in conformity with the Constitution of the United States in all respects, framed by a convention of delegates elected by the male citizens of said State twenty-one years old and upward, of whatever race, color, or previous condition, who have been resident in said State for one year previous to the day of such election, except such as may be disfranchised for participation in the rebellion, or for felony at common law, and when such constitution shall provide that the elective franchise shall be enjoyed by all such persons as have the qualifications herein stated for electors of delegates, and when such constitution shall be ratified by a majority of the persons voting on the question of ratification who are qualified as electors for delegates, and when such constitution shall have been submitted to Congress for examination and approval, and Congress shall have approved the same, and when said State, by a vote of its legislature elected under said constitution, shall have adopted the amendment to the Constitution of the United States, proposed by the Thirty-ninth Congress, and known as article fourteen, and when said article shall have become a part of the Constitution of the United States, said State shall be declared entitled to representation in Congress, and Senators and Representatives shall be admitted therefrom on their taking the oaths prescribed by law, and then and thereafter the preceding sections of this act shall be inoperative in said State: *Provided,* That no person excluded from the privilege of holding office by said proposed amendment to the Constitution of the United States shall be eligible to election as a member of the convention to frame a constitution for any of said rebel States, nor shall any such person vote for members of such convention.

Sec. 6.   That until the people of said rebel States shall be by law admitted to representation in the Congress of the United States, any civil governments which may exist therein shall be deemed provisional only, and in all respects subject to the paramount authority of the United States at any time to abolish, modify, control, or supersede the same; and in all elections to any office under such provisional governments all persons shall be entitled to vote, and none others, who are entitled to vote under the provisions of the fifth section of this act; and no person shall be eligible to any office under any such provisional governments who would be disqualified from holding office under the provisions of the third article of said constitutional amendment.

Passed March 2, 1867.

Albion Tourgée, a North Carolina Republican, Later Condemns Congress's Reconstruction Policy, 1879

So it must have been well understood by the wise men who devised this short-sighted plan of electing a President beyond a peradventure of defeat, that they were giving the power of the re-organized, subordinate republics, into the hands of a race unskilled in public affairs, poor to a degree hardly to be matched in the civilized world, and so ignorant that not five out of a hundred of its voters could read their own ballots, joined

From Albion Tourgée, *A Fool's Errand* (Harper and Row Torchbook Edition, 1966 [1879]), pp. 136–137.

with such Adullamites among the native whites as might be willing to face a proscription which would shut the house of God in the face of their families, together with the few men of Northern birth, resident in that section since the close of the war,—either knaves or fools, or partaking of the nature of both,—who might elect to become permanent citizens, and join in the movement.

Against them was to be pitted the wealth, the intelligence, the organizing skill, the pride, and the hate of a people whom it had taken four years to conquer in open fight when their enemies outnumbered them three to one, who were animated chiefly by the apprehension of what seemed now about to be forced upon them by this miscalled measure of "Reconstruction"; to wit, the equality of the negro race.

It was done, too, in the face of the fact that within the preceding twelvemonth the white people of the South, by their representatives in the various Legislatures of the Johnsonian period, had absolutely refused to recognize this equality, even in the slightest matters, by *refusing to allow the colored people to testify in courts of justice* against white men, or to protect their rights of person and property in any manner from the avarice, lust, or brutality of their white neighbors. It was done in the very face of the "Black Codes," which were the first enactments of Provisional Legislatures, and which would have established a serfdom more complete than that of the Russian steppes before the *ukase* of Alexander.

And the men who devised this plan called themselves honest and wise states-men. More than one of them has since then hugged himself in gratulation under the belief, that, by his co-operation therein, he had cheaply achieved an immortality of praise from the liberty-lovers of the earth! After having forced a proud people to yield what they had for more than two centuries considered a right,—the right to hold the African race in bondage,—they proceeded to outrage a feeling as deep and fervent as the zeal of Islam or the exclusiveness of Hindoo caste, by giving to the ignorant, unskilled, and dependent race—a race who could not have lived a week without the support or charity of the dominant one—equality of political right! Not content with this, they went farther, and, by erecting the rebellious territory into self-regulating and sovereign States, they abandoned these parties like cocks in a pit, to fight out the question of predominance without the possibility of national interference. They said to the colored man, in the language of one of the pseudo-philosophers of that day, "Root, hog, or die!"

It was cheap patriotism, cheap philanthropy, cheap success!

ESSAYS

These two essays investigate the degree to which the congressional Republicans' approach to-ward the South was radical. The term *radical Reconstruction* is often used, but its accuracy is often questioned. In the first piece, Michael Les Benedict of Ohio State University claims that Republican policy was in fact far from radical; rather, it was characterized by conciliation and conservatism. The second essay, by Eric Foner of Columbia University, examines the views and policies of Thaddeus Stevens, one of the best known and probably the most consistently radical of the Republicans in Congress. It suggests that the positions he took, especially his ad-vocacy of confiscation of Confederates' land, were live possibilities under discussion within the party.

The Conservative Basis of Radical Reconstruction

MICHAEL LES BENEDICT

. . . [The purpose of this article is to] help explain why Reconstruction failed to achieve its goals and why so many Republicans appeared so quickly to abandon the struggle after 1869. [Indeed] historians may be mistaken when they refer to a retreat from Reconstruction [because t]he distaste of many Republicans for federal intervention in the South was manifest in the Reconstruction program itself. Although they insisted on guarantees for the security of loyal whites and blacks in the South and passed laws and constitutional amendments which appeared to delegate power to the national government to secure citizens' rights, most Republicans never desired a broad, permanent extension of national legislative power. Republicans framed the most limited, conservative Reconstruction possible, adhering until 1868 to the position that their legislation was merely a temporary aberration in the federal system. When continued violence in the South after 1868 forced many Republicans to endorse some permanent broadening of national power—a constitutional position which was truly radical—most Republicans tried to limit the degree of the expansion, and many others refused to make this new departure at all. Nor is it accurate to charge that the courts in interpreting Reconstruction legislation betrayed the principles and purposes of the Republicans who had framed it; rather they carried over to the judicial arena Republicans' reluctance to alter fundamentally the federal system.

Even as the exigencies of war forced the national government to exert broad, new powers, most Republican legalists justified wartime measures in such a way as to preserve the old balance of the Constitution. Rather than admitting that the war had precipitated a fundamental alteration in the federal system, they argued it merely had forced a suspension of peacetime constitutional provisions. Unionists reached this conclusion by different routes. Francis Lieber, the leading student of government in mid-nineteenth-century America, espoused the first interpretation: "The whole Rebellion is beyond the Constitution," he insisted. "The Constitution was not made for such a state of things. . . . [T]he life of a nation is the first substantial thing and far above the formulas [for government] which . . . have been adopted." The Constitution had been intended to serve a nation forged by a common heritage and experience before and during the War for Independence. That nation had to be preserved even if the Constitution was violated. A second school argued that the Constitution itself incorporated virtually unlimited war powers through the clause vesting in Congress the power to prosecute war (Art. 1, sec. 8). These powers were as much a part of the Constitution as its peacetime provisions, but in a state of war the war powers naturally became more prominent while other provisions receded into the background.

By justifying the massive wartime expansion of the national government's power in this way, Republicans believed they had preserved the Constitution from contamination. With war's end, the occasion for using the war powers—whether under the Constitution's authority or outside it—would cease. The limitations of the peacetime fundamental law would regain their sway.

The desire to preserve the federal system's prewar balance weighed heavily on the minds of leading Republicans. As early as 1861, a worried Republican Senator James

W. Grimes wrote fellow Senator Lyman Trumbull: "We are gradually surrendering all the rights of the states & functions & shall soon be incapable of resuming them." Five years later, as one of the respected members of the prestigious Joint Committee of Fifteen on Reconstruction, Grimes was insisting that "During the prevalence of the war we drew to ourselves here as the Federal Government authority which had been considered doubtful by all and denied by many of the statesmen of this country. That time, it seems to me, has ceased and ought to cease. Let us go back to the original condition of things, and allow the States to take care of themselves as they have been in the habit of taking care of themselves."

This kind of constitutional conservatism left Republicans ill prepared to cope with the complex problems of Reconstruction, which so clearly called at minimum for long-term national protection of citizens' rights. By 1865, Republicans had become so committed to the proposition that the national government's power would shrink to prewar dimensions at war's end that an immediate recognition of continued southern statehood upon the surrender of the rebel armies would have restored prewar state rights virtually intact, rendering the national government powerless to secure any guarantees of loyalty from the South. Because Republicans had refused during the war to acquiesce in a permanent expansion of national power at the expense of the states, they were in 1865 and 1866 forced to deny that the southern political organizations were as yet entitled to the rights of states. Therefore, the great constitutional controversy between President Andrew Johnson and his supporters and the Republican party centered on the constitutional issue of the status of the former southern states. . . .

Students of Reconstruction history are familiar with the theories of Reconstruction outlined by [William A.] Dunning, [John W.] Burgess, and other historians and recapitulated in most textbooks—the "southern," "presidential," "conquered provinces," "state suicide," and "forfeit rights" theories. Each of these was designed to fix the status of the former southern states and the degree of national power over them. All but the southern theory maintained that the southern states were either out of the Union *de facto* or had ceased to exist at all. Only if southern state organizations remained out of normal federal relations would the Republicans' claim of power for the national government over the South in Reconstruction be consistent with their wartime constitutional conservatism. Thus, Republicans clearly acknowledged that once the government recognized the restoration of the southern states they would enjoy the same relations with the national government as existed before the war. . . .

Having defined the status of the rebel states in a way that denied them immediate restoration to prewar rights, Republicans turned to three sources of national power over them. Thaddeus Stevens enunciated one alternative suggesting that, "as there are no symptoms that the people of these provinces will be prepared to participate in constitutional government for some years, I know of no arrangement so proper for them as territorial governments." [Then,] "They would be held in a territorial condition until they are fit to form State Constitutions, republican in fact not in form only, and ask admission into the Union as new States." In a certain sense, Congress' power over the South would indeed expand if Stevens' scheme were adopted. Congress had absolute control over territorial property of the United States subject only to the few general prohibitions the Constitution imposed on congressional power. In the 1860s Congress generally allowed territories to govern themselves through territorial legislatures, but their powers were derived from and subject directly to that of Congress. And territorial governors were appointed by the President with the advice and consent of the Senate. But this power over the South would not be permanent; it would cease with statehood. In fact, it was precisely because Congress lost its power once the "territories" were readmitted as states that special care had to be taken to see that they had learned their lessons: "If Congress approve their Constitutions, and think they have done works meet for repentance they would be admitted as new states," suggested Stevens. "If their Constitutions are not approved of, they would be sent back, until they have become wise enough so to purge their old laws as to eradicate every despotic and revolutionary principle. . . ." Nor could Congress force permanent changes on an unwilling people. The sole hope for a permanent rearrangement of the southern political, economic, and social order lay in southerners themselves voluntarily agreeing to such changes in return for statehood. "If they are to be admitted as new States they must form their own constitutions; and no enabling act could dictate its terms," Stevens insisted.

Although many Radicals preferred Stevens' territorial policy to establish congressional control over the South, his program met with such a negative response from non-Radical Republicans that when he presented a Reconstruction bill to the House in 1867 it bore no resemblance to his earlier suggestion.

Republicans discerned a second source of congressional power over Reconstruction in Congress' war powers. Building consciously on the legal-constitutional justifications for expanded national power developed during the war, these Republicans suggested that, although peace would indeed restore the sway of peacetime constitutional limitations on the national government, it was up to the government to decide precisely when peace had arrived. In that case the government might demand that the rebel states meet certain conditions in return for recognition that peace was restored. This view was popularized by the conservative Richard Henry Dana in a speech delivered in Faneuil Hall on June 21, 1865: *"The conquering party may hold the other in the grasp of war until it has secured whatever it has a right to acquire,"* he maintained. This theory was received with favor in Boston. Ohio's new governor, Jacob D. Cox, House speaker Schuyler Colfax, Senator Fessenden, Representative George S. Boutwell, also named to the Reconstruction Committee, Representative William Lawrence of the House Judiciary Committee, and Carl Schurz all expressed views similar to Dana's.

Like the theory of temporarily expanded national power in time of war from which it sprang, the grasp of war doctrine was designed to protect the federal system from fundamental, permanent change as a result of crisis. The federal system, Dana warned, "is held together by a balance of powers—centripetal and centrifugal forces. Let not their balance be destroyed." By simply continuing military occupation this danger could be avoided. "If we should undertake to exercise sovereign civil jurisdiction over those States, it would be as great a peril to our system as it would be a hardship upon them."

So like Stevens' territorial scheme, the grasp of war policy gave no permanent power to Congress. Dana had proposed a consciously conservative program. As he wrote to Charles Francis Adams, Jr., immediately after his speech, "It would be an irreparable mischief for Congress to assume civil and political authority in state matters, but it is not an irreparable mischief for the general government to continue the exercise of such war powers as are necessary until the people of those States do what we in conscience think necessary for the reasonable security of the republic. . . ."

Not only did Congress gain no power under Dana's doctrine, but even while the South remained in the "grasp of war," Congress' prerogatives were strictly limited. The people of the southern states themselves were "voluntarily" to give guarantees of security through their own legislation. This might be done under the pressure of continued exclusion from the Union, but the guarantees were to be achieved through state rather than national legislation. Thus, both Stevens' and Dana's proposals not only left ultimate power to protect citizens' rights with the states, but even during the period of Reconstruction maintained a fiction of voluntarism around state action in meeting conditions for a restoration of peace and normal relations. Even during the crisis Congress could not presume to dictate state action.

Republicans found a third source of congressional power in the duty the Constitution imposed on the national government to guarantee to the states republican forms of government. Republicans who argued that the southern states had ceased to exist during the war particularly favored this theory. If there were no state governments at all in the South, then "manifestly, the first step after the war ended was for someone to establish a local government there." And this duty the guarantee clause placed on the national government.

This was the only constitutional basis for Reconstruction which could promise the national government permanent power, even after the rebel states were restored to normal relations. Some Republicans felt it assumed a standard of republicanism and gave the national government power to enforce that standard whenever a state—any state—fell short of it. But few Republicans endorsed such a radical expansion of national power. In 1867 the House of Representatives agreed to a resolution instructing the Judiciary Committee to investigate "whether the States of Kentucky, Maryland, and Delaware now have State governments republican in form." Such resolutions normally passed without Republican opposition as they embodied no actual legislation, but on this occasion twenty-two Republicans joined Democrats in opposition. The committee took testimony and evidence but let the matter die. Several Republicans proposed bills based on the guarantee clause in efforts to extend universal male suffrage and protect its exercise throughout the Union, but none passed or even won endorsement by a committee.

Although Republicans regularly pointed in campaign speeches to the guarantee clause as somehow sanctioning their Reconstruction policy, they were reluctant to base their actual legislation on it. Instead they used it as a vague guide in setting the conditions that southern states had to meet before Congress would recognize them as entitled to normal state rights. Most Republicans relied on the grasp of war doctrine to justify their Reconstruction legislation, and in so doing they employed the narrowest, most conservative theory of the three available—the one which virtually sanctified "the federal system as it was."

Republicans twice formulated conditions for the southern states to meet before Congress would recognize their restoration. Each time they conditioned restoration on the voluntary passage of state legislation, stolidly preserving the states as the primary authors of legislation, firmly refusing to force compliance through exercise of national power. And southern reaction demonstrated that this "voluntarism" was more than illusory.

The first set of conditions were the propositions embraced in the Fourteenth Amendment to the Constitution, framed in 1866. Holding that "the conquered rebels were at the mercy of the conquerors," the Joint Committee on Reconstruction offered the amendment under "a most perfect right to exact indemnity for injuries done and security against the recurrence of such outrages in the future." Written by Fessenden, the committee's report closely paralleled Dana's views. The report emphasized the temporary nature of the exclusion of the southern states and conceded the "distracting and demoralizing" tendency of such a state of affairs. The dangerous situation would end, the committee implied, when the southern states signified their agreement to the conditions embodied in the Fourteenth Amendment by ratifying it.

More than the mere method of proposing the Fourteenth Amendment manifested Republicans' fundamental constitutional conservatism. By the very terms of the Fourteenth Amendment, Republicans once again demonstrated their overriding desire to preserve for the states the primary responsibility for the protection of citizens' rights. The initial section, which for the first time defined American citizenship and guaranteed citizens' rights, did not itself expand the national government's jurisdiction in areas traditionally left to the states. Its language recognized implicitly that states continued to be the primary source of the legislation which regulated citizens' rights and duties. The amendment limited states' alternatives in framing and possibly administering laws involving these rights; it did not transfer to the national government the power to frame all laws touching on them. No longer could states pass laws which denied or abridged the privileges and immunities of United States citizens, or which deprived any person of life, liberty, or property without due process of law, or which denied equality before the law. Possibly, states could not informally administer laws unequally. But this interpretation trod upon the farthest limit of the amendment. So long as the states did none of these things, the national government had no more power in areas of traditional state jurisdiction than it had before the war. "The political system of this Republic rests upon the right of the people to control their local concerns in their several states . . . ," affirmed Carl Schurz in a speech defending the Amendment. "This system was not to be changed in the work of reconstruction."

Republicans understood the dangers inherent in their first, conservative Reconstruction plan. Many of them feared that, without political power, blacks might be victimized by restored governments in the hands of former rebels. Given the political situation in spring 1866, however, Republicans felt they could not retain power if they presented more extreme conditions for restoration. In an effort to minimize the danger, they passed two bills which appeared to mark radical changes in the relations between the states and the national government.

The Freedmen's Bureau bill and the Civil Rights bill both seemed to place the rights of the newly freed slaves under the protection of the national government. Yet, even with the prospect of restored, white, former rebel-dominated state governments facing them, Republicans refused to offer blacks the permanent protection they realized was needed. Offered by the conservative constitutionalist Lyman Trumbull, the Freedmen's Bureau bill was avowedly a temporary measure, based primarily on Congress' war powers, a measure the authority for which would cease soon after the southern states were restored to the Union, the very time the freedmen would need its protection most. Despite this conservatism, Republican Senate leader Fessenden barely could bring himself to support the measure, acquiescing in its passage only after personal discussions with Trumbull.

The Civil Rights bill promised to stir even more doubts. It was manifestly a peacetime measure, to be passed by virtue of Congress' power under the second section of the Thirteenth Amendment to enforce emancipation by appropriate legislation. As originally presented, the bill declared the inhabitants of every state and territory entitled to certain fundamental rights without regard to color or previous status and made it a crime for anyone to deny these rights under the cover of law. All violations of the bill were to be tried in United States district courts. Most important, any person who could not secure the rights guaranteed under the bill in state or local courts could transfer his case to the United States district or circuit courts in his locality. Other sections of the bill outlined enforcement procedures. Later Trumbull added a provision conferring citizenship on all persons of African descent born in the United States.

On its face the Civil Rights bill radically expanded national power. For the first time the national government accepted the responsibility for protecting the rights of its citizens. Under the bill national courts might try cases of every description, civil and criminal, wherever state and local courts did not grant all citizens equal protection in the rights guaranteed by the bill. This broad, apparently radical bill was patently inconsistent with Trumbull's political conservatism on Reconstruction matters and his constitutional conservatism generally. But in fact Trumbull had found a way to preserve rather than alter the old federal system.

Although theoretically Trumbull's bill vastly expanded the duties of the national government, in fact these new duties would not be permanent. The bill was to provide the threat of national assumption of jurisdiction over civil rights in order to force states to fulfill that role themselves. Court jurisdiction was the key to the bill's real purpose. Jurisdiction would be taken from the state courts only so long as they enforced state laws or court procedures which discriminated in the rights guaranteed to all inhabitants by the first section of the Civil Rights bill. Once the states enforced these rights equally, there could be no removal of jurisdiction from state to national courts. Thus there would be great pressure on states to change their laws in order to regain their old spheres of jurisdiction. There would be no point in resisting. Retain unequal law or procedures and blacks would simply take their cases into the federal courts.

Trumbull had found a way to force the states themselves to alter their discriminatory laws. Once they did, they would regain jurisdiction over all their citizens, and the balance of power between the state and national governments would remain unchanged. Trumbull emphasized this in his defense of the measure:

> [The bill] may be assailed as drawing to the Federal Government powers that properly belong to "States"; but I apprehend, rightly considered, it is not obnoxious to that objection. It will have no operation in any State where the laws are equal, where all persons have the same civil rights without regard to color or race.

The goal of the first Republican program of Reconstruction was to protect freedmen's rights in the South with the minimum possible coercion of white southerners and least possible alteration of the traditional boundaries of state and federal jurisdiction. Despite its manifest conservatism, southerners rejected this first offer of conditions precedent to restoration; only Tennessee chose to ratify the proposed constitutional amendment, and Republicans quickly responded by recognizing the state's return to normal rights and privileges in the Union.

Faced with southern intransigence and growing public impatience, Republicans framed a second plan of Reconstruction in February 1867. In 1866 the Reconstruction Committee had been willing to restore the rebel-dominated state organizations erected under the guidance of President Johnson in return for ratification of the constitutional amendment. In the Military Government bill, which the committee reported to Congress in 1867, the Johnson governments were expressly disavowed and the southern people remanded to the direct control of the military authorities (who could utilize civil tribunals and officers if they wished, however). The plan seemed to justify Stevens' conquered province theory of southern status, but in fact it was proposed by two conservative Republicans, Senator George H. Williams and Representative Roscoe Conkling. Stevens fought for this bill so tenaciously that possibly he saw it as an opening wedge for his views on "territorialization," but other Republicans believed, with Representative Augustus Brandegee, that it simply "holds those revolted communities in the grasp of war until the rebellion shall have laid down its spirit, as two years ago it formally laid down its arms," until, in John A. Bingham's words, "those people return to their loyalty and fealty in such a manner as shall satisfy the people of the United States, . . . represented in Congress, of their fitness to be restored to their full constitutional relations."

Fearing the Military Government bill might lead to a long period of exclusion, conservative Republicans in the House, led by Bingham and James G. Blaine, offered an amendment "to notify [southern whites] in the most solemn form . . . that . . . all they have to do, in order to get rid of military rule and military government, is to present to the Congress of the United States a constitutional form of State government in accord with the letter and spirit of the Constitution and laws of the United States, together with a ratification of the pending constitutional amendment." Defeated in the House, the so-called "Blaine amendment" succeeded in the Senate where it was offered by the conservative Republican Senator John Sherman. The bill as finally passed promised restoration on four conditions: the people of each southern state had to frame a new constitution at a convention elected by universal male suffrage; the constitution had to be ratified in a second election; the new constitution had to provide for equal male suffrage; and the state legislature elected under the new constitution had to ratify the Fourteenth Amendment.

Dana happily recognized in this bill the vindication of his doctrine of Reconstruction. "[I]t is on the principle which I had the honor to be the first to lay down in my Faneuil Hall speech of June, 1865,—what my flattering friends call my 'Grasp-of-war Speech',," he wrote proudly. "Not that my speech had any agency in the result, but that the result justifies it." Hardly a constitutional defense of the bill was made that did not justify it on these grounds.

Like the first Reconstruction plan, the Reconstruction Act called for voluntary state action under the threat of continued exclusion and military government if the state refused. As [Representative James A.] Garfield put it, "Congress shall place civil Governments before these people of the rebel States, and a cordon of bayonets behind them."

The major conditions Congress demanded the southern states meet before being released from "the grasp of war" were the ratification of the Fourteenth Amendment and the enfranchisement of their male black citizens. Because the Reconstruction Act required black suffrage historians have generally viewed it as a true embodiment of radical principles. By imposing Negro suffrage on recalcitrant southerners, historians have believed, Radical Republicans demonstrated their willingness to disregard traditional lines of state and national authority. But in fact by 1867 the argument for black suffrage was distinctly conservative. Republicans were unwilling to leave black Americans at the mercy of former rebels; they were equally unwilling permanently to extend the power of the national government to protect them. As Edwin L. Godkin, editor of the

Nation, explained, "our Government owes to those who can get it no other way that one thing for which all governments exist . . .—security for person and property. This . . . we can supply either by the provision of a good police or by the admission of the blacks to such a share in the management of state affairs that they can provide a police for themselves. The former of these courses is not strictly in accordance with the spirit of our institutions; the latter is."

The enfranchisement of black men in the southern states, then, was the one measure which would provide security for the Union and its loyal southern supporters and yet allow Reconstruction to continue on a conservative constitutional basis. "Far from desiring centralization repulsive to the genius of this country, it is in the distinct interest of local self-government and legitimate State rights that we urge these propositions," wrote Schurz, "and nothing can be more certain than that this is the only way in which a dangerous centralization of power in the hands of our general government can be prevented." As the *Nation* pointed out, Negro suffrage "though brought forward as a radical remedy . . . is anything but radical."

Only as the Reconstruction process neared completion did many Republicans finally realize its essential weakness. As southerners met Congress' conditions and pressed for restoration in 1868, Republicans suspected that their compliance with the Reconstruction acts was more apparent than real. "You are hastening back States where rebelism is pervading them from end to end," complained an outspoken Radical. The grasp of war theory had worked too well, perhaps. In many states southerners had met the conditions set forth in the Reconstruction acts not out of reawakened loyalty or new devotion to racial justice but out of a simple desire to be rid of the national presence. Radicals who recognized the weakness of the loyal forces in the South urged delay in restoration. In reality, "there are not ten men in this Senate who believe it is a safe thing to do at this time," Timothy Otis Howe charged. Other Radicals agreed, but political necessities required readmission.

Realizing the futility of trying to delay restoration, many Republicans finally decided on an effort to guarantee permanence to the new political order in the South. As a new "fundamental condition" for readmission, Republicans insisted southern states agree never to alter the basis of suffrage in their new constitutions. For the first time Republicans were trying to gain a measure of permanent power for the national government to protect the rights of its citizens in the South. In doing so, they were forced to abandon the grasp of war theory under which they had thus far proceeded. Some, like the respected constitutionalist, Senator George F. Edmunds, turned at last to the guarantee clause. The power to guarantee republican forms of government to states, he argued, was "plenary and absolute," and therefore Congress clearly had the power "to put that government in such a form that it shall 'stay put'. . . ." But the guarantee clause justification implied a sweeping alteration in national-state relations. Radical Illinois Senator Richard Yates brought this home to his colleagues in his defense of the guarantee clause:

> When the question arises whether a constitution is republican in form, who decides it? Congress. May not Congress say that no constitution is republican in form which excludes any large class of people from voting . . . ?
> If New York excludes any portion of her citizens who bear arms and pay taxes from the right of suffrage, hers is not, according to our republican theory, a government republican in form. Congress, not the States, decide that question.

But most Republicans who favored the imposition of new fundamental conditions preferred a more restrained justification. Led by William M. Stewart, the second-ranking Republican on the Senate Judiciary Committee, they drew a parallel between the restoration of the southern states and the admission of new states, insisting that Congress had regularly exacted concessions from petitioning territories in return for grants of statehood. Although these unhappy Republicans perceived that their new theory inevitably implied expansion of national power, they intended to keep that expansion to the absolute minimum. Republicans did not include any provisions for enforcing the conditions if violated, hoping they would be self-enforcing. Even Stewart finally conceded that "I do not pretend to say that the insertion of this declaration in the bill [to restore the southern states] will alter either the constitution of the State or of the General Government." It was merely "a declaration of principle, which has generally been respected."

This hesitant, timorous attempt to provide permanent national power to protect rights precipitated the first of the series of intra-Republican confrontations on constitutional questions which would mark Reconstruction legislation of the post-1868 era. Conservative constitutionalists in the Republican party, including the very architects of congressional Reconstruction—Fessenden, Trumbull, and Conkling—were unprepared to cooperate in this new attempt to limit state prerogatives. "[T]he States have the right to alter or amend their Constitutions at pleasure . . . ," they insisted. Once restored to the Union, a southern state "will have the same power to regulate the question of suffrage that the State of New York has, unquestionably." A motion to eliminate the "fundamental conditions" from the resolution restoring Arkansas to the Union failed by only one vote in the Senate, despite the overwhelming Republican majority there. . . .

Republicans never shook off their state-centeredness. In passing the Force Act of 1871—constitutionally far more radical than previous legislation—they progressed to the position that Congress could step in to protect citizens' rights when states failed to do so as well as when states positively discriminated, but Republicans would not agree to the proposition that Congress had acquired direct, permanent jurisdiction over citizens' rights through the Fourteenth Amendment. Republicans were circumscribed not only by their continuing reluctance to alter the balance of federalism but by their past conservatism as well. They remembered how carefully they had limited the scope of the constitutional amendments, how tender their concern had been to preserve old areas of state jurisdiction. When Bingham was finally driven to new ground by southern intransigence and argued for the broadest interpretation of congressional powers under the Fourteenth Amendment, James A. Garfield gently reminded him, "My colleague can make but not unmake history." The limits on congressional power had been set by Republicans' earlier conservatism. Those limits could not be undone. Even Radical Charles Sumner, struggling to pass his new, broad Civil Rights bill from 1870 until his death in 1874, had to argue that the discrimination he sought to eliminate in inns, theaters, carriers, and cemeteries was somehow sanctioned by state law. Given this continuing conservatism, it appears that historians might characterize Republicans' final decision in 1877 to cease attempting to protect citizens' rights in the South through national power more aptly as a consequence than a betrayal of their principles of 1865–1868.

The disastrous consequences of Republican conservatism in Reconstruction legislation are readily apparent. Congress withdrew its protection of southern citizens in 1877, unwilling any longer to exercise powers Republicans had so purposefully tried to avoid before 1868. The federal courts followed suit. Judges and justices, most of whom as

Republicans remembered well the circumstances surrounding the passage and ratification of the constitutional amendments, carefully preserved the state jurisdiction upon which Republicans had been so unwilling to encroach. Accepting the Republican position that the national government could protect citizens whose rights to equal protection of the laws were deprived either through state action or failure to act, lower federal courts and ultimately the Supreme Court rigorously scrutinized congressional legislation to make certain it stayed within those boundaries. And when the loosely worded Force Act of 1871 and Civil Rights Act of 1875 came before them, the perhaps overly cautious courts found both to exceed the constitutional limits with which their framers had intended to comply. Even today, it is only with the utmost reluctance that our national government will intervene to protect citizens' rights within states. After 100 years, the constitutional conservatism which prevented Republicans from protecting adequately the rights of citizens remains a part of American political character.

Thaddeus Stevens, Confiscation, and Reconstruction

ERIC FONER

In the history of American politics, Thaddeus Stevens is something of an anomaly. As a self-proclaimed radical, he seemed out of place at the center of a political system which—with the glaring exception of the Civil War—has perennially prided itself on its ability to resolve disputes without resort to extreme measures. Historians have found Stevens a baffling figure, whose unusual complexity of motivations and unique blend of idealism with political opportunism made him almost impossible to categorize. The most perceptive of his contemporaries described him simply as a revolutionary—or at least the closest thing to one imaginable in American politics. To a British observer, he was "the Robespierre, Danton, and Marat of America, all rolled into one." And a leading American newspaper attributed his influence in the 1860s to the nation's having undergone a political and social revolution which "demanded revolutionary qualities" of its leaders—qualities Stevens seemed to have in abundance.

Only an unparalleled crisis like the Civil War could have brought a man like Stevens to the fore. His personal characteristics—cynicism, courage, imperviousness to criticism or flattery, brutal honesty, and willingness to use daring and even outrageous means to achieve his ends—were as necessary in wartime as they seemed inappropriate in peace. And Stevens's combination of genuine idealism with a pragmatism learned in the school of Pennsylvania politics enabled him to recognize and articulate the policies which Union victory required. While Lincoln declared his conviction that the war must not degenerate into "a violent and remorseless revolutionary struggle," Stevens saw that this was precisely what it must become. From the outset he insisted that only the seemingly draconian measures of freeing and arming the slaves and seizing the property of the leading rebels could produce victory. In Congress, as chairman of the House Committee on Ways and Means, Stevens became "the master-spirit of every aggressive movement . . . to overthrow the Rebellion and slavery." By the end of the war he had acquired a national reputation as the radical of radicals, and at an age when most men have retired

From *The Hofstadter Aegis: A Memorial* by Stanley Elkins and Eric McKitrick, eds. Copyright © 1974 by Alfred A. Knopf, Inc. Reprinted by permission of the publisher.

from active pursuits—he was seventy-three in 1865—Stevens embarked on the most important phase of his career.

Any attempt to analyze Stevens's role in Reconstruction is immediately confronted with a paradox. Many historians of the period have depicted him as the dictator of the House and the major architect of Reconstruction. Even such hard-headed contemporary political leaders as James G. Blaine and Justin Morrill viewed him as "the animating spirit and unquestioned leader" of the House of Representatives. Stevens was certainly a master of parliamentary tactics. More than once he bullied the House into passing measures by choosing just the right moment to call the previous question, cutting off debate and forcing a vote. His quick tongue and sarcastic wit, moreover, made his colleagues of both parties consciously avoid tangling with him in debate. As one of them remarked, "I would sooner get into difficulty with a porcupine."

And yet if Stevens was a political "dictator," his power was strangely limited. In Pennsylvania he was never able to challenge the Republican kingpins, Simon Cameron and Andrew Curtin, for control of the party machinery; and even in the House, as one puzzled newspaper observed, "no man was oftener outvoted." In addition, as recent research has made clear, the major Reconstruction legislation was the work of no one man or faction but the result of a complex series of legislative compromises and maneuvers in which moderate Senators and Congressmen had as much influence as radicals like Stevens.

Stevens was in fact not a dictator, but neither was he just another Republican politician. In a period of intense political and ideological crisis, his function was to outline a radical position toward which events would force the party to move, and to project the conditions under which change would occur. At a time when every Congress witnessed a high turnover of Representatives, Stevens had a career of service stretching back into the 1850s. He could remind younger colleagues that he had been through the revolution from the beginning, and could speak of the times when southerners like "the mighty Toombs, with his shaggy locks, headed a gang who, with shouts of defiance, rendered this a hell of legislation." Throughout the Civil War, Stevens would stake out a position, confidently predicting that the nation would move leftward and adopt it within a year or two, and usually he was right. As a newspaper in his home district in Pennsylvania declared, "In all the leading questions of the late war, Mr. Stevens has been in advance of his compeers, but the Government has eventually seen the necessity of giving practical effect to his views of the national policy."

Stevens, then, was "a man absolutely convinced, and in a sense rightly, that he and history were for the moment in perfect step." His record of having been proved right by events helps explain why, when Stevens rose to speak, the House fell uncommonly quiet, the galleries quickly filled, Senators often dropped their work to attend, and, as a freshman Congressman commented, "everyone expects something worth hearing." And yet by the very nature of his leadership Stevens was most effective in providing his party with means, rather than ends. During the Civil War, Republicans eventually came to agree with Stevens that freeing and arming the slaves was the only way to achieve the unquestioned goal of Union victory. And during Reconstruction, Stevens would be most successful when his proposals seemed to provide ways of moving toward the party's commonly held goals of Republican ascendancy in the national government, protection of the basic rights of the freedmen, and reorganization of southern governments under the control of genuinely loyal men. Thus as events convinced Republicans that Stevens's proposals, including civil rights and suffrage for the freedmen, a period of military rule in the South, and even the impeachment of the President, were necessary for the achievement of their basic aims, they would follow Stevens—or at least move to the positions he had outlined. But Stevens failed completely in pressing for the confiscation and redistribution of the lands of the leading rebels, because he was unable to convince his party that such a policy was either an essential goal or an acceptable means to other ends.

The issue of confiscation had roots stretching back to the first years of the Civil War, when abolitionists and radical Republicans first linked the goal of landownership for southern blacks with that of emancipation. And as the war progressed, increasing numbers of Republicans were converted to the view that the confiscation of rebel property would be a legitimate war measure. The first Confiscation Act, of August 1861, was directed only against property used in aid of the rebellion, but in 1862 Congress enacted a far more sweeping measure, declaring all property of rebels liable to confiscation. President Lincoln, who strongly opposed widespread confiscation, forced Congress to pass an explanatory resolution, limiting the seizure of land to the lifetime of the owner. Only a handful of Republicans, Stevens among them, voted in opposition. The debates of 1862 indicated that while a majority of Republicans were willing to use confiscation as a war measure and a way of attacking slavery, far fewer envisioned a sweeping revolution of land tenure in the South.

As the war progressed, however, the idea of permanent land confiscation gained wider support. In 1864 and 1865, Stevens and the veteran land reformer George W. Julian led a fight in Congress to repeal the joint resolution of 1862 and authorize the permanent seizure of rebel lands. By the end of the war both Houses, by narrow margins and in votes on different measures, had repealed the 1862 resolution. But no joint measure was ever enacted. The Freedmen's Bureau bill, passed in March 1865, did contain a provision assigning to freedmen and white refugees forty acres of confiscated or abandoned land, although the land was to be rented for three years and there was no promise of permanent ownership. Meanwhile, though the Lincoln administration had left the Confiscation Act of 1862 virtually unenforced, thousands of acres of abandoned land had fallen into government hands, and General Sherman's famous order settling freedmen on such land in South Carolina and Georgia seemed to some to presage a general policy of establishing the blacks on homesteads.

At the outset of Reconstruction, therefore, the Republican party had taken some steps toward Stevens's goal of providing land to the freedmen from the estates of the planter aristocracy. But even in wartime the party had not overcome its inhibitions about such a policy, and once Union victory had been achieved, the notion to many Republicans became unthinkable. For confiscation flew in the face of too many basic tenets of the ideology which had carried the Republicans into the Civil War and which had emerged unchanged, even strengthened, by the war experience. To a party which believed that a free laborer, once accorded equality of opportunity, would rise or fall in the social scale on the strength of his own diligence, frugality, and hard work, confiscation seemed an unwarranted interference with the rights of property and an unacceptable example of special privilege and class legislation.

And yet there were values and aspirations, shared by most Republicans, to which Stevens could and did appeal in an attempt to build a pro-confiscation coalition. Republicans were committed to restricting the power of the planters, protecting the rights of the freedmen, and transforming the South into a democratic (and Republican) society. During the congressional debates of 1865–67 most radical Republicans, and an increasing number of moderates, viewed black suffrage as the most effective means of achieving these goals and of obviating the need for massive federal intervention in the South. Stevens, however, challenged the idea that the impoverished and despised former slaves could immediately become independent voters. As he admitted to the House early in 1866, Stevens did not want Negro suffrage enacted for a few years. If the southern states were readmitted to the Union before the federal Constitution was altered to guarantee black rights and before the freedmen were given the economic wherewithal to establish their independence from economic coercion, the verdict of the Civil War would be undone: "They will give the suffrage to their menials, their house servants, those that they can control, and elect whom they please to make our laws. This is not the kind of suffrage I want."

Stevens thus insisted that it was unrealistic to expect the freedmen to challenge effectively the political dominance of the South's traditional ruling class. John Andrew, the war governor of Massachusetts, who shared Stevens's perception, drew from it the inference that the only stable basis of reunion was an understanding between Republican leaders and "the natural leaders of opinion in the South"—a preview of the policy which would end Reconstruction in 1877. Stevens drew precisely the opposite conclusion. Realizing that emancipation had not destroyed the planter class, whose wealth rested not only on slaveholding but on control of prime black belt lands, he urged that such lands be confiscated. The franchise by itself, he insisted, would not really touch the blacks' basic problems: "homesteads to them are far more valuable than the immediate right of suffrage, though both are their due." Most Republicans would reverse the proposition, as did the radical Congressman James Ashley of Ohio. "If I were a black man," Ashley declared, "with the chains just stricken from my limbs, without home to shelter me or mine, and you should offer me the ballot, or a cabin and forty acres of cotton land, I would take the ballot." Only George Julian, Wendell Phillips, and, occasionally, Benjamin F. Butler and Charles Sumner, stressed the land question, and none did so as consistently and forcefully as Stevens. Phillips, indeed, did not come around to this view until 1866, though when he did, he argued it much in the way Stevens had done: "You cannot govern the South against its educated classes, with their social prestige. If they cannot be hung nor exiled, they must be flanked. . . . Four millions of uneducated negroes, with none of that character which results from position, with none of that weight which comes from one or two generations of recognized manhood, cannot outweigh that element at the South."

Confiscation, for Stevens, thus had two related goals. One was to destroy the power of the planter class; the other, to create a new class of black and white yeomen as the basis of future southern political and social power, and as allies of the Republican middle class of the North. Revolutionary as such a proposal may have been, it could be defended as the corollary of a traditional, widely shared value—the conviction that democratic institutions must rest on an industrious middle class. Stevens had always paid homage to the ideal of the yeoman republic. As he declared in 1850, "the middling classes who own the soil, and work it with their own hands, are the main support of every free government." Stevens's complete lack of racial prejudice was evident in his assumption that distributing land to blacks would make them middle-class yeomen; that their social position, morals, and psychology were the outgrowth of slavery, not of racial inferiority, and could therefore be altered. But he also recognized that in view of the legacy of slavery and the hostility of southern whites, the traditional American ideal of success through thrift and hard work simply could not apply while the former slaves remained under their present disadvantages. But confiscation, he argued, could achieve a whole panoply of results central to the Republican ethos:

> Nothing is so likely to make a man a good citizen as to make him a freeholder. Nothing will so multiply the productions of the South as to divide it into small farms. Nothing will make men so industrious and moral as to let them feel that they are above want and are the owners of the soil which they till. . . . No people will ever be republican in spirit and practice where a few own immense manors and the masses are landless. Small independent landholders are the support and guardians of republican liberty.

There were other arguments as well [for] confiscation. For one thing, the seizure of planter lands would be a fitting punishment for the architects of the rebellion, those "who have murdered our brothers, our fathers, and our children." If the lands of the planter class, moreover, were seized and forty acres allotted to each freedman, there would still remain hundreds of millions of acres—90 per cent of the land, in fact—which could be sold to help pay the national debt, reduce taxes, and provide pensions for Union soldiers and reimbursement for loyal citizens whose property had been destroyed during the war (of whom there were many in Stevens's home area of southern Pennsylvania). It would be, moreover, in Wendell Phillips's words, merely "naked justice to the former slave," whose uncompensated labor had cleared and cultivated the southern land and who was certainly entitled to "a share of his inheritance." But Stevens's basic appeal was to the remodeling of southern society: the transformation of an alien, undemocratic, severely stratified social order into a prosperous, democratic, and loyal republic. "The whole fabric of southern society," he declared in 1865, "*must* be changed, and never can it be done if this opportunity is lost."

Stevens seems to have assumed that such a desire was widely shared in the Republican party. And there was certainly some evidence for that assumption. Long before the Civil War, anti-slavery northerners had developed an extensive critique of the southern social order and had declared their wish that the South might be transformed into a society more akin to that of the North and West. And most Republicans in the early years of Reconstruction shared Carl Schurz's view that "a free labor society must be established and built up on the ruins of the slave labor society." But far fewer were prepared to accept confiscation as the means to this end, both because Stevens's plan conflicted with some basic Republican values and because the creation of a black yeoman middle class was not what important elements of the party had in mind for the economic future of the South. Republicans in Boston, New York, and Philadelphia (the ante-bellum centers of the cotton trade), as well as other northerners who hoped to invest in the post-war South, tended to favor the speedy revival of the cotton plantation system, with northern capital and migrants supplanting the former slaveholders. Blacks would remain an essentially propertyless plantation labor force, whose basic legal rights would be recognized but who would hardly be in a position to challenge propertied whites for political and economic dominance. When the New York *Times,* the leading spokesman for this view, spoke of the South's need for a "prosperous yeomanry," it was quick to add, "very many of them will be northerners."

Another group of Republicans, more willing to grant complete legal and political equality to the freedmen, looked to a wider economic transformation of the South, including the creation of a diversified, industrializing economy. But again, the South was to be rebuilt under the auspices of northern capital and settlers. This was the view, for instance, of Horace Greeley's New York *Tribune,* the *Nation,* and spokesmen for Pennsylvania's iron industry. Greeley insisted that what the South needed most was not talk of confiscation, which would paralyze investment and economic development, but an influx of northern capital, settlers, and industrial skills. And Congressman William "Pig Iron" Kelley of Pennsylvania, after touring the South in 1867 and extolling the region's economic resources and latent wealth, concluded, "The South must be regenerated and we of the North must do it."

Stevens was never able to make confiscation palatable to such Republicans. He feared, indeed, that the quick economic reconstruction of the South under northern auspices was likely to leave the freedmen no better off than under continued planter domination. He may have been influenced by the arguments of George Julian, who in 1864 and 1865 repeatedly pointed to the danger that confiscated and abandoned lands would be swallowed up by northern speculators. In Louisiana, under the direction of General Nathaniel P. Banks, freedmen had been put to work on plantations controlled by such men in "a system of enforced and uncompensated labor." If this was any indication of the economic future of the South, it appeared that "in place of the slaveholding landowner . . . we shall have the grasping monopolist of the North, whose dominion over the freedmen and poor whites will be more galling than slavery itself."

That Stevens was less interested than other Republicans in speedy southern economic development under northern auspices was amply demonstrated during Reconstruction. He fought unsuccessfully in 1866 for a constitutional amendment authorizing an export tax on cotton—hardly the sort of measure investors in southern cotton plantations were likely to support. When Kelley pleaded for aid to a northern-owned railroad, on the ground that railroad development would aid the destitute freedmen of the region, Stevens scoffed: "May I ask my friend how many of these starving people he thinks are stockholders in this road?" And in 1868 he and Julian endorsed a measure, which passed the House but was killed in the Senate, declaring federal land grants to railroads in four southern states forfeited and open to black and white settlers.

Because he was an iron manufacturer and supporter of a protective tariff, many historians have pictured Stevens as a conscious agent of northern capitalism, bent on establishing the North's economic hegemony over the South. But northern business interests did not see it that way. As one Philadelphia businessman complained, after learning of Stevens's opposition to a federal bankruptcy law to aid business in the South, "he seems to oppose any measure that will not benefit the *nigger.*"

The combination of ideological and economic obstacles to confiscation became fully apparent after Stevens, in September 1865, outlined his views on Reconstruction in a widely reprinted speech. Only a handful of Republicans endorsed his program, the most cordial reaction being that of an editor who told Stevens that the speech itself had been well received, "with the exception of your extreme views on confiscation. Some object to going as far in that measure as you purpose." Stevens, however, was not the sort to be disheartened by criticism. When Congress convened in December 1865, he introduced and the House quickly passed a resolution directing General O. O. Howard, superintendent of the Freedmen's Bureau, to report how much property under his jurisdiction had been returned to its owners, and "under what pretense of authority." Stevens's purpose was to make plain that President Johnson's lenient pardon and amnesty policies and his insistence that all land which had not been sold be returned to its pardoned owners were leading to wholesale evictions of blacks from abandoned lands on which they had been settled. Howard's reply, which was not ready until April, made the impact of Johnson's policies plain: virtually all the land under Bureau authority had been restored to the former rebels, while the amount in black hands was minuscule.

Even before Howard's report had been received, Stevens introduced a confiscation measure in the House. The occasion was the bill extending the life of the Freedmen's Bureau. Introduced by the moderate Senator Lyman Trumbull, the bill had wide support among Republicans, and Johnson's eventual veto of it would be a decisive step in his break with the party. As drafted by Trumbull, the bill set aside three million acres of public land in the South for homesteading by freedmen and white refugees, affirmed for three years the title of freedmen to the lands set aside for them by General Sherman, and authorized the Bureau to buy lands for resale to blacks. In Stevens's view, none of these provisions was satisfactory. The public domain in the southern states consisted largely of hill and swamp lands, and the impoverished freedmen did not possess the capital necessary to establish homes and farms there, or to buy land from the Bureau. And there was no promise of permanent ownership of the Sherman lands. The bill did not touch the economic power of the planters, nor did it give freedmen access to the black belt land which was the key to the southern economy. When it came to the House, Stevens declared, "I say that this bill is a robbery."

When the Trumbull bill reached the House floor early in February [1866], Stevens proposed a substitute measure, adding "forfeited estates of the enemy" to the land open to settlement, making certain that the land could be purchased by blacks on easy terms, and making permanent their possession of the Sherman lands. When this substitute came to a vote it was overwhelmingly defeated, 126 to 37; Republicans divided 37 in favor, 86 opposed, with 10 abstentions, and many of the House's leading radicals, including Ashley of Ohio and Kelley of Pennsylvania, opposed it.

The tangled complexities of the land question were further illustrated two days after Stevens's substitute was rejected and the Freedmen's Bureau bill passed, when the House with virtually unanimous Republican support passed Julian's Southern Homestead Act, opening all public land in the South to settlement and giving blacks and loyal whites preferential treatment until 1867. Republicans were thus quite willing to offer freedmen the same opportunity to acquire land which whites had received under the Homestead Act of 1862; they simply refused to take land from the planters to make farmers of blacks. As Stevens had foreseen, the Julian bill was a dismal failure. The land involved was so inferior, and the freedmen so lacking in capital, that by 1869 only four thousand black families had even attempted to take advantage of the Act, and many of these subsequently lost their land.

These votes of February 1866 posed a dilemma for Stevens. He could have accepted them as defining for all practical purposes the limits to which Republicans were willing to move toward providing blacks with land and reorganizing southern society. As William McFeely has pointed out, the Freedmen's Bureau bill despite its limitations did hold out the possibility of a gradual but far-reaching change in the South's land system. It established federal responsibility for giving blacks access to land, and for assisting them in purchasing it on credit. Because the policy did not involve severe punishment of the planters, a complete upheaval of southern society, or special privilege for the blacks, it commanded wide support in Republican ranks. Had Stevens thrown his weight behind the measure as an acceptable alternative to massive confiscation, it might have become, in effect, official Republican policy on the land question. Yet Stevens's whole experience in the 1860s predisposed him not to accept these votes as a final verdict. The conservative New York *Herald* could exult over his defeat ("thus we see . . . the real strength of the Jacobins in the House"), but Stevens might have retorted that when he first proposed a measure for the use of black troops it had received only thirty votes. He had always been ahead of his party, he once remarked during the war, but "I have never been so far ahead . . . but that the members of the party have overtaken me."

Stevens's strategy was based on the judgment that a prolongation of the national crisis would push the Republican party to the left. The longer the crisis lasted, he thought, the more radical the final settlement was likely to be. Throughout 1866 and 1867, Stevens bided his time on the land question, devoting his energies to the Fourteenth Amendment and Negro suffrage, while trying to delay a final settlement. The leftward drift which Stevens counted on as the dynamic element of the political situation was explained by the *Nation* during the hectic debates of February 1867: "Six years ago, the North would have rejoiced to accept any mild restrictions upon the spread of slavery as a final settlement. Four years ago, it would have accepted peace upon the basis of gradual emancipation. Two years ago, it would have been content with emancipation and equal civil rights for the colored people without the extension of suffrage. One year ago, a slight extension of the suffrage would have satisfied it." Now, in March 1867, the Republicans succeeded in passing the first Reconstruction Act, temporarily forcing the planter class from participation in politics and imposing Negro suffrage on the South. And, just as southern intransigence had swelled the ranks of the Republican party in the 1850s and forced it to embrace emancipation and the arming of the slaves during the Civil War, Stevens could hope that if southern whites again obstructed northern goals, the party would move to an even more radical measure—confiscation. Yet the passage of the Act revealed the weakness of Stevens's strategy. As the New York *Times* had observed in 1866, Stevens's program "presupposes the continuance during peace of a public opinion which acquired force under the excitement and perils of war." Inevitably, however, the impulse for a return to normal, for an end to the crisis, had grown in the Republican party—and Stevens, though unhappy with the new Reconstruction measure, had been powerless to block it. Now, the political initiative in effect passed to southern whites. If they accepted the new situation "in good faith," they could destroy whatever chance Stevens's more radical policies might have had.

Although most historians of Reconstruction have not emphasized the fact, confiscation was very much a live political issue in the spring and summer of 1867. But while the debate was very animated, it soon became clear that the fears aroused by Stevens's proposals far outweighed any attractions the plan contained. When Congress reconvened in March 1867, Stevens, ill and too weak to speak, had a colleague read a long speech and a bill providing forty acres to freedmen from confiscated land. "To this issue," he announced, "I desire to devote the small remnant of my life." At the same time, Charles Sumner pressed the issue in the Senate, and outside of Congress Benjamin Butler, Wendell Phillips, and the American Anti-Slavery Society endorsed Stevens's proposals.

The moderate majority of Republicans, however, were determined that Congress should embark upon no new Reconstruction experiments until the success or failure of the recently enacted measures had become clear. Stevens's bill was postponed to December, and Sumner's resolutions were handily defeated. William P. Fessenden, perhaps the most powerful Senate Republican, informed Sumner, "This is more than we do for white men." To which Sumner responded, "White men have never been in slavery."

The farthest some Republicans would go was a warning to the South. If the recently adopted Reconstruction plan did not achieve satisfactory results, several highly respectable Republican journals declared, confiscation would be the logical next policy. Surprisingly, only the generally conservative Philadelphia *North American,* a self-proclaimed spokesman for the manufacturing interests of Pennsylvania, seemed genuinely sympathetic to confiscation. The key question of Reconstruction, the *North American* announced, was the fate of the "plantation oligarchy," and those who opposed Stevens's proposals "must find some other means of destroying this landed aristocracy." The journal also emphasized that the creation of a yeoman class in the South would greatly benefit northern industry (which in 1867 was suffering from the post-war recession). "Just in proportion as the freedmen rise in the social scale will they consume more of the fabrics we sell to the South. Just in proportion as the South refuses to let them rise . . . do we suffer in our trade." If small farms replaced plantations as the basis of southern agriculture, the South would "buy ten dollars of merchandise off us for every one it now takes. . . ."

The prospect of the confiscation and redistribution of planter lands, the Boston *Advertiser* reported in June 1867, "has taken possession to a large extent of the mind of the loyal population of the South—the poor whites and land-lack negroes." This was hardly to say, however, that there were not strong Republican elements in the South which opposed such a measure. As each southern state went through the process of organizing a Republican party in the spring of 1867, virtually every convention found itself divided between "confiscation radicals" and more moderate Whiggish elements. The results were not comforting to moderate and conservative northern Republicans. In Alabama the Union League resolved that if former rebels did not accept the new political situation "in good faith," Congress should confiscate their lands. In North Carolina a Republican mass meeting called on Congress to enact Stevens's latest measure. Most disturbing was the situation in Virginia, where black delegates at the state convention almost to a man demanded a confiscation plank. Most white Republicans, led by the venerable John Minor Botts and other one-time Whig Unionists, opposed the plan, but the blacks were supported by certain white radicals such as the Reverend James Hunnicutt, the editor of a Richmond newspaper. In the end, an uneasy compromise was reached, in a resolution threatening confiscation if planters tried to intimidate black voters.

Northern Republicans, including many radicals, were alarmed at the apparent influence of men like Hunnicutt among the freedmen. "Nothing could be more ominous of disaster," declared the Boston *Advertiser,* ". . . than such an array of class against class in the Southern States" as Hunnicutt and others sought. To counteract pro-confiscation influence, three Republican orators, all considered radical in the North, visited the South in the late spring, addressing gatherings of freedmen. Horace Greeley spoke at a large meeting at Richmond's African Church. "I beg you to believe," Greeley told the blacks, "that you are more likely to earn a home than get one by any form of confiscation. . . . Confiscation shrivels and paralyzes the industry of the whole community subjected to its influence." Senator Henry Wilson brought the same message to Virginia and South Carolina, and William D. Kelley also visited the South, praising its potential for economic development and informing the freedmen that "they can have homes of their own by working hard and saving what they earn—not otherwise."

From Washington, Stevens looked on as the gospel of work was brought to the freedmen. Late in April, he denounced Wilson's Virginia speech and warned that "no man should make promises for the party. . . . Who authorized any orator to say that there would be no confiscation?" In May, he reiterated his criticism of the "Republican meteors" pursuing their "erratic . . . course" through the South, and in June he announced his intention of pushing the confiscation plan at the next session of Congress. But by the end of May it had become apparent that Greeley, Wilson, and Kelley were far closer to the mainstream of Republican opinion than was Thaddeus Stevens. Speaker of the House Schuyler Colfax and Senate leader Fessenden publicly supported Wilson against Stevens's criticisms, and a committee of Congressmen charged by the Republican caucus with overseeing political developments in the South declared that the rights of property would not be infringed (although it did piously urge landholders to offer land for sale to blacks at reasonable rates). It was apparent, in short, that whatever southern Republicans desired, the party in the North was hardly prepared to embrace confiscation. Consequently, as the summer progressed, talk of confiscation subsided in southern Republican conventions.

By the end of 1867, the leftward drift which had characterized the Republican party since the beginning of the Civil War had definitely come to an end. The party suffered a series of reverses in the state elections of 1867, which many Republican leaders blamed squarely on Stevens, the radicals, and their "extreme theories." The election returns greatly strengthened the hand of Republicans like the Ohio banker Henry Cooke and Boston's liberal industrialist Edward Atkinson, who were determined to "put down" the "ultra infidelic radicals" and "prevent the creation of an exclusive black man's party [in the South] and also kill the scheme of confiscation." As the party turned toward respectability, conservatism, and Grant, it appeared certain that, as an Ohio politician observed, "the Negro will be less prominent for some time to come."

By August 1868, when he died, Stevens's political influence was at low ebb. In his characteristically cynical way he had told an interviewer, "I have no history. My life-long regret is that I have lived so long and so uselessly." He died aware that planters were already beginning to use economic intimidation to counter black voting power and that sharecropping and the crop lien—a new "system of peonage," as he called it—were spreading in the black belts, threatening to keep the freedmen permanently dependent on the planters. Stevens was nonetheless still a formidable figure, venerated by the freedmen and by millions of other Republicans, and his death produced a public expression of grief second only to the funeral of Lincoln. It marked in some ways the end of an era, symbolizing the transition from ideology to political expediency as the guiding force of the Republican party. Though the Philadelphia *Press* declared, "He dies at the moment when the truths for which he fought a long and doubtful battle have permanently and almost universally triumphed," James G. Blaine, one of the rising politicos who would control the party's destinies in the 1870s, saw it differently. "The death of Stevens," Blaine observed, "is an emancipation for the Republican party."

Between 1860 and 1868 revolutionary changes had taken place, changes for which contemporaries gave Stevens more than an average share of the credit. Slavery had been abolished, the freedmen granted civil and political equality, and democratic institutions established in all the southern states. But the final step of the Second American Revolution, the provision of an economic underpinning to the blacks' newly won freedom, had not been taken. The failure of Stevens's campaign for confiscation, his demand that society confront the basic economic questions which the abolition of slavery had entailed, exposed the limitations of the Republican party's middle-class ideology. At the same time, it exposed the vulnerability of Stevens's anomalous position as a radical in politics. Lacking a political base outside the Republican party, Stevens could be successful only so long as his proposals posed no fundamental challenge to the values and interests of the Republican mainstream. Possibly a more flexible man than Stevens, one willing to talk less flamboyantly of punishing traitors, revolutionizing southern society, and destroying social classes, one prepared to accept some form of limited, compensated expropriation of land and its sale on credit, might have achieved more for the cause of black landowning than did Stevens. Probably, however, the very idea of confiscation violated too many of the basic Republican verities for the party ever to become reconciled to it.

Stevens's failure, indeed, revealed the limits to what a bourgeois capitalist culture, even in its most radical phase, will voluntarily yield to radicalism. What is actually most striking about the confiscation debate is the way it prefigured the disillusionment which would soon overtake radical Reconstruction. The same fears aroused by confiscation—special privilege, corruption, black domination, dramatic social upheaval by government fiat, a general undermining of the principles of good government—would shortly come to be associated with Reconstruction itself. The arguments used against Stevens between 1865 and 1867 would eventually justify the entire abandonment of Reconstruction.

F U R T H E R   R E A D I N G

Richard H. Abbott, *The Republican Party and the South, 1855–1877* (1986)

Herman Belz, *Reconstructing the Union: Theory and Policy during the Civil War* (1969)

——, *Emancipation and Equal Rights: Politics and Constitutionalism in the Civil War Era* (1978)

Michael Les Benedict, "The Rout of Radicalism: Republicans in the Election of 1867," *Civil War History* 18 (1972), 334–344

——, *A Compromise of Principle: Congressional Republicans and Reconstruction* (1974)

W. R. Brock, *An American Crisis: Congress and Reconstruction 1865–1867* (1963)

Dan T. Carter, *When the War Was Over: Self-Reconstruction in the South, 1865–1867* (1985)

Stanley Coben, "Northeastern Business and Radical Reconstruction," *Mississippi Valley Historical Review* 46 (1959) 67–90

LaWanda Cox and John Cox, *Politics, Principle and Prejudice, 1865–1866* (1963)

David Donald, *Charles Sumner and the Rights of Man* (1970)

Harold M. Hyman, *A More Perfect Union: The Impact of the Civil War and Reconstruction on the Constitution* (1973)

Peyton McCrary, *Abraham Lincoln and Reconstruction: The Louisiana Experiment* (1978)

Eric L. McKitrick, *Andrew Johnson and Reconstruction* (1960)

Michael Perman, *Reunion without Compromise: The South and Reconstruction, 1865–1868* (1973)

——, *Emancipation and Reconstruction, 1862–1879 (1987)*

James E. Sefton, *Andrew Johnson and the Uses of Constitutional Power* (1980)

Hans Trefousse, *The Radical Republicans: Lincoln's Vanguard for Racial Justice* (1969)

——, *Thaddeus Stevens: Nineteenth Century Egalitarian* (1997)

C. Vann Woodward, "Seeds of Failure in Radical Race Policy," in C. Vann Woodward, *American Counterpoint: Slavery and Racism in the North-South Dialogue* (1971), 163–183

CHAPTER 12

Political and Economic
Change in the
Reconstruction South

ᕤ

By June 1868, all of the former Confederate states—except Virginia, Mississippi, and Texas, where the process took a little longer—had been reconstructed and readmitted to the Union. This had been accomplished under the terms of the Reconstruction Act of March 1867. These terms required, first, that all adult male African Americans be entitled to vote and that leading Confederates be disfranchised as well as disqualified from holding office. Second, this transformed electorate in each state was then to elect a new government and ensure that a new constitution was written. When each state had met these conditions, it was readmitted to the Union.

Naturally enough, these reorganized state governments were to be controlled by loyal elements that supported Reconstruction and were Republican in party affiliation. To keep the South out of disloyal as well as Democratic hands had, after all, been essential to an effective federal policy for the defeated section. But electing and installing these governments was just the beginning. If Reconstruction was to endure and thereby introduce much-needed economic, political, and even social changes in the South, these Republican administrations had to be sustained and remain in power. Yet most citizens viewed them as alien and illegitimate, and even those who voted for them and held office under them gave them little respect. Moreover, the kinds of reforms and innovations that the Reconstruction governments had to introduce were certain to provoke vigorous, even violent, opposition from the planter class and its allies, who dominated Southern society. Intense opposition was likely because the mandatory agenda included such goals as a broadening of political participation, the passage of civil rights legislation, the creation of a free and independent labor force, and the development of railroads and industry.

Nevertheless, the new governments went ahead and introduced many changes in the region's life. Participation in politics and government was expanded through the introduction of universal male suffrage and the reduction of financial qualifications for officeholding. The responsibilities of government were also increased by the creation of new penal, charitable, and welfare institutions as well as public school systems, which were groundbreaking initiatives for the Southern states. In addition, these Republican governments enacted civil rights laws. And they provided aid to encourage the building of railroads. Many, if not most, of these initiatives were limited in scope and impact, but they should not be discounted as inconsequential. Had these reforms been little more than lip service, much of the opposition to the Reconstruction governments would have evaporated.

Meanwhile, changes occurred in the economy as a result of emancipation and the new postwar order. No longer tied to a master, the former slaves now had some control over how many members of their household would work, and they could move in search of better employment and then negotiate its terms. This caused a significant rearrangement in the way labor was employed and the plantation system was organized. Other changes arose within agriculture as a result of developments unrelated to emancipation, such as the increasing demand for cotton and new methods of furnishing farmers with their supplies and of marketing their crops. Also not to be forgotten was the emergence during Reconstruction of some manufacturing and the building of new cities in some parts of the region.

Even though the South was not completely transformed politically and economically—Reconstruction was, after all, short-lived—, reforms were introduced and changes did occur. Just because some of these changes were not as enduring or as far-reaching as had initially been hoped does not mean that the South experienced stasis and continuity in its political and economic life during Reconstruction.

D O C U M E N T S

The primary sources for this chapter cover the three areas discussed by the essays that follow. These are, first, the mobilization of new voters, especially African Americans, and the passage by the Republican-controlled governments of a number of reforms demanded by their supporters; second, the changes in the role in the household and in the labor force of women who had formerly been slaves; and last, the emergence of a rearranged plantation system worked by free laborers. The documents will be presented chronologically rather than topically, however.

The first selection is a petition to Congress by the Colored People's Convention of South Carolina of November 24, 1865, that shows African Americans calling public meetings to present their demands immediately after the war was over and several years before they had the vote. The second item is a short, undated extract in which a freed slave, Mattie Curtis, recalls how she fared in the post-emancipation years. In the third piece, an African American named Henry Adams observes in 1867 how black women reacted to working in the fields after they were freed. The fourth document is a speech by a black South Carolina legislator who would later be elected to Congress, Richard H. Cain. Cain was addressing the state's constitutional convention on February 17, 1868, on behalf of his ultimately unsuccessful petition to Congress for a loan of $1 million to purchase land for the freedmen.

The fifth document, from Edward King's book *The Great South* (1875), describes the labor system that King observed in operation on the plantations in the Natchez District during his extensive tour of the South. And the sixth and final item is Albert T. Morgan's positive evaluation of his own work as sheriff of Yazoo County, Mississippi, which is taken from his memoir of his grim experiences during Reconstruction, entitled *Yazoo; Or, On the Picket Line of Freedom in the South* (1884).

South Carolina African Americans Present Their Demands, November 1865

Memorial to the Senate and House of Representatives of the United States in Congress Assembled

Gentlemen:

We, the colored people of the State of South Carolina, in Convention assembled, respectfully present for your attention some prominent facts in relation to our present condition, and make a modest yet earnest appeal to your considerate judgment.

We, your memorialists, with profound gratitude to almighty God, recognize the great boon of freedom conferred upon us by the instrumentality of our late President, Abraham Lincoln, and the armies of the United States.

"The fixed decree, which not all Heaven can move,
  Thou, Fate, fulfill it; and, ye Powers, approve."

We also recognize with liveliest gratitude the vast services of the Freedmen's Bureau together with the efforts of the good and wise throughout the land to raise up an oppressed and deeply injured people in the scale of civilized being, during the throbbings of a mighty revolution which must affect the future destiny of the world.

Conscious of the difficulties that surround our position, we would ask for no rights or privileges but such as rest upon the strong basis of justice and expediency, in view of the best interests of our entire country.

We ask first, that the strong arm of law and order be placed alike over the entire people of this State; that life and property be secured, and the laborer free to sell his labor as the merchant his goods.

We ask that a fair and impartial instruction be given to the pledges of the government to us concerning the land question.

We ask that the three great agents of civilized society—the school, the pulpit, the press—be as secure in South Carolina as in Massachusetts or Vermont.

We ask that equal suffrage be conferred upon us, in common with the white men of this State.

This we ask, because "all free governments derive their just powers from the consent of the governed"; and we are largely in the majority in this State, bearing for a long period the burden of onerous taxation, without a just representation. We ask for equal suffrage as a protection for the hostility evoked by our known faithfulness to our country and flag under all circumstances.

We ask that colored men shall not in every instance be tried by white men; and that neither by custom nor enactment shall we be excluded from the jury box.

We ask that, inasmuch as the Constitution of the United States explicitly declares that the right to keep and bear arms shall not be infringed and the Constitution is the Supreme law of the land—that the late efforts of the Legislature of this State to pass an act to deprive us of arms be forbidden, as a plain violation of the Constitution, and unjust to many of us in the highest degree, who have been soldiers, and purchased our muskets from the United States Government when mustered out of service.

From South Carolina African Americans' Petition, November 24, 1865, in James S. Allen, *Reconstruction: The Battle for Democracy, 1865–1876* (International Publishers, 1937), Appendix, pp. 228–229.

We protest against any code of black laws the Legislature of this State may enact, and pray to be governed by the same laws that control other men. The right to assemble in peaceful convention, to discuss the political questions of the day; the right to enter upon all the avenues of agriculture, commerce, trade; to amass wealth by thrift and industry; the right to develop our whole being by all the appliances that belong to civilized society, cannot be questioned by any class of intelligent legislators.

We solemnly affirm and desire to live orderly and peacefully with all the people of this State; and commending this memorial to your considerate judgment.

Thus we ever pray.

Charleston, S. C., November 24, 1865
Zion Presbyterian Church.

Mattie Curtis Remembers Her Struggle after Emancipation (Undated)

I got married before de war to Joshua Curtis. I always had craved a home an' plenty to eat, but freedom ain't give us notin' but pickled hoss meat an' dirty crackers an' not half enough of dat. Josh ain't really care 'bout no home but through dis land corporation I buyed dese fifteen acres on time. I cut down de big trees dat wus all over dese fields an' I hauled out de wood an sold hit, den I plowed up de fields an' planted dem. Josh did help to build de house an' he worked out some. All of dis time I had nineteen chilluns an' Josh died, but I kep' on.

I'll never fergit my first bale of cotton an' how I got hit sold. I was some proud of dat bale of cotton, an' atter I had hit ginned I set out wid hit on my steercart for Raleigh. De white folks hated de nigger den, 'specially de nigger what was makin' something so I dasen't ax nobody whar de market wus. I rid all day an' had to take my cotton home wid me dat night 'case I can't find no place to sell hit at. But dat night I think hit over an' de next day I axes a policeman 'bout de market.

I done a heap of work at night too, all of my sewin' and such and de piece of lan' near de house over dar ain't never got no work cept at night. I finally paid for de land.

Henry Adams Reports on Women and Fieldwork, 1867

I seen on some plantations on Red River where the white men would drive colored women out in the fields to work, when the husbands would be absent from their home, and would tell colored men that their wives and children could not live on their places unless they work in the fields. The colored men would tell them they wanted their children to attend school; and whenever they wanted their wives to work they would tell them themselves; and if he could not rule his own domestic affairs on that place he would leave it and go somewhere else. So the white people would tell them if he expected for his wife and children to live on their places without working in the field they would have to pay house rent or leave it; and if the colored people would go to leave, they would

From Mattie Curtis in *We Are Your Sisters: Black Women in the 19th Century,* Dorothy Sterling, ed. (Norton, 1984), p. 323.

From Henry Adams in *We Are Your Sisters: Black Women in the 19th Century,* Dorothy Sterling, ed. (Norton, 1984), p. 322.

take everything they had, chickens, hogs, horses, cows, mules, crops, and everything and tell them it was for what his damn family had to eat, doing nothing but sitting up and acting the grand lady and their daughters acting the same way, for I will be damn if niggers ain't got to work on my place or leave it.

Richard H. Cain of South Carolina Stresses the Importance of Land, February 1868

. . . *Mr. R. H. Cain.* I may be mistaken, but I watched very closely the arguments made by the gentleman last Saturday, and I distinctly understood him to say he was in favor of taxing the lands so as to compel the sale of them, and throw them into the market. The poor would then have a chance to buy. I am unqualifiedly opposed to any measure of taxation for the simple purpose of compelling the owners to sell their lands. I believe the best measure to be adopted is to bring capital to the State, and instead of causing revenge and unpleasantness, I am for even-handed justice. I am for allowing the parties who own lands to bring them into the market and sell them upon such terms as will be satisfactory to both sides. I believe a measure of this kind has a double effect: first, it brings capital, what the people want; second, it puts the people to work; it gives homesteads, what we need; it relieves the Government and takes away its responsibility of feeding the people; it inspires every man with a noble manfulness, and by the thought that he is the possessor of something in the State; it adds also to the revenue of the country. By these means men become interested in the country as they never were before. It was said that five and one-seventh acres were not enough to live on. If South Carolina, in its sovereign power, can devise any plan for the purchase of the large plantations in this State now lying idle, divide and sell them out at a reasonable price, it will give so many people work. I will guarantee to find persons to work every five acres. I will also guarantee that after one year's time, the Freedman's Bureau will not have to give any man having one acre of land anything to eat. This country has a genial clime, rich soil, and can be worked to advantage. The man who can not earn a living on five acres, will not do so on twenty-five. I regret that another position taken by gentlemen in the opposition, is that they do not believe that we will get what we ask for. I believe that the party now in power in the Congress of the United States, will do whatever they can for the welfare of the people of this State and of the South. I believe that the noble men who have maintained the rights of the freedmen before and since their liberation, will continue to do everything possible to forward these great interests. I am exceedingly anxious, if possible, to allay all unpleasant feeling—I would not have any unpleasant feeling among ourselves.

I would not have any unpleasant feelings between the races. If we give each family in the State an opportunity of purchasing a home, I think they will all be better satisfied.

But it is also said that it will disturb all the agricultural operations in the State. I do not believe if the Congress of the United States shall advance one million of dollars to make purchase of lands, the laborers will abandon their engagement and run off. I have more confidence in the people I represent. I believe all who have made contracts will fulfill those contracts, and when their contracts have expired, they will go on their own lands, as all freemen ought to go. I claim it would do no harm. It would be a wonderful concatenation of circumstances indeed, to find that because the Government had appro-

From Richard H. Cain, speech, February 17, 1868, in *Proceedings of the South Carolina Constitutional Convention of 1868,* pp. 420–421.

priated one million of dollars for the purchase of lands, to see all of four hundred thousand people, rushing pell mell down to Charleston to get a homestead. I know the ignorance of the people with whom I am identified is great. I know that four hundred years of bondage has degraded them, but I have more confidence in humanity than to believe the people will leave their homes and their families to come to Charleston just to get five acres of land.

If I understood the speaker in the opposition this morning, he offered it because he said it was simply a scheme for colored men. I wish to state this question right. If there was one thing on which I thought I had been specific, it was on that point. The clock had struck two and I had dashed down my pen when the thought struck me it might be misunderstood. I retraced my steps and so shaped the petition as simply to state the poor of any class. I bore in mind the poor whites of the upper districts. I saw, not long ago, a poor white woman walk eighteen miles barefooted to receive a bag of corn and four pounds of meat, resting all night on the roadside, eating one-half and then go away, living on roots afterwards and half starved. I desire that class of people to have homes as well as the black man. I have lost long since that hateful idea that the complexion of a man makes any difference as far as rights are concerned. The true principle of progress and civilization is to recognize the great brotherhood of man, and a man's wants, whatever he may be, or whatever clime he comes from, are as sacred to me as any other class of men. I believe this measure will advance the interests of all classes.

Edward King Describes the Postwar Plantation System in the Natchez District, 1875

. . . The region which finds its market and gets its supplies in Memphis, Vicksburg, and Natchez, is probably as fair a sample of the cotton-producing portion of the South as any other, and I found in it all the ills and all the advantages complained of or claimed elsewhere. Imagine a farming country which depends absolutely for its food on the West and North-west; where every barrel of flour which the farmer buys, the bacon which he seems to prefer to the beef and mutton which he might raise on his own lands, the clothes on his back, the shoes on his feet, the very vegetables which the poorest laborer in the Northern agricultural regions grows in his door-yard—everything, in fact,—has been brought hundreds of miles by steamer or by rail, and has passed through the hands of the shipper, the carrier, the wharfmen, the reshipper (if the planter live[s] in a remote section), and the local merchant!

Imagine a people possessed of superior facilities, who might live, as the vulgar saying has it, on the fat of the land, who are yet so dependent that a worm crawling over a few cotton leaves, or the rise of one or two streams, may reduce them to misery and indebtedness from which it will take years to recover! Men who consider themselves poorly paid and badly treated in Northern farming and manufacturing regions live better and have more than do the overseers of huge plantations in this cotton country. If you enter into conversation with people who fare thus poorly, they will tell you that, if they raise vegetables, the "niggers" will steal them; that if times were not so hard, and seasons were not so disastrous, the supply system would work very well; that they cannot organize their labor so as to secure a basis on which to calculate safely; and will finally end by declaring that the South is ruined forever.

From Edward King, *The Great South* (Louisiana State University Press, 1972 [1875]), pp. 272–273.

These are the opinions of the elders mainly. Younger men, who see the necessity of change and new organization, believe that they must in [the] future cultivate other crops besides cotton; that they must do away with supply-merchants, and try at least to raise what is needed for sustenance. There are, of course, sections where the planter finds it cheapest to obtain his corn and flour from St. Louis; but these are small items. There are a hundred things which he requires, and which are grown as well South as North. Until the South has got capital enough together to localize manufactures, the same thing must be said of all manufactured articles; but why should a needless expenditure be encouraged by the very people whom it injures and endangers?

There are many plans of working large plantations now in vogue, and sometimes the various systems are all in operation on the same tract. The plan of "shares" prevails extensively, the planter taking out the expenses of the crop, and, when it is sold, dividing the net proceeds with the negroes who have produced it. In some cases in the vicinity of Natchez, land is leased to the freedmen on condition that they shall pay so many bales of cotton for the use of so many acres, furnishing their own supplies. Other planters lease the land in the same way, and agree to furnish the supplies also. Still others depend entirely upon the wages system, but of course have to furnish supplies at the outset, deducting the cost from the wages paid hands after the crop is raised. Sometimes the plantation is leased to "squads," as they are called, and the "squad leader" negotiates the advances, giving "liens" on the squad's share of the crop and on the mules and horses they may own. This plan has worked very well and is looked upon favorably.

Under the slave *régime,* the negroes working a large plantation were all quartered at night in a kind of central group of huts, known as the "quarters"; but it has been found an excellent idea to divide up the hundred or five hundred laborers among a number of these little villages, each located on the section of the plantation which they have leased. By this process, commonly known as "segregation of quarters," many desirable results have been accomplished; the negro has been encouraged to devote some attention to his home, and been hindered from the vices engendered by excessive crowding. On some plantations one may find a dozen squads, each working on a different plan, the planters, or land owners, hoping in this way to find out which system will be most advantageous to themselves and most binding on the negro. . . .

I took a ride one morning in this same Concordia parish [on the west bank of the Mississippi River] for the purpose of conversing with the planters, and getting testimony as to the actual condition of the laborers. Concordia was once the garden spot of Louisiana; its aspect was European; the fine roads were bordered with delicious hedges of Cherokee rose; grand trees, moss-hung and fantastic in foliage, grew along the green banks of a lovely lake; every few miles a picturesque grouping of coarsely thatched roofs marked negro "quarters," and near by gleamed the roof of some planter's mansion. In this parish there was no law and but little order— save such as the inhabitants chose to maintain. The negroes whom I met on the road were nearly all armed, most of them carrying a rifle over their shoulders, or balanced on the backs of the mules they were riding. Affrays among the negroes are very common throughout that region; but, unless the provocation has been very great, they rarely kill a white man.

In a trip of perhaps ten miles I passed through several once prosperous plantations, and made special inquiries as to their present condition. Upon one where six hundred bales of cotton were annually produced under slave culture, the average annual yield is now but two hundred and fifty; on another the yearly average had fallen from one thousand to three hundred bales; and on two others which together gave the market fifteen hundred bales every year, now barely six hundred are raised. The planters in this section thought that cotton production had fallen off fully two-thirds. The number of negroes at work on each of these plantations was generally much less than before the war. Then a bale to the acre was realized, now about one bale to three acres is the average. Much of this land is "leased" to the negro at the rate of a bale of cotton weighing four hundred and thirty pounds for each six acres.

The planters there raise a little corn, but are mainly supplied from the West. The inundation was upon them at the epoch of my visit, and they were in momentary expectation of seeing all their year's hopes destroyed. The infamous robberies, also, to which they had been subjected by the Legislature, and the overwhelming taxation, had left them bitterly discouraged. One plantation which I visited, having sixteen hundred acres of cleared land in it, and standing in one of the most fertile sections of the State, was originally valued at one hundred dollars per acre; now it could not be sold for ten dollars. In Madison parish recently a plantation of six hundred improved acres, which originally cost thirty thousand dollars, was offered to a neighboring planter for *seven hundred dollars.* . . .

While there is no doubt that an active, moneyed, and earnest immigration would do much toward building up the southern portion of the Mississippi valley, it is evident that so long as the negro remains in his present ignorance, and both he and the planter rely on other States for their sustenance, and on Providence never to send them rainy days, inundations, or caterpillars, the development of the section will be subject to too serious drawbacks to allow of any considerable progress. All the expedients, the tenant systems, and years of accidental success will not take the place of thorough and diversified culture, and intelligent, contented labor resulting from fair wages for fair work. Nothing but the education of the negro up to the point of ambition, foresight, and a desire to acquire a competence lawfully and laboriously, will ever thoroughly develop the Lower Mississippi valley. As the negro is certainly to inhabit it for many years at least, if not forever, how shall he learn the much-needed lesson?

On the other hand, the whites need to be converted to a sense of the dignity of labor, to learn to treat the laboring man with proper consideration, to create in him an intelligent ambition by giving him education. Something besides an introduction to political liberties and responsibilities is needed to make the negro a moral and worthy citizen. He is struggling slowly and not very surely out of a lax and barbarously immoral condition. The weight of nearly two centuries of slavery is upon his back. He needs more help and counsel. An old master will tell you that he can discover who of his employés has been a slave, "for the slave," he says, "cannot look you in the eye without flinching." . . .

Albert T. Morgan of Mississippi Recalls His Achievements As Sheriff, 1884

The reader has already seen what was accomplished by "the enemy" during the years of its control prior to the war, and in the four years which followed that event, in the way of county public improvements. In this chapter I shall endeavor to faithfully set down what was accomplished by "we all radicals," in the six years of my "dictatorship." By the beginning of the year 1875, the requisite repairs upon the county highways and

From Albert T. Morgan, *Yazoo, Or, On the Picket Line of Freedom* (Russell and Russell, 1968 [1884]), pp. 416–417, 422.

bridges had been completed, and new bridges built, so that in that respect the county had never before enjoyed equal facilities. Improvements upon the poor-farm buildings had been made, the farm put in cultivation, system and order enforced in its management and among its inmates, and the institution had become nearly self-sustaining.

The capacity and security of the jail had been enlarged by the addition of safe, iron cells.

A new court-house, costing quite seventy thousand dollars, had been erected and paid for as the work progressed, and had been "accepted" by a committee of the oldest and best members of our Yazoo bar association. Everybody said it was a credit to the county.

The county indebtedness had at no time exceeded the annual levy for current expenses. The finances had been managed in such a way that within the first year of our control, county warrants went up to par, and remained there during the entire period, with only short exceptional occasions. At the close of 1873 there were outstanding obligations amounting to quite thirty thousand dollars, but nearly if not quite the entire sum would be absorbed by the tax-levy of that year, the collection of which had been interfered with by the "insurrection."

Yazoo City was an incorporated town, its government was under the control of the Republicans, who were in a majority. As in the county so it was here; extensive improvements had been wrought; new side-walks, pavements, and gutters, had been made, and, above all, perhaps, a new steam fire-engine had been provided. Our Yankee postmaster, aided by a few public-spirited fellow-citizens, was foremost in all these good works.

We had failed, it is true, to get a railroad to our town, but that was by no fault of "we all Yankees." Three lines had been chartered, and at one time the prospect was very bright indeed that we would have one. But the great panic [of 1873] spreading throughout the North had interfered with our plans. Mississippi hardly felt the great shock, it is true, but as we were depending largely upon Northern capital for our road, and as the panic wrecked for a season all such prospects, our proposed railroad withered and shrank so far away that it had not yet reached Yazoo City, nor even Mississippi.

On all these improvements our party leaders had been practically a unit, and the great body of the freed people had stood squarely by us. I am sorry to say that there was not the same harmony among "we all Republicans" upon the school question. . . .

At the outset the free-school idea met the determined hostility of the irreconcilables, the faint acquiescence of the conservatives in the ranks of the enemy, the lukewarm adherence of the Unionists, the sympathy and active co-operation of the Northerners and the unanimous and greedy support of the "freedmen, free negroes and mulattoes."

But in spite of all the obstacles in the way of its growth, in 1875 the system in Yazoo was a complete success, a fact acknowledged by all except possibly a handful of the most violent of the irreconcilables.

It had become so popular that old and wealthy planters often came personally to the superintendent or members of the board, and pleaded for a school on their own plantations, declaring that they not only wished it as a means of improving the freed people, but also, because they had observed that the laborers on other plantations where schools were, or who were in the neighborhood of schools, were more contented and worked better.

It was found impossible to supply the demand. To have done so at once would have so greatly increased the taxes that it would have been burdensome to the government.

It is with a feeling of no little pride and gratification that I am able to add here, at the close of this account of my stewardship, that the tax-levy at no time during the entire period exceeded two and one-half per cent, and in 1875, was but two and one-fifth per cent for all purposes.

E S S A Y S

For this chapter on changes and developments that occurred in the South during Reconstruction, the essays focus on three areas in particular, which are also represented in the documents. The piece by Eric Foner of Columbia University describes the remarkable upsurge of political activity on the part of African Americans, not only after they obtained the vote, but even before. Jacqueline Jones of Brandeis University discusses the ways in which African American women changed their role and behavior, both in the household and in the fields. This extract is from her book on black women and the family from the era of slavery to the present. And finally, Harold D. Woodman of Purdue University describes the system of agricultural labor that emerged after the war. Even though the plantation survived the war and emancipation, both the way it was organized and the labor force it relied on became, in his view, very different.

Black Reconstruction Leaders at the Grass Roots

ERIC FONER

In November 1869, in Greene County, Georgia, disguised Klansmen forced Abram Colby into the woods "and there stripped and beat him in the most cruel manner, for nearly three hours." Born a slave and freed in 1851, Colby earned his living as a minister and barber. Since the end of the Civil War he had taken an active part in black political life, organizing "one of the largest and most enthusiastic" branches of Georgia's Equal Rights Association in 1866 and winning election to the state legislature two years later. According to the local agent of the American Missionary Association, Colby was whipped because he had recently appealed to Governor Rufus Bullock to protect the county's black population, and his assailants "had besides as they said, many old scores against him, as a leader of his people in the county." Eighteen months later South Carolina Klansmen whipped Samuel Bonner, an unassuming black sharecropper, along with his mother and sister. Before the assault Bonner was asked if he were a Republican. "I told them," he later recalled, "I was that, and I thought it was right."

Minor episodes in the history of Reconstruction, these incidents nonetheless illuminate larger themes of its political culture and the nature of grass-roots black leadership. Colby exemplifies the humble social status of local black leaders; although free before the Civil War, he was illiterate and, according to the 1870 census, owned no property. His experience in the legislature reveals the fragility of black-white cooperation in Reconstruction politics, for white Republicans were among those who voted to expel Colby and other blacks. Bonner's willingness to assert his convictions in the face of violence epitomizes the depth of commitment that animated the Reconstruction black community. These small dramas guide us into the world of local black politics, its organization, ideology, and leadership during Reconstruction.

Southern black politics, of course, did not begin with the Reconstruction Act of 1867 [act of Congress reorganizing politics in the southern states by creating new Republican-controlled state governments and providing suffrage for African American males], as Abram Colby's career illustrates. Before the end of the Civil War, black political organizations had appeared in such Union-occupied areas as New Orleans. And in 1865 and 1866, in black conventions throughout the southern states, future Reconstruction leaders like James T. Rapier and William H. Grey first came into prominence. By and large, however, the tone of these early conventions was moderate. Throughout the South, 1865 was a year of labor conflict, with freedpeople refusing to sign contracts and some seizing plantations and staking a claim to the soil. But the free-born mulattoes, ministers, and northern blacks who dominated the conventions all but ignored the land question.

Whatever the accomplishments of these conventions (and one delegate told the 1866 gathering in Tennessee that his constituents believed "we do nothing but meet, pass resolutions, publish pamphlets, and incur expenses"), the process of selecting delegates politicized black communities. Some delegates were elected by local mass meetings; others were sent by churches, clubs, and black army units stationed in the South. In the fall of 1866, two black men held "a regular canvass" in Greene County, North Carolina; an organized election followed to choose a delegate to the state's second black convention. The local chapters of the Georgia Educational Association, established at the state's January 1866 black convention, became "schools in which the colored citizens learn their rights." Nonetheless, this first phase of political organization was spotty and uneven— large areas of the black belt remained untouched by organized political activity.

It was in 1867, the *annus mirabilis* of Reconstruction, that a wave of political activism swept across the black belt. Itinerant lecturers, black and white, brought their message into the heart of the rural South. A black Baptist minister calling himself Professor J. W. Toer toured parts of Georgia and Florida "with a magic lantern to exhibit what he calls the progress of reconstruction. . . . He has a scene, which he calls 'before the proclamation,' another 'after the proclamation' and then '22nd Regt. U.S.C.T. Duncan's Brigade'." Voting registrars held public meetings to instruct blacks on the nature of American government and "the individual benefits of citizenship in the nation and in the state." In Monroe County, Alabama, where no black political meetings had occurred before 1867, freedpeople crowded around the registrar shouting "God bless you," "Bless God for this." Throughout the South there were complaints of blacks neglecting plantation labor: "they stop at any time and go off to Greensboro or any other place to attend a political meeting" complained a white Alabamian. So great was the enthusiasm for politics that, as one former slave minister later wrote, "politics got in our midst and our revival or religious work for a while began to wane." Although suffrage was restricted to men, black women and even children often played a vocal part in political gatherings. One plantation manager summed up the situation: "You never saw a people more excited on the subject of politics than are the negroes of the south. They are perfectly wild."

The meteoric rise of black political activity was reflected in the growth of the Union League. Few developments of this period are more tinged with irony than the metamorphosis of a loyalist club, developed among the respectable middle classes of the Civil War North, into the political expression of impoverished freedpeople. An earlier generation of historians tended to dismiss the Union League by portraying it as a vehicle through which carpetbaggers [a pejorative term coined by southern whites to vilify northerners involved in Republican party politics in the Reconstruction South] manipulated the votes of gullible blacks, who were attracted to its meetings by secret passwords and colorful initiation rites. In fact, its purposes were far more complex: the league served simultaneously as "a political school for the people," as a North Carolina teacher described it, a vehicle for the emergence of a greatly expanded class of black political leaders, and an institutional structure blacks could utilize for their own purposes and through which they could articulate their own aspirations.

Even before 1867, local Union League branches had sprung up among blacks in some parts of the South, and the order had spread rapidly among Unionist whites in the Alabama, Georgia, and Tennessee hill country. In 1867, as blacks poured into the league, many white members either withdrew or formed segregated local chapters. Many local leagues were all-black or all-white, but integrated leagues also existed, in which black and white Republicans achieved a remarkable degree of interracial harmony. In Union County, North Carolina, a racially mixed league met "in old fields, or in some out of the way house, and elect[ed] candidates to be received into their body."

By the end of 1867 it seemed that virtually every black voter in the South had enrolled in the Union League, the Loyal League, or some equivalent local political organization. Meetings were generally held in a black church or school, or at the home of some prominent black individual, or, if necessary, secretly in woods or fields. In Paulding, Mississippi, a hundred or more blacks, along with a few whites, met monthly at the home of Jim Cruise, a black house carpenter. Usually, a Bible and a copy of the Declaration of Independence and the Constitution lay on a table, a minister opened the meeting with a prayer, new members took an initiation oath, and there were pledges to support the Republican party and uphold the principle of equal rights.

The main function of these meetings, however, was political education. "We just went there," related Henry Holt, an illiterate black league member from North Carolina, "and we talked a little; made speeches on one question and another." Republican newspapers were read aloud, candidates were nominated for office, and political issues were debated. One racially mixed league discussed at various meetings the organization of a July 4 celebration, cooperation between the league and the Heroes of America (a secret white Unionist organization dating from the Civil War), and issues like disfranchisement, debt relief, and public education which were likely to arise at the forthcoming constitutional conventions. In Maryville, Tennessee, the Union League held weekly discussions on the issues of the day—the impeachment of President Johnson, the national debt, and such broader questions as, Is the education of the female as important as that of the male? Should students pay corporation tax? Should East Tennessee be a separate state? Although mostly white in membership in a county only one-tenth black, this league called for Tennessee to send at least one black to Congress. In 1868 its members elected a black justice of the peace and four blacks to the seven-member city commission.

It would be an error, however, to assume that the Union leagues were "political" only in the sense of electoral politics. Their multifaceted activities reflected what might be called the politicization of everyday life during Reconstruction. Colleton County, South Carolina, league members (led by a freedman with the venerable Palmetto State name Wade Hampton) marched in a body to the local magistrate demanding the arrest of a white man who had injured a black with a slingshot. A local North Carolina league official—a minister describing himself as "a poor Colord man"—proposed to Governor Holden that the league "stand as gardians" for blacks who "don't know how to make a bargain . . . and see that they get the money." In Alabama's black belt, league organizer

George W. Cox was besieged by freedpeople requesting information about suing their employers, avoiding fines for attending political meetings, and ensuring a fair division of crops at harvest time. Two of the most militant collective actions by blacks during Georgia Reconstruction, the Ogeechee uprising of 1869 and Cudjo Fye's "rebellion" of 1870, were sparked by the arrest of league members by white authorities.

In 1867 and 1868 Union League activity reached its zenith. By 1869 it had begun to decline in many parts of the South, disrupted by Klan violence or absorbed into the burgeoning apparatus of the Republican party. "It is all broke up," said one black member from Graham, North Carolina, an area of rampant Klan activity. In Texas, Republican chieftain James Tracy moved to assimilate the leagues into a more disciplined party structure, evoking strong protests from militant black leaders like the legislator Matthew Gaines. But in wide areas of the black belt, the tradition of local political organization embodied in the leagues persisted throughout Reconstruction. Sometimes the names changed, but the structure and purposes remained the same. In Abbeville County, South Carolina, the Union League was succeeded by The Brotherhood, the United Brethren, and finally, in 1875, the Laboring Union; as former slave A. J. Titus explained, "they was all laboring men, you see." In the Vicksburg region a successor to the Union League, called the "council" by blacks, met until 1874 to discuss self-protection and Republican politics. Its members, armed with pistols and shotguns, unsuccessfully resisted white efforts to oust black sheriff Peter Crosby in the Vicksburg crisis of December 1874.

In this hothouse atmosphere of political mobilization, the Union leagues generated a new class of local black political leaders. Local leaders in the black belt, where few free blacks had lived before the Civil War, and especially outside Louisiana and South Carolina, with their large and politically active freeborn communities, tended to be former slaves of very modest circumstances. Many were teachers and preachers or other individuals who possessed a skill of use to the community. Former slave Thomas Allen, a Union League organizer elected to the Georgia legislature, was a propertyless Baptist preacher, shoemaker, and farmer. But what established him as a leader was literacy: "In my county the colored people came to me for instructions, and I gave them the best instructions I could. I took the New York Tribune and other papers, and in that way I found out a great deal, and I told them whatever I thought was right." In occupation, the largest number of local black leaders appear to have been artisans, men whose skill and independence marked them as leaders but who were still deeply embedded in the life of the black community. There were others, apparently lacking in distinctive attributes of status, respected for personal qualities—oratorical ability, a reputation for moral standing, or simply good sense, honesty, or a concern for the welfare of their neighbors. Calvin Rogers, a black constable murdered by the Florida Klan, was described by another freedman as "a thorough-going man; he was a stump speaker, and tried to excite the colored people to do the right thing. . . . He would work for a man and make him pay him." Others were men who had achieved prominence as slaves before emancipation, like Louisiana justice of the peace Hamilton Gibson, a "conjurer."

In his study of social and political organizations among Memphis blacks, Armstead Robinson has identified a fairly sharp distinction between political leaders, who tended to be prosperous and light of skin, and religious/benevolent leaders, who were generally unskilled former slaves. In the less-stratified rural black belt, however, lines of occupation and social function frequently overlapped: preachers and teachers earned their living in part as artisans or laborers, politicians helped establish churches, meetings of fraternal organizations discussed political events, and Union leagues raised money for black schools. This was a world suffused with politics, in which local leaders gave articulate expression to the multiplicity of grievances and the timeless aspirations of their humble constituents.

In Union leagues, Republican gatherings, and impromptu local meetings, black and white Republicans in these years debated the basic question of the polity—What was the meaning of freedom and citizenship in republican America? Black leaders drew upon a broad range of experiences and ideas, some derived from slavery itself and others grounded in the traditions of the larger society, in defining the bounds of black politics. The language of American republicanism suffused black political culture. As Rev. J. M. Hood put it at the North Carolina Constitutional Convention of 1868, "the colored people had read . . . the Declaration [of Independence] until it had become part of their natures." A petition of eleven Alabama blacks complaining in 1865 of contract frauds, injustice before the courts, the refusal of whites to rent land to freedpeople, and other abuses, concluded with a revealing masterpiece of understatement: "this is not the pursuit of happiness." And ten years later, a group of Louisiana freedpeople felt it appropriate to open their petition for the removal of a hostile local official with these well-known words: "We the people of Louisiana in order to establish justice, insure domestic tranquility, promote the general welfare . . . do ordain and establish this Constitution."

There was much more here than simply accustomed language; blacks, freeborn and slave, were staking their claim to equal citizenship in the American republic. To them the republican inheritance implied the rights to vote and to education, the free exercise of religion, access to the courts, and equal opportunity in all the avenues of economic enterprise—every right already enjoyed by whites. As one black delegate to the Virginia Constitutional Convention put it, no civil right "ever enjoyed by citizens prior to the year 1861" could now justifiably be denied to blacks. Anything less would be a violation of the principles upon which the nation had been founded. As Louisiana's Oscar J. Dunn insisted, "it is the boast and glory of the American republic that there is no discrimination among men, no privileges founded upon birth-right. There are no hereditary distinctions." Continued proscription of blacks, Dunn warned, would undermine the republic and "open the door for the institution of aristocracy, nobility, and even monarchy."

At their most utopian, blacks in Reconstruction envisioned a society purged of all racial distinctions. This did not mean the abandonment of race consciousness—there is abundant evidence that blacks preferred black teachers for their children as well as black churches and ministers. But in the polity, blacks, who had so long been proscribed because of their color, defined equal citizenship as colorblind. Thomas Bayne told the Virginia Constitutional Convention that his constituents expected him to help draft a constitution "that should not have the word black or white anywhere in it." Politicians seeking to arouse a sense of racial self-consciousness sometimes found black audiences unreceptive to their message. Martin Delany, the "father of black nationalism," discovered in South Carolina that it was "dangerous to go into the country and speak of color in any manner whatever, without the angry rejoinder, 'we don't want to hear that; we are all one color now.'" He was astonished to find that the freedpeople did not share his belief in the necessity of electing blacks (particularly Martin Delany) to office. Rather, they believed "that the Constitution had been purged of color by a Radical Congress."

The black claim to equal citizenship was grounded in more than a restatement of republican principles, however. Repeatedly in Reconstruction it was linked as well to black participation in the Civil War. Indeed, while blacks revered Lincoln as the Great Emancipator, it was also an article of faith that they had helped emancipate themselves. "They say," an Alabama planter reported in 1867, "the Yankees never could have whipped the south without the aid of the negroes." At the same time, the secular claim to citizenship was underpinned by a religious messianism deeply rooted in the black experience. As slaves, blacks had come to think of themselves as analogous to the Jews in Egypt, an oppressed people whom God, in the fullness of time, would deliver from bondage. They viewed the Civil War as God's instrument of deliverance, and Reconstruction as another step in a divinely ordained process. Black religion reinforced black republicanism, for, as Rev. J. M. P. Williams, a Mississippi legislator, put it in an address to his constituents in 1871, "my dear friends, remember this, of one blood God did make all men to dwell upon the face of the whole earth . . . hence, their common origin, destiny and equal rights." Even among nonclerics, secular and religious modes of political discourse were virtually interchangeable. One example is a speech by North Carolina black Edwin Jones, as reported by a justice of the peace in 1867: "He said it was not now like it used to be, that . . . the negro was about to get his equal rights. . . . That the negroes owed their freedom to the courage of the negro soldiers and to God. . . . He made frequent references to the II and IV chapters of Joshua for a full accomplishment of the principles and destiny of the race. It was concluded that the race have a destiny in view similar to the Children of Israel."

Republicanism, religious messianism, and historical experience combined to produce in black political Reconstruction culture a profound sense of identification with the American polity. The very abundance of letters and petitions addressed by ordinary freedpeople to officials of the army, the Freedmen's Bureau, and state and federal authorities revealed a belief that the political order was open to black participation and persuasion. Blacks enthusiastically embraced that hallmark of the Civil War era, the rise of an activist state. With wealth, political experience, and tradition all mobilized against them in the South, blacks saw in political authority a countervailing power. On the local and state level, black officials pressed for the expansion of such public institutions as schools and hospitals. And in proposing measures (generally not enacted) for free medical care and legal assistance for the poor, government regulation of private markets, restrictions on the sale of liquor, and the outlawing of fairs and hunting on Sunday, they revealed a vision of the democratic state actively promoting the social and moral well-being of its citizenry.

It was the national government, however, that blacks ultimately viewed as the guarantor of their rights. Those whose freedom had come through the unprecedented exercise of federal authority were utterly hostile to theories of state rights and local autonomy. As Frederick Douglass put it, until Americans abandoned the idea of "the right of each State to control its own local affairs, . . . no general assertion of human rights can be of any practical value." Blacks did not share fears of "centralism" common even in the Republican party; like white Radical Republicans, black leaders found in the guarantee of republican government—the "most pregnant clause" of the Constitution, Robert B. Elliott called it—a grant of federal power ample enough to promote the welfare and protect the rights of individual citizens. Throughout Reconstruction, black political leaders supported proposals for such vast expansions of federal authority as James T. Rapier's plan for a national educational system, complete with federally mandated textbooks.

The course of events during Reconstruction reinforced this tendency to look to the national government for protection. The inability of state and local authorities to control violence prompted demands for federal intervention. "We are more slave today in the hand of the wicked than we were before," read a desperate plea from five Alabama blacks. "We need protection . . . only a standing army in this place can give us our right and life." Blacks enthusiastically supported the Enforcement Acts of 1870 and 1871 and the expansion of the powers of the federal judiciary. One black convention went so far as to insist that virtually all civil and criminal cases involving blacks be removable from state to federal courts, a mind-boggling enhancement of federal judicial authority. To constitutional objections, most blacks would agree with Congressman Joseph Rainey: "Tell me nothing of a constitution which fails to shelter beneath its rightful power the people of a country."

Republican citizenship implied more than political equality overseen by an active state, however. It helped legitimize the desire for land so pervasive among the freedpeople, for a society based upon a landed aristocracy and a large propertyless lower class could not be considered truly republican. "Small estates are the real element of democracy," wrote the *New Orleans Tribune*. "Let the land go into the hands of the actual laborers."

In 1865 and 1866 the claim to land found little expression at statewide black conventions. In 1867, however, the situation was very different. At the grass roots, demands for land among blacks and, in some areas, poor whites animated early Republican politics. The advent of suffrage and Thaddeus Stevens's introduction of a confiscation bill in the House rekindled expectations that had, in most areas, subsided after January 1866. A northern correspondent reported that "Thad Stevens' speech has been circulated among those of them who can read and fully expounded to those of them who cannot." As southern Republican parties were organized in the spring of 1867, virtually every convention found itself divided between "confiscation radicals" and more moderate elements. In Mississippi, a black delegate proposed that the party commit itself to the confiscation of Confederate estates and their distribution to freedpeople. At a black mass meeting in Richmond, a freedman announced that large holdings belonging to rebels should be confiscated for the benefit of poor, loyal blacks. The issue was most divisive in North Carolina, where local demands for land were voiced by both black Union leagues and loyalist whites in the Heroes of America. One delegate told the state Republican convention, "the people of this State have a hope in confiscation, and if that is taken away the Republican party [will] give away the power they have gained."

The outcome of the confiscation debate reveals a great deal about the limits within which black politics could operate during Reconstruction. No state convention endorsed the idea, although a few called for planters voluntarily to sell land to impoverished freedmen. The obstacles to confiscation were indeed immense. National Republican leaders, including long-time Radicals like [U.S. Senator] Henry Wilson, publicly condemned Stevens's initiative. "Let confiscation be, as it should be, an unspoken word in your state," Wilson advised North Carolina black leader James H. Harris. Democratic victories in the 1867 northern elections reinforced the conviction that Reconstruction had gone far enough; more radical policies would jeopardize Republican electoral chances in 1868 and beyond.

Even among southern Republicans there was strong opposition to the confiscation idea. Most white Republican leaders were committed to what [historian] Mark Summers calls the "Gospel of Prosperity," believing that their party's prospects hinged on a program of regional economic development and diversification. While envisioning the eventual demise of the plantation system, this "gospel" called for respect for individual enterprise and desired to encourage northern investment in the South, both seemingly incompatible with confiscation. Then, too, most white Republicans fully embraced the free labor ideology, insisting that while possession of land was unquestionably desirable, the freedpeople, like all Americans, would have to acquire it through hard work. Alabama carpetbagger C. W. Dustan solemnly announced that lands "cannot be owned without being earned, they cannot be earned without labor. . . ." (Dustan did not exactly follow this free labor prescription in his own life: he acquired a sizable holding by marrying the daughter of a Demopolis planter.)

Of course, as [historian] Thomas Holt has demonstrated, the black community itself was divided on the land question. The free labor ideology, with its respect for private property and individual initiative, was most fully embraced by two sets of black leaders—those from the North and the better-off southern free Negroes. Prominent northern blacks like Jonathan Gibbs and James Lynch would insist during Reconstruction that the interests of labor and capital were identical. Among "black carpetbaggers" only Aaron A. Bradley became actively involved in the land struggles of the freedpeople. So, too, the free black leadership of Charleston and New Orleans rejected confiscation. At Louisiana's Republican state convention, "all the freedmen, *save one,* were in favor of confiscation, and the measure would have been adopted . . . had it not been for the energetic exertions of the white and free born colored members." Their own experience convinced successful free blacks that freedpeople required not governmental largesse but only an equal chance. . . .

Alone among the nations that abolished slavery in this hemisphere, the United States accorded its former slaves legal and political equality within a few years after emancipation. The unprecedented character of this development, the sense among blacks that their newly won rights were constantly at risk, the refusal of large numbers of Democrats to acknowledge freed blacks as part of the "political nation," helps explain the abnormal aspects of Reconstruction politics—the high degree of political mobilization in the black community, the burdens placed upon black leaders by their constituents, and the widespread use of violence and economic coercion as political weapons.

In the spring of 1868 a northern correspondent, reporting on election day in Alabama, captured the sense of hope with which Reconstruction opened, the conviction among the enfranchised black voters that politics could indeed change their lives. "In defiance of fatigue, hardship, hunger, the threats of employers," blacks had flocked to the polls. Not one in fifty wore an "unpatched garment," few possessed a pair of shoes, yet they stood for hours in line in a "pitiless storm." Why? "The hunger to have the same chances as the white men they feel and comprehend. . . . That is what brings them here" to vote. With the overthrow of Reconstruction, politics could no longer serve as an effective vehicle for expressing such aspirations. The emerging black political class was devastated by Redemption—murdered or driven from their communities by violence or deprived of the opportunity to hold office, except in a few exceptional areas of the South. Black politicians ceased to exercise real power, apart from a handful of men dependent on federal patronage and on prominent politicos who advised Republican presidents on token appointments for blacks. Men of ambition in the black community now found other outlets for their talents, whether in education, business, the church, or the professions.

Nearly a century would pass before the southern black community was again as fully galvanized at the grass roots by political activity.

The Political Economy of the Black Family during Reconstruction

JACQUELINE JONES

The northerners' hope that black workers would be able to pursue their interests as individuals did not take into account the strong family ties that bound black households tightly together. More specifically, although black women constituted a sizable proportion of the region's labor force, their obligations to their husbands and children and kin took priority over any form of personal self-seeking. For most black women, then, freedom had very little to do with individual opportunity or independence in the modern sense. Rather, freedom had meaning primarily in a family context. The institution of slavery had posed a constant threat to the stability of family relationships; after emancipation these relationships became solidified, though the sanctity of family life continued to come under pressure from the larger white society. Freedwomen derived emotional fulfillment and a newfound sense of pride from their roles as wives and mothers. Only at home could they exercise considerable control over their own lives and those of their husbands and children and impose a semblance of order on the physical world.

As soon as they were free, blacks set their own work pace and conspired to protect one another from the white man's (and woman's) wrath. Plantation managers charged that freed people, hired to work like slaves, were "loafering around" and "lummoxing about." More than one postwar overseer, his "patience worn plum out," railed against "grunting" blacks (those "pretending to be sick") and others who sauntered out into the fields late in the day, left early to go fishing, or stayed home altogether; "damd sorry work" was the result. Modern economic historians confirm contemporary estimates that by the 1870s the amount of black labor in the fields had dropped to one-quarter or one-third preemancipation levels.

The withdrawal of black females from wage-labor—a major theme in both contemporary and secondary accounts of Reconstruction—occurred primarily among the wives and daughters of able-bodied men. (Women who served as the sole support for their children or other family members had to take work wherever they could find it.) According to a South Carolina newspaper writer in 1871, this development necessitated a "radical change in the management of [white] households as well as plantations" and proved to be a source of "absolute torment" for former masters and mistresses. The female field hand who plowed, hoed, and picked cotton under the ever-watchful eye of an overseer came to symbolize the old order.

Employers made little effort to hide their contempt for freedwomen who "played the lady" and refused to join workers in the fields. To apply the term ladylike to a black woman was apparently the height of sarcasm; by socially prescribed definition, black women could never become "ladies," though they might display pretensions in that direction. The term itself had predictable racial and class connotations. White ladies remained cloistered at home, fulfilling their marriage vows of motherhood and genteel domesticity. But black housewives appeared "most lazy"; they stayed "out of the fields, doing nothing," demanding that their husbands "support them in idleness." At the heart of the issue lay the whites' notion of productive labor; black women who eschewed work under the direct supervision of former masters did not really "work" at all, regardless of their family household responsibilities.

In their haste to declare "free labor" a success, even northerners and foreign visitors to the South ridiculed "lazy" freedwomen working within the confines of their own homes. Hypocritically—almost perversely—these whites questioned the "manhood" of husbands whom they charged were cowed by domineering female relatives. South Carolina Freedmen's Bureau agent John De Forest, for example, wrote that "myriads of women who once earned their own living now have aspirations to be like white ladies and, instead of using the hoe, pass the days in dawdling over their trivial housework, or gossiping among their neighbors." He disdained the "hopeless" look given him by men told "they must make their wives and daughters work." George Campbell, a Scotsman touring the South in 1878, declared, "I do not sympathize with negro ladies who make their husbands work while they enjoy the sweets of emancipation."

Most southern and northern whites assumed that the freed people were engaged in a misguided attempt to imitate middle-class white norms as they applied to women's roles. Even recent historians have suggested that the refusal of married women to work in the fields signified "conformity to dominant white values." In fact, however, the situation was a good deal more complicated. First, the reorganization of female labor resulted from choices made by *both* men and women. Second, it is inaccurate to speak of the "removal" of women from the agricultural work force. Many were no longer working for a white overseer, but they continued to pick cotton, laboring according to the needs and priorities established by their own families.

An Alabama planter suggested in 1868 that it was "a matter of pride with the men, to allow all exemption from labor to their wives." He told only part of the story. Accounts provided by disgruntled whites suggest that husbands did often take full responsibility for deciding which members of the family would work, and for whom: "Gilbert will stay on his old terms, but withdraws Fanny and puts Harry and Little Abram in her place and puts his son Gilbert out to a trade," reported a Georgia plantation mistress in January 1867. However, there is good reason to suspect that wives willingly devoted more time to childcare and other domestic matters, rather than merely acquiescing in their husbands' demands. A married freedwoman, the mother of eleven children, reminded a northern journalist that she had had "to nus' my chil'n four times a day and pick two hundred pounds cotton besides" under slavery. She expressed at least relative satisfaction with her current situation: "I've a heap better time now'n I had when I was in bondage." *

The humiliations of slavery remained fresh in the minds of black women who continued to suffer physical abuse at the hands of white employers and in the minds of freedmen who witnessed or heard about such acts. . . . [I]t is important to note only that freedmen attempted to protect their womenfolk from rape and other forms of assault; as individuals, some intervened directly, while others went to local Freedmen's Bureau agents with accounts of beatings inflicted on their wives, sisters, and daughters. Bureau records include the case of a Tennessee planter who "made several base attempts" upon the daughter of the freedman Sam Neal (his entire family had been hired by the white man for the 1865 season). When Neal protested the situation, he was deprived of his wages, threatened with death, and then beaten badly by the white man and an accomplice. As a group, men sought to minimize chances for white male–black female contact by removing their female kin from work environments supervised closely by whites.

At first, cotton growers persisted in their belief that gangs afforded the most efficient means of labor organization because they had been used with relative success under slavery and facilitated centralization of control. Blacks only had to be forced to work steadily. However, Charles P. Ware, a Yankee cotton agent with [Edward] Philbrick on the Sea Islands, noted as early as 1862, "one thing the people are universally opposed to. They all swear that they will not work in a gang, i.e., all working the whole, and all sharing alike." Blacks preferred to organize themselves into kin groups, as evidenced by the "squad" system, an intermediary phase between gang labor and family sharecropping. A postwar observer defined the squad as "a strong family group, who can attach other labour, and bring odd hands to work at proper seasons"; this structure represented "a choice, if not always attainable, nucleus of a 'squad.'"

Described by one scholar as a "non-bureaucratic, self-regulating, and self-selecting worker peer group," the squad usually numbered less than a dozen people (seven was average), and performed its tasks under the direction of one of its own members. In this way kinship patterns established under slavery coalesced into work relationships after the war. Still, blacks resented an arrangement under which they continued to live together in old slave quarters grouped near the landowner's house and lacked complete control over the work they performed in the field.

In the late 1860s this tug of economic and psychological warfare between planters determined to grow more cotton and blacks determined to resist the old slave ways culminated in what historians have called a "compromise"—the sharecropping system. It met the minimal demands of each party—a relatively reliable source of labor for white landowners, and, for freed people (more specifically, for families), a measure of independence in terms of agricultural decision making. Sharecroppers moved out of the old cabins and into small houses scattered about the plantation. Contracts were renegotiated around the end of each calendar year; families not in debt to their employers for equipment and fertilizer often seized the opportunity to move in search of a better situation. By 1870 the "fifty-fifty" share arrangement under which planters parceled out to tenants small plots of land and provided rations and supplies in return for one-half the crop predominated throughout the Cotton South.

According to historians and econometricians who have documented the evolution of sharecropping, the system helped to reshape southern race and class relations even as it preserved the "stagnant" postbellum economy. The linking of personal financial credit to crop liens and the rise of debt peonage enforced by criminal statutes guaranteed a large, relatively immobile labor force at the expense of economic and social justice. In increasing numbers, poor whites would come under the same financial constraints that ensnared black people. But, for the purposes of this discussion, the significance of this "almost unprecedented form of labor organization" lies in its implications for black family life.

Although 1870 data present only a static profile of black rural households in the Cotton South, it is possible to make some generalizations (based on additional forms of evidence) about the status of freedwomen five years after the war. The vast majority (91 percent) lived in rural areas. Illiterate and very poor (even compared to their poor white neighbors), they nonetheless were not alone, and shared the mixed joys of work and family life with their husbands, children, and nearby kin. Fertility rates declined very slowly from 1830 to 1880; the average mother in 1870 had about six or seven children. The lives of these women were severely circumscribed, as were those of other family members. Most of the children never had an opportunity to attend school—or at least not with any regularity—and began to work in the fields or in the home of a white employer around the age of ten or twelve. Young women found it possible to leave their parents' home earlier than did the men they married. As a group, black women were distinguished from their white neighbors primarily by their lower socioeconomic status and by the greater reliance of their families on the work they did outside the realm of traditional domestic responsibilities.

Within the limited public arena open to blacks, the husband represented the entire family, a cultural preference reinforced by demographic and economic factors. In 1870, 80 percent of black households in the Cotton Belt included a male head and his wife (a proportion identical to that in the neighboring white population). In addition, most of the husbands were older than their wives—in more than half the cases, four years older; in one out of five cases, at least ten years older. Thus these men exercised authority by virtue of their age as well as their sex.

Landowners, merchants, and Freedmen's Bureau agents acknowledged the role of the black husband as the head of his family at the same time they encouraged his wife to work outside the home. He took "more or less land according to the number of his family" and placed "his *X* mark" on a labor agreement with a landowner. Kin relationships were often recognized in the text of the contract itself. Indeed, just as slaveholders had opportunistically dealt with the slave family—encouraging or ignoring it according to their own perceived interests—so postbellum planters seemed to have had little difficulty adjusting to the fact that freedmen's families were structured "traditionally" with the husband serving as the major source of authority. Patrick Broggan, an employer in Greenville, Alabama, agreed to supply food and other provisions for wives and children—"those who do not work on the farm"—"at the expense of their husbands and Fathers," men who promised "to work from Monday morning until Saturday night, faithfully and lose no time. . . ."

The Freedmen's Bureau's wage guidelines mandated that black women and men receive unequal compensation based on their sex rather than their productive abilities or efficiency. Agents also at times doled out less land to families with female (as opposed to male) household heads. Moreover, the bureau tried to hold men responsible for their wives' unwillingness to labor according to a contractual agreement. For example, the Cuthbert, Georgia, bureau official made one black man promise "to work faithfully and keep his wife in subjection" after the woman refused to work and "damned the Bureau" saying that "all the Bureaus out cant make her work."

A black husband usually purchased the bulk of the family's supplies (either in town or from a rural local merchant) and arranged to borrow or lease any stock animals that might be needed in plowing. He received direct payment in return for the labor of a son or daughter who had been "hired out." (It is uncertain whether a single mother who operated a farm delegated these responsibilities to her oldest son or another male kin relation, or took care of them herself.) Finally, complaints and criminal charges lodged by black men against whites often expressed the grievances of an entire household.

Thus the sexual division of labor that had existed within the black family under slavery became more sharply focused after emancipation. Wives and mothers and husbands and fathers perceived domestic duties to be a woman's major obligation, in contrast to the slave master's view that a female was first and foremost a field or house worker and only incidentally the member of a family. Women also worked in the fields when their labor was needed. At planting and especially harvest time they joined their husbands and children outside. During the late summer and early fall some would hire out to white planters in the vicinity to pick cotton for a daily wage. In areas where black men could find additional work during the year—on rice plantations or in phosphate mines or sugar mills, for example—they left their "women and children to hoe and look after the crops. . . ." Thus women's agricultural labor partook of a more seasonal character than that of their husbands.

The fact that black families depended heavily upon the field work of women and children is reflected in the great disparity between the proportion of working wives in Cotton Belt white and black households; in 1870 more than four out of ten black married women listed jobs, almost all as field laborers. By contrast, fully 98.4 percent of white wives told the census taker they were "keeping house" and had no gainful occupation. Moreover, about one-quarter (24.3 percent) of black households, in contrast to 13.8 percent of the white, included at least one working child under sixteen years of age. The figures related to black female and child labor are probably quite low, since census takers were inconsistent in specifying occupations for members of sharecropping families. In any case, they indicate that freedmen's families occupied the lowest rung of the southern economic ladder; almost three-fourths of all black household heads (compared to 10 percent of their white counterparts) worked as unskilled agricultural laborers. By the mid-1870s no more than 4 to 8 percent of all freed families in the South owned their own farms.

The rural *paterfamilias* tradition exemplified by the structure of black family relationships after the Civil War did not challenge the value and competence of freed-women as field workers. Rather, a distinct set of priorities determined how wives and mothers used their time in terms of housework, field labor, and tasks that produced supplements to the family income. Thus it is difficult to separate a freedwoman's "work" from her family-based obligations; productive labor had no meaning outside the family context. These aspects of a woman's life blended together in the seamless fabric of rural life.

Since husbands and wives had different sets of duties, they needed each other to form a complete economic unit. As one Georgia black man explained to George Campbell in the late 1870s, "The able-bodied men cultivate, the women raise chickens and take in washing; and one way and another they manage to get along." When both partners were engaged in the same kind of work, it was usually the wife who had stepped over into her husband's "sphere." For instance, Fanny Hodges and her husband wed the year after they were freed. She remembered, "We had to work mighty hard. Sometimes I plowed in de fiel' all day; sometimes I washed an' den I cooked. . . ." Cotton growing was labor-intensive in a way that gardening and housework were not, and a family's ability to obtain financial credit from one year to the next depended upon the size of past harvests and the promise of future ones. Consequently the crop sometimes took prece-dence over other chores in terms of the allocation of a woman's energies.

Age was also a crucial determinant of the division of labor in sharecropping families. Participation in household affairs could be exhilarating for a child aware of her own strength and value as a field worker during these years of turmoil. Betty Powers was only eight years old in 1865, but she long remembered days of feverish activity for the whole family after her father bought a small piece of land in Texas: "De land ain't clear, so we 'uns all pitches in and clears it and builds de cabin. Was we 'uns proud? There 'twas, our place to do as we pleases, after bein' slaves. Dat sho' am de good feelin'. We works like beavers puttin' de crop in. . . ." Sylvia Watkins recalled that her father gathered all his children together after the war. She was twenty years old at the time and appreciated the special significance of a family able to work together: "We wuked in de fiel' wid mah daddy, en I know how ter do eberting dere ez to do in a fiel' 'cept plow. . . ."

But at least some children resented the restrictions imposed by their father who "raised crops en made us wuk in de fiel." The interests of the family superseded individual desires. Fathers had the last word in deciding which children went to the fields, when, and for how long. As a result some black women looked back on their years spent at home as a time of personal opportunities missed or delayed. The Federal Writers Project slave narrative collection contains specific examples of fathers who prevented daughters from putting their own wishes before the family's welfare during the postbellum period. Ann Matthews told a federal interviewer, "I didn't go ter schul, mah daddy wouldn' let me. Said he needed me in de fiel wors den I needed schul." Here were two competing "needs," and the family had to come first.

The status of black women after the war cannot be separated from their roles as wives and mothers within a wider setting of kinship obligations. Herbert Gutman has argued that these obligations probably assumed greater significance in nineteenth-century Afro-American life than in immigrant or poor white communities because blacks possessed "a distinctive low economic status, a condition that denied them the advantages of an extensive associational life beyond the kin group and the advantages and disadvantages resulting from mobility opportunities." Indeed, more than one-third of all black households in the Cotton Belt lived in the immediate vicinity of people with the identical (paternal) surname, providing a rather crude—and conservative—index of local kinship clusters. As the persons responsible for child nurture and social welfare, freedwomen cared not only for members of their nuclear families, but also for dependent relatives and others in need. This postemancipation cooperative impulse constituted but one example of a historical "ethos of mutuality" developed under slavery.

The former slaves' attempts to provide for each other's needs appear to have been a logical and humane response to widespread hardship during the 1860s and 1870s. But whites spared from physical suffering, including southern elites and representatives of the northern professional class, often expressed misgivings about this form of benevolence. They believed that any able-bodied black person deserved a "living" only to the extent that he or she contributed to the southern commercial economy. Blacks should reap according to the cottonseed they sowed.

Soon after she returned to her family's Sea Island estate in 1866, Frances Leigh thought there was nothing else "to become of the negroes who cannot work except to die." In this way she masked her grief over the death of slavery with professed concern for ill, young, and elderly freed people. But within a few months she declared with evident irritation, ". . . it is a well-known fact that you can't starve a negro." Noting that about a dozen people on Butler's Island did not work (in the cotton fields) at all and so received no clothes or food supplies, the white woman admitted that she saw "no difference whatever in their condition and those who get twelve dollars a month and full rations." Somehow the field workers and nonworkers alike managed to take care of themselves and each other by growing vegetables, catching fish, and trapping game. Consequently they relied less on wages paid by their employer. The threat of starvation proved to be a poor taskmaster in compelling these freed people to toil for Frances Leigh.

Too many blacks, according to bureau agent John De Forest, felt obliged to look after "a horde of lazy relatives" and neighbors, thus losing a precious opportunity to get ahead on their own. This tendency posed a serious threat to the South's new economic order, founded as it was, in De Forest's view, on individual effort and ambition. He pointed to the case of Aunt Judy, a black laundress who barely eked out a living for herself and her small children. Yet she had "benevolently taken in, and was nursing, a sick woman of her own race. . . . The thoughtless charity of this penniless Negress in receiving another poverty-stricken creature under her roof was characteristic of the freedmen. However selfish, and even dishonest, they might be, they were extravagant in giving." By calling the willingness to share a "thoughtless" act, De Forest implied that a "rational" economic being would labor only to enhance her own material welfare.

The racial self-consciousness demonstrated by black women and men within their own kin networks found formal, explicit expression in the political arena during Reconstruction. As Vincent Harding and others have shown, freedmen actively participated in postwar Republican politics, and leaders of their own race came to constitute a new and influential class within black communities (though rivalries among members of this group could at times be intense). Class relationships that had prevailed before the war shifted, opening up possibilities of cooperation between the former slaves and nonelite whites. The two groups met at a historical point characterized by landlessness and economic dependence, but they were on two different trajectories—the freed people on their way up (no matter how slightly) from slavery, the poor whites on their way down from self-sufficiency. Nevertheless, the vitality of the political process, tainted though it was by virulent racial prejudice and violence, provided black men with a public forum distinct from the private sphere inhabited by their womenfolk.

Black men predominated in this arena because, like other groups in nineteenth-century America, they believed that males alone were responsible for—and capable of—the serious business of politicking. This notion was reinforced by laws that barred female suffrage. However, black husbands and fathers, unlike their white counterparts, perceived the preservation and physical welfare of their families (including protection from terrorists) to be distinct political issues, along with predictable measures like land reform and debt relief. In political activity, freedmen extended their role as family protector outside the boundaries of the household. One searches in vain for any mention of women delegates in accounts of formal black political conventions held during this period—local and state gatherings during which men formulated and articulated their vision of a just postwar society. Freedwomen sometimes spoke up forcefully at meetings devoted to specific community issues, but they remained outside the formal political process. (In this respect white women occupied a similarly inferior position.) The sight of black wives patiently tilling the soil while their husbands attended political conventions, at times for days on end, convinced at least one white teacher that freedwomen deserved to participate more actively in the community's public life. Elizabeth Botume wrote in 1869:

We could not help wishing that since so much of the work was done by the colored women,—raising the provisions for their families, besides making and selling their own cotton, they might also hold some of the offices held by the men. I am confident they would despatch [*sic*] business if allowed to go to the polls; instead of listening and hanging around all day, discussing matters of which they knew so little, they would exclaim,—

"Let me vote and go; I've got work to do."

In praising black women and their potential for political leadership, Botume denigrated black men. Like so many northerners, she could hardly express positive sentiments toward one sex without belittling the other.

It is true that freedmen monopolized formal positions of power within their own communities during Reconstruction. But that did not necessarily mean that women quietly deferred to them in all matters outside the home. For example, in some rural areas two sources of religious authority—one dominated by men, the other by women—co-existed uneasily. At times formal role designations only partly reflected the "influence" wielded by individuals outside their own households. In the process of institutionalizing clandestine religious practices formed during slavery and separating them from white congregations, freed people reserved church leadership positions for men. In other ways, individual congregations fashioned a distinctly inferior role for women; some even turned women out of the sanctuary "before the men began to talk" about matters of church policy. On the Sea Islands, whites reported the public censure of freedwomen who had committed marital transgressions by showing a lack of proper respect for their husbands' authority. The biblical injunction "Wives submit yourselves to your husbands" provided preachers with a succinct justification for church-based decisions that seemed arbitrary or unfair to the women involved.

These examples must be contrasted with equally dramatic cases of women who exercised considerable influence over their neighbors' spiritual lives, but outside of formal religious bodies and, indeed, of Protestant denominationalism altogether. Elderly women in the long line of African and Afro-American conjurers and herb doctors were often eagerly consulted by persons of both sexes. They included the African-born Maum Katie, "a great 'spiritual mother', a fortune-teller, or rather prophetess, and a woman of tremendous influence over her children," as well as other women whose pronouncements and incantations were believed to be divinely inspired. Rural communities had two (in all probability competing) sources of spiritual and secular guidance—one a male, and formal, the other female, and informal—and this pattern magnified the sex-role differentiation within individual households.

In rejecting the forced pace of the slave regimen and embracing a family-based system of labor organization, freed people exhibited a preference for work patterns typical of a "traditional" rural society in which religious, regional, and kinship loyalties are the dominant values, as opposed to personal ambition or the nationalistic goal of social and economic "progress." Indeed, very soon after emancipation black households emerged—set within larger networks of kin and community—that closely conformed to the "premodern" family model. In this case the terms traditional and premodern are misleading, however, because the sharecropping family that lived and worked together actually represented an adaptation, or response, to postwar conditions rather than a clinging to old ways. This development, initiated so boldly by blacks, was particularly significant because it contrasted sharply with trends characteristic of late nineteenth-century northern society, in which making a living was increasingly carried on by individuals, apart from family life.

The Reconstruction of the Cotton Plantation in the New South

HAROLD D. WOODMAN

Substantial evidence supports the view that continuity is the major theme in nineteenth-century southern history. It would appear, therefore, that . . . use of the term "revolutionary" to describe the effects of the Civil War and emancipation is completely inappropriate. At best it might be used to describe the possibility for change favored by some who ultimately did not prevail. Freedmen received neither land nor mules, and they failed to keep their political rights. Freedom became a mockery when the lyncher's rope replaced the slaveowner's lash, debt servitude replaced slavery, and racism justified repression just as it had justified slavery. King Cotton remained on his throne, and the South, except in a few scattered places, did not experience the rapid industrial and commercial expansion that took place elsewhere in the nation.

That there is considerable evidence for continuity in the nineteenth-century South should not be surprising. The Civil War neither destroyed nor dispersed the people, black and white. Obviously, the world these people built after the war was heavily influenced by the legacy of the antebellum world, the only one they knew. Indeed, it is my argument that the only way to understand social and economic reconstruction is to appreciate the importance of this legacy as it affected the course of a fundamental and revolutionary transformation of the South. The task is not to compare a list showing changes with another showing continuity in order to determine which one best characterizes the nineteenth-century South. Comparing such lists inevitably leads to the convenient and liberal-minded conclusion that there was both continuity and change, a resolution that merely leaves the question unanswered.

Instead of chronicling quantity, we must rather assess quality: the problem is not how *much* change but what *kind* of change. Those who count persisting planters and Whigs, or list persisting evidences of racism or persisting patterns of coercion, are not so much wrong as incomplete in their analyses, because they ignore the social revolution initiated by and required by emancipation: a slave society had to be transformed into a bourgeois, free labor society. The Civil War and emancipation achieved only half a revolution; they destroyed an old economic system but created nothing to replace it. Moreover, this destructive half of the revolution, although it had supporters within the South (most notably the blacks but also some whites), did not result from an internal upheaval by a class armed with the experience, the ideology, and the vision of a new society. It was imposed from the outside. Thus, the remaining half of the revolution, the building of a free labor economy and society, had to be achieved by a population that had not initiated the revolution in the first place—indeed, by a population that included large numbers who actively and violently opposed it. This alone would explain evidences of continuity.

But these elements of continuity do not signal counterrevolution. Slavery was gone. Slaves who had been chattel became free workers; planters who had been slaveowners producing a single crop for a world market, and a food supply that made their plantations self-sufficient rural centers of power, became businessmen, employers of free labor, and investors in agricultural, industrial, and commercial enterprises; whites who had never owned slaves, who had produced a rude if ample self-sufficiency on their small farms, became commercial farmers, mill hands, and industrial workers. Such massive social changes can only be described as revolutionary.

To say that slaves became free workers is not to deny that they were subjected to violence, intimidation, and other forms of coercion; or that their freedom of choice was often the choice between one kind of work and starvation; or that their living and working conditions were wretched. But such language could also be, and was, applied to the condition of the working class in the North, in England, in France, and elsewhere at the time. A casual glance at the reformist literature of the late nineteenth century makes it clear that the South had no monopoly on coercing and underpaying workers, or on company stores and company towns. Even if it could be shown that the treatment of blacks was worse than that of northern workers, it would not follow that blacks were not free workers. That they were "free" means that they were no longer property to be bought, sold, traded, and moved at the whim of their owners, and that they were no longer wealth to serve as collateral for loans or as symbols of prestige and power. Only if we equate free labor with freedom in its democratic and equalitarian sense will we have difficulty seeing and appreciating the importance of the change from slavery to free labor.

That the change, when stated in this way, seems obvious does not make it unimportant. That former slaveowners had difficulty accepting the change, or that freedmen understood it quite differently from their former owners and their northern liberators, does not mean it did not take place. Emancipation created the necessary condition for the rise of a free labor system, but it was not sufficient in itself to create that system immediately. Such a system requires that there be a market for labor power rather than for laborers themselves, but this in turn requires a set of institutions and perceptions and an ideology that allow that market to function. The conflicts and struggles in the postwar South may be best understood as arising from tensions between an inherited ideology based on slavery and the need to forge the institutions necessary for a free labor system. If we start with the obvious yet fundamental change from slavery to free labor and then recognize that southerners, black and white, had to complete the revolution begun by emancipation by building a free labor society, we can begin to make sense of the confusing and often contradictory evidence we find in our investigations of the postwar years: the great variety of early tenure forms; the tentativeness and variability in early laws regarding liens and tenancy; the conflicts among merchants, planters, yeomen, and blacks over rights and duties; the nature and extent of violence and coercion. What appears to be confusion often approaching anarchy becomes comprehensible when we recognize that people held varying views shaped by a past experience that had become irrelevant. They were looking backward as they stumbled uncertainly into the future.

For many of the victorious northerners, the future did not seem uncertain—at least not at first. Those who went south to work with the freedmen were filled with enthusiasm and confidence. Once released from the shackles of slavery, the blacks, they thought, would respond like free people everywhere, would be eager to work because they would now reap the benefits of their toil. True, slavery had kept them in the grossest ignorance and had linked labor and servitude, but proper schools and adequate returns from their work would help them overcome slavery's pernicious legacy quickly and easily. Motivated by an evangelical humanitarianism, they came south, opened schools, and (in

Horace Mann Bond's words) provided the blacks with "moral homilies . . . in the best New England Sunday School style," reflecting the "youthful industrialism of the North" in the prewar generation in which they had grown up.

The benefit of hindsight informed Bond's cynicism about Sunday School homilies, but his recognition of the source of these ideas remains a significant insight. By the mid-nineteenth century, a free labor ideology had become pervasive in the North. It was a view that stressed the dignity of labor and the opportunities available to those who worked hard and were honest and faithful. It described the system itself; as [the historian] David Montgomery, has noted, "the nation's economic system was not called 'capitalism' but the 'free-labor system.'" And this system, northerners insisted, stood in marked contrast to that in the South. As [another historian,] Daniel T. Rodgers, observes, northerners "saw themselves as a society of hard-working and economically independent farmers, mechanics, and tradesmen, defending the cause of a worker's freedom against the inroads of the Southern master-servant economy." . . .

. . . But when it came time to create a free labor system in the South, differences arose among advocates of free labor. [Some] envisioned a South of small, independent farmers and merchants, while others, equally ardent supporters of a free labor system, emphasized the need to get southerners back to work producing the valuable staple crops, particularly cotton. . . .

The basic assumption in the free labor ideology was that people would work without physical compulsion because it was in their own interest to do so. Slavery was socially debilitating because slaves worked merely to avoid punishment. Free people worked harder and more reliably than slaves because they reaped the benefits of their work. With each individual working for his own gain, the entire society would benefit from the resulting increase in total output and wealth. Thus, what Adam Smith had called the "invisible hand" would guide the South to the end that [the New England businessman Edward] Atkinson had described.

The means to get the process underway seemed obvious, at least to [most] north-erners. . . . Southerners had the land, the labor, and the knowhow to produce cotton. Prices for the staple were high, indicating strong demand. Given such conditions, the rest would be automatic. This explains Atkinson's initial enthusiasm, but it does not explain what actually happened.

If the general proposition were true that people will voluntarily work for their own benefit (even if that benefit be merely the avoidance of starvation), "it did not follow," as [the historian] Thomas C. Holt has put it, "that freedmen would apply themselves to the production of plantation staples or that their labor would be disciplined and reliable." Nor did it follow that their potential employers, the planters who had owned them as chattel, would know how to deal with the freedmen as employees. . . .

From all over the South, Freedmen's Bureau officials reported much the same story. Although they retained their faith in the free labor system, their work in the field demonstrated that the system was not easily applied. "It is a subject of congratulation," reported John C. Robinson from North Carolina, "to see the great good that has been accomplished in the elevation of a race of people to a sphere which their habits and education, and the opposition of their former owners made it extremely difficult for them to understand." Similarly, R. K. Scott concluded his report from South Carolina by noting that the "free labor of the past year in this State, notwithstanding the ignorance of the freedmen, the want of capital, and the impracticable views of land owners, has demonstrated the fact that the same incentive which prompts the white man of the north and other countries to labor will apply to the freedmen of the south."

It was apparent that the mere absence of slavery did not ensure the presence of a liberal bourgeois economy. The free market would operate only if people acted as they were supposed to. But, alas, southerners—black and white—did not. Slavery turned out to be more than a legal relationship; it had social and psychological dimensions that did not disappear with the passage of a law or a constitutional amendment. People had to learn how to respond—perhaps even be coerced.

Such was the conclusion of one Captain Charles Soule, head of a "Special Commission on Contracts with Freedmen at Orangeburg, S.C.," who in mid-1865 called together the local freedmen and read them a carefully prepared speech designed to explain the duties and responsibilities of free people and to disabuse them of a number of pernicious ideas that the blacks, in their naiveté, might confuse with freedom. He told the assembled freedmen that their duty was to work hard and obey orders. He warned them not to expect that freedom would automatically ensure the good life: "You are now free," he said, "but you must know that the only difference you can feel yet, between slavery and freedom, is that neither you nor your children can be bought or sold. You may have a harder time this year than you have ever had before; it will be the price you pay for freedom."

Blacks might have wondered about the value of freedom that had such a high price. Their wonder probably increased when Soule informed them that they not only had to work harder but had to do much the same work they had done as slaves. "Do not think, because you are free you can choose your own kind of work," he warned, explaining that "every man has his own place, his own trade that he was brought up to, and he must stick to it." For blacks, this place was work as fieldhands or house servants. There was no shame in such labor: "If a man works, no matter in what business, he is doing well. The only shame is to be idle and lazy."

Soule then went on to provide a cogent analysis of how the free labor system worked:

> You do not understand why some of the white people who used to own you, do not have to work in the field. It is because they are rich. If every man were poor, and worked in his own field, there would be no big farms, and very little cotton or corn raised to sell; there would be no money, and nothing to buy. Some people must be rich, to pay the others, and they have the right to do no work except to look out after their property. It is so everywhere.

The assembled blacks were probably surprised to learn that "it is so everywhere," for the free labor system that Soule described seemed no different from the slave system from which they had expected to be freed. But Soule noted what to him was a big difference: "Perhaps," he explained, "by hard work some of you may by-and-by become rich yourselves."

Soule sent a copy of his speech to Maj. Gen. O. O. Howard, the head of the Freedmen's Bureau. In a covering letter he explained to Howard that their experiences as slaves had failed to equip blacks with the proper attitudes. They refused fair contracts for work, took time off from their labors, were generally idle and often vicious—all vices that he attributed "not so much to their race, as to the system of slavery under which they had lived." The rigorous discipline of the plantation is gone, he explained, leaving blacks with nothing but the vices associated with slavery. Therefore, the new regime required a new "code of laws and punishments" to destroy slavery's vices and to teach the blacks by experience new patterns of behavior. "Only actual suffering, starvation, and punishment will drive many of them to work."

Soule found no reason to be apprehensive about the attitude of the former slaveowners. Deprived of their slaves, they had no choice but to turn to free labor to work their fields—and this, he said, was exactly what they were trying to do. He admitted that deep in the countryside some planters continued to treat the blacks as slaves, but such behavior would disappear as soon as the blacks became responsible workers, aware of their obligations.

Soule patterned his vision of the future of the South on his perception of the good' society in the North—a disciplined, responsible, and energetic working class, adequately but not extravagantly paid, willingly and cheerfully accepting the direction of employers. He was not advocating a return to slavery; he would have been outraged if so charged. He was advocating a thoroughly bourgeois relation between capital and labor. The planters' offers of housing, food, clothing, and sometimes a small portion of the crop were certainly fair and adequate wages, he argued. After all, he explained, laborers in the North usually spent their entire wages for food, clothing, and house rent. If the freedmen received more, "the relation between capital and labor would be disturbed." Critics in the North were already terming such conditions "wage slavery," but no such idea troubled Soule.

General Howard, both more sensitive and more perceptive than his subordinate, congratulated Soule for his efforts "to secure harmony and good will in society." He did not object to Soule's advice to the freedmen, but added mildly that "while we show the freedmen how freemen support themselves at the North by labor, we ought to let him [*sic*] taste somewhat of the freeman's privileges." The planters, he warned, wanted to deny the freedmen those privileges by imposing a "despotism" that was very close to slavery, and they expected the federal authorities to grant them the necessary authority and backing to do so. He gently chided his subordinate for being deceived by the planters' "sophistries," suggesting that they too required attention. If former slaves lacked the experience of free workers and needed Soule's earnest advice, former slaveowners were "mostly ignorant of the workings of free labor," and needed advice as well: "You had better therefore draw up an address to them also explaining their duties and obligations."

The Civil War and emancipation had destroyed traditional lines of authority, leaving the chaos and uncertainty that so troubled people such as Soule. Emancipation without any form of payment or other support for the freed slaves (beyond the temporary relief offered by the army and the Freedmen's Bureau, relief that was niggardly to begin with and withdrawn as quickly as possible for fear of weakening the work ethic among blacks) meant that the ex-slaves had no choice but to go to work on the farms and plantations of their former owners. Northerners saw this as the first step in the creation of a free labor society—even after they recognized that the change would not proceed as smoothly as they had hoped and expected, and even when they disagreed about the sources of the problems that arose. New lines of authority had to be established, but by whom and to what end remained uncertain.

The old planters found their accustomed authority challenged from every direction—by blacks, by Freedmen's Bureau officials, by enterprising merchants, by [Republicans] in the state legislatures, by Washington, and—most debilitating of all—by their own inability to cope with changed conditions. Hiring laborers cost money, which the factors upon whom they had always relied were often unable to supply, especially after initial crop failures made it impossible to repay loans. The blacks frequently proved unreliable, leaving the fields at crucial times to work for others who promised higher pay—an action that seemed reasonable enough to those learning the oft repeated lessons about the operation of the free labor market, but completely unreasonable to those with a crop to care for and no workers in the fields.

In an attempt to improve the situation, planters offered to pay workers a share of what they produced instead of a monthly cash wage. They thought that workers would be more industrious if they shared in the output and would not leave before the harvest for fear of forfeiting their wages. Furthermore, under this arrangement planters could proceed with a minimum of operating expenses because most of the workers' wages would not be paid until the crop was picked and sold. As this system became popular, it intensified the problems instead of solving them and created new and unexpected difficulties. When crop failures meant that there was nothing to be divided, employees became understandably reluctant to contract again on the same terms. Many workers complained that planters, despite the agreements, failed to pay them their share or drove them away after the crop was made but before the sale and division of proceeds. Planters, for their part, charged that workers would steal cotton from the fields and trade it for goods at local stores, where the merchants gave little thought to who owned the cotton they were buying in small parcels, often in the dead of night.

Other problems, new and confusing, arose. Workers insisted that their contracts called for the making of a particular crop, and they refused to do extra work—fencing, ditching, and other general maintenance as well as preparation of the fields for the next season—without extra pay. When planters sought to include these services in the contracts, the blacks simply declined to work for them. In brief, the blacks expected freedom to mean that they would no longer be treated like slaves. They opposed the planters' demands that they work the same hours, exert the same effort, and obey the same rules as they had as slaves. They demanded the right to work fewer hours, to allow their women to remain at home, to come and go as they pleased, and even to have a voice in the management of production—arguing that if they shared in the output, they should have a share in decisions that influenced that output. Some went so far as to claim that not only were they no longer slaves, but neither had they become employees or tenants; rather their new status made them partners in the enterprise.

Planters, to their disgust and chagrin, found themselves competing for the services of their former slaves by offering higher wages or a larger share of the crop, by promising to provide a school on the plantation, by providing food and clothing for both the men and their families, even when the women and children did not work in the fields. Workers resisted gang labor under close supervision as being no improvement over slavery. Unable to secure their own land, they sought increased independence in other ways, and learned to organize and withhold their labor until their demands were met. Some organized "companies," agreeing to work as a group on a particular parcel of land under their own supervision. Others sought to rent or lease land and work it themselves. Many refused to live in the old slave-quarter cabins, preferring to live in town, in their own communities, or scattered on the lands they worked.

Edwin De Leon, an ardent and early advocate of the "New South," presented a gloomy picture of conditions in 1874. The causes of the general social disorganization, he perceptively noted, "have been partly political and partly produced by the effects of the earthquake shock which overturned the whole system of Southern life and labor, and the struggle to substitute a new one." Southern progress, he insisted, depended upon social stability. "The great, the vital question for the Southern cotton and sugar-growing region is the question of labor, and its regulation so as to make it profitable to employer and employed." Although he could not predict how this "vital question" would be solved, he did find hopeful signs, the most important being the fall of the [Republican] state governments.

Although they might not have been clear to De Leon, writing in 1874, changes were already underway. Hindsight allows us to see the growth and consolidation of a new dominant class made up of some elements of the old planter aristocracy and some newcomers who were able to capitalize on the new conditions. A number of historians have noted what they call the "persistence" of planters in the new South and have found this to be the basis for what they consider the persistence of old South values and perceptions in the new South. But such a view ignores the fundamental change that was taking place. More important than the genealogy of the new class was the changed ideology of its members and their changed relationship to the means of production. Planters—at least those who survived and prospered—became businessmen, as did a growing merchant class that acquired large landholdings in the countryside. For many such capitalist landlords, land became but one in a portfolio of investments that included stores, gins, compresses, lumbering operations, and other businesses, as well as holdings in railroads, banks, and factories and speculation in the market, especially in cotton futures. Although this new class owed its wealth primarily to the agricultural sector (which remained overwhelmingly the most important in the southern economy), its orientation was urban, toward market and trade centers. Some were absentee landlords, living in town and relying on others to supervise their lands and collect rents, while they devoted their energies to other economic pursuits. Others resided in the rural areas, turning dusty little crossroads villages into nerve centers for the direction of agricultural production, financing, marketing, and research.

Corresponding to these changes were similarly significant changes in the working class. The first step in solving what De Leon called "the great, the vital" problem of the South—the organization and discipline of the labor force—was in a very real sense a compromise: the recognition and acceptance of the fact that the blacks would not continue to work in gangs under strict supervision as they had as slaves. Wage labor on plantations of the prewar type gave way to what can be called share wages, whereby workers were paid a share of what they produced, but as I have already noted, this system did not have the results the planters expected. Gradually, in some instances, share wages evolved into tenancy; that is, payment *by* the landlord of a portion of the crop as wages became payment *to* the landlord of a portion of the crop as rent. Other, less unusual forms of tenancy also arose: payment of a set amount of cotton for use of the land (standing rent), and payment of an agreed amount of cash per acre for use of the land (money rent). At the same time, in other instances, share wages came to be called sharecropping. The sharecropper was not a tenant but a wage worker whose wages—a share of what he produced on a given parcel of land—were paid *to* him by the landowner.

Changes came gradually, piecemeal, experimentally; they were compromises between landowners, eager to get their lands worked, and blacks, eager to get away from the slavelike gang labor system and achieve something approaching the independence of the small farmer. Blacks worked specified plots of land, earning a portion of the income from them; they moved away from the old slave quarters and, they expected, the watchful eye of the planter.

But if blacks expected that tenancy and sharecropping would put management decisions in their hands, the landlords—at least some of them—expected to provide that management. The resulting conflict concerned the familiar problems of labor-management relations in a free labor, capitalist economy: rates of pay, hours of work, degree of supervision. The particular conditions in the South posed in addition questions of the mix of crops to be grown; the disposition of the crops after harvest; the tenure arrangements on the land; the source, amount, and cost of credit; and, usually, living conditions as well, because housing, rights of fishing and hunting, use of land for gardens and livestock grazing, and rights to woodlots for fuel were a part of agreements between landowners and workers.

How these problems would be solved—or to use more specific terms, what the outcome of the class struggle would be—would depend upon the relative strength of the contending forces. The rapid decline in the activities of the Freedmen's Bureau and the demise of the [Republican] governments ended the minimal protection that such agencies had afforded blacks. The increased power of the planters in the legislatures and the courts provided additional opportunities to solve the labor question. With civil government in their hands and with the black vote controlled by intimidation and fraud, the landlords had the law and the police to secure their interests; and they had little fear of punishment should it be necessary to use extralegal means to control their labor force.

Gradually, the new free labor system had taken shape. Put succinctly, what finally emerged in the southern countryside was capitalistic agriculture. To be sure, capitalism in the South differed from that in the North in a number of important ways that cannot be ignored, but in its basic class structure and its organization of production, it resembled the North more than it differed. Furthermore, in its evolution over time, southern capitalism paralleled that of the North, exhibiting in some areas the same features of concentration and centralization of production.

At the heart of the change in the countryside was the reemergence of the plantation. Not until 1910 did the census bureau recognize what had happened. Since 1870 the census had considered all farming units, whether operated by an owner or a tenant, as separate farms; when it realized that this was misleading, the bureau collected data on "plantations in the South," which were published as a chapter in the 1910 census and then separately in an expanded version in 1916. At about the same time, agencies in the United States Department of Agriculture were compiling information concerning farm management in the South, as were various state departments of agriculture and extension stations.

From this information it is possible to see that the organization of agricultural production took three very different forms. No clear line separated one form from another, and at any given moment an area might be in the process of change and therefore impossible to classify with precision. Nevertheless, by the end of the nineteenth century, the three forms were clearly apparent.

In some places, notably the Delta region and some of the old black-belt areas, there arose large-scale, centrally organized production units that may be best termed "new business plantations." Resident managers and supervisory personnel made all production decisions, owned the land and all tools of production, and owned and controlled the entire output. The work force, primarily black sharecroppers, in practice and in law were considered wage workers who received as pay the value of a portion of what they produced on a parcel of land assigned to them.

A second form of organization was the tenant plantation. Although often large, it was not a centralized production unit. Absentee landlords only casually and intermittently supervised tenants, who paid their rent in money, a proportion of the crop, or a set amount of the crop. Each tenant family worked its individual plot, made its own production decisions, and owned and controlled the output, all subject to liens required by landlords and merchants to guarantee the payment of rent and any loans of money or supplies needed to produce the crop. Both blacks and whites were tenants, the blacks predominating in the old black belt, the whites in the upland regions.

The third form of organization was that of the small landowners. Although they owned their own land, these producers, like the tenants, had to provide liens in order to secure necessary advances. In addition, many mortgaged their land, which meant that when times were bad, they lost their property and fell into the ranks of tenants. Some small landowners were black but most were white, the descendants of the antebellum yeomen farmers.

By recognizing these general trends we can resolve a number of contradictions that have vexed historians. Evidence concerning such matters as the degree of supervision of workers, the power and influence of merchants, and the effects of the lien laws appears contradictory only when the controlling assumption is that of a static agricultural economy displaying minor variations over time and place and by race and class. Once this static view is replaced by what I suggest is a more realistic dynamic picture, apparent contradictions or random variations can be seen as the different characteristics of different systems of production. . . .

To insist, as I have, that the Civil War and emancipation brought a revolutionary change to the South is not to insist that the new South shed all the baggage of the past in creating a free labor system. My point is that if we fail to recognize the fundamental change and its effects, we cannot fully understand the nature of the society and the economy of the post-emancipation South. The new business elite that emerged in the postwar South dominated a stunted, static capitalism which, if it made some fortunes, made more poverty by choking off opportunities and stifling economic development. Workers and tenants learned to obey, but they did not learn the responsibilities of entrepreneurship, and they lacked the ability to organize and win political allies to improve their situation. Indeed, their experiences systematically stifled such qualities and in the process destroyed even hopes and dreams. Franklin D. Roosevelt was certainly correct when, in 1938, he called the South "the nation's No. 1 economic problem." That problem was the unfortunate legacy of the massive changes following the Civil War.

FURTHER READING

Eric Anderson and Alfred A. Moss, Jr., eds., *The Facts of Reconstruction: Essays in Honor of John Hope Franklin* (1991)

W. E. B. Du Bois, "Reconstruction and Its Benefits," *American Historical Review* 4 (1910), 781–799

———, *Black Reconstruction in America, 1860–1880* (1935)

Michael W. Fitzgerald, *The Union League Movement in the South* (1989)

Eric Foner, *Reconstruction: America's Unfinished Revolution, 1863–1877* (1988)

John Hope Franklin, *Reconstruction: After the Civil War* (1961)

Steven Hahn, *The Roots of Southern Populism: Yeoman Farmers and the Transformation of the Georgia Upcountry, 1850–1890* (1983)

Thomas C. Holt, *Black Over White: Negro Legislators in South Carolina During Reconstruction* (1977)

Peter Kolchin, *First Freedom: The Response of Alabama's Blacks to Emancipation and Reconstruction* (1972)

Peggy Lamson, *The Glorious Failure: Black Congressman Robert Brown Elliott and the Reconstruction in South Carolina* (1973)

Leon Litwack, *Been in the Storm So Long: The Aftermath of Slavery* (1979)

Carl H. Moneyhon, *Republicanism in Reconstruction Texas* (1980)

———, *The Impact of the Civil War and Reconstruction on Arkansas: Persistence in the Midst of Ruin* (1994)

Howard N. Rabinowitz, ed., *Southern Black Leaders of the Reconstruction Era* (1982)

Julie Saville, *The Work of Reconstruction: From Slave to Wage Laborer in South Carolina* (1994)

Michael Wayne, *The Reshaping of Plantation Society: The Natchez District, 1860–1880* (1983)

Joel Williamson, *After Slavery: The Negro in South Carolina during Reconstruction, 1861–1877* (1965)

Gavin Wright, *Old South, New South: Revolutions in the Southern Economy since the Civil War* (1986)

CHAPTER 13

Southern Republicans and the Problems of Reconstruction

By early 1877 the Republicans had lost control of every Southern state. Some states, among them Georgia, North Carolina, Texas, and Virginia, had fallen to the Democrats a few years after being reconstructed. Others, such as South Carolina, Louisiana, and Florida, were held until the disputed election of 1876–1877, when, in exchange for their presidential support, the Republican candidate Rutherford B. Hayes let the Democrats of those three states regain power. Southern Reconstruction, which had been started as a crusade to bring progress and democracy to the region, was therefore brought to a close in one of the most notorious political capitulations in American history. What had happened?

Of course, it could be said that nothing much at all had happened, that the Reconstruction governments had been so vulnerable from the outset that their demise was only a matter of time. But if the means they were provided with were predictably inadequate, what was the point of reconstructing the South in the first place? Surely Reconstruction was important enough that it would not have been undertaken with the expectation of certain failure.

Perhaps it can be assumed, therefore, that these Reconstruction governments had a good chance of success. After all, they had the political support and military protection of the federal authority. Furthermore, the Republicans in each state did control the administrative and legal apparatus as well as the legislative branch of government. Besides, were there not thousands of white Southerners who would be drawn to a party that could offer a new deal; that is, an agenda that would appeal both to those who had been deprived and exploited by the plantation regime and to those who wanted the South to become modern and prosperous? Since these administrations still collapsed, it is reasonable to conclude that mistakes and shortcomings on the part of the Republicans themselves could have accounted for the collapse of Reconstruction.

There is, however, an alternative explanation. It can be argued that the opposition mounted by the former Confederates, who were now arrayed in the Democratic party, was so skillful or so relentless that only a far more firmly established political organization could have withstood the onslaught. In that case, the blame for Reconstruction's downfall is shifted away from the Republicans, in the South as well as in Congress, and onto the Southern Democrats, often referred to by their admirers as Redeemers because they redeemed, or saved, the South.

Historians still debate this issue, and two questions seem to be the focus of the discussion. First, was Reconstruction doomed from the start, or did it have a reasonable chance of success? Second, assuming that there was a chance for its success, which contributed more to its unattainability—Republican inadequacies or Democratic resistance?

☞ D O C U M E N T S

Contemporary views about the Republicans and the governments they ran are presented in these documents, as are the reactions by the Republicans themselves to the violent measures resorted to by their Democratic opponents.

The first item is an extract from the testimony given by James L. Orr, South Carolina's governor from 1866 to 1868, before the Ku Klux Klan Investigating Committee in Washington on June 6, 1871. A prominent Unionist in the 1850s who associated with the Republican party in his state after it was established in 1868, Orr showed a great deal of understanding of the difficulties facing the new party and its African American supporters. The second piece is from a speech in the House of Representatives on June 8, 1874 by L. Q. C. Lamar of Mississippi attacking the Northerners who had come to his state and, he claimed, taken over the Republican party. The third document is an official proclamation by William P. Kellogg, the Northerner who was governor of Louisiana from 1872 to 1876, describing the assassination at Coushatta of Republican officials in Red River Parish and offering a reward for information about their assailants. It was issued on September 3, 1874.

The fourth document is a defense of Northerners' activities in the Republican party offered in the House on February 4, 1875 by Representative Alexander White, who was himself a native Southerner and a Republican. The fifth piece is an indictment of the Mississippi Republicans by Charles Nordhoff, a Northern journalist who toured the South in 1875 and later published his observations as *The Cotton States in the Spring and Summer of 1875* (1876). Nordhoff is also, it should be added, quite critical of the Democrats and their provocative attitudes and actions. The sixth selection is a letter from Governor Adelbert Ames of Mississippi to his wife, Blanche, who was the daughter of Benjamin F. Butler, a famous congressman and general. Ames was himself a Union general and Freedmen's Bureau agent who decided to stay in the South after the war. He became a leading Republican and served as U.S. senator from 1870 to 1874. In his letter of September 5, 1875, Ames describes the violence being stirred up by the Democrats prior to the state election of 1875. The "white liners" he refers to were the extreme element in the Democratic party who used race to arouse white Democrats and then employed violence to intimidate black Republicans, and thus win the election.

Former Governor James L. Orr Defends South Carolina's Republican Government, June 1871

By MR. VAN TRUMP [Democrat]:

Question. In regard to those eighty colored members of the house of representatives, if I understood correctly your answers to some of General Blair's [Congressman Frank Blair of Missouri] questions, you have some fears that there is some truth in the charges of bribery?

From James L. Orr, testimony before the Klan Investigating Committee, June 6, 1871, in *Ku Klux Klan Report,* Vol. 3, pt. 1, pp. 9–15. This selection is also available in *Reconstruction, the Negro and the New South,* LaWanda and John H. Cox, eds. (Harper & Row, 1973), pp. 249–255.

Answer. I think they are true as to some of them.

Question. Is it not the fact in regard to negroes of that character, (uneducated and who have been slaves,) that wily white men, approaching them with money, can seduce them into violating their official obligations?

Answer. I think that is according to our experience and knowledge of men of all classes; it would apply as well to whites as to blacks. I have no doubt they are more susceptible to such influences than if they had a high moral training and good intellectual culture.

Question. You say that the law, so far as your region of the State is concerned—I suppose you speak of your judicial circuit—is fully administered?

Answer. Yes, sir.

Question. In regard to the violations of law, of which you have spoken, could not the State power control them without asking for or resorting to the Federal power to come there and subdue them?

Answer. That is one of the difficult questions I had in my mind when I replied to a question of the chairman, as to how those disturbances could be best suppressed. If there was, in those localities, a healthy public opinion among the substantial men of the country, if they were determined to put down these disorders, I think the law there is abundantly sufficient to put them down.

Question. The law, without resort to armed force?

Answer. Yes, sir. You could not very well resort to State militia, because there is no system that I know of by which you mingle the two races together in a military organization without running a greater hazard than even to allow marauding to go on. If you were to attempt to unite the two races in a military company, you could not get it done by volunteering, and you would fail if you attempted to do it by compulsion.

Question. Then you think that the attempt at a half-white and a half-negro government is a failure?

Answer. I think it has been a very difficult experiment. . . .

By MR. STEVENSON [Republican]:

Question. You have spoken of corruption in the legislature. Do you mean to say that it was confined to colored men?

Answer. I do not think it was, from what I heard. I have no positive information upon the subject; I have been very little in Columbia, but I have heard a great deal. I think in all probability a portion of the whites are just as culpable as the colored men; whites in the legislature and also whites outside of the legislature.

Question. Lobbyists?

Answer. Lobbyists are more responsible, perhaps, than anybody else, as is generally the case.

Question. Is it your opinion that this corruption, of which you have heard, is confined exclusively to either party?

Answer. No, sir; I am sorry to say that it is not.

Question. A majority of the people of South Carolina are colored men, are they not?

Answer. Yes, sir; about 120,000 majority colored population.

Question. Yet I infer from what you say that a majority of office-holders, taking the importance of the office also into consideration, are white.

Answer. Yes, sir. . . .

Question. Speaking in regard to the disposition of the negroes in South Carolina, I would like to ask you whether, in your opinion, if the old white citizens had taken part in reconstruction and had manifested a disposition to accept the situation, as the phrase is, to take part in administering the government of the State under the reconstruction acts, would the negroes have been willing to support them and elect them to office?

Answer. My answer to that would be this: Freedom was considered by the negro a great boon, and he naturally felt very grateful to that particular party that he supposed had given him his freedom. From the very outset he was made to believe that the republican party, as a party, had done that for him; that Mr. Lincoln, in September, 1862, issued the proclamation providing for their freedom on the 1st of January, 1863. Then there was the legislation of Congress afterwards, the civil rights bill and the Freedmen's Bureau bill; then the constitutional amendments, &c., &c. That was all explained to him; and it required a very short argument to be addressed to the most ignorant negro in the State to satisfy him that his attachment to the republican party should be greater than to the democratic party. It was charged publicly by his orators, those whom he had confidence in, that the democratic party had resisted all that legislation; that the democratic party had declared that reconstruction was unconstitutional, revolutionary, and void; and that if the democrats were reinstated in power very many of these privileges would be taken away from the colored people. I thought at the time that it was very unreasonable to imagine for a moment that the colored population could be induced to vote for a party from whom they apprehended such results, and against a party that had done them such service. I have no doubt in the world that if the white element of the South would turn republican, would consent to support the republican party instead of the democratic party—although in the republican party there has been a very pernicious element, there is no doubt of it—I have no doubt if they should support the republican party instead of the democratic party, then the white population of the South would obtain absolute control of affairs there. In the contest of 1870, and it will be the same thing in 1872, the great bulk of the whites thought the democratic party was the party nearest to them. The colored men think the republican party the party nearest to them. . . .

Representative L. Q. C. Lamar of Mississippi Assails Reconstruction, June 1874

When, in order to consummate your policy, you divided the southern country into military districts, your military commanders, distrusting the purposes of the southern people and knowing the negroes were incompetent to manage the affairs of government, called to their aid and installed into all the offices of the States, from the highest to the lowest, a set of men from the North who were strangers to our people, not possessing their confidence, not elected by them, not responsible to them, having no interest in common with them, and hostile to them to a certain extent in sentiment.

I am not going to characterize these men by any harshness of language. I am speaking of a state of things more controlling than ordinary personal characteristics. Even if it were true that they came to the South for no bad purposes, they were put in a position which has always engendered rapacity, cupidity corruption, grinding oppression, and taxation in its most devouring form. They were rulers without responsibility, in un-

From L. Q. C. Lamar, speech in the House, June 8, 1874, *Congressional Record,* 43 Cong., 1 Sess., Vol. 2, pt. 6, p. 429.

checked control of the material resources of a people with whom they had not a sentiment in sympathy or an interest in common, and whom they habitually regarded and treated as rebels who had forfeited their right to protection. These men, thus situated and thus animated, were the fisc of the South. They were the recipients of all the revenues, State and local. Not a dollar of taxes, State or local, but what went into their pockets. The suffering people on whom the taxes were laid could not exercise the slightest control, either as to the amount imposed or the basis upon which they were laid. The consequence was that in a few short years eight magnificent Commonwealths were laid in ruins. This condition of things still exists with unabated rigor in those Southern States. For when, by your reconstruction measures, you determined to provide civil governments for these States, the machinery by which these men carried their power over into those civil governments was simple and effectual. Under your policy generally—I repeat, my purpose to-day is not arraignment—under that policy you disfranchised a large portion of the white people of the Southern States. The registration laws and the election laws in the hands of these men kept a still larger proportion away.

But there was an agency more potent still.

By persistent misrepresentation a majority in Congress was made to believe that the presence of the United States Army would be necessary not merely to put these governments in force, but to keep them in operation and to keep them from being snatched away and worked to the oppression and ruin of the black race and the few loyal men who were there attempting to protect their rights. Thus was introduced into those so-called reconstructed civil governments the Federal military as an operative and predominant principle. Thus, with a quick, sudden, and violent hand, these men tore the two races asunder and hurled one in violent antagonism upon the other, and to this day the negro vote massed into an organization hostile to the whites is an instrument of absolute power in the hands of these men. These governments are in external form civil, but they are in their essential principle military. They are called local governments, but in reality they are Federal executive agencies. Not one of them emanates from the uncontrolled will of the people, white or black; not one which rests upon the elective principle in its purity. They have been aptly styled by a distinguished statesman and jurist in Mississippi, (Hon. W. P. Harris,) State governments without States, without popular constituencies. For they are as completely insulated from the traditions, the feelings, the interests, and the free suffrages of the people, white and black, as if they were outside the limits of those States. Where is the public sentiment which guides and enlightens those to whom is confided the conduct of public affairs? Where is the moral judgment of a virtuous people to which they are amenable? Where is the moral indignation which falls like the scathing lightning upon the delinquent or guilty public officer? Sir, that class and race in which reside these great moral agencies are prostrated, their interests, their prosperity jeopardized, their protests unheeded, and every murmur of discontent and every effort to throw off their oppression misrepresented here as originating in the spirit which inaugurated the rebellion. Sir, the statement that these southern governments have no popular constituencies is true, but they nevertheless have a constituency to whom they bear a responsibility inexorable as death. It is limited to the one point of keeping the State true and faithful to the Administration; all else is boundless license. That constituency is here in Washington; its heart pulsates in the White House. There is its intelligence and there is its iron will. I do not exaggerate when I say that every one of these governments depends, every moment of their existence, upon the will of the President. That will makes and unmakes them. A short proclamation backed by one company determines who is to be governor of Arkansas. A telegram settles the civil magistracy of Texas. A brief order to a general in New Orleans wrests a State government from the people of Louisiana and vests its control in the creatures of the Administration. . . .

Governor William P. Kellogg of Louisiana Demands Punishment for the Coushatta Assassins, September 1874

Proclamation—The Assassination of Red River Parish Officers

State of Louisiana,
Executive Department,
New Orleans, September 3, 1874.

Whereas, during the morning of Sunday, August 30, 1874, at the McFarland plantation, in the parish of Bossier, about forty miles east of the Texas line, Homer J. Twitchell, Robert A. Dewees, Clark Holland, W. J. Howell, Frank S. Edgerton, and M. C. Willis, peaceful and law-abiding citizens of this State, were cruelly murdered in cold blood by a body of armed and mounted men, claiming to belong to an organization known as the White League of Louisiana:

Now, therefore, I, William Pitt Kellogg, governor of the State of Louisiana, with a view, if possible, of bringing the perpetrators of this great outrage to justice, and of preventing the repetition of such crimes in the future, do issue this my proclamation, offering a reward of $5,000 each for such evidence as shall lead to the arrest and conviction of the said murderers, or any of them.

Given under my hand and the seal of the State hereunto attached this 3d day of September, in the year of our Lord 1874, and of the Independence of the United States the ninety-ninth.

William P. Kellogg.

By the governor:

P. G. Deslonde, Secretary of State.

A Statement to the Public

Having felt it my duty to issue my proclamation offering a large reward for the apprehension and conviction of the murderers in the Coushatta outrage, and to the end that the law-abiding citizens of the State may fully comprehend the magnitude of the crime committed and be induced to render more active assistance to the officers of the law, I deem it proper to make the following statement.

These facts are gathered from reliable information received at the executive department:

On or about the 28th day of August, 1874, a body of persons belonging to a semi-military organization-known as the White League of Louisiana assembled in the town of Coushatta, parish of Red River, in this State, for the purpose of compelling, by force of arms, the State officers of that parish to resign their positions.

William P. Kellogg, Proclamation regarding Coushatta massacre, September 3, 1874, in "Condition of the South," *House Reports,* No. 261, 42 Cong., 2 Sess., pp. 1003–1004.

These officers were men of good character, most of them largely interested in planting and mercantile pursuits. They held their positions with the full consent of an admittedly large majority of the legal voters of the parish, this being a largely republican parish, as admitted even by the fusion returning-boards.

The only known objection to them was that they were of republican principles. Frank S. Edgerton, the duly qualified sheriff of the parish, in strict compliance with the laws of this State and of the United States, summoned a *posse comitatus* of citizens, white and colored, to assist him in protecting the parish officers in the exercise of their undoubted rights and duties from the threatened unlawful violence of the White Leagues. His posse, consisting of sixty-five men, was overpowered by a superior force, assembled from the adjacent parishes, and finally, after several colored and white men had been killed, surrendered themselves prisoners, with the explicit guarantee that their lives would be spared if the more prominent republicans would agree to leave the parish, and those holding office would resign their positions.

These stipulations, though unlawfully exacted, were complied with on the part of the republican officials, who were then locked up in the jail for the night.

The following-named persons were among those so surrendering and resigning:

Homer J. Twitchell, planter and tax-collector of Red River, and deputy United States postmaster in charge of the post-office at Coushatta; Robert A. Dewees, supervisor of registration, De Soto Parish; Clark Holland, merchant and supervisor of registration, Red River Parish; W. J. Howell, parish attorney and United States commissioner; Frank S. Edgerton, sheriff of Red River Parish; M. C. Willis, merchant, and justice of the peace.

On the following morning, Sunday, the 30th day of August, these persons were bound and conducted by an armed guard to the McFarland plantation, just over the parish line of Red River, within the boundaries of Bossier Parish, about forty miles east of the Texas line. There they were set upon and deliberately murdered in cold blood. Their bodies were buried near where they fell, without inquest or any formality whatever.

On the night preceding the surrender, a body of forty members of the White League of Caddo Parish, mounted and armed, left the city of Shreveport, and were seen riding in the direction of the place where the murder was subsequently committed.

William P. Kellogg, Governor.

Representative Alexander White of Alabama Defends "Carpetbaggers," February 1875

... These white republicans are known by the contemptuous appellation of carpet-bagger and scalawag, names conferred upon them by the chivalry, in whose political interest prowl the bands of Ku-Klux and White League assassins in the South, and as such, especially the carpet-bagger, they have become a by-word and reproach. We of the South are not responsible for them; they are a northern growth, and unless going South expatriates them, they are still northern men, even as you are—bone of your bone, flesh of your flesh. But who are they? I can speak for my State, for I think I know nearly all

From Alexander White, speech in the House, February 4, 1875, 43 Cong., 2 Sess., Vol. 3, pt. 3, Appendix, pp. 14–24.

in the State, and there are a good many of them. Most of them have titles, not empty titles complaisantly bestowed in piping times of peace, but titles worthily won by faithful and efficient service in the Federal armies, or plucked with strong right arm from war's rugged front upon the field of battle. Many of them bear upon their bodies scars of wounds received while fighting under your flag for the nation's life and the country's glory. These men either went South with the Union armies and at the close of the war remained there, or went there soon after, in the latter part of 1865 or early in 1866, to make cotton. The high price of cotton in 1865 and 1866, and the facility with which cheap labor could be obtained, induced many enterprising northern men, especially the officers in the Federal armies in the South who had seen and become familiar with the country, to go or remain there to make cotton. Many purchased large plantations and paid large sums of money for them; others rented plantations, in some instances two or three, and embarked with characteristic energy in planting. This, it should be remembered, was before the civil-rights bill or the reconstruction acts, before the colored people had any part in political matters, and two years before they ever proposed to vote or claimed to have the right to vote at any election in the Southern States.

When the political contests of 1868 came on in which the colored people first took a part in politics, as near all the native population in the large cotton-growing sections were opposed to negro suffrage and opposed to the republican party, they very naturally turned to these northern men for counsel and assistance in the performance of the new duties and exercise of their newly acquired political rights, and they as naturally gave them such counsel and became their leaders, and were intrusted with official power by them.

This brief summary will give you a correct idea of the manner in which, as I believe, nine-tenths of those who are called carpet-baggers became involved in political affairs [in the] South, and dispose of a very large part of the slanders which have been promulgated against them not only by their political enemies at the South, but by the treacherous northern knaves who, under the pretense of being republicans and as correspondents of so-called republican papers at the North, have gone down South prepared in advance to stab the cause of justice and of truth, of humanity and freedom, of the law and the Constitution, to the heart. Could these miserable miscreants have known with what ineffable contempt they were regarded by the very men whose credulous dupes they were, with what scathing scorn they regarded northern men who would lend themselves to traduce whole classes of northern men, who would allow themselves to be used as the tools to break down the political party to which they professed to belong, it would have diminished much the self-complacency with which their work was done. They could have realized that southern men, though bold and often reckless of the means by which they seek to attain political ends, that earnest and vehement, ardent and high-spirited, under the influence of one great ultimate aim to which all else is subordinated, they may reach politically to the parallel of the dogma which once prevailed in the religious world, "there is no faith to be kept with heretics," yet they can never be brought to descend to sympathy with or respect for such low-browed infamy as theirs.

These two classes, the carpet-baggers and scalawag[s], are the object of peculiar assault by the democracy, for they know that these constitute the bulwark of the republican party in the South. Without their co-operation and assistance the colored republicans could neither organize nor operate successfully in political contests, and without them the party would soon be extinguished in the Southern States. . . .

Charles Nordhoff Censures Mississippi Politicians, 1875

. . . Mississippi is, politically, in a melancholy condition. . . . [The state] has a colored majority in its voting population of probably fifteen thousand, and possibly twenty thousand. To these must be added about nine thousand or ten thousand white Republicans, of whom at least two-thirds are natives of the State. About five thousand negroes are counted on to vote the Democratic ticket. . . .

That there have been wastefulness and corruption in the government of Mississippi there is no doubt. I am so weary of official grand and petit larceny that I do not mean to go at any length into Mississippi finances. It is enough to say that the State debt is trifling; there have been no great railroad swindles; a constitutional provision wisely forbids the loan of the State credit. But there has been gross financial corruption in many counties; officers with high salaries have been needlessly multiplied; there have been notorious jobs, such as the State printing; and the ruling powers, the Ames Republicans, have unscrupulously used the ignorance and greed of the negroes to help them in their political schemes. Controlling the negro vote, and using it as a solid mass, they have put into such offices as county supervisors and treasurers, as well as into the Legislature, negroes who were often not only unable to read and write, but who were notoriously corrupt and corrupting demagogues. For instance, the late treasurer of Hinds County, in which the State capital lies, was a negro who could neither read nor write, and who was killed by another negro a few weeks ago for a disgraceful intrigue. In the last Legislature were several negroes who could neither read nor write. It has happened that the members of a grand jury were totally illiterate. A city government was to be elected last August in Vicksburg, and the Republicans nominated for mayor a white man at the time under indictment for twenty-three offenses, and for aldermen seven colored men, most of them of low character, and one white man who could neither read nor write, the keeper of a low groggery. This ticket was denounced by General M'Kee, Republican member of Congress, in a public speech, and, with the help of the Republicans, was beaten. Of the present supervisors of Warren County (Vicksburg), the president and two others cannot read. It is a notorious fact that Governor Ames has appointed to judicial places men ignorant of law, and that he has used his appointing power to shield criminals, who were his adherents, and to corrupt the judiciary of the State. . . .

Such men as Barksdale, Wharton, Lamar, and hundreds of other prominent Democrats, have clean hands and are men of honor; but there is an undoubted propensity to corruption among some Democratic as well as among Republican leaders. For instance, Vicksburg has been, since August, under Democratic rule; but the expenses of the city government, I am told, have increased, and order is not as well maintained under Democratic rule as formerly.

Nor, if the Democratic leaders were fair, would they omit to tell their people that the expenses of State and county governments have necessarily increased, for the colored people being free give business to the courts and the officers and institutions of justice; they must have schools; and in other ways the cost of government is increased. That a very large balance of waste and theft and high taxation remains, is perfectly true, and of that all may rightfully complain, as well as of other and graver wrongs which I have mentioned above.

From Charles Nordhoff, *The Cotton States in the Spring and Summer of 1875* (Burt Franklin, 1965), pp. 75–77.

It is a complaint, also, of the Democrats that their opponents have, for corrupt purposes, maintained the color-line in politics. It is true that the Ames men cultivate the negro vote by corrupt means; but it is also true that the Democrats have helped them. In Arkansas and Louisiana, I do not remember having once heard of the negro except as a part of the body politic, ignorant, to be sure, but a good worker, and, as was often said to me by Democrats, "not to be blamed that he went wrong under bad advice." But in Mississippi the commonest topic of discussion is the "damned nigger." A dozen times, at least, prominent Democrats told me he was a peculiar being, not possessing the virtues of the Caucasian race, and not fitted by nature to vote, or to sit on jury, or to bear witness—a creature admirably fitted to make cotton, and so on. I have heard such discussions going on in the presence of colored men, who naturally listened with all the ears they had.

Now, the negro is not an idiot. He would be if he voted for and with men who habitually call him a "nigger," and often a "damned nigger," and who openly assert his incapacity by nature to perform the functions of a citizen. When the "most respectable citizen in Vicksburg" blustered about the postmaster appointing a "damned nigger," he was heard by at least twenty-five colored men and women. Yet, in that very town leading Democrats groan about the impossibility of breaking the color-line. One would have a contempt for such politicians were not their course a constant injury to the State in which they are so foolishly noisy, and in which the quiet, sensible, and orderly people seem to have almost entirely resigned the power and supremacy which belong to them.

The thing which was oftenest said to me in Mississippi by Democratic politicians was this: "Our only hope is in the Democratic success in the next Federal election. The Democratic successes last fall gave us our first gleam of light." But when I asked how a Democratic administration could help them, the reply was, "Because then we can disorganize the colored vote. They will not vote without white leaders to organize them." And when I asked one of the white leaders of the "white-line" movement, whose object is to draw the color-line strictly, how he could hope to get all the white people, with their strongly diverging views, into his movement, his reply was, "We'll make it too damned hot for them to stay out."

Now, to me this does not look like the American way of carrying an election. It is a method of bluster and bullying and force. The honest Republicans whom I asked whether the white-line movement could possibly draw in all the white voters, all replied in the affirmative. It would silence opposition at any rate, they said. . . .

Governor Adelbert Ames Deplores the Violence in Mississippi, September 1875

Jackson, Miss., September 5, 1875

Dear Blanche: I had finished my letter to you yesterday and was looking for George to mail it when Capt. Fisher came to me out of breath and out of heart to tell me of a riot which had just taken place at Clinton (a village ten miles west of here) and from which he had just escaped, with his wife. He was speaking when the riot began. It was a

Letter, Adelbert Ames to wife, September 5, 1875, in *Chronicles from the Nineteenth Century: Family Letters of Blanche Butler and Adelbert Ames* (Clinton, Mass., 1957), vol. 2, pp. 163–164.

premeditated riot on the part of the Democracy which resulted in the death of some four white men and about the same number of Negroes and quite a large number of Negroes wounded. There were present at a Republican barbecue about fifteen hundred colored people, men, women, and children. Seeking the opportunity white men, fully prepared, fired into this crowd. Two women were reported killed, also two children. As the firing continued, the women ran away with the men in many instances, leaving their children on the ground. Today there are some forty carriages, wagons and carts which were abandoned by the colored people in their flight. Last night, this morning and today squads of white men are scouring the county killing Negroes. Three were killed at Clinton this morning—one of whom was an old man, nearly one hundred years old—defenseless and helpless. Yesterday the Negroes, though unarmed and unprepared, fought bravely and killed four of the ringleaders, but had to flee before the muskets which were at once brought onto the field of battle. This is but in keeping with the programme of the Democracy at this time. They know we have a majority of some thirty thousand and to overcome it they are resorting to intimidation and murder. It is cold-blooded murder on the part of the "white liners"—but there are other cases exactly like this in other parts of the state. You ask what are we to do. That is a question I find it difficult to answer. I told you a day or two ago that the whole party has been opposed to organizing the militia and furthermore I have been unable to find anyone who was willing to take militia appointments.

The Mansion has been crowded all day long with Republican friends and Negroes from the field of battle. I have run off to the northwest chamber for my daily chat with you, leaving a crowd in the other rooms. There has also been a crowd at the front gate all day long. The town is full of Negroes from the country who come to escape harm. The whites here are afraid of the Negroes who have come in. A committee of white men have just waited on me and offer to keep the peace so far as may be in their power. The Sheriff has selected a number of them to act as a posse to go out into the country and arrest those who are murdering Negroes. This last step has caused a subsidence of the excitement felt by the whites as well as blacks.

I anticipate no further trouble here at this time. The "white liners" have gained their point—they have, by killing and wounding, so intimidated the poor Negroes that they can in all human probability prevail over them at the election. I shall at once try to get troops from the general government. Of course it will be a difficult thing to do.

I send a world of love.

Adelbert

ESSAYS

The downfall of the Reconstruction governments in the South is approached from two different angles in the essays that follow. The first, by Lawrence N. Powell of Tulane University, offers an insightful account of the Northerners who joined the Republican party—pejoratively called "carpetbaggers" by their Democratic opponents—and their contribution to the party's difficulties and ultimate collapse. And the second essay is by the editor of this anthology, Michael Perman of the University of Illinois at Chicago, who explains the methods and strategies employed by the Republicans' opponents, the Democrats, in their campaign to overthrow Reconstruction.

Carpetbaggers and the Problems of Republican Rule in the South

LAWRENCE N. POWELL

It is now beginning to dawn on historians of Reconstruction that Southern Republicans during those years were inordinately addicted to factional quarrels. In fact, the infighting probably had more than a casual bearing on the eventual collapse of Reconstruction, which makes it frankly bewildering and hard to explain. Though the party was admittedly composed of wildly disparate elements, Southern Republicans had more reason to hang together than did any comparable group of politicians in American electoral history. Their political opponents, known variously as Conservatives or Democrats or Conservative-Democrats, were not a "loyal opposition" in any ordinary sense. They favored a "rule or ruin" policy and did not scruple to employ the methods of fraud, terror, and assassination in order to achieve their ends. But Southern Republicans were sometimes slow to catch on. At the very moment when their existence as a viable political party was at stake, they often seemed to devote less energy to fighting the opposition than to fighting one another. They appear to have been incapable of *"party discipline* and self control," to quote a typical complaint they made about themselves. What explains this puzzling failure of Republicans in the Reconstruction South to pull together in the face of common adversity? Why was the Southern wing of the party of emancipation unable "to create a political culture in which solidarity was a virtue?"

A look at the experience of carpetbaggers provides a partial answer. Over the past twenty-odd years we have been taught to view these Northern Republicans in the South more objectively and charitably, and we have learned in addition a great deal that is informative about their background, their political creed, their voting behavior, and their typical constituency. Yet few have taken the time to explore the question of why they entered and remained in Republican politics in the first place. The answer is revealing on several scores. Northern newcomers became Republican politicians in the South partly because they had to make a living that could not be easily earned at that time in the usual ways. That is to say, carpetbaggers in the Lower South, which for the purposes of this essay includes Alabama, Florida, Georgia, Louisiana, Mississippi, and South Carolina (where most of them were concentrated), were in a worse predicament than the ordinary American politician ever finds himself in. They relied on office not only for power and prestige but for economic survival. This dependence upon politics for their livelihood in turn greatly aggravated the factional weaknesses to which Southern Republicans were already prone.

No attempt is being made here to resurrect the Redeemer myth that the carpetbaggers were low-flung, penniless adventurers who came South originally for the purpose of living off of office. Every modern study of Reconstruction politics demonstrates conclusively that the carpetbaggers scarcely fit the caricature of them that used to pass for historical truth. They were, as a class, fairly well educated, a large proportion of them having attended college, and they came from backgrounds that were solidly middle class.

They were not the jetsam and flotsam of Northern society. Nor did they come South strictly for the sake of office. The fact is, as Richard N. Current reminded us several years ago, the overwhelming majority of carpetbaggers arrived in the region well before congressional enactments in 1867 made Republican politics a live possibility and officeholding a thing to be pursued. The few Northern newcomers who did hunger after office during presidential Reconstruction soon learned that Andrew Johnson preferred Southern men for federal appointments, and that Southern men frowned on Northern men who meddled in local politics without an invitation. In short, most Northerners who later ended up as carpetbaggers did not anticipate this aspect of their careers at all. They came to the former Confederacy for reasons other than politics.

Of course, what mostly attracted Northerners to the South, or tempted them to remain or return there after their discharges from the military, were the manifold opportunities of a business nature that the region held forth in the years just preceding and following Appomattox. Land speculators and developers from the Old Northwest were sure that the former Confederacy would be the next frontier to roll into vision. Merchants and jobbers were just as positive that their special talents would find full scope in the consumer market that emancipation had recently enlarged. Lawyers for their part sensed that there might be "much litigation growing out of the Confiscation Act[s] of the U.S. Congress, [and] also out of the Sequestration Act of the late Confederate Congress and other matters connected with the war." In addition to all these types were those countless Northerners, numbering possibly in the tens of thousands, who believed that cotton growing at prices then prevailing was the quickest way imaginable to secure a financial "competency" of the sort that most men in nineteenth-century America envied and aspired to. In a word, economic, not political, motives impelled most carpetbaggers originally to move to the South. And it remains to say that the newcomers were scarcely impecunious when they first put in their appearance. They invested thousands of dollars in the Southern economy, and in all likelihood they brought more money into the former Confederacy than they took out.

If carpetbaggers originally came South for financial reasons, and if some of them abandoned whatever political ambitions they had not long after arrival, why then did they become involved in the Southern Republican party at the time they did? What were those "conditions which none of [them] could control" and which before long caused them to find themselves "up to [their] eyes in politics"? The answers that have been given by revisionist historians cannot be lightly dismissed. It is undoubtedly true that the enfranchisement of the former slaves in the spring and summer of 1867 brought with it not only "political opportunity" but "political responsibility" as well, and that more than a few carpetbaggers seized both the opportunity *and* the responsibility out of a sense of duty. In fact, some carpetbaggers had to be called to the colors, if not by the freedmen then by the native whites or, more common still, by the military commanders who were charged with putting the congressional plan of Reconstruction into motion. Union generals were often unable to find white Southern natives who could take the Ironclad Oath, so they simply selected many of their voting registrars and judicial officers from among "the late volunteer officers of our army when it [was] practicable. . . ." Though the summons to office caught a few by surprise, the newcomers usually overcame initial reservations about officeholding and concluded that it was their solemn duty to assist the government and the newly enfranchised in the grand experiment about to be launched. No explanation of the origins of carpetbaggers can do full justice to the subject if it disregards the feelings of public altruism and patriotic duty that were awakened in many Northerners by the birth of the Southern Republican Party.

Yet there was another motive that tended to draw many Northerners into Republican politics. It often had little to do with idealism and civic-mindedness, though it was by no means inconsistent with these virtues. This other motive was the practical one of how to earn a living. It figured rather large in the calculations of many soon-to-be carpetbaggers. For, although the majority of the carpetbaggers were anything but penniless at the time they arrived in the South, they were very nearly penniless at the time they became Republican politicians, which is more than partly why they chose that occupation when they did. They needed to secure a livelihood.

The truth is, the Southern Republican party was born in the midst of hard times, and the bitter circumstances of its birth profoundly affected the style of politics to which it would be prone. To understand why this was so we need only consider for a moment the experiences of Northern cotton planters. Practically all of them were financially strapped when Radical Reconstruction commenced in the South. Every year since 1864 they had been planning to make a fortune, and every year since that time they had been going broke, casualties of agricultural disasters that, like misfortune, never came singly. By the beginning of 1867 they were on the ropes; at the end of the year they were on the canvas, for the price of cotton had fallen to levels that did not cover the cost of cultivation. Individual losses commonly ran into the tens of thousands of dollars. Henry W. Warren, a Yankee planter who later became Republican speaker of the Mississippi House of Representatives, summed up cotton raising as "an occupation that proved disastrous." . . .

Yankee planters were certainly not alone among carpetbaggers in viewing Republican politics in the South as a source of livelihood. They were only more conspicuous in this regard, having been heavy losers in the crop failures of 1866–67. Yet everyone in the Lower South, at least, felt the reverberations of these cotton losses, and most everyone had to adjust his plans accordingly. As one Indiana native explained of a fellow Mississippi carpetbagger in distress, "Like nearly all of us northern men in the South, he is broken up financially. . . ." Individual instances of what he meant can be found in a variety of occupations. A Northern lawyer in Mobile, Alabama, for example, who counted several former Confederates among his personal friends, said his clients were so poor, "I can't make anything." He wanted to be appointed recorder of deeds and mortgages in New Orleans. Attorneys for the freedmen were in financial straits just as dire, if not more so. John Emory Bryant, a former Freedmen's Bureau agent in Georgia who had tried without success to make a living as a lawyer for the ex-slaves, saw in the Republican party a future that might bring him "position and money." Northern teachers in the South also had pecuniary motives for a change of occupation. "I am tired of the schoolroom," one of them wrote the commanding general in Alabama in 1867, "and I would like to have an appointment . . . which will pay me liberal wages." Northern-born editors of Republican sheets likewise found themselves in "financial distress" and in need of political assistance. They would continue to find themselves in this predicament throughout Radical Reconstruction, for it was nearly impossible to support a Republican journal in the South during these years except by means of state or federal printing contracts.

At a time when business in general was flat and decent prospects were lacking, the financial attractions of political positions in the South could not be taken for granted.

The prosaic duty of registering voters under the military Reconstruction acts of 1867, for instance, paid a commission fee of thirteen to forty cents a voter and could bring in several thousand dollars in some districts. These were not low wages for the time, and several Northerners who actively sought out registrar appointments apparently sensed as much. Fees available to sheriffs and tax collectors, moreover, often added up to more than pocket change; salaries of $5,000 to $20,000 a year were not unheard of. State legislators were not paid so liberally, but ordinarily they could supplement their incomes with generous per diem and travel expenses, and in other ways. State officers, on the other hand, from the governor on down, were usually—though not always—well remunerated, and federal officeholders were everywhere handsomely rewarded. To name one case, registers in bankruptcy, a newly created federal position that did a brisk business in the Reconstruction South, earned annual incomes that ranged from $5,000 to $12,000. George E. Spencer, a future carpetbagger U.S. senator, landed one of these for Alabama's fourth congressional district. The position made him feel, as he put it, "that my duty is to remain here and help reconstruct this God forsaken and miserable country." . . .

That this style of politics lasted for as long as it did was owing in large measure to the stark reality of Southern poverty, on the one hand, and the unpleasant reality of pervasive ostracism, on the other. The two realities seem to have worked in tandem to reinforce the attitude that political patronage was indispensable to personal financial well-being. The poverty can scarcely be exaggerated. Never during Reconstruction—or for the remainder of the century, for that matter—did the former Confederacy enjoy anything like true prosperity. The years 1868–72 saw a return of commercial health and a quickening of business energies, but this was a prosperous period only in comparison with the economic desperation of the immediate past and future. When the panic of 1873 struck, triggering a depression that reversed such small gains as had been registered since the surrender, cotton prices had already commenced a long-term, though fluctuating, decline that before it ended would further impoverish white yeomen and black freedmen and leave the planters more land poor than ever. Added to these problems was the handicap the South faced in the form of inadequate banking capital and currency, which the National Banking Act [of 1863] and supplemental congressional legislation did much to create. . . .

Hardly less effective in reinforcing the same attitude [of political patronage as being indispensable for personal financial well-being] was the ostracism to which carpetbaggers were subjected. The proscription of Northern Republicans was as prevalent as it was relentless, and it ranged in intensity from the cold shoulder and the audible insult to the coarser techniques of terrorism, bullyism, and plain assassination, which was favored by the Ku Klux Klan and similar groups. Commercial ostracism was also popular, and sometimes went forward on an organized basis. A Democratic editor in Alabama recommended it as superior to violence. "STARVE THEM OUT!" was the advice he gave for bringing white Republicans to heel. "Don't put your foot in the doors of their shops, offices, and stores. Purchase from true men and patronize those of known Southern sympathies." The effect was merely to add an extra weight to the burden of economic difficulties carpetbaggers were already shouldering in their efforts to make a living in the Reconstruction South, particularly if they were business and professional men or otherwise dependent on the goodwill of the surrounding community. Their only clientele, the freedmen, were the most poverty-stricken of all Southerners, which partly explains why one Northern physician in Florida found it necessary to moonlight as a clerk of court (the position paid $5,000 annually). . . .

It is admittedly misleading, not to say unfair, to stress the pecuniary preoccupations of the carpetbaggers to the exclusion of other motives. The Southern Republican party had more than its share of Northerners who became carpetbaggers not because they loved money less, but humanity more. After all, Albert T. Morgan and his brother entered Republican politics not simply to secure to themselves a financial "restoration," but also to secure to the freedman "the right to life, liberty and pursuit of happiness." Who is to say which motive was the controlling one? In the case of Albert Morgan, who kept faith with his principles long after it was popular or safe to do so, it was probably the idealistic motive that was dominant. He once passed up an opportunity to be sheriff of Yazoo County, a position "worth in fees and commissions six to ten thousand per year," because he wished to remain in the state legislature, where he thought he would "be able to do more good." And what are we to make of the fact that Albion Tourgée ran for a seat in the North Carolina Constitutional Convention and later welcomed a state judgeship because his private business affairs were in disarray and he needed the money? Surely to say this about him is to leave a lot unsaid. To the list of high-minded carpetbaggers should be added the names of John Emory Bryant in Georgia, Reuben Tomlinson in South Carolina, Leonard G. Dennis in Florida, and that skillful nepotist himself, Marshall H. Twitchell in Louisiana. They and many like them were all committed to the proposition that racial and social justice were things worth dedicating one's life to. Their motives may have been complex, even contradictory at times, but this is no argument against either their integrity *or* their accomplishments, which were real and considerable. It is no part of wisdom to sneer at sincere purpose even when it is difficult to dissociate from economic motivation. . . .

Which brings us back to the subject of Southern Republican factionalism. A substantial amount of it appears to have originated in the financial weaknesses of the organizational leadership; otherwise there is no explaining why Southern Republicans fought about nothing so much as the loaves and fishes of office. By all accounts patronage was usually *the* issue over which the Reconstructionists quarreled the most. To be sure, a certain degree of internecine feuding was to be expected in a party composed of former slaves and former slaveholders, wealthy landlords and impoverished tenants, former Whigs and former Democrats, wartime Unionists and original secessionists, black-belt planters and hill-country yeomen, blacks and whites, and, not least, the victor and the vanquished. Once the Reconstructionists in the Deep South wrote into law their minimal reform agenda, these incongruent elements began to war among themselves over who should run the party and in whose interests. Did more need to be done in the way of racial integration and black economic uplift, or did wisdom dictate slighting the black vote in order to enlarge the white vote? If the latter was the case, which whites should be appealed to, the masses or the classes? And what of reform in general? Should it be in the direction of greater economic democracy or diversified economic development? Over the question of leadership the debate often became sulfurous. Many carpetbaggers, as we have seen, believed they had special claims to dominance. Several scalawags, as native white Republicans were called, replied that they were "opposed to newcomers occupying prominent positions either in the State or general government." They felt they deserved preeminence by virtue of their pre-war residence, wartime sufferings, or high antebellum status, as the case might be, or in recognition of the fact that they had sometimes been the first to come forward as party organizers in their respective states. Black Republicans also excelled at special pleading, especially in the latter phases of Reconstruction. Since they supplied the bulk of the votes, they reasoned they should receive a fair share of the offices. Especially hard words were exchanged between quondam Whigs and Democrats, and the recriminations that ex-Confederates and persistent Unionists hurled at one another could not always be repeated in polite company. Factionalism along these lines and over these issues was altogether natural, and when and where Southern Republicans enjoyed comfortable legislative and electoral majorities, it thrived nearly unchecked.

Yet, what gave these antipathies of race, class, section, and party an edge they might not otherwise have had was the financial indigence of so much of the rank-and-file Republican leadership. The simple truth is that carpetbaggers were by no means alone in their reliance upon political office for a livelihood. Numerous scalawags appear to have been in similar straits. Several pre-war officeholders in Mississippi, for instance, converted to Republicanism largely for economic purposes. "I am in need of employment which would give me some remuneration," one of them confessed. J. Madison Wells, the Johnsonian governor of Louisiana who later joined the Republican party, offered this explanation as to why his son should receive a federal appointment: "All things being equal, I think preference should be given to those 'of the manor born' and who have lost everything by the war." A desire to secure a steady income was admittedly not the only—or even the major—reason many scalawags identified with the party of black rights. Their motives for becoming Republicans were probably more mixed than were those of the carpetbaggers, ranging from reform to revenge and including opportunism of the broadest kind. But poverty and proscription worked upon native white Republicans with particular severity; in Alabama, at least, "scalawags were much more bitterly hated than carpetbaggers," and the financial effects of persecution caused many wartime Unionists to scurry for Republican appointments. Of course, no class of Republican politician was more financially needy than were black office-holders. As we now know, many were artisans and small tradesmen and thus singularly vulnerable to the economic reprisals the white community was especially prone to bring down upon maverick black citizens. W. McKee Evans explains their situation best: "Once a Negro acquired the reputation of being a politician, for better or for worse, he became dependent upon political jobs for a livelihood." Negro and native white Republicans also felt constrained to employ the various unethical means carpetbaggers relied on to supplement their incomes. Honest and dishonest graft were not a Northern import but generally selective adaptations for survival in the hostile Southern environment. . . .

In their motives for seeking office, in their reasons for holding on to office, and in their methods of living off of office, carpetbaggers in the Deep South illustrate a tragic truth about Republican Reconstruction that is unpleasant to acknowledge. If several carpetbaggers went into politics in order to secure a livelihood, if they grabbed for as many offices as they could in order to protect that livelihood, and if they tried by factionalist means to retain those offices because public and private poverty and economic and social ostracism made it necessary for them to do so, the Northern newcomers only throw into sharp relief the formidable handicaps that the Reconstructionists were up against. Those handicaps were the colonial economic status that the defeated Confederacy was sliding into, the weak social base of the party that the abandonment of land reform did nothing to strengthen, and the utter unwillingness of the conquered to concede legitimacy, not to mention fellowship, to the party of black rights. Between the poverty that resulted from the former two handicaps and the economic coercion that resulted from the latter, Southern Republicans could find little room to maneuver save by cannibalizing one another in patronage fights that they could ill afford. The experience of carpetbaggers in the Lower South makes the factionalism that brought the Republicans to grief a little more comprehensible.

Reconstruction under Attack

MICHAEL PERMAN

In the reconstructed South, there were two political parties but no two-party system. This was because one of the existing parties refused to accord legitimacy to the other. The opponents of Reconstruction, that is, the Democrats, would not acknowledge that the Republican party had a right to participate in southern political life. First of all, it was the partisan instrument of a Reconstruction policy that had been framed and imposed by a northern Congress and, second, its support was based essentially on the votes of the former slaves.

This denial of legitimacy was even more serious because it extended beyond the political party to encompass state government as well, since the Republicans controlled and ran it. This amounted to a renunciation of the authority of the state. In effect, the Republicans were viewed as an occupying force whose authority was rejected. Nevertheless, because they were a political party, not an army, they had to govern by consent. Thus, they had to obtain legitimacy, and this would only be done by breaking down disrespect and converting it into political support at election time. As evidence that legitimacy was indeed the issue at stake, historians have customarily categorized these Republican administrations as "regimes" and their defeat as their "overthrow," descriptive terms not applicable under normal circumstances.

From the outset, the Republicans worked energetically to acquire legitimacy. They lavished attention and patronage on politically prominent white Southerners who, despite the risk of shame or censure, chose to affiliate with the suspect new party. Indeed, so eager was the party to please them as well as advertise their defection that many were given the most prestigious positions it could bestow. Some were even appointed chief justice of the state supreme court, like Joseph E. Brown in Georgia, Richmond Pearson in North Carolina, and Samuel Rice in Alabama, while others such as Mississippi's James L. Alcorn, Alabama's William H. Smith, and Georgia's Rufus Bullock became governor. Also, the Republicans' policy of railroad building was pursued with an almost obsessive determination and generosity because it was thought to be the "open sesame" to success and respectability. By contrast, the party leadership quickly relented on policies that would have been punitive to well-to-do whites, like land redistribution and political proscription. And, finally, the party tried to disarm white opposition with reassurances about the limited role and influence of blacks within its ranks. . . .

Besides its own internal difficulties and shortcomings, the Republican party was beset by a relentless foe. After the war, the former Confederates had fought for over two years to reject, or at least evade, the terms proposed by the victorious North. They had tried to maneuver around Johnson's policy in 1865; they had flatly rejected Congress' Fourteenth Amendment a year later; and they had attempted to undermine the requirements of the Reconstruction Act from 1867 to 1868. Although failing to avert Reconstruction, their resistance did, nevertheless, make Congress' task extremely difficult. Paradoxically, however, their refusal to accept these proposals forced Congress to introduce terms that were increasingly severe. Finally, in 1868, a last desperate attempt to forestall Reconstruction was made when, with the Klan operating unofficially and independently as a weapon of last resort, they mobilized all their political resources to prevent the election of Ulysses Grant.

In Georgia and Louisiana, they were successful, although at a cost of about 1,000 lives in the Louisiana election alone, according to the report of the Ku Klux Klan Investigating Committee of 1871. This questionable feat was not enough, however, since Grant was elected president and every southern state was reconstructed and came under Republican control. Accordingly, the Democrats—as the anti-Reconstructionists had begun to identify themselves—had to reassess their strategy. In a dramatic about-face after 1868, they decided to eschew confrontation and try instead to defeat the Republicans in the normal competition of party politics—that is, by winning electoral majorities peacefully. Behind this judgment was the conviction that continued resistance could only keep the region in a state of political turmoil detrimental to its social stability and economic recovery. Persistent confrontation would also force the federal government to intervene constantly in southern affairs, while simultaneously scaring off much-needed northern capital. This change of course, which paralleled a similar shift by the national Democrats in 1871, was called the New Departure. Under it, the party accepted the finality of Reconstruction and acknowledged the actuality of black suffrage.

Their accommodation to the new political order in the South enabled the Democrats to become involved in the emerging political and economic developments of the region. Since they could no longer be dismissed as out-of-touch obstructionists, the Democrats hoped to attract support from economic and financial interests that might otherwise have been won over by the Republicans because of their promotion of internal improvements as well as their ties to the federal authorities and to northern capital. Also, former Whigs who might have resisted affiliation with their prewar political enemies, particularly if the Democrats were disruptive and resistant to change, would reconsider. Besides helping to retain white support, the New Departure provided a means of making inroads into the Republicans' black constituency. This may appear a rather unlikely proposition, but the Democrats had great hopes for it. By their acceptance of the right of blacks to vote, the party might no longer be seen as unalterably opposed to the political gains made by the freedmen. Moreover, as their employers, Democrats could bring pressure on the ex-slaves to realize that, politically, their best interests lay in appeasing their bosses rather than antagonizing them by voting Republican. So Zebulon B. Vance, the war-time governor of North Carolina, urged party members to "act so as to make them sick of the yankees, and show them that their old masters and themselves are natural allies." Meanwhile, the leading Democratic paper in the state, the Raleigh *Sentinel,* recommended that "Those who work daily with the negro can exercise great influence over him." If this maneuver were successful, two worrisome developments would be forestalled. Political parties would not be racially exclusive and the relations between white capital and black labor would not be aggravated by political polarization. To the Democrats, therefore, biracial parties could defuse the threat of racial friction posed by the introduction of the Republican party into the South.

The New Departure enabled the Democrats to stem the defection of whites, but it enticed only a smattering of blacks away from the Republicans. More effective at breaking down black support was the tactic of encouraging Republican dissension and then forming electoral alliances with factions of the party that bolted. Some black votes came with the bolters, but the main advantage of these fusion arrangements was that the Republicans were weakened by the split. In addition, the Democrats were benefited because they could disguise their identity in strong Republican districts through endorsement of and voting for bolting opposition candidates. Fusion and the New Departure had their greatest opportunity in 1872 with the Liberal Republican defection. But its disastrous outcome encouraged critics of the strategy within the party to demand yet another reconsideration of its priorities.

Thus commenced the third phase in the postwar struggle on the part of the region's traditional leaders to regain political control. The critics of the New Departure were described by contemporaries as Bourbons, not a reference to whiskey but to the French royal family that returned to the throne after Napoleon, having learned nothing and forgotten nothing. They insisted that the Democrats repudiate their recently adopted strategy of playing down the differences between the parties and accentuate instead their own party's distinctive identity, interests, and constituency. The New Departure, the Bourbons claimed, had tried to falsify the dichotomies in southern politics. In so doing, it had failed, not only to win over Republicans but, more seriously, to arouse the Democratic party's own supporters. The remedy was to shun fusion and to campaign instead as straight-out, unabashed Democrats. Simultaneously, the racial differences between the two parties were to be emphasized. With whites leaving the Republicans rapidly after 1872 and with blacks refusing to be lured by the Democrats, the reality of the racial polarization of southern politics seemed increasingly difficult to refute. So, after four years of obfuscation and evasion, race became politicized in 1873–74.

As campaign issues, race and white supremacy were extremely problematic for the Democrats, however. In states like Texas and Arkansas that had heavy white majorities, an appeal to race was not necessary because a well-organized straight-out campaign might win anyway. In fact, with the collapse of the Republicans' railroad schemes and the accompanying indebtedness, a focus on fiscal questions was as likely to succeed as race. Not only was it less disruptive but it was an issue with broad appeal that might encourage many Republicans to switch their vote because of dissatisfaction with their own party's economic record. Indeed, there is strong evidence that lower expenditures and therefore reduced taxes appealed to taxpayers regardless of party, since they were becoming very aware and angry that taxes had risen steeply under the Republicans. Particularly aggrieved were small landowners who paid significantly more now that the levy on slaves was abolished because the tax had been transferred to land. Since they were operating on a close margin anyway, the increased taxation pushed them to the brink. Therefore, it was quite probable that fiscal issues were more effective vote getters than race. Indeed, the Democrats captured Texas in 1873 and Arkansas in 1874 without basing their campaigns exclusively on white supremacy.

In those states where, by contrast, blacks were in a majority, a racial canvass seemed to guarantee defeat for the party of white supremacy. Indeed, that was the major reason why the Democrats had previously shied away from it. But the Bourbons conceived of race as an appeal so electrifying that it would rally whites who had previously been apathetic and confused when faced with the perplexing fusion politics of the New Departure. With their natural constituency stimulated and polling a full vote, they argued that the Democrats' chances would be considerably enhanced. The case for a race-based campaign was presented most graphically by Nathaniel B. Meade, a leader in James L. Kemper's successful straight-out canvass for governor of Virginia in 1873. "To save the state," he suggested, "we must make the issue *White and Black* race against race and the canvass red hot—the position must be made so odious that no decent white man can support the radical ticket and look a gentleman in the face." If, in addition, black Republicans could be intimidated into not voting, then victory was quite conceivable. Indeed, organized terror and intimidation was to be the military complement to the Bourbons' political strategy. Accordingly, the White League in Louisiana in 1874, the Rifle Clubs in Mississippi in 1875, and the Red Shirts in Wade Hampton's gubernatorial campaign of 1876 in South Carolina were mobilized to spread such fear among black Republicans that the party became demoralized.

In Louisiana, the White League attacked government buildings and assaulted officials in outlying Republican-held districts in order to shatter the party's local control. Two violent clashes revealed the bloody lengths to which organized terror would resort. One was at Colfax in Grant parish in 1873 when about one hundred blacks were murdered, most in cold blood, after their attempt to hold on to the besieged courthouse had failed. The other occurred at Coushatta in Red River parish, near Shreveport, a year later when six white Republican officials and two of their black associates were seized by a mob of a thousand whites from Coushatta and its vicinity. Despite promises to leave the town, they were all murdered by their captors, thereby eliminating the men who had run the parish under the leadership of a courageous Northerner, Marshall Twitchell, who, by chance, was not in town on the day of the massacre. Meanwhile, in New Orleans, the League fought a pitched battle with the Metropolitan Police and black militia at Liberty Place in September 1874. The Mississippi, Alabama, and South Carolina campaigns developed a common pattern of intimidation and violence. During the summer before the election, a racial affray was provoked in which blacks were attacked and hunted down as occurred at Clinton, Mississippi, in 1875 and at Hamburg, South Carolina, a year later. These incidents were followed by military drilling and nighttime terror in selected black counties. Meanwhile, Democratic politicians warned whites of their responsibility to their race for driving out the black man's party. So effective was this grim tactic in Alabama in 1874 that Walter Bragg, the Democratic state chairman, observed gloatingly: "The spirit of our people is roused to the highest pitch that will admit of control—the negroes sink down before it as if stricken with awe." With the Republicans staggering under these violent assaults and with whites responding eagerly to the Democrats' call for white supremacy, the outcome was the final defeat of Reconstruction in the Deep South states after 1874.

Drawing the color line between the two parties was the weapon that finally toppled the Republicans. . . . Since racial subordination was at the core of southern society and culture, race was obviously an ever-present element during Reconstruction, especially because the Republican party with its black constituency threatened to disturb the existing racial order. But, until the mid-1870s, the Democrats had deliberately chosen not to make race the issue dividing the two parties. Instead, they had relied on a strategy aimed at denying the Republican party credibility and legitimacy. With its northern origins and extensive black support in the South and with its far-from-perfect perform-ance in office, there was plenty of ammunition available to keep the party off-balance and weaken it electorally. Besides, racial polarization was sure to provoke federal displeasure and intervention and also, quite probably, disrupt labor relations and frustrate economic revival. Thus, while it was understood that the parties were racial in essence, the Democrats were not willing to act upon this awareness politically. In actual fact, neither could the Republicans, because they were desperately eager to secure the votes and recognition of whites. Once it was clear that the Republicans could not attract a significant amount of white support, while, at the same time, it was apparent that the Democrats themselves could not win the Deep South without polling a greater white vote than they had previously been able to obtain, then it was both safe and necessary to play the race card.

As soon as the genie was out of the bottle, race became the issue defining the two parties, not only in those states where it had been employed as a last resort to redeem them from Republican rule, but throughout the entire region. Because theirs was the party that had uprooted Reconstruction and restored white supremacy, the Democrats now claimed what was tantamount to an unquestioned right to rule. But appearances were deceptive. After its return to power, the white man's party seemed to hesitate and belie its new, exultant identity. For it did not proceed right away to repeal the Republicans' civil rights legislation or to remove all black officials from power. The reason for the Democrats' reluctance was that a frontal assault was unnecessary. The Democrats had regained political dominance anyway and they did not need to vindicate their racial credentials by eradicating every gain that blacks had made under Reconstruction. Indeed, such action was almost certainly counterproductive, since it would provoke the federal authorities and also thwart the serious and effective overtures that, in a move reminiscent of the New Departure, the Democrats began making to reassure blacks and win over their votes. In effect, the Democratic leadership was concerned to quiet down the racial friction that had been generated during the "white supremacy" campaigns. Therefore, there was to be no further overt hostility toward blacks. Rather, they were to be reassured that the rule of white men "to the manor born" would be benevolent. As Governor Wade Hampton explained patronizingly to black South Carolinians in 1878, they had no reason to fear the return of the Democrats because "We propose to protect you and give you all your rights."

So there was no intention of removing blacks' legal rights, and they were accordingly left alone. Instead, other kinds of problems concerned the Democrats more. The first was the consolidation of the party's political control. This was achieved by the removal of the most important Republicans who still held office in the executive and judicial branches and by the reapportionment of the legislature so as to reduce Republican representation significantly. Next, in most states between 1874 and 1879, the Democrats called conventions to rewrite the Reconstruction constitutions of 1868. In these conventions, which they dominated, the Democrats prohibited the use of state aid for internal improvements and repudiated most of the debts incurred by the Republicans. In addition, the responsibilities and the cost of government were drastically reduced, as was the rate of taxation. Besides being a reaction against the presumed extravagance of Reconstruction, this initiative also represented a reassertion of the traditional laissez-faire, minimal government doctrines of the Democracy that were being urged on the party by its Bourbon purists. As it returned to power, the Democratic party was therefore also returning to its original identity and principles.

The third of the initiatives taken by the resurgent Democrats was their passage of laws aimed at tightening the existing controls over the plantation labor force. The target of this legislative activity was the modicum of autonomy that laborers, particularly black sharecroppers, still possessed under the newly emergent, but legally imprecise, labor system. A series of repressive ordinances gave landlords virtually uncontested control over their laborers. The first of these were laws prohibiting tenants and croppers from selling, without their employer's permission, the cotton they were growing on his land. The impact of these measures, called "sunset to sunrise" bills because they were intended to outlaw nighttime trading with local stores, was to prevent croppers from disposing of their share of the crop in whatever way and whenever they wished. Another step the state legislatures took drastically increased the severity of existing legal sanctions against theft and trespass. A third type of measure imposed restrictions on the laborer's ability to move around and bargain for better terms through what were called anti-enticement laws forbidding employers from competing for each other's workers. Frequently, states also levied taxes on labor agents in an attempt to curb their activity among the farm labor force. The ultimate device for ensuring the landlord's control over his laborers was the redrafting of the existing crop lien laws so as to give the landlord's lien for rent and supplies indisputable primacy over those of the laborer and, most important, of the merchant with whom the cropper may have been dealing for supplies and the sale of his cotton. By these measures, the landowners secured dominance over the post-Emancipation agricultural system and over the increasingly dependent labor force. Gone was the plantation worked by gangs of slaves. In its place, there had arisen a system that was repressive and labor-intensive and that, furthermore, possessed few of the features thought to be characteristic of free labor.

With the return of the Democrats to power in the late 1870s, the priorities of Reconstruction itself, not just the Republican party, had been substantially overthrown. As is invariably the case, however, the break with the recent past was not a clean one. Some of the features and priorities of Reconstruction persisted. The civil and political rights that blacks had won were retained on the statute books and would remain there until segregation and disfranchisement were made law at the turn of the century. Also a powerful segment of the Democratic party still pursued railroad building and pressed for the development of manufacturing, though neither could now expect public subsidization. But the discontinuities were far more noticeable, as the triumphant Democrats reduced governmental activism to a minimum, consolidated the region's repressive system of land and labor, and vindicated their claim to be the restorers of white supremacy. Reconstruction had pointed the way to a New South: its overthrow ensured that whatever was new about the South in the last quarter of the nineteenth century would be severely circumscribed by old practices and priorities.

FURTHER READING

Richard N. Current, "Carpetbaggers Reconsidered," in Kenneth M. Stampp and Leon Litwack, eds., *Reconstruction: An Anthology of Revisionist Writings* (1969), 223–240
———, *Those Terrible Carpetbaggers: A Reinterpretation* (1988)
Eric Foner, "Reconstruction and the Crisis of Free Labor," in Foner, *Politics and Ideology in the Age of the Civil War* (1980)
James T. Moore, "Redeemers Reconsidered: Change and Continuity in the Democratic South, 1877–1900," *Journal of Southern History* 64 (1978), 357–378
Elizabeth S. Nathans, *Losing the Peace: Georgia Republicans and Reconstruction, 1865–1871* (1968)

Otto H. Olsen, "The Ku Klux Klan: A Story of Reconstruction Politics and Propaganda," *North Carolina Historical Review* 39 (1962), 340–362

——, ed., *Reconstruction and Redemption in the South* (1980)

Michael Perman, *The Road to Redemption: Southern Politics, 1869–1879* (1984)

Lawrence N. Powell, *New Masters: Northern Planters during the Civil War and Reconstruction* (1980)

George C. Rable, *But There Was No Peace: Violence and Reconstruction* (1984)

Mark W. Summers, *Railroads, Reconstruction and the Gospel of Prosperity: Aid under the Radical Republicans, 1865–1877* (1984)

J. Mills Thornton, III, "Fiscal Policy and the Failure of Reconstruction in the Lower South," in J. Morgan Kousser and James M. McPherson, eds., *Region, Race, and Reconstruction* (1982), 349–394

Allen W. Trelease, *White Terror: The Ku Klux Conspiracy and Reconstruction* (1971)

Ted Tunnell, *Crucible of Reconstruction: War, Radicalism, and Race in Louisiana, 1862–1877* (1984)

Jonathan Wiener, *Social Origins of the New South: Alabama, 1860–1885* (1978)

C. Vann Woodward, *Origins of the New South, 1877–1913* (1951)

——, *Reunion and Reaction: The Compromise of 1877 and the End of Reconstruction* (1951)

Richard Zuczek, *State of Rebellion: Reconstruction in South Carolina* (1996)

CHAPTER
14

The Northern Retreat
from Reconstruction

Between 1865 and 1870, the Republican party in Congress had struggled mightily to formulate and implement terms for reconstructing the defeated South. Yet, within a few years, the governments they had brought into existence there began to collapse and/or be overthrown until, by 1877, Reconstruction was effectively over. And Northerners, including even the Republicans themselves, accepted this disastrous outcome with apparent calm. What had happened to let this reversal be tolerated?

The abandonment of Reconstruction is one of the most puzzling aspects of the entire episode. If it was so vital to reconstruct the South after the war, how could the policy be so readily forsaken? Part of the answer can be found by looking more closely at the initial policy itself. The terms for readmission of the Southern states envisioned no active or continuing role for the federal government in the South. The assumption behind both of the proposals passed by Congress in 1866 and 1867 was that the Southern states would be self-governing. Indeed, as members of a federal union of equal states, they should be able to take care of themselves without outside interference. Readmission to Congress—that is, reunion—was therefore predicated upon the existence of independent and effective governments in the Southern states. When these had been established, federal supervision, civil as well as military, would be withdrawn as rapidly as conditions allowed. But, in the years immediately following readmission, the Reconstruction governments found it necessary to ask for help in dealing with resistance and lawlessness. The federal government often responded but it never committed itself to a deep and continuing involvement.

Despite its avowed purpose of phased withdrawal as the situation allowed, the federal government found itself constantly drawn back in because the predicament of the Republican regimes in the South worsened, as did that of their supporters, the freedmen, and those whites who voted Republican. With the Democrats likely to return to power and with their own experiment in reorganizing the South in danger of collapse, the Northern Republicans had a political interest in sustaining Reconstruction as well as a moral obligation not to abandon their allies. Instead of increasing their involve-

ment in Reconstruction, however, the party's leaders hewed to their original course. Why was that?

Even if, as we have been arguing, the abandonment of Reconstruction in 1877 was not a departure from the approach the congressional Republicans took at the outset, was not the situation in the mid-1870s sufficiently threatening to require a reassessment and a change of course? If the political needs of the Republicans nationally had remained the same as in the immediate aftermath of the war, then they might have been compelled to reconsider their stance toward the South. But, by the mid-1870s, they had more to lose by supporting the Republican governments in the South than by abandoning them. Equally, attitudes toward the idea of reconstructing the South politically and economically had undergone considerable change in the preceding five to ten years. One element in this shift was a growing unwillingness to allow the fate of the national Republican party to be tied to the black voters of the South. Rather than allies, they were now seen as dependents who needed the Republicans more than the Republicans needed them. These changing attitudes in the North contributed strongly to the willingness of the Northern people and the federal government to end Reconstruction.

D O C U M E N T S

The retreat from Reconstruction is illustrated in various ways by the selections that follow. In the first, Senator Charles Sumner, the leading radical Republican in the Senate, tells the abolitionist, Gerrit Smith, that he will not support Grant for reelection in 1872. Grant's attempt to acquire Santo Domingo (Haiti) over Sumner's objections as chairman of the Senate Foreign Relations Committee was one reason; the other was the president's handling of the South, which Sumner felt was feeble and irresponsible. The second document is from a speech by Carl Schurz, a Republican senator from Missouri who was active in the Liberal Republican movement of 1872. In this speech, Schurz calls for amnesty and conciliation toward the South. The speech was delivered in the Senate on January 30, 1872. A short extract from James S. Pike's *The Prostrate State* is the third item. Published in 1873, Pike's book was a blistering indictment of South Carolina's Republican government during Reconstruction. Pike was an influential northern journalist who had favored a strong policy toward the defeated South but, like many others, he turned on Reconstruction soon after it ran into difficulty.

A speech in the House of Representatives by the Speaker, James G. Blaine of Maine, on January 10, 1876, is the fourth item. In the small extract printed here, Blaine, who caused a sensation by urging that Jefferson Davis alone be excluded from the final amnesty act, points out that the Republicans' offer of amnesty to leading Confederates had been remarkably ungrudging and fulsome, and yet it had produced only antagonism on the part of its beneficiaries. The fifth document is from Rutherford B. Hayes's letter accepting the Republican nomination for president in July 1876. After stating his policies on civil service reform, government expenditures, and the currency, he presented his views on the Southern question. The sixth item is a dispatch from President Grant to Governor Daniel H. Chamberlain of South Carolina, telling Chamberlain that, despite anti-Republican and anti-black violence such as the Hamburg riot, he could not continue to expect the support of the federal government. Grant's reply to Chamberlain's request for help is dated July 26, 1876.

Senator Charles Sumner Can No Longer Support President Grant, August 1871

private

Nahant—Mass. 20th Aug. '71

My dear friend [Gerrit Smith],

Yr note & its enclosure reached me at this retreat where I am with my friend [the poet, Henry Wadsworth] Longfellow. I regret much that I cannot see the Presidential question as you see it.

I know few politicians who think that Grant can be re-elected. Greeley told me last week that he looked upon his defeat as inevitable. Forney, who is friendly to him & has just accepted the collectorship of Phila., told me that he did not see how he could be re-elected, although he thought he would obtain the nomination;—to which I replied that he could not be nominated if it appeared that he could not be re-elected.

Therefore when you ask me to withdraw opposition to Grant, you ask me to aid in the defeat of the Republican Party. I have too much interest in this party to do any such thing.

But waiving the question of his success—he does not deserve the nomination. "One term" is enough for any body—especially for one who, being tried, is found so incapable,—so personal—so selfish—so vindictive, & so entirely pre-occupied by himself. All who have known him best testify to his incapacity. . . .

It is hard to see the Ku Klux raging & good people dying through his luke-warmness & indifference. It is my solemn judgt, which at the proper time I shall declare, that the much-criticized Ku Klux legislation of the last Congress would have been *entirely unnecessary,* if this Republican President had shown a decent energy in enforc-ing existing law & in manifesting sympathy with the oppressed there. *On him is that innocent blood,*—which flowed while he circulated at entertainments, excur-sions, horse-races. Instead of being at Long-Branch [Grant's home in New Jersey] a good Presdt. would have been at Savannah & Mobile or at least he would have made himself felt in those places.

Consider, then, the insincerity of his message about St Dom [Santo Domingo]. One million of blacks are now kept in anxiety & terror by the Republican Presdt, whom you hail as representing "moral ideas"! Instead of abandoning his ill-omened Scheme,—he is now pressing it—working at home, like Hamlet's ghost, under ground & at the island with a most expensive fleet. His war-dance about the island has cost several millions. Instead of making peace between the two contending parties, & setting each on its legs, in the spirit of disinterested benevolence, he sends money to Baez under pretense of a sham treaty to keep alive civil war. Nothing has aroused me more since the Fug. Sl. Bill & the outrages in Kansas. The same old spirit is revived in the treatment of the Haytian Republic.

And I am asked to help the re-nomination of such a man. Impossible! I love the Republican [party]—love my country too well to have a hand in such a thing.

In these conclusions I am governed by no personal feelings—more than I had to Franklin Pierce or James Buchanan! How can I, an old public servant, devoted to a

From Charles Sumner to Gerrit Smith, in *The Selected Papers of Charles Sumner,* Beverly Wilson Palmer, ed. (Northeastern University Press, 1990), Vol. 2, pp. 569–570.

cause, turn aside on any personal feelings?—No,—my dear friend, I write in sadness & sincerity, hoping yet to do something by which the cause of our country shall be saved. Think of five years under his vindictive imperialism! Surely *you* must hesitate. . . .

Senator Carl Schurz of Missouri Condemns Reconstruction, January 1872

. . . But the stubborn fact remains that they [Southern black voters and officeholders] *were* ignorant and inexperienced; that the public business *was* an unknown world to them, and that in spite of the best intentions they *were* easily misled, not infrequently by the most reckless rascality which had found a way to their confidence. Thus their political rights and privileges were undoubtedly well calculated, and even necessary, to protect their rights as free laborers and citizens; but they were not well calculated to secure a successful administration of other public interests.

I do not blame the colored people for it; still less do I say that for this reason their political rights and privileges should have been denied them. Nay, sir, I deemed it necessary then, and I now reaffirm that opinion, that they should possess those rights and privileges for the permanent establishment of the logical and legitimate results of the war and the protection of their new position in society. But, while never losing sight of this necessity, I do say that the inevitable consequence of the admission of so large an uneducated and inexperienced class to political power, as to the probable mismanagement of the material interests of the social body, should at least have been mitigated by a counterbalancing policy. When ignorance and inexperience were admitted to so large an influence upon public affairs, intelligence ought no longer to so large an extent have been excluded. In other words, when universal suffrage was granted to secure the equal rights of all, universal amnesty ought to have been granted to make all the resources of political intelligence and experience available for the promotion of the welfare of all.

But what did we do? To the uneducated and inexperienced classes—uneducated and inexperienced, I repeat, entirely without their fault—we opened the road to power; and, at the same time, we condemned a large proportion of the intelligence of those States, of the property-holding, the industrial, the professional, the tax-paying interest, to a worse than passive attitude. We made it, as it were, easy for rascals who had gone South in quest of profitable adventure to gain the control of masses so easily misled, by permitting them to appear as the exponents and representatives of the National power and of our policy; and at the same time we branded a large number of men of intelligence, and many of them of personal integrity, whose material interests were so largely involved in honest government, and many of whom would have cooperated in managing the public business with care and foresight—we branded them, I say, as outcasts, telling them that they ought not to be suffered to exercise any influence upon the management of the public business, and that it would be unwarrantable presumption in them to attempt it.

I ask you, sir, could such things fail to contribute to the results we read to-day in the political corruption and demoralization, and in the financial ruin of some of the Southern

From Carl Schurz, speech in Senate, January 30, 1872, in *Speeches, Correspondence and Political Papers of Carl Schurz*, Frederic Bancroft, ed. (G. P. Putnam's & Co., 1913), pp. 326–327.

States? These results are now before us. The mistaken policy may have been pardonable when these consequences were still a matter of conjecture and speculation; but what excuse have we now for continuing it when those results are clear before our eyes, beyond the reach of contradiction? . . .

James Shepherd Pike Offers a Liberal Republican View of Reconstruction, 1873

. . . The State really bears a foreign yoke; not one imposed by its own people, or by an authority which has arisen of itself among themselves. And this is the anomaly of the situation. It is a so-called democracy sustained by external force. In other words, it is a government that the intelligent public opinion of the State would overthrow if left to itself. It may be called self-government, or republican or democratic government, but in no just sense is it either. It is a government which in the very nature of things could never rise to control, of itself, in any community. It is not an outgrowth of power and authority in the regular order. It is a hybrid born of unnatural connections, offensive alike to God and man; and, wherever the retributive responsibility of it fairly belongs, it is clear that it does not belong to the generation now rising upon the stage of action in the South, and who alone will be in the near future the sole victims of its oppressions. And this is the class whose just rights must be considered, whose hardships must be mitigated and removed by the power which holds the actual control of the situation, or another and yet another political and social convulsion will inevitably ensue, till disorder and revolution become chronic in our affairs. Not till absolute justice is established can we look for peace and tranquillity in our political system anywhere. . . .

The Federal Government could do much, if it would take the necessary pains, toward correcting some of the worst practices of this corrupt travesty of a government. It did something in the appointment of Governor Orr as minister to Russia. It was at least an expression of sympathy with those who made an effort at reform at the last election. But it accomplished nothing of real value. In fact, by sending a leading supporter of the Administration, who was an opponent of corruption, 5,000 miles out of the country, it took away an influence which might, on occasion, deter the rogues from some of their more nefarious acts.

The only authority to which these miscreants pay the least deference is the Federal Government; for its power and its countenance are requisite to the success of many of their own operations. It makes large appropriations for new public edifices in the State, as is attested by those which are now going up in Charleston and Columbia. It appoints to office the large body of revenue officers, both internal and external, the numerous postmasters, the Federal judges, attorneys, and special agents, and it keeps bodies of Federal troops in the State, which are everywhere welcome for the money they disburse. Through these and kindred influences, the Federal Government holds vast sway over the State. That for some reason it has not exercised its influence to any appreciable extent in the interest of good government, is evident. It might do much toward repressing many corrupt practices and raising the moral tone of the State government. It has not done this. And yet it would seem to be its interest to do it. Why should the Republican party of the country, composed so largely as it is of its best and most conscientious citizens, be

From James Shepherd Pike, *The Prostrate State: South Carolina Under Negro Government* (New York: Loring & Massey, 1935), pp. 82–87.

compelled to endure the foul stain inflicted by the robberies and outrages of caitiffs, who deserve the State-prison? Some of the leaders of affairs are men who have merely adopted Republicanism as a cloak for their villainies. South Carolina to-day rejoices in a Republican Representative in Congress who once made a formal proposition in the State Legislature to reduce all the free blacks to slavery, and it has a Republican Governor [Franklin J. Moses] who tore down the American flag from Fort Sumter, and, treading it under foot, hoisted the Confederate ensign in its place. Dancing at negro balls and issuing "pay certificates" as Speaker is said to have been the means whereby he has condoned his offenses. One turns with inexpressible loathing and disgust from such wretched demagogues. They cover Republicanism with reproach, and, what is worse, they depress and extinguish the hopes of philanthropic men who wish to see the capacity and better qualities of the black man fairly tested in the bold experiment of his sudden emancipation and enfranchisement. . . .

Speaker James G. Blaine Points Out the Results of the Republicans' Generous Amnesty Policy, January 1876

. . . Well, that disability [the Fourteenth Amendment's third clause] was hardly placed upon the South until we began in this Hall and in the other wing of the Capitol, when there were more than two-thirds republicans in both branches, to remit it, and the very first bill took that disability off from 1,578 citizens of the South; and the next bill took it off from 3,526 gentlemen—by wholesale. Many of the gentlemen on this floor came in for grace and amnesty in those two bills. After these bills specifying individuals had passed, and others, of smaller numbers, which I will not recount, the Congress of the United States in 1872, by two-thirds of both branches, still being two-thirds republican, passed this general law:

> That all political disabilities imposed by the third section of the fourteenth article of amendments of the Constitution of the United States are hereby removed from all persons whomsoever, except Senators and Representatives of the Thirty-sixth and Thirty-seventh Congresses, officers in the judicial, military, and naval service of the United States, heads of Departments, and foreign ministers of the United States.

Since that act passed a very considerable number of the gentlemen which it still left under disability have been relieved specially, by name, in separate acts. But I believe, Mr. Speaker, in no single instance since the act of May 22, 1872, have the disabilities been taken from any man except upon his respectful petition to the Congress of the United States that they should be removed. And I believe in no instance, except one, have they been refused upon the petition being presented. I believe in no instance, except one, has there been any other than a unanimous vote. . . .

As to the general question of amnesty, Mr. Speaker, as I have already said, it is too late to debate it. It has gone by. Whether it has in all respects been wise, or whether it has been unwise, I would not detain the House here to discuss. Even if I had a strong conviction upon that question, I do not know that it would be productive of any great good to enunciate it; but, at the same time, it is a very singular spectacle that the

From James G. Blaine, speech in the House, January 10, 1876, *Congressional Record,* 44 Cong., 1 Sess., Vol. 4, pt. 1, pp. 324–325.

republican party, in possession of the entire Government, have deliberately called back into public power the leading men of the South, every one of whom turns up its bitter and relentless and malignant foe; and to-day, from the Potomac to the Rio Grande, the very men who have received this amnesty are as busy as they can be in consolidating into one compact political organization the old slave States, just as they were before the war. We see the banner held out blazoned again with the inscription that, with the united South and a very few votes from the North, this country can be governed. I want the people to understand that is precisely the movement; that that is the animus and the intent. I do not think offering amnesty to the seven hundred and fifty men who are now without it will hasten or retard that movement. I do not think the granting of amnesty to Mr. Davis will hasten or retard it, or that refusing it will do either.

Rutherford B. Hayes Describes His Southern Policy for the 1876 Presidential Campaign, July 1876

The condition of the Southern States attracts the attention and commands the sympathy of the people of the whole Union. In their progressive recovery from the effects of the war, their first necessity is an intelligent and honest administration of government which will protect all classes of citizens in their political and private rights. What the South most needs is peace, and peace depends upon the supremacy of the law. There can be no enduring peace if the constitutional rights of any portion of the people are habitually disregarded. A division of political parties resting merely upon sectional lines is always unfortunate and may be disastrous. The welfare of the South, alike with that of every other part of this country, depends upon the attractions it can offer to labor and immigration, and to capital. But laborers will not go and capital will not be ventured where the Constitution and the laws are set at defiance, and distraction, apprehension, and alarm take the place of peace-living and law-abiding social life. All parts of the Constitution are sacred and must be sacredly observed—the parts that are new no less than the parts that are old. The moral and material prosperity of the Southern States can be most effectually advanced by a hearty and generous recognition of the rights of all, by all—a recognition without reserve or exception. With such a recognition fully accorded it will be practicable to promote, by the influence of all legitimate agencies of the general Government, the efforts of the people of those States to obtain for themselves the blessings of honest and capable local government. If elected, I shall consider it not only my duty, but it will be my ardent desire, to labor for the attainment of this end.

Let me assure my countrymen of the Southern States that if I shall be charged with the duty of organizing an administration, it will be one which will regard and cherish their truest interests—the interests of the white and of the colored people both, and equally; and which will put forth its best efforts in behalf of a civil policy which will wipe out forever the distinction between North and South in our common country.

With a civil service organized upon a system which will secure purity, experience, efficiency, and economy, a strict regard for the public welfare solely in appoint-

Letter, Rutherford B. Hayes to Edward McPheron et al., June 8, 1876, in Charles Richard Williams, *The Life of Rutherford B. Hayes* (Houghton Mifflin, 1914), Vol. 1, p. 462.

ments, and the speedy, thorough, and unsparing prosecution and punishment of all public officers who betray official trusts; with a sound currency; with education unsectarian and free to all; with simplicity and frugality in public and private affairs; and with a fraternal spirit of harmony pervading the people of all sections and classes, we may reasonably hope that the second century of our existence as a nation will, by the blessing of God, be preeminent as an era of good feeling and a period of progress, prosperity, and happiness.

Very respectfully, your fellow citizen,
R. B. Hayes

To the Hons. Edward McPherson, Wm. A. Howard, Jos. H. Rainey, and Others, *Committee of the National Republican Convention.*

President Grant Disclaims Responsibility for Reconstruction in South Carolina, July 1876

Executive Mansion,
Washington, D.C., July 26th.

Dear Sir:—I am in receipt of your letter of the 22d of July, and all the inclosures enumerated therein, giving an account of the late barbarous massacre at the town of Hamburg, S. C. The views which you express as to the duty you owe to your oath of office and to citizens to secure to all their civil rights, including the right to vote according to the dictates of their own consciences, and the further duty of the Executive of the nation to give all needful aid, when properly called on to do so, to enable you to ensure this inalienable right, I fully concur in. The scene at Hamburg, as cruel, blood-thirsty, wanton, unprovoked, and uncalled for, as it was, is only a repetition of the course which has been pursued in other Southern States within the last few years, notably in Mississippi and Louisiana. Mississippi is governed to-day by officials chosen through fraud and violence, such as would scarcely be accredited to savages, much less to a civilized and Christian people. How long these things are to continue, or what is to be the final remedy, the Great Ruler of the universe only knows; but I have an abiding faith that the remedy will come, and come speedily, and I earnestly hope that it will come peacefully. There has never been a desire on the part of the North to humiliate the South. Nothing is claimed for one State that is not fully accorded to all others, unless it may be the right to kill negroes and Republicans without fear of punishment and without loss of caste or reputation. This has seemed to be a privilege claimed by a few States. I repeat again, that I fully agree with you as to the measure of your duties in the present emergency, and as to my duties. Go on—and let every Governor where the same dangers threaten the peace of his State go on—in the conscientious discharge of his duties to the humblest as well as the proudest citizen, and I will give every aid for which I can find law or constitutional power. A government that cannot give protection to life, property, and all guaranteed civil rights (in this country the greatest is an untrammelled ballot) to the citizen is, in so far, a failure, and every energy of the oppressed should be exerted, always within the law

From Ulysses Grant to Daniel Chamberlain, July 26, 1876, in Walter Allen, *Governor Chamberlain's Administration in South Carolina* (Books for Libraries Press, 1969 [1888]), pp. 325–326.

and by constitutional means, to regain lost privileges and protection. Too long denial of guaranteed rights is sure to lead to revolution—bloody revolution, where suffering must fall upon the innocent as well as the guilty.

Expressing the hope that the better judgment and co-operation of citizens of the State over which you have presided so ably may enable you to secure a fair trial and punishment of all offenders, without distinction of race or color or previous condition of servitude, and without aid from the Federal Government, but with the promise of such aid on the conditions named in the foregoing, I subscribe myself, very respectfully, your obedient servant,

U. S. Grant.

To the Hon. D. H. Chamberlain,
Governor of South Carolina.

E S S A Y S

The waning of interest and commitment in the North played a significant part in the collapse of Southern Reconstruction. The two essays on this topic both focus on the Republican party, though on different aspects of it. In the first, Richard H. Abbott of Eastern Michigan University surveys the performance of the Republican political leadership in Washington as it dealt with the Southern question during the presidency of U. S. Grant. The extract reprinted here begins with the election of 1872 and continues with Grant's second term. The accompanying piece, by Michael Les Benedict of Ohio State University, examines an increasingly influential group within the party who referred to themselves as Liberals. Although they were mainly thinkers and writers, rather than politicians and party activists, they nevertheless influenced the party considerably, pushing it in a conservative direction, away from its earlier, more radical embrace of Reconstruction.

Reconstruction Winds Down: The Grant Years, 1869–1877

RICHARD H. ABBOTT

Despite the evidence from the election of 1868 that the Southern Republican party was weak, lacked significant white support, and was receiving little Northern assistance, some Northern Republicans continued to harbor optimism about their Southern prospects. With Grant in the White House they would no longer have to contend with an obstructionist president; both executive and legislative branches of the federal government were firmly in their hands. Northern Republicans also hoped that with their victory in 1868 Southern Democrats and Conservatives would cease their violent opposition to Reconstruction measures, recognizing that the Republicans would hold power in Washington for at least four more years. Thus peace and order would return to the South, and many hoped that in an atmosphere of stability the party would have a chance to build on its base there. Perhaps Southern whites who had resisted the Republicans up to this point might reconsider their position and join the party.

From Richard H. Abbott, *The Republican Party and the South, 1855–1877: The First Southern Strategy* (The University of North Carolina Press, Chapel Hill and London, 1986). Copyright © 1986. Reprinted by permission of Richard H. Abbott.

In the wake of optimism following Grant's election, many Northern Republicans believed their work in the South was done. Confident that Grant's presidency would restore order in the South, Benjamin Butler proclaimed early in 1869 that "we will want no army [there] after the 4th of March next." Butler had already been telling Southern Republicans that after the Reconstruction Acts had been implemented, they should expect no more help from the North: "Now you must help yourselves." Horace Greeley agreed, informing the Southern Republicans that it was time they ceased "hanging around the neck of the North." In Massachusetts, Edward Atkinson and other members of the Massachusetts Reconstruction Association, arguing that "the election of Grant settles the Southern question," disbanded the group, and in Washington, the Republican Congressional Committee was no longer as active as it had been in overseeing Southern affairs.

Unfortunately for the Republicans, this optimism concerning the future of the South proved misplaced. The problems the party faced there before the election did not go away, but instead grew worse. Although the Republicans reelected Grant in 1872, by the end of his second term the party had lost control of every state in the South. The overthrow of the Republican party in the South was largely the result of Southern conditions, but it also came about because the Northern Republicans, for the most part, continued to be inattentive to the Southern party's needs. They saw the South as an unlikely region in which to build a permanent party able to contest with the Democrats for control.

President Grant and his fellow Northern Republicans were not blind to their party's needs in the South. The executive branch under Grant was more active than it had been under Lincoln or Johnson in promoting Republican fortunes below the Mason-Dixon line. For its part, Congress amended the Constitution again to ensure the permanence of Negro suffrage and then in 1870 and 1871 passed legislation to enforce the amendment. Nonetheless the policies the Northern Republicans followed in the South after 1868 were inconsistent and plagued by frustrations and disappointments. They continued to wrestle with problems that had appeared during and after the implementation of the Reconstruction Acts: whether to give amnesty to Southerners still under political disqualifications, whether to bolster the party's appeal among blacks, especially by appointing more to office and enacting new civil rights laws, and whether to use the federal government to protect black voters from white terrorism. Northern Republicans also continued to ignore or slight Southern Republican needs by not providing them with enough patronage, campaign funds, or federal economic assistance to help promote the party there. Instead, the national party continued to follow the pattern it had already set of giving top priority to maintaining its base among Northern voters, even if this meant sacrificing the interests of party colleagues in the South. . . .

[Omitted is a discussion of Republican policy toward the South during Grant's first term, 1868–1872, focusing on such matters as enforcing voting rights under the Fifteenth Amendment, putting down Klan violence, and offering amnesty to former Confederates still unpardoned.]

By 1872 [many] Republicans' discontent with their party's Reconstruction policies was reaching major proportions. [Liberal Republicans such as Horace Greeley, Jacob D. Cox, Carl] Schurz, Samuel Bowles of the *Springfield Republican,* and others condemned the party for failing to repeal the ironclad oath and offer the South universal amnesty. They were also opposed to continued federal regulation of Southern elections through the Enforcement Acts and wanted an end to military intervention there. The Liberals were also horrified at scandals that surfaced implicating some of Grant's subordinates and were eager for civil service reform that they hoped would bring honesty and efficiency to government bureaucracy. In addition, many Liberals were opposed to the protective tariff policies of the Republican administration. When the Republican party renominated Grant for president in 1872, the dissidents broke with their fellows and chose Horace Greeley to run as an independent on a Liberal Republican platform. The Democrats, despite their enormous distaste for Greeley, a lifelong Republican who had denounced their party for years, decided to support him instead of running a candidate of their own. Because the Democrats were most interested in home rule for the South and Greeley had little interest in civil service reform and was opposed to tariff reduction, the campaign centered on amnesty and self-government for the South.

Even though the main issues in the campaign were related to Southern conditions, the Republicans believed, as they had in past years, that they would win or lose the election in the North, and they devoted most of their attention to that section. The institutions that were at hand for the party in 1868 to use in the campaign in the South were now missing. The Freedmen's Bureau had been largely withdrawn from the South after the election of 1868. The Union League, which the Republicans had used extensively in the South in 1867 and 1868 to organize voters, was now defunct in the North and virtually destroyed by Klan violence in the South. The Congressional Committee, which had closely supervised Southern developments while the Southern states were undergoing the Reconstruction process in 1867–69, no longer continued this responsibility and no longer maintained speakers and agents to send into the South. Once the Republicans had organized in each of the Southern states, the state parties were expected to be self-sufficient.

Northern Republicans once again made North Carolina the major exception to their policy of stressing Northern priorities over Southern needs. The state's August elections were the first to be held in the presidential year, and many considered them to be an early indicator of voter loyalties for the fall. Hence Republican leaders recognized the importance of winning the state. When the Republican national convention met that summer, Judge Thomas Settle, one of North Carolina's most prominent white Republicans, was chosen chairman of the gathering. During the summer the Department of Justice redoubled its efforts to indict suspected Klan members in the state. Most significantly, the Northern Republicans made a major concession to the state in their allocation of campaign funds and speakers. The Republican National Committee agreed to send $10,000 to the state to help it carry the election. The committee also sent Northern speakers into the state, including cabinet secretaries George Boutwell and Columbus Delano and Senator Henry Wilson.

Republicans both North and South were heartened when the Republican gubernatorial candidate in North Carolina won a narrow victory. But Republican success in that state did not encourage the national committee to send any more money southward. Instead, it resumed its customary policy of emphasizing campaigns in the Northern states. As Southern politics proved volatile and unpredictable, Republican hopes continued to rest on the states that had formed the party in 1855 and had elected Lincoln and Grant in the last three presidential canvasses. John Murray Forbes, an important fund-raiser for the now defunct Massachusetts Reconstruction Association, declared that the only way to protect black Republicans in the South was "by a united Republican North," and most party leaders agreed with him.

As in previous elections, the national committee paid particular attention to the crucial Northern states that held state elections in October. The national committee spent at least as much in Maine as it had in North Carolina and sent $75,000 into Pennsylvania; the party leaders especially believed if they could carry that state, "the fight is over." By September, the committee's members were struggling to raise the funds needed to pursue a vigorous campaign in the "closely contested states," but they ultimately raised enough funds to send $40,000 to Indiana and at least $10,000 to Ohio.

In the meantime, party committees in the South sent urgent pleas to the North for campaign funds. Edwin Morgan, chairman of the national committee, told the Southern petitioners that they could expect no money until the October states in the North were secured for the party. He also indicated that states like Tennessee, Georgia, and Virginia, which were in Conservative hands, could expect almost no help. Most Republican leaders in the South were understanding, realizing that, as before, they stood little chance of holding their states if Northern voters deserted the Republican party. Nonetheless, they urged Morgan and William E. Chandler to supply them with whatever aid they could.

In late September, feeling more confident about the upcoming elections in the North, Morgan agreed to send $2,000 to Alabama and an equal amount to Florida, with promises of more aid if it could be raised. After the Republicans swept the October states, and thereby apparently sealed Grant's victory in November, Morgan found it almost impossible to raise further funds. Southern party chairmen, realizing that Grant did not need their states' electoral votes, still asked for aid, justifying it as necessary to keep the party alive until the next presidential election. One Georgia Republican importuned Chandler, asking for as little as $100 or "even a letter of sympathy." Senator James Harlan, a member of the Congressional Committee, told Chandler that he believed that Grant would win in November without the South. Nonetheless, he still professed "deep solicitude" for the party's "feeble friends" there and hoped that the national committee could send them a little help, arguing that "the moral effect would be very great."

Morgan admitted that because of demands for funds in the North, the committee had "done but little for the Southern states." Later in October, because some pledged money was still coming to his committee, Morgan managed to send another $1,000 to Alabama; he also distributed small amounts to Virginia, Arkansas, and Mississippi. Altogether, however, the Southern states, with the exception of North Carolina, had received less aid than that given to the single Northern state of Maine. Although the party did send more Northern speakers into the South than it had in 1868, the Republicans still kept their best orators before Northern audiences, at least until the October elections were over. In addition, the party brought some of its Southern speakers North to convince Northern voters of the existence of continued lawlessness in the South that could be quelled only by Grant's reelection.

Once again, the Republican party in a national election had revealed that its Southern concerns were secondary to maintaining its Northern base. Southern Republicans were once again disappointed with the encouragement and assistance they received from the national party. The Northern strategy did pay off for the Republicans, as it had in 1860, 1864, and 1868; this time Grant swept the North, and with it the election. In 1872 he also carried all the former Confederate states except Georgia, Texas, and Tennessee, and in the border he won Delaware and West Virginia. In large part Grant was successful in the nation and in the South because of Greeley's weakness as a candidate; he won fewer electoral votes and a smaller percentage of the popular vote than the Democrats had won in 1868. In fact, his electoral vote and popular vote percentage totals were the lowest of any candidate between 1860 and 1892. Grant won six of his ten Southern states by narrow margins. There his success was owing not only to Democratic weakness but to the steadfast support of black voters, who were protected at the polls in many instances by the operation of the Enforcement Acts, which for the time being had stayed the hand of Southern vigilante groups like the Klan. Indeed, the election of 1872 was one of the most peaceful and democratic in Southern postbellum history.

Although the 1872 election results in the South demonstrated the continued potential of the black vote for the Republican party, after Grant was reelected the Northern public and the Republican administration showed less and less interest in enforcing civil and political rights in the South. During Grant's second term, he authorized federal intervention in Arkansas and Louisiana but could not prevent the Conservatives from taking control of the former state. In Texas, Alabama, and Mississippi, he abstained from involvement in behalf of the Republican governments, and by the end of 1875 all of them were lost to the party. Communications between Northern and Southern Republicans, which had already begun to decline rapidly after Grant was elected in 1868, picked up momentarily in 1872 but fell off after the presidential election and never resumed the level matched during the period when the Republican party was organizing in the South. Financial aid from the party continued to dwindle, and few Northerners visited the South.

This lack of support for Southern Republicans was reflected in Congress's continued failure to recognize their requests for federal patronage and economic assistance. The Northern Republicans had already set this pattern in the years 1867–68, when the Reconstruction program of Congress was being implemented in the South. Congress proved willing then to put troops in the South, enfranchise blacks, and create an environment in which the Republican party could emerge, but did nothing to provide economic assistance that might have increased the party's appeal to both races. Because blacks already were committed to the party through its advocacy of the Fourteenth and Fifteenth amendments, Republicans in the North saw the need to bid for white support in the South, but they were indicating as early as 1867 that they were not willing to provide whites with much incentive for voting Republican. This pattern was continued in both Grant administrations. Southern Republican petitions for patronage, for financial assistance in the way of railroad aid and levee improvement, or for currency redistribution or inflation were either ignored or barely recognized. Even though the Republicans advertised themselves to the South as the party of material progress and social improvement, they did little on the national level to give substance to those claims.

Even though Southern states were now fully represented in Congress, Southern Republicans did not get recognition in filling the important congressional committee posts. Nor did they get their fair share of federal patronage. During Grant's presidency no Southerners were appointed to the seven vacancies that appeared on the Supreme Court. Nor did any Southerner except Amos Akerman of Georgia serve in Grant's cabinet. After Akerman's appointment, the patronage of his office did not meet Southern expectations. A prominent Georgia Republican reprimanded Akerman for not giving "sufficient importance to the Federal patronage," reminding him that Southern Republicans "must be aided by the party." In 1872, Robert B. Elliott, a black congressman from South Carolina, complained to Grant himself about leaving the Republicans of his state to stand "self-sustained without any appreciable aid from official patronage."

During Grant's administration Congress returned to many of the economic issues of concern to the South that had been raised in the Fortieth Congress, which had presided over the drafting and execution of the Reconstruction Acts. At that time Congress had turned a deaf ear to Southern pleas for federal aid for levee rebuilding, railroad construction, tax relief, and a redistribution of national bank currency that would provide badly needed circulating medium for the South. The four succeeding Congresses that sat while Grant was president did little more than their predecessor in answering these pleas.

From the time the South reentered Congress, Southern Republican congressmen sought federal aid for river and harbor improvements. As the South gained full representation, Congress did begin to appropriate such funds, particularly for harbor improvement, but Southerners still objected that the Great Lakes states of Michigan and Wisconsin got more funds for such purposes than the entire South. Southern representatives from states bordering on the Mississippi River were particularly concerned about getting federal aid for levee rebuilding; some virtually staked their political careers on acquiring it. James Lusk Alcorn, a white Mississippian who had helped organize the Republican party in his state and was its first Republican governor, was elected to the U.S. Senate in 1871 and worked mightily for federal funds for levee reconstruction. Not until 1881, however, did Congress agree to the expenditure, and by then the aid was too late to help the Republican party in the South.

The Republican Congresses of the 1870s were of little more use to the Southerners when it came to appropriating funds or granting lands for railroad construction. Southern Republicans made a major issue of the importance of railroad building to the prosperity of the South and eagerly looked to Congress for federal aid. They knew that the North had benefited greatly from federal land grants to railroads during and after the war, especially for building transcontinental lines from the Mississippi to the Pacific; they thought it was now the South's turn for such largesse. They also argued that providing the South with such land grants would prove to white Southerners that the Republican party cared about their needs. Unfortunately for Southern hopes, however, the Congress had decided to end the policy of railroad land grants. The South did win one victory in 1871, when the Forty-first Congress agreed to a land grant to aid in the building of the Texas and Pacific, the South's only transcontinental project. Even then the grant was smaller than that accorded previously to Northern lines, was not accompanied by any loan guarantees, and required that the road be built on the Northern gauge, which limited its usefulness to Southern cities that hoped to connect with it.

Congress also turned a largely deaf ear to Southern pleas to adjust the revenue and currency structure of the nation to bear less heavily on the South. Southerners still resented the cotton taxes collected in the South from 1862 to 1868 and in 1873 sought to have the government refund $57 million in taxes collected in this manner. Southern representatives voted 60–3 for the proposal, but Northern Republicans voted 3–74 against it, and the proposal was easily defeated. The Congress was slightly more receptive to renewed pleas from the South that the country make more currency available to the South, which was sadly lacking in a circulating medium after the war. Southerners hoped to get a redistribution of existing currency, but Northerners defeated such proposals, fearing loss of bank notes from their own states. In 1870 the South did get some relief when Congress approved a law that would increase new bank note issues and allow a redistribution of $25 million worth of currency. Southerners continued, for the most part, to seek currency expansion, either through more bank notes or through more liberal use of greenbacks; in 1874 Congress agreed to expand greenback circulation, but Grant vetoed the measure. Southern Republicans were embarrassed by the president's action, but by then the party was on its last legs in the few Southern states where it remained.

When Southern Republicans requested federal aid for education, this plea also fell on deaf ears in Washington. In 1870 and again in 1871 a number of petitions reached

Congress asking for federal aid for schools; the requests all came from the South, primarily from North Carolina and Tennessee. The proposal for federal aid for Southern schools was not new. As early as 1867 Charles Sumner recommended it, and in the same year Greeley's *New York Tribune* endorsed the idea. As Negro suffrage in the South became a fact, and particularly after the Fifteenth Amendment was ratified, other Northern Republicans, concerned about the advisability of enfranchising a largely uneducated race, began to consider federal aid to schools in the South more seriously. When President Grant sent a special message to Congress in 1870 applauding the ratification of the Fifteenth Amendment, he recommended legislation to promote education in the South. In that year Republican Congressman George F. Hoar of Massachusetts introduced a bill to promote schools in the South, stating that he preferred such a measure to enactment of further force acts. Hoar's proposal got nowhere, but in 1871 several Republicans, including Henry Wilson, introduced a bill to grant revenue from federal land sales to states needing support for their educational systems. In 1872 such a measure passed the House, but the Senate failed to act on the bill. Not until 1880 did the Republican party platform commit the party to the support of federal aid for schools, but legislation was never approved.

In most cases, Northern Republicans did not vote down Southern proposals out of malice or vengeance toward the South. By the 1870s the general mood in the North was opposed to providing more federal aid for internal improvements no matter what section of the country was to be affected. Party and regional lines tended to blur when matters of currency and finance were raised in Congress, and the South could count on support from Western Republicans in working for currency inflation and banking reform. The proposal for federal aid to education brought opposition from the Democrats, who feared such legislation would allow the federal government to encroach on the domain traditionally assigned to the states, and many Republicans agreed. There was a precedent, however, for federal aid in the form of the Morrill Land Grant Act of 1862, which appropriated revenues from public land sales to help finance agricultural and mechanical colleges in the states; when the South rejoined the Union it was given funds under this program. In 1873, when Henry Wilson tried to amend a bill providing for the further support of land-grant colleges so as to extend federal aid to the common schools of the South, the Senate rejected his proposal.

Although some of the unwillingness of Northern Republicans to aid their Southern brethren was based on considerations of public economy or state rights, another reason was Northern distrust of all things Southern. Northern Republicans had never felt comfortable with their Southern allies, black or white, as they made clear particularly in their attitude toward Southern Unionists. During and after the war the Southern whites who were most active in organizing the Republican party claimed to have opposed the Confederacy and supported the Union. Some Northern Republicans took these claims literally and hoped to build their party in the South on such support, but they soon developed misgivings about the numbers and convictions of such Unionists. The history of the Southern Claims Commission provides an excellent illustration of the power of this Northern suspicion of the South. After the war Southern Unionists asked the government to recognize their claims for the loss of property used by the federal armies during the conflict. Congress dragged its feet on the matter; Republican leaders frequently indicated that they feared if they did establish a commission to consider such claims, it would invite a raid on the U.S. Treasury. Southern Republicans pushed for the commission, claiming that the Unionists loyal to the federal government during the war deserved justice and also that the Republican party could gain political dividends among white voters by approving such a measure.

In 1871 the Forty-first Congress, in addition to passing the Texas and Pacific railroad bill, recognized Southern concerns by creating the Southern Claims Commission. Under its terms Southerners filed a total of 22,298 claims against the U.S. government, totaling more than $60 million. The Congress was so suspicious of Southern Unionism, however, that it required exceedingly stringent tests for claimants to establish their loyalty. The process of making and supporting a claim became arduous and costly. One Southerner complained to Benjamin Butler that "persons of limited means cannot afford to prosecute claims, consequently the Commission is of no benefit to us, *politically.*" The commission fell far behind in its processing of the claims; as late as 1877, 11,282 cases, or 50 percent of those filed, were still unconcluded. When all accounts were finally closed, in 1880, the commission reported that it had approved a total payment of $4,636,920, or less than 10 percent of the amount claimed.

By 1875 James G. Blaine, Republican Speaker of the House, was vehement in his denunciations of alleged Southern Unionists and their claims against the government. After the war was over, he recalled, Washington became "the resort of those suffering patriots from the South who through all Rebel persecutions had been true to the Union and the number was so great that the wonder often was where the Richmond Government found soldiers enough to fill its armies." Unless one were in the capital, he stated, it was impossible to appreciate "the beggars, the swindlers, and the scalawags wherewith the average Congressman is evermore afflicted." Blaine's contempt for Southern white Republicans is reflected in his willingness to use the word "scalawag" for them, a term of opprobrium invented by the Conservatives. By then Northern Republicans had also begun to appropriate the Conservative epithet for Northern Republicans in the South, whom they called carpetbaggers. Northern Republican use of such terms was a measure of the lack of esteem in which they held their Southern colleagues. But at no time had they been hearty advocates of Southern Republicans.

Much of the Northern Republicans' distaste for their Southern white allies continued to stem from their ignorance of Southern conditions. Benjamin Butler, a leading Northern Republican who did give a good deal of attention to the South, confessed to an Alabama correspondent that he could not understand the state's politics. Rarely did Northerners meet with their Southern colleagues except in Congress, and almost never did Republican politicians venture into the South to assess conditions there for themselves. And when they did they often returned with even less commitment to their Southern allies.

By the early 1870s some of the Republican governments in the South deserved condemnation in the North because they ran up state debts and entered railroad deals that were often corrupt. The state of South Carolina acquired a particularly unsavory reputation for corruption. William Sprague, Republican senator from Rhode Island, claimed that his financial agent in South Carolina could buy himself a Senate seat from that state for $75,000 and that consequently he "distrusted the whole batch of carpetbag senators." One of the white Republicans of South Carolina insisted that his state had saddled the national party with a heavier burden than all the other Southern states combined. Another Republican from South Carolina complained that the state "has received nought but abuse from the party generally" and asked the Northern Republicans to give his party "able counsel and gallant leading, instead of upbraiding us so continually." Even Henry Wilson, a staunch defender of Southern Republicans, admitted by 1874 that affairs in the Southern states had hurt the party nationally. Indeed, a growing concern in the party about the political liabilities of continuing to intervene in the South to protect Republican regimes that were perceived in the North as corrupt was a major reason Grant stopped such interventions.

Northern Republicans, for the most part, were no more enthusiastic about their black allies in the South than they were about their white supporters. The party had only reluctantly endorsed Negro suffrage in the South, and from the beginning of Reconstruction many Republicans had expressed doubts about the reliability of black voters who were uneducated, politically inexperienced, and subject to white domination. Many who became Liberal Republicans in 1872 felt this way. In 1868 Horace Greeley asked the editor of the Republican newspaper the *Independent* to prepare a stirring address to the "colored rabble of the South" explaining why they should vote Republican. Greeley believed that "many of the blacks are quite ignorant and credulous. They like to vote with those they have been accustomed to regard as gentlemen whenever they deem it safe to do so." Carl Schurz, who had supported universal suffrage, was contending by 1871 that the blacks "tend to blindly follow demagogues" and added that the carpetbag governments they helped elect "have often been scandalous." Liberal Republican criticism of black voters reached its epitome in the vitriolic pen of James Shepherd Pike, a Northern Republican journalist who stated that "the nigger is a porcupine who fills with quills everybody who undertakes to hug him." Pike visited South Carolina and returned to publish an article in the *New York Tribune* in which he condemned the Republican government of the state for holding its white population "under the heel of 400,000 pauper blacks, fresh from a state of slavery and ignorance the most dense."

Pike, Greeley, and Schurz were all Liberals who broke with Grant and the Republicans; but even regular party members grew more vocal in expressing their doubts about black voters. In 1869 the editors of the *New York Independent,* the same paper that Greeley had asked to exhort black voters to vote Republican, wondered if the party could trust the "ignorant loyalty" of the freedmen. William E. Chandler, who was largely responsible in 1868 and 1872 for directing the Republican national campaigns, told Ben Butler in 1869 that he feared the Democrats would soon control every Southern state: with "the negroes deceived, coaxed or bullied" and the former Confederates voting solidly with the Democrats, "there can be but one result." William T. Sherman warned his brother John, senator from Ohio, that "negroes were generally quiescent and could not be relied on," and John Murray Forbes told Charles Sumner that "you cannot really understand what children most of them are." Such views spread even to ardent advocates of black rights. The editor of the *Boston Commonwealth,* a newspaper that long had supported Reconstruction, endorsed James S. Pike's condemnation of South Carolina's black legislators; by 1876 the paper was arguing that blacks, not habituated to arms or political agitation, were too docile and inoffensive in the face of white violence. This view was echoed by Benjamin Butler, who said in late 1875 that blacks would have to defend themselves against white terrorists: "So long as they will submit to be killed by every marauding white man who will do so, so long there will be no help . . . from the United States."

Despite continued doubts about the reliability of black voters, the fact remained that they were the mainstay of the Republican party in the South; as the Republicans lost control of Virginia, Tennessee, Georgia, North Carolina, and the border states, they relied even more heavily on the large numbers of black votes in the Deep South. It was largely because of pressure from black voters, who had begun to doubt the Republican party's commitment to equal rights, that the Senate agreed in 1874 to pass a new civil rights bill. The measure was sweeping, requiring that blacks be given equal access to public accommodations, schools, institutions, colleges, and cemeteries, as well as the right to serve on juries. The bill had originally been drafted and introduced in the Senate by Charles Sumner on several occasions from 1870 through 1872. At those times he sought to add it as an amendment to amnesty bills, arguing that if whites were to be forgiven, blacks should be guaranteed racial justice. Sumner's proposal put his Republican colleagues in a bind. If they rejected his bill, they would risk alienating black voters in all sections of the country, and particularly in the Deep South, where they provided almost all of the party's votes. But if they passed it, whites would be offended, not only in the South but in the North as well. It provided a classic illustration of the problems the Republicans faced in trying to organize a biracial party.

Although some Northern Republicans in the Senate either abstained or absented themselves from votes on the bill, it did pass that body twice, in 1872 and again in 1873, but was killed in the House. Several Senate Republicans voted for the measure, apparently in the hope that it would not pass the House. In the spring of 1874, in the wake of Sumner's death in March, the Senate again took up his proposal and passed it, and again the House failed to consider the bill. Nonetheless, by acting favorably on the measure, the Senate had projected the issue of civil rights into the fall congressional campaigns, and many Republicans feared that the party would suffer the consequences. The danger of white backlash against civil rights was especially great in the South. A number of Southern congressmen either abstained or voted against it. When Southern Republicans held a convention in Chattanooga, Tennessee, before the November elections, they were concerned about the adverse effects of the bill. A Mississippi Republican, writing to the president of the convention, warned that "it would be a bad exchange to secure success in a few southern states, on the agitation of the Civil Rights bill, at the sacrifice of Republicanism everywhere." The convention delegates agreed and did not discuss or endorse the Senate bill.

When the totals from the election were counted, the Republicans had indeed suffered badly in the South: Democrats won control of thirty-seven of the fifty-four congressional seats available in the Southern states. Appalachian whites in the mountains of Virginia, North Carolina, Tennessee, and Kentucky deserted the Republican party in droves. Southern Republicans condemned their Northern allies for saddling them with the burden of the civil rights bill. A leading Republican judge in Kentucky accused the national party leaders of proposing a measure designed to keep the party from gaining a foothold among Southern whites. According to Albion Tourgée of North Carolina, the folly of the civil rights bill again proved that the Republican legislators in the North did not understand the South.

The civil rights bill took its toll of Northern Republican votes as well. Civil rights did not furnish quite the issue in the North that it did in the South, but it was still a concern for voters in the Midwestern states. The backlash against civil rights, Northern dissatisfaction with the Grant administration's policy in dealing with the Panic of 1873, and a growing disillusionment with Reconstruction and Republican regimes in the South all led Northern voters to repudiate the Republicans. The party suffered its worst defeat in its two-decade history, losing a total of eighty-nine seats in Congress and consequently losing control of the House to the Democrats for the first time since the Civil War began.

Ironically, in the wake of the 1874 election the lame-duck Republican House did take up and pass the civil rights bill, but only after weakening it by removing the provisions on integrating schools and cemeteries and by relaxing some of the Senate bill's enforcement clauses. Many Republicans voted for the bill on the assumption that the Senate would refuse to accept weakening it and it would never pass both houses. To their surprise, the Senate accepted the House changes, and Grant signed the measure on March 1, 1875. The law, which passed almost ten years after the end of the Civil War, at a time when there was almost no support left for using federal intervention for black rights, proved to be a dead letter, as most legislators expected it would. Thus, although the Republicans did enact a law aimed directly at the interests of Southern blacks, it was done at least in part from cynical motives and proved to be meaningless. Its only effect was to alienate Southern whites from the Republican party and threaten the party's base of support in the North.

The same lame-duck session also considered a new enforcement act to renew some expired provisions of earlier laws authorizing the president to suspend the writ of habeas corpus and enacting vague, wide-ranging provisions to allow increased federal supervision of elections. Once again Republicans debated the wisdom of such legislation; its proponents argued that it was necessary to save the South for the party in 1876, and its critics claimed it would alienate Northern voters and cost the party support there. Speaker James G. Blaine believed that the bill could not save the South in any case and that it was better to "lose the South and save the North than to try through such legislation to save the South and thus lose both North and South." The House did pass the measure, but it failed to meet with approval in the Senate.

Blaine's definition of his sectional priorities matched that of his party. Since its origins the Republicans had stressed building their Northern base rather than extending their party into the South, and whenever the Northern and Southern needs conflicted the latter always lost. In 1875 President Grant himself furnished an example of this regional priority, when he refused the pleas of Mississippi Governor Adelbert Ames to send troops to protect black voters during state elections there, arguing that if he did he would alienate Ohio voters who were about to go to the polls in that state. As a result, the Mississippi government was overthrown, leaving only Florida, South Carolina, and Louisiana still in Republican hands.

By 1876 Republicans had virtually no hope of carrying any of the Southern states. In the presidential campaign, the national party again followed its usual procedure of emphasizing the canvass in the Northern October states. Republicans also again waved the bloody shirt in an effort to rally their Northern supporters behind the party ticket. This time, however, the October results were inconclusive, and for the first time since the Republican party entered the South, it seemed that Southern electoral votes might make the difference in the presidential campaign. In November, thanks to state returning boards that certified election results in the three states still in Republican hands, the party was able to claim all its electoral votes and contest what appeared to be a certain Democratic victory. As a result of the dispute over the election of 1876, compromises were arranged for counting the electoral vote and declaring a winner. The votes of Florida, South Carolina, and Louisiana were added to the Republican column, making the party's candidate, Rutherford B. Hayes, president by a single vote.

Thus at the very time the Republican party was about to disappear in the South, Southern votes helped make a Republican president. In return for those votes, however, Hayes withdrew federal troops from the South, and the last three Republican regimes quickly collapsed. The Southern Republicans had made their last sacrifice for the interests of the national Republican party. Republicans would not reappear in these states, or in any other Southern state, in significant strength for the next one hundred years.

Reform Republicans and the Retreat from Reconstruction

MICHAEL LES BENEDICT

In 1961, John Hope Franklin published one of the earliest and most influential of the studies that completely revised earlier interpretations of the origins of so-called Radical Reconstruction. Most of these works concentrated on the development of reconstruction policy; none analyzed closely the *decline* of Republican radicalism, which decline was attributed variously to the death of radical leaders, northern racism, and commitment to federalism or laissez faire.

Historians long have recognized that the defection of self-consciously reform-oriented Republicans played an important part in the decline of radical Republicanism and the abandonment of southern Republicans in the 1870s. The reformers included academicians such as Charles W. Eliot, David A. Wells, Francis Lieber, and Amasa Walker; littérateurs and editors such as Horace White of the Chicago *Tribune,* Edwin L. Godkin of the New York *Nation,* James Russell Lowell and Charles Eliot Norton of the *North American Review,* George William Curtis of *Harper's Weekly,* and Parke Godwin and Charles Nordhoff of the New York *Evening Post;* and intellectually inclined businessmen and lawyers such as Edward Atkinson, John Murray Forbes, Dorman B. Eaton, and Richard Henry Dana. These men identified themselves as an intellectual elite—"the best men"—who bore a special responsibility to the nation but who also were entitled to special deference. During the war and the early years of Reconstruction, most of them had been firm supporters of radical antislavery action, providing an intellectual foundation and political support for radical Republican demands for emancipation and equal rights. As Franklin complained, however, when the final Republican Reconstruction policy took shape, these "former advocates of strong measures against the South turned their fire on those attempting to carry out the strong measures." By 1870, most of the reformers were clearly hostile to much of the leadership of the Republican party and were helping to create the movement, already known as "liberal Republicanism," that would sap the party of much of its intellectual vigor and its crusading spirit.

Liberal Reformers and Laissez-Faire Morality

Historians have recognized the importance of the liberal reformers' defection, but they have not explained it very well. The most common viewpoint attributes the desertion to racism. It is difficult, however, to see how the reformers' racism differentiated them from other Republicans. Few Republicans during the war or Reconstruction believed blacks to be the equals of whites. Republicans had insisted only that the freedmen be secured equality in basic civil and (after some hesitation) political rights, not that they be conceded what was called at the time "social equality." Even Thaddeus Stevens said that he had "never held to that doctrine of negro equality . . . in all things—simply before the law." The radical Republican Ignatius Donnelly expressed the outlook that most Republicans shared: "If it be true . . . that the negro belongs to an inferior race . . . the more reason is there why he should be protected by equal laws." Or as a California Republican legislator put it when he voted to eliminate the state's ban on black testimony, "It is not elevating the negro to give him justice."

To understand what did alienate liberal reformers from Republican reconstruction policy after 1869, one must assess their ideas in the context of the almost idolatrous faith in science that swept European and American intellectuals in the nineteenth century. Science made sense of a physical world that for millennia had been rationalized through superstition or religion. By the mid-nineteenth century, educated men clamored for the application of the same tool to human relationships. They were convinced that these relationships were subject to laws just as certain as those that governed the physical universe. The new "social science," as it was called, would ferret out these laws. Charles Francis Adams, Jr.'s recollection of his scientific awakening indicates science's almost mystical attraction. The revelation occurred while he lay abed in Europe in 1865, recovering from the rigors of his Civil War service and reading an essay by John Stuart Mill on Auguste Comte. "That essay of Mill's revolutionized in a single morning my whole mental attitude," Adams remembered. "I emerged from the theological stage . . . and passed into the scientific."

In no area were reformers more certain that scientific truth had been discovered than in economics—the "science of wealth," as one of its most influential students called it. Not only did economics (or "political economy," as it also was called) belong "to the same class of sciences with mechanics, astronomy, optics, chemistry, [and] electricity," but its laws already were known and needed only to be applied to specific circumstances. They were laws "like those of other sciences," laws "universal and invariable in their operation."

Most nineteenth-century economists concluded that because natural laws of economics existed, they were beyond human interference. The clergyman-economist Lyman Atwater put it most trenchantly: "Legislation cannot alter the laws of nature, of man, of political economics." Moreover, contemporary economists confused the notion of *interfering* with economic laws with that of *harnessing* them. It was no part of economics, as the reformers understood it, to study how human economic activities might be modified to achieve some social goal. Rather, political economy was, as Godkin put it, the science of "what man, as an exchanging, producing animal, would do, if let alone." That was "a real science," in Godkin's estimation. Years later his point of view had changed, and he lamented that political economy "has assumed the role of an advisor, who teaches man to make himself more comfortable through the help of his government"; it had "no more claim to be a science than philanthropy." Thus economists, and the reformers who so ardently had popularized their conclusions, laid upon government the famous injunction *laissez-nous faire,* which the influential American astronomer and financial writer Simon Newcomb translated as the "let-alone principle."

As the historian Sidney Fine has observed, "Free trade and liberty were synonymous to the foes of protection." He might have said the same of almost every position the laissez-faire liberal reformers took, whether on the tariff, finances, taxation, or labor legislation. Despite its scientific trappings, the laissez-faire economic theory was in essence a commitment to liberty as the theorists perceived it—that is, to the "right of every man to employ his own efforts for the gratification of his own wants." Therefore, the social science that the reformers worshiped was shot through with value judgments that would be considered inappropriate by modern scientific standards. It was not unusual for a "scientific" reformer to insist, for example, that "any honest man" could understand financial questions "because they are also, and equally, moral questions."

The great threat to liberty lay in the temptation to use the power of the state to promote the interests of one group at the expense of others—that is, to enact "special" or "class" legislation. The struggle against kings and aristocrats had been waged to free the people from the inordinate power that enabled such persons to use the state to levy special, monopolistic exactions from the rest of society. Such power also had been the essence of the slave system in the South, where the entire weight of the state was thrown behind the expropriation of the labor of black workers by white masters. "The highest right of property is the right to freely exchange it for other property," reformers insisted. "Any system of laws which denies or restricts this right for the purpose of subserving private or class interests, reaffirms . . . the principle of slavery." . . .

Thus at the heart of the reformers' laissez-faire ideology lay a continued adherence to the notion of "equal rights" that had fueled Jacksonian resistance to "special privilege" in economic areas and Republican opposition to privilege based on race. With the establishment of majoritarian democracy by Jacksonian Democrats and radical Republicans, however, the great threat to equal rights no longer seemed to emanate from above, but from below. Weak-minded sentimentalists or corrupt demagogues would promise ignorant or venal voters benefits that could be acquired only by invading the rights of those whose abilities had lifted them above the crowd. "The problem," one reformer wrote, "is, to make men who are equal . . . in political rights and . . . entitled to the ownership of property . . . content with that inequality in its distribution which must inevitably result from the application of the law of justice." . . .

Not surprisingly, the reformers' convictions had serious implications for their attitudes toward democracy. The reformers believed that "the highest allegiance of every man is due to liberty and civilization. . . . The possession of the suffrage by anybody . . . is but a means to these ends," not an end in itself. If this belief alone were not enough to undermine their commitment to democracy, to it was added their conviction that there was a science of society—and the more one perceives measures to govern society to be matters of science, the less they can be matters of public opinion. As Frances Lieber put it while agitating for free trade, "Truth is not settled by majorities." So the reformers did not conceive politics to be the mechanism by which the will of the majority was translated into action. Instead, it was "the art by which the teachings of social science are put into practice." Legislators at all times had to keep in mind the "laws of social order and well-being," laws as "immutable as that of gravitation."

It followed that, as Henry Adams put it, "the great problem of every system of Government has been to place administration and legislation in the hands of the best men"—those with "the loftiest developments of moral and intellectual education." As Adams perceived, this conviction "clash[ed] with our fundamental principle that one man is as good as another." Although Adams admitted, at least at first, that he did not know how to escape this dilemma, most reformers were unabashedly elitist. "It is curious, that, in a country which boasts of its intelligence, the theory should be so generally held that the most complicated form of human contrivance . . . can be worked at sight by any man able to talk for an hour or two without stopping to think," James Russell Lowell wrote. "Experience would have bred in us a rooted distrust of improvised statesmanship, even if we did not believe politics to be a science, which . . . demands the long and steady application of the best powers of men as . . . [can] master even its first principles." To a reformer like Lowell, democracy was "after all, nothing more than an experiment," to be judged by whether it fulfilled its function of elevating "the best men" to leadership.

Convictions like these naturally led the liberal reformers to endorse proposals to reform the civil service so as to make ability the criterion for appointment and to make tenure independent of politics. Of course, there was a good deal of self-interest in this. Well-educated and certain of their own talents, the liberal reformers could not help but be convinced that under such standards the jobs would go to men like themselves—a conviction reflected in Atkinson's brash affirmation to David Wells: "If you or I or any other honest economist ever seeks office, we should get it." Several historians of the civil service reform movement have noted that liberal reformers' interest in such reform blossomed when they failed to receive appointive offices for which they believed themselves particularly suited.

Other specific policies followed logically from the reformers' scientific under-standings and moral convictions. The first of these involved the money question. The reformers were convinced that political economists had demonstrated that the value of goods and services was determined by their supply and the demand for them. That intrinsic value could not be affected by changes in how it was measured. To insure a stable economy, however, people needed a stable standard, free of fluctuation, by which to measure value so that they could compare the value of one kind of goods with that of another. In the opinion of nearly all American economists—and of the liberal reform-ers—experience had proved "scientifically" that only gold could serve that function, although a few believed silver also might do. "Money," the medium of exchange, therefore had to be based on gold, or perhaps gold and silver, in order to reflect the real value of goods.

To repeat, one could not alter the intrinsic value of goods, that is, the value determined by supply and demand, by changing the standard by which it was measured—for example, by inflating the amount of money in circulation irrespective of the availability of gold to back it. Such artificial inflation was no different from trying to change the weight of goods by altering the scales, "as if more hay scales would mean more hay," the liberal reformer-businessman John Murray Forbes scoffed. Such an effort would make people uncertain of the value of the money, not increase the value of the goods, and thus it would introduce serious instability into the economy.

As always with the reformers, however, beyond the question of the expediency of tampering with the standard of value was that of its morality. Speculative fever associated with inflation would lead to "the diffusion of a taste for luxury, dissipation, and excess," not to mention "gambling . . . scoundrelism and effrontery." Moreover, as the supply of money grew, its purchasing power would depreciate. Creditors, who in good faith had lent money to those seeking it, would be repaid in currency of less value. Thus, a policy of inflation was a dangerous example of state action that threatened liberty. When debtors pressed for such a policy, they were seeking to use state power to benefit themselves at the expense of creditors, since inflation amounted to an appropriation of the property of one group for the use of another. Following this reasoning, the liberal reformers perceived currency based on gold to be "honest money" or even "moral money." During the Civil

War, the government had been forced to issue "legal tender notes"—the so-called greenbacks—backed by no more than a promise to repay them in gold or silver someday. After the war, the reformers favored steady "contraction" of the currency—that is, a steady reduction in the amount of greenbacks circulating—and they believed deeply that those who agreed with them were "the friends of sound money and sound morals." Those who pressed for "easy money" presented "the bald issue whether the nation shall be a liar and a thief or not."

Closely linked to the currency question was the issue of how to repay the national debt incurred in suppressing the rebellion. Those who pressed for inflation also generally urged that the debt be repaid in the paper currency in which it had been incurred. Of course, this policy would keep paper money in circulation, as the inflationists wanted, and therefore would violate the same fundamental economic laws that inflation did, in the opinion of the liberal reformers. Moreover, the reformers thought that the moral question was put even more starkly on this issue than on inflation. They insisted that refusal to repay the debt in gold amounted to its repudiation.

Another violation of scientific principles and republican liberty was the protective tariff. Laissez-faire economists and their liberal reformer allies were certain that, if left alone, people would exchange those goods they could produce at least cost for other goods produced more cheaply elsewhere. The "great laws of human nature which are the natural forces of the science" of economics would accomplish this as surely as "universal gravitation will construct the solar system as it is." Such free trade would benefit both parties and permit the widest distribution of goods, since goods always would be produced where this could be done most cheaply, thereby keeping prices low.

Besides flatly scorning arguments that protective duties were necessary to promote American industrial development, laissez-faire economists and liberal reformers once again raised an even more compelling moral objection: protection imposed higher prices on American consumers so that the capitalists and laborers of a particular industry might survive foreign competition. Like inflationary schemes, the protective tariff was but an effort to use the power of government to enrich one group in the community at the expense of another. A petition for tariff protection, wrote Atkinson, ought to read as follows: "Whereas we, the undersigned, are desirous of establishing certain branches of industry . . . for which we have neither the capital nor the skill, we ask that our countrymen shall be compelled to purchase our products at such prices as it may be found necessary for us to impose, while we are learning our trade and accumulating wealth at the cost of our said neighbors."

Reformers and Radicals

Historians generally have perceived the defection of the reformers to have begun after the restoration of most of the southern states to normal relations in the Union and the election of Ulysses S. Grant to the presidency in 1868, culminating in the Liberal Republican bolt of 1872. Yet on all counts, from general principles to specific policies, future liberals began to drift away from their radical allies and toward the more conservative elements of the party as early as 1867. In doing so, the reformers robbed radical politicians of one of the strongest elements of their appeal, for the alliance with the reformers had given radicals something of a cachet, of somehow being more than "mere" politicians. By the 1870s, the more radical Republicans seemed no more virtuous than any other politicos—less so, in fact, than those who had replaced them in the reformers' affections.

The reformers' conviction that one can arrive at a science of society was, as Godkin recognized, "based on the theory that society is not an artificial arrangement regulated by contract like a business partnership, but an organism that grows in accordance with certain laws." This evolutionary sociology approximated the central principle of Burkean conservatism, and the statement itself embodied a none-too-subtle slap at the traditional American notion, rooted in the nation's Lockean heritage, that men enter into society by free acts of will, which in turn implies equality of rights within society. Thus, the radical Republican argument that all men, including black men, had certain rights by virtue of their entering society was nonsense. A community's understanding of what rights individuals and groups possessed grew naturally out of its earlier development, and no one had an abstract right to anything more. Within the framework of American development, individual liberty had become a paramount value, and the extension of legal and political equality to the former slaves had been an appropriate method of securing liberty to them. But this was a matter of expedience and egalitarian tradition, not of right, and if the consequences were evil, no theory of abstract rights could stand in the way of a different solution to the problem of the freedmen's status.

The reformers' commitment to new "scientific" ideas about social relations made enthusiasm for any major social or economic reform suspect. For if society was governed by natural laws, there were distinct limits to the possibilities of social improvement through drastic "artificial" changes imposed by human will. Reformers scoffed at the "inordinate belief, common among the half-educated, in the potency of legislation." Thus the new social science was profoundly conservative. "Social science," Godkin wrote, "seeks to convince people that in sociology, as in medicine, all vendors of panaceas are quacks, that anybody who goes about saying that either equality, or freedom, or female suffrage, or prohibition, or common schools, or the ballot will make the world what it ought to be, should no more be listened to than the patent pill-man."

Their disagreements with radical politicians over specific issues disturbed reformers even more than the growing divergence between the two groups' general understanding of society and reform. By 1867, Republicans were engaged in a bitter struggle over financial and tariff policy, barely hidden by the facade of unity imposed by their battle with President Johnson and the Democrats over reconstruction. Manufacturing interests in developing industries, bankers who had not joined the newly established national banking system, western bankers, capitalists who were inclined to aggressive investment program, railroad promoters, agrarians, and labor reformers pressed for easy money and high tariffs. Merchants involved in international trade (and their local agents and independent wholesalers), manufacturing interests in established industries, and leading bankers urged contraction of the currency and reduction of tariff rates.

Blind to the economic self-interest that motivated the hard-money, low-tariff forces, the liberal reformers allied with them as a matter of "scientific" and moral principle. The reformers were dismayed, however, to find the most important Republican radicals among the leading proponents of soft money and high tariffs. Thaddeus Stevens, Benjamin F. Butler, William D. Kelley, Benjamin F. Wade, and Zachariah Chandler all were tainted. Many of the reformers shared the feelings of the Ohio Republican congressman Rufus P. Spalding, who complained: "It would seem that no man can come fully up in these days to the standard of radicalism unless he be prepared to put a tariff upon foreign goods that shall amount to a prohibition, and to open and extend the paper circulation of the country without limitation."

In fact, the reformers' fear was misplaced; radical Republicans were not united on these issues. But the identification of key radical leaders with soft money and high tariffs was so strong that the differences among less prominent radicals were overlooked. Even Charles Sumner came under suspicion until he proved his financial orthodoxy in 1868, and several historians have suggested that there was an implicit radical Republican "ideology" in which soft money, high tariffs, and racial liberalism were manifestations of an underlying egalitarianism.

The liberal reformers were shocked by the early successes of the soft-money, high-tariff forces. In 1867 the soft-money, protariff lobby persuaded Congress to repeal the authority under which Secretary of the Treasury Hugh McCulloch had been restricting the circulation of greenbacks since 1866. Congress also had come close to passing a general upward revision of tariff rates and had succeeded in increasing the tariff on wool and wool products. Support seemed to be growing for a proposition to pay the national debt in greenbacks. Early in 1867 the worried special commissioner on revenue, David A. Wells, wrote an intimate, "I am afraid the extremists and inflationists will have it pretty much their own way."

Aware of the reformers' concern, conservative Republicans worked assiduously to widen the break. "There is not a man who fought against us in the rebellion in whom I have not more confidence and for whom I have not more respect than I have for Mr. B. F. Butler . . . [and] Thad. Stevens is no better than Butler," Iowa's conservative Republican senator, James W. Grimes, wrote Atkinson. "The great question in American politics today is the financial question," he insisted, and he believed that this question "ought to override . . . reconstruction." As radicals attacked Republican conservatives such as William Pitt Fessenden, senator from Maine, as "clogs and obstructions" to a thoroughly just reconstruction program, Grimes warned, "Let . . . 'clogs and obstructions' be removed from Congress and Thad. Stevens and Butler be in controul [*sic*] as they then would be with their revolutionary and repudiating idea in the ascendancy and our government would not last 12 mos."

The implications of a radical victory within the Republican party for its position on financial and tariff issues drove the reformers into a de facto alliance with Republican conservatives. On the money question, the reformers joined the conservatives in praising the contractionist policies of Secretary McCulloch, in a campaign that culminated in highly publicized plans for a testimonial dinner in McCulloch's honor in Boston. The movement was a public rebuke to the radicals, who bitterly opposed extending honors to anyone openly supporting Johnson's reconstruction policy. As arranged, McCulloch declined the invitation but used the opportunity to defend his hard-money policies in a letter that was then broadcast by the Boston group.

The reformers' cooperation with McCulloch cooled their ardor for one of the most important radical proposals, the impeachment of Andrew Johnson for his obstruction of congressional reconstruction policies. If Johnson were removed from office, the high-tariff, inflationist Ben Wade, president *pro tem* of the Senate, would succeed him. McCulloch certainly would lose his position as secretary of the treasury, and an inflationist just as surely would replace him. Moreover, the circumstance would give Wade a crucial boost in his quest for the 1868 Republican presidential nomination.

The radicals' flirtation with a policy of land confiscation and redistribution in the South, along with southern radicals' endorsement of former Confederate disfranchisement and courtship of black voters through promises of further change, also alienated the reformers. Land confiscation and redistribution was, of course, the quintessential case of using state power for the benefit of one group at the expense of another. When radicals justified such a policy on the grounds that "a landed aristocracy is fatal to the advance of the cause of liberty and equal rights," the hitherto sympathetic, reformer-linked Boston *Advertiser* asked: "Why a *landed* aristocracy? This mode of argument is two-edged. For there are socialists who hold that any aristocracy is 'fatal to the advance of the cause of liberty and equal rights'—socialists who would not hesitate to say that . . . large income places [one] . . . in the ranks of an aristocracy." Driving the same point home, the conservative Cincinnati *Commercial* gleefully began to refer to Butler and Stevens as the "Red Rads."

The liberal reformers also felt threatened by southern radicals' appeals to the former slaves for their main support and by their desire to disfranchise large numbers of formerly Confederate southern whites. The reformers shared the certainty of nearly all white Americans that blacks were incapable of the intellectual achievements of whites, or at least of Anglo-Saxon and Germanic whites. Therefore, black enfranchisement, although just and necessary, was dangerous. As James Russell Lowell put it, "What is bad among ignorant foreigners in New York will not be good among ignorant natives in South Carolina." Like lower-class white northerners, especially Irish immigrants, southern blacks easily might be subject to manipulation. Charles Francis Adams, Jr., was expressing a common concern among reformers when he wrote that Americans were lifting voting restrictions despite the development of a "Celtic proletariat on the Atlantic coast, an African proletariat on the shores of the Gulf, and a Chinese proletariat on the Pacific." Disfranchisement of the white southern "intelligent class" would only make things worse.

As they pondered these prospects, reformers found southern radicals themselves something less than attractive. The radicals' campaigns for black support on such issues as confiscation, civil rights laws, expanded public services, and hostility to the white "upper class" seemed the obvious counterpart to those of such freebooters as Ben Butler and the Tammany Hall Democrats in the North. Godkin thought it was "plain" that the freedmen were "in danger of falling into the hands of demagogues who will use them without scruples for purposes which will finally prove disastrous to the race," and he demanded that "the national leaders of the party . . . find some means of liberalizing the party managers at the South."

To counter the danger, Massachusetts reformers organized the Massachusetts Reconstruction Association at about the same time they endorsed Johnson's treasury secretary McCulloch. The association's purpose was to "prevent the creation of an exclusive black men's party and to kill the scheme of confiscation," Atkinson informed McCulloch. Not coincidentally, its organizers also hoped "to secure the election of a southern [congressional] delegation who shall not be under Thad Steven[s'] lead on tariff and currency questions." The New York *Nation* quickly endorsed the effort. "We need not urge such men to see to it that nothing is done to excite the freedmen to feelings of revenge or with delusive hopes of direct benefits from Government," Godkin noted with satisfaction. What the freedmen needed, and what the Reconstruction Association would provide, was a crash course on the laws of political economy. "The more demagogues rave and rant, the more car-loads of teachers and books we ought to send off," Godkin urged.

Thus, by the summer of 1867, Republican conservatives and liberal reformers were allied in a bitter war upon the radicals. As the conservative organs blasted radical "one idea men, fanatics," Godkin's *Nation* echoed them, in its genteel way, with a new definition of "True Radicalism": "Many well-meaning persons . . . are so anxious to be considered 'radical' in their views that they fear to stop even when they have attained all that is really desirable or practicable." Efforts to transform southern society overnight by further radical legislation were doomed to failure because social science taught that social institutions evolve naturally. "The wise radical is content to wait . . . and slowly to build up when the work of pulling down is properly over." Henry Adams began to refer to himself, Richard Henry Dana, and their allies as representing the "conservative liberalism of New England." By late August, the Chicago *Tribune* editor Horace White also found himself in an anamolous position. "I call myself a Radical," he mused, "and yet find myself more in harmony with those . . . style[d] Conservatives than with any other branch of the party." . . .

The reformers understood that the radical Republicans had secured their positions by appealing to the antislavery sentiment of the Republican rank and file. The reconstruction issue was the natural outgrowth of the antislavery movement, and it tapped the same underlying sentiment. The reformers and their conservative allies understood very well that if they could eliminate the "Negro question" from politics, they would deprive the radicals of the vehicle by which they had driven to power in the party. With the restoration of all but three of the southern states to normal status in the Union in 1868, the election of Ulysses S. Grant to the presidency in the same year on a platform of "Let Us Have Peace," and the passage in 1869 of the Fifteenth Amendment, securing black suffrage, the reformers insisted that the old issues were dead and would be superseded by questions of finance, taxation, and reform in government administration. The implications for the future leadership of the Republican party were plain, as James Russell Lowell made clear in a January, 1869, article designed to serve as the keynote of the reformers' campaign for power. In the fight over slavery and equal rights, Lowell observed, "ethics have been called on to perform the function of jurisprudence and political economy"; consequently, "an easy profession of faith is getting to be the highest qualification of a legislator." But the times dictated a change: "The Republican party, so long accustomed to deal largely with problems into which morals entered largely and directly, is now to be tried solely by its competency for other duties." The point was clear. The new problems required the expertise of the reformers rather than the sentimental moralism of the radicals.

All this implied a new attitude toward southern whites. As early as 1866, Horace White had looked forward to a post-Reconstruction, free-trade alliance between West and South, a prospect apparently endangered by what conservatives thought was the protariff bias of southern Republican radicals. Moreover, hostility toward the former rebels played into the hands of the radical southern "demagogues" who were courting black support by stressing the differences between the interests of southern blacks and whites. As a result, by 1867 reformers and conservative Republicans already were urging Republican leaders to conciliate white southerners by stressing the moderation of Republican Reconstruction policy and by disavowing radical demands for further change. Reconciliation with white southerners remained a staple of the liberal-reform program throughout the 1870s.

The liberal reformers' sympathy for southern whites was based on more than political calculation, however. It was reinforced by their perceptions of politics in the South under Republican governments—and in this connection the reformers' racism came into play. It was not that the reformers' growing sympathy with conservative white southerners was founded on race hatred, nor did racism ever lead them, as it did most white southerners and northern Democrats, to justify legal discrimination against black people. Rather, the reformers' belief in black intellectual and moral inferiority led them to perceive the freedmen as posing the same threat to liberty in the South that the so-called "dangerous classes" of whites posed in the North—the threat of oppressive "class legislation." Having slight faith in blacks' political intelligence or political integrity, the reformers were quick to respond to the pleas of southern whites, who as early as 1868 were charging that the reformers' fears already had come true.

By the 1870s, most southern Conservatives [usually Democratic voters]—particularly those moderate Conservatives with whom the liberal reformers most closely identified—no longer framed their criticism of Republican Reconstruction in terms of white supremacy. That was the coin of the White League and color-liners, whose extremism more moderate whites claimed to resist. Promising acquiescence in the political and legal equality guaranteed by the Reconstruction amendments, moderate Conservatives lambasted scalawags and carpetbaggers, who "control the politics of the State through the control which they have obtained over the colored man." The result of this control, they charged, was a massive system of class legislation. Penniless blacks elected governments that taxed whites to support bloated payrolls, expensive and corrupt building and internal-improvement programs, inefficient and largely black schools, and unnecessary public services. Whereas "all persons in the community who receive the benefits of government ought to contribute equally according to their means," southern Republicans "boast that one class of the population is required to bear only a small share of the burdens of taxation," the Conservatives claimed. "Taxation is robbery, when imposed for private gain, or to build up monopolies for the benefit of the few at the expense of the many." No complaint could have been better framed to win the reformers' sympathy.

Controlling the nation's leading intellectual organs, the liberal reformers ultimately had an immense influence upon the intellectual currents of the United States, and their distaste for the redistributive policies of the southern Republican regimes spread through the North. By the mid-1870s, it would be a common sentiment that, in the words of the conservative Republican New York *Times,* "these freedmen must be convinced that public affairs must not be managed solely for pillage and oppression." Many Republicans came to believe that even black suffrage and Republican control of the South were at best necessary evils, justified only by the threat southern Conservatives posed to freedmen's civil rights and to the Union. To stress that threat, Republican leaders desperately employed the rhetoric that came to be known as "waving the bloody shirt." But as southern Conservatives pledged to protect black rights under Conservative regimes and as charges that white southerners continued to nurture treasonous designs against the nation became ever more fatuous, national Republican support for southern Republicanism became less and less tenable.

The change seriously affected power relationships within the Republican party. During the Civil War and Reconstruction years, ambitious Republicans had sought to harness the radicalism of most party activists and the rank and file in order to advance their party careers. Pressure from such radicals often had forced intraparty rivals toward radicalism in self-defense. But under the reformers' attack, radicalism lost much of its appeal to activists and rank and file. Moreover, many established leaders were identified thoroughly with the results of radical Reconstruction and, as the reformers had recognized earlier, could hardly be dislodged on that issue. By the 1870s, liberalism was a more attractive position from which to attack factional rivals than radicalism. Allying with the reformers, ambitious challengers insisted that Republicans had to replace the reconstruction issue with others that would mobilize the rank and file and reconcile "the best men" to the party.

Just as established leaders had been pushed toward radicalism by such challenges in the 1860s, many were pushed toward conservatism in the 1870s. While some hard-liners urged firmness, the more flexible of the Republican leaders searched for new issues. After the terrible Republican defeats in the elections of 1874, that search became desperate. In the state elections of 1875, some Republican candidates experimented with a mix of support for hard money, anti-Catholicism, and attacks on agrarian and labor radicalism—all of which resonated with the laissez-faire morality of the liberal reformers. The experiment proved especially successful in the key state of Ohio. There Republicans demonstrated how to win victories on new issues, electing a governor who by virtue of his triumph came to be perceived as the embodiment of the possibilities—the flexible Rutherford B. Hayes.

F U R T H E R   R E A D I N G

Michael Les Benedict, "Southern Democrats in the Crisis of 1876–1877," *Journal of Southern History* 46 (1980), 489–524

Paul H. Buck, *The Road to Reunion* (1937)

David Donald, *Charles Sumner and the Rights of Man* (1974)

Sidney Fine, *Laissez faire and the General Welfare State: A Study of Conflict in American Thought, 1865–1901* (1956)

William Gillette, *Retreat from Reconstruction, 1869–1879* (1979)

Morton Keller, *Affairs of State: Public Life in Late Nineteenth-Century America* (1977)

William S. McFeely, *Grant: A Biography* (1981)

Allan Peskin, "Was There a Compromise of 1877?" *Journal of American History* 60 (1973), 63–75.

Terry L. Seip, *The South Returns to Congress: Men, Economic Measures and Intersectional Relationships, 1868–1879* (1983)

Nina Silber, *The Romance of Reunion: Northerners and the South, 1865–1900* (1993)

Brooks D. Simpson, *The Political Education of Henry Adams* (1996)

———, *The Reconstruction Presidents* (1998)

John B. Sproat, *"The Best Men": Liberal Reformers in the Gilded Age* (1968)

Irwin Unger, *The Greenback Era: A Social and Political History of American Finance, 1865–1879* (1964)

C. Vann Woodward, "Seeds of Failure in Radical Race Policy," in Woodward, *American Counterpoint: Slavery and Racism in the North-South Dialogue* (1971)

CHAPTER 15

The Impact and Significance of the
Sectional Conflict

Appropriately enough, this final chapter attempts to assess and evaluate the conflict between the two sections that occurred in mid-nineteenth-century America. After the examination of the conflict in its three phases—the coming of the war; the conduct, or
fighting, of the war; and the consequences of the war during Reconstruction—there
now comes the all-important summing up. What did the war accomplish? What was
its impact? What significance did it have? This inquiry is far more difficult to undertake and certainly more uncertain in its conclusions than the question of what caused
this particular, or any, historical event or episode. Unlike causes, consequences do not
culminate in a single event. Rather, they ramify beyond the event in all directions, and
they have no obvious terminal point chronologically. Historians therefore feel much
more comfortable and confident dealing with causes than with consequences. Another
reason why the causes are less problematic is that they do not necessarily raise the difficult issues of judgment and evaluation that are central to any investigation of the consequences of a historical episode.

Despite these problems and difficulties, the consequences of the Civil War and Reconstruction have to be examined. Otherwise, there is no way of deciding whether the
conflict was worth all the trouble it caused, what its legacy for future generations was,
and so on.

Some historians have concluded that the conflict had little long-term impact. Arguing that the war was "repressible" or "avoidable" or "needless," they found, naturally, that it produced minimal results, save ending a dispute that should never have
been allowed to go as far as it did. This view was especially common in the 1940s and
1950s. A more significant and influential position has claimed that the contest was
about limited goals, and that these were, to a large degree, achieved. After all, the Union, which had dissolved into two hostile sections, was reunified. Furthermore, the federal system, whose structure and operation the Southern states had seriously
questioned, was reorganized and revised as a result of the war and Reconstruction.
And finally, slavery was abolished because the war had resulted in the defeat of the
South. Thus, a conflict that had arisen out of real and important issues had ended with
most of them resolved.

There is a third way of looking at the Civil War and Reconstruction. A struggle
that preoccupies a country for almost half of a century and produces a four-year mili-

tary contest of unprecedented size and scope might well have considerable, even extraordinary repercussions. Such a conflict might bring about developments well beyond the issues that precipitated it. For instance, in addition to ending slavery, the emancipation of the slaves may have produced major changes in race relations and in the system of labor and agriculture in the Southern states. Also, the defeat of the cotton-producing and cotton-exporting states may well have removed economic and political barriers to the development of manufacturing and industry throughout the country. Class relations, too, may have changed quite drastically as plantation owners and their landed and paternalistic allies in the Northern states were pushed aside by a bourgeois manufacturing class whose rise was stimulated by the war and made possible by Southern defeat. And, of course, the postwar reunification may well have reconstructed the Union, making it more unified and centralized than ever before. In effect, a nation-state may have been created out of the loose confederation formed during the Revolutionary era. Maybe these kinds of changes, if indeed they occurred, justify describing the sectional conflict as a transforming, or revolutionary, event. And if the Civil War and Reconstruction was revolutionary, in what way was it so? Was it a revolution like the American Revolution of the 1770s and 1780s? Or was it more like the French, or even the Russian, Revolution?

Once historians begin to make such comparisons, their horizons widen. When the sectional conflict is related to other dramatic events occurring at different times, it is possible to compare it to the American Revolution, the Depression and New Deal, or even, to a lesser extent, the civil rights movement, which has often been termed the "Second Reconstruction." Comparison with broadly similar episodes happening not in the United States but outside it offers other yardsticks for measuring and assessing this period of American history. Both revolutions and civil wars in other countries can be compared with the conflict in the United States. So can secession movements elsewhere or movements for national liberation or wars of national unification. Equally revealing are attempts to discern similarities and differences in the way nation-states were formed elsewhere, especially during the late nineteenth century in Europe and South America. Meanwhile, race relations systems in which one race dominates another can also be juxtaposed, using such societies as the United States, South Africa, Cuba, and Brazil as points of comparison. As historians begin to place events and developments in America's history in a comparative context, all sorts of interesting insights emerge. This awareness of larger arenas and of parallel developments adds new dimensions, but it also makes for increasing complexity. An already difficult problem for historians becomes compounded, as consequences now ramify across space as well as time.

E S S A Y S

Three quite different assessments of what the sectional conflict was all about are presented in the essays for this chapter. The first is the viewpoint of James M. McPherson of Princeton University that, because of the extensive changes it brought about, to characterize the Civil War as a "Second American Revolution," as Charles A. Beard put it, would be quite accurate. A different approach is taken by Carl N. Degler of Stanford University, who considers the American conflict in the context of other nineteenth-century civil wars, causing him to conclude that it was a war to consolidate and unify a nation-state which, until that time, had been quite decentralized and unformed. The final contribution to this discussion comes from Steven Hahn of the University of California at San Diego. He also places the conflict and its aftermath in a comparative context. In this case, he compares the Southern landed and slaveholding elite to its contemporary counterparts in Europe and South America and finds that the war and emancipation reduced the Southern planters' power enormously. In this sense, the conflict's impact was radical and decisive, perhaps even revolutionary.

The Second American Revolution

JAMES M. McPHERSON

During the fateful years of 1860 and 1861, James A. Garfield, a representative in the Ohio legislature, corresponded with his former student at Hiram College, Burke Hinsdale, about the alarming developments in national affairs. They agreed that this "present revolution" of southern secession was sure to spark a future revolution of freedom for the slaves. Garfield quoted with approval William H. Seward's Irrepressible Conflict speech predicting a showdown between the slave South and the free-labor North. Garfield echoed Seward's certainty of the outcome. The rise of the Republican party, they agreed, was a "revolution," and "revolutions never go backward." If civil war followed from secession, wrote Garfield, so be it, for the Bible taught that "without the shedding of blood there is no remission of sins." Or as Hinsdale put it: "All the great charters of humanity have been writ in blood. . . . England's was engrossed in that [the blood] of the Stuarts—and that of the United States in [the blood] of England." Soon, perhaps, the slaves would achieve their charter of freedom in the blood of their masters.

When the war came, Garfield joined the Union army and rose eventually to the rank of major general. For him the war was, quite literally, the second American Revolution. In October 1862, he insisted that the conflict of arms must destroy "the old slaveholding, aristocratic social dynasty" that had ruled the nation, and replace it with a "new Republican one." A few months later, while reading Louis Adolphe Thiers's ten-volume *History of the French Revolution,* Garfield was "constantly struck" with "the remarkable analogy which the events of that day bear to our own rebellious times."

In December 1863, Garfield doffed his army uniform for the civilian garb of a congressman. During the first three of his seventeen years in Congress, he was one of the most radical of the radical Republicans. In his maiden speech to the House on January 28, 1864, Garfield called for the confiscation of the land of Confederate planters and its redistribution among freed slaves and white Unionists in the South. To illustrate the need for such action, he drew upon the experience of the English revolution against the Stuarts and the American Revolution against Britain. "Our situation," said Garfield, "affords a singular parallel to that of the people of Great Britain in their great revolution" and an even more important parallel to our forefathers of 1776. "Every one of the thirteen States, with a single exception, confiscated the real and personal property of Tories in arms." The southern planters were the Tories of this second American Revolution, he continued, and to break their power we must not only emancipate their slaves, "we must [also] take away the platform on which slavery stands—the great landed estates of the armed rebels. . . . Take that land away, and divide it into homes for the men who have saved our country." And after their land was taken away, Garfield went on, "the leaders of this rebellion must be executed or banished. . . . They must follow the fate of the Tories of the Revolution."

From James McPherson, "The Second American Revolution," *Hayes Historical Journal,* Spring 1992. Copyright © 1992 by James M. McPherson. Reprinted by permission of the author and the Rutherford B. Hayes Presidential Center.

These were harsh measures, Garfield admitted, but "let no weak sentiments of misplaced sympathy deter us from inaugurating a measure which will cleanse our nation and make it the fit home of freedom. . . . Let us not despise the severe wisdom of our Revolutionary fathers when they served their generation in a similar way."

Garfield later receded from his commitment to confiscation and his belief in execution or banishment. But he continued to insist on the enfranchisement of freed slaves as voters, a measure that many contemporaries viewed as revolutionary. He linked this also to the ideas of the first American Revolution. The Declaration of Independence, said Garfield in a speech on July 4, 1865, proclaimed the equal birthright of all men and the need for the consent of the governed for a just government. This meant black men as well as white men, he said, and to exclude emancipated slaves from equal participation in government would be a denial of "the very axioms of the Declaration."

In 1866, Congress passed the Fourteenth Amendment to the Constitution as a compromise that granted blacks equal civil rights but not equal voting rights. When the southern states nevertheless refused to ratify this moderate measure, Garfield renewed his call for revolutionary change to be imposed on the South by its northern conquerors. Since southern whites, he said in early 1867, "would not co-operate with us in rebuilding what they had destroyed, we must remove the rubbish and rebuild from the bottom. . . . We must lay the heavy hand of military authority upon these Rebel communities, and . . . plant liberty on the ruins of slavery."

This rhetoric of revolution was hardly unique to Garfield. Numerous abolitionists, radical Republicans, and radical army officers were saying the same things. The abolitionist Wendell Phillips was the most articulate spokesman for a revolutionary policy. He insisted that the Civil War "is primarily a social revolution. . . . The war can only be ended by annihilating that Oligarchy which formed and rules the South and makes the war—by annihilating a state of society. . . . The whole social system of the Gulf States must be taken to pieces." The congressional leader of the radical Republicans, Thaddeus Stevens, was equally outspoken. We must "treat this war as a radical revolution," he said. Reconstruction must "revolutionize Southern institutions, habits, and manners. . . . The foundations of their institutions . . . must be broken up and relaid, or all our blood and treasure have been spent in vain." The colonel of a Massachusetts regiment stationed in the occupied portion of South Carolina during 1862 said that the war could be won and peace made permanent only by "changing, revolutionizing, absorbing the institutions, life, and manners of the conquered people."

European radicals also viewed the American Civil War as a revolution. In London, Karl Marx followed the American war with intense interest. He wrote about it in articles for a Vienna newspaper and in private letters to his colleague Friedrich Engels. Marx described the war for the Union against the "slave oligarchy" as a potentially "world transforming . . . revolutionary movement" if the North would only seize the moment to proclaim the abolition of slavery. When Lincoln did so, Marx was ecstatic. "*Never* has such a gigantic transformation taken place so rapidly" as the liberation of four million slaves. "Out of the death of slavery" would spring "a new and vigorous life" for working-class people of all races, wrote Marx, for "labor with a white skin cannot emancipate itself where labor with a black skin is branded. . . . Workingmen of Europe feel sure that as the American War of Independence initiated a new era of ascendancy for the middle class, so the American Antislavery War will do for the working classes." Georges Clemenceau of France, future leader of the French Left and premier of France in the later stages of World War I, was the American correspondent of a radical French newspaper from 1866 to 1869. In articles written from Washington, where Clemenceau came particularly to admire Thaddeus Stevens, the young French journalist described the abolition of slavery and enfranchisement of the freedmen as "one of the most radical revolutions known in history." A British writer chimed in with a description of Stevens as "the Robespierre, Danton, and Marat of America, all rolled into one."

Hostile contemporaries concurred with this appraisal of the Civil War's revolutionary impact. The conservative and pro-Confederate *Times* of London described the radical Republicans as the Jacobins of the second American Revolution, a label picked up by subsequent historians who used it as an epithet to portray the radicals as bloodthirsty fanatics. A Democratic newspaper in Boston likewise compared radicals to "the 'Committee of Twelve' of the days of the Reign of Terror." A few weeks after Appomattox the *New York Herald,* notorious during the war for its hostility to Republican war policies including emancipation, concluded that by destroying both slavery and "the domineering slaveholding aristocracy . . . this tremendous war has wrought in four years the revolutionary changes which would probably have required a hundred years of peace." An anguished editor in Memphis declared in 1865 that "the events of the last five years have produced an entire revolution in the entire Southern country." And two years later a South Carolina journalist, reacting to the enfranchisement of the freedmen, pronounced it "the maddest, most infamous revolution in history."

Among historians the notion of the Civil War as the second American Revolution is identified most closely with Charles A. Beard. But in Beard's view, slavery and emancipation were almost incidental to the real causes and consequences of the war. The sectional conflict arose from the contending economic interests of plantation agriculture and industrializing capitalism. Slavery happened to be the labor system of plantation agriculture, Beard conceded, but apart from that it was not a crucial issue in and of itself except for a handful of abolitionists. In effect, the war was a class conflict between a Yankee capitalist bourgeoisie and a southern planter aristocracy. "Merely by the accidents of climate, soil, and geography," wrote Beard, "was it a sectional struggle." The triumph of the North under the leadership of the Republican party, which represented the interests of northern capitalism, brought about "the unquestioned establishment of a new power in the government, making vast changes in the arrangement of classes, in the distribution of wealth, in the course of industrial development." If the overthrow of the king and the aristocracy by the middle classes of England in the 1640s was to be known as the Puritan Revolution, and the overthrow of king, nobility, and clergy by the middle classes and peasants of France as the French Revolution, maintained Beard, then "the social cataclysm in which the capitalists, laborers, and farmers of the North and West drove from power in the national government the planting aristocracy of the South" was the "Second American Revolution, and in a strict sense, the First"—the first because the Revolution of 1776 had produced no such changes in the distribution of wealth and power among classes.

Beard's interpretation was a modern variant of Marx's perception of the Civil War, with the question of slavery—which was of central importance for Marx—shunted into the wings. Although not strictly a Marxist, Beard was influenced by reading Marx. Avowed Marxian historians such as Herbert Aptheker and James S. Allen (the pen name of Sol Auerbach) have emphasized more than did Beard the issue of slavery. For them, the outcome of the Civil War was not merely a triumph of northern industrial capitalism over plantation agriculture; it was also a victory of the radical bourgeoisie in alliance with the black proletariat and elements of the white proletariat over the southern aristocracy. That a large percentage of the white "proletariat" in both North and South either supported the Confederacy or opposed emancipation, however, is something of an embarrassment to the Marxian interpretation.

A scholar whose work owes much to Marxian analytical categories is Barrington Moore, who has portrayed the Civil War as "the last Capitalist Revolution." Moore's argument is subtle and complex, hard to summarize briefly without distortion. He sees the revolutionary dimension of the war not simply as a triumph of freedom over slavery, or industrialism over agriculture, or the bourgeoisie over the plantation gentry—but as a combination of all these things. Plantation agriculture in the South was not a form of feudalism, Moore insists; rather, it was a special form of capitalism that spawned a value system and an ideology that glorified hereditary privilege, racial caste, and slavery while it rejected bourgeois conceptions of equality of opportunity, free labor, and social mobility. Thus the war was a struggle between two conflicting capitalist systems—one reactionary, based on slave labor, and fearful of change; the other progressive, competitive, innovative, and democratic. Although the slave system presented no obstacle to the growth of industrial capitalism as an *economic* system (here is where Moore differs from Beard), it did present a "formidable obstacle to the establishment of industrial capitalist democracy . . . at least any conception of democracy that includes the goals of human equality, even the limited form of equality of opportunity, and human freedom. . . . Labor-repressive agricultural systems, and plantation slavery in particular, are political obstacles to a *particular kind* of capitalism, at a specific historical stage: competitive democratic capitalism we must call it for lack of a more precise term." In this sense the free-labor ideology of the Republican party in the Civil War era was heir to the radical bourgeois ideologies of the English and French Revolutions; the triumph of this ideology in the 1860s was therefore the "last revolutionary offensive on the part of what one may legitimately call urban or bourgeois capitalist democracy. . . . It was a violent breakthrough against an older social structure."

The number of historians as well as contemporaries who have perceived the Civil War as a revolutionary experience would seem to have established something of a consensus on this question. But in the 1960s and 1970s several historians questioned the idea that the Civil War accomplished any sort of genuine revolution, and some even denied that it produced much significant change in the social and economic structure of the South or in the status of black people.

The initial challenge to Beard's thesis of the war as an economic revolution came from economic historians in the 1960s. They argued, first, that the basic developments which produced the industrial revolution in the United States—the railroad, the corporation, the factory system, the techniques of mass production of interchangeable parts, the mechanization of agriculture, and many other aspects of a modernizing industrial economy—began a generation or more before the Civil War, and that while the war may have confirmed and accelerated some of these developments, it produced no fundamental change of direction. Economic historians demonstrated, second, that the decade of the 1860s experienced an actual slowing of the rate of economic growth, and therefore the war may have retarded rather than promoted industrialization.

The first of these arguments is well taken. Crucial innovations in transportation, technology, agriculture, the organization of manufacturing, capital formation, and investment did take place in the first half of the nineteenth century. The Civil War did not begin the modernization and industrialization of the American economy. But this truth actually supports rather than contravenes the Beard and Moore theses. Most of these antebellum modernizing developments were concentrated in the North. The South remained a labor-intensive, labor-repressive undiversified agricultural economy. The contrasting economic systems of the antebellum North and South helped to generate the conflicting proslavery and antislavery ideologies that eventually led to war. Northern victory in the war was therefore a triumph for the northern economic system and the social values it had generated. The war discredited the economic ideology and destroyed the national political power of the planter class. In this sense, then, the Civil War produced a massive shift toward national domination by the northern model of competitive democratic free-labor capitalism, a transformation of revolutionary proportions as described by Beard and Moore.

This ties in with the second point concerning the slowdown in the rate of economic growth in the 1860s. It is true that growth during the decade which included the war was lower than in any other decade between the 1830s and 1930s. But these growth data include the South. The war accomplished a wholesale devastation of southern economic resources. If we consider the northern states alone, the stimulus of war production probably caused a spurt in the economic growth rate. It was the destruction of the southern economy that caused the lag. After the war the national economy grew at the fastest rate of the century for a couple of decades, a growth that represented a catching-up process from the lag of the 1860s caused by the war's impact on the South.

Let us take a closer look at that impact. Union invasion of the Confederacy and the destruction of southern war industries and transportation facilities, the abolition of slavery, the wastage of southern livestock, and the killing of one-quarter of the South's white male population of military age made an economic desert of large areas of the South. While the total value of northern wealth increased by 50 percent during the 1860s, southern wealth *decreased* by at least 60 percent. In 1860 the South's share of national wealth was 30 percent; in 1870 it was only 12 percent. In 1860 the average per capita income of southerners, including slaves, was two-thirds of the northern average; after the war the southern average dropped to less than two-fifths of the northern, and did not rise above that level for the rest of the nineteenth century.

The withdrawal of southern representatives and senators from Congress when their states seceded also made possible the passage of Republican-sponsored legislation to promote certain kinds of economic development. For years the southern-dominated Democratic party had blocked these measures. But Congress during the war enacted higher tariffs to foster industrial development; national banking acts to restore part of the centralized banking system destroyed in the 1830s by Jacksonian Democrats; land grants and government loans to build the first transcontinental railroad; a homestead act to grant 160 acres of government land to settlers; and the land-grant college act of 1862, which turned over federal land to the states to provide income for the establishment of state agricultural and vocational colleges, which became the basis of the modern land-grant universities.

The war had a crucial impact on the long-term sectional balance of power in the nation. Before 1861 the slave states, despite their declining percentage of the population, had used their domination first of the Jeffersonian Republican party and then the Jacksonian Democratic party to achieve an extraordinary degree of power in the national government. In 1861 the United States had lived under the Constitution for seventy-two years. During forty-nine of those years the president had been a southerner—and a slaveholder. After the Civil War a century passed before another resident of the South was elected president. In Congress, twenty-three of the thirty-six speakers of the House down to 1861, and twenty-four of the thirty-six presidents pro tem of the Senate, were from the South. For half a century after the war, *none* of the speakers or presidents pro tem was from the South. From 1789 to 1861, twenty of the thirty-five Supreme Court justices had been southerners. At all times during those years the South had a majority on the Court. But only five of the twenty-six justices appointed during the next half-century were southerners.

These sweeping transformations in the balance of economic and political power between North and South undoubtedly merit the label of revolution. But this was a revolution in an *external* sense. It was only part of what contemporaries meant when they described the war as a revolution. More important, in the eyes of many, was the *internal* revolution: the emancipation of four million slaves, their elevation to civil and political equality with whites, and the destruction of the old ruling class in the South—all within the space of a half-dozen years. This was what the disgruntled South Carolinian quoted earlier meant when he deplored Reconstruction as "the maddest, most infamous revolution in history." It was what Georges Clemenceau meant when he spoke of "one of the most radical revolutions known to history." This was what freed slaves meant in the 1860s when they said jubilantly, "the bottom rail's on top."

But during the later 1960s and 1970s—in the climate of disillusionment produced by the Vietnam War and the aftermath of the civil rights movement—a number of skeptical historians maintained that the bottom rail never was on top and that a true internal social revolution never took place. Some argued that the Republican party's commitment to equal rights for freed slaves was superficial, flawed by racism, only partly implemented, and quickly abandoned. Other historians maintained that the policies of the Union occupation army, the Freedmen's Bureau, and the national government operated in the interests of the white landowners rather than the black freedmen, and that they were designed to preserve a docile, dependent, cheap labor force in the South rather than to encourage a revolutionary transformation of land tenure and economic status. And finally, another group of scholars asserted that the domination of the southern economy by the old planter class continued unbroken after the Civil War. By such devices as the crop lien system, debt peonage, sharecropping, and a host of legal restrictions on black labor mobility, the planters kept their labor force subservient and poor in a manner little different from slavery. Thus, in the words of historian Louis Gerteis, the war and Reconstruction produced no "fundamental changes" in the "antebellum forms of economic and social organization in the South." No "social revolution" took place because the abolition of slavery produced no "specific changes either in the status of the former slaves or in the conditions under which they labored."

These studies left the question of the Civil War's revolutionary dimensions in considerable doubt and confusion. Part of the problem stemmed from the elastic meaning of the word "revolution." The term is often thrown around with careless abandon. The concept has almost become trivialized. In our own time we have lived through the technological revolution, the cybernetic revolution, the sexual revolution, the black revolution, the green revolution, the feminist revolution, the youth revolution, the paperback revolution, and the revolution of rising expectations—to name but a few.

By such standards the Civil War was indeed a revolution—but so was just about everything else in American history. If we turn for help to the large scholarly literature on revolutions, we find almost as wide a variety of meanings as in common parlance. Definitions range from such brief statements as: Revolution "connotes a sudden and far reaching change, a major break in the continuity of development"; or "a sudden overthrow of established authority, aimed at a fundamental change in the existing social order"; to more complex and sweeping definitions, such as "a Revolution is a rapid, fundamental, and violent domestic change in the dominant values and myths of a society, in its political institutions, social structure, leadership, and government activity and policies." Some analysts, mainly political scientists and political historians, focus on revolutions that overthrow existing governments. For one such analyst, revolution is a "sudden and violent change in the political system and government of a state," while another defines it as "the drastic, sudden substitution of one group in charge of the running of a territorial political entity for another group." But for other scholars, especially but by no means exclusively those influenced by Marxist thought, even a violent overthrow of political institutions or rulers is not a genuine revolution unless, in Marx's words, it produces "a social transformation in which the power of the obsolescent class is overthrown, and that of the progressive, revolutionary class is established in its place."

Faced with such a bewildering variety of definitions, one is tempted to agree with the French historian who decided that the only way to study revolutions was to "accept as revolution what men of a certain period experienced as revolution and so named it themselves." But since many contemporaries called the American Civil War a revolution, that would not help us with the analytical problem raised by historians who deny that it really *was* a revolution. Let us instead adopt a common-sense working definition of revolution, and then return to the question whether the Civil War meets this definition. Let us define revolution simply as the overthrow of the existing social and political order by internal violence. Does the Civil War qualify? Certainly it does on the grounds of violence. It was by far the most violent event in American history. The 620,000 soldiers killed in the Civil War almost equals the number of American fighting men killed in all the country's other wars combined. What about the overthrow of the existing social and political order? As noted earlier, in an external sense the war did destroy the South's national political power, so thoroughly crippled the region's economy that it took nearly a century to recover, and by abolishing slavery undermined the basis of the antebellum social order. In these respects, the Civil War overthrew the *ancien régime* about as thoroughly as any previous revolution in history had done.

But we must still confront the arguments that the war and Reconstruction did not accomplish a genuine revolution in race relations or labor relations in the South. To a considerable degree, these arguments are flawed by presentism, by a tendency to read history backwards, measuring change over time from the point of arrival rather than the point of departure. Such a viewpoint looks first at the disabilities and discrimination suffered by black Americans in the twentieth century and concludes that there must have been little or no change since slavery. But this is the wrong way to measure change. It is like looking through the wrong end of a telescope—everything appears smaller than it really is.

A few statistics will illustrate the point. When slavery was abolished, about 90 percent of the black population was illiterate. By 1880 the rate of black illiteracy had been reduced to 70 percent, and by 1900 to less than 50 percent. From the perspective of today, this may seem like minimal progress. The illiteracy of almost half the black population in 1900, compared with less than a tenth of the white population, may seem shameful. But viewed from the standpoint of 1865 the rate of literacy for blacks increased by 200 percent in fifteen years and by 400 percent in thirty-five years. This was significant change. Or take another set of educational data: in 1860 only 2 percent of the black children of school age in the United States were attending school. By 1880 this had increased to 34 percent. During the same period the proportion of white children of school age attending school had grown only from 60 to 62 percent. From one viewpoint, the proportion of black school attendance was still only half the proportion of white in 1880. But the change since 1860 was dramatic—indeed, revolutionary. The relative proportions of blacks and whites attending school had jumped from one-thirtieth to more than one-half. No other period of American history witnessed anything like so great a rate of relative change.

Or let us look at the economic condition of the freed slaves in the generation after emancipation. This is the issue that has attracted most of the attention of historians who deny the existence of meaningful change. The grim reality of sharecropping and rural poverty in the South seems at first glance to confirm their argument. But studies of the economic consequences of emancipation by Roger Ransom and Richard Sutch provide evidence for a different conclusion. In the first place, Ransom and Sutch point out, the abolition of slavery represented a confiscation of about three billion dollars of property— the equivalent as a proportion of national wealth to at least three *trillion* dollars in 1990. In effect, the government in 1865 confiscated the principal form of property in one-third of the country, without compensation. That was without parallel in American history—it dwarfed the confiscation of Tory property in the American Revolution. When such a massive confiscation of property takes place as a consequence of violent internal upheaval on the scale of the American Civil War, it is quite properly called revolutionary.

The slaves constituted what economists call "human capital." Emancipation transferred the ownership of this capital to the freed slaves themselves. This had important consequences for the new owners of the capital, according to Ransom and Sutch. They calculate that under slavery, the slaves in the seven cotton states of the lower South had received in the form of food, clothing, and shelter only 22 percent of the income produced by the plantations and farms on which they worked. With the coming of freedom, this proportion jumped to 56 percent, owing to the ability of free laborers to bargain for higher wages—in the form of money or a share of the crop—than they had received as slaves. This did not mean that the overall standard of living improved quite so dramatically for blacks, because the postwar poverty of the southern agricultural economy meant that the average per capita income in the region declined. Blacks were getting a bigger share of the pie, but it was a smaller pie. Nevertheless, Ransom and Sutch conclude that between 1857 and 1879 the average per capita income for blacks in southern agriculture increased by 46 percent, while the per capita income of whites declined by about 35 percent. Put another way, black per capita income in these seven states jumped from a relative level of only 23 percent of white income under slavery to 52 percent of the white level by 1880. Thus, while blacks still had a standard of living only half as high as whites in the poorest region of the country—the negative point emphasized by the historians cited earlier—this relative redistribution of income within the South was by far the greatest in American history.

Or consider the question of land ownership, a vital measure of wealth and status in an agricultural society. Again, at first glance the picture seems to confirm the argument of the "no change" historians. Abolitionists and Republicans like Garfield had urged the confiscation of land owned by wealthy Confederates and the allocation of part of this land to freed slaves. This would have been a truly revolutionary act. But confiscation was too radical for most Republicans, and even if they had tried it the Supreme Court might have ruled it unconstitutional. There was no meaningful land reform in the South. Planters lost their slaves but not their land. In this respect the war accomplished only half a revolution. Nevertheless, there were significant changes even in the matter of land ownership. In 1865 few blacks owned land in the South. But by 1880, 20 percent of the black farm operators owned part or all of the land they farmed (the rest were renters or sharecroppers). By 1910, 25 percent of the black farmers owned land. At the same time the proportion of white farmers who owned land was decreasing from more than 80 percent at the end of the war to 60 percent in 1910. Here again, while blacks remained far below whites, the war made possible a large and important relative change.

Finally, let us look at one more index of change within the South—political power. At the beginning of 1867 no black man could vote in the South. A year later, blacks were a majority of registered voters in several ex-Confederate states. No black man yet held political office. But three or four years later, about 15 percent of the officeholders in the South were black—a larger proportion than in 1990. In 1870, blacks provided three-fourths of the votes in the South for the Republican party, which controlled the governments of a dozen states in which five years earlier most of these black voters had been slaves. It was this phenomenon, more than anything else, that caused contemporaries to describe the events of those years as a revolution.

It has also caused the historiographical pendulum in the 1980s to swing back toward a perception of the Civil War and Reconstruction as a revolutionary experience. Two books [*Nothing but Freedom* and *Reconstruction*] by Eric Foner have been instrumental in this process. Foner points out that the United States was unique among post-emancipation societies in granting freed slaves equal political rights. This revolutionary act had important consequences for social and economic relations in the new order. "The Second American Revolution," writes Foner, "profoundly if temporarily affected the relationship of the state to the economic order. . . . The freedmen won, in the vote, a form of leverage their counterparts in other societies did not possess. . . . Radical Reconstruction stands as a unique moment when . . . political authority actually sought to advance the interests of the black laborer." As a South Carolina planter complained in 1872, "under the laws of most of the Southern States ample protection is afforded to tenants and very little to landlords."

In Foner's judgment, this exercise of political power was more important than land redistribution would have been. The experience of freed slaves and of non-white peoples in the Caribbean, Africa, and other regions demonstrates that nominal ownership of land does little to foster economic independence "where political power rests with classes that are at worst hostile and at best indifferent to the fate of the rural population." Reconstruction legislatures enacted certain taxes, mechanic's and renter's lien laws, measures concerning credit and the like that protected the interests of sharecroppers and wage-earners against landlords and employers. The "Redeemer" governments that overthrew Reconstruction in the 1870s reversed the relationship. A few examples will illustrate the point. In 1865–66 southern state governments had adopted "Black Codes" to keep black labor in a state of dependence and subjection as close to slavery as possible. The Freedmen's Bureau and federal courts suspended these codes; Republican state governments repealed them during Reconstruction; Redeemer governments in effect restored some of them in the form of landlord's liens, vagrancy laws, contract labor laws that amounted to peonage, anti-enticement laws to limit labor mobility, criminal statutes rigged against blacks, and a pattern of law enforcement that favored white over black and landlord over cropper. During Reconstruction the state of South Carolina set up a land commission that sold land to 14,000 black families on easy terms; the Redeemer government retained the commission but changed its administration in such a way as to foreclose on the properties of most of these families and transfer the land to white ownership. When Republicans controlled the South Carolina government, black rice workers struck for higher wages in 1876 and won; across the Savannah River in Georgia, where Democrats ruled, wages on the rice plantations averaged less than half the level in South Carolina.

In 1868 a black speaker at a political meeting in Savannah declared that "a revolution gave us the right to vote, and it will take a revolution to get it away from us." That, unfortunately, is what happened. For freed slaves the second American Revolution turned out, in Foner's words, to be "America's unfinished revolution" because many of its gains were reversed by what Vice-President Henry Wilson described in 1874 as "a Counter-Revolution." The Civil War *did* partially overthrow the existing social and political order in the South—overthrow it at least as much as did the English Revolution of the 1640s or the French Revolution of the 1790s. Neither of those revolutions totally destroyed the *ancien régime,* and both were followed by counterrevolutions that restored part of the old order, including the monarchy. But scarcely anyone denies the label revolution to those events in English and French history. The events of the 1860s in the United States equally deserve the label revolution. It also was followed by a counterrevolution, which combined white violence in the South with a revival of the Democratic party in the North and a growing indifference of northern Republicans toward the plight of southern blacks. The counterrevolution overthrew the fledgling experiment in racial equality. But it did not fully restore the old order. Slavery was not reinstated. The Fourteenth and Fifteenth Amendments were not repealed. Blacks continued to own land and to go to school. The counterrevolution was not as successful as the revolution had been. The second American Revolution left a legacy of black educational and social institutions, a tradition of civil rights activism, and constitutional amendments that provided the legal framework for the second Reconstruction of the 1960s.

One among Many: The Civil War and National Unification

CARL N. DEGLER

More than a century ago, between the years 1845 and 1870, the world witnessed a widespread efflorescence of nation-building, in the midst of which was the American Civil War. Some of those instances of people's seeking national identity and statehood remind us of the Confederacy inasmuch as they failed to achieve independence. The revolt of the Hungarians against their Austrian masters in 1848 under the leadership of

From "One Among Many: The United States and National Unification," by Carl N. Degler, from *Lincoln the War President: The Gettysburg Lectures,* edited by Gabor S. Boritt. Copyright © 1992, 1994 by Gabor S. Boritt. Used by permission of Oxford University Press, Inc.

Louis Kossuth was one such failure, though within two decades Hungarian nationalism achieved a kind of acknowledgment of national identity in the dual empire of Austria-Hungary. A more crushing failure was the experience of the Poles who rose in 1863 against their Russian rulers, at the very same time that the United States was struggling to suppress its own uprising in the South. Contrary to the Confederacy's fate, the Polish defeat would be reversed at the end of the First World War.

Other instances of nation-building achieved their aims. In 1847 the Swiss cantons concluded their war for a Union under a new federal constitution and with a fresh and enduring sense of nationality. In 1860, Camillo Cavour of the kingdom of Sardinia with the assistance of France and the military help of Giuseppe Garibaldi brought into being the first united Italy since the days of ancient Rome. During that same decade of the 1860s a united Germany came into existence for the first time as well. Nor were the nationalist outbursts of that quarter-century confined to Europe. They also erupted in Asia, where a new Japan emerged in the course of the Meiji Restoration, in which feudal power was forever subordinated to a centralized state that deliberately modeled itself after the nation-states of Europe.

Looking at the American Civil War in the context of contemporary efforts to establish national identity has the advantage of moving us beyond the often complacent concern with ourselves that I sometimes fear is the bane of United States historians. The Civil War is undoubtedly a peculiarly American event, one central to our national experience. In its endurance, the magnitude of its killing, and the immense extent of its arena it easily dwarfs any other nationalist struggle of its century. Yet if we recognize its similarity to other examples of nation-building of that time we may obtain fresh insights into its character and its meaning, then and now.

First of all, let me clear the ground by narrowing our comparisons. Although the European and Asian instances of nation-building in the years between 1845 and 1870 are comparable to the American experience in that they all involve the creation or the attempt to create a national state, not all of them are comparable on more than that general level. The Meiji Restoration, for example, was certainly the beginning of the modern Japanese state but the analogy stops there since it did not involve a military struggle. The Polish and Hungarian national uprisings bear closer comparison to the Confederate strike for independence, but the differences in nationality between the oppressors and the oppressed (Austrians versus Hungarians; Russians against Poles) render dubious any further analogy to the Confederacy. After all, both the Hungarians and the Poles had been conquered by foreigners; each enjoyed a national history that stretched deep into the past, something totally missing from the South's urge to separate from the United States.

The Italian experience in nation-building comes closer to the North's effort to preserve the Union. A united Italy did emerge eventually from the wars of the Risorgimento and Garibaldi's conquests of Sicily and the Kingdom of Naples. Pertinent, too, is that Garibaldi, as an internationally recognized hero of Italian unification, was entreated by the Lincoln Administration to become a leading officer in the Union army. Yet, neither event offers much basis for comparison. The unification of all of Italy was, as English statesman William Gladstone remarked, "among the greatest marvels of our time," and simultaneously a kind of accident.

It was a marvel because Italy's diversity in economy, language, culture, and society between North and South and among the various states into which the peninsula had been divided for centuries made unification seem most unlikely. Cavour, who is generally considered the architect of Italian unification, came late to the idea of uniting even northern Italy much less the whole peninsula. That he always wrote in French because his Italian was so bad further illustrates the marvelous character of Italian unification. That the whole of the peninsula was united at all resulted principally from the accident of Giuseppi Garibaldi and his famous Thousand. Cavour had tried vigorously to prevent the irrepressible Genovese from invading Sicily only to have Garibaldi within a matter of months present Cavour's own King Victor Emmanuel of Sardinia with not only Sicily, but the Kingdom of Naples as well. Historian Denis Mack Smith has suggested that the limited energy expended in achieving the Kingdom of Italy is measured in the statistic that more people died in a single day of the Franco-Prussian War than died in all of the twenty-five years of military campaigns to unify Italy. In that story there is little to remind us of the crisis of the American Union.

Can a better analogy be drawn between our war for the Union and the story of German unification? When Otto von Bismarck in 1871 finally brought together into a single nation the heretofore independent states of Germany a new country was thereby brought into existence. The United States, on the other hand, had come into existence almost a century earlier. In 1861 it could hardly be counted as a fledgling state on a par with the newly created German Empire. To make that observation, however, is to read the present back into the past, that is, to assume that the Union of 1787 had created a nation. That, to be sure, is the way Lincoln viewed the Union and, more important, it is the way in which many of us envision the Union, for which a war was necessary in order to excise the cancer of slavery threatening its survival. The unexpressed assumption here is that a *nation* had been endangered, that a sense of true nationhood already embraced the geographical area known as the United States. It was, as noted already, the assumption from which Abraham Lincoln operated. That is why, to respond to a comment made by Robert Bruce, Lincoln, unlike many other American political figures of his time, from whom Professor Bruce quoted, never predicted a war over the Union. A nation does not go to war with itself.

Lincoln's view, however, was not that held by many people of the time, and especially not by Southerners. Suppose we look, then, at the era of the Civil War from the standpoint of the South, and not from the standpoint of him who conquered the region, and denied its essential difference from the rest of the United States. Southerners, it is true, unlike Poles or Hungarians, had originally agreed to join the Union; they were neither conquered nor coerced and they shared a common language, ethnicity, and history. Indeed, the South's sons were among those who drafted the Constitution of the Union, headed the resulting government, and even came to dominate it. Yet, as the early history of the country soon demonstrated, that Union was just a union of states, and not a nation in any organic sense. Paul Nagel in his study of the concept of Union points out that in the first twenty-five years of the country's existence the Union was generally seen as an experiment rather than as an enduring polity. It was, he observes, more a means to achieve nationhood than a nation itself.

Certainly the early history of the country reflects that conception of the Union. Within ten years of the founding of the new government one of the architects of the Revolution and an official of the administration, Thomas Jefferson, boldly asserted a state's right to nullify an oppressive act of Congress. Five years later those who objected to the acquisition of Louisiana talked openly of secession from the Union as a remedy for their discontent, and within another fifteen years even louder suggestions for getting out of the Union came in the course of the war against England. The most striking challenge to the permanence of the Union, of course, came not from New England, but from the South, from South Carolina in particular during the nullification crisis of 1828–33. Just about that time, Alexis de Tocqueville recognized that if the Union was intended to "form one and the same people," few people accepted that view. "The whole structure of the government," he reported "is artificial," rather than organic. . . .

We call the struggle the Civil War, some Southerners who accepted the Southern view of the Constitution, call it the War Between the States, and officially it is the War of the Rebellion. But it was, of course, really the War for Southern Independence, in much the same league, if for different historical reasons, as Poland's and Hungary's wars of national liberation around the same time. We know, too, that the South's determined struggle revealed how wrong Lincoln had been to believe in a broad and deep sense of Unionism among Southerners.

European observers of the time well recognized the incomplete nature of American nationalism, if Lincoln did not. William Gladstone, the English Chancellor of the Exchequer in 1862, could not conceal his conviction, as he phrased it, that "Jefferson Davis and other leaders of the South have made an army; they are making, it appears, a navy; and they have made what is more than either, they have made a nation." Soon after the war the great liberal historian Lord Acton, in a letter to Robert E. Lee, explained why he had welcomed the Confederacy. "I saw in State Rights," Acton wrote, "the only availing check upon the absolutism of the sovereign will, and secession filled me with hope, not as the destruction but as the redemption of Democracy. . . . I deemed that you were fighting the battles of our liberty, our progress, and our civilization; and I mourn the stake which was lost at Richmond more deeply than I rejoice over that which was saved at Waterloo."

In short, when the South seceded in 1860–61 that fact measured not only the failure of the Union, but, more important, the incomplete character of American nationalism. Or as historian Erich Angermann has reminded us, the United States in 1861, despite the Union of 1787, was still an "unfinished nation" in much the same way as were Italy and Germany.

True, a deep sense of nationhood existed among Americans, but it was confined largely to the North. Indeed, to acknowledge that nationalism is probably the soundest way to account for the remarkable explosion of popular support that greeted Lincoln's call for volunteers to enforce the laws in the South after the fall of Sumter. When we recognize that in 1860 only a truncated nationalism existed among Americans despite the eighty-year history of the Union, then the American Civil War suddenly fits well into a comparison with other nation-building efforts of those years. The Civil War, in short, was not a struggle to save a failed Union, but to create a nation that until then had not come into being. For, in Hegel's elegant phrase "the owl of Minerva flies at dusk," historical understanding is fullest at the moment of death. International comparison throws into relief the creative character of war in the making of nations, or, in the case of the Confederacy, in the aborting of nations.

For one thing, all of the struggles for national unification in Europe, as in the United States, required military power to bring the nation into existence and to arm it with state power. This was true not only of Italy and Germany, but of Switzerland as well, as I hope to show a little later. As Ernest Renan wrote in his 1882 essay "What Is a Nation?," "Unity is always realized by brute force. The union of North and South in France," he pointed out, "was the result of a reign of terror and extermination carried on for nearly a century" in the late Middle Ages. "Deeds of violence . . . have marked the origin of all political formations," he insisted, "even of those which have been followed by the most beneficial results."

The Italian wars of national unity may not present much of an analogy with the American war, but the course of German unification is revealing. Everyone is familiar with the role of the Franco-Prussian war in the achievement of the unification of Germany in 1871. Equally relevant for an appreciation of the American Civil War as a struggle for nationhood was the Seven Weeks War between Austria and Prussia, which preceded the war with France and which culminated in Prussia's great military victory at Königgrätz or Sadowa in 1866. That war marked the culmination of Bismarck's determined efforts to exclude Austria from any united Germany in order that Prussia would be both the center and the head. By defeating Austria and creating the North German Confederation under the leadership of Prussia, Bismarck concluded what many observers at the time and historians since have referred to as a *Bruderkrieg,* a German civil war. For it was neither foreordained by history nor by the power relations among the states of central Europe that a *Kleindeutschland* or lesser Germany from which Austria was excluded would prevail over a *Grossdeutschland* or greater Germany in which Austria would be the equal or even the superior of Prussia.

At that stage in the evolution of German nationhood, the closest analogy to the American experience puts Prussia in the position of the Southern Confederacy, for it was in effect seeking to secede from the German Confederation, created at the time of the Congress of Vienna and headed by Austria. Just as Bismarck had provoked Austria into war to achieve his end, so Jefferson Davis and the South were prepared to wage war against their long-time rival for control of the North American Union.

Despite the tempting analogy, however, Jefferson Davis was no Bismarck. His excessive constitutional scruples during the short life of the Confederacy make that crystal clear. (If anything Bismarck was just the opposite: slippery in regard to any constitution with which he came into contact.) Davis's rival for domination of the North American continent—Abraham Lincoln—came considerably closer to Bismarck, including the Bismarck who by his innovative actions within the North German Confederation had laid the foundations of German industrialization.

Historians of the United States have not liked comparing Bismarck and Lincoln. As historian David Potter once wrote, "the Gettysburg Address would have been as foreign to Bismarck as a policy of 'blood and iron' would have been to Lincoln." It is certainly true that the Gettysburg Address could not have been a policy statement from Bismarck, though he boldly introduced universal manhood suffrage and the secret ballot in the new Germany, much to the horror of his conservative friends and to the consternation of his liberal opponents. And it is equally true that the Junker aristocratic heritage and outlook of the mature Bismarck stands in sharp contrast to the simple origins and democratic beliefs of Abraham Lincoln. But if we return to seeing the war and Lincoln's actions at the time from the standpoint of the South then the similarities become clearer. Once we recognize the South's disenchantment with the transformation in the Union of its fathers and its incipient nationalism, which slavery had sparked, we gain an appreciation of the incomplete nature of American nationalism. Lincoln then emerges as the true creator of American nationalism, rather than as the mere savior of the Union.

Given the immense carnage of the Civil War, not to mention the widespread use of iron in ordnance and railroads, that struggle in behalf of American nationality can hardly escape being described literally as the result of a policy of blood and iron. The phrase fits metaphorically almost as well. Reflect on Lincoln's willingness to risk war in 1861 rather than compromise over the issue of slavery in the territories. "The tug has to come, and better now, than anytime hereafter," he advised his fellow Republicans when the Crittenden compromise was before Congress. Like Horace Greeley, Lincoln was determined to call what he considered the South's bluff, its frequent threat over the years to secede in order to extract one more concession to ensure the endurance of slavery. Convinced of the successful achievement of American nationhood, he counted on the mass of Southerners to rally around the national identity, only to find that it was largely absent in the region of his birth. Only military power kept even his native state within the confines of his nation. Bismarck had to employ no such massive power to bring the states of south Germany into his new Reich in 1870–71. Rather, their sense of a unified Germany bred over a quarter-century of common action brought Catholic Bavaria, Württemberg, and Baden immediately to Protestant Prussia's side when France declared war in 1870.

But then, unlike Bismarck, Lincoln was seeking to bring into being a nation that had lost whatever sense of cohesion its Union of 1787 may have nurtured. His task was more demanding and the means needed to achieve the goal were, for that reason, harsher, more deadly, and more persistently pressed than the creation of a new Germany demanded of Bismarck. Lincoln's commitment to nationhood rather than simply to the Union comes through quite clearly in an observation by James McPherson. In his First Inaugural, Lincoln used the word "Union" twenty times; "nation" appears not at all. (That description of the United States, of course, had long been anathema to the South.) Once the South had seceded, however, the dread word began to appear in his texts: three times in his first message to Congress. By the time of the Gettysburg Address, the term "Union" appeared not at all, while "nation" was mentioned five times. In his Second Inaugural, Lincoln used Union only to describe the South's actions in disrupting the Union in 1861; he described the war as having saved the "Nation," not simply the Union.

In deeds as well as in words, Lincoln came closer than Jefferson Davis to Bismarck. There is nothing in Lincoln's record that is comparable to Bismarck's famous "Ems dispatch" in which he deliberately edited a report on the Prussian king's reaction to a demand from the French government in such a way as to provoke the French declaration of war that Bismarck needed in order to bring the south German states into his unified Germany. Over the years, the dispute among United States historians whether Lincoln maneuvered the South into firing the first shot of the Civil War, has not reached the negative interpretation that clings to Bismarck's Ems dispatch. Yet Lincoln's delay in settling the issue of Sumter undoubtedly exerted great pressure upon the Confederates to fire first. To that extent his actions display some of the earmarks of Bismarck's maneuvering in 1870. For at the same time Lincoln was holding off from supplying Sumter he was firmly rejecting the advice of his chief military adviser, Winfield Scott, that surrendering the fort was better than provoking the Confederates into beginning a war. Lincoln's nationalism needed a war, but one that the other side would begin.

The way in which Lincoln fought the war also reminds us at times of Bismarck's willingness to use iron, as well as shed blood, in order to build a nation. Throughout the war Lincoln denied that secession was a legal remedy for the South, yet his own adherence to constitutional limits was hardly flawless. If Bismarck in 1862 in behalf of his king's prerogative interpreted parliamentary government out of existence in Prussia for four years, Lincoln's interpretation of the American Constitution followed a similar, if somewhat less drastic path. As Lincoln scholar James G. Randall remarked years ago, Lincoln employed "more arbitrary power than perhaps any other President. . . . Probably no President has carried the power of proclamation and executive order (independently of Congress) as far as did Lincoln." Randall then proceeded to list those uses of power: freeing slaves, accepting the dismemberment of Virginia by dubious constitutional means, providing for the reconstruction of states lately in rebellion, suspending the writ of habeas corpus, proclaiming martial law, and enlarging the army and the navy and spending public money without the necessary Congressional approval. "Some of his important measures," Randall points out, "were taken under the consciousness that they belonged within the domain of Congress. The national legislature was merely permitted," Randall continues, "to ratify his measures, or else to adopt the futile alternative of refusing consent to accomplished fact." Lincoln himself justified his Emancipation Proclamation on the quite questionable ground "that measures otherwise unconstitutional might become lawful by becoming indispensable to the preservation of the Constitution through the preservation of the nation."

That slavery was the spring and the river from which Southern nationalism flowed virtually dictated in Lincoln's mind that it must be extirpated for nationalist as well as humanitarian reasons. For many other Northern nationalists the fundamental role slavery had played in the creation of Southern nationalism must have been a prime reason for accepting its eradication. Few of them, after all, had been enemies of slavery in the South, much less friends of black people. Indeed, hostility to blacks on grounds of race in the 1860s was almost as prevalent in the North as in the South.

What the war represented, in the end, was the forceful incorporation of a recalcitrant South into a newly created nation. Indeed, that was exactly what abolitionist Wendell Phillips had feared at the outset. "A Union," he remarked in a public address in New York in 1860, "is made up of willing States. . . . A husband or wife who can only keep the other partner within the bond by locking the doors and standing armed before them, had better submit to peaceable separation." The United States, he continued, is not like other countries. "Homogeneous nations like France tend to centralization; confederations like ours tend inevitably to dismemberment."

A similar objection to union by force had been advanced by none other than that old nationalist John Quincy Adams. "If the day should ever come (may Heaven avert it)," he told an audience celebrating the jubilee of the Constitution in 1839, "when the affections of the people of these states shall be alienated from each other; when the fraternal spirit shall give away to cold indifference . . . far better will it be for the people of the disunited states, to part in friendship from each other, than to be held together by constraint." In Lincoln's mind, it was to be a stronger and more forceful nation, one which would mark a new era in the history of American nationality, just as Bismarck's proclamation of the new German Empire in the Hall of Mirrors at Versailles in January, 1871, constituted both the achievement of German unity and the opening of a new chapter in the history of German nationality.

The meaning of the new American nationhood as far as the South was concerned was its transformation, the rooting out of those elements that had set it apart from

Northern nationalism. In the context of nation-building the era of Reconstruction can best be seen as the eradication of those aspects of the South that had lain at the root of the region's challenge to the creation of a nation. That meant ridding the South not only of slavery, but also of its undemocratic politics, its conservative social practices, its excessive dependence upon agriculture, and any other habits that might prevent the region from being as modern and progressive as the North.

Nowhere does this new nationalism appear in more strident form than in an essay by Senator Charles Sumner deceptively entitled "Are We a Nation?." The title was deceptive because there was no doubt in Sumner's mind that the United States was indeed a nation, and had always been. The essay was first given as a lecture in New York on the fourth anniversary of Lincoln's delivery of the address at Gettysburg. Sumner was pleased to recall Lincoln's reference to "a new nation" on that previous occasion, causing Sumner to remark that "if among us in the earlier day there was no occasion for the Nation, there is now. A Nation is born," he proudly proclaimed. That new nation, he contended, was one in behalf of human rights, by which he meant the rights of blacks, which the South must now accept and protect.

Interestingly enough, in the course of his discussion of nationhood, Sumner instanced Germany as a place where nationhood had not yet been achieved. "God grant that the day may soon dawn when all Germany shall be one," he exclaimed. In 1867 he could not know what we know today: that the defeat of Austria at Königgrätz the year before had already fashioned the character and future of German unity under Bismarck.

No single European effort at creating a new sense of nationhood comes as close to that of the United States as Switzerland's. Although the Swiss Confederation, which came into existence at the end of the Napoleonic era, lacked some of the nationalist elements of the American Constitution, it constituted, like the United States, a union of small states called cantons, which, again like the states of the American Union, had once been independent entities. And as was the case in the American Union, the cantons of the Swiss Confederation were separated by more than mountainous terrain. The role that slavery played in dividing the United States was filled among the Swiss by religion. The Catholic cantons of Uri, Schwyz, and Unterwalden had been the original founders of the confederation in the days of William Tell, while the Protestant cantons were not only the more recent, but more important, the cantons in which the liberal economic and social ideas and forces that were then reshaping European society had made the most headway.

Among the intellectual consequences of that modernity was a growing secularism, which expressed itself in 1841 in the suppression of all religious orders by the Protestant canton of Aargau. The action was a clear violation of the Federal Pact of 1815, but none of the Protestant cantons objected to it. The Catholic cantons, however, led by Lucerne, vehemently protested the overriding of their ancient rights. In this objection there is a striking parallel with the South's protest against the North's attacks on slavery and refusal to uphold the fugitive slave law; both slavery and a fugitive slave law, of course, were embedded in the original United States Constitution.

The Catholic cantons' response to the violation of the Confederation's constitution was that Lucerne then invited the Jesuit Order to run its schools, much to the distaste of the Protestants in Lucerne and the Protestant cantons in general. Some of the Lucerne liberals then set about to organize armed vigilantes or *Freischaren* to overthrow the governments in the Catholic cantons. The American analogy for these military actions that leaps to mind, of course, is "bloody Kansas." Nor was the guerrilla violence in Switzerland any less deadly than that in Kansas. When the canton government of Lucerne sentenced a captured *Freischar* to death, a group of his supporters invaded the canton and triumphantly carried him off to Protestant Zürich. More than one hundred died in the escapade.

Like "Bloody Kansas," the guerrilla phase of the Swiss conflict between old (Catholic) and new (Protestant) cantons deepened a sense of alienation between the two contending parties, which, in turn, led, almost naturally, to a move for separation from the Confederation. In December, 1845, seven Catholic cantons, including, interestingly enough, the three founding cantons of ancient Switzerland, formed what came to be called the *Sonderbund* or separatist confederation. Unlike the Southern states in 1860–61, the cantons of the *Sonderbund* did not proclaim secession, though they clearly saw themselves as resisting violations of traditional constitutional rights. Indeed, under the rules of the Swiss Confederation regional agreements among cantons were permissible, but the army the *Sonderbund* cantons brought into being, and the public stands they announced, strongly suggested to the rest of Switzerland that secession was indeed their intention. And so in July, 1847, the Diet of the Confederation ordered the *Sonderbund* to dissolve, an act that precipitated the departure of the delegates of the *Sonderbund* cantons. Again, like the Confederacy, the *Sonderbund* sought foreign support (particularly from Catholic and conservative Austria), but it was no more successful in that respect than the Confederacy. In early November the Diet voted to use force against the *Sonderbund;* civil war was the result.

Although each side mustered 30,000 or more troops under its command, the war was brief and light in cost; it lasted no more than three weeks and fewer than 130 men lost their lives. The victory of the Confederation's forces resulted in the rewriting of the constitutional relations among the cantons. The new national government was to be a truly federal republic deliberately modeled after that set forth in the Constitution of the United States. The immediate postwar era in Switzerland exhibited little of the conflict that we associate with the Reconstruction era. But then, the Swiss civil war was short and if not sweet, at least not very bloody. Yet there, too, as in the United States, the winners deemed it essential to extirpate those institutions that had been at the root of the disruption of the Confederation. Before the cantons of the *Sonderbund* were accepted back into the Confederation they were compelled to accede to barring the Jesuit Order from all the cantons. The acceptance of the Order into Lucerne had been, after all, a major source of the cantonal conflicts that led to the civil war. A measure of the depth of the religious issue in the Swiss conflict is that almost a century and a half passed before the Jesuit Order was readmitted to Switzerland. And in that context it is perhaps worth remembering that a century passed before a president of the United States—Lyndon B. Johnson—could be elected from a state of the former Confederacy.

As happened with the Civil War in the United States, the *Sonderbundkrieg*—the war of the Separatist Confederation—marked the long-term achievement of nationhood. So settled now was the matter of Swiss national identity that when Europe erupted in 1848 in wars of national liberation and revolution, the new Swiss Federation, the embodiment of Swiss nationality, escaped entirely from the upheaval. No longer was there any question that Switzerland was a nation; just as after 1865 there could be no doubt that the United States was a nation. In both instances, war had settled the matter for good. . . .

Class and State in Postemancipation Societies

STEVEN HAHN

The experience of the Old South's planters cannot fail to impress by comparison [with the landed classes of Europe and South America]. At a time when the use of bound labor was coming under attack throughout the Atlantic world, the slave South underwent a spectacular geographic and economic expansion that thrust the chattel institution from the eastern seaboard out to Texas, helped unify the interests of the elite (chiefly as a result of the short-staple cotton boom), and created the largest slave population in the Western Hemisphere. Granted, slaveownership was broad based, slaveholding units normally were small, and even large-scale slaveholders paled by the standards of the Caribbean and Brazil. But Stuart Schwartz has recently demonstrated that small slaveholders predominated numerically almost everywhere and that slaveowning was more highly concentrated in the mid-nineteenth-century South than in the colonial Brazilian northeast. More to the point, in the Lower South by 1860, farms and plantations containing at least twenty slaves accounted for well over 60 percent of the black labor force and over 60 percent of the cotton produced. In that year, the twelve wealthiest counties in America were to be found in the slave states, and, although the economic development of the South lagged behind that of the North, the Southern elite built an infrastructure and enjoyed a period of economic growth—largely because of the tremendous demand for cotton—that would have been the envy of any rural society in the world.

At the same time, there were signs for concern. Over the course of the antebellum period, the planters' share of Southern wealth and slaves grew, albeit unevenly. In 1800, one-third of the white families in the region owned slaves; in 1860, only one-quarter did, and social stratification seemed more pronounced. During the 1850s, some plantation districts saw growing numbers of propertyless white laborers, while larger towns and cities witnessed a significant influx of European immigrants, who soon dominated the skilled trades and resented slave competition. Slaveholders and their spokesmen thus turned more attention, in speeches and in print, to explaining "the interest of nonslaveholders" in the slave regime. Some warned of imminent class and racial conflict. Despite such trends, until secession itself, the Southern planter class presided over the most stable and prosperous servile order in modern history.

In the political arena, notwithstanding an increasing defensiveness during the antebellum period, the Southern landed elite retained both a remarkable degree of control over its own affairs and a strong voice in national politics. The planters were the first slaveholding class in the hemisphere to gain independence; they did not have a monarch with whom to contend over labor policies or on whom they had to depend for financial support; they helped write a constitution that not only sanctioned slavery while limiting federal jurisdiction over it but also rewarded slaveholders with more representation than other Americans; and they had no need for the standing armies that sapped the resources and talents of their counterparts in war-torn Europe. In fact, freedom from British imperial restraints and a subsequent loose federalism opened the way for the westward migration that bolstered the slave system. Until 1850, Southerners held the presidency for all but thirteen years, occupied half the seats in the Senate, and wielded great power in the House of Representatives as a result of their influence in the Democratic party. The South thereby managed to circumscribe federal authority and unfavorable economic policies. When the free states came to outnumber the slave in the 1850s, Southern interests gained protection from sympathetic Northern Democrats in the White House, even greater control of the Democratic party, and a decisive majority on the Supreme Court. Before 1860, nearly 60 percent of all Supreme Court justices were Southerners, and the South had parity or, more often, a majority on the court for all but eleven years between the ratification of the Constitution and the onset of the Civil War.

Historians frequently allude to the democratic character of antebellum Southern politics (for white men) to distinguish the tendencies and world-view of the planter class from landed elites elsewhere in the Americas and Europe. There is no denying the contention; Southern planters were not culturally akin to Brazilian sugar planters, Prussian Junkers, or Russian noble landowners (*pomeshchiki*), although the work of Shearer Davis Bowman and Peter Kolchin suggests important similarities. Nonetheless, the Southern political system long exhibited patron-client features that were, in several respects, broadened and reinforced by the tide of Jacksonian democratization, buttressing the hegemony of the planter class. Above all, we must recognize the conservative and anti-democratic trajectory of the slave regime as a whole, as well as the new dimensions of struggle for state power that the sectional conflict encouraged. Many Northerners certainly did. The suppression of abolitionist literature, censorship of the mails, the enactment of the gag rule and a tougher fugitive slave law, the decision in the Dred Scott case, and the demand for federal protection for slavery in the territories did more than signal the South's increasingly reactionary role in national life. They also made plain that the South, in a shift of stance, sought to use the national government for its own purposes and that the maintenance of slavery would commit federal resources to socially and politically repressive policies. Northerners feared the expanding "slave power," and with good reason: politically prominent Southerners called for the nullification of all personal liberty laws in the North, and there are grounds to believe that, were it not for secession, the Supreme Court might have effectively "nationalized" slavery by invalidating all obstacles to slave transit.

It is in light of the strength of the Southern landed elite in national affairs and the histories of other landed classes that the unfolding of emancipation and unification in the United States must be considered. What then becomes strikingly apparent is not the persistence of the Southern planters' power but rather its dramatic and irreversible decline. After all, the South was not alone among servile societies in resisting emancipation, however much secession and civil war lent it a distinctive aspect. No landed elite easily accepted emancipation. Recalcitrance prevailed at the very least; violence, upheaval, or military crisis normally occurred before the deed was done. There can be no separating the abolition of slavery and other servile relations in the West from the great Christmas uprising of 1831 in Jamaica, the Ten Years' War in Cuba, the Paraguayan War and slave flight from the plantations in Brazil, the revolutions of 1789 and 1848 in France, the Napoleonic wars and the Revolution of 1848 in Prussia, the Crimean War in Russia, and peasant unrest in many parts of the Continent. Still, aside from St. Domingue, no landed elite was wholly toppled by the emancipation process; in most areas—the South included—various forms of extra-economic compulsion, both new and old, continued to shape rural labor relations for some time thereafter.

Only in the United States and St. Domingue, however, did abolition come in the midst of a massive shift in power away from the landed classes. Elsewhere, their objections, protests, and threats notwithstanding, the elites were able to define the boundaries of emancipation policy and supervise its implementation. Either they were compensated for their losses or awarded state subsidies to attract new labor and buffer the transition. In any event, they retained direct control over the countryside and wide prerogatives to regulate freedpersons. In the British Caribbean, the planters received a share of the £20,000,000 distributed throughout the empire, a temporary apprenticeship system, and a large measure of home rule. In Brazil, the coffee growers benefited from a state-financed program to import free workers even before slavery ended. And, in Europe, landed proprietors extracted indemnification from the peasantry that often delayed by years the peasants' full emancipation.

Whatever the shortcomings of federal emancipation and reconstruction policy, in the United States alone it was formulated without the landed elite's direct influence, and, as a consequence, proved the most sweeping and far-reaching. Nowhere else were so many servile laborers liberated in one stroke or soon after provided equivalent civil and political rights. Indeed, for some time, it seemed that a major program of land reform might be initiated. Even with the failure of land reform, black enfranchisement and the active organizing of the Republican party presented a serious political challenge to planters who had already suffered military defeat and heavy economic losses. The freedmen pressed their claims, came to sit in Southern state legislatures, and—in numerous plantation belt counties—took command of the local government. To many whites, it appeared nothing less than a world turned upside down.

The radical changes and inversions did not endure. A massive counteroffensive, made possible by a limited and flagging federal commitment to revolutionizing the South, rolled back many of the freedmen's gains, rapidly in some areas and gradually in others. And as a growing number of local studies are demonstrating—studies that have contributed to various "continuity" theses—the planters did maintain or reassert their dominance over much of the Southern countryside. Evidence from virtually every ex-Confederate state shows that the rate at which plantation owners persisted from 1860 to 1870 differed little from the previous decade and that the landed elite of the 1870s had firm roots in the antebellum era. No doubt a considerable turnover in land titles took place during the postwar years, and we need to learn more about its extent. Even so, its implications are not readily obvious: very high turnover rate among Junker estates in parts of mid-nineteenth-century Prussia, for example, failed to bring about a significant weakening of traditional landed power. Capital from the North and abroad did make its way into Southern agriculture, though not for some time after emancipation, and it went chiefly into the prairie rice, sugar, and Mississippi Delta cotton sectors. Merchandisers, for the most part Southern-born and filling the vacuum left by the eroding factorage system, did begin to establish a strong foothold in rural districts and move into the ranks of substantial landed proprietors, although they did so most prominently in heavily white, nonplantation counties. The Black Belt, from Virginia to Texas, by and large saw not so much the displacement as the bourgeois metamorphosis of older planter families and their holdings.

Although we still know less about the social bases of Southern politics after the war than before it, there is also good reason to believe that the landed elite retained the upper hand, albeit uneasily, into the twentieth century. Thrown on the defensive by freedmen, merchants, industrial interests, and Republicans generally during Reconstruction, planters fended off its worst effects and led the movement to overthrow Republican regimes. Redeemer constitutions of the 1870s then restricted state-supported economic development, while state legislatures of the period enacted a variety of measures that strengthened the hands of landlords, amplified the voice of rural counties, established state agricultural departments, provided tax benefits to plantation districts, and brought railroad companies under scrutiny. Dissension continued to strain the Democratic party, with its unwieldy factions; but, within the shifting party coalitions, the large landowners usually functioned as the anchors. In short, it is difficult to argue that the post-bellum South came under the control of a new urban and industrial ruling class.

From a national and international vantage point, however, the position of the postwar Southern landed elite appears far less sanguine, and the dominant political bloc coming to govern the country far more exceptional. In the United States, as in other Western countries, emancipation helped usher in the final stages of national unification and nation building: the absorption of regional elites and labor systems into capitalist nation-states. In this regard, the Civil War and Reconstruction formed part of a much larger socio-political process that completed what Eric Hobsbawm has called "the global triumph of capitalism." Yet the process was by no means uniform in character, pace, or outcome; the examples of Brazil and Germany highlight important contrasts with America.

The Brazilian case presents some particularly novel features when compared with the United States. To begin with, slavery prevailed throughout the country. As late as the 1870s, every province had its slaves, and on the eve of emancipation all but northernmost Amazonas and Ceará still held them. Furthermore, the establishment of the First Republic in 1889, almost immediately after abolition, brought about political and administrative decentralization, the reverse of the trend almost everywhere else. What linked these features was the nature of the class and region assuming the dominant position in the new Brazilian state.

Between the achievement of independence and the onset of the republic, Brazil was held together, tenuously at times, by a constitutional monarchy that concentrated policy making in the hands of the monarch (known as the emperor) and the institutions (appointive and elective) that oversaw the imperial system. Although the emperor ultimately depended on the support of the rural slaveholding elites and could seldom enforce his will on questions of national importance, he nonetheless had to perform a difficult balancing act: juggling the demands of troubled sugar planters in the northeast, rising coffee growers of the south-central region, Portuguese-born merchants and courtiers, a small urban middle class, and the abolition-minded British, who also played a pivotal role in the export economy. Local revolts, which flared sporadically before 1850, testified to the tensions within the empire. Relative peace then followed until the American Civil War and, especially, the traumatic Paraguayan War (1865–1870) gave impetus to an indigenous, urban-based antislavery movement that viewed abolition as a necessary step toward modernization. While Emperor Dom Pedro II comprehended its political complexities, his sentiments leaned toward the side of emancipation reform.

Few Brazilian slaveholders unequivocally embraced abolitionism. They proved least reluctant in the northeast, where slavery had been in long-term decline as a result ⸍th manumissions and the internal slave traffic, although they expected emancipation ₊radual and bring compensation. Far more resistance could be found in the south, notably in the Paraíba valley, where the coffee economy was expanding and heavily dependent on slave labor. Even the Paulista planters [from the São Paulo region], whose rise began as the Atlantic slave trade terminated and the slavery crisis escalated, showed little desire to hasten slavery's demise. Yet, as early as the 1840s, some Paulista planters experimented, for the most part unsuccessfully, with free labor. By the 1880s, they had enlisted the aid of the provincial and imperial governments in financing an immigrant labor program. Thousands of workers began to stream in, and by May 1887 recently arrived Italians already outnumbered slaves working on Paulista coffee plantations (*fazendas*). Seven months later, as large numbers of fleeing slaves prompted some owners to grant freedom in return for continued labor, the most prosperous planters accepted abolition. Shortly thereafter, in 1888, the more-than-three-century reign of slavery came to an end.

Having emerged as the most vital of Brazilian regions by the 1870s, São Paulo suffered under a centralized regime in which its political power was not commensurate with its economic power. While the province's income increased rapidly, it remained grossly underrepresented in the ministries and council of state as well as in the senate. A budding urban bourgeoisie and the growth of manufacturing further exposed the outmoded quality of the imperial structure and helped to inspire a republican movement. But opposition to the monarchy intensified as abolitionists pressed for land reform as an accompaniment to emancipation. For the Paulista planters, attracted by the idea of federalism, also feared that a weakened emperor and a chaotic political system might be unable to resist such a radical assault. Thus the coffee growers, especially the more advanced section in the west, sided with the republicans and were ultimately joined by northeastern sugar planters disgruntled over the empire's failure to provide indemnification for their liberated slaves. Once the military abandoned the monarchy, its days were numbered; a bloodless coup toppled it in 1889.

The ensuing federal republic greatly improved the position of São Paulo and its coffee planters, while securing the power of rural elites in less developed areas. It thereby revealed the decisive imprint of landed wealth and export agriculture. On the one hand, each of the twenty Brazilian states received considerable measures of self-government, including the right to tax exports and borrow abroad, which worked to the advantage of São Paulo and Minas Gerais, the two major coffee-producing states, as well as the sugar-growing northeast. On the other hand, the national government itself soon came under the sway of an alliance between São Paulo and Minas by virtue of an agreement that granted state governors and bosses essential autonomy over their own domains in return for Paulista and Mineiro control over the presidency and other strategic federal posts. As a result, although their will did not go uncontested and the implementation of policy could require extended negotiation, the coffee planters collected sufficient revenues to propel the growth of their own states and won federal support to prop up the export economy. Not only was further assistance for immigrant labor forthcoming but, when coffee prices slumped in the late 1890s, a federal-state valorization scheme was fashioned whereby government-secured foreign loans underwrote the stockpiling of coffee for more opportune sale, a program that buoyed the planters in choppy market waters for the next two decades.

So it was that, in the course of emancipation and nation-building, the landed classes throughout Brazil retained their property, control over labor, and local prerogatives. The coffee planters, furthest along the road of capitalist agriculture, also succeeded in using the resources of the state to advance their interests. The overwhelmingly immigrant urban bourgeoisie, despite some real gains, failed to establish an independent base: they aligned with the coffee planters, who in turn spearheaded much of the industrial investment. Indeed, the substantial industrial growth experienced by São Paulo in the late nineteenth and early twentieth centuries came chiefly under the auspices of a class whose major economic foundation was export agriculture and whose economic policies served to weaken federal finances, inhibit the importation of essential machinery, deny other exporting regions much-needed capital, and impede the expansion of the domestic market. The price would be limited economic development for the nation as a whole and increased foreign influence over the financial sector. . . .

[The German case has been omitted.]

Viewed from the perspective of Germany and Brazil, and for that matter of most Western nations during the nineteenth century, the American experience of unification is strikingly different. Much currency has been accorded the notion that the South and its landed elite "lost the war but won the peace." And, insofar as the notion speaks to the limits of federal reconstruction—defined in terms of its most far-reaching possibilities—and to the conservative drift of the Republican party after 1867, particularly the attempts to align with whiggish Southern whites at the expense of freedmen and small producers generally, it is compelling. Although some interpretive controversy surrounds the events that led directly to the Republican acceptance of "home rule" for the South in 1877, it surely stands as a signal event in American political history. More remarkable from a comparative vantage point is the fact that a coalition (a "solidarity bloc," as Alexander Gerschenkron calls it) of big agriculture in the South and big industry in the North did not emerge. The political bloc coming to dominate the new nation-state scarcely included the Southern landed elite.

For some time now, economists and economic historians have been questioning what was once a conventional wisdom: that the Civil War played a central role in speeding the course of American industrialization. The issues remain in dispute. But there can be little doubt that the war decisively affected the *political economy* of industrialization. With most of the Southern states out of the Union, the Republican party enacted banking, monetary, tariff, land, and tax policies that established the sovereignty of the federal government, helped channel capital to heavy industry at the expense of other economic sectors, and greatly enlarged the domestic market for industrial goods. In light of the longstanding opposition of the South to such federal initiatives, which set the boundaries of national economic policy before 1861, the shift in power and authority was all the more dramatic. Even Robert Sharkey, who effectively demolished the portrait of a united business-Republican front, has insisted that wartime legislation clearly "tipp[ed] the class and sectional balance" in favor of the East over both the South and West. This, he claimed, was "*the* momentous change" between 1850 and 1873: a change that enabled large industrialists and bankers to consolidate and reorganize after the ensuing depression.

The Republican hold on the national polity was not, however, firmly secured by the war and Reconstruction. Party competition intensified during the 1870s and, together with widespread social and economic dislocations, threatened Republican control over the state. In 1874, Democrats won a majority in the House of Representatives for the first time since 1858; a revitalized labor movement pressed for the eight-hour day and contributed to the appearance of new political parties and independent tickets at the local, state, and national levels; a severe depression produced massive unemployment and mounting social strife; and in 1877 the most destructive labor conflict of the nineteenth century engulfed railroads from the Middle Atlantic through the Midwest, bringing the intervention of federal troops. Having established a national framework of market relations and having largely purged its radical wing in the North and South, the Republicans might then have looked to the "classic conservative coalition" to maintain their rule.

Despite flirtations in that direction, no American analogue to the German "marriage of iron and rye," linking the Rhineland and East Prussia, or to the Brazilian alliance of *café com leite,* linking São Paulo and Minas Gerais, ever emerged. Republicans offered limited encouragement and few resources, even to sympathetic Southerners during the postwar period. And the party had enough influential leaders who "waved the bloody shirt" and kept "sectional issues" alive to circumscribe further overtures southward while fanning the hostility of cotton planters and their supporters. Federal subsidies for internal improvements did figure importantly in the Republican strategy to attract whiggish Southern Democrats and build a stable political base in the South, but the events of 1877, when assistance to the Texas and Pacific Railroad failed to materialize, showed the strategy to be problematic under what seemed the best of circumstances. Subsequent Republican administrations and presidential aspirants vacillated in their "southern policy." For the most part, they sought to build up their protectionist, sound-money bloc through tariff appeals to industrialists and to sugar, rice, and tobacco planters on the Southern periphery rather than through compromise with the cotton interest in the Southern heartland. Even these efforts came to little.

Propelled by what Richard Franklin Bensel has termed the "military pension-tariff engine of national development," the Republicans forged a coalition that included substantial sections of the skilled industrial working class, commercial farmers relying on the domestic market, a great many Civil War veterans, and pietistic Protestants, who tended to be found among the other groups or the urban middle class. But the party's policy-making core was composed of heavy industrialists, national bankers, and textile manufacturers. The South, particularly the cotton-growing landed elite, remained within the Democratic low-tariff coalition, which included financiers and exporters on both coasts, as well as farmers looking chiefly to overseas markets and ethnic groups in urban areas—an alliance that mixed internationalist and localist concerns. While the Democrats obtained popular pluralities in all save one presidential election from 1876 to 1892 (although on only two occasions won the presidency) and normally commanded the House with the Southern faction looming largest, almost even major policy conflict was resolved in favor of big industry. Even when the South and West joined forces on key issues like the money supply, industrial interests usually effected a suitable compromise. Thus the Bland-Allison Act of 1878 not only avoided the unlimited coinage of silver (which Southern farmers and planters generally wanted) but also received the firm support of the congressional delegation from iron-producing Pennsylvania. During the 1890s, when economic depression and the merger movement permitted the triumph of the agrarian free-silver wing within the Democratic party, once-loyal investment and commercial bankers jumped to the Republicans and completed the political bloc that would govern the "System of 1896." As one scholar of comparative politics remarked, "In no other country did [industrialists] share power so little."

The failure of the "classic conservative coalition" to emerge, and, therefore, of the southern landed elite to retain significant influence over national life, is further evidenced by the region's relative exclusion from a number of strategic positions that had been virtual Southern preserves before the Civil War. While Southerners had dominated the presidency, the Supreme Court, the speakership of the House of Representatives, and the diplomatic corps during the antebellum period, they claimed but a handful of such posts thereafter: between 1865 and 1912, only 7 of 31 Supreme Court appointments, 2 of 12 House speakerships, 14 of 133 cabinet positions, and, excepting the rather unusual case of Andrew Johnson, not even one presidential or vice presidential nomination, let alone an office. "Never in the history of the country, and rarely in the history of any country," C. Vann Woodward wrote, "had there been a comparable shift in the geography of political power." The presence of landed aristocrats in European and Latin American governing circles into the twentieth century (well into the century, in some instances) stands as a stark contrast. So, too, does what has variously been called the "gentrification," "nobilization," or "feudalization" of the bourgeoisie in the wake of other Western unification struggles. The cult of the "Lost Cause" and the romanticization of plantation life had more than sectional appeal in postwar America, as did a racism etched into national law by the end of the nineteenth century. An antimodernism that occasionally celebrated the Middle Ages and the pastoral ideal also found an audience amid the teeming cities of the industrial North. But antimodernism, as T. J. Jackson Lears has demonstrated, ultimately contributed to the remaking and reinforcing of bourgeois values and class hegemony. Except for the brief Northern planter movement of the middle to late 1860s, there was no important American counterpart to the bourgeois acquisition of landed estates and noble titles.

The dramatic setbacks suffered by the South and its planters on the national front did not bring much in the way of compensation regionally. Indeed, the national setbacks both promoted and accentuated Southern woes of the postwar decades. This is not to discount the internal factors that made for poverty and limited development in the post-bellum South: the physical repercussions of the war, the traditionalism of many large landowners, the exploitative practices of merchants and landlords, and a rampant racism, to name but a few. Nor is it to paint a portrait of general stagnation, for the postwar period saw the refashioning of social relations in the plantation districts, the integration of the white yeomanry into the staple market, the rapid growth of towns and cities, and the appearance of new industrial enterprises in rural and urban areas alike. It is not to suggest that the North simply plundered the South. Rather, it is that the fate of the Southern economy cannot be understood apart from the shape of the national political economy.

Planter resistance to industrialization in the South was not inconsiderable. It had a long history and a sound logic. Before the Civil War, cities and industries were often viewed as antithetical to the stability of the slave regime; after the war, industrial development was commonly seen as a threat to planter control of the free black labor force. Not by accident did Southern textile manufacturers depend chiefly on white operatives or railroad and mining companies look to the leasing of convicts. But it is easy to exaggerate the planters' hostility to modernization and their conflicts with industrialists. More than a few wealthy landowners and their kin adjusted to the postwar world by seeking innovations in agriculture and by investing in merchandising, mills, mines, lumbering, and railroads. Their prospects, however, continued to rest heavily on the health of a cotton economy that came to dominate more and more of the region; and the cotton economy entered a state of gradual and, save for some brief upturns, irreversible deterioration. Thus, although figures for the post-bellum South as a whole show relatively rapid recovery in output and, after 1880, rates of economic growth similar to the North, the cotton states experienced both sharper declines following the war and slower resuscitation.

The direct effects of the Civil War, coupled with longer term unfavorable conditions in the international market, including a leveling off in the demand for cotton, accounted for many of the region's economic problems. But the fall of the South from national power and the contours of the new political economy made them all the more difficult to overcome. Protectionism forced cotton growers to sell cheap and buy dear; the national banking system institutionalized a scarcity of regional capital and produced high interest rates; and the structure of postwar revenue collection, before the implementation of income and corporate taxes, placed fiscal burdens most heavily on consumers and landowners. Together, these policies funneled surplus income out of the South, hampered investment, and helped put the region in a quasi "colonial" status in relation to the North by the end of the nineteenth century. The lack of adequate capital stymied the transition to wage labor and a more general reorganization of production in the countryside, thereby contributing to the spread of tenancy and sharecropping, and it decidedly limited the options of aspiring manufacturers and entrepreneurs, who were left to rely on a local, highly personal, and shallow financial market. In 1880, per capita bank deposits in the South represented only one-fifth the figure for the entire nation, and, as late as the first decade of the twentieth century, interest rates were systematically higher than in any other region. Southern planters charged, moreover, that federal economic policies, especially high tariffs, amounted to sectional taxes that promised to usurp their property. But there was no significant relief forthcoming. Southern Democrats pressed for monetary inflation, repeal of the 10 percent tax on state bank notes, reduction of the tariff, and an income tax—and lost. As the majority faction in the Democratic party, the South did make its presence felt in Congress; yet, until the twentieth century was well advanced, only home rule could be secured. . . .

There was nothing inevitable about the outcome of these political developments. The war for the Union could well have failed much as did the revolutions of 1848 in Europe, postponing unification and strengthening the Southern landed elite when unification ultimately occurred (presuming that it would occur). However much historians tend to assess the impact of the Civil War and Reconstruction in terms of the most progressive possibilities and however tempting it may be to speculate about the repercussions of a more "radical" Reconstruction, the likely alternatives within the national and international context of the mid-nineteenth century were all in the other direction. Indeed, as Barrington Moore, Jr., has suggested, we might well ponder what anything short of a total Union victory would have meant for American society.

That the Southern landed elite managed to remain a dominant force within the South depended on a cross-sectional community interest of property and race created by cotton, mounting labor unrest nationwide, and the intellectual and political currents of a new age of imperialism. Few Northerners imagined that the postwar South would not continue to be a cotton-producing region, and more and more came to believe that white planters were best suited to run it. The granting of "home rule" in part confirmed this. But if home rule enabled the big landowners to recapture a significant measure of regional power, it did not enable them to recapture substantial national power. And their failure on the national level contributed to the erosion of their regional base. In comparative perspective, what stands out in the course of emancipation and unification is the swift and dramatic decline in the fortunes of the Southern planter class.

☞ *F U R T H E R   R E A D I N G*

Arthur Bestor, "The American Civil War as a Constitutional Crisis," *American Historical Review* 69 (1964), 327–352

Gabor S. Boritt, ed., *And the Civil War Came* (1996)

David Herbert Donald, *Liberty and Union* (1978)

Eric Foner, "The Causes of the American Civil War: Recent Interpretations and New Directions," *Civil War History* 20 (1974), 197–214

Elizabeth Fox-Genovese and Eugene D. Genovese, *Fruits of Merchant Capital: Slavery and Bourgeois Property in the Rise and Expansion of Capitalism* (1983)

Barrington Moore, Jr., "The American Civil War: The Last Capitalist Revolution," in Barrington Moore, Jr., *Origins of Dictatorship and Democracy* (1966), 111–155

Allan Nevins, *Ordeal of the Union*, 4 vols. (1947–1950)

——, "A Major Result of the War," *Civil War History* 5 (1959), 237–250

Frank L. Owsley, "The Fundamental Cause of the Civil War: Egocentric Sectionalism," *Journal of Southern History* 7 (1941), 3–18

Philip S. Paludan, "The American Civil War as a Crisis of Law and Order," *American Historical Review* 77 (1972), 1013–1034

——, "The American Civil War: Triumph through Tragedy," *Civil War History* 21 (1975), 254–260

Peter J. Parish, *The American Civil War* (1975)

David M. Potter, "The Civil War in the History of the Modern World," in Potter, *The South and the Sectional Conflict* (1968)

James G. Randall, "The Blundering Generation," *Mississippi Valley Historical Review* 27 (1940), 3–28

James G. Randall and David H. Donald, *The Civil War and Reconstruction* (1969)

John S. Rosenberg, "The American Civil War and the Problem of 'Presentism,' " *Civil War History* 21 (1975), 242–253

Arthur M. Schlesinger, Jr., "The Causes of the Civil War: A Note on Historical Sentimentalism," *Partisan Review* 16 (1949), 969–981

Richard H. Sewell, *A House Divided: Sectionalism and Civil War* (1988)

William G. Shade, " 'Revolutions May Go Backwards': The American Civil War and the Problem of Political Development," *Social Science Quarterly* 55 (1974), 753–767

Kenneth M. Stampp, "The Irrepressible Conflict," in Stampp, *The Imperiled Union* (1980),191–245

Geoffrey Ward, with Ric Burns and Ken Burns, *The Civil War: An Illustrated History* (1990)